1

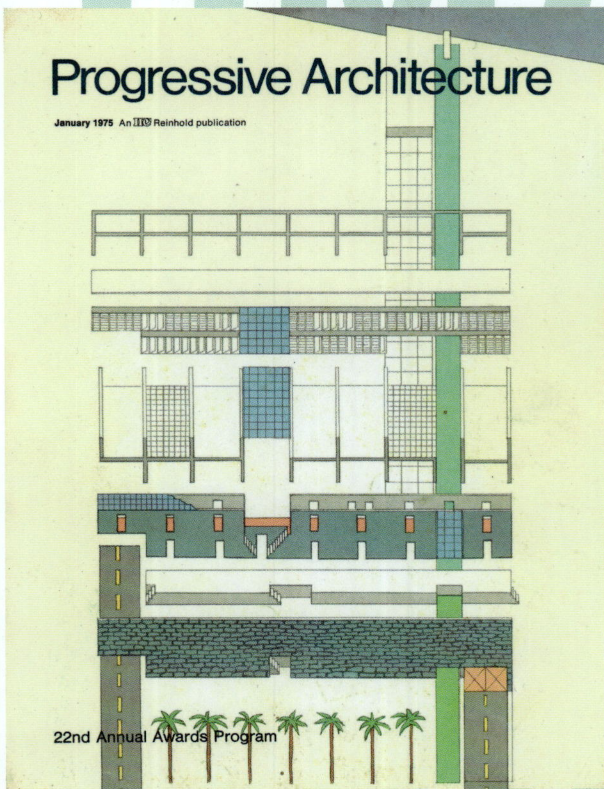

2

3

OMA REM KOOL-HAAS

A CRITICAL READER

CHRISTOPHE VAN GERREWEY (ED.)

BIRKHÄUSER
BASEL

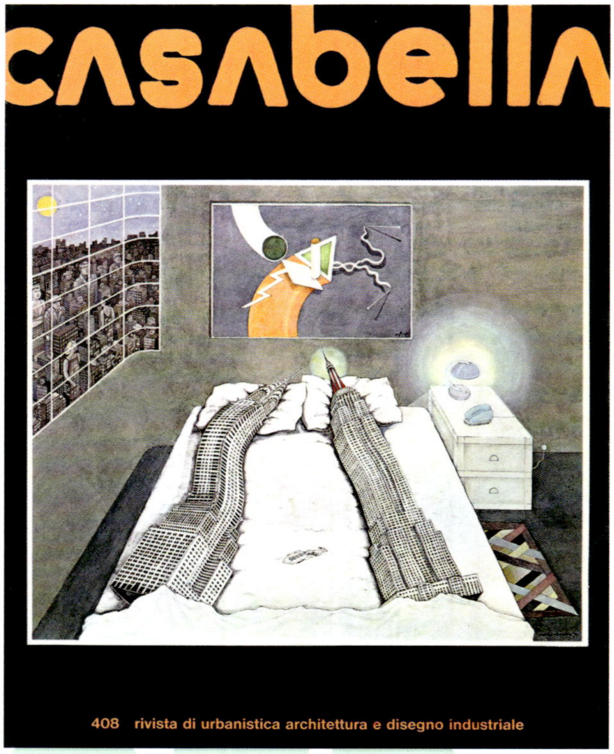

4

1973–
1977

5

6

1 *Casabella* 378 (1973) / Exodus or The Voluntary Prisoners of Architecture: A Sunset at the Allotments, 1972 **2** *Progressive Architecture* 1 (1975) / Spear House, Miami, 1974 / Rem Koolhaas, Laurinda Spear **3** *Progressive Architecture* 6 (1975) / Egg of Columbus Center, New York, 1973 / Elia and Zoe Zenghelis **4** *Casabella* 408 (1975) / *Après l'amour,* 1974 / Madelon Vriesendorp **5** *L'Architecture d'Aujourd'hui* 186 (1976) / *Ecstasy of Mrs Caligari,* 1974 / Madelon Vriesendorp **6** *Casabella* 418 (1976) / *The Story of the Pool,* 1974 / Madelon Vriesendorp **7** *Architectural Design* 5 (1977) / *Welfare Palace Hotel: The Raft of the Medusa,* 1975–1977 / Madelon Vriesendorp **8** *Soho Weekly News* 8 (1978) / *Dream of Liberty,* 1974 / Madelon Vriesendorp **9** *wonen-TA/BK* 11 (1978) / Welfare Palace Hotel, 1975–1977

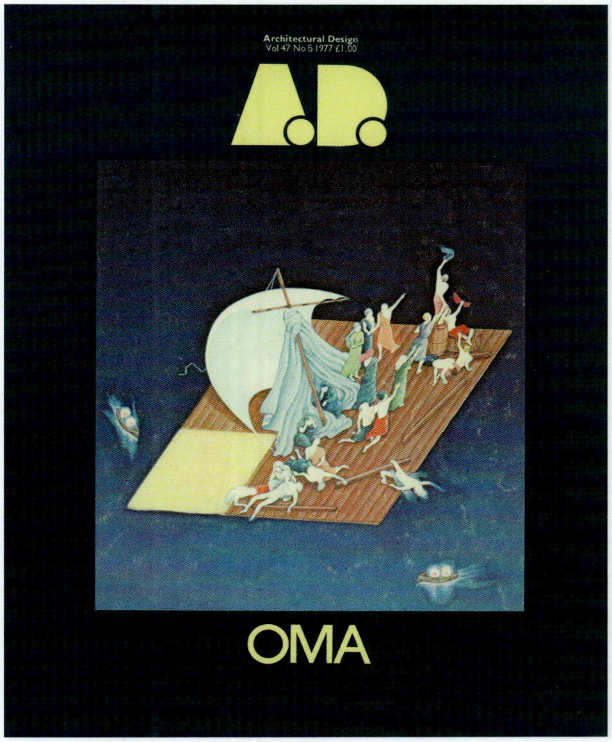

7

8

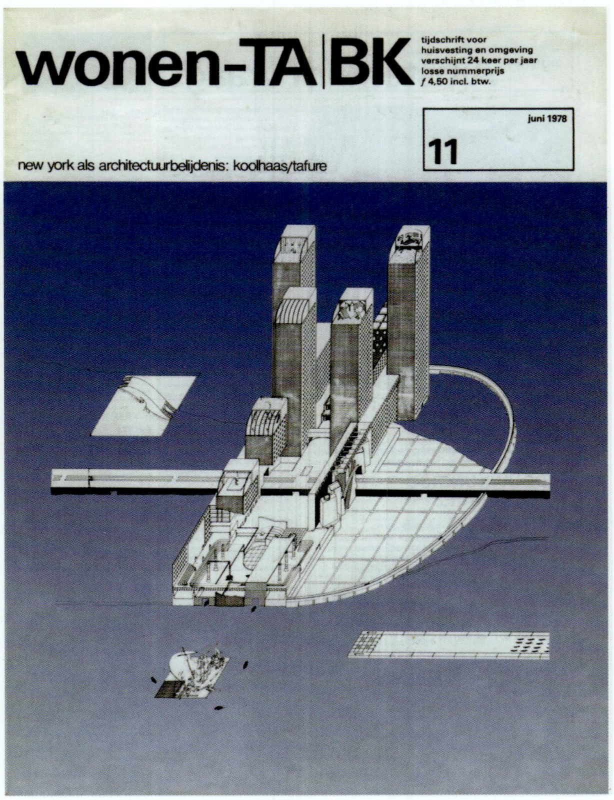

9

DEARCHITECT
PRIJSVRAAG
IN DE VERNIELING
VAKTIJDSCHRIFT VOOR ARCHITECTUUR
78 11
NUMMER 11
NOVEMBER 1978
ARCHITECTENRESEARCH 50
WONINGBOUW TE LONDEN 68
DE ROL VAN SCULPTUUR 74
STADHUIS VOOR SNEEK 81
GOTISCHE NICOLAÏKERK GERESTAUREERD 85
MAANDBLAD - JAARGANG 9 - TEN HAGEN BV

10

DEARCHITECT
KOOLHAAS' ONTWERP VOOR UITBREIDING VAN DE TWEEDE KAMER
VAKTIJDSCHRIFT VOOR ARCHITECTUUR
80 5
NUMMER 5
MEI 1980
STEDEBOUW EN GELUID 38
DECADENTIE IN OLDENZAAL 41
MONTESSORISCHOOL
JAN VERHOEVEN 72
HET SCHRIKBEELD
VAN LIVERPOOL 82
COMPUTER EN BOUW 95
EEN FATALE TRECHTER 106
MAANDBLAD - JAARGANG 11 - TEN HAGEN BV

11

TRANSITION
volume 1 No. 4
october 1980
3 interviews: Graves,
Koolhaas, Baird.
The romance of High Tech.
DISCOURSE ON ARCHITECTURE
REGISTERED FOR POSTING AS A PUBLICATION—CATEGORY B

12

OMA
PROJECTS 1978-1981

13

1978–1980

14

15

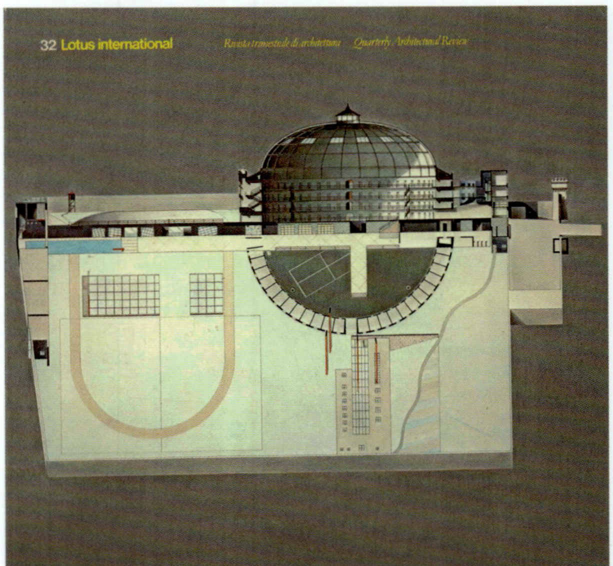

16

10 *De Architect* 11 (1978) / Dutch Parliament Extension, The Hague, 1978 **11** *De Architect* 11 (1980) / Dutch Parliament Extension, The Hague, 1978 **12** *Transition* 4 (1980) / Discourse on Architecture: Michael Graves, George Baird, Rem Koolhaas **13** Robert Maxwell, ed., *OMA: Projects 1978–1981* (London: Architectural Association, 1981) / Facade in the Strada Novissima, Venice Architecture Biennale, 1980 **14** *Architecture Mouvement Continuité* 54–55 (1981) / Boompjes with Witte Huis (1898), Rotterdam, 1980 **15** *Archithese* 5 (1981) / Boompjes, Rotterdam, 1980 (with green sketch by Aldo van Eyck) **16** *Lotus international* 32 (1981) / Arnhem Panopticon Prison, 1980

17

18

1982

17 *Lotus international* 36 (1982) / IJplein Housing: Urban Studies for Amsterdam, 1981 **18** *L'Architecture d'Aujourd'hui* 223 (1982) / Boompjes, Rotterdam, 1980 **19** *Dutch Art + Architecture Today* 12 (1982) / Boompjes with Willemsbrug, Rotterdam, 1980 **20** *Express Extra* 2 (1982) / Boompjes, Rotterdam, 1980 **21** *De Groene Amsterdammer* 43 (1982) / Boompjes, Rotterdam, 1980 **22** *Skyline* 5 (1982) / Boompjes: Viewing Tower, Rotterdam, 1980

19

20

SPECIAL ISSUE LIMITED EDITION

$4.00

EXPRESS
EXTRA

THE OFFICE FOR
METROPOLITAN
ARCHITECTURE

27 oktober 1982, nr. 43 f 3,00

De Groene Amsterdammer

Onafhankelijk weekblad sedert 1877. 106de jaargang. Westeinde 16, 1017 ZP Postbus 353, 1000 AJ Amsterdam. Telefoon 020-23.08.64

Kapitalistische revival?

Het zag er zo veelbelovend uit, vonden de ondernemers. In sneltreinvaart kwam het rechtse kabinet naderbij. Eindelijk dan een regering die de ekonomie echt zou durven hervormen. Toen stapte Van Agt van zijn troon, en de nieuwe prins heet Lubbers. Een man die naar de zin van de werkgevers veel te veel belang hecht aan 'het sociale gezicht' van het CDA. De kapitalistische revival opnieuw uitgesteld. Pagina 3.

De Cuba-krisis

Twintig jaar geleden, eind oktober 1962, stond de wereld bijna een week lang aan de rand van een atoomoorlog. De Verenigde Staten ontdekten dat de Sovjetunie bezig was kernraketten te plaatsen op Cuba, op enkele honderden kilometers van het Amerikaanse vasteland. Voor het eerst daagde de Sovjetunie de Verenigde Staten uit en nog wel in haar eigen invloedssfeer. Het konflikt werd in cowboystijl uitgevochten. De laatste grote krisis van de Koude Oorlog, op pagina 10 en 11.

En verder:

Laat er alsjeblieft een rechts kabinet komen, pag. 2
Hans Achterhuis en het misbruik dat rechts van zijn ideeën maakt, pag. 5
Amerikaanse verkiezingen in het teken van de angst, pag. 9
Drie kongsi's strijden in Polen om de macht, pag. 13
Wat is er mis aan Saters 'Verkilling'? pag. 17
De odyssee van een Palestijn, pag. 20

Architektonische tegenspraken

Rotterdam riep hem te hulp bij de invulling van de Maasboulevard; hij zette er onder andere de Maasbrug voor op zijn kop.
In Amsterdam-noord wordt in nauw overleg met de toekomstige bewoners een 'stedelijk dorp' gebouwd door een architekt die zich altijd heeft uitgesproken tegen inspraak. Tegenspraken te over op het IJplein. Architekt Rem Koolhaas laat zich erdoor inspireren tot spannende ontwerpen. Worden de bewoners van Amsterdam-noord door hem belazerd of heeft Koolhaas zich eindelijk aangepast? Pagina 14 en 15.

21

Skyline

The Architecture and Design Review May 1982 $2.50

The Office for Metropolitan Architecture

Plus: Neutra in Vienna, Frampton in Japan (2), Interview with Cesar Pelli, Insider's Guide to Architecture Schools, and More Emerging Voices

OMA: Rem Koolhaas with Stefano de Martino and Kees Christiaanse. Two Structures for Rotterdam; project, 1980–81. Viewing tower on the bridgehead.

22

1982–1983

23

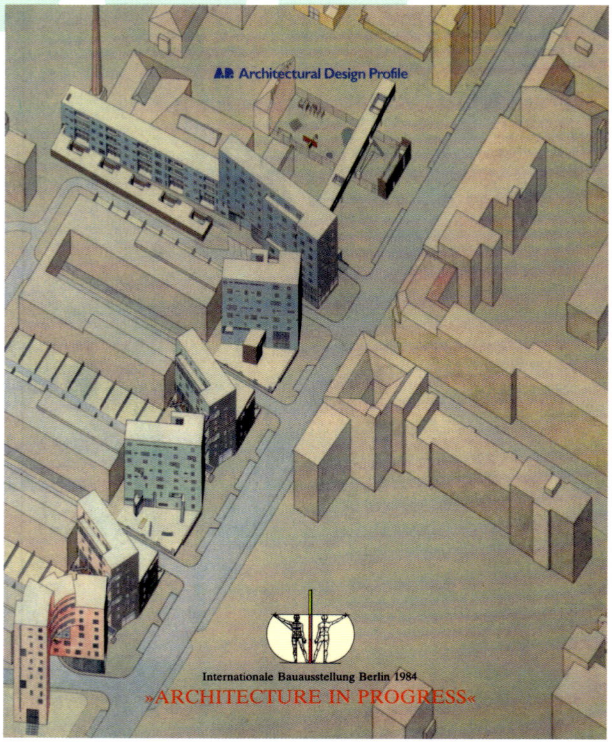

24

25

26

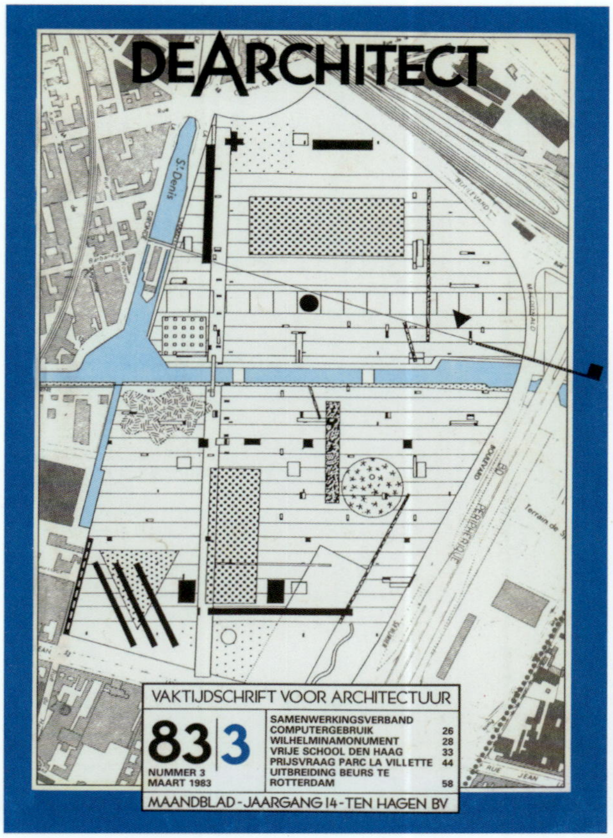

27

28

23 *wonen-TA/BK* 13–14 (1982) / Boompjes, Rotterdam, 1980 **24** Frank Russell, ed., *Architectural Design Profile: Architecture in Progress—International Bauaustellung Berlin 1984* (London: Architectural Design, 1983) / Lützowstrasse Housing, Berlin, 1980 **25** *Casabella* 492 (1983) / Parc de la Villette, Paris, 1982 **26** *De Architect* 3 (1983) / Parc de la Villette, Paris, 1982 **27** *Modo* 58 (1983) / Boompjes: View from the Interior, Rotterdam, 1980 **28** *Architecture Mouvement Continuité* 6 (1984) / Parc de la Villette, Paris, 1982

29 *De Architect* 4 (1984) / Netherlands Dance Theater: First Version for Scheveningen, 1983 **30** *L'Architecture d'Aujourd'hui* 238 (1985) / Netherlands Dance Theater, The Hague: Still from Model Video, 1985 **31** *Haagse Post* 50 (1985) / Rem Koolhaas with a Model for Byzantium, Stadhouderskade Amsterdam (1985–1991) **32** *Vlees & Beton* 4 (1985) / Rem Koolhaas lecturing with Geert Bekaert in Rotterdam **33** *Arkitekten* 18 (1986) / Irish Prime Minister's Residence, Dublin, 1979 **34** *De Architect Thema: Het Beheer van de Stad (City Management)* 25 (1986) / Bijlmermeer Redevelopment, Amsterdam, 1986

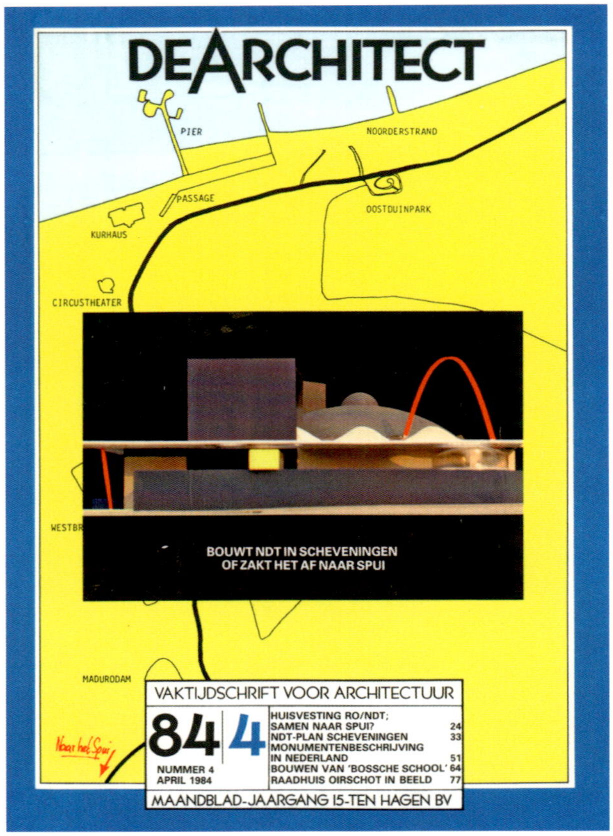

29

30

31

1984–1986

32

33

34

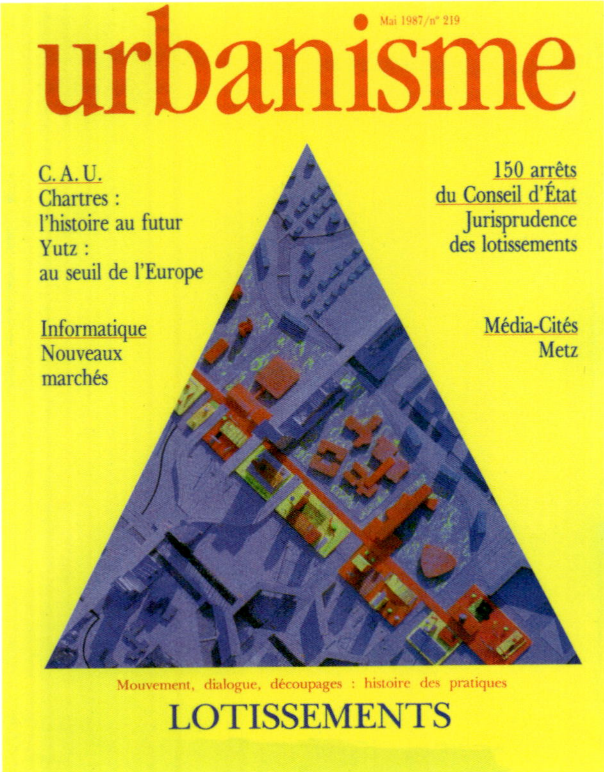
Mai 1987/n° 219
urbanisme
C.A.U.
Chartres :
l'histoire au futur
Yutz :
au seuil de l'Europe
Informatique
Nouveaux
marchés
150 arrêts
du Conseil d'État
Jurisprudence
des lotissements
Média-Cités
Metz
Mouvement, dialogue, découpages : histoire des pratiques
LOTISSEMENTS

35

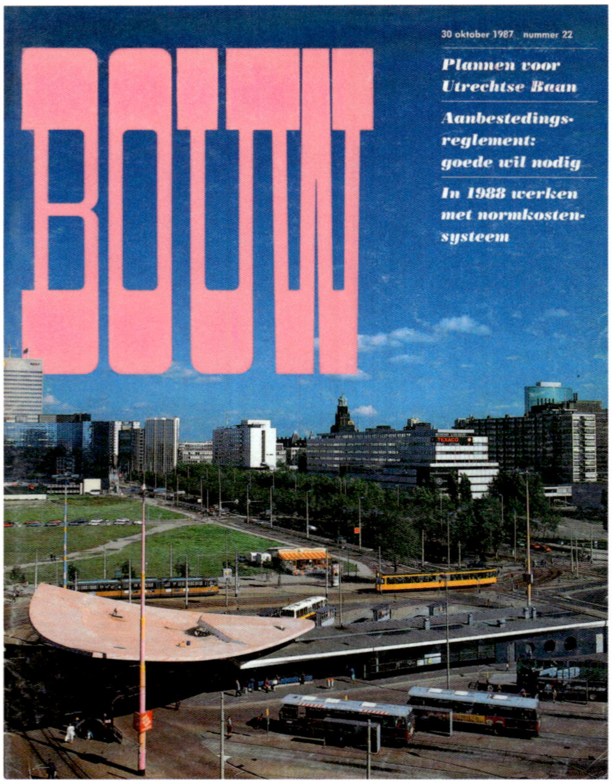
30 oktober 1987 nummer 22
BOUW
Plannen voor
Utrechtse Baan
Aanbestedings-
reglement:
goede wil nodig
In 1988 werken
met normkosten-
systeem

36

AMC
N° 18 / DECEMBRE 1987
REVUE D'ARCHITECTURE
90 F
I.M.A.
L'Institut du Monde Arabe
O.M.A. TRAVAUX DE
REM KOOLHAAS
Le théâtre de danse
de La Haye
JOURDA PERRAUDIN
L'école d'architecture
de Lyon
DES IMMEUBLES VILLAS / YANNIS KOKKOS / THÉÂTRE DES CHAMPS-ÉLYSÉES / DU BESSET-LYON-MORITA

37

1987–1988

38

39

40

35 *Urbanisme* 219 (1987) / Bijlmermeer Redevelopment, Amsterdam, 1986 **36** *Bouw* 22 (1987) / Central Station Bus Terminal, Rotterdam, 1985–1987 **37** *Architecture Mouvement Continuité* 18 (1987) / Netherlands Dance Theater, The Hague: Skybar, 1987 **38** *De Architect* 18 (1987) / Netherlands Dance Theater, The Hague, 1987 **39** *Quaderns d'arquitectura i urbanisme* 175 (1987) / Netherlands Dance Theater, The Hague: Rear Facade, 1987 **40** *A+U* 217 (1988) / Netherlands Dance Theater, The Hague, 1987

1988

41

ARCHITECTURAL
RECORD
Business Design Engineering
A McGraw-Hill Publication, Seven Dollars
April 1988

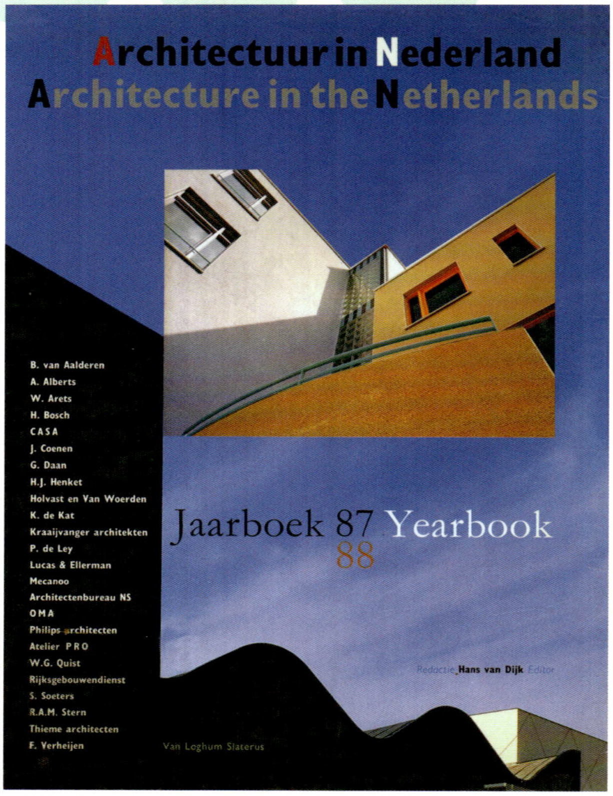
Architectuur in Nederland
Architecture in the Netherlands
B. van Aalderen
A. Alberts
W. Arets
H. Bosch
CASA
J. Coenen
G. Daan
H.J. Henket
Holvast en Van Woerden
K. de Kat
Kraaijvanger architekten
P. de Ley
Lucas & Ellerman
Mecanoo
Architectenbureau NS
OMA
Philips architecten
Atelier PRO
W.G. Quist
Rijksgebouwendienst
S. Soeters
R.A.M. Stern
Thieme architecten
F. Verheijen
Jaarboek 87 88 Yearbook
Redactie Hans van Dijk Editor
Van Loghum Slaterus

42

REVUE · INTERNATIONALE · D'ARCHITECTURE · ET · DE · DESIGN
techniques &
ARCHITECTURE
380
ÉMERGENCES DU PROJET
Art, philosophie, architecture, biologie, musique, scénographie
SIX ISSUES A YEAR. ISSN 0373-0719
INTERNATIONAL · REVIEW · OF · ARCHITECTURE · AND · DESIGN

43

41 *Architectural Record* 4 (1988) / Netherlands Dance Theater, The Hague: Box Office, 1987 **42** Hans van Dijk, ed., *Architecture in the Netherlands: Yearbook 1987–1988* (Rotterdam: NAi Publishers, 1988) / Netherlands Dance Theater, The Hague, 1987 **43** *Techniques & Architecture* 380 (1988) / Netherlands Dance Theater, The Hague: Axonometric Drawing, 1987 **44** *Blueprint* 44 (1988) / Boompjes, Rotterdam, 1980 **45** Carolina De Backer, ed., *Office for Metropolitan Architecture* (Antwerp: deSingel, 1988) / Netherlands Architecture Institute, Rotterdam: Model, 1988 **46** *Architectuur/Bouwen* 4 (1988) / Netherlands Architecture Institute, Rotterdam, 1988

44

45

46

47

1988–
1989

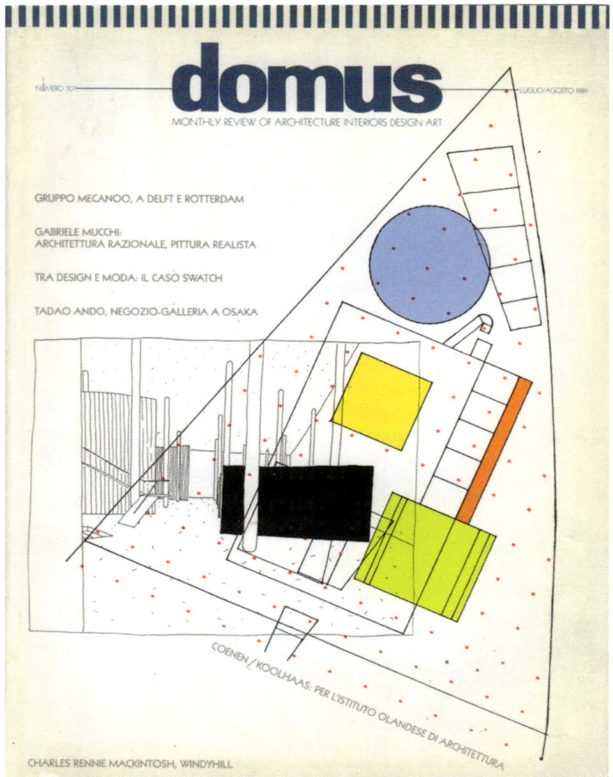

48

49

50

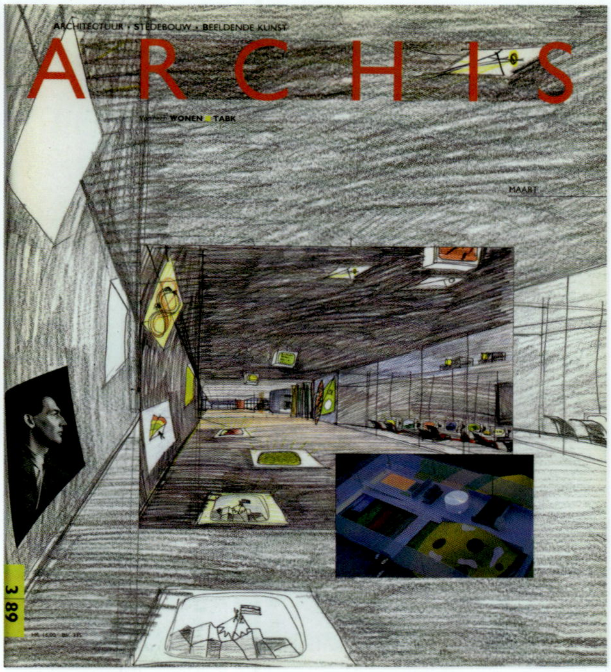

51

52

47 *De Architect* 7 (1988) / Netherlands Architecture Institute, Rotterdam, 1988 **48** *Domus* 707 (1989) / Netherlands Architecture Institute, Rotterdam, 1988 **49** *A+* 105 (1989) / Projects for Sea Trade Center, Zeebrugge, 1989: Bob van Reeth, Charles Vandenhove, Aldo Rossi, OMA/Rem Koolhaas, Fumihiko Maki **50** *Architecture Mouvement Continuité* 4 (1989) / Sea Trade Center, Zeebrugge, 1989 **51** *Archis* 3 (1989) / Sportmuseum, Flevohof, 1988 **52** *Bauwelt* 1–2 (1989) / Netherlands Dance Theater, The Hague: Lighting Bridge, 1987 / Photo Hans Werleman, Hectic Pictures

53

54

55

53 *Wiederhall* 9 (1989) / Villa dall'Ava, Paris, 1984–1991 / Drawing Madelon Vriesendorp **54** *Arquitectura Viva* 12 (1990) / Central Station Bus Terminal, Rotterdam: Interior, 1985–1987 **55** Josep Lluis Mateo, ed., *Rem Koolhaas: Urban Projects (1985–1990)* (Barcelona: Quaderns d'Arquitectura i Urbanisme, 1990) / Ville Nouvelle Mélun-Senart, 1987 **56** *De Architect* 5 (1990) / Checkpoint Charlie Apartments, Berlin, 1980–1990 **57** *Werk, Bauen + Wohnen* 3 (1990) / Très Grande Bibliothèque, Paris, 1989 **58** *De Architect Thema: Badcultuur (Bath Culture)* 42 (1991) / Casa Palestra, Milan Triennale, 1985–1986 **59** *Archis* 8 (1991) / Byzantium, Stadhouderskade Amsterdam, 1985–1991

56

57

58

1989–1991

59

LE MONITEUR
ARCHITECTURE
AMC
PAYSAGE
LE PARC DE CHAMPIGNY
DÉTAILS
LES MENUISERIES EN ACIER
TRIBUNE
VENTURI AUJOURD'HUI
LILLE
Une métropole européenne
LE MENSUEL VILLE ARCHITECTURE DESIGN

60

Themanummer 44 – Ten Hagen bv – september 1991
de Architect
HOTEL
METRO
Stationsgebieden

61

Jaargang 22 – Ten Hagen bv – december 1991
de Architect

62

1991

64

60 *Architecture Mouvement Continuité* 19 (1991) / Lille Grand Palais, 1990–1994   **61** *De Architect Thema: Stationsgebieden (Station Areas)* 44 (1991) / Euralille: Espace Piranésien, 1989–1994   **62** *De Architect* 22 (1991) / Nexus World Housing, Fukuoka, 1988–1991   **63** *Domus* 730 (1991) / Nexus World Housing, Fukuoka, 1988–1991   **64** *Progressive Architecture* 8 (1991) / Nexus World Housing, Fukuoka, 1988–1991   **65** Jacques Lucan, ed., *OMA/ Rem Koolhaas: Architecture 1970–1990* (New York: Princeton Architectural Press, 1991). Published in French, German and Italian editions. / Bijlmermeer Redevelopment, Amsterdam, 1986

63

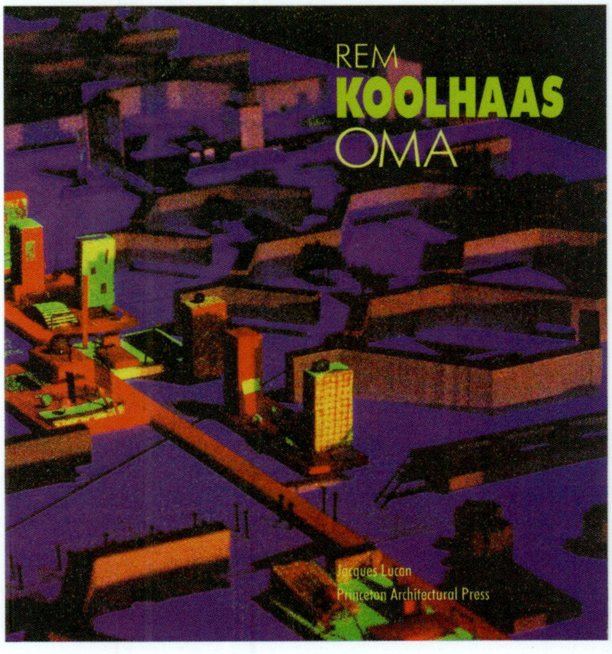

65

Arquitectura Viva
mero 23
Marzo-abril 1992
1.000 ptas
oolhaas y Holl: Fukuoka
entro penitenciario de Bonell / Rius
rtigues / Sanabria en Vallvidrera
Gallego en Sada: residencias
asas de Norten y Jiménez
istorias del cuerpo,
e Rotterdam a Chicago
icente Verdú: el hogar
El cuerpo doméstico
Cárceles y casas, anatomías habitables

66

ENGLISH SUMMARY
DiseñoInterior
INTERIOR ARCHITECTURE AND DESIGN FOR LIVING
FUKUOKA
EL EXPERIMENTO DE ISOZAKI
Holl, Koolhaas, Mack, Ishiyama,
Portzamparc y Tusquets
SILLAS
La generación del 92
OCTOPUS
La pieza clave de De Dur Lo
FERIAS
Europa, de Luminaire a Colonia

67

1992

L'ARCHITECTURE
D'AUJOURD'HUI
REM KOOLHAAS . LILLE
GROUPE EXPANSION
AV 92 N 280

68

69

70

71

66 *Arquitectura Viva* 23 (1992) / Nexus World Housing, Fukuoka, 1988–1991 **67** *Diseño Interior* 12 (1992) / Nexus World Housing, Fukuoka, 1988–1991 **68** *L'Architecture d'Aujourd'hui* 280 (1992) / Euralille, 1989–1994 **69** *El Croquis* 53 (1992) / Lille Grand Palais, 1990–1994 **70** *Architects' Journal*, March 11, 1992 / Villa dall'Ava, Paris, 1984–1991 **71** *Architecture Mouvement Continuité* 28 (1992) / Villa dall'Ava, Paris, 1984–1991

Jaargang 23 – Ten Hagen bv – maart 1992
de Architect

72

GA
Global Architecture
HOUSES
36

73

MARCH 1992
$4.00
HG
HOUSE & GARDEN
A Romantic Garden in Provence
Setting the Table with Style
Picasso's Still Lifes

74

NEWSLINE
COLUMBIA UNIVERSITY AVERY HALL NEW YORK NEW YORK 10027
SEPT/OCT '92
COLUMBIA
ARCHITECTURE
PLANNING
PRESERVATION
THIS ISSUE:
REM KOOLHAAS 2
LILLE IN NEW YORK
Open Forum
PIRANESI 3
PRESERVATION AT RISK
LAURETTA VINCIARELLI 4
MUSEUM OF MODERN ART
Exhibition Announcements
STANLEY ALLEN 5
On Projection
JULIUS POSENER
SASKIA SASSEN 6
NEW FACULTY
OF NOTE 7
SEMESTER SCHEDULE
AVERY EXHIBITIONS
REVIEW 8
Sexuality and Space
Review by Thomas Keenan
EXHIBITION NOTES
FALL LECTURES/EVENTS

75

72 *De Architect* 23 (1992) / Jean Nouvel visiting the Villa dall'Ava, Paris / Photo Hans Werleman, Hectic Pictures **73** *GA Houses* 36 (1992) / Villa dall'Ava, Paris, 1984–1991 **74** *House & Garden* 3 (1992) / Villa dall'Ava, Paris, 1984–1991 / Photo Hans Werleman, Hectic Pictures **75** *Newsline Columbia University*, September–October 1992 / Zentrum für Kunst und Medientechnologie, Karlsruhe, 1989, and Très Grande Bibliothèque, Paris, 1989 **76** *HP/De Tijd*, October 23, 1992 / Rem Koolhaas in the Kunsthal, Rotterdam ("The Sad Contradiction of a World-Famous Architect") **77** *Archis* 1 (1993) / Kunsthal, Rotterdam, 1988–1992 **78** *De Architect* 1 (1993) / Kunsthal, Rotterdam, 1988–1992

76

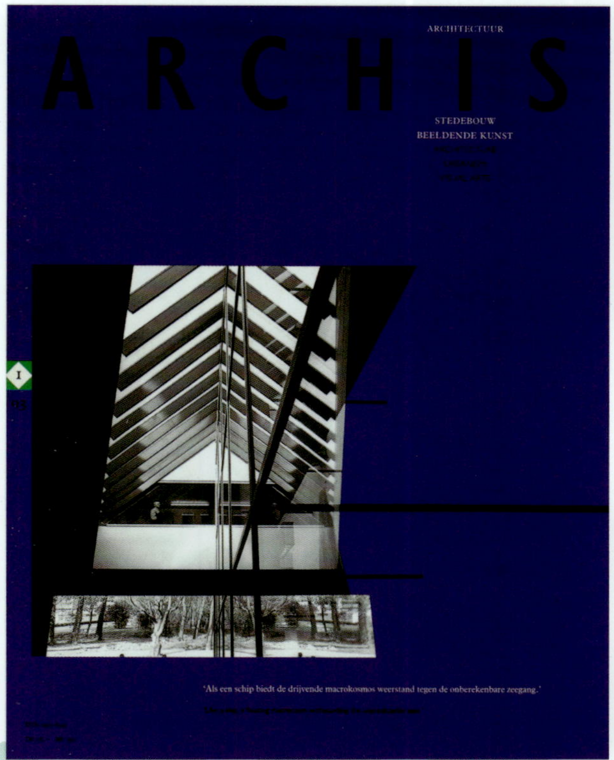

77

1992–1993

78

1993–1994

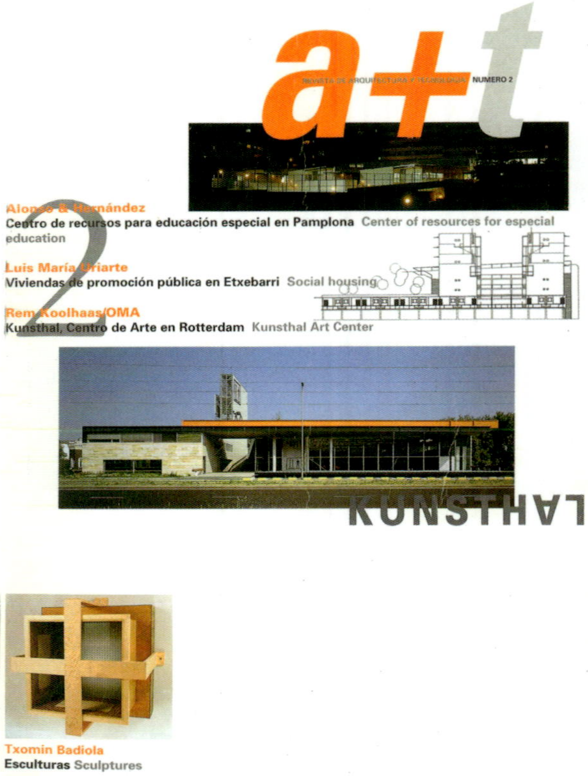

79

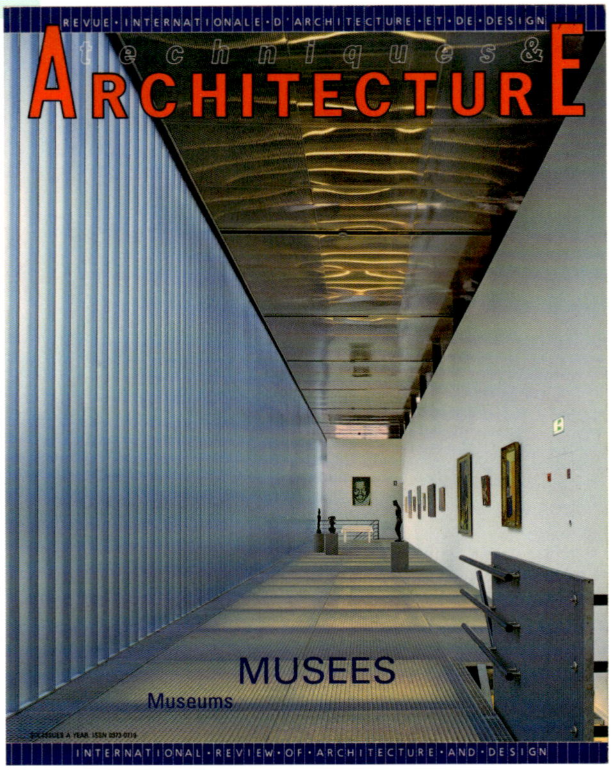

80

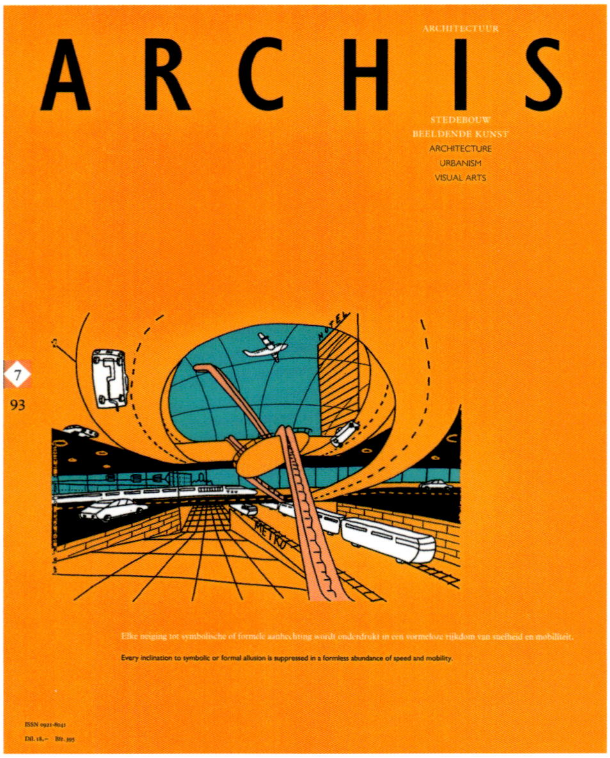

79 *a+t* 2 (1993) / Kunsthal, Rotterdam, 1988–1992
80 *Techniques & Architecture* 408 (1993) / Kunsthal, Rotterdam, 1988–1992 **81** *Archis* 7 (1993) / Euralille: Espace Piranésien, 1989–1994 **82** *AA Files* 26 (1993) / Jussieu—Two Libraries, Paris, 1992 **83** *ARCH+* 117 (1993) / Jussieu—Two Libraries, Paris, 1992 **84** *Artforum* 12 (1993) / Jussieu—Two Libraries, Paris, 1992
85 *De Architect* 1 (1994) / Jussieu—Two Libraries, Paris, 1992

81

82

AA files
JOURNALS OF THE ARCHITECTURAL ASSOCIATION SCHOOL OF ARCHITECTURE
26

83

ARCH+
Rem Koolhaas
Die Entfaltung der Architektur
Unfolding Architecture
Zeitung:
Kollhoffs
Bekehrung
Baumarkt:
Bad und Küche
117
Juni 1993
DM 24

ARTFORUM
INTERNATIONAL

84

85

Jaargang 25 – Ten Hagen & Stam bv – januari 1994
de Architect

86

建築と都市
Architecture and Urbanism
August 1994
No. 287
94:08
サナクセンアホ、グループ、
ジョヴァニーニ、ドメニル、
ツィフコヴィチ/コノリィ、ハイド/
リース、メイヤー/ファン・
ショーテン、コールハース、ウッズ
Sanaksenaho, Group,
Giovannini, deMenil,
Zivkovic/Connolly, Heide/Reese,
Meyer/van Schooten,
Koolhaas/OMA, Woods
a+u

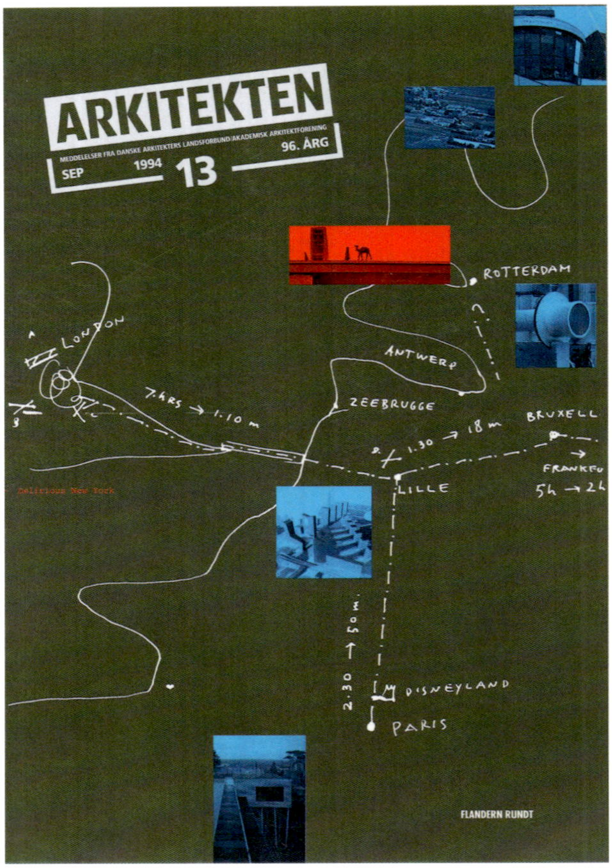
ARKITEKTEN
MEDDELELSER FRA DANSKE ARKITEKTERS LANDSFORBUND/AKADEMISK ARKITEKTFORENING
SEP
1994
13
96. ÅRG
ROTTERDAM
LONDON
ANTWERP
ZEEBRUGGE
BRUXELL
LILLE
DISNEYLAND
PARIS
FLANDERN RUNDT

87

THE LEADING MAGAZINE OF ARCHITECTURE & DESIGN • NOVEMBER 1994 • £3.50 • NO 112
BLUEPRINT
HEAVEN, HELL
AND REM
KOOLHAAS
ARRIBAS • CHALAYAN • DAY • HERRON • MIRALLES • MORRIS • WITTGENSTEIN

88

86 *A+U* 287 (1994) / Kunsthal, Rotterdam, 1988–1992
87 *Arkitekten* 13 (1994) / Euralille: Future Context, 1989–1994
88 *Blueprint* 112 (1994) / Lille Grand Palais: Interior, 1990–1994
89 *De Architect* 12 (1994) / Lille Grand Palais: Interior, 1990–1994 **90** *Werk, Bauen + Wohnen* 11 (1994) / Lille Grand Palais: Construction Site, 1990–1994 **91** *GA Houses* 43 (1994) / Dutch House, Holten, 1992–1995

90

1994

89

91

92

3-1995 APRIL
arkitektur
JO COENEN
KOOLHAAS
OMA
DERLÄNDERNA
MECANOO

CASABELLA
623
Nel paesaggio umbro: progetti di Francesco Cellini. A Graz: il nuovo aeroporto di Florian Riegler e Roger Riewe. A Città del Messico: la Scuola Nazionale di Teatro di TEN Arquitectos. Servizio su OMA a Euralille: le strategie progettuali dello sviluppo. Bruno Fortier sulle "amate città". Inizia, con Roma, una serie di ricognizioni sulle politiche urbane in Italia. Editoriale sul silenzio in architettura.
Rivista internazionale di architettura
International Architectural Review

93

ARCHITECTURAL RECORD
3/1995

94

1995–1996

95

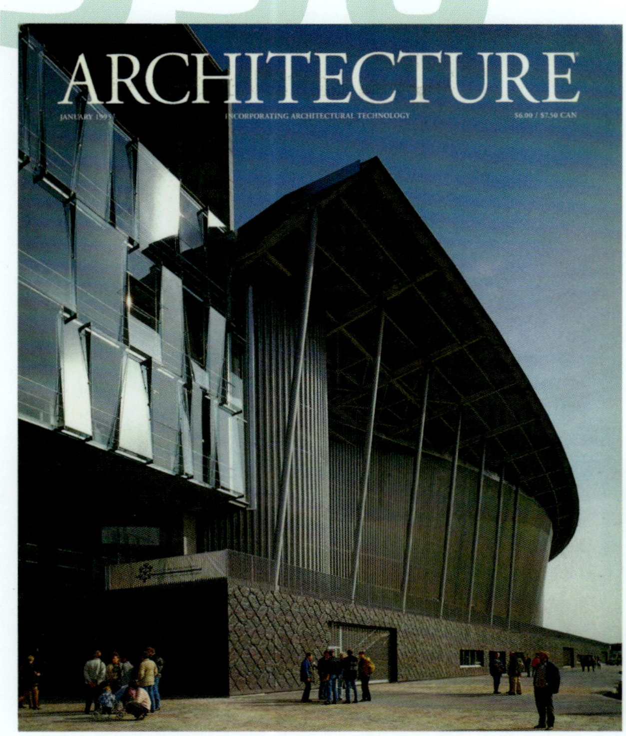

92 *Arkitektur* 3 (1995) / Kunsthal, Rotterdam, 1988–1992 / Photo Hans Werlemann, Hectic Pictures **93** *Casabella* 623 (1995) / Euralille, 1989–1994 **94** *Architectural Record* 3 (1995) / Lille Grand Palais, 1990–1994 **95** *Architecture* 1 (1995) / Lille Grand Palais, 1990–1994 **96** *d'Architectures* 60 (1995) / Lille Grand Palais, 1990–1994 **97** *Architecture Today* 55 (1995) / Lille Grand Palais: Vauban Auditorium, 1990–1994 **98** *Daidalos—Magic of Materials II* (1995) / Lille Grand Palais, Detail Facade, 1990–1994 **99** *Baumeister* 4 (1995) / Lille Grand Palais, 1990–1994 **100** *El Croquis* 79 (1996) / Rem Koolhaas

97

96

DAIDALOS
MAGIE DER WERKSTOFFE MAGIC OF MATERIALS II

98

bAUMEISTER
■ Thema: Wächst alles zusammen, werden wir international? Oder bauen nur bekannte und etablierte Architekturbüros überall dort ihre unverwechselbaren Standards, wo man sie läßt? **Große Europäer** allemal? Fünf aktuelle Bauten zwischen Den Haag und Leipzig stehen für die Vielfalt der Auffassungen ■ Fokus: Kostenermittlung durch EDV-Einsatz ■ Recht: Rechnungsstellung ■ Exkursion: Neue Architektur in Karlsruhe
Zeitschrift für Architektur 4 April 1996

99

1992 1996
oma / rem koolhaas
EL croquis
79

100

OMA / REM KOOLHAAS

A CRITICAL READER FROM *DELIRIOUS NEW YORK* TO *S,M,L,XL*

OMA REM KOOL-HAAS
A CRITICAL READER

CHRISTOPHE VAN GERREWEY (ED.)

BIRKHÄUSER
BASEL

INTRODUCTION: SUSPENDED MEANING

Thought alone, the fruit of labor, is transmissible.
Le Corbusier, *Mise au Point*

His work cannot be categorized merely as historical, like anyone else's, but it intended to be so and understood itself as such.
Walter Benjamin, *Charles Baudelaire: A Lyric Poet in the Era of High Capitalism*

The most important task of architecture is to provoke writing and thinking. If this is true, then the work of Rem Koolhaas and his many collaborators is extraordinary. The activities of Koolhaas as a writer and a (paper) architect have received reaction, mediation, and interpretation, even before the foundation of the Office for Metropolitan Architecture in January 1975. The work of OMA has been talked and written about in the languages of Western architecture culture, to the extent that it can be regarded as the foundation of an ever-growing Tower of Babel, consisting of diverse texts, commenting on specific projects but reaching out to a variety of topics.

This is not exclusively an achievement of the work itself. The first twenty-five years of OMA's existence coincide with the efflorescence of combinations of theory, history, and criticism to approach architecture, with the proliferation of journals and exhibitions, and with a growing general interest in the discipline. Architecture seemed close to becoming a full-fledged part of culture, as one of the manifestations, within the arts, of intellectual achievement regarded more or less collectively. In 1981 French philosopher Hubert Damisch ascertained this evolution in *Architecture Mouvement Continuité*, in an issue with OMA's project for Boompjes in Rotterdam on the cover. "At the point where we are in this century," Damisch wrote, "things have the merit of being clear: either architecture will become an integral part of culture, or we can cross out one and the other."[1] Whether this prediction has become true is another matter, but the oeuvre of OMA, or more precisely its variegated reception, does prove it: during the 1970s, 1980s, and 1990s the promise of architecture as an equal part of culture—on a par with, let's say, literature, visual art, or film—loomed on the horizon, while the academic research of architecture as an autonomous field of knowledge continued to grow, though not to the levels of specialization, away from contemporary practice, experienced since the turn of the century. The work of OMA, for many reasons, nearly begged to be understood and analyzed in an historical time frame—defined by relative prosperity, an unproblematized hegemony of the Western world, and a public sphere with the printed word as the main location of intellectual authority—in which the conditions to consume, to enjoy, and to discuss architecture were more than favorable.

While it is not difficult to develop, for these reasons, some kind of nostalgia for the final decades of the twentieth century, it is important to remember that this situation was substantially criticized at the moment it came into being. Although he only once referred to OMA—mentioning the "'jokes' of Koolhaas"[2] in an enumeration of practices—Manfredo Tafuri's analysis of the new spheres of architectonic production in the 1970s remains essential to understand the context in which Koolhaas & Company started to work. In an article entitled "The Ashes of Jefferson," published in 1976 in an issue of *L'Architecture d'Aujourd'hui* with a drawing from the *New York* series by Madelon Vriesendorp on its cover, Tafuri reflected on the New York scene that was developing around the Institute for Architecture and Urban Studies, where Koolhaas became a research fellow in 1973 and would work on *Delirious New York*. These architects from the 1970s, Tafuri wrote, had become part of "an intellectual elite" that necessarily reduced its activities to a solipsistic conversation about formal and linguistic problems. The organization of labor had gradually secluded architects into an isolated bubble. "Once high levels of comprehensive integration in the determining sectors have been reached, it becomes possible to maintain well-defined cultural spaces, entrusted with the task of pleasurably entertaining a highly select public."[3] This analysis more or less sealed the fate of what has become known, to this day, as "contemporary architecture": an intellectual and cultural activity that seems to have no profound consequences for the organization of society. Tafuri argued how architects had been exiled to a kind of deer park, while the rest of the world carried on with business as usual. "New circuits of production and use do come to be created: architecture comes to be exhibited in its own *cinemas d'essai*. But there is no hope for architecture to influence structures or relations of production: no reformative hypothesis appears to have the right of sanctuary in the new monasteries in which patient monks transcribe and comment upon the codices of the modern tradition."[4]

Koolhaas and OMA have without a doubt tried to expand both the audience and the tools of architectonic production to such a degree that one can wonder if what we talk about when we talk about OMA can still be considered architecture. But despite differences in temperament, preferences, and strategy, OMA does share Tafuri's assumption—following the classic Marxist divide between base and superstructure—that architecture is always a consequence of economy and politics; vice versa, architecture can't change the way things are in a capitalist society. The crucial distinction is, however, that for Koolhaas this subordination of architecture should not be a tragedy. On the contrary: freed from the old humanist obligation to improve upon the world, as well as from nostalgia or nihilism, architecture can develop on its own terms, as an activity that is exciting, provocative, and stimulating, not only for the architect, but also for the many "patient monks" who are prepared to comment upon its qualities and meanings. Belgian critic Geert Bekaert, who was one of the first to write extensively on OMA in Koolhaas's mother tongue, has commented on the possibilities this created, in an interview in 2001 with Pier Vittorio Aureli and Saskia Kloosterboer: "Koolhaas's merit is his ability to free himself, in an unbelievably intelligent manner, from outdated theoretical standpoints. To see architecture as a sort of self-evident discipline at the service of a concrete problematic. Koolhaas's charm was that he gave the impression that there was no problem in architecture."[5]

1 Hubert Damisch, "Pourquoi le XXe siècle," *Architecture Mouvement Continuité* 54–55 (1981), 134.
2 Manfredo Tafuri, "The Ashes of Jefferson," in *The Sphere and the Labyrinth: Avant-Gardes and Architecture from Piranesi to the 1970s* (Cambridge, MA: The MIT Press, 1987), 300. The reference to Koolhaas was absent in the French version of the article published in *L'Architecture d'Aujourd'hui* 186 (1976), 53–58.
3 Ibid., 293.
4 Ibid.
5 Pier Vittorio Aureli and Saskia Kloosterboer, "No History as History, No Theory as Theory: Conversation with Geert Bekaert," *Hunch* 4 (2001), 44.

Although OMA is part of a generation of architects who accepted the conditions of this architectonic "boudoir,"[6] it is not an exaggeration to claim that Koolhaas tried to occupy its walls and stretch its boundaries, if only to hold up to his fellow architects a funhouse mirror or a deadly serious one, depending on one's point of view. To do so, the work of OMA had to be, from the beginning, provocative, elusive, and ungraspable. The texts collected in this anthology can be summarized as the search for answers to one and the same question: What could it all possibly mean? That some architects presented their work as an open invitation to interpretation was nothing new, but it did become explicit during the 1960s, as is shown for example by the seminal essay from 1967, "*La Dimension Amoureuse* in Architecture" by George Baird, an important early OMA interpreter.[7] It had become impossible for architects to maintain, Baird argued, that their projects had a fixed and intentional meaning, communicable in a transparent and rational way. The "enamored dimension in architecture"—the staging of the desire for meaning, which should never be completely fulfilled—would become dominant in the work of Koolhaas's generation, and of that of OMA in particular. On a methodological and theoretical level, this implied a growing importance of semiology (the study of how signs produce meaning) and of structuralism (the uncovering of the defining but often invisible interrelations between human activities)—an evolution that can be traced comprehensively by applying the writings of literary critic and theoretician Roland Barthes to architecture, or by reconstructing how they have been applied. To explore the work of OMA and its critical reception, Roland Barthes is still the best guide, which also indicates how architecture—and its criticism, theory, and history—shifted in the direction of literature in the period in which Koolhaas started working. In a text published in the *Times Literary Supplement* in 1963, Barthes tried to answer the question "What Is Criticism?" He argued that it can never be the critic's task to reveal the one and only truth of a work of art or literature, for example by naively reconstructing the intentions of the author or the artist. Work that one-dimensionally lends itself to this kind of activity is boring and bad; work that, on the contrary, "is never entirely non-signifying (mysterious or 'inspired'), and never entirely clear" can claim the label "good," exactly because it "accedes to critical scrutiny." This kind of work "is, one may say, a *suspended meaning*: it offers itself to the reader as an avowed signifying system yet withholds itself from him as a signified object."[8]

This act of both offering and withholding meaning is typical for architecture culture during the second half of the twentieth century, and for the work of OMA in particular: it does not stop provoking questions—and texts with attempts to answer them. Tafuri was, again, rather skeptical about this interplay between architects and critics. In "The Ashes of Jefferson," he, too, referred to Barthes, to indicate how this erotic play of question and answer may have intellectual merits, but, unfortunately, "no 'social' value." Nevertheless, he argued that these architectures did "reveal to the very depths the condition in which he who still wants to make 'Architecture' is confined."[9] Revelation, and the production of thought and of knowledge—no matter

6 To refer to another article of Tafuri about the fate of contemporary architecture in the 1970s, see "L'architecture dans le boudoir," also included in *The Sphere and the Labyrinth*, 276–90 (see note 2).

7 George Baird, "'La Dimension Amoureuse' in Architecture," in *Meaning in Architecture*, ed. Charles Jencks and George Baird (New York: George Braziller, 1969), 79–99.

8 Roland Barthes, "What Is Criticism?" in *Critical Essays*, trans. Richard Howard (Evanston: Northwestern University Press, 1972), 259.

9 Manfredo Tafuri, "The Ashes of Jefferson," 302 (see note 2).

how uncertain, subjective or unstable—is what the collaboration between an architect like Koolhaas and his critics did offer to society.

If the work of OMA asks to be interpreted, then the result of this activity inevitably reflects the way things are. Dealing with Koolhaas means dealing with contemporaneity, modernity, and history. In a conversation in 1994, Oswald Mathias Ungers—a teacher of Koolhaas in the US during the early 1970s, and an architect whose initials are supposed to have inspired the naming of OMA,[10] has spoken without restraint about his former pupil. "I regard him highly as an intellectual, as a writer, and as an architect. But he tries to be a 'modern man.' He tries to transform the consumer-attitude into an artistic expression. He will never end this because he is always concerned with updating."[11] OMA projects have tried to formalize and even exaggerate changes by means of architecture, rather than to oppose them, although this does not mean that the work of OMA hasn't been reactive or critical toward architectonic developments. *Il faut être absolument moderne*—it is true for Koolhaas, but only following this definition of Peter Sloterdijk: "The real foundation of modernity is not revolution, but explicitation."[12] The strategy of OMA is to make things architectonically visible—to imagine the immediate future *just before it takes place*. The famous aphorism by Karl Krauss that Manfredo Tafuri applied to the American work of Mies van der Rohe—"Since the facts have the floor, let anyone who has anything to say come forward and keep his mouth shut"[13]—can be adjusted to the case of Koolhaas: "Since the facts have the floor, let's talk about them while talking about the work of OMA."

It is a welcome advantage of this method that everything that happens, no matter how terrible, seems in retrospect—it is the main strategy behind *Delirious New York*—to be coauthored or ghostwritten; facing the consequences of your own creation is always preferable to having to deal with a fait accompli. If Koolhaas is a voluntary prisoner of architecture (to refer to the subtitle of "Exodus" from 1972), he will never allow himself to be a victim of history. This implies that the work of OMA is not modern in the more idealistic (and less conservative) sense: it does not express a devout faith in that other kind of modernity—of trying to modernize society, improve everyone's living and working conditions, combat inequality, and emancipate or even liberate as many people as possible. Another definition of modernity can be inserted here, by Roland Barthes, from 1973: "Being modern means to know what is no longer possible."[14] Koolhaas not only tracks down the impossibilities caused by the storm of progress, but also shows them by developing the options that he already deems unavoidable—options that are, of course, often (but not always) quite productive for an architectural office. This can be tied to OMA's wish to remain avant-garde—to abandon previous achievements and to reveal what is new for a specific era without worrying too much about the value of these "cutting-edge" developments.

The tendency to shelve Koolhaas and everything he and his office did as capitalist, neoliberal, and reprehensible is therefore not only a one-sided reaction that sidesteps theoretical and historical considerations—it also misses the point. The work of

10 See Lara Schrijver, "OMA as Tribute to OMU: Exploring Resonances in the Work of Koolhaas and Ungers," *The Journal of Architecture* 3 (2008), 235–61.

11 Ole Bouman, Roemer van Toorn, "Le Style, c'est l'homme: A Conversation with Oswald Mathias Ungers," in *The Invisible in Architecture* (London: Academy Editions, 1994), 58.

12 Peter Sloterdijk, *Sphären III: Schäume* (Frankfurt am Main: Suhrkamp, 2004), 87.

13 Manfredo Tafuri, *Modern Architecture*, trans. Robert Erich Wolf (New York: Harry N. Abrams, 1979), 339.

14 Roland Barthes, "Requichot et son corps," in *Oeuvres complètes* (Paris: Seuil, 2002), 4:397.

OMA from the 1970s, 1980s, and 1990s remains, together with its critical reception, highly suitable for an understanding of the decades that immediately precede—and explain—life in the twenty-first century. Koolhaas made architecture—together with everything that touches upon it—negotiable and discursive, without clearly indicating how all these negotiations and conversations could lead to a better world. But as both Antonio Negri and Pier Vittorio Aureli have suggested, the kind of historical knowledge this work can yield might nevertheless be a prerequisite for change.[15]

The open work of OMA welcomes criticism. Koolhaas has allowed critical interpretation, sometimes with indignation about superficial results, and sometimes with a remarkable reticence. In a conversation with Bart Verschaffel and Camiel van Winkel in 2004, he refused to answer a question about intentionally empty and unusable spaces in OMA projects: "That's a statement from a critic. I recognize what you're saying and what you're aiming at, I believe. But I won't say: yes, that's right. I don't want to banalize your role. Sometimes you're totally right, sometimes totally not. In both cases it's an enrichment."[16] Despite this generosity (of granting validity to opposing interpretations), the work of OMA has been overshadowed by the words of Koolhaas himself—a paradoxical situation of which the eloquent and self-conscious architect is well aware. "This is in a way the difficulty of my whole career," Koolhaas confessed to Enrique Walker in 2013, "that it has been mostly defined in my own words, rather than in the words of others. Which I think is a real problem."[17] Not only is Koolhaas the only author of the essays in OMA's massive career overview *S,M,L,XL*, he has always (supposedly) delivered the key concepts and stories to understand his work in essays but also (and probably more dominantly) in countless interviews.

At the same time, Koolhaas has tried to be faster than his own shadow, or to leave no shadow at all. Looking back on past achievements—or inviting others to do so—is something Koolhaas seldom does. Instead of folding back on past realizations and wielded strategies, and to properly theorize or criticize them, Koolhaas has often chosen to hurl OMA into an uncertain future. On this continuous urge for renewal, this fear of boredom and the desire for molting that results from it, his former partner and cofounder of OMA Elia Zenghelis said in 2005: "When I asked Koolhaas why we had to turn our back so fast on what we had just done so well, his answer was that it was necessary to be ahead of being consumed."[18]

The major disadvantage of this swiftness is that OMA has likewise stayed ahead of being properly and comprehensively understood. This certainly doesn't mean that there haven't been attempts at interpreting the work of OMA—on the contrary—but it does imply that the contemporary reception took place in very different contexts and languages (in both the literal and figurative sense), at a high speed (*S,M,L,XL* was, for example, already reviewed even before it was published), and without many well-organized moments "to catch its breath" by looking back.[19] In an essay about the work of Jeff Wall, Tom Holert has argued that critics writing about an artist form a "discourse society," a term from Michel Foucault's inaugural lecture at the Collège de France in 1970.[20] Around every major artist (or architect) a group of

15 Antonio Negri, "On Rem Koolhaas," trans. Arianna Bove, *Radical Philosophy* 154 (2009), 48–50; Pier Vittorio Aureli, "Architecture and Counterrevolution: OMA and the Politics of the *grands projets*," *OASE* 94 (2015), 44–52.

16 Bart Verschaffel, Camiel van Winkel, "'Ik ben verbluft over de rechten die het artistieke zich aanmeet': Vraaggesprek met Rem Koolhaas," *De Witte Raaf* 109 (2004), 4.

17 "Rem Koolhaas in Conversation with Enrique Walker: Amsterdam, October 16, 2013," in *The Ordinary: Recordings*, ed. Enrique Walker (New York: Columbia Books on Architecture and the City, 2018), 13.

18 Elia Zenghelis, "Text and Architecture: Architecture as Text," in *Exit Utopia: Architectural Provocations 1956–76*, ed. Martin van Schaik and Otakar Mácel (New York: Prestel, 2005), 262.

19 One exception is the volume edited by Jacques Lucan, with contributions by Jean-Louis Cohen and Hubert Damisch, published in French in 1990, and translated in 1991 in English as *OMA/Rem Koolhaas: Architecture 1970–1990*, ed. Jacques Lucan (New York: Princeton Architectural Press, 1991).

critics is formed, and together they define the major, often conflicting themes and motives that circulate around this oeuvre. In the case of Koolhaas, and especially in the years prior to 2000, one could say that instead of a discourse society there is a kind of "lost civilization"—a very diverse collection of people that was never effectively assembled, but that nevertheless "collectively" wrote (and read) about OMA's work. Only the king himself of this civilization is today still communicative, well-known, and addressed, while the texts of its members are forgotten, dispersed, and hidden in archived journals, out-of-print essay collections, and nondigitalized magazines; a large part of them has never been available in English. This situation has led to a kind of amnesia in the more recent (and post-2000) reception of OMA, both in the academic world and in general culture. Only a few interviews, well-known notions, and classic anecdotes return—not coincidentally almost without exception derived from *Delirious New York*, *S,M,L,XL*, or the two (self-curated) OMA issues of *El Croquis* from 1992 and 1996.

20 Tom Holert, "Interview with a Vampire: Subjectivity and Visuality in the Works of Jeff Wall," in *Jeff Wall: Photographs*, ed. Achim Hochdörfer (Vienna: Museum Moderner Kunst Stiftung Ludwig, 2003), 132.

The selection of texts in this anthology is based on this paradoxical predicament: we are dealing with an architectonic oeuvre that lends itself to a nearly endless deciphering and discussion, that is narrowed down to a set of intentions, pronunciations, reproaches, catchphrases, and clichés. To face this situation, a proper and multilingual critical bibliography of OMA was drawn up, composed of texts written—more or less—in between the publication of *Delirious New York* (1978) and *S,M,L,XL* (1995). All of these texts are contemporary: they are written as immediate (or almost) reactions to the projects, books, or buildings under review. These texts don't benefit or suffer from an historical distance, and they are the result of the decision of one or more authors to confront the recent cultural production of OMA/Rem Koolhaas—to try to divest meaning from it, to evaluate, understand, compare, contextualize, or historicize it, to use it as a lens to get a better look at contemporary culture—and, in the end, to love or to hate it. The reasons to limit this selection to the period between the early 1970s and the late 1990s are diverse. This series of texts is literally bookended between two books and their reception: *Delirious New York* and *S,M,L,XL*—arguably (and for instance compared to the somewhat cynically produced *Content* from 2004) the most important written achievements of Koolhaas to date, and unsurpassed as theoretical statements on (or next to) OMA's production. Secondly, there is more than enough material available from these twenty-five years, certainly when the aim is to give a detailed, exact, but still compact overview. And thirdly: there is a curious unity to this period, not only content-wise but also in terms of the nature of the texts. Simply put, after *S,M,L,XL*, the conditions for architectural production and for architectural criticism changed rather drastically. As Andrew Leach has argued, the publication of *S,M,L,XL* in 1995 defined "a new pragmatism in architecture against which the idea of the postcritical defined itself: not spurring criticality in architecture, but reuniting criticism with architectural production in terms that negated the institutional positioning of architectural criticism."[21] Although this might (again) appear to be an analysis with nostalgic un-

21 Andrew Leach, "It's Not Me, It's You," in *On Discomfort*, ed. David Ellison and Andrew Leach (London: Routledge, 2017), 105.

dertones, the culture of magazines and books—on paper—is intertwined with this institutional idea of criticism, and the advent and success of the Internet is inversely proportional to profound critical writing and collective reception. Since 2000, in an evolution that was put in motion (or at least announced) by *S,M,L,XL*, architectural discourse is split between a not so much contemporary but rather simultaneous reception and reproduction online, and an academic industry that has, in an ongoing process of scientification and rationalization, drained both contemporary architecture as a subject as well as the critical distinction between good or bad options.

The questions posed to sift the more or less 600 substantial texts on OMA published in the twentieth century (or at least dealing with projects included in *S,M,L,XL*, as well as with the book itself), were the following. Does the author reveal aspects of the work of OMA that weren't previously under consideration? Are things being told that can be important for the (theoretical but also factual) understanding of the reviewed projects, and that haven't been collected or noted elsewhere? Does the text mark a kind of event—is it a moment of reception that has introduced a new phase in OMA's oeuvre to a particular audience, or that has ended such a phase, possibly for Koolhaas himself? Has the publication a kind of anecdotal but at the same time historical value, because it occurred in a surprising, popular, or unusual "circuit of production"? In the case of an interview, is Koolhaas (without a doubt, in this period, a very outspoken commentator on his own work but also on that of colleagues) confronted with unexpected questions that make it impossible to recite rhetorically his concerns at that moment? Does the author take a moral, philosophical, political, or aesthetic position in order to defend or praise Koolhaas or to condemn and reject his choices as dangerous, unethical, or troublesome? And is architectural criticism deployed as a scalpel rather than as a stethoscope, not to listen but to cut to the heart of the matter—of OMA's work, of the art of building, but also of the world and of modern life in general?

Based on these criteria, about 150 texts—book reviews, interviews, reportages, round tables, essays, exhibition reviews, editorials, opinion pieces, letters, introductions, building appraisals, competition reports and pieces of journalism—were selected and reproduced on the following pages, often in abbreviated form to avoid factual repetitions or well-known insights. A third has been translated for this occasion; for reasons of comprehension and accessibility, some have been retitled—the original title is available in the bibliography. The texts are divided into ten groups and chapters, devoted to one project (Spear House, Dance Theater The Hague, Villa dall'Ava, and Kunsthal Rotterdam), to one period (1978–1985, 1986–1989, 1989–1996), or to one book or essay (*Delirious New York*, "Bigness," and *S,M,L,XL*). Each chapter is introduced to summarize the historical context, to explain interpretative challenges and critical strategies, and to refer to more recent literature. The anthology concludes with a full critical bibliography of the work of OMA/Rem Koolhaas up to (and including) *S,M,L,XL*.

As will be clear by now, this is not a book about images—on the contrary. The images to illustrate these texts are exactly one hundred cover shoots—the result of, each time, an editorial decision to put a work of OMA (or in a few cases a picture of Koolhaas) in pole position. The magazine cover is a phenomenon that largely belongs to a previous stage of our image culture, in which the image itself was not the goal, but only the invitation to browse through the pages, to read, and to consider the ideas behind the image. For anyone familiar with the history of OMA, it is not surprising that it takes almost fifteen years before a photograph of a building is featured on a cover, rather than a drawing or a collage. But this also indicates that architecture and its reception shouldn't be limited to built projects: in the case of OMA, the most trenchant notions and unexpected views—and the best texts—are often the result of aborted or theoretical proposals.

The first time I was introduced to the work of OMA/Rem Koolhaas it was, if I remember well, with a warning. As a first-year architecture student at Ghent University, Belgium, in 2000, eighteen years old, I attended the course "Architectural Actualia" of professor Mil De Kooning. For an entire semester, he discussed and criticized late-twentieth-century oeuvres—no architectural education should start without a profound introduction to contemporary architecture. De Kooning confessed that he had been talking, earlier that day, with his colleague Bart Verschaffel about the lecture on Koolhaas he was about to give. "Tell them," Verschaffel had said with a grin, "that they should never trust him." This introduction made the enigmatic work of OMA all the more attractive, as did the many texts on OMA that I was about to read during my education the following five years, if not written by De Kooning or Verschaffel then provided by them. It was also under their guidance that I made a PhD on the work of the late Belgian critic Geert Bekaert, whose both disinterested and passionate approach to architecture, as well as to life itself, remains an example, challenging and comforting at the same time. Without the three of them this book wouldn't exist.

I don't remember when the idea occurred for the first time to critically anthologize OMA, but conversations with many people precede that primary intuition. I have fond memories of OMA exchanges—both very theoretical and very frivolous, but not necessarily less enlightening—with Pier Vittorio Aureli, Jeroen Beerten, Roger Conover, Cynthia Davidson, Michiel Dehaene, Maarten Delbeke, Benjamin Eggermont, Job Floris, Adrian Forty, Xaveer De Geyter, Andrew Leach, Maarten Liefooghe, Willem Jan Neutelings, Joan Ockman, Freek Persyn, Daniël Rovers, Jan De Ruyver, Francis Strauven, Léa-Catherine Szacka, Thomas Weaver, and Rem Koolhaas himself. Many texts and images in this book couldn't have been collected (and digitized) without now and then a slight bending of library rules, and I would like to thank in particular Rik Vanmoerkerke and Mieken Osselaer from the library at the Department of Architecture and Urban Planning at Ghent University. It was a privilege to edit in 2015 an issue of *OASE* on OMA's First Decade together with Véronique Patteeuw, and this collection is both a sequel to and an extension of *What Is OMA?*, the volume she edited in 2003.[22]

It was Kersten Geers who convinced me to start working in 2015 at EPFL in Lausanne, where the work on this book was funded, but I owe him much more than that, and our talks about (among many other things) OMA—sometimes (and quite fittingly) before, after, or even during swimming sessions—were always reveal-

22 *What Is OMA? Considering Rem Koolhaas and the Office for Metropolitan Architecture*, ed. Véronique Patteeuw (Rotterdam: NAi Publishers, 2003).

23 Roberto Gargiani, *Rem Koolhaas/OMA: The Construction of Merveilles* (Lausanne: EPFL Press, 2008).

ing. Among my other colleagues in Switzerland, I would like to mention Roberto Gargiani, whose book from 2008 has become the bible for OMA studies,[23] and Luca Ortelli, who guided me throughout academic life. The study of the Kunsthal in Rotterdam that Tibor Pataky is conducting under my supervision as a PhD student has provided me more insights than I am aware of, and the same goes for the philosophical explorations of André Patrão. The office of Iannis Goerlandt (D'onderkast) has taken care of Dutch, French, German, and Italian translations; Nele Noppen translated from the Japanese. The results now and then seem to outrank the original texts. During the last stages of the conception of this book, Stéphanie Savio has carefully read and commented upon the manuscript, and her editorial assistance—in contacting the authors involved, for example, but also in tracing down Japanese articles—has been indispensable. Finally, I would like to thank everyone at Birkhäuser, Alexander Felix and Regina Herr in particular.

In daily life, the support of my parents and of Evelien is so fundamental that it is all too easily forgotten—without the three of them, I wouldn't exist. But if this anthology wants to prove something, it is also that the distinction between daily and professional life, or between living, architecture, criticism, history, and theory is—or should be—a false one. Why would we occupy ourselves with architecture, if it wouldn't be for biographical, personal, daily, and existential reasons—to deal with problems that are very much our own, and to find concepts, ideas, and words to at least understand them? In a world and in an architecture culture that seems dominated on the one hand by research, science, big data, tech transfers, peer review, the quest for funding and the striving for unambiguous correctness and transparency (which is the striving for meaninglessness) and on the other by Instagram posts, tweets, comments, digital images, updates, headlines, likes, and dislikes, this book is an homage to (architectural) writing and reading.

Christophe Van Gerrewey, March 2019

SPEAR HOUSE (1975): A GREAT DISAPPOINT-MENT OR A VERY MARVELOUS THING

1

OMA was founded in London on January 1, 1975, by Rem Koolhaas, Madelon Vriesendorp, and Elia and Zoe Zenghelis. Their first project predates the office: its members had been collaborating since 1971 on "Exodus, or the Voluntary Prisoners of Architecture," officially considered as the first work of OMA/Rem Koolhaas. "Exodus" was submitted to the competition *La città come ambiente significante*, organized in the autumn of 1971 by the Associazone per il Disegno Industriale of Milan and the Italian magazine *Casabella*, that published the project on its pages and its cover in June 1973.[1]

Another kind of debut is marked by someone else's criticism—by external interpretation and public analysis. The first time a project by Koolhaas and a collaborator was discussed at length, in a text of nearly 1,000 words and in a form presented for posterity, is marked by the 22nd Annual Awards Program in 1974 of *Progressive Architecture* and the American Institute of Architects. The program received 737 submissions, with 611 in the category for architectural design, 101 for planning and urban design, and 25 for applied research. The architecture jury consisted of Peter Chermayeff, Peter Eisenman, Eberhard H. Zeidler, and Paul Rudolph as chairman—a set of very different personalities, and none of the six awards and seven citations were unanimous. One entry was put in pole position and published (in the form of an expanded projection) on the cover of *Progressive Architecture* in January 1975—a design for a house on the waterfront in a suburban neighborhood in Florida (the other awarded teams were led by Don M. Hisaka, Marvin Hatami, Myers and Bennett, MLTW/Turnbull, and Booth & Nagle).

This project was made by Remment Koolhaas and Laurinda Spear, one of Koolhaas's students at Columbia University. It looks like a domestic small-scale and doubled version of Exodus, as a set of four walls in different materials (natural stone, ceramic panels, aluminum louvered doors, and glass brick), placed parallel to the water, creating three different zones. It is one of the most rationalist projects Koolhaas has collaborated on, as an attempt to prove the laconic and almost shocking geometric simplicity architecture—and the activity of dwelling—could endure, in an exaggerated and nearly parodistic version of early-twentieth-century abstraction and repetition. If it was true, as was becoming conventional wisdom during the 1970s, that modernist architecture had failed, Koolhaas claimed that this was the case not because it had been too radical, cerebral, or inhospitable, but because its intellectual, imaginary, and cultural potential had only been partially explored.

As usual with any debut, it is possible to retrieve motives and obsessions that will return in later work, although the Spear House (it was commissioned by Laurinda's parents) is also an apotheosis of earlier and contemporary OMA strategies and obsessions: a rectangular swimming pool, perpendicular to the strips, stretches out from the site boundary to the bay, and is crowned by a double diving board offering "the choice between the fresh water of the pool or the salt water of the sea"[2]; a car could use the house unhindered as a drive-through; program and form might become exchangeable thanks to a stacked organization; walls are uninterrupted planes, clad in single homogeneous materials; domesticity is defined as turning away from the immediate environment, blocking it out; and—given the cell-like character of the different spaces—members of a family should not be forced to meet, but rather bump into one another in a generously sized but equally oneiric circulation space.

The jury comments show how the project was perceived as a provocation, and how it was defended by Peter Eisenman, whose role in the development and the presence in American architecture culture of OMA during the 1970s cannot be underestimated. It turns this first text on the work of Koolhaas into a witty and moving read, because the members of the jury—with Eisenman partly as an exception—have no clue who they are dealing with, and how the oeuvre of one of the architects of this house will develop. Paul Rudolph, inclined to not take the project seriously, lets himself be persuaded; he does conjecture something extreme is going on, and that he is dealing with an architect who will struggle for more than a decade with his image as a "paper architect." "If this design were carried out," Rudolph concludes the round table, "it obviously would be something very different. It might be a great disappointment or it might be a very marvelous thing."

The design was carried out, but in a different version and without Koolhaas, which turns this debut, fittingly for a nontraditional architect, into an ironic comment on the classic career trajectory. Spear had associated herself in 1977 in Miami with Bernardo Fort-Brescia to form Arquitectonica. The Spear House—redubbed Pink House—was completed in 1978. As John Morris Dixon wrote in *Progressive Architecture*, the first version was "more ambitious. [...] The pool, which pierced dramatically through the earlier design, now runs parallel to the layers in a sheltered location that makes it more private and comfortable."[3] The house, in its brighter incarnation with more *couleur locale*, did capture Miami's atmosphere at the beginning of the 1980s: it became a widely published icon of its tropical but cool and slightly dangerous lifestyle. As if to prove the ability of an architectural project to take on different connotations, it was used as the house of a wife-beating arms dealer played by Bruce Willis in a 1984 episode of *Miami Vice*.

1 For a reinterpretation of Exodus, see Lieven De Cauter and Hilde Heynen, "The Exodus Machine," in *Exit Utopia: Architectural Provocations 1956–1976*, ed. Martin van Schaik and Otakar Máčel (New York: Prestel, 2005), 263–76.

2 Rem Koolhaas, "House in Miami/ 1974," *Architectural Design* 5 (1977), 352.

3 John Morris Dixon, "Layers of Meaning," *Progressive Architecture* 12 (1979), 70. See also Susan Grant Lewin, "Color Blazes a Trail," *House Beautiful* 10 (1979), 158–63; Fulvio Irace, "The Dream of a House," *Domus* 616 (1981), 11–12; and "Living Color," *Life Magazine 3* (1981), 62–68.

REMMENT KOOLHAAS, LAURINDA SPEAR: AWARD
Peter Eisenman, Peter Chermayeff, Paul Rudolph, Eberhard H. Zeidler *Progressive Architecture* 1 (1975), 46.

pe: I think this makes a genuine statement about houses. It's one of the few statements about suburban living and it's obviously, for me, a very iconic statement. It's one of the few that seems to be making that kind of gesture—it's the attitude, the metaphoric content. I believe architecture traditionally served a critical function in society; that is, in its critique of society and of architecture. This house is above all a critical gesture at architecture today and at society. In that alone, in telling society to take another look at itself, is its great strength. It represents an attitude toward the developer's house which I think is refreshing. Also, it's one of the few projects that shows a site plan in its context.

pc: It's turning an absolutely ruthlessly blank space to the public world, and then it opens up completely to the outside, in a refreshing simplicity. I find it intriguing and disturbing, but I can accept it because it's so utterly rational; it's an entirely rational plan in the way the house is zoned and in the way he separates family, which is a very good idea. It really isn't developed yet as architecture. It's a poetic diagram; actually, it could be called a very rational poetic statement. Yet it's not so rational if it's all air-conditioned. All the glass brick and skylight create a tremendous load problem. But it starts to become poetic in some of its extreme statements. He's a mad poet in the way he's stretched it out; taken the drawings and laid them down like a child's cutouts. It doesn't look like the hand of an architect, though.

pr: Well, you realize what it is. It's some guy who never built anything and has no feeling for materials. One can be beguiled by the drawings and by what one reads into them, and that's all fine, but building it would be an entirely different matter. The whole notion of the structure ... a column in one place and not in another; he depends on a wall ... is that really the way you want to make a house? It's not the work of an architect, yet he may become an architect.

ehz: It's a very controversial building, and that's what I like about it. It's so much at the edge of absolute disaster, yet it has such fantastic poetry.

pr: One can be beguiled by such things, but they're not to be taken seriously.

pe: But I have to take it seriously because there's nothing else, for me, searching for that feeling. I think someone has go to recognize that search. It breaks from the Corbu tradition; there's no Venturi, no Giurgola, none of that; it's astylistic, and that's what I like about it. It's one of the few submissions that makes a comment about the suburb, the private house, the way it occupies space, about the metaphorical nature of our personal lives. It's a kind of utopistic gesture in the midst of this awful middle-class suburbia; it thumbs its nose at the middle class, and in the end it's a poetic gesture of the sort you can perhaps only do in a private house.

ehz: It's quite beautiful; it's either very great or very, very bad. The funny part about the whole thing is that it's so weakly done, yet it's such a strong statement. The way it's drawn is unbelievable. It's very consistent in the way it's presented and in the way it's drawn, but there is something of an unsureness in the way the pencil lines are drawn and in the way the spaces are created, and yet they are so unbelievably romantic; they are very appealing, and it would be a wonderful house to be in. While it uses very minimal elements, their sequence creates a totally new space feeling that I haven't seen before. You feel that, given time, and that someone would buy or build a house like that, whoever drew that up should be capable of fulfilling the promise in there. It's a promise at the moment, nothing more. It definitely needs far more work to realize that house than the other things we've seen, because all of the elements have to be reinvented, the details have to be reinvented.

pr: I think I can agree with what's been said. It does have a surrealistic quality which one cannot put one's finger on; it has a kind of power which is inexplicable. If one tried to imagine it built, however, it's another matter. One of the very good things about it is one could use one's own imagination with regard to what it would be like. I can never just look at drawings; I can only look at them in terms of what something would be like. If it were carried out, it obviously would be something very different. It might be a great disappointment or it might be a very marvelous thing.

THE SPARKLING METROPOLIS & DELIRIOUS NEW YORK (1978): A REPOSITORY OF FORMS AND ACTIVITIES

2

Delirious New York: A Retro-Active Manifesto for Manhattan was published on November 16, 1978, the day before Rem Koolhaas's thirty-fourth birthday. Reactive and progressive at the same time, the book argued how the most modern metropolis in the world came about without the help of canonized architects, and nearly without theoreticians' noticing. Nevertheless, it was a deliberate determination of a position by a young architect. Koolhaas interpreted Manhattan as a pure, younger, and reckless version of the kind of urbanity Europe could only dream of—as a dense, hedonist, different, and exciting city that should be enjoyed instead of being condemned. *Pleasure* was a keyword, just like *sex* and *subversion*, possibly thanks to the maintenance of taboos without obeying them, and the constant creation (and recreation) of "ingenuous architectural arrangements for ever new forms of human interchange," as Koolhaas expressed it in 1996, at a moment when the red-light district of Forty-Second Street, "an Empire of Tawdriness," was about to be scrubbed away.[1]

The anatomy of *Delirious New York* mimics the autonomous blocks of Manhattan; its structure, as Martino Stierli has argued, is based on the montage of seemingly unrelated elements and concepts.[2] In writing defined by the combination of enthusiasm and skepticism, it marks the start of the self-fashioning of a practitioner of architecture who would continue to question that very activity. In a language full of unexpected metaphors, unfathomable anecdotes, and risky speculation—with a boldness and a lack of restraint that might be due to the fact that the author wasn't writing in his mother tongue—Koolhaas set out to construct an unconservative place, both imaginary and real, where he could start working as an architect, seemingly freed from the constraints of history, ideology, and politics. One of the rhetorical strategies consisted in defining another kind of modern architecture, as if to show that the father figure of Le Corbusier could indeed be killed, but without necessarily regressing to the postmodern historicism or the sterile self-examination that intellectual architects had started to profess, nor succumbing to the condemnation of architecture as lip service to capitalism (and thus inequality and oppression), as Manfredo Tafuri had been proclaiming. Already in 1976, as a short text in *Architectural Design* by Camilla Ween shows, Koolhaas was perceived as an alternative for an architectural avant-garde "fiddling with increasing intensity," while the problems of New York became all the more urgent. Less than a year later, an entire issue of *Architectural Design* was devoted to OMA, after mediation by Charles Jencks. It was a talent of Koolhaas to know the right people in the right places at the right moments, although these people also became "right" partially because of their contribution to OMA's early fame.

It is too easily forgotten how essential the work of Madelon Vriesendorp was for the genesis of *Delirious New York*. Koolhaas acknowledged how the book owed her "a special debt of inspiration and reinforcement,"[3] and in a way, her cover painting, showing two of the world's most famous skyscrapers in a postcoital condition, was the embryo of the text.[4] In the years in which architectural drawings emerged as aesthetic objects and coveted commodities, the first incarnation of OMA survived financially by selling the work of Vriesendorp and Zoe Zenghelis.[5] On the evening of November 16, 1978, the exhibition *The Sparkling Metropolis* opened on the top floor of the Guggenheim Museum, while below a retrospective exhibition by Mark Rothko was taking place. This time, the role of go-between was filled in by Hubert Damisch, an acquaintance of Guggenheim curator Margit Rowell. In five categories, fifty-four works were shown: "Projects for London" (including Exodus, but also a Railway Hotel and Museum by Zaha Hadid, who had joined OMA in 1977), "The Secret Life of Buildings" (Vriesendorp's psychoanalytical and humorous paintings), "Projects for New York" (such as The City of the Captive Globe and Hotel Sphinx), "The Story of the Pool," and one "Elevation of All New York Schemes."

The Sparkling Metropolis functioned as a month-long book launch; it was nearly impossible—and this wouldn't change in the history of OMA—not to confuse the authorship nor the meaning of the texts with that of the projects. The book and the exhibition were reviewed more or less together and sometimes in opposition. Peter Blake, author of *God's Own Junkyard* from 1964 but also of *Form Follows Fiasco: Why Modern Architecture Hasn't Worked* from 1977, concluded his book review with praise for the exhibition (and with a tease at Frank Lloyd Wright): "I wish it could be kept up on those rather Freudian walls forever." Paul Goldberger criticized Koolhaas for his bad scholarship, while he praised "Vriesendorp's exquisite and witty drawings," concluding that "one cannot escape the feeling that the pictures make Koolhaas's point far better than do his words." Critics who didn't mind Koolhaas's openly operative historiography considered him nostalgic: Reyner Banham coined the term *Manhattalgia*. Others focused on Koolhaas's nationality, and saw everything OMA did as a result of the centuries-old relationship between the US and Europe. Most of all, and probably in line with Koolhaas's intentions, the multifaceted paperwork of OMA was regarded as a means to imagine a future for architecture, in ways that buildings could not (or not yet). What would architecture look like if it would be made according to this version of New York and its "culture of congestion"? Could OMA build? And if so, how would their projects intervene in reality—what were the intentions of these architects, and would they be understood?

In 1980, Bernard Tschumi dismissed this question—and its underlying duality—when he offered a critique of critiques, indicating—as a like-minded contemporary of Koolhaas—that *Delirious New York* wasn't to be judged as the new Ten Commandments of architecture, but as "a repository of forms and activities that await a possible meaning."[6] With this structuralist analysis that nailed the character of the work of OMA, Tschumi seemed to indicate how the true modernity of architecture—defined by the inevitably elusive character of its significations—had only very recently begun.

1 Rem Koolhaas, "Regrets," *Grand Street* 57 (1996), 137.

2 Martino Stierli, *Montage and the Metropolis: Architecture, Modernity, and the Representation of Space* (New Haven: Yale University Press, 2018), 228–67. For a conversation with Koolhaas on the writing of the book, see Cynthia Davidson, "Rem Koolhaas: Why I Wrote *Delirious New York* and Other Textual Strategies," *ANY* 0 (1993), 42–43.

3 Rem Koolhaas, "Acknowledgments," in *Delirious New York* (Oxford: Oxford University Press, 1978), 263.

4 Beatriz Colomina, "Disaster Follows Ecstasy like Form Follows Function," in *The World of Madelon Vriesendorp*, ed. Shumon Basar and Stephan Trüby (London: AA Publications, 2008), 42–43.

5 Shumon Basar and Stephan Trüby, "Worrying Kindness and Ultimate Wisdom," in ibid., 262. For the first OMA exhibitions in galleries, see Jordan Kauffman, *Drawing on Architecture: The Object of Lines, 1970–1990* (Cambridge, MA: The MIT Press, 2018), 264–66.

6 Bernard Tschumi, "On Delirious New York: A Critique of Critiques," *International Architect* 3 (1980), 68. Bernard Tschumi asked for a separate introduction for the partial republication of his text, a request the editor unfortunately could not comply with.

FIDDLING WHILE NEW YORK BURNS

Camilla Ween
Architectural Design 10 (1976), 630.

While New York City burns—both financially and literally—the architectural avant-garde fiddles with increasing intensity. [...] The New York scene is attacked abroad for the incestuous milieu of such cultural institutions as Urban Design Group, the Institute for Architecture and Urban Studies, and the Cooper Union, all of which form a basis of support for New York's new generation of cult architects. These architects can be accused of not really opening any new doors and of widening the gulf between the ruling classes and the newly urbanized poor.

The rivalry between the two bands, the Whites and the Grays, continues, though the issues have become more hazy. Both movements are elitist, which could be construed as the common ground from which they diverge, though the Grays like to consider themselves populist. The Whites adhere to a classical approach of strict academic formalism, which amounts to an attempt to update the Modern movement. The guru of the Whites is Colin Rowe; their spokesman is Peter Eisenman, the whitest of them all.

In contrast, the Grays take up an eclectic position. Architectural references to many different sources, particularly American shingle style, are thrown together to produce a great richness and excitement. The Godfather of the Grays is Vincent Scully, and their fellow traveler in Philadelphia, Robert Venturi, has spread the word of populism around the world. In New York the Grays' case is presented by Robert Stern, who advocates Postmodernism as opposed to Eisenman's Postfunctionalism. [...]

Rem Koolhaas plays another tune. His work, rife with humor, exposes the uninitiated to the opulence of a city once imaginary, continually hysterical, and finally delirious. His fantasy drawings, curiously emanating from the White enclave (the Institute for Architecture and Urban Studies) are featured in a number of foreign magazines. An infection of its source would be a welcome event. Could it depict an end to the battle of the isms between Whites and Grays?

LES EXTRÊMES QUI SE TOUCHENT

George Baird
Architectural Design 5 (1977), 326–28.

In my view, the work of OMA constitutes one of current architecture's most provocative revisionisms. To show this, one needs only to set OMA's position against two or three other important current tendencies. Colin Rowe, for example, has in his introduction to *Five Architects* conceded the contemporary irrelevance of the social programs of modern architecture, and pondered for us, with mixed feelings, the residue of forms—the physique without the morale. OMA, on the other hand, argues instead that it is the forms that are moribund; and elaborates a new formal vocabulary around precisely those "social condensers" which once formed the core of modern architecture's program.

To take another important case, the current status of the reputation of Mies van der Rohe—surely, except for

Ludwig Hilberseimer, today's least fashionable modern architect. Figures such as Van Eyck and Rykwert would deplore his influence—even Arthur Drexler, his earliest American promoter, now speaks of Charles Garnier! Yet OMA reasserts the pertinence of the work of Mies—and the grid, the curtain wall, and the sheer plane surface all make their significant reappearance in OMA's work. Or again, Robert Venturi's plea for a less ambitious but more effacing modern architecture than that practiced by his predecessors. To this, OMA responds by positing the continuing relevance of visionary projects.

By virtue of these oppositions alone, OMA's position must be regarded as significant. It is a highly complex revisionism, bringing together such a diverse set of heroes as the aforementioned Mies van der Rohe, together with Ivan Leonidov, Salvador Dalí, John Portman, Wallace Harrison, and Norman Bel Geddes. What is more, it also involves, in a more intimate way, the concepts of OMA's sometime mentor/sometime collaborator, O. M. Ungers. All of this produces an architecture of a nature which is, for today, quite astonishing. For it turns out to be visionary at the same time as it is implementable; surreal at the same time as it is commonsensical; puritanical at the same time as it is luxurious. And it possesses a revolutionary character which lies precisely in its untypical—for a modern architecture—loyalty to an historical tradition of the metropolis.

To be sure, the demeanor of enfants terribles plays a certain exorcist role in OMA's polemic. For example, insofar as it lauds Leonidov's heroism and spurns Le Corbusier's, the polemic relies for its impact on the relative unfamiliarity of the former, as opposed to the latter. Insofar as it raises to the level of heroes such contentious figures as Harrison and Portman, the OMA polemic, in large measure, strives merely to *épater*—not this time *les bourgeois*, but rather, today's complacent arbiters of respectable taste. Insofar as it reveals for our astonishment "the secret life of buildings," it lastly demonstrates the iconic barrenness of most contemporary architectural debate. But even allowing for a certain rhetorical tone after all, Koolhaas has himself advised us of the methodological implications of the paranoid critical method—there remains for more serious, and more substantial examination, the fascinating set of conceptual polarities outlined above, manifested in the work itself.

Let us take them in turn. First, an architecture which is visionary at the same time as it is implementable. OMA's work presents an image of the metropolis which is itself indisputably visionary. Its luminous profiles and gleaming towers both represent an ideal city. What is more, the projects propose the most elaborately disposed and equipped social condensers seen in modern architecture since the Heroic Period. Yet at the same time that all of this is true, the projects involve no tours de force of engineering, no mile-high skyscrapers, no transformations of extant urban patterns of public and private space. From time to time, buildings span streets (Hotel Sphinx) or bridges become buildings (Welfare Palace Hotel) in a fashion which would necessitate the entrepreneurial initiative of a Haussmann or a Robert Moses, but save for these exceptional cases, these iridescent drawings depict eminently—if surprisingly—buildable buildings.

Second, an architecture which is surreal at the same time as it is commonsensical. In its most elaborate and most voluptuous details, OMA's work indeed evokes a secret life of buildings. Yet, following Art Deco precedents, such details tend to concern quite specifically the tops, bottoms, and edges of buildings. The principal volumes in between these limits in most cases display a quite evidently "dumb and ordinary" neutrality which is not exceeded by that of Robert Venturi's Guild House or Brighton Beach competition entry. So commonsensical in fact are these forms that it may be surmised how the projects, if built, would be regarded as less exceptionable by the lay public than they would be by informed architects.

Third, as architecture which is puritanical at the same time as it is luxurious. This is perhaps the most fascinating of OMA's polarities. On the face of it, the projects seem to offer up the most hedonistic of social possibilities—"eating oysters, naked, with boxing gloves" may serve as a definitive example. Yet it is significant to what degree the programmatic roles of OMA's social condensers are athletic and/or sublimating, rather than sedentary or gratificatory. Indeed, so true is this that I find it difficult to see OMA's commitment to the metropolitan tradition revolving around flaneurs as originally conceived by Walter Benjamin. Rather, I see OMA's metropolitans, as they proceed serenely through architectural spaces of intense drama and luxury, as somewhat Corbusian Supermen, nonchalant and daring, but somewhat reserved, in their ongoing confrontation with metropolitan destiny.

Last, an architecture which is revolutionary at the same time as it is evolutionist. In its definitive commitment to the metropolis, OMA announces what must be seen as a clear caesura in the history of modern architecture. For there is nowhere in the orthodox history even a leaning toward such an heretical sympathy. (Even OMA's hero, Leonidov, did not accept congestion as the hallmark of modern urbanity.) But OMA has not only made an unprecedented commitment to the principle of the metropolis; it has also given urban form to that commitment through its absorption in the matter of urban morphologies characteristic of, and appropriate to, the metropolis itself. (It is, of course, not possible to discuss morphologies without citing the name of Ungers, and I can only assume that this input to the work of OMA is Ungers's major contribution—even to the projects in which he is not an active collaborator.) But of course, insofar as it is morphological in urban intention, OMA's work is necessarily evolutionist, since no morphological enterprise can proceed independently of a grasp of the generic form of any given urban entity. Hence, as a morphological commitment to the metropolis, the work of OMA is revolutionary and evolutionist at the same time.

As I have said, all these aspects of their work can be interpreted as a highly significant revisionism. Yet it remains to be seen what the ongoing impact will be of OMA's polemic on OMA's production. For it is here that certain major reservations arise, for me, in respect to the possibility of sustaining all the polarities addressed. When they succeed, OMA's synthesizations of polarities manifest a liberating and exhilarating potential. We may take as dramatic, existential instances two of which—typically enough—are concerned with swimming. In the project for a house in Miami there is proposed the double diving board, from which one can choose either the salt water of the ocean, or the fresh water of the pool. In the Hotel Sphinx, the tower swimming pool extends at one point right to the edge of the building, so that it is possible, from the water, to savor the view of the metropolitan skyline beyond. In these exuberant circumstances, the heroic optimism of OMA's vision is precisely crystallized. Yet there is a rhetorical countercurrent to the work, in which the synthesis attempted remains unfulfilled. One may, for instance, cite the precedents of Electric Bathing, and Barrels of Love, in which the hedonistic gratifications are so automatistic in nature, and so unsublimated, as to be unconvincingly behaviorist. Or, alternatively, despite the relentlessly outward-looking orientation of all the facilities of the Hotel Sphinx—to such a degree that the view itself risks absorption into the cycle of consumption. In this perspective, we may return to the Story of the Pool, which—swimming again—arises out of its own paradoxical polarity of swimming in a floating pool. In the heroic—if fortuitous—locomotion of the constructivist architect/lifeguards, hedonism, and puritanical rigor—to employ Koolhaas's own terms—really do converge, and the implications astonish. Yet in the rhetorical invocations of metropolitanism, these convergences are not always sustained, and specters of legitimated kitsch and soulless gratification reemerge.

Still, if in all of the work of OMA, the paradoxical extremes of experience appropriated do not always touch, I, for one, am nevertheless prepared to wait. For, with such ambitious syntheses as are attempted here, it will be worth it.

TWO OR THREE THINGS I KNOW ABOUT THEM: A NOTE ON MANHATTANISM

Kenneth Frampton

Architectural Design 5 (1977), 315–18.

A pedestrian knew how to display his nonchalance provocatively on certain occasions. Around 1840 it was briefly fashionable to take turtles for a walk in the arcades. The flaneurs liked to have turtles set the pace for them. If they had had their way, progress would have been obliged to accommodate itself to this pace. But this attitude did not prevail; Taylor, who popularized the watchword, "Down with dawdling!" carried the day. — Walter Benjamin[1]

The return to meaning in architecture begins to take on the form of a collective reflex—the flight from history. The mind distressed by the absence of significance ransacks the intellect in search of a new lexicon. Frustrated, it posits a music that sings of itself, or an icon of archetypal force. It seeks, above all, the lost image of the city: for the metropolis of the nineteenth century—now dissipated, or for that of the twentieth—aborted at birth. Like King—it dreams of New York—or like Campanella, of the sun! The mind imagines a citadel comprising a new nature perpetually flooded with light. It reinvents the future with the past. It stands transfixed before the Rockettes and the pyrotechnic display of Radio City. Like Baudelaire or Fourier it compensates for its alienation with arcades of infinite length, or like Kahn with spaces full of wonder, white and gold.

Yet for OMA, the city is paved, like Kraus's Vienna, not with gold but with culture. Theirs is an Amerika of archetype and nostalgia. A world to be read at the level of narrative and myth, or simultaneously at the level of both. The palette is Vista-color;

the format—the postcard, the still and animated film. A Dreisenberg moon; Gatsby transfixed before the mooring lights of Oyster Bay; the Chrysler Building gleaming viridian in an atomic dawn.

The paranoid-critical method ranges in its achievements from divine vengeance to cosmic disaster; from the glaciation of an entire city to the inundation of the sea with sand. Moments are refracted in the prism of delirium. Time is stripped of its fatal sequence by nostalgia. Translux consorts with the Transrational on Welfare Island.[2] Leonidov and Jarry combine in mid-stream to fabricate *une piscine célibataire*—a critical image of profound ambivalence, devoid of pleasure. The *Sur-mâle* and the Stakhanovite.[3] The industrialization of athletics assists the genius of Taylor in creating a collective Prometheus. As night descends over the city Géricault's *The Raft of the Medusa* slips, with imperceptible relief, into the dark of the East River. The last migration before the flood. "Your tired, your hungry and your poor, your teeming masses yearning to breathe ..."—the sequestered of Ellis Island. The ship of fools or the image of salvation, hallucination at the point of death—*The Bird of Paradise* and *The Painted Word*.[4]

The extraordinary richness and delicacy of OMA's work defy description. Its scintillation reminds one of the lost art of the miniature. A sensuous imagination of dissent emanates from these projections against a background of positivistic production and populist kitsch. At the same time its reductive manipulation and consumption of images borders on a kitsch of its own. It looks to Dalí for its cargo-cult reduction of culture to a commodity.[5]

What then are we to make of this illuminated gloss on Manhattan; its landscape stripped of reality, its monuments converted into cryptic icons? The hermetic nature of the total gesture defies interpretation. To claim it as another kind of music is hardly plausible given its low level of formal order. The exceptions to this are evident, but they are posited at a realizable level: the house in Florida, the housing for Roosevelt Island, and the museum for Amsterdam. To assert the rest in the name of the surreal establishes little by way of meaning—for what after all did the ideology of surrealism ultimately intend?

The degree to which modern art has been about the destruction of traditional culture leads to the conclusion that the imagination has its own autonomy; a natural Rousseauesque sovereignty, by which it is guaranteed a certain freedom from reason and reality. Yet this essentially Romantic perspective only acquires its full significance if the argument is taken to its logical end; that is to say, if desire is consciously reinstated in the very center of our existence and this André Breton was prepared to do. "From this point of view," he wrote, "it was to be expected that sexual desire—which up to that time was more or less repressed in an anxiety-ridden or a guilt-ridden conscience because of taboos—should prove to be (in the last analysis misleadingly) the dizzying and invaluable "world on this side of eternity" in whose endless purlieus human dreams have built all "worlds beyond." It need merely be pointed out that here Surrealism deliberately departs from most traditional doctrines, according to which carnal love is a mirage, and passionate love a deplorable intoxication by astral light, insofar as this latter love is said to be prefigured in the serpent of Genesis. Provided that this love corresponds in every particular to the word *passionate*, that is to say presupposes election in all the rigor of that term, it opens the gates of a world where by definition it can no longer be a question of evil, of a fall, or of a sin."[6]

As illuminated by Breton, the highly ambivalent production of OMA laminates distinctly into two different levels of meaning, whose consequence I would argue, must vary to the degree that they emerge from the "illusion" of painting or the "reality" of architecture. On the one hand the highly hermetic sublimation of the unconscious and on the other, the direct projection of a hedonistic world whose meaning—as form—would coincide, if built, with the actual fulfillment of desire. That moment projected by Baudelaire where all would be *luxe, calme, et volupté*.

The critical significance of OMA's contribution surely resides here, beyond the surface brilliance of the work itself which by virtue of its status remains contained within the domain of art. As art it conceals beneath its sparkle a strange form of *embourgeoisement*—the unworldly concerns of art on the frontier of compensatory therapy; the sublimatory ends of folk culture masked by a subtle disguise. Yet beneath this gratuitous distraction the work gravitates toward the fundamental conundrum of the century; to that central dilemma as to which will have the ultimate authority: man/machine or machine/man: to that issue formulated by Marcuse as Eros versus Thanatos.

In its overt celebration of the utopian enthusiasms of the early twentieth century, OMA looks with delight on the gleaming towers of Babylon-Translux, but without once losing sight of the fearful depths of production as an end in itself. In as much as it projects the image of an alternative reality this work embodies a radical potential which is as critical of communism in its ascendancy as it is of capitalism in its decline. For that "positivistic" consensus who, irrespective of their particular hue, must, however, embrace the given reality and hence perforce pass negative judgment on every act of anarchic creation, this has already been cause enough to disclaim the work as reactionary. But for those who remain unconvinced by the populist cultural policies of the Welfare State and who shrink from its Benthamite reduction of the human condition to the metabolic criteria of production and consumption, to the gratification of "need" and the manipulation of social behavior, this work retains its challenging appeal.

1 Walter Benjamin, *Charles Baudelaire: A Lyric Poet in the Era of High Capitalism* (London: New Left Books, 1973), 129. The reason for making this reference is threefold: it establishes the link of the work of OMA to the imagery of Baudelaire; it introduces the quintessential metropolitan figure of the flaneur to whom OMA's work is dedicated; through the kaleidoscopic insight of Benjamin, it opposes this antihero to the merciless rule of Taylorized production; to that "machine" that holds nothing sacred, least of all the city.

2 Translux and Transrational are references to the curious juxtaposition of the two images in the Welfare Island rendering. Translux alludes to the ocean liner designed by Norman Bel Geddes in 1932, which while never built, is envisaged here as docking beside a Suprematist skyscraper by Kasimir Malevich dating from 1923. Malevich had in fact once collaged this image on to a postcard of the Manhattan skyline. See Jiri Kroha, Jiri Hruza, *Sovetska architektonicka avantgarda* (Prague:

Odeon, 1973). While Translux is a "patent" term deriving from a chain of Art Deco cinemas in New York, it sums up better than any other term I know the idea of transatlantic luxury culture that Art Deco often attempted to express. [...] Transrational on the other hand is a reference to Russian *zaum* poetry: that is, to that invented, otherworldly language that was not so much irrational as it was *transrational*. This was largely the invention of Alexi Kruchenykh, whose play, *Victory of the Sun*, produced in the Luna Park of St Petersburg in 1931, was the occasion and inspiration for Malevich's invention of Suprematism.

3 The floating swimming pool or *piscine célibataire* is of course a play (for me) on Marcel Duchamp's *Large Glass*—the bottom of the boat is even made of glass. It seems to be an unconscious comment on Harald Szeemann's extraordinary exhibition, *La Machine Célibataire*, which revealed the *Large Glass* as being the quintessential "bachelor machine." [...] Additional note should be taken of the Downtown Athletic Club, New York of 1931 designed by Starrett and Van Vleck. This skyscraper was nothing if not a "social condensor" and a "bachelor machine" combined; the "bachelors" bringing their bodies to peak condition on the lower floors of the structure and rising after the mandatory workout to associate with the "brides" who, strictly restricted to the lounges of the upper levels, were to attend their arrival before an aerial panorama of the city. This link between eroticism and the useless production of Taylorized athletics finds its back-breaking productive opposite in the Stakhanovite movement; those heroes of the Soviet Union who after 1935 attempted to follow the "time and motion" example of the coal miner Alexei Stakhanov, who overnight managed to increase the productive norm by fourteen times.

4 These references to books by R. D. Laing and Tom Wolfe are not, of course, present in the work itself; but the image of Géricault's *The Raft of Medusa* of 1818 was sufficient to suggest them. While this is an image of salvation and wonder it is hardly without its ambiguous overtones; for after the horror of cannibalism who or what can be saved? While the choice of their image may have been intuitive, the pain of reality and the fragility of the illusion that it implies are enough to invoke Laing's unbearable portrait of Glasgow, given under the title *The Bird of Paradise*. As for illusion itself, that is to say, art, Wolfe's promotion of *photo realism* and his simultaneous mid-cult attack on critical interpretation is a sufficiently reflexive comment for all concerned.

5 I am at a loss to know where the anthropological term *cargo cult* comes from, but the phrase appeals to me and I understand that it refers to the imposition of cultural form through repeated patterns of trade (see Alison and Peter Smithson, *Without Rhetoric* [London: Latimer, 1973]). I associate the painted production of Salvador Dalí—as opposed to his films—with this idea of art transformed and transported by trade. Dalí's apoliticality and his cynical pursuit of publicity, his habit, that is, of working with one eye obsessively fixed on the market, were sufficient to bring about his final rift with Breton's Surrealist movement in 1936.

6 See André Breton, *Manifestoes of Surrealism* (Ann Arbor: The University of Michigan Press, 1969), 302. This quote is from a text from 1953 entitled "On Surrealism in its Living Works." Breton was to make his political position unequivocally clear on numerous occasions throughout the mid-1930s.

PANDORA'S BOX

Demetri Porphyrios

Architectural Design 5 (1977), 359–64.

[...] Scanning the tradition of ideal urban schemes, from Ledoux's Salt Works to Fourier's Phalanstère, or from Jules Borie's Aérodomes to Le Corbusier's Plan Voisin, or even from Archigram's Instant City to Superstudio's Continuous Monument, one clearly discerns the deep parenthood of Exodus, the first representational statement of Koolhaas and Zenghelis which won them recognition in the *Casabella* competition in 1974. Intrinsically an ideal city, Exodus is a dropped-in deus ex machina which forces London into a gradual but sure extinction. The tips of this ideal urban strip are the points of ideological friction between the old and the new, while the nine squares of the city proper refer to its collective ideological rituals: the ideology of private property (the Square of the Private Allotments), of ceremonial festivities (the Ceremonial Square), of civic initiation (the Reception Hall), of historical consciousness (the preservation of Nash London), of sensuous pleasurability (the Baths), of the artificial alternative to nature (the Park of the Four Elements), of cure and immortalization (the Hospital), and of scientific knowledge (the University Square).

There is, of course, nothing new featuring in the permissive ideological coexistence of these squares of bourgeois reification. The old dream of Ledoux for erecting a city comprising Temples to Love, Memory, Knowledge, etc., or that of Fourier for founding an ideal brotherhood, or that of Jules Borie for allowing the traditional city to wither away while its inhabitants escape to the crystalline dropped-in aerodromes, or that of Le Corbusier for the perpetual warfare that the Plan Voisin would initiate, or that of Archigram for an overnight physical transformation of the world, or that of Superstudio for an uninterrupted crystalline monument meandering around the globe—all these dreams and still many others are present in Exodus, yielding with their superimposition a Freudian tableau of contemporary urban memory.

But the architectural gaze is now organized in a new way. It is no longer the gaze of the redeemer, as was the case with all urban idealizations from the nineteenth century onward. The effort now is not to single out the ills of contemporary cities, nor to propose solutions for their cure. In that sense, there is no intention for unburying the debate about problems and solutions so popular in the tradition of the 1950s and 1960s. Interestingly enough, Zenghelis, though a student of Smithson at the AA, never returned to the positivist tradition of bubble diagrams, nor to the "scientist" assumption that thorough analysis is the mandatory precedent for design. All the nuances of positivist consciousness—from Christopher Jones, Christopher Alexander, Lionel March and [Philip] Steadman, or the long list of behavioral scientists—are here denied any legitimacy with the implicit accusation of pseudo-scientism.

Instead, the task so obvious in Exodus is to plunge straight into pure ideology and comprise for the first time an inventory of today's urban episodes; a clinical description of the various unquestioned habits which have become mundane realities and without which it would be inconceivable to date our lifestyles. This portraiture, however, is not a mere depiction: on the contrary, by analyzing, patterning, and articulating the metropolitan imagery, it has the power to link our knowledge of things across the dimension of history, while at the same time attempting a reinterpretation of that history and a possible materialization. In that sense it would be untrue, no doubt, to see in Koolhaas's and Zenghelis's work a mere annihilation of design long burdened with the tradition of conceptual art. It is not even a question of a displacement of the traditional means and media of design, or of the denial to draw—as was the case, for example, with the advocacy planning movement in the late 1960s. Instead, in constituting anew the composite portrait of contemporary urban life, OMA gives birth to a new representational tactic which gradually formalizes itself to the point of becoming a modus vivendi. [...]

The first consequence that the portraiture of the metropolis has had is the unreserved preoccupation with sensuous imagery. From the first sketches of Exodus, the Hotel Sphinx, or the City of the Captive Globe, it became obvious that mere architectural delineation—no matter how intricate in detail or overburdened with axonometric projections—would be incapable of capturing an urban portrait. Color and above all secondary nonarchitectural information was needed. In Exodus one finds it impossible to grasp the pictorial implications of the childish drawing of the Square of the Private Allotments, or that of the Park of the Four Elements, were it not for the adjunct images borrowed from daily experience. In the City of the Captive Globe, one is not merely confronted with the towers of the Plan Voisin, or with the expressionist shells, or the constructivist tower of Lissitzky, but rather with the vast regions of theoretical debate and practical implementation that they stand for. This incessant reference to an associational density and to the whole profusion of adjunct and complementary images defines a representational tactic far removed from the orthodox modernist ethos, and very similar to that of the nineteenth-century École des Beaux-Arts. Against Modernism's positivist dream of an architecture with no memory (at least not an explicitly discussed one), Koolhaas and Zenghelis will insist on a sensuously corporeal architecture that is capable of triggering an unlimited flow of associations. In their visible, tactile and almost hedonistic status, the highway, the pigeon-hole window, the escalator, or the so many metropolitan fragments that animate their vision are by no means abstract and universal names (as, for example, the column, line or plane were for Modernism), but on the contrary they carry with them a spontaneous unfolding of representation (like, for example, the ionic column, the traveated pediment, or the Louis Quatorze window did for the Beaux-Arts mind).

These sensuous clues which open up whole regions of references owe their power to the very sensuousness they possess. Bereft of their color, crispness, harshness, or delicacy, they become impotent three-dimensional gestures with no parenthood or horizon of descendancy. And it is not without significance that such preoccupation with the corporeality of architectural elements coincides with a general rebirth of a decorative architectural consciousness. Since the pioneering work of Venturi in the mid-1960s, and with the gross popularization of semiological tools among architectural circles [...] architecture thought it possible to return to the nineteenth-century sensibility of decoration as significatory clothing. It is true that such thought must have crossed the architectural mind as early as the postwar years, for otherwise the excesses of Brutalism, or the stylistics of corporate design (for example, Yamasaki or Portman) would have been unintelligible. Yet it was not until the early 1970s that such a proposition was clearly stated and theoretically formalized without the implicit fear of stepping onto morally risky ground. [...]

At the moment when it became possible to denounce the commemoration of scientism and consumerism, Koolhaas and Zenghelis were establishing an alliance at once tangled and extremely vague with a number of nonarchitectural disciplines: literature, painting, and psychology. The innumerable references to a Brave New World, the *en bloc* transposition of pictorial thematics as with the romantic story of the Raft of Medusa, the ingenious fabrication of the legend of the Pool, the direct allusions to the pictorial tradition of color postcards of the 1920s and 1930s, the polemic and irritative tone of the language in their texts, the Dadaesque quality of their pictorial narratives, or even still their almost medieval determination to produce by hand a second or third copy of the same colorful drawing for an exhibition or a museum purchase—all there are sure indices of minds that have accepted the notion of interdisciplinary quotation. In this way they outwitted in advance the positivist attempts of their contemporaries to insert architecture's chronology within that of science, technology, or consumerism, and sanctioned instead the inverse endeavor to align the experience that man has of things with the knowledge he has acquired of them through a psychological internalization. This leads to a significant temptation: to make psychology into a sort of general tactic of design. On the horizon of their architectural thinking there is the project of bringing consciousness back to its real conditions, of restoring it to the contents and forms that brought it into being. This is why the problem of the unconscious—its possibility, status, mode of existence, the means of knowing it and bringing it to light—is not simply an excuse for a formal exercise, but it is a problem that is ultimately coextensive with the very ability to imagine, draw, and build. In setting themselves the task of restoring the domain of the psychological, Koolhaas and Zenghelis tactily imply that the unveiling of the unconscious is posited in its greatest clarity—as with Vriesendorp's metropolitan tableaux—the better the work becomes, demarcating in an unambiguous way an architecture with the task of making the discourse of the unconscious speak through consciousness. [...]

A MORE EXPANSIVE SPECTRUM OF FUNCTIONALISM

Hans van Dijk
wonen-TA/BK 11 (1978), 17–20.

[...] **hvd:** OMA's kind of positive attitude toward the metropolis is rare in modern architecture, unlike in say film or literature.

rk: I have never understood why modern architecture is not enthusiastic about it. It is a riddle I would like to someday solve. The metropolis is a mutation so radically different from everything that came before that it has shaken up the entire traditional terrain of architectural discourse, history, knowledge, and so forth. In that sense, "large urban cities" are indeed a threat to architecture as it has been traditionally understood. Big cities need their own kind of architecture, which has yet to be developed. And architects are obsessed with exercising control; but a metropolis makes any kind of control totally impossible. So if architects truly devote themselves to big cities, they have to relinquish many of their accustomed pretensions.

hvd: What kinds of pretensions do you mean exactly?

rk: One clear example is the Kriers. They still pretend to have the capacity to organize huge swaths of the city. And surprisingly enough, it's true that under certain regimes in this day and age, such as a socialist one, that is indeed possible. But the products of that are generally regarded as monstrosities—monstrosities which are a combination of misplaced pretensions on the part of the architect and too much control on the part of the state. That combination gets in the way of the realization that the metropolis cannot be controlled—is, in fact, distinctly uncontrollable.

hvd: The modernist movement has mostly asserted that the city causes nothing but disease, isolation, crime, and suicide, and it calls on architects to eradicate the causes of these afflictions. The Manhattanism formulated in your book *Delirious New York* maintains that urban stress can be compensated by intensifying these things.

rk: No, what I want is to exploit the stress that inherently exists in a positive way instead of desperately trying to fight against it. I don't believe at all that it can or needs to compensate for anything.

hvd: *Delirious New York* can be compared to the Venturis' *Learning from Las Vegas*, in that both books take up popular images that have been ignored by architecture. The difference is that the Venturis set out to teach lessons, whereas you have written a manifesto for what you encountered, like Duchamp attached a title to a urinal and then exhibited it.

rk: That's true, yes, except that New York is no urinal. [...] On the one hand I see myself as Manhattan's ghostwriter, but on the other I'm its architect, in the sense that I distill principles and a certain form of architecture out of it.

hvd: The Venturis wrote about Las Vegas, Banham about Los Angeles, and now you've written about New York. Do you think every metropolis of significance deserves to have a manifesto written for it?

rk: No, it's limited. Every city had its time when that could be done. It would've been possible for Paris in the nineteenth century or London, but not now. Banham's book is indeed a manifesto too, just not for Los Angeles. It's a camouflaged, chauvinistic tribute to London. His chameleon-like disguise as Angeleno is completely false. Nevertheless, it was clearly written from an ideological standpoint—which is unusual for an Englishman—and that makes it enjoyable anyway. The same holds true for the Venturis; the deficiency of their book is that their primary aim, in the end, is to make the billboards even better, more beautiful and more "responsible." In the same way that Marie Antoinette played the shepherdess, they are acting out a populist American myth. Except for their truly artistic, pretentious buildings, the things they make are lifeless and weak; they're either boring or truly very ugly.

hvd: You said just now that you distilled certain principles from your study of New York. Does Manhattanism have a theoretical core that could be relevant in other situations? I'm thinking of the so-called archipelago theory.

rk: When the creators of New York are pressed to reveal the theoretical model for their city, they talk about a "modernized Venice": Manhattan was an archipelago, every block an island, and the architecture established miniature states on each island, each with its own aims, laws, and reality. A city like that is not based on cohesion, but rather heterogeneity. In the neutrality of the great archipelago model, each block or fragment has its own model. And that kind of archipelago is implicit in many cities. [...] There is no homogenous strategy that works for the city. For the older sections, you can't assume that everything must be preserved, with the traditional folk living there and barriers setting them off. You have to be able to constantly introduce new elements, which allows for forming new relationships with and within the existing situation. What we're hoping to do with Ungers in Berlin includes purposely not preserving certain blocks that are already halfway gone. That's the difference with someone like Krier, who mercilessly restores everything.

hvd: And you just accept the trend for clearing out the inner city?

rk: The inner cities are stagnant anyway. That's what awaits all of Europe. I don't view it as tragic, but rather as a process that opens up its own new possibilities. Designing that clearing out—I'd say that's a good formula for what we are doing.

hvd: There are, of course, large groups of people opposed to that.

rk: You mean the locals? I think there are very few true locals in the Netherlands anymore. They have long since evolved into a fake army of public input monsters trained in a specialized form of terror.

hvd: My question about that theoretical core of Manhattanism was also prompted by how different your book is from all those ruminations on architecture shoved full of theory and references to contemporary philosophers.

rk: Yes, I did purposely avoid that, though I too know all those philosophers. That kind of architectural criticism often comes across as a form of intimidation. People use every big name who ever lived to further their own agenda. And you don't learn anything; at least I've rarely experienced any actual relevance. My book is about the material itself. It presents a host of precedents, which are reduced to their purest formula. This series of formulas and tactics thus constitutes more of a handbook than a theory, in a way.

[...]

hvd: You call *Delirious New York* a manifesto, and with that deliberately tread into the realm of ideology. It is a constructed twentieth-century myth.

rk: Yes. I want to emphasize that I have put this Manhattan forward not as a literal phenomenon but as an analogy. It is certainly not a call for it to be recreated.

hvd: But you mystify Manhattan and you do it quite deliberately. That makes it an attack on critics and architects who want to arrive at an ideological tabula rasa before starting on something and want to demystify everything.

rk: You mean people like Tafuri? Sure, annoyance and anger at their production was an important source of energy.

hvd: Is that because in those quarters every architectural undertaking is essentially judged in the context of economic and social issues? For example, Benjamin's question about the position of the architect's intellectual work within the apparatus of production or the extent to which it, to use Brecht's word, refunctionalizes the means of production.

rk: I have always had an almost physical incapacity to think in those terms and, thus, also to contravene them. It is my strong impression that Tafuri and his followers hate architecture. They have declared architecture dead. Architecture to him is a row of corpses in the morgue. Yet even though those corpses are dead, they won't leave them alone; they are vain enough to presume to be the experts of the morgue. They name-drop their way through it. Every now and then, they'll pull out a corpse and say something about it before shoving it back in, but on the whole it's really all intolerable—with the exception of Aldo Rossi, for some inexplicable reason.

hvd: Who also rants against Tafuri, by the way.

rk: Yeah, well, if you're the only survivor for someone who has declared everyone else dead, I would be nervous, too. I focused on New York because to me it represents an apogee in the culture of our century. I have never seen a map in Tafuri's articles on skyscrapers. To him they are totems of the downside of capitalism, and he would naturally be mortified to discover that something else is going on. I hope I have proven that skyscrapers do in fact advance a certain—occasionally impressive—vision of social life, which they sometimes even achieve.

hvd: Is that where the connection you make to the "social condensers" in the Soviet Union after 1917 comes from?

rk: The similarities are indeed discernible and astonishing. What is masochistic about today's official discourse is that pure, unbuilt ideas are taken seriously, whereas those same ideas are ignored once they are built by Wall Street bankers—for their own enjoyment.

[...]

hvd: Charles Jencks's book *The Language of Post-Modern Architecture* is basically one long argument in favor of metaphors. Are you insulted or relieved that your work wasn't included in it?

rk: No comment. But the metaphors he references are all puerile, such as Ronchamp with its resemblance to a nun's hat or a duck. Any metaphors I use are deliberate and literary. I believe that buildings of a certain scale incontrovertibly need literary themes that can be evoked through other than purely architectural means.

hvd: Both Jencks and Venturi legitimize their use of metaphors by proposing it as a form of irony for revealing some of our less admirable social values.

rk: I hate irony in architecture; it's like humor in music. I try to avoid it as much as possible. I will admit that my work is occasionally critical, but I think irony is too ineffectual to tackle anything.

hvd: Besides the metaphorical aspect, there is also the utilitarian aspect of your work.

rk: *Utilitarian* is and will always be a beautiful word. The best formulation to that side of my work is "puritanical hedonism." What it comes down to is that I really want things to serve a particular function and the metaphors are part of that. They allow you to cover a more expansive spectrum of functionalism.

hvd: Yet it is in your smaller, "rectangular" projects that that utilitarian aspect is more pronounced.

rk: Do you really think so? I have discovered, through my work, that the metaphors become more abstract when you are working on small things. In a house, you can use a "boat" as a theme, but then it becomes infantile. In a large building, one part can be a boat and another can be something else. That gives you a much broader range of possibilities.

hvd: Are you attempting in those small projects to develop a sort of poetics of utilitarianism?

rk: Yes, because I consider myself a descendant of the true Moderns. With the floating pool, I consciously tried to imagine their poetry of utilitarianism in its most extreme and simplest form. I am not at all affected by the unpopularity of modern architecture these days. When I worked in London, Peter Cook called me a "boring fascist" because I drew rectangular plans. People like Mies van der Rohe, Hilberseimer, and Leonidov are true heroes for me; I have a great, serious respect for them. I love the word *utilitarian* because I think programmatic intentions and usability are important. Eisenman eschews those intentions and I don't believe in that. The whole reason I went into architecture was to shake that guilty feeling of operating on a purely gratuitous level. I used to write film scripts but those were not useful in the same way. Architecture in use is consumed in an authentic manner.

hvd: At a symposium on the avant-garde in Eindhoven, Alexander Tzonis used your work to illustrate his theory that many architects these days are taking refuge in drawings and models because of a lack of building commissions due to the economic decline. What do you think of that interpretation?

rk: Crudely materialistic. I won't deny that I sometimes find it exasperating not to have any work, but that is a ridiculous hypothesis about cause and effect. What exactly is he accusing me of?

hvd: Tzonis said: "The latest response represents the desire of the architect to rise above the present malaise and view himself as unique, necessary, and almighty. We could call this phase narcissistic, in a psychoanalytical sense, because this defense can only exist in the mind by denying the dividing line between reality and desire."

rk: I often don't see or experience any such dividing line. You could indeed see my New York book as a denial of that dividing line, as proof that desire and reality can certainly coalesce. What is the Chrysler Building if not pure desire? That dividing line is a means by which the humanists pursue their own course with impunity. Desire and reality can coalesce in otherwise very professional, objective circumstances. I have always gotten what I wanted, not from being indulged, but because it's a question of how intensely you want something. And I consider myself an inalienable part of reality. Very few architects have that feeling. They think they are somehow removed from it.

hvd: Tzonis also said: "Buildings have to be inhabitable, and fantasies won't make them inhabitable."

rk: But that's the same kind of crude, materialistic thinking. Every building is both inhabitable and a fantasy. It does not make any logical sense to say that a building was not once a fantasy. Show me an uninhabitable building and I'll show you an unjealous academic. That shows the absurdity of his argument.

hvd: But don't you share the fear that architects will be priced out of the market and that much more of the process will be left up to developers and consortia of banks and contractors? There's no denying that trend, is there?

rk: No, and it's hardly a gratifying trend. But it seems to me that it is actually the government that is the cause of that nasty trend. The big problem is that all of the decisions are concentrated within a single group—and they only care about the money. Because what it boils down to is that those project developers are cheaper.

hvd: I doubt whether the government is the main culprit. In England, with its moribund social democracy, architects are awarded a large share of the work, whereas in capitalist America, the percentage is much lower.

rk: You mean the fact that only something like 3 percent of the total built volume there is done by architects? But that 3 percent is concentrated in places where it matters. The rest is a form of ultra-logical, utilitarian architecture. The reason that doesn't work here is, again, state control. In a climate in which the state discourages road-building one minute and encourages it the next—in other words, constantly changes its mind—the arbitrariness is just getting worse. The problem is that certain people are no longer responsible for certain places. That is also one of the reasons that Team 10 became somewhat creepy. The architects are no longer confronted with an individual client with whom to wage the campaign, as it were, through which the building comes into being. There is no longer any Nietzschean conflict underlying it all. The only thing that matters is being able to talk up the public servants, and then you can do whatever you want.

hvd: You referred earlier to the Bijlmermeer. In *Werk/Archithese* you called it the Strip, except it's not the Las Vegas Strip, but that of the social democratic welfare state. Why do you have such great admiration for it in spite of everything?

rk: The interesting thing about the Bijlmer is that it is a reversal of the oedipal formula in architectural history, whereby one generation must always murder the previous one. There you see—due to the delay in its inception—the CIAM forefathers engaging in a polemic against their successors. The Bijlmer is the result of total state control, even though the descendants of Modernism use every means at their disposal to suggest an architecture of variation derived from spontaneity, improvisation, and input, thereby rejecting all of the forces currently at work. If you look at it that way, the Bijlmer is simply less hypocritical.

hvd: Some would say that the Bijlmer is an example of an architecture that has been silenced through its dissolution into a rational urban planning process. But you see the Bijlmer as being full of meaning?

rk: Yes, because of the intention. In that regard, I don't agree with Jencks's criticism of modern architecture. I find the intention behind the Bijlmer noble and idealistic, and it was largely realized, too. What could you have against that? I consider it outrageous meddling. All the more so because the people who live there are patently satisfied and happy.

[...]
hvd: But apart from the simulation and inspiration, you could also see it as a certain desirable quality for the built environment. Hertzberger, echoing Mitscherlich, talks about "accommodation."

rk: I do not believe at all in the therapeutic quality of architecture. That became a sick aberration after the Second World War, which saw the rise of an architecture that declared everyone an invalid, whether they liked it or not: too old, or mentally or physically handicapped, or single mother. Everyone belonged to one of those categories of needy citizens; everyone was in need of help and thus in need of architecture. I get insulted to the core of my being when someone tries to do something for "my own good." That's what I mean when I say that architecture has become a sort of therapy that diagnoses me as someone in need of accommodation.

hvd: You reject any humanistic justification for your architectural activities?

rk: Everything done by people is humane. But the humanity of architecture is a distant echo that architects have all too readily laid claim to. No one ever examined what those concepts, "humane" and "humanity," really entailed after they were formulated. It just became a facile formula, a cheap public service announcement that granted architects good intentions by default, which allowed them to do what they liked as they saw best.

hvd: If you could build something in the Netherlands, what would you propose in its stead?

rk: I would be inclined to ignore it more than propose something in opposition. Otherwise I would be forced to do the opposite and I don't believe in that. In any event, I wouldn't build something for orphans or the elderly. I would like to build something for ordinary people, with a whiff of nostalgia for the struggle of life.

hvd: You work in New York at the Institute for Architecture and Urban Studies, in London at the Architectural Association School, and in Delft at the Faculty of Architecture. Would you be willing to present a comparison of those educational situations?

rk: About Delft, I'll say that it's the most degenerate educational situation I've ever encountered in my life. The overwhelming atmosphere is one of mutual disregard. On top of that, that very emphasis on the human side, conviviality, being socially and politically conscious has led to a complete lack of any awareness of architecture as a formal endeavor. That's why all of the formal theories here are so unbelievably primitive. The so-called Dutch Structuralism is unbelievably blunt and naive, don't you think? The great pretext about the human side of things has overtaken everything. In New York people aren't bothered by that at all, which is a relief. But the drawback there is their slavish adherence to certain masters and that students often purposely dedicate themselves to prima donnas. So Princeton only produces mini Graves and Cooper Union mini Hejduks; or big ones—same difference. The AA in London has this sort of lovely anarchy, where you can at least do your own thing. If you don't want to be with people, you don't have to; if you want to, you can. But to be honest I'm bothered by the whole educational system at the moment. I find it disturbing to think that you inspire people and maybe permanently destroy their ability to function normally.

hvd: But doesn't a school serve a purpose if it pursues a particular stream of ideas?

rk: Yes. As far as that's concerned, I'd say that the climate in New York and London is very favorable to that. In the Netherlands, it's hopeless—and embarrassingly bad, actually, because ignorance is passed off as a virtue here; purposely not knowing things, as an ideology. In Delft I have to explain to 99 percent of the students who Krier is, for example. They have absolutely no ability to put things in context. And it seems to me that people like Aldo van Eyck and Hertzberger definitely encouraged that. Are you familiar with the term *polder blindness*? Because of the absence of points of reference in the polder, a hare can appear as large as a cow. The Netherlands is suffering from the same phenomenon in an architectural sense. Van Eyck and Hertzberger represent an explosion of genius here, and there is no criticism whatsoever of them or others. Hardy is still talking about putting flamingos instead of house numbers at the front door. And Hertzberger actually never talks about anything other than that you need a special brick on the doorstep to set the milk bottle on, right? Even your average porn film has more nuanced ideas about housewives and milkmen. I recently heard one of his colleagues speak about "the public realm." Lot of slides of gray paving stones and concrete blocks; otherwise it was taken word-for-word from a lecture in London seven years ago. Your classic Montessori terrorism. It's like those people have a scorched-earth policy. I honestly do not think we are going to find solutions to our critical problems from Africa, be it from the Dogon or the kasbahs. We have no choice but to follow the course that has been set—toward even more antinaturalism.

hvd: You mean an ongoing perpetuation of the uneasy balance of the metropolis?

rk: I'm afraid so, yes.

GUGGENHEIM UNVEILS SURREALIST CITY VIEWS

Paul Goldberger
New York Times, November 17, 1978.

[...] OMA actually works as an architectural office but has achieved most of its renown for a number of theoretical projects. More than fifty drawings of these projects go on display today at the Guggenheim Museum, tucked into the top of the spiral ramp, above the museum's huge Rothko retrospective, where they will remain until December 17. This exhibition, entitled *The Sparkling Metropolis*, does not offer a total picture of a new kind of city. Rather, it is a collection of elements, some of which are literal and others purely figurative. Some of the OMA drawings are richly colored, lavish visions of what the city might be, while others are comments about what the city now is, and still others are witty, insightful observations about architecture in general.

The show includes a number of schemes for New York, which range from an entry into the 1975 competition for new housing for Roosevelt Island that is presumably real and buildable to more visionary projects such as a vast hotel, called the Sphinx Hotel because of its shape, for the middle of the north end of Times Square; a monumental egg as the centerpiece for an urban-renewal project on the East River, and an almost purely metaphorical City of the Captive Globe, a vision of block after block of Manhattan, each block with a different kind of architecture sitting on a base that looks like a marble sculpture pedestal. The last scheme is an exceptionally beautiful drawing, rich in color and texture, and it is hardly meant to be taken literally. What Mr. Koolhaas and his colleagues are telling us here is that the city—at least the City of New York—is an assemblage of objects that bear little stylistic relation to one another, save for what Mr. Koolhaas sees as a common desire to be exuberant, to be theatrical, to be daring.

All the styles come together on Manhattan Island; everything is there for the picking. It could all be chaos, but for the strength and order of the grid of the city's streets, which holds it all together. Now these are not new ideas, but they have never been expressed better in visual terms than in this drawing. Suddenly it is clear to us that each building is a performer and is playing a role in an architectural ensemble in which its responsibility is to a larger whole as well as to its own impulse. In a sense, the OMA architects are also dealing here with our unconscious view of the city. With the images of the city we carry deep in our minds. The OMA schemes exaggerate certain things, such as theatricality, congestion, and living drama. There are elements here like a huge plastic Raft of the Medusa, floating off Roosevelt Island, and a Freud Unlimited Club atop a hotel tower as a means of reminding us how we really live in the city.

Some of the best explorations of the unconscious are the drawings of Madelon Vriesendorp, which are surely the wittiest and perhaps the finest things in the entire exhibition. In an altogether remarkable piece, Miss Vriesendorp places the Chrysler Building and the Empire State Building in bed together—the two greatest fantasy skyscrapers of the 1930s are locked in romance as the RCA Building, sign of the impending Modernism that was to put an end to their joyous affair, bursts in the door like a detective catching them in the act. It is a picture of grace and wit and expresses perfectly a notion of Mr. Koolhaas's—that the spirit of intense theatricality of New York has been lost to a banal modern dreariness. The picture was used for the jacket of his new book, *Delirious New York,* which is being published this month by the Oxford University Press to coincide with the Guggenheim show.

Like Miss Vriesendorp's piece, many of the finer things in the exhibition can stand on their own as works of art. In a section of the show documenting an early and powerful, if horrifying, imaginary project for a vast linear structure to be built across London over a path many city blocks wide, there is a collage that is remarkably moving on its own. It has a photograph of the Berlin Wall with a cluster of Empire State Building spires on the other side, with a group of tiny figures running toward them. The collage calls to mind associations as diverse as Franz Kafka and the set for *The Wiz*; like all of the work of the Office for Metropolitan Architecture, it is a reminder of the power of architecture to sway minds.

FREUDIAN WALLS
Peter Blake
New York Magazine,
December 18, 1978.

I once wrote in this magazine that it might be a great idea if Manhattan were operated by Walt Disney Productions—an organization that had built the only successful New Towns in the United States since the Second World War, Disneyland and Walt Disney World. Now that Ed Koch has taken my advice and decided to turn this city into a vast tourist resort, *Delirious New York* might, conceivably, serve as a guidebook to the centerpiece of the city—Manhattan Island, the New Atlantis!

The architect Rem Koolhaas, who wrote this marvelously unintelligible Baedeker, absolutely worships New York. Oblivious to natives bemoaning the squalor, ugliness, violence, pollution, and general rottenness of the city, Koolhaas has opened our eyes to a panoply of absolutely staggering dimension, form, color, and vivid imagination. He has a wonderful sense of humor and a most perceptive eye.

There is one thing, however, that would keep *Delirious New York* from becoming the official guide to any city, especially one run by Walt Disney: It is the first X-rated architecture book. The cover, just for starters, shows Manhattan's two most prominent phalluses—the Chrysler and the Empire State—in bed together, but not, apparently, all that much in love. On the bedside table there is this Miss Liberty lamp, and Chrysler is ogling her, while Empire State is rigidly jealous. Rockeller Center is spying on them from a nearby closet.

Take two: We are now on pages 66 and 67. Chrysler and his friend seem to be a lot cozier, and there is this deflated and exhausted Goodyear blimp on the bedsheet between them. Rockefeller is not in sight at this moment.

Take three: On pages 198 and 199, the plot has thickened, to put it mildly. The bed has been replaced by all of Manhattan, which is now an air-mattress-type of bed floating in a sea of blue. In the drink are the three phalluses. Now Chrysler is chasing Rockefeller, while Empire State is about to drown in grief—or, anyway, in the general vicinity of Spuyten Duyvil. Madelon Vriesendorp, who did these paintings and who is Mrs. Koolhaas in what passes for Real Life, calls this scene "Freud Unlimited." So, you see, I am not making any of this up [...]

What Koolhaas has done in this book is not *entirely* innovative. A lot of people—for example, Robert Rauschenberg—have long told us about Manhattan's utterly chaotic and wonderful skyline and announced that Times Square was America's greatest work of art. But not until this book came along did we have all the facts, all the quotations, and all the beautiful images in one place.

There is an exhibition of all these fantasies, and many more, at the Guggenheim, until December 17. I wish it could be kept up on those rather Freudian walls forever.

ARCHITECTURAL EXTRAVAGANZA

Gilbert Millstein
New York Times, December 24, 1978.

The reader of this book will probably find it significant that the author is a European (a Dutchman, as it happens) and that he was first a screenwriter and only after that an architect. Historically, cultivated Europeans have tended to regard New York City either as Armageddon or as Paradise, but unquestionably as epitome or culmination (the living end?). In that last, Rem Koolhaas is no exception, and, of course, he is right. The city is, even in its decline of the last fifteen years or so, still the scale on which all other cities must be measured, precisely because of the destruction it has wreaked on itself, precisely because of the insane, unbalanced behavior of those who run it, tear it down and build it, and decide what shall happen to it. Enough of it survives—anxious, short of breath, by turns arrogant and cringing—so that the world (gladly or grudgingly) must say of New York that it is the paradigm of every city.

Now, it seems to me that *Delirious New York* is a motion picture script (indeed, Mr. Koolhaas describes himself as "Manhattan's ghostwriter") on the order of something turned out by one of the epic-makers of Hollywood past. That is, its historical research and the illustrations chosen to accompany it are absolutely first-rate—from the photographs of the three great lost amusement parks at Coney Island, to Murray's incredible "Roman Gardens" on West Forty-second Street (I wish he had been able to find pictures of the weird complex of theaters, roof gardens, and restaurants built by the first Oscar Hammerstein on Longacre Square), to Hugh Ferriss's romantic, terrifying visions of what New York should look like. When he is quoting from solid sources, the reader knows it, and when he is quoting from the bunkum of press agentry, the reader is told so, too. But in the end, what Mr. Koolhaas has given us is a Hollywood costume production and, like one of them, it is chock-full of pseudo-philosophy, heavy breathing, cloudy epigrams ("Manhattan is a utilitarian polemic") and similar pretensions. And we disagree on things. For example, Mr. Koolhaas sees Coney Island as the precursor of the Manhattan that came to be, a "foetal Manhattan" as he puts it. I think what happened is far different. The men who built Coney Island could never have put up their wild fantasies of Steeplechase, Luna, and Dreamland in Manhattan. They couldn't have paid for the land or made enough money out of what they had in mind. I believe that whatever elements of Coney may have been incorporated into the Manhattan skyscrapers were less the influence of Coney's extravagances than of the Beaux-Arts background of Manhattan's architects. Also, they were doing such things years before late-nineteenth-century Coney.

One has only to look at the catalogues of parts—parts, mind you!—for cast-iron buildings or facades. They were not simply extravagant extrapolation of classical models, but they made building more extravagant (in terms of architecture) because a builder could select half a dozen different forms out of the catalogues for a single building, ranging from Corinthian columns (sometimes painted to simulate marble) to Italianate lintels and sills between Gothic arches and French Renaissance cornices. Take a look in SoHo if you don't believe it. Mr. Koolhaas takes up a lot of space to say, "Wallace Harrison is Manhattan's last genius of the possible. It is his tragedy that after the Second World War the possible coincides no longer with the sublime. No longer can architects count on the businessmen's phantom calculations that make the impossible inevitable. The postwar architecture is the accountants' revenge on the prewar businessmen's dreams. [...] The result is the disintegrating curtain walls of the cheap skyscraper." It would have been simpler to say that the International Style won out, that it had become too expensive to put ornament on buildings, and that the cost of men and materials became prohibitive after the Great Depression. (In fact, Mr. Koolhaas points out that one good reason for Rockefeller Center is the Depression drop in cost of everything.)

Finally, he has an "Appendix: A Fictional Conclusion," and I am glad he called it that. It consists of a number of projects for Manhattan and Roosevelt Island that even the controversial architect John Portman wouldn't fool around with. On the other hand, you never know. Last summer, I visited the Beaubourg in Paris and saw the exhibit called "Paris-Berlin, 1900–1933." It contained many architects' drawings for projects not realized. Then I spent a couple of days walking around Défense and Nanterre, west of Paris. And I realized, with a sinking heart, that all the nonsense thought up by those faraway and long-ago architects in Paris and Berlin had come to be in La Défense and Nanterre. They are nightmarish places. The smell of lifelessness pervades them, as it does deserted movie sets. And, sooner than have the Koolhaas "fictional conclusion" achieve reality, I would settle for what is, bad as a lot of it is. I don't use the word *kitsch* much any more, but that is what La Défense and Nanterre and the "fictional conclusion" are.

A CONVERSATION WITH HUMAN ACTIVITIES

Marc Balet
Andy Warhol's Interview 2 (1979), 29.

rk: Architecture is a conversation with human activities in a precedented pattern.

mb: What is your favorite building?

rk: Rockefeller Center. I'd like to live at the Waldorf Astoria.

mb: What about loft living?

rk: It's corny and passé.

mb: Should form follow function?

rk: It couldn't, even if it should.

MANHATTALGIA

Reyner Banham
New Society, April 12, 1979, 98–99.

Delirious New York is a latecomer to the apparently still-profitable market for Manhattalgia, that rose-tinted retrospect of the skyscraper-crusted island which many people still seem to think of as the capital of America. The present wave of Manhattalgia runs from the Batman TV programmer of 1966–67 to *Superman*—the Movie—and is fundamentally camp-an'-Art-Deco Appreciation Society.

Not that the present wave lacks works of serious scholarship—*The Skyscraper Style* by Cervin Robinson and Rosemary Bletter, or Carol Krinsky's *Rockefeller Center*—but the camp and the serious always run back together; Robinson had a sizeable photo credit on *Superman*, Krinsky's book came out on the day "they saved the Rockettes," and what could be more camp than that proposal to preserve the Radio City chorus line as a civic monument?

Delirious New York is also serious and camp; and innovative, silly, penetrating, cheeky, infuriating, diverting, well researched, badly organized, far too pleased with itself, and marvelously recondite. In other words, Koolhaas is a genuine original who would have written this book had the present wave of skyscraper nostalgia never happened. Nevertheless, the more self-indulgent aspects of his thesis are at least partly attributable to current camp. Yet more are due to the fact that the whole project was initially developed in and around the Architectural Association in London, that academic Theater of the Absurd where anyone with two ideas to rub together is guaranteed a large and uncritical audience.

Koolhaas is also Dutch, which means that his is—among the present wave—a uniquely European and offshore view. Appropriately, then, he actually begins on the Atlantic Coast at "Coney Island, the technology of the fantastic" and works his way inward from there to finish at the centerpiece of the 1964 World's Fair, a skeletal globe where "like charred pork chops, the continents cling desperately to the carcass of Manhattanism."

And for the purposes of this book, Manhattanism is "the one urbanistic ideology that has fed, from its inception, on the splendors and miseries of the metropolitan condition—hyperdensity—without once losing faith in it as the basis for a desirable modern culture. Manhattan's architecture is a paradigm for the exploitation of congestion."

Well, it's a good try—the only trouble is that the ideology was so unstated and little understood back in the 1920s that it hardly deserves the name of ideology. Indeed, the fact that Koolhaas has had to write a "retroactive manifesto for Manhattanism" suggests that it may never have existed as a real "-ism" until he identified and named it.

The identifying and naming—however instructive—must remain largely symbolic. If you add up his case studies and his heroes—Rockefeller Center, the Waldorf, the Empire State Building, the Downtown Athletic Club, and Samuel Lionel Rothafel ("Roxy" of Radio City), Raymond Hood (architect of key skyscrapers around 1930), Salvador Dalí, Le Corbusier, and John D. Rockefeller, for instance—they account for such a small part of the land surface and real estate values of this actually rather low-density island-city that you have to wonder if the whole skyscraper thing is not just a figment of a fevered imagination.

Not necessarily Koolhaas's, but that of Hugh Ferriss, the real hero of the book. Ferriss was a brilliant architectural perspectivist for whom skyscraper New York was the natural stamping ground. He promoted fantasies of his own (*The Metropolis of Tomorrow*) and he converted other people's financial calculations into profiles of "buildings like mountains." His was the vision of a Manhattan that might have been (but for the slump and a few other things) and happened only in fragments, of which the last is the United Nations Building.

Obviously fascinated, Koolhaas calls him "The Prince of Darkness," but that really won't do. Too slick, too limiting. Ferriss was a minor architectural luminary who shone the brighter for concentrating his talents within a relatively tiny problem—the kinds of buildings that might be built within a couple of blocks of Wall Street, and in Midtown along Park and Fifth. What makes him so typically Manhattan is the intensity of his obsessive parochialism.

All right—the parish in question was then the financial capital of the world, and therefore of the utmost fascination to Europeans (*Geldzentrum, Weltzentrum,* cooed Eric Mendelsohn in tones of religious awe), but it was still a very little parish architecturally, in spite of the size of the individual structures (which Le Corbusier deemed "too small" in a brilliant preemptive quip to conceal his own awe-struck provincialism).

Is Koolhaas, too, trapped in some European parochialism and convinced that he understands when he does not; or does his easily impressed provincialism give him genuine insights into the skyscraper jungle that a true cosmopolite from, say, Rome or Leningrad or Edinburgh, might never possess? The book, alas, is not well enough thought out nor well enough written for us to know; everything (or nearly everything) is surface, sharply observed but delivered in flip aphorisms like: "Man's rush to the n-th floor is a neck-and-neck race between plumbing and abstraction."

But still, it's a load of fun; the pictures (except the projects by his own little coterie) are fascinating and some are real finds, like the drawings for a hotel in "Manhattan by the legendary Antonio Gaudí, the last past-master of Art Nouveau." But when Koolhaas proposes an "affinity between Gaudí's hysteria and Manhattan's frenzy," he really camps his case to pieces. Gaudí's design is not "an ideal skyscraper" but a Gothic Tower of Babel; put it alongside one of Ferriss's renderings, and it looks clumsy, pretentious, and nothing to do with Manhattanism "as a paradigm for the exploitation of congestion." Treat the book, therefore, as a marvelous postcard album of a fossil future, and save its alleged arguments for a night when the TV is on the blink.

HE'LL TAKE MANHATTAN

Paul Goldberger
New York Review of Books 10 (1979), 15–17.

[...] *Delirious New York* is a morality play masquerading as architectural history. This is too bad, really, because the right and noble side—the exuberant towers of a prewar Manhattan—is worth praising. Indeed, what Koolhaas admires is almost always worth admiring and what he damns is almost always worth damning. The problem is that so much else goes with Koolhaas's judgments. Setting the story of Manhattan into the frame of a struggle between the forces of irrationality (good) and the forces of rationality (evil) has led Koolhaas to be so selective in his facts as to make the book virtually useless as history, and what we are left with is merely polemic. And polemics are always more effective when they attack the future, where nothing can be proven, than when they turn backward and tangle with scholarship.

[...] Congestion is a magical concept here, but it is never fully explained. In his belief that vitality is a product of density, Koolhaas aligns himself with what has, by now, become conventional urban theory. Jane Jacobs would doubtless agree when Koolhaas tells us that "only congestion can generate the modernized automotive Venice," but he ignores the fact that Los Angeles and Houston, both cities of startling vitality, are places of relatively low density, their population spread widely across the landscape. Houston in particular seems today to have all of the aggressiveness and self-pride Koolhaas ascribes to New York, and does so with relatively little conventional congestion at all.

[...] Koolhaas ignores the negative meaning of congestion for the poor, just as he ignores the implications electronic technology has for the forms of cities. On the other hand, there are a number of observations in this book that are intelligent, and not a few that are also fresh—though Koolhaas's insistent hyperbole and exclusive use of the present tense often undermine them. Koolhaas is right, for example, in believing that the grid plan of streets is crucial to Manhattan's identity; it holds this irrational city in check, providing a subtly rational counterpoint to the city's mad impulses. But does that make the 1811 plan in which the grid was laid out "the most courageous act of prediction in Western civilization"? And if, as Koolhaas says, "subjugation, if not obliteration, of nature is [the grid's] true ambition," it hardly follows that the grid "makes the history of architecture and all previous lessons of urbanism irrelevant."

This last remark suggests the thesis, so often promoted by other romantic historians of Manhattan, that everything in New York was directed toward the new, toward the obliteration of everything old in favor of things that had never existed before. But is was never so simple: culture was never seen to begin with a truly fresh slate, even in the ruthlessly energetic New York of the early twentieth century, which was so passionately committed to growth. Koolhaas himself quotes from Benjamin de Casseres's *Mirrors of New York*: "We take from you what we need and we hurl back in your face what we do not need. Stone by stone we shall remove the Alhambra, the Kremlin, and the Louvre and build them anew on the banks of the Hudson." This more accurately reflects the attitude toward history that existed in the early years of this century—New York wanted history desperately, but without any of the ideological baggage that came along with it.

The notion was, in effect, to use architecture as a way of owning the past as no other culture had done before. The Gothic Revival of the nineteenth century, immersed in moral fervor as it was, was more dominated by the Gothic style than a style on its own; in twentieth-century New York, freedom from the ideologies of these different styles had been achieved not by abandoning them all to Modernism, as Le Corbusier urged, but by taking them, and using them freely, hedonistically even, with scant regard for their original meanings. A Roman bath for a train station, a Gothic crown for an office building, a Georgian manor for an apartment house—how better, in the absence of confidence in any indigenous tradition, to assert the superiority of one's own culture over all the others, now made architectural captives? Visual pleasure was the goal, and history was seen as a vast smorgasbord, each style there for the picking.

This is not entirely inconsistent with Koolhaas's view; his very point is to prove that New York was hedonistic. But he errs in seeing this hedonism as central to the city's physical development. The city's image in the early decades of this century was one of consummate theatricality, but this was always balanced by hardheaded, no-nonsense business. Skyscraper tops in New York may have been flamboyant—one could never imagine the Chrysler

Building in Chicago, the city of rational skyscrapers—but they sat on top of straightforward rentable space. There was nothing hedonistic about the Equitable Building which Koolhaas so much admires—it was a cynical attempt to get a lot of rentable space onto a small amount of land, no different in intention, really, from the boring glass boxes that line Third Avenue today.

[...] Koolhaas's acknowledgment of the rest of New York is so brief as to invite quotation in full: "A blueprint does not predict the cracks that will develop in the future; it describes an ideal state that can only be approximated. In the same way this book describes a *theoretical* Manhattan, a *Manhattan as conjecture*, of which the present city is the compromised and imperfect realization" (italics his). A lawyer writing liability disclaimers could not get his client off the hook more neatly: if there is not enough evidence to support the theory, he is saying, well, just remember that the world is imperfect and full of compromises, and that the theory is true anyway. Not only is this not good scholarship, it is barely even good polemic.

There is, however, an enormous amount of useful information here, even if it is often twisted to be made compatible with Koolhaas's "manifesto." Much of it is visual—there are superb photographs of early skyscrapers, and a truly remarkable array of documents of unbuilt projects, such as the early scheme by Wallace Harrison joining all of Lincoln Center's buildings by a common curvilinear lobby (I do not believe that this has ever been published), a fine set of illustrations of the early versions of Rockefeller Center, and a 1906 proposal by Theodore Starrett for a 100-story building. There are also splendid color plates of the projects which Koolhaas and his associates have done to encourage Manhattan to return to its irrational ways, and these are often quite beautiful and powerful.

The best is The City of the Captive Globe, a metaphorical Manhattan in which countless architectural styles, and much of architectural history, sit on a granite base, each piece filling its own private block of the grid and turning the city literally into a gallery of the history of architecture. Finally there are Madelon Vriesendorp's exquisite and witty drawings of skyscrapers as living beings, one of which, a view of the Empire State Building and the Chrysler Building in bed together, adorns the cover. All of the illustrations in the book suggest a Manhattan of great beauty and drama, and one cannot escape the feeling that the pictures make Koolhaas's point far better than do his words.

THE CULTURE OF PROFESSIONAL ARCHITECTURE

S. Frederick Starr

Architectural Design 5–6 (1979), 136–39.

It will be interesting to see how the avant-garde establishment handles this book, which assaults most of the precepts upon which that school has been based since the days of Gropius and Le Corbusier. It will be no less instructive to observe the response of the emerging counterestablishment, which rejects the avant-garde's tired addiction to socialized fish tanks, but retains its faith in the leadership of a verbalizing, self-advertising high culture elite in architecture. The safest tactic for both would be to ignore *Delirious New York*. Alternatively, they might compliment the author on his droll style and tip their hats to his wife, Madelon Vriesendorp, for her Vitruvian-porno architectural paintings which adorn the pages of Koolhaas's study. They might even take note of the pioneering historical scholarship that has recalled from oblivion major landmarks in American architecture of the period 1890–1940. But either camp will find it difficult to accept the argument that Koolhaas's material poses with such clarity and rationality, for that argument is utterly subversive of the notion of architecture as it has been practiced for most of our century.

In *The Painted Word*, Tom Wolfe argued that modern painting is in fact not painting at all, but a series of verbal manifestoes translated into nonverbal artifacts and then deciphered back into the original verbal texts by critics. According to Koolhaas, modern architecture is in much the same predicament. For three score years, architects have piled up ringing declarations, evocative slogans, and verbal calls to arms. Occasionally, these have been translated into buildings, though rarely into cities or complete environments. The best remains on paper, which has replaced brick and mortar as the prime medium for the architectural sophisticate.

[...] Those seeking in *Delirious New York* a definition of Manhattanism as a specific style will be disappointed. Manhattanism embraces a myriad of mutually incompatible styles, often arrayed on the same building. Having found no single stylistic stamp that constitutes Manhattanism, Koolhaas turns his back on the entire critical method that has prevailed since Wölfflin, according to whom the history of architecture is a study in the morphology of style. Nor does Koolhaas accept the technological determinism that holds that Manhattan's new architecture was created in response to the possibilities offered by new materials and techniques. New York was as omnivorous with regard to technologies as it was to style, turning any technologies to its own ends rather than becoming their slave, and concocting surrogate technologies and materials when the "real" ones had not yet been invented. Least of all does Koolhaas find that the architecture of Manhattan was created according to some preconceived dogma. The skyscraper, for example, came into being with "no manifesto, no architectural debate, no doctrine, no law, no planning, no ideology, no theory." Other emanations of Manhattanism were similarly unconscious.

Koolhaas's New York is dumb, unreflective. And how could it have been otherwise? A closet Nietzschean, Koolhaas holds that for a doctrine to be fully realized it cannot be openly stated, that self-consciousness arises only when the period of greatest creativity is passed—in short, that the owl of Minerva flies only at night.

[...] Who devised and penetrated this expansive program on Manhattan Island? A major contribution of Koolhaas's study is that it brings to the fore a group of brilliantly innovative architects who, though they did not themselves acknowledge it, functioned as a school above schools, bound together only by their adherence to this program. The names of such diverse figures as Raymond Hood, Harvey Wiley Corbett, Frederic Thompson, and William H. Reynolds may not dominate the annals of modern architecture, but they should, and very likely will, thanks to this book. Dedicated above all to deeds, rather than words, these men worked quietly but decisively to create the world's greatest city. To a man, they understood that the elegant *architect-poseur* is one who has failed as architect-builder. They therefore shunned the personal style of the architect-aesthetes, with their velvet jackets and portfolios of hothouse conceptions. They were, as Koolhaas observes, a cabal of sophisticated architects masking themselves as philistines.

To see just how much further these pioneers went than their better-known aesthete contemporaries, compare Hugh Ferriss with the Polish-Russian avant-gardist Kasimir Malevich. Malevich, it will be recalled, developed a series of visionary *Arkhitektons* on the basis of his own Suprematist experiments and his second-hand contact with New York. Some of his earliest drawings of *Arkhitektons* were, in fact, imposed on photographs of the real world of Manhattan skyscrapers as they then existed. Several years earlier, however, Ferriss had grappled with the program imposed by New York's 1916 zoning law and devised a series of expressionistic *Arkhitektons* of his own which, unlike Malevich's, were destined to serve as the basis for a series of actual buildings by Ferriss and others.

If members of Koolhaas's cabal outstripped their contemporaries at the drawing board, they surpassed all but the most visionary utopians of the modern era in the boldness of their psychological and social insights. In this respect Koolhaas's chapter on Coney Island is particularly instructive. On that "clitoral appendage at the mouth of New York's natural harbor" a succession of home-grown Fouriers devised buildings and whole environments with no purpose other than to provide pleasure. In the same year Freud was writing his *Interpretation of Dreams*, Senator William H. Reynolds set out to build at Coney a Dreamland, replete with a Boullée-like "Blue Dome of Creation"; an Incubator Building, where a tamed technology would save premature infants for the new society; and a Lilliputia, the miniaturized laboratory where notions later implemented on Manhattan itself were first essayed.

[...] It is not surprising that the Schilleresque playfulness of Manhattanism was immensely popular with the public. Indeed, nowhere on Earth did modern architecture have a mass following as it did in New York. Nor is this mere supposition on Koolhaas's part. In a particularly imaginative investigation into popular culture, the author presents some of the thousands of contemporary postcards depicting New York monuments, many based on designs released by the architects but others actually anticipating the architects' fantasies, as if the public was impatient with the designers' restraint and caution. The messages to the folks back home scrawled by American tourists on the backs of such cards attest to the intense engagement with modern architecture that existed on Manhattan during the so-called age of the avant-garde.

It need scarcely be said that the mass popularity of Manhattanism sharply contradicts the European and Russian conception of modern architecture as being imposed "from above" by an enlightened elite. To be sure, the architects of the Bauhaus and the Russian Constructivists proclaimed their concern for the public at large, but they did so on the basis of an ideological image of "the proletariat" (to which they obviously did not belong) rather than on an actual involvement with its social and psychological aspirations. No wonder that in both Germany and Russia, the avant-gardists were swept aside by *volkish* or proletariat architects, who denounced Modernism and its advocates as an arrogant conspiracy against public taste. Meanwhile, Manhattan was surging to its zenith in the 1930s.

Some years ago Robert Venturi shocked architectural highbrows by suggesting that they could actually learn something from Las Vegas. This outrageous proposal served as a timely corrective to an avant-gardism which demurely covered its elitism with the fig leaf of radical rhetoric. But the positive ideal that Venturi advanced turned out to be quite limited in its possibilities, and rather tacky besides.

Not so with Koolhaas's Manhattanism. Because at bottom it is a worldview rather than a style, a method of design, or a complex of technologies, Manhattanism opens far more doors than it closes. For this reason most of the leading ideologists of the avant-garde were fascinated by it, though for them to have acknowledged their fascination would have meant virtually to have declared their own bankruptcy. Koolhaas writes: "It is Le Corbusier's all-consuming passion to invent and build the New City commensurate with the demands and potential glories of the new machine civilization. It is his tragic bad luck that such a city already exists when he develops this ambition, namely Manhattan."

[...] Koolhaas's Manhattan was completed by 1940. Since then, he admits, it has been in decline. One may well enquire into the causes of this reversal of New York's fate, since they may have implications for any post-Manhattanism, if such should arise. Regrettably, Koolhaas devotes far less attention to the fall of Manhattan than to its rise, and his explanation is not fully satisfactory. Avoiding the obvious socioeconomic factors, he argues that Manhattanism was exported to Europe at an early date and came back to America after the war, cleaned up, civilized, and denatured. Meanwhile, many of New York's best architects had died, taking their testament with them to the grave. Manhattan "became an enigmatic heritage that the next generation could no longer decipher." Koolhaas claims that the bacillus of avant-gardism that had been unable to take root in the healthy organism of pre-1940 New York architecture now spreads through the bloodstream like measles among the Indians. It caused imagination to atrophy and the wholesome playfulness to give way to moralistic earnestness.

Unlike the rest of the book, this line of argument is not well grounded in the historical evidence. Surely the problem was not merely that the architects had lost their nerve (even as they became more visible); rather, the patrons, too, had gone square, losing their sense of adventure and the close engagement with public imagination upon which true Manhattanism had fed for two generations.

In the conclusion of *Delirious New York,* Koolhaas steps out of the role of historian and assumes his more customary role as a card-carrying visionary architect. [...] The project for a City of the Captive Globe is particularly important because it indicates more clearly than the rest of the book just where Koolhaas himself stands in relation to his subject. In this fantasy he assembles on a grid plan the architectural manifestations of most of the leading ideologies and beliefs, from Communism, Capitalism, and Christianity to Surrealism, Suprematism, and Technocratism. Like the exhibits at Coney Island, each is allotted its own block on the grid and each is allowed and even encouraged to realize itself to the fullest extent possible on that territory. The liberated egos working to elaborate each "ism" are utterly free, thanks to the grid. They are far freer, in fact, than would be possible on a more thoroughly planned design or, by implication, in a less pluralistic society. But the grid also prevents conflict. Just as at Coney Island it was inconceivable that Dreamland should invade the territory of Luna Park, so is it out of the question for one ego in the pluralistic grid to impinge on the territory allotted to another. And because there is no conflict, no ego is able fully to realize itself and, in the end, nothing is truly real except the grid.

Thus, Koolhaas's City of the Captive Globe—of modern civilization—is that this fact is fully understood by the faceless crowd thronging its streets. The Metropolis might seek to replace nature, but the man on the street, whether in Coney Island or the City of the Captive Globe, understands full well the unreality of the man-made environment which he admires as a spectator. No "ism," no Ego in the modern city is fully realized because the democratic grid has relativized them all out of existence.

The average person does not take the competing theories and ideologies seriously because they are not real, and they are not real because he knows they exist only thanks to, and within the protective framework imposed by, the grid. It goes without saying that the designers who conceived the grid also appreciate this, just as the greenhouse keeper knows that his orchids and cacti would expire at once without the artificial protection offered by the film of glass overhead.

Who, then, does not understand the true nature of things? Koolhaas responds: the thinkers, theorists, polemicists, and ideologists who constitute the "critically thinking intelligentsia." In the last analysis, Koolhaas's book is a savage attack on the naiveté of this group as it has existed in the modern era. It is an attack on architects who, having joined the verbalizers, spend their days talking about hypothetical new worlds when real ones are springing up all around. It is an attack on the pomposity of false revolutionaries who won't acknowledge that genuine ones are to be found in anonymous office buildings and on the streets of the modern Metropolis.

If *Delirious New York* can be said to have a program it is this: to transform the very culture of professional architecture so as to rescue it from the position of utter ineffectuality to which it condemned itself when it adopted the doctrine of avant-gardism. Such a program renders this otherwise delightful book subversive.

REMIFICATIONS
Patrick L. Pinnell
Skyline 6 (1979), 8.

"When correctly viewed, anything is lewd," Tom Lehrer used to sing. Rem Koolhaas's working premise in *Delirious New York* is not far from that. When correctly viewed, *anything* can be a metaphor, and existence's random slosh and wash can be willed apart to reveal the bottom-patern below the choppy surface of events. There is a plot, Koolhaas says, in Manhattan's apparently chaotic tale; *Delirious New York* is nothing less than an attempt to sketch the secret psychohistory of the City. It would also like to be political and polemical, exactly as the subtitle implies, and that is a real problem. Nothing is wrong with taking a well-chosen extreme position: architecture these days could use a good bit more of that. But *Delirious New York*'s dual aspirations turn out to be mutually exclusive.

[...] The most important virtue is the illustrations. Koolhaas's interest, though he never acknowledges it, must be not only in Manhattan as a theoretical demonstration, but as an often bizarrely beautiful phenomenon, for he has collected a bookful of images which reflect exactly that. The pictures are the author's best friends and worst enemies. They, if anything, will sell the book, but they are of such interest themselves as to make the "Manifesto" of the book's subtitle almost invisible.

Another asset is the writing, which in more than a few places is very good indeed. It is all present-tense and sorts out into discrete episodes with single-word titles (Dos Passos, anyone?). At its best this gives the book a good, driving narrative pace. But with everything in one tense, and all episodes about the same length, the whole has a certain heated monotony to it, even if a large cryptobiographical shape is apparent.

But problems of overall form are outweighed by Koolhaas's gift for making imaginatively stunning individual episodes. Each little tale has its own Aristotelian unities of time, place, and action, and is usually based on some wild extrapolation of a simple fact or act into an all-encompassing generality. Some of this invention is shaggy-dog, some pointed and wickedly funny.

[...] The title and, more than that, the very existence of *Delirious New York* confirm the suspicion that an important shift has occurred in what architects and critics feel to be basic to making a building. In their time the historians Sigfried Giedion and Nikolaus Pevsner, assisted by a host of architects, argued that the fundamental necessity for architecture was to reflect faithfully some immanent spirit of the age, some zeitgeist. David Watkin's *Morality and Architecture* has lately made it its mission to discredit zeitgeist and all its nasty consequences; there has also been a notable increase in publications with location-oriented titles, like *Summer Places, People in Places, The Place of Houses*. *Delirious New York* must be counted with the others as indicating that a change has occurred away from the Giedion-Pevsner Modern tendency to explain architecture as a manifestation of some pervasive character of its age, and toward looking at it as a more or less direct consequence of its location. Genius loci has replaced zeitgeist in the creation myth of architecture.

The phenomenon seems to be one different in kind from the "regionalisms" which in the 1940s and 1950s used to square dance in and out of trade magazines. Current concerns are both more site-specific and more—well, basically, mystical and irrational. This is not to argue that the real old Greek sense of the genius loci is abroad in the land—we are not back to the point of planting our Parthenons only where we're sure there's a Sybil just below the footings—but Charles Moore's care for "making places," and Robert Venturi's concern for physical, cultural, and historical context begin to look like early aspects of a desire to see buildings and cities as the expressions of the unique combination of forces at work on a given site. Energy conservation alone cannot nearly account for the number of buildings now designed to dig deeply into their ground, and which make a special point of their rootedness; nor does the fashion for gardens fully explain the equal number of designs where the architecture does a topiary weave into the site vegetation. The urge takes many forms, but it is apparent that for many architects location, locus, is all.

Delirious New York would be significant if only because it is the clearest single expression so far of this general tendency. Koolhaas's Manhattanism marks a state of mind precisely contrary to that in the idea of an International Style. No more universal space-time; instead, the will of the place, Manhattan Island or wherever. Style, be it good, bad, ugly, historicist-eclectic, or ruthlessly, unreferentially postfunctional, is no longer in this view an important issue. In Manhattanism *every* style can coexist within the grid. Perhaps most interestingly the idea of a governing genius loci denies Modern's utopian program of universal social and political perfection any possibility of success.

[...] *Delirious New York* is absorbingly imaginative, well-written, wonderfully illustrated, poorly made—at thirty-five dollars it should not have a hot-pink hard cover which curls up at the corners—and, at the level of polemic to which Rem Koolhaas admirably enough aspires, fundamentally dubious.

ENMESHED IN IRRESOLUTION

Richard Munday

Transition 4 (1980), 46–48.

[...] There need be no doubting that *Delirious New York* is a work of intensity and purpose, and for that matter, sincerity. Koolhaas, and his colleagues in OMA [...] do appear to be actively cognizant of, and have chosen—as have few of their contemporaries in architecture—to comprehensively confront in their work the particular questions concerning the nature of existence which still face the twentieth-century artist. *Delirious New York* may have failed, it may have offered no resolution, but as an attempt to involve architecture in the problems which have been faced in other art forms, it is an impressive achievement. [...]

Sigmund Freud—that opening wedge in the twentieth-century collapse of faith—is not a new consideration, either in art or in the formulations of popular mythology, but Koolhaas does not appear to be convinced that society has encompassed him yet. Through the interplay between the subject of Koolhaas's writing and the language and manner of the writing, this issue is directed plainly though unclearly to our attention. Abundant sexual metaphors suggest that civilization is no more than a diaphanous veil, while the extension of the terminology into the psychiatric serves to call into question the sanity of the world which is being portrayed. (The lifting of skirts by the writing also suggests the nature of its own commerce vis-a-vis the subject matter and the writer's intentions.) The heroes of Koolhaas's New York, those whom he credits with acts of genius, and who go almost unmentioned in other histories, are in the main also portrayed as shrewd opportunists, gamblers, and showmen, people who exploit and mislead a society, which colludes eagerly in its own debasement. Further, the fragmented episodic structure enables Koolhaas to suggest quite plausibly—but without having to furnish evidence—hidden connections between ideas, events, and people, simply by virtue of their location on a page.

By such means a theme of alienation develops. Society is portrayed as irrational, coarse, even cruel, and this is applauded. Values are inverted and become suddenly meaningless. This impression contextualizes and undermines the positivism endemic in urban and architectural ideology and implicit in the forms of both the historical analysis and the manifesto which comprise the structural substance of the book, and in this lies a hidden proposition: to see and recognize a reality, and to formulate values more comprehensive than those which earlier sufficed as a basis for action. [...]

Delirious New York is a rich and complex statement. The writing is a tableau which attempts to represent issues that Koolhaas believes to be ineluctably bound to architecture, and which he would have the reader see as he sees, and in a way that somehow takes into account the implications of unconsciousness and the chronic partiality of vision. However, its obfuscatory intentions are often so irritatingly obvious that it is almost not worth the effort. The book is a departure from familiar exposition and almost unique in architectural literature. Consequently it has and will continue to be grievously misunderstood. It is open to the widest interpretation.

Madelon Vriesendorp's paintings are clever and painstaking, and the OMA projects, which range right across Modernism, from J. J. P. Oud and the Russian Constructivists, to a very strong debt to Robert Venturi (even for the cadence of the project explanations) offer a valuable synthesis which alone make the book, itself enmeshed in irresolution, worthwhile.

AN ABRUPT DEPARTURE FROM THE NEW HOPELESSNESS

Gert Jonker

Bouw 24 (1980), 24–25.

For two months, in two of its galleries, the Stedelijk Museum in Amsterdam will be exhibiting work by the Office for Metropolitan Architecture—a conglomerate domiciled, to the best of my knowledge, in London, though that is not reported in any of the documentation. Professor Ungers was part of the group for a while but has since left. OMA currently consists of Rem Koolhaas, Elia Zenghelis, Madelon Vriesendorp, and Zoe Zenghelis. Concurrent to this, a new gallery in Amsterdam located a stone's throw from the museum—the Van Rooy gallery at Willemsparkweg 36—is showing a single work by OMA in detail. That work is titled Exodus.

In a particularly lucid statement accompanying the exhibition, Rem Koolhaas writes that neither his projects for Manhattan and an adjacent island nor any of his other designs are meant to be "utopian," in the sense of being unfeasible. But since these American plans have no clients, the attendant design art is indeed a sort of "paper architecture" (Koolhaas calls it a recently invented category). "But the danger exists that drawing becomes a vicarious activity and the 'paper' reputation of its maker in the end stands in the way of realization," according to Koolhaas. "His activity becomes a kind of fertilizer for 'real' architecture."

The opening at Stedelijk Museum on November 6 drew a huge crowd; one could have walked across the, primarily architectonic, heads of those in attendance. Anyone as yet not aware of it might be tempted to surmise that the OMA method is "in." Koolhaas's 1978 book *Delirious New York* may well have contributed to this, but there is obviously more to it than that.

The explanation could lie in the fact that OMA fits almost seamlessly in with the New Despair, which I consider a better name than "postmodern," "neorealism" or "neorationalism." The group of New Despairers is extremely heterogeneous and includes extraverts such as Johnson alongside coquettish introverts such as Venturi, yakheads such as Aldo Rossi (to introduce you to some new terms), neomonumentalists such as Stirling and many others. What they have in common is their despair, because things cannot continue as they are. The movement bears all the characteristics of a counterreformation—including all the unsavory ones. Of course the New Romanticism of cozy domesticity was also counterreformational, albeit without the onerous consequences of Ignatius. [...] In that sense, the New Despair is counter-counterreformational. That may well yield it a level of temporary success, since we live in a time of despair on just about every front.

Innovations in (and outside of) architecture are almost always part of the endless seesawing between styles, not much different than the move from long skirts to short skirts, bullet bras to braless and so on. To the extent they are captured in words, they consist of an untenable vilification of that which came before and an indemonstrable deification of the new, with some obfuscation of the fact that the new is not so new after all.

When Koolhaas explains his ideas for Manhattan with the assertion that Manhattan is already a hotchpotch conglomeration and his plans are intended to transform it into an "archipelago of ideological islands," that hardly sounds new at all. The concept of more or less autarkic buildings lined like headstones along a network of roadways (which would naturally be obsolete between autarkies) is not a new one. The watered-down versions once built in this vein made for unlivable environments and the designers of these *villes radieuses* could claim that their uninhabitability was the result of half-hearted execution. Never a shortage of excuses.

It is not evident from the works exhibited whether they would have any architectural merit in reality. That trick with the bird's-eye view (compare Stirling's worm's-eye view) provides a pictorial charm that deflects from the issue of whether all those New Neurenberg-esque toys would have any intrinsic value close-up. Looking at the drawing City of the Captive Globe, one sees a collection of literally every skyscraper totem ever conceived or conceivable, some imbued with a superficial plasticity, some only visible to plane passengers, many displaying their patent unfeasibility, though in other cases at the very least suggesting their unnecessariness.

New Welfare Island (1975–76) shows a collection of linen cupboards scattered in a desolate expanse, which, if memory serves with regard to that landscape, the urban planners will first have to create. The pièce de résistance is a collection of six towering, somewhat quarter-barrel tipped, poles that to my mind evoke Sert's Miró museum in Barcelona and Gropius's Bauhaus Archive for Darmstadt (now in West Berlin). Evocations of Sert are of course understandable; his apartment building with analogous poles—in the form of stairwells—is nearby. But of course OMA is counting on America's demolishing everything every twenty-five years from now on—so that explains it.

All of this is nice enough as a pithy debate presentation, but I find myself wondering why it is automatically associated with architecture. In recent years Koolhaas and his ilk have turned their sights toward Europe and a greater degree of reality, "alarmed," as he says in his statement, "by the abundance of 'theoretical' projects—an almost overflowing reservoir of unproven claims and pretensions."

We would include in that category a design for the revitalization of the old dome prison in Arnhem. It contains plans for expanding the building with a basement story in the cylindrical void—no longer intended, apparently, for roughing up prisoners out of sight but to house sporting and other beneficial activities. A cruciform trench in the ground provides access to the underworld: excessively dramatic and, in an erstwhile Christian country, not in the best of taste. Other holdovers from modern prison thinking are incorporated in the wedge-shaped and other extensions along the outer circle, all neatly executed in the still immortal idiom of the International Style.

The second object in the "European gallery" is, of course, the design for the extension to the Dutch Parliament complex at the Binnenhof in The Hague. "Only through a clear-sighted reimagining of the process of constant revision to which all institutes are exposed can the new be made believable once again," says the designer. To that end he offers us a denuded unplaza at the mouth of the Spui, with an orthogonal strip of buildings along one side that penetrates the Binnenhof square from Lange Poten street.

In the nearby Van Rooy gallery, Exodus is exhibited in its entirety, although not through January 4 but only until December 25. This closer inspection does not yield any truly new insights, however. OMA's work is essentially urban planning in the sense the term once long ago held as the physical shaping of the outdoor space to such an extent that all that is left for architecture are the detailing and interiors. Anyone unable to embrace the external world molded by OMA can perhaps find solace in the fact that OMA itself also disregards this aspect. The "building," the "thing," appears to be only the vehicle for the "expressive form" of innovation.

None of that has anything to do with architecture as the (for my part, utopian) design and expression of human behavior. It is spectacle, presumably much better than its built realization—and therein lies the crux: true architecture is always better than its pictures. For all that, at the new gallery people can at least enjoy the fact that there is a place where architectural drawings are displayed and offered for sale.

This is noted, however, with certain reservations. When I saw the highly pictorial works of Koolhaas/Vriesendorp and several others hanging on the wall for several thousand guilders apiece over the past few weeks there, the existence of this new viewing locale indicated to me above all the existence of a new market. The "unproven claims and pretensions" may just be, if sufficiently masterful and self-involved, a new field for collectors and traders that could lead to a whole new "circuit" of prestige. Painting, sculpture, and land, environmental, and conceptual art have all long been caught in such circuits, which decide what is or will be "in." With a bit of luck, we are now getting an architecture circuit that state architects, beer manufacturers, and, in due course, housing corporations will not be able to ignore.

FIRST DECADE, FIRST HALF (1978–1985): HOPE HAS RETURNED

3

At the end of the 1970s, OMA came back to Europe, and in 1980 the Rotterdam headquarters was established, following the commission for a social housing project in Amsterdam. The office had already made a second start in 1978, after its foundation in 1975, by submitting a proposal to the competition for an extension to the Dutch Parliament in The Hague. The design was a joint effort of Koolhaas, Zenghelis, and Zaha Hadid, a student of theirs at the Architectural Association in London. It marked the beginning of OMA's First Decade—as the retrospective exhibition in Rotterdam in 1989 would be called—but it was also a declaration of intent. After learning from Manhattan, OMA would concentrate during the next decade on Europe—exposing its nostalgic neuroses and slow inefficiency—and more particularly on the Netherlands, where Koolhaas detected many mendacious, patronizing, and dull tendencies in Dutch structuralist architecture. A consensus was growing in the debate on the European city: a confrontation with the historical urban fabric was no longer considered desirable, and what was needed was a careful and recognizable construction. OMA's project for the Dutch Parliament was a blatant and brutal attack on these *idées reçues* concerning conservation, city renewal, and political representation.

This is true for most of their unbuilt proposals from this period, and critical reception followed suit. OMA's innovative and polemical projects were interpreted as necessary electroshocks for a self-centered, conformist, and depressed architecture, but they were also considered too confrontational to be implemented—not by critics but by decision-makers and administrations. The strategies partly discovered, partly created in *Delirious New York*—dealing with instability, entrepreneurship, speed, novelty, humor, and entertainment, but also with both unexplored and self-evident formal architectonic possibilities—enabled OMA to shake the old continent, and critics from the Netherlands, Belgium, the United Kingdom, France, Switzerland, and Italy were grateful for the chances architecture was offered to survive as a stimulating, surprising, and relevant discipline, that didn't simply tried to satisfy or soothe its public. OMA appeared to be a strange, fascinating, and somewhat secret bunch of architects, and real resistance to their approach did not yet occur. The opposite is true: "The traditional idea of architecture has vanished," French theoretician Françoise Choay wrote, full of praise for the project for La Villette in Paris (a competition OMA lost against Bernard Tschumi); Belgian architecture critic Geert Bekaert concluded his first long essay—published in a Dutch periodical—on OMA with the promising words: "Hope has returned." To understand this conclusion, it is necessary to understand the economic, social, political, and cultural crisis of the 1970s in Europe. In architectural theory, it came to the fore most clearly in Manfredo Tafuri's pessimism (and in his conviction that architecture should accept its marginal position by remaining silent and suspending every form of communication or projection). The sense of despair was also present, however, in other domains of culture and society, and found concise expression in, for example, the lyric "No future / No future for you" by the Sex Pistols, but also in the poem "Remembrance" by German poet Hans Magnus Enzensberger from 1980, in which the 1970s are dismissed with the line "That anyone should think of them with leniency / would be asking too much." OMA proved how it was possible to leave that dreadful decade behind by developing future-oriented scenarios in the form of architectural projects.

OMA did not yet build, but the office continued to exhibit—at the Stedelijk Museum in Amsterdam (1980), the Architectural Association in London (1981) and the Max Protetch Gallery and the Institute for Architecture and Urban Studies in New York (1982). In his review of the two latter events, Paul Goldberger indicated OMA's idiomatic way of designing contextually: "These romantic, machine-like objects have been shaped to relate to what is around them, to take into account the needs and textures of the existing city and landscape." This is also true on a conceptual level, and the reception of the early work shows that national architecture cultures reacted differently, according to their own problems and cultural histories. While in the United Kingdom, writing about OMA remained limited to the vicinity of the Architectural Association, in France Koolhaas became part of a struggle for the values and techniques of modernist architecture which were aligned with the achievements of French modernity and of the French Revolution. It is no coincidence that *L'Architecture d'Aujourd'hui* published a theme issue on OMA in 1985, including an interview with Koolhaas entitled "The Second Chance for Modern Architecture." Already in 1982, forty young French architects had been assembled in Paris in the exhibition *La modernité, un projet inachevé*—also the title of Jürgen Habermas's text, written in reaction to the twenty facades in the Strada Novissima at the Venice Architecture Biennale of 1980, as a defense of "what assisted the spontaneously self-renewing historical contemporaneity of the zeitgeist to find its own objective expression."[1] For Habermas, postmodernist architecture, based on a straightforward, deliberate but superficial reuse of the past, had abandoned the necessary task of modernizing society. Habermas didn't take into consideration OMA's contribution to the 1980 biennale—a nonfacade in the form of a translucent screen that went against the grain of the exhibition, and that can be regarded both as an emblematic project and as a clear sign how the work of OMA was received by critics, not only as a reckoning with the 1970s but also as an alternative to the increasingly dominant Postmodernism of the 1980s.[2]

1 Jürgen Habermas, "Modernity: An Unfinished Project," trans. Nicholas Walker, in *Habermas and the Unfinished Project of Modernity*, ed. Maurizio Passerin d'Entreves and Seyla Benhabib (Cambridge: Polity Press, 1996), 39.
2 On OMA's contribution to the Strada Novissima, see Léa-Catherine Szacka, *Exhibiting the Postmodern: The 1980 Venice Architecture Biennale* (Venice: Marsilio, 2016), 153–54.

SHEDDING OF THE SHACKLES
Cathy Peake, Grant Marani, Ian McDougall, and Richard Munday
Transition 4 (1980), 14–18.

[...] *Does your fascination with Manhattan lead to a fascination with the fine line between the moral and the immoral, or good and evil?*

I'm a kind of Nietzschean and so there are kind of amoral, hedonistic drives which I follow to their logical conclusion. I think that's exhilarating, but I don't see it really as a struggle between good and evil. What is Nietzsche's book called—*The Gay Science*? I consider that *Delirious New York* is also *The Gay Science* for architecture. A kind of shedding of the shackles. Everyone else is running back to the shackles. [...] To understand the present scene you have to understand one thing. Modernity was invented on the continent, and it was almost totally ignored by the Anglo-Saxon world until the mid- to late 1930s. Then with the war, it kind of stepped over to England, first in the person of the émigrés, but in England also, some people became interested. There, a circle developed which consisted of Colin Rowe and others. They became the avant-garde of modernity in architecture in England. But they hated its idealism. They liked the formal intricacies and the language of modernity, but they hated its content. So, from the beginning, they have always tried to divorce the content from the appearance. Rowe worked on that. In the 1940s he went to the US and became an extremely influential teacher, and, at some point, all of the New York Five came under his influence. So they all performed the same lobotomy between content and appearance. And Rowe, with his horribly cynical way of discussing it, enjoyed the physique without being embarrassed by the morality. In Rowe's book *Collage City*—his final statement—he says it is all directed toward "the enjoyment of utopian aesthetics without suffering the embarrassment of utopian politics": that's a direct quote. He's very frank, very interesting. But that attitude accounts for a lot of their relentlessness about form. They have been programmed by someone who hated that idealism about content.

Scully would say that American architecture has always taken the forms of European architecture and translated them into its own forms without the content.

Yes, but at least he would say that they substituted another content. And that is the whole point. I think the strange consequence of Rowe's people was that they really became against content. So that is why you see Peter Eisenman struggling like crazy to avoid content. And why, in a completely different way, you also see Michael Graves being extremely shy about content—really staying with the surface.

Last night you were criticizing Eisenman's way of operating.

No, I wasn't criticizing it.

Well, how do you approach his work?

I think that he is somebody who has completely fabricated an architecture, out of nothing, almost.

I find his architecture poses a very human challenge.

Yes, me too. Out of nothing he started to apply a series of rules and volatile substance. By sheer logic he makes it into impulse and in the end it leads to objects that are very dense with willpower. He manages to be a sort of Super 8 movie in his work. But I both like him and admire his work. Actually, it is a lot nicer than you would think. Those houses, if you are inside, really are very nice, to the point of cuteness.

[...]
Do you see the artist as a dissident? And as subversive?

No. There are also some very good nondissident artists. I don't even think the artist necessarily has to be subversive. I think, in a way, the idea of subversion is a fallacy of the avant-garde. But it has to be new.

[...]
Do you think there are any parallels between you and Venturi? He went to Las Vegas, you went to New York as the archetypal metropolis of the twentieth century.

I will continue to be a speculative architect; you have to devise or develop significant metaphors which structure the whole situation. But as far as Venturi goes, *Learning from Las Vegas* came out just as I was working for my book. I was terribly afraid that it would preempt anything I had to say. When I read it, I was very pleased that it didn't. Because again, it is a work which completely disregards content. There is nothing at all about what happens inside those buildings in Las Vegas, which I think is legitimate, in a certain sense. But there are parallels—the difference is that my book is more of a book than his. Mine has more claims to literature than it has to being a book strictly about architecture. His book addresses an architectural audience. I am not necessarily interested in that in the first place.

What do you think has happened to our ideas about the future?

I don't know. They are gloomy. We are now so undisciplined that we can be thrown by the slightest obstacle in our path. I notice that in architecture it is not professional to claim that there is a future.

[...]

Last night we were talking about your perverse interests in architecture and the perverse way you look at things.

No. People have always called me perverse but I have never understood why. Maybe that perverseness has something to do with me becoming a chameleon in reverse—if everybody is thinking one thing I have to think the opposite. I have to be careful with this because at times people make sense and I have to avoid thinking the opposite.

[...]

What was the central figure in your development as an architect?

I would say Leonidov. In the beginning. Without any doubt. But I hope to exorcize that by publishing a book some time next year. And then, people like Hood and Mies.

[...]

Who was your best critic? You spoke about Jencks picking you up off the street.

Two people have picked me up off the street in my life. One was Jencks and the other was Eisenman. Eisenman was a good critic. And he said, "You have no sense of architecture at all." The pool analogy is really addressed to Eisenman—he would always say there is no shift, no tension, no ... "architecture is aaargh" of my work. They were both good at establishing human relations. I think George Baird has insights that are very sophisticated, very developed. I value him very much too, especially for his accuracy.

CELEBRATION OR CRITICISM

Robert Maxwell
OMA: Projects 1978–1981, ed. Robert Maxwell (London: Architectural Association, 1981), 3–7.

[...] It would be possible to see these earlier works of OMA as either a celebration of capitalist fantasy or a criticism of its heartlessness. The Raft of the Medusa and the Floating Pool are not proposing commercial propositions on a par with James Wines' disintegrating supermarkets but suggest an underlying polemic which is metaphysical rather than ironic. As with many surrealist propositions, the results are hardly legible as imitation of life or propaganda for a lifestyle—but rather call for an appreciation of the sheer autonomy of the aesthetic: the impossible story is resolved only on a level of pure poetry—the aim has been to create poeticity itself—or, in the case of OMA, pure architecturality.

But not anymore, it seems. In these new offerings we find a certain modification of the story. Although the architectural forms remain wholly consistent, they are no longer proposing a life beyond life, but a here and now. In the proposal for the extension of the Dutch Parliament, the contrast between the Modern movement slabs and the gabled and turreted old buildings is total, yet the two are proposed as a complete working organism, a functional solution which combines old and new. It would be possible to present the project in the Rob Krier style—the old on its own, then the separate system of the new, finally the new superimposed on the old. They combine meaningfully, and the new acts of building are clearly conceived as contextualist, yet the resulting combination is not one of a near homogeneous entity, but of a collagist composition of extreme contrast.

This is something new. It allows the possibility that the new, in weaving its way into the old, need not adopt false identities or assume thin surface masks. It can remain true to its own time, or at least to a spirit of modernity; to the enjoyment of an architecturality of purist forms. We had thought that modern architecture was antipathetic to old urban texture, to the continuation of the city. But of course, the modern architecture in OMA's scheme of things is not Ville Radieuse rationality, nor Hilberseimian sobriety, nor megastructural systematicity. It is already a quasi-historical modernity which harks back to the decade of the 1920s in Russia and in America. It recalls the abstractions of Malevich and Lissitzky, the idealities of Chernikov and Leonidov, the sheer adventurousness of Raymond Hood. It is sensuous, wayward, and episodic in a way which has not been seen since the early days. All that strange variety of modern architecture in the days before Pavilion Suisse defined the canon of rationality and commercial expediency once and for all, returns now in OMA to haunt us with the possibilities of a future which we had already thought was over.

[...] The residential scheme for Lützowstrasse in Berlin is another case of contextualism and historicism. It recognizes the need for privacy for the low-rise residential blocks—already built at the heart of the site—yet resists the "new" dogma of perimeter blocks following the street as a wall, and closing off the interior of the city block. Instead, pairs of short slab buildings maintain the overall shape of the main street, while funneling its space into the public side streets and at the same time shielding the private back gardens. These variations of angle, and some playful extensions, give rise to a series of interesting buildings which are full of particularity, even whimsy, without ever losing the discipline of relating to function and use. The range and variety of window shapes, remaining always within modernity, is a challenge to the false vernacularism of folksy motifs. It touches a point near to the reduced classicism of la rue des Hautes-Formes; and the combination of large and small-scale elements eventually also touches on the scale contrasts of Léon Krier, showing that behind the apparent eclecticism there is a spirit of today.

In all these schemes we are contained in a drawn world. It is superbly controlled, aligned, colored, gathered, dispersed, allowed to rest, reanimated, brought to a point. It remains a drawn world, a vision in search of a patron.

But it enables us to picture a "modern movement," which began in the enthusiasm of revolution, continuing in enthusiasm, inventing, retrieving, realigning itself, accepting the vernacularity of being modern, showing itself now lean and hungry, now fat and contented, now static, now dynamic. A rich adventure of form which offers, not the deadness of a rational utopia, but the liveliness of a dream.

For Malevich, red squares were never just patterns, but were suffused with meaning. This architecture has taken the emotion from Russian Constructivism and extended it into a celebration of its revolutionary discoveries to a point where it reaches the possibility of actually being constructed and entering into everyday life. To adjust Rem Koolhaas's pithy comment on Raymond Hood's McGraw Building of 1931: it is the fire of Modernism raging within the iceberg of street architecture.

AN INVITATION TO ROTTERDAM FOR LEONIDOV

Stanislaus von Moos
Archithese 5 (1981), 57–62.

1. Rem Koolhaas is seen as a "paper architect." This is due to the fact that, until recently, he and his Office for Metropolitan Architecture have primarily produced — as Taut is meant to have said — "consciously utopian" projects. Koolhaas's book *Delirious New York* is well known. It most closely fits the genre of the architectural fable (a genre that was practiced, by way of example, in the fifteenth century by Antonio Averlino Filarete, and in the 1960s by Adolfo Natalini and his Superstudio, in both instances in Florence). However, although Koolhaas's book concerns itself with the fabulous, it is composed of hard facts: of historical close-up views and essayist aperçus on the American metropolis as a colossal machine for living and working, a machine for transportation and enjoyment.

[...] Like every fable, there is a moral to the story of *Delirious New York*. And if underlying the architectural fantasies of Koolhaas and Madelon Vriesendorp is a mix of almost tortured love for the paradox and an audacious naiveté, then the moral is both paradoxical and simple. It consists approximately (briefly stated) in Manhattan embodying a model form of coexistence for the future, but not having gained traction in this respect, because the theory on which it is based has never been made explicit, has never been put forward as a manifesto.

It may well be pedantic to test a fundamentally poetic conception of the urban for practical validity, and yet the inconsistencies of Koolhaas's proposition, if one is to take it at its word, are all too evident to be ignored. The first noticeable paradox lies in the fact that Koolhaas conceived of the system of urban density, such as is embodied in New York, precisely at the moment when he needed to substantiate his theory and siphon it off into programmatic "units," since New York was threatening again to founder on the rocks of its, that is, his, as Koolhaas emphasizes, never explicitly formulated theory. And, for the very reason — this is the second paradox — that the urban nature of the metropolis in the case of New York was achieved by the "hard technology" of highly developed skyscraper engineering, whereas for decades it could have been created more cheaply and more efficiently (and for the "middle class" ostensibly more attractively) using the "soft technologies" of private automobile traffic and electronics.

In other words, the metropolis, made comprehensible in an architectonic image, had long since transmuted itself into a "global village"; Los Angeles ("urban sprawl") had long ago won the day over New York (a major urban center in a confined space) — that sophisticated urbanites again want to live in Greenwich Village does not disprove the trend. The tax-paying inhabitants of this city are dispersed across the wider region surrounding New York (and not just New York), and Koolhaas's attempt, at the very least, to distill Manhattanism from the endangered vital nerve of the metropolis is, within this context, akin to a late (dilatory, and thus merely ritual) salvage operation. Whereby what is meant to be salvaged is, ultimately, less a special form of urbanism and more the idea of architecture itself, or rather the idea of a city defined by buildings. Or even by towers — that is, the potentiality of architecture.

In as far as this New York fable represents a kind of fevered mythological compensation for the actual, unstoppable decline of architecture as an institution, as a cultural factor, and for the withdrawal of the American middle classes from city centers, it is probably closer to the often equally feverish, although hardly less amusing, postmodern fairy-tale cities than Koolhaas himself would like.[1] However, OMA's fantasy operates on entirely other dimensions of urbanism; in essence, even if it reverses certain premises, it is further developing Bakema's in many respects no-less-fantastic dream as expounded in *Architecture—Urbanism*. In fact, Koolhaas does not want to be classified as postmodern, and, for that reason, he constantly superimposes his Manhattanism with images from the arsenal of the European avant-garde's enthusiasm for America. He contrasts—as he himself says—the "built unconsciousness of America with the unbuilt consciousness of Europe": Malevich, El Lissitzky, Leonidov, Le Corbusier, and Mies.[2] Is Koolhaas fascinated by Manhattan then, because this city, "without knowing it," embodies the most audacious Soviet avant-garde *Kollektivhaus* utopia? Or is he under the spell of Leonidov because this architect "knew" the future would be constructed only with, not against, American super-pragmatism in the technological fitting out of the metropolis? What is certain is that peeping out from behind OMA's invented futurology is a particular kind of nostalgia; "this is," as Kenneth Frampton says, "an America of archetype and nostalgia."

2. However speculative the architectural fantasies were with which OMA made its name in the 1970s, the projects with which the team have been trying to gain a foothold in Europe, in the Netherlands, are suddenly decidedly realistic and feasible. OMA commenced its Dutch comeback with a project proposal to extend the seat of the Dutch parliament in The Hague (1978). The intention was to divide the Binnenhof, the apple of the eye of the Netherlands' architectural conservation program, the restored historical core of The Hague and the center of legislative and executive state power, by means of a narrow, ovoid, fully glazed block. It referred to this intervention as a razor-sharp juxtaposition of "old" and "new."[3]

Its contrast with the then current ideals for a contextualizing "harmonization with the existing" fabric, evident in the majority of competition entries, could not have been more pointed. There was not even any effort made to "democratize" the business of parliament and the national administration by means of architecture in its proposal, as many participants in the competition had attempted by employing an architectural language giving the impression that involvement in interpersonal "communication" and "encounters" was really the raison d'être of these bodies of state. OMA appeared instead to work on the basis that the work of parliament and the civil service was de facto (and they may well have been correct in this) formalized to a very great degree and subject to the bureaucratic rules of the game. Of course, an obvious polemical barb was implicit in the decision explicitly not to resort to themes of "communication" and "encounter" in this building, a building that by definition has to do with representing democracy, which has, since the days of *Forum*, been one of the core principles of architecture seen as progressive and humane in Holland, but instead to recoup older notions of social progress informed by the architecture of New Objectivity and Constructivism.

Koolhaas anticipated the debate as to whether this "revenge" of heroic Modernism[4] was modern or postmodern in terms of its structure, when he separated architecture that "laid claim to the centers of historical cities as its territory" from contemporary work: from contextualism, rationalism, and structuralism. He reserved particular derision for contextualism: "The central moment of the contextualist epiphany is the collision of a projected ideal with an 'empirical necessity.' From the way in which the latter transforms the former and dampens its utopian tendencies, the contextualist derives not only aesthetic pleasure, but also—more importantly—a degree of anti-metaphysical comfort."[5]

Of course, such demarcations, especially when they are presented with such delicate, logistical acrobatics, are also symptoms of a connectedness, and, it is for this reason that the name of Léon Krier, for instance, almost inevitably comes to mind as a synonym for many things associated with OMA's cause on its route to direct negation.

On the subject of rationalism, Koolhaas believes that its appeal lies "in the abstinent economy of imagination that it postulates"—a suspicion that one perhaps maintains about several of his own projects (such as, for instance, his house in Miami or the design for a museum of photography in Amsterdam). Above all, however, he castigates the exclusivity with which rationalism gives precedence to certain typologies and morphologies borrowed from the "elevated sphere" of Classical architecture, considering them dogmatic and "ominous," which puts him alongside Robert Venturi, who summarized his critique of the "advice" as follows: "Total architecture" (here Venturi alludes to Gropius's term *total design*) "is not worse than its opposite: exclusive architecture; that is, the limiting of choice of building types to those on which the program of public and monumental architecture is based, its traditional function following its Classical form, and assenting to a restricted culture of taste: libraries, yes, supermarkets, no!"[6]

[...] That OMA had to isolate itself against the "new frumpiness," that is, against the almost compulsive fixation, for a time, of the Dutch architectural scene on small-scale, segmented forms, supposed to epitomize the humane, is obvious. The practice considered it nonsense that small-scale modules should represent democracy. It ascribed the idea of achieving democratic transparency by dividing institutions into smaller components—which played a major role in many entries for the parliamentary competition—to Aldo van Eyck—or more precisely, to his Burgerweeshuis in Amsterdam: "Where Van Eyck divided a group of orphans into 'families' and created a metaphorical correspondence between these 'families' and the 'little houses' in which they lived, this context was completely lost in the later iterations of the theme, where division became a simple affectation."[7]

However, the actual irritant, which Koolhaas termed "classic Montessori terrorism," was the claim that architecture, since the days of *Forum*, was proffering its services as social hygiene therapy, and was thus turning society as a whole into a sick bay and architects into social medicine practitioners and spiritual directors. [...] Koolhaas found this fixation of architecture on themes, such as old people's homes, orphanages, and homes for unmarried mothers treacherous. Of course, he was tactful enough to keep his opinions to himself as to which buildings he meant here. [...] How ironic then that the first substantial commission that OMA is presented with in Holland turns out to involve an extreme case of a therapeutic social institution: a prison! And what an argument in favor of the relevance of Koolhaas's skepticism about any kind of therapeutic role for architecture, when the "humanism" of a building aimed at "encounter" and "communication" should be in a field where it would seem to be turned into precisely its opposite, that inevitably seems to suggest itself as an experimental terrain: that is, the "humanization of the penal system." Will the contracting authorities allow themselves to be persuaded that there are situations—and one involving a prison seems to be just such a case—where the "humanization" of communal life might have something to do with the fact that architecture is withdrawing from its role of creating architectonic "space," as architects always have it (instead of human "places" as demanded by the architecture of pastoral care understood as social hygiene)?

The design for Arnhem also presents itself, with its drawings, in which Lissitzky's *Prouns* vibrate to the surface, as a kind of revenge of constructivist Modernism from the pre-CIAM years on later, "humanist" postwar Modernism. The same applies to the high-rise residential scheme for Rotterdam, that is about to be built, and—in order to carry the irony to the extreme—alongside a wide cluster arranged around a skyscraper pinnacle by Piet Blom, of all places. The entire complex is, of course, also a salute to Manhattan, the international harbor city on the other bank of the water, which sparked OMA's interest in the metropolis. And the crane-like, slightly canted, high-tower framework in front of it is an homage to El Lissitzky's Lenin Tribune and Leonidov's Lenin Library.[8]

However, while citation from the arsenal of iron construction embodied an industrial future for El Lissitzky and Leonidov, here it is a relic from Rotterdam's past: literally, a colossal ready-made. A piece of an iron bridge shifted to the vertical from the horizontal, and thus repurposed as a watch tower. Recently, as with Manhattanism, visual themes belonging to a fifty-to-sixty-year-old constructivist avant-garde have merged with a reality that has lost its historical bearings (in order to become a monument, the bridge had first to be closed to traffic and replaced with another bridge constructed immediately alongside it). Lately, it has been possible to perceive the status quo, the city, just as it is, as a spectacle, to give it a voice, by means of a conceptual recourse to the avant-garde. Recently, the utopia of ancient history has served to expose the utopia of yesteryear with its shallow romanticism, and to thrust the reality of today into the spotlight.

A couple of young members of the OMA team, who are studying architecture at Delft, have turned the events circa 1978 into a neo-Dadaist film grotesque on the subject of Rotterdam. In it, toward the end, a large neon sign appears in a football stadium with the words: "ROTTERDAM INVITES THE EIFFEL TOWER." As Mayakovsky said in his poem, "Eiffel Tower": "Come to Moscow, here is vastness!" Here the Eiffel Tower, which even in Mayakovsky's time was a piece of industrial archaeology, is recycled again within the frame of an architectonic avant-garde.

3. In all of this, neither "delirious New York" nor the transatlantic myths that served as a foundation and as an unachievable goal for the European avant-garde of the 1920s have been forgotten. Since in Manhattanism in *Delirious New York*, there is, it turns out, not only an extravagant mix of utopia and nostalgia, but also a decisive pragmatism and a goal-oriented engagement in acknowledging the status quo of architecture and the city. The project to redevelop the area around Kochstrasse/Friedrichstrasse in Berlin can serve as an example. OMA proposes an open development with small villas and patios for the quarter that intersects Kochstrasse and Friedrichstrasse with planar residential blocks for rent, instead of the traditional frontage development around inner courtyards so emphatically gentrified again as part of the IBA.[9]

Why not return to a "historic city"? Because, OMA seems to reply, the current postmodern notions of the "historic city," still in the lap of the IBA, are based on a fiction that the history of the city came to an end in the nineteenth century, whereas—it almost seems like a provocation to utter it—Mies's skyscraper project for Friedrichstrasse (1919) and Hilberseimer's proposed development for Friedrichstadt (1925) also belong to the historical context of architecture in Berlin. And because the notions of the historic city current today, overlook the fact that the existing development in the Kochstrasse/

Friedrichstrasse quarter, in as much as it has any kind of historical identity, owe this, above all, to the lax redevelopment of the 1950s and the Berlin Wall immediately adjacent to it.

OMA's pragmatism can indeed be identified most readily if one once again calls upon the widespread and widely misused term, viz. that of *history*. It is not unimportant that Koolhaas has writing in the blood (his father is one of the best-known authors and essayists in the country) and was a filmmaker and worked as a journalist for an extended period for the *Haagse Post*. If "history" for him as an architect (as for other architects, too) is a "better past," for which it is worth ensuring a future, then it is composed for him, as the reporter and writer he also is, of stories, facts, and everyday situations. Seen in this light, architecture becomes viable to the extent that it links to the everyday and even trivial "histories" of the city.[10]

Despite their curiosity about the gray zones of normality, do OMA's eyes have Dutch blinkers on?—Are they spellbound by the heroic relics of the 1920s? Even their recent projects testify to this. To reclaim their formal world for today, in light of the "degenerate" Modernism of the postwar boom, Koolhaas must stop lamenting and must be prepared to learn. [...] Where he had to subject his redevelopment of Bijlmermeer near Amsterdam to the same "learning to like it" that Venturi did for his Co-op City near New York, he must hold out against the idealistic and voluntary humanism of Team 10 and *Forum* with something like Laurids Ortner's "Amnesty for built reality."

What else are we to understand by the slogan "retroactive manifesto," the subtitle of *Delirious New York*, other than a reference to history? What does the Manhattan "manifesto" consist of here, if not its own history reduced to didactic formulae?—Encoded within this slogan is both a critique of modern architecture and an attempt at rehabilitating it. A critique, in as much as high modernist architecture has largely kept its eyes open while trusting in the necessity of the tabula rasa and has continued to ask whatever questions may arise about the how and why of the status quo of cultural sociology. An attempt at rehabilitation in as much as Modern architecture, in the actual circumstances of its implementation—however suspect—represents an undeniable reality. To this degree, it has reclaimed the terrain that it has had to forfeit as a utopia, thanks to its simple presence, and now constitutes the parameter within which a future for architecture is conceivable at all.

1 One thinks of Rob and Léon Krier as well as the group around Maurice Culot in Brussels and its call, made up of no less phantasmagorical images, for a reconstruction of the city—even if, in this case, it means the European city.

2 Rem Koolhaas, "Urban Intervention: Dutch Parliament Extension, The Hague," *International Architect* 3 (1980), 50. In his commentary on Koolhaas's book, Kenneth Frampton constructs a further network of references between American "reality" and European "utopia," but he takes it too far—see "Two or Three Things I Know About Them: Note on Manhattanism," *Architectural Design* 5 (1977), 315–18.

3 For a summary of the competition, see Hans van Dijk, "'Demokratische Symbolik'—oder Architektur?," *werk/Archithese*, 25–26 (1979), 7–11.

4 The image of revenge comes from Koolhaas himself. He considers the notorious Bijlmermeer development as a kind of revenge of the fathers of Modern architecture on their sons, a revenge of the Charter of Athens on Team 10—a reverse Oedipus situation; see "Bijlmermeer-Strip," *Werk/Archithese* 5 (1977), 17–19.

5 Koolhaas, "Urban Intervention," 51 (see note 2).

6 Robert Venturi, "Learning the Right Lessons from the Beaux-Arts," *Architectural Design* 1 (1979), 31.

7 Koolhaas, "Urban Intervention" (see note 2).

8 Koolhaas has engaged extensively with the work of Leonidov; see Rem Koolhaas and Gerrit Oorthuys, "Ivan Leonidov's Dom Narkorntjaziprom, Moscow," *Oppositions* 2 (1974), 95–103.

9 The contextualism of the IBA seems to have been defined as programmatic by Josef Paul Kleihues, "Berliner Baublöcke: Grundriss einer Typologie," *Werk/Archithese* 31–32 (1979), 18–27.

10 Here the efforts of OMA also touch most notably on those of Venturi and his team. The concept of the city in the case of Venturi and his team are also heavily determined by scientific and artistic visual effects, which they employ in their environmental studies—such as, for example, urban sociology and pop art. My attempt at a brief account of this appears in "Architektur als Bilderbogen: Graphik und Photo-Graphik bei Venturi and Rauch," in *Jahrbuch für Architektur 1980/81*, ed. Heinrich Klotz (Braunschweig/Wiesbaden: Vieweg, 1980), 95–100. On the city as "paysage urbain," see, for instance, Jean-Pierre Keller, *Pop Art et évidence du quotidien* (Lausanne: L'âge de l'homme, 1979), 15–19.

A EUROPEAN WITHOUT HUMOR

Patrice Noviant
Architecture Mouvement Continuité 54–55 (1981), 59.

The history of the Modern Movement, particularly the history of German modernism, is filled with renunciations through which a symbolic or expressionist architect—whatever one would like to call him, but in any case an architect weary with form and its overabundance—intensifies his work by reducing it to the essential. Bruno Taut's work in Berlin-Britz, as well as that of Hugo Häring in Siemensstadt, demonstrate the tense quality that arises when an architect is dynamically involved in world reform. Minimal housing is not an act of stripping, but a dynamic act, a tension: the positive renunciation, typical of functionalism, is the ascetic means by which the artist-architect achieves renewed socialization, leading to the paradoxical production of work that still haunts the architectural memory. On this fertile soil, which might even be called mystical, teaching was established, academism and production. The conviction was: we have found our theory, now let's just wait for its application ...

We know the results. Born after the war, our experience was precisely built on the foundation of this teaching and this production. We were the sons of an objectivity that was no longer radically new but established, no longer ascetic but almost eclectic—an objectivity that, in the end, had retained from the 1920s above all a good conscience. We have struggled to come out of that state of trance; we looked around, to appreciate the qualities of the historical city, to notice the popular failure of contemporary architecture, particularly in its main form of the *Grand Ensemble*, and to begin to question ourselves, and to criticize, almost unknowingly, the Modern Movement. Having realized that we have been criticizing the masters, today we could be in this passionate situation in which everyone acknowledges the existence of the "mistakes of the Modern Movement." We would have to part ways with it, after having evaluated whether it was positive—or not, obviously ...

Rem Koolhaas, through his determination to put the issue of "program" back on the table, suggests a fortunate shift in this rhetorical debate. In order to affirm that the modern cannot persist without a social project, without the desire to change the habits and ways of societal life, or at least without the desire to actively participate in ongoing transformations, Koolhaas asserts the need to restore modernity in its not strictly formal—or even architectural—definition, which was precisely what caused its historical break.

It is true that during the 1930s, the modern had lost much of its programmatic radicalism, and that its internal debate had become a debate on legitimate style. The central question was whether one could "go beyond" purism, accept Alvar Aalto, bricks and wood, etc. It resulted in a very broad concept of modernism that benevolently considered its own static history, generously including Mendelsohn's Einstein Tower by considering it as modern as his Universum Cinema. Postmodernism would be only one more step, the naive-cynical stage in which each project is the conscious result of the long, eclectic, cheerfully multifaceted process of considering modern architecture as style. [...]

Rem Koolhaas is, first of all, the author of *Delirious New York*, this murky praise of life's diversity and of metropolitan happiness. Now, Rem Koolhaas, the merry New Yorker, returns home. From his London retreat, it is toward Holland that his interest goes. The competition for the expansion of the parliament in The Hague is almost won—it is for the moment suspended. Other projects followed, and already a practice is established by OMA that escapes the personal work of Koolhaas. For those who incorrectly read *Delirious New York* as praise for spontaneity—although it was impossible to read it correctly, as the book was as fascinatingly ambiguous as the metropolis itself—the precise dryness of the projects for the Netherlands comes as a shock. Koolhaas now appears to be a "European without humor." We should reread *Delirious New York* to find that dryness of the soul that has been previously overlooked.

What could be the meaning of the use of what may appear a useless, aggressive loyalty to the forms of the avant-garde from the 1920s? An emotional feeling of nostalgia must have led our hero to convoke the whole of this European architecture. However, if we think that Rem Koolhaas's accuracy is in opposition rather than aligned with the stylistic discourse about the modern, that is because he reactivates modern architecture in its dimension of social project, with a fascination for the most radical approaches of, among others, Leonidov-Rimbaud, Le Corbusier-Verlaine, and the young Mies van der Rohe.

We might add that the revival of modern architecture as a sign of a desire for social change is sought through the use of a vocabulary without specific qualities, in which architecture becomes absolutely legitimate again, absolutely justified in the object itself. Rem Koolhaas trembled before architecture and the discourse of power upon which it is built; the moment when it has almost disappeared, when it is almost only practical is also the moment when it is almost absolutely legitimate. His ideal architecture is shown by the drawing in *Delirious New York*, when naked, gloved boxers eat oysters in a locker room, establishing by themselves the tangencies of architecture. Beyond transparent walls, the tense juxtaposition of practices. Obviously, the other emblem is the floating swimming pool, whose ideal state would have a water level at the same height of the river or sea on which it floats.

By coming to Europe, Rem Koolhaas takes a step that leads from the tense, sensuous asceticism of the bodies in Manhattan to the almost bourgeois evidence of the Boompjes building in Rotterdam. His play on quiet reflections, his explicit desire to soothe and order the city's chaotic debate by proposing towers that become bars—all this participates in the desire to see architecture become more objective, stripped of ideology, the enemy standing near: the damp humanism from Dutch anthropo-structuralism, represented by Bakema and Piet Blom. [...]

ENTER THE PROPHETS OF NEW SOBRIETY

Deyan Sudjic
Building Design
549 (1981), 2.

"The time for paper architecture is past," says Elia Zenghelis, half of the public face of the Office for Metropolitan Architecture. Which is why he and his partner, Rem Koolhaas, two of architecture's most indefatigable manifesto writers, have decided to come off the academic fence, get their boots dirty, and actually build something. But before they do that, they are treating us to an exhibition at the Architectural Association of where their designs have got to now.

"We decided that if people were going to take us seriously we would have to take the plunge, stop teaching, and start building," says Zenghelis. What they want us to take seriously is Modernism. Not the Modernism of a Rogers or a Foster but a Modernism that contains a hefty chunk of nostalgia for the Russian Constructivists and the 1920 skyscraper builders of Manhattan. "We are wary of the Sainsbury Center, its blatant know-how without much know-why. If we had that kind of technological know-how it would be great. You feel that it's applied without any outside context."

Looking at the OMA's exhibits on the walls of the AA, you certainly can't help feeling that they could do with a bit of technology. They are brilliantly good at suggesting the kind of urbanity and vitality that is entirely lacking in the flaccid imagery of everybody from the English new-towners to the neo-vernacularists. What they are not so good at is suggesting that they would be able to achieve what their drawings promise, even if they had the chance.

Even on the opening night of the AA show, one of their exhibition panels sheared loose from its supporting cables and came crashing down into the crowd.

Their flat, diagrammatic perspectives have a curious, dreamlike, insubstantial quality about them. Nevertheless, OMA is building a group of houses in Greece and seems to have a good chance of realizing one or other of its projects in Holland.

According to Zenghelis, OMA is trying to do something about "architecture's claustrophobic language, incomprehensible to most people." OMA by contrast aims to provide a more understandable and relevant alternative. "Both the so-called Postmodernists and the Neorationalists look back to the repetition of the past. We have consistently held that Modernism is the appropriate cultural response to our age—anything else is an insult to our present-day life." The Postmodernists "presume that everyone reads Goethe and listens to

Wagner; we design for people who listen to Capital Radio. We are not populists, but we do respond to people," says Zenghelis.

All of which is admirable, refreshing, and in its own way convincing enough. Yet how much will the people get out of the AA exhibition? Not much I suspect. They will be treated to a series of delicately colored drawings of projects ranging from an unsuccessful competition design for the Irish Prime Minister's house to a study for the rehabilitation of Holland's last remaining panopticon prison. Pretty they may be, but accessible to a general audience they certainly are not. [...]

LIGHT IN THE DARKNESS

Sander Wissing
Hard Werken 10 (1982), 47.

In a previous issue of this periodical I wrote about the doom and punishment that awaits Rotterdam, born out of a pitiful and sad conspiracy of Mr. P. Blom and the rulers of this city. Now: attention for OMA, that took the bold step of developing a beautiful, daring, complete, and well-substantiated plan. This group, and Rem Koolhaas in particular, has previously shown to dispose of an authentic and free vision that I really appreciate. Their plan includes, among other things, putting upright a part of the old Willemsbridge, but this, I assume, the interested reader knows. Another part of the plan, without a doubt equally important, is a large and high apartment building, that will reinforce the effect of the standing bridge. The emphasis is on metropolitanism, the image and its attractiveness, which is good.

Didn't the regents of Rotterdam decide that it should become a city on the river? But what happens? We stuff the Leuvehavenkade and the Blaak with fifteenth-hand tinkering, with squiggles on a board—no big gesture, no allure at all, only unsalable ugly rotten luxury apartments. When will all this misery stop? This plan, nota bene commissioned by the municipality, gives the gentlemen-administrators the opportunity to finally shake off the mantle of mediocrity—the big challenge: the end of a grizzled and terrible era of bullshitting and postponing. So we decide unanimously that the entire plan will be carried out, we don't establish talk groups, no evaluation committees, no consultation rounds that always give the same result ... "Hm, Mister Koolhaas, wouldn't it be nice to put on the head of the old bridge a big picture of for example that beautiful model of the plan, so that all Rotterdam ..."—and so on.

Dear citizens of Rotterdam and other fanciers, I don't care if the plan is expensive, useless, nonsensical or elitist, it's good and it HAS TO be executed because little by little we are dying here of BOREDOM.

THE ODYSSEY OF AN ENLIGHTENED ENTREPRENEUR

Geert Bekaert

wonen-TA/BK 13–14 (1982), 50–57.

On demande un Colbert.
Le Corbusier

La mariée mise à nu par ses célibataires, même.
Marcel Duchamp

Rem Koolhaas established OMA in Rotterdam. It wouldn't have been possible anywhere else in the Netherlands. Everything has to fit perfectly into the discourse. The precision of its internal coherence is the source of its reality, and its power of fascination derives from the real itself. *De la séduction.* A city such as Rotterdam, suffering from chronic imagelessness and constantly in search of an identity (which, by the way, is a concept he detests), has the potential, like New York or any other metropolis, to absorb many stories. Stories about Amsterdam are all fairly similar. The same could never be said of Rotterdam. Besides, Rem Koolhaas did not just settle down in any old Rotterdam location. And has he really settled down? He occupies a floor, a loft, in an office building in the old harbor district, with a view of what remains of the old Willemsbrug (he'd like to do something with that). A white oasis in the midst of activity and color. A void that exists by virtue of what surrounds it. A secret headquarters in a strange, disorganized territory where everything is one great writhing mass. Coherence is elsewhere. In the white office, perhaps? Any given floor has no idea what is happening on the next one up or down. Even the doorman doesn't know. "Delirious" is a strong word, but there is plenty of technology and congestion, and the imagination runs free. And there is not a trace of social stability. There are no crèches or homes for the elderly in the neighborhood (though Koolhaas's new design for the area envisages some nearby), no shelters for single mothers. In the end, everyone stands alone.

Rem Koolhaas has installed himself in a world of utility and efficiency, a world whose logic is perfectly irrational but highly effective. No lapse of attention goes unpunished. It's one long, enervating high-wire act. No freedom. No values. What matters is knowing the rules of the game, and that means knowing how to use them in your favor. Machiavelli discusses this in *Il Principe.* No whining. And no criticism. Criticism means frustration.

Does architecture belong in this world? As Koolhaas sees it, this is the kind of question one would expect from an architect: an utterly meaningless one. Where else would architecture belong? An architect is an entrepreneur who produces programs. "Paper architecture," it has been called. But Koolhaas has no interest in either paper or architecture. He could not care less where the boundaries of architecture may lie. As a professional entrepreneur, he markets products that are usable—which is to say that they appeal to the imagination. His hero is Samuel Lionel Rothafel, aka Roxy, the Radio City Music Hall man. An entrepreneur has ideas, not preconceptions. His finest quality is his imagination, which allows him to conjure up forms of coherence for his public. Rationality lies with the public, as Laugier once declared to architects. And is there anything more public than architecture?

By allowing architecture and enterprise to run together, Rem Koolhaas has shown himself to be not only an enlightened architect, but also an enlightened entrepreneur. The natural connection between the two is, for whatever reason, often suppressed, and architects feel obliged to wear the mantle of idealism.

Rem Koolhaas has shed that mantle. He knows that entrepreneurs are after the most rational, efficient, and useful manifestation of the irrational. Hence his admiration for Roxy, the prototypical entrepreneur, and for Radio City Music Hall, the social paradigm of the irrational. The entrepreneur is the entertainer of modern society, successor to kings and priests. It is he, rather than the state or religion, who generates the artificial needs that give direction to social life and supplies the technology that can satisfy these needs in artificial paradises. With this simple philosophy (for Koolhaas, everything is simple), firmly rooted in the European tradition, he hitches his wagon, as it were, to the claims of the Modern movement, which presented its architecture not as a formalistic game but as a social necessity. This places him in a comfortable polemical position with regard to the many forms of so-called Postmodernism, which still suffer from avant-gardism and desperately try to make that the foundation of their identity. Koolhaas's identity is perfectly secure; his *différence* is unmistakable. However interchangeable the product may be, it must remain distinctive.

By revealing the true character of Modernism, Koolhaas differentiates his position in yet another way, thus escaping (as he himself puts it) the dreary succession of fashions that dominates the world of architecture. He stands above the internecine quarrels between frustrated architects who have had enough. He has discovered the Archimedean point, yet again. The entrepreneur is always on the right side of the argument. The public awaits him as if awaiting a redeemer.

Exodus (1972) marked the beginning of Rem Koolhaas's public life as an architect. Just as exactly fifty years earlier Le Corbusier's Plan Voisin provided the inevitable solution not only to the problem of the modern city, but to that of modern society in general, as demonstrated by the example of Paris, so did Exodus, when applied to the sleepwalking metropolis of London, provide the inescapable model for our present-day society. We have moved beyond history. We live in a state of closure and completion. Exodus is an outstanding textbook for those who seek to understand the Plan Voisin and, conversely, Exodus becomes clear when read in the light of the Plan Voisin. In this case, the paranoiac-critical method does the job efficiently. Voisin is "the name of the famous makers of aeroplanes and automobiles who (along with Monsieur Frugès) provided financial support to the architects of the Pavillon de l'Esprit Nouveau just when the situation had become absolutely desperate." (Le Corbusier) The architect and the entrepreneur know how to find each other. Politics can only get in the way.

In the Plan Voisin, Le Corbusier does no more than formulate what the people of Paris had long been demanding. The city center is no longer inhabitable, he argues, and the threat of a complete exodus is looming. But all that is needed is for a strong leader to step forward—"On demande un Colbert"—and everyone, regardless of age, race, or intelligence, will recognize the utility of the enterprise and march into the new city cheering, in a spontaneous reverse exodus, as "voluntary prisoners of architecture." [...] Everything imaginable has been provided for. Ah yes, and thinking is no longer necessary in the modern metropolis. There is so much going on that no one has time for it. The only person who does not take part in this stimulating arrangement, because he has assumed the task of thinking on behalf of the metropolitan public, is the architect, the entrepreneur. That is because he must ensure that his "instrument of genuine modernity" functions properly and that its "human choreography" proceeds entirely according to plan.

[...] Fifty years later, Koolhaas overlaid the Plan Voisin with his own Exodus. But utopians learn from one another. Le Corbusier had such confidence in his public that he assumed that it would appreciate the benefits of his plan without any form of instruction and would have no difficulty seeing itself as part of it. He believed that the scales would fall from people's eyes spontaneously.

Koolhaas understands that he must protect his public from itself. In Exodus, following the example of the Berlin Wall, he screens off his artificial paradise from the dormant city. Two walls run east to west through the heart of historical London, clearing a zone consisting of a series of successive squares—each with its own program and scenario—in which it is possible to enjoy both total privacy and intense community experiences. Unlike the Plan Voisin, the Strip in Exodus is not only strictly walled off from the rest of the city, but also has a clear sense of direction, a therapeutic, pedagogical purpose. Le Corbusier's endless cycle is ultimately devoid of excitement and prospects. Its voluntary prisoners are trapped in an eternal satisfaction, without desire or hope. In Exodus there is a course of events, a substitute for history, an intensification culminating (at the Institute of Biological Transactions) in an exciting adventure: will the prisoner be selected by the capricious doctors for deliverance and for further training by a gang of lunatics, or conveyed directly to the cemetery? In Exodus, the prisoner has prospects. Le Corbusier has no such exciting scenarios to offer. His range of social services is limited. He never thought of building a Park of Aggression, even though the idea goes back to the Romans. Nor did he think of using lunatics as therapists—but what does it matter? Fundamentally, both Exodus and the Plan Voisin are architectural metaphors for modern society, as arresting as they are ambiguous. Despite the contrasts between the two metaphors, they do more to reinforce each other than to cancel each other out. Even if we consider Exodus as a parody, read it with the aid of a Surrealist, Dadaist, or other interpretation model, view it as the architectural presentation of a literary fiction, or view it in all these ways at once—as Koolhaas once described a project by Leonidov, "a building, a manifesto, and a Russian novel"—it is the building, the manifesto, the story of an architect-entrepreneur, Dutch and Calvinist. Compare it to the fantasies of Superstudio, which provide Exodus with a source of inspiration and a target of opposition.

The implacable eye of the outsider sees all and weaves, in and around its field of vision, forms of coherence that reduce all the autonomous fragments to a text, thus creating a world whose legibility makes it superior to the blind machinery of fate in which ordinary mortals are constantly bumping into each other. Foucault's "order of discourse" or "eye of power," the perspectival eye, remains fascinated by all the chaos, and works to develop methods not to understand it, cultivate it or learn to live with it, but to organize, reduce, program, and manipulate it, hence obliterating its own object. Chaos is not experienced through an interpretive writing, a method that goes back to Greek tragedy and has been attempted and reattempted right up to the present day. Instead, it is catalogued and stripped of its absurdity. By its nature, this method is precise in its use of both visual and written media, which, it should be added, correspond perfectly. The illusion of coherence must be consummate. The system must not show the slightest fracture through which the author reveals a glimpse of himself. He does not belong there. The system is as implacable as science. Everything is drawn up with anatomical precision. But every trace of life is gone. It is not surprising that the aloof bird's-eye perspective is so widely used. It is not surprising that every project is accompanied by such massive reams of commentary. Every alternative interpretation must be ruled out. There is a very real danger that the chaos will regain its freedom. A message from one of the voluntary prisoners of architecture can never reach us. *The Fun Never Sets.*

The method of inversion, which sparks so much ingenuity in Exodus, is put to further use in the retroactive manifesto *Delirious New York*. The architect is no longer concerned with walls. In New York, the exodus has already happened, though the city dwellers are unaware of it.

The voluntary prisoner no longer realizes that he is a prisoner. The sleepwalking metropolis should not be restored here. Or should it? In New York, again, Koolhaas arrived too late to join the party. The blissful period of unconsciousness had ended, once and for all. Manhattanism was dead, the flaneur no more than a museum piece. All that Koolhaas could do was to learn from history and restore the corpses of past architecture to life in an unbridled flight of fancy. In *Delirious New York,* a hermeneutic mill grinds the history of New York into an insane product. The aloof eye is a quasi-natural fact, integral to the metropolis itself. Not only have the age of the metropolis and the distinction between the ideal and the real been abandoned, but furthermore, the view from above, from the top of the skyscraper, is readily available. Like each zone in the London Strip, each building has its own program and scenario within the framework of the grid. Yet the Strip's sense of direction is now absent. Just as in the case of the Plan Voisin, the excitement has dissipated. The buildings stand or lie around as if in a colossal house of wax, as if they were actual individuals. Not only the existing ones, the familiar ones, but also the new ones. For Koolhaas would not be Koolhaas if he remained a mere man about town, content to experience and contemplate the city. He intervenes. He completes it. He brings it to an end. The City of the Captive Globe, from the same prolific year as Exodus, gets to the bottom of what New York truly is, through the image of what it once wished to be; New York and modern architecture are reconciled. The incomplete project is completed, Modernism liberated from its frustrations. It must have pleased Philip Johnson, this vision of New York as a contemporary cosmology in miniature. *La mariée mise à nu par ses célibataires, même.* The Earth conquered in the imagination of technology, the imagination of architecture. An archaeological print to be displayed on every classroom wall. A modern-day Pompeii, with the Welfare Palace Hotel on its outskirts for inquisitive tourists.

The end of the world has never been charted so carefully. It could not be more dead. Any resistance that could give rise to life has been abandoned, every precondition for imagination destroyed. The Plan Voisin collapses like a house of cards. But, as in any good apocalyptic scenario, there is hope. There is the threat of the globe (yet again a prisoner); as Koolhaas puts it, "its ageless pregnancy survives." That threat is the only kind of future available after the "terminal stage of Western civilization" indicted by Koolhaas in *Delirious New York.*

Beyond the dream of Modernism, all the illusions of which are unmasked here, we revert to the state of the "natural man" as described by Jean-Jacques Rousseau. Koolhaas could have supplied *Émile ou de l'éducation* as bedtime reading on the nightstands of the Welfare Palace Hotel. But then one must read nature as a metropolis, but one does so automatically, since the big city, after all, is nothing more than artificial nature, improved by the technology of the imagination or the imagination of technology, nothing more than human factory farming. "Un nouveau contrat social."

"It is you, my teacher," Émile says to his tutor, "who have made me free by teaching me to yield to necessity." And of his own free will, like a voluntary prisoner of architecture, Émile yields to the laws of nature, distrusting the weak, who need a society to protect them. The lonely man is strong. He creates his own religion. "A thousand new religions" are on offer in The City of the Captive Globe. Who knows? Perhaps the lonely couple dancing in the spotlights on the Raft of the Medusa are talking about Émile and his teacher's charitable deeds.

Yet it is more probable that they are talking about architecture, that magical human invention whose benefits they are in the act of reaping. Filarete, who once wrote a retroactive manifesto of his own, for the Italian Renaissance city, noted: "Building is nothing more than a voluptuous pleasure, like that of a man in love. Anyone who has experienced it knows that there is so much pleasure and desire in building that however much a man does, he wants to do more. When a man is in love ..." The remarkable thing about Koolhaas's story, like Filarete's, is that in a direct manner, as if it were the most ordinary thing in the world, they discuss architecture in the way that one discusses a fantastic, exciting affair. This is not about milk bottles or kitchen cupboards. But Koolhaas, unlike Filarete, is only able to accomplish this by abstracting the architecture that he discusses to a purely "conceptual-metaphorical" level and arranging things so that a cut-and-dry moral lesson emerges. He topples Le Corbusier from his pedestal only to take his place, wagging his finger, uninhibited by any Oedipus complex. His true kindred spirit is not Leonidov, Malevich, Mies van der Rohe, Hilberseimer, or whoever else he may have up his sleeve, but Le Corbusier. The two men both base their approaches on the same conception of reality, for which Koolhaas has developed a whole slew of terms along the lines of "Spartan hedonism."

This conception of reality recognizes no dividing line between reality and desire, as Koolhaas himself says. [...] This point is proven by his "realistic" projects; for the sake of convenience, let us include competition entries in this category. His housing proposal for the Roosevelt Island competition (1975) predates the Welfare Palace Hotel proposal (1976–77). This implies that there is, in any case, no chronological dividing line. The dividing lines are not between fantasy and reality, but in the imagination itself, which in this proposal seems to have suddenly dried up. To the extent that there is a scenario at all, it consists of the simple repetition of "vulgar materialist" elements. Adieu, Dalí and Mies van der Rohe. As if there were nothing wrong, Koolhaas and his staff persist in their affirmative linguistic style, derived from "concepts and strategies that have evolved on the mother island—Manhattan," but Manhattanism is dead. The crudest of architectural terms have been dragged in to replace it: "genuine street life," "communal and private gardens" and "unimpeded view," to mention just a few. Even Richard Plunz knew what to say about this in his later analysis of New York City housing. Congestion, social instability, technological fantasies, alternative modernities, ideological islands, incoherence—forget about it. Everything exhilarating has vanished. There is still the quasi-systematic use of "synthetic brownstones" and the effect of mirrors. But that's where it ends. The iconographic tension is no longer present; the art of memory is severely impoverished. Icarus has fallen into the sea next to the raft of the Medusa, and everyone has leisurely turned away.

[...] The derivative quality of the Roosevelt Island proposal may stem from the fact that it has to do with dwellings, and "dwelling" is simply a frustrating concept that, as Loos once suggested, transcends architecture. But in the case of Koolhaas, what was probably even more significant is the lack of any polemical stimulus. Koolhaas himself went on to fill this gap. In the Nietzschean arena of the metropolis, he had already shot his last bolt. Supporters of his retroactive manifesto did not stand a chance as designers in New York. He was forced to retreat to less metropolitan, more provincial areas—the Netherlands, for instance.

In 1978, OMA took part in a competition for the extension of the parliament buildings in The Hague, part of a historic complex with the evocative name of the Binnenhof (literally "Inner Court"). There could have been no better opportunity for Koolhaas to demonstrate his architectural ideology. The proposal that he submitted is as clear as one could possibly wish and responsive to all groups: politicians, architects, sociologists, and so forth. Its inverse symbolism made the building ideally suited to its function—not the building that had been requested, but one that had been eagerly anticipated all the same. It is deeply regrettable that the jury did not award the proposal the first prize and recommend that it be built. The Netherlands missed a unique opportunity to live up to its reputation as a forward-looking nation and uphold its tradition of modern institutional architecture. [...] It would have been a milestone in architectural history. The very idea is fascinating.

At the same time that Koolhaas was working on the design for the Binnenhof, he also had an actual commission to investigate the possibility of renovating the panopticon prison in Arnhem in line with the current needs and views of the penal system. The project seemed tailor-made for Koolhaas. It was almost as if—in fine, traditional style—he was choosing his commissions himself. There was plenty of room for controversy, especially given recent experiences with prison-building in the Netherlands.

In Exodus, Koolhaas had toyed with the ambiguity of terms such as *voluntary* and *prisoner*. In the Arnhem project, these terms took on a more than metaphorical significance. But Koolhaas no longer waded into the ideological fray. By this time, his concern was the ideology of architecture itself. [...] In this project, everything really does converge: all the manifestoes, all the ideas about the potential and the limits of architecture and the architect. We have not examined any projects in depth, but it is now very tempting to succumb to this refreshing lyricism. Only ill will could inspire the claim, made by some architects, that the proposal could never be carried out—unless this reaction should be interpreted as an expression of the fear that these brilliant drawings would lose too much of their charm if transformed into actual buildings.

[...] The real-world character of the panopticon project is absent from the design for a residence and guest house for the Taoiseach (Prime Minister) of Ireland, but the project did present an opportunity—the most explicit one thus far—to elaborate on the specifics of Koolhaas's view on architecture: architecture as action, or, in his own terms, as scenario. If he speaks of a program, it is not in the usual sense. His architecture does not have a program; it is a program. An official residence is an ideal illustration of this point, even more so than a prison. Only a mansion for a Middle Eastern oil sheik could outdo the display of luxury in this project. But the Middle East has not yet discovered Koolhaas. Just as we compared Exodus to the Plan Voisin, we could compare this residence to the Villa Savoye. [...] The point, Le Corbusier explains, is a true architectural walk, constantly revealing new, varied, unexpected, and sometimes wondrous facets of the building. Elsewhere he says: "Un édifice est comme une bulle de savon." But besides the walk in the soap bubble, there are many other points of comparison: the unhealthy quality of nature, for which architecture is a remedy, hygiene, the body, traffic routes and idleness. No dwellings, no voices. A machine for motion, undisturbed by thoughts or feelings, unconstricted. Far removed from politics of all kinds: trade union leaders visit the prime minister. The only thing missing is Le Corbusier's sunlight. Koolhaas's light is artificial.

It is a big step from the Irish prime minister to the IJplein public housing development in Amsterdam, but Koolhaas takes it with the greatest of ease. Architecture is architecture. Even on the highest throne in the world, we are still sitting on our ass, as Montaigne pointed out. The eccentricities of the Roosevelt Island proposal, intended to convert us to Manhattanism, are now absent, and instead we find Piet Blom-style declarations about "rural urbanity" and even stronger stuff about the "individuality of the neighborhood," calculated to underscore the

Amsterdam character of the project. But the truly remarkable thing is not these volte-faces, but the fact that Koolhaas remains true to himself and does exactly what he means to do. The volte-faces are among the techniques of persuasion indispensable to any entrepreneur. They could also be interpreted as delightful parodies of the arbitrary nature of architectural discourse.

Koolhaas certainly spares no effort to put the irrationality of architectural decision-making on display. He produces lengthy reports in which, for instance, he might present all existing models that could conceivably apply to the project, one after another, in order to facilitate the evaluation of his project. Van Loghem, Stam, Duiker, Bakema, Garnier, Le Corbusier, Hilberseimer, Mies van der Rohe, Gropius, Leonidov, Cerdá, Ungers and even Krier each present their solution. Then, without any form of argumentation, Koolhaas concludes with his own proposal for row housing with a few towers. Incidentally, as Koolhaas might say, it's a good plan, with many of the same strengths as the Binnenhof and Arnhem proposals. In an academic mode, with shadow diagrams, planting concepts, potential areas for sports and games, and convergence lines, it is presented as truly inevitable architecture, not in need of any commentary whatsoever. It is, in fact, evocative—though not derivative—of the master architects mentioned earlier in the report, but it has little to do with Amsterdam. Like The Hague and Arnhem, Amsterdam is used to affirm Koolhaas's own identity and uphold the spirit of Modernism. Apparently, this is possible even outside Manhattan. The proposal for a dance theater in Scheveningen is directly related to the one for Amsterdam. In one of the numerous reports accompanying this project [...] Koolhaas explicates his methods in more detail: first he takes stock of the available information and the possibilities that it entails, and then he draws up a proposal that reinforces the existing context and reclaims essential themes that had been neglected and might even have been in danger of being lost. Again, these reports do not go into unseemly detail about the form that the project will take. The postmodern debate is nonexistent. [...] The form is derived from the objectives, the function, and the terms of reference, and in that sense, it is free. We never find out what became of the formal oppositions in The City of the Captive Globe. Or are we meant to assume, in the spirit of Le Corbusier (quoted above), that this is a question of personal taste that has nothing to do with the essence of architecture?

Judging by Koolhaas's proposal for Berlin, this is by no means the case. Flouting the principles of Hood and the Moderns, Koolhaas does not derive form from function in a scientific manner. He does not derive his forms at all. He chooses them from the modernist repertoire, though he does so inventively and does show certain preferences. Like a performer, he consummates the work conceived by others. He consummated New York, he is consummating Berlin, and soon he will consummate Rotterdam. Modernism has an aftertaste of endings. It is a kind of clearance sale; the stock will never again be replenished. All that can be achieved is a new combination. [...] The great monument to Koolhaas's war of attrition with architectural form was unveiled at the Venice Architecture Biennale in 1980, where he was placed amid an antimodernist mob. In a restored street, he designed a frontage alongside those of the other participating architects. Though he was assigned the very last plot and almost excluded entirely, he did not entirely escape the story of architecture. Even his nonfacade became a facade, albeit one bearing a distinctive Koolhaas signature: an OMA sign in fiery red neon letters (at least, when there was electricity).

This sign jutted out of his shop front like the red plaque on the parliament building in The Hague. The shop itself was closed off with a sheet of canvas that displayed the suppleness of the material in a fixed, rigid form, just as nature is perfected in the metropolis. Behind the canvas, protected from the busy posturing of the postmodern street, the real architecture of the projects presented at the Biennale was on display, in a typically Koolhaasian display of humble arrogance. The oeuvre thus far culminates in the Boompjes project in Rotterdam, which had the lofty purpose of rescuing Rotterdam from its recent degeneration and the attempt to humanize it, and restoring the city to its original purity. Koolhaas was in a similar position with this project as he had been at the Venice Biennale, but this time the city was on his side. He was not trapped in the unnatural isolation of an exhibition. In Rotterdam, he himself could select the vulnerable point at which he, in his exemplary, unique way, could administer his therapy, a point that seemed to be lost to architecture, that no commissioning party had ever dared propose to an architect. He chose the point where city and harbor, land and water, and the sky above them meet. "The city's window on the water," envisaged in the original plan but never realized, was to become "the hinge between the city and the river," with myriad internal structural echoes. Just as in London, New York, Berlin, and even Amsterdam, Koolhaas did not think on the scale of the building, but on the scale of the city. He turned the remaining section of the old Willemsbrug (no small structure) into an upright signal in the form of a pleasure tower. He then established the architectural feel of the project by means of a massive building, a synthesis of a slab and towers, which amid the surrounding motion—and there is nothing but motion there—takes on protean forms, constantly imbued with new identities. It is a pure monument to the real Rotterdam, which is more than just neighborhoods with sweet little houses, a monument to the modern metropolis. Meanwhile, a floating swimming pool built by Russian Constructivists was passing through Rotterdam on its odyssey and found a home port in the shadow of this monument. Hope has returned.

TOWARD AN ARCHITECTURE OF CONGESTION

Haig Beck

Express Extra 2 (1982), 3.

[...] OMA has been operating on a much more pragmatic plane. For more than three years now, their efforts have been concentrated on translating the experiments into real building. Working first from their base in England, but now with offices in Holland and Greece as well, they have a body of rational work to challenge the so-called Rationalist efforts to recover the urbanity of the European city.

The shift from conceptual investigation to experimental application begins with The Hague Parliament competition in 1978. This scheme, done by the old OMA line-up of Hadid, Koolhaas, and Zenghelis, defied the pastiche of contextualism with a building that dared to be as modern as its historic neighbors had once been. It is a Malevich-like architectonic housing the colisive programs of the parliament, connecting the existing urban fabric with a sequence of discrete penetrations and extrusions.

[...] Their projects in 1980 show other themes investigated with the same willful rationality. The most important of these is the ongoing Rotterdam housing, which occupies a breach in the dam of modern buildings that rings the harbor. Koolhaas, De Martino, and Kees Christiaanse have for almost two years refined an architectonic envelope intended for housing, once the Rotterdam Council has found a developer. Consequently, this building, with no specific program, still has no detailed plans—only the public interior spaces (there has to be something to show the potential client). But as the IAUS show reveals, these have been two busy years with hundreds of study sketches, computer simulated perspectives, color studies, sunlight projections, transparency exercises, and investigations of the kinetic effects of sky and canal reflections.

At the same time, Zenghelis and Koolhaas (since the departure of Zaha Hadid to her own London practice) have exercised more independent roles within OMA. For the Berlin Building Exhibition, each of them submitted separate schemes, under the collective title of OMA. Koolhaas, along with De Martino, chose to experiment with the courtyard house as a reactivated Berlin type on their Kochstrasse/Friedrichstrasse site in the shadow of the Berlin wall. Elia Zenghelis, with Ron Steiner, proposed a sequence of architectonics to restructure the disintegrating Lützowstrasse. Rather than build a wall of public housing to screen the luxury "town" houses laid out along cross streets on the site behind, they opened each of their buildings toward the entries to these cross streets forcing the private into a dialogue with the public. It is only when looking along the Lutzowstrasse that the buildings align to define the street.

Two further projects by the Zenghelis team at OMA demonstrate a certain independence of mind that can be traced back to the Hotel Sphinx. One, for a site with several small holiday villas at Antiparos in Greece, looks at first like the litterings of some suprematist Greek god; but on closer inspection it reveals the traces of a grand platonic geometry hidden in wall planes of the houses and fragments of the site's topography. The other, for the Therma Hotel in the Bay of Gera on the Island of

Lesbos, is even more startling: at first the plan gives the impression of uncoordinated fragmentation; but the elements of the hotel mount up with an unrelenting architectonic logic in the compelling aerial perspectives drawn by Steiner and rendered in oils by Zoe Zenghelis.

These two tendencies within OMA confront each other across the gallery at Protetch: to one side the sun-drenched palette of Zoe Zenghelis's renderings of Steiner perspectives; to the other, the somber prison interiors of De Martino's colored charcoals. With Madelon Vriesendorp's early New York paintings mediating on the wall between.

At the Institute (in a space that still pines for the marvelous curving walls Koolhaas erected there for his Wallace Harrison exhibition) there is a much more pragmatic presentation. It underscores the extent to which OMA is prepared to experiment before finalizing their researches into the presentation renderings to be seen at Protetch. Mounted here (not at Protetch) is the Amsterdam-Noord public housing scheme. On a site in the heart of Amsterdam, Koolhaas and Jan Voorberg—with the rigorous logic of rational experimentalists—subjected the site to twenty-three different studies based on housing ideologies ranging from Hilberseimer to Krier, before submitting their own. It won the approval of the Amsterdam council by deftly controlling the combatting tensions between central urban development and the popular call for a low profile. Now OMA have been appointed supervising architects to the site—responsible for the work of six other architects.

Contradictions are evident in the work—the Arcadian tendencies of Zenghelis in particular—but even these can be interpreted as part of OMA's opportunistic determination to build their experiments. The Amsterdam and Rotterdam schemes, however, are explicitly urban propositions. And it is this fact that will come as the greatest shock to many who will see the recent work of OMA for the first time: it is still an architecture of congestion, as conceptionally experimental as ever, even more finely rendered than before, but now about to break ground.

EXHIBIT POINTS UP VIEWS ON CONTEXT OF A BUILDING

Paul Goldberger
New York Times,
March 28, 1982.

The notion that buildings in cities should pay attention to what is around them—should fit into the context, to use the currently prevailing phrase—has been achieving wider and wider acceptance. But this can mean a lot of very different things, as the work of the Office for Metropolitan Architecture, a group of young, European-based architects, makes clear. A large selection of the group's recent work has just gone on display at the Max Protetch Gallery, at 37 West Fifty-seventh Street, and at the Institute for Architecture and Urban Studies, at 8 West Fortieth Street. It provides an important counterpoint to the ethos of contextualism that is becoming more and more the American way of designing.

As contextualism has become more of an established principle and less of a quirky idea, it has been interpreted, in this country at least, more and more literally. We have come increasingly to think that if buildings look like the ones around them they fit in, and if they look different they do not fit in. What this yields is a kind of literal contextualism, a way of designing almost by imitation—a classical building goes onto a street of classical buildings, a Spanish Colonial house goes into a village of Spanish Colonial houses. If nothing else, this is a refreshing change from the arrogant stance of anticontextualism that Modernism tended to take, and it has brought us some good architecture. To defer to what has come before is frequently correct, and it is almost always a civilized way in which to design.

But it is not all there is to contextualism, welcome as it may be as a general attitude. The work of OMA is as firmly committed to contextualism as anything being done in the United States. But it is just as firmly nonimitative. It is an articulate statement for a kind of architecture that is determinedly modern in its form, but respectfully postmodern in its attitude. The buildings designed by OMA are crisp and precise modernist forms, recalling, most of all, the early modernist work of the constructivist and De Stijl architects of the 1920s. But they do not stand alone as pure, abstract objects, as so much modern architecture has done. These romantic, machine-like objects have been shaped to relate to what is around them, to take into account the needs and textures of the existing city and landscape. They are an attempt to tell us that contextualism is much more than style—that it can be achieved through the articulation of a building shape, through the acceptance of neighboring buildings and the attempt to integrate new and different forms into them. [...]

DRAWING CONCLUSIONS

Michael Sorkin
Village Voice, April 20, 1982.

The Rotterdam-based Office for Metropolitan Architecture typifies the trajectory of a generation strongly molded by the events of May 1968. For many of them, beginning the practice of architecture coincided with a moment when both its ideological and visual foundations were severely undermined, a moment when every fundamental seemed to need reinvention. The times demanded not building but polemic, the creation of images and analyses which could make critical breaks with a recently untenable present.

The early work of OMA (whose principals are Rem Koolhaas and Elia Zenghelis) had a strong polemical orientation. It joined the debate over the redescription of urbanism which opposed Modernism's repudiation of traditional cities. Their major work was *Delirious New York*, written by Koolhaas and illustrated with projects by the office. Intended as a "retroactive manifesto," the book aimed to adduce a sort of systematic urbanism based on the author's reading of Manhattan, itself a delirious enthusing of the type which only Europeans seem able to produce. The accompanying projects—while resolutely conceived with winning irony and brilliantly drawn—had a problematic dimension. One might say that they knew too much. *Delirious New York* celebrated buildings and architects (Coney Island, Raymond Hood, Wallace Harrison) which found their daring precisely in their failures of systematic self-consciousness. OMA, having written the manifesto, was forced to live up to it. After arguing that "Manhattanism" was possible because its outrageous basis remained implicit, OMA, by spilling the beans, had to outrage.

The work was boxed in, victim of the tension between the will to polemicize and the will to draw buildings. Hypothetical projects like the Hotel Sphinx and a housing scheme for Roosevelt Island were striking architecture but could not, by definition, be exemplary of an argument centered on crazed diversity. A series of designs directly meant to illustrate particular insights (some in fable form) had a more comfortable relationship to the text. Still, the City of the Captive Globe or the Floating Pool, while seductive as images, remained exegetic. Only the brilliant paintings of Madelon Vriesendorp were happily true to the demands of the polemic. These looked neither to illustrate nor intervene but to force a shift of vision by an almost mad animation. Her work brought buildings to life, metaphorically eroticizing the city by allowing its structures sex. The Chrysler and Empire State buildings lie together in bed, spent after making love, a crumpled condom in the form of the Goodyear blimp lying on the floor beside them. In another scene they are caught in flagrante by the RCA Building which bursts through the door.

The growth of gallery architecture forces a kind of schizophrenia: what are we talking about here, drawings or buildings? This split is neatly acknowledged (if not precisely accommodated) by two current New York shows, one of which is at a commercial gallery (Max Protetch) and the other at an academic institution (The Institute for Architecture and Urban Studies). In the former, the work is for sale and much of it has surely been prepared with this intention. The gorgeous technique which animated polemic compellingly aligns itself with the shift to the real. OMA is wonderful at presenting architecture, and commands a broad but consistent range of media, learned both from the conventions of architectural drawing and (via close participation of artists such as Vriesendorp) from those of the fine arts. Perspectives are presented in scrupulous oils, axonometrics are surreally distorted, roofs fly entrancingly away from cutaway views. Over at the institute, however, the emphasis is directed away from presentation toward what is being presented, the "architecture" simulated. Here, there are reproductions of more technically descriptive drawings, rough sketches showing the development of architectural ideas, explanatory labels.

In the new work currently on exhibit, OMA has undergone a change in direction, the result of a decision to undertake only "real" projects. This, too, is a typical switch. Over the last decade or so, architecture has been very much talked about, so much so that many architects have found themselves talked into a corner. OMA sensed this danger both in an anxiety over a practice remote from daily life and in the risk of a looming classification of their work as "fantastic" or "visionary," and of themselves as surrealists, naughty but lacking that critical measure of seriousness. They recoiled, in Zenghelis's phrase, from risking the charge of "poetical opportunism." The risk was very real. In the period of its theoretical preoccupations, OMA emerged among the cream of image-makers, acquired graphic technique both singular and striking, came out at the very top in the architectural drawing wars. Unlike many other combatants, however, one always had the sense that OMA were designers first.

Although none of this work has been built (some is under construction) the connection between drawing and buildings is especially strong for OMA: their sensibility as designers has a direct relationship to the page. It connects with a specific architectural tradition which was highly concerned with two-dimensional composition. Constructivism, De Stijl, the European Mies, all sought to poeticize geometry by arraying it in accord with rules not of mathematics but of the eye. More than anything else, it is this ability to compose that gives OMA its particular sheen. In project after project, architecture's bits—whether rooms, walls, surface materials, or individual buildings—are assembled with assurance, clear both in the "artistic" work emphasizing this layer of abstraction, as well as in the more technical presentations where an awareness of function sustains the artistry.

[...] There's a funny kind of warped Jamesianism in OMA's history. Finding their work in America threateningly abstract and detached, too theoretical, they returned to Europe to recover the practical and to exhume their roots. The choice seems to have been a wise one. Along with others, they are involved in making an architecture that is very specifically European, in continuing a modernist tradition cut off in its prime. Because it is grounded in a critical stance, their Modernism is explicit; more than a critique, an embrace. Their interest in a catalogue of particulars is not constraining but liberating, precisely because it runs deep. By stripping European Modernism bare of a polemic that was really never its own, OMA have helped to recover its usefulness. And, in their work, they have redeemed and enriched its future.

THE IRONY OF METROPOLIS

Anthony Vidler

Skyline 5 (1982), 18–21.

The idea of a "modern" architecture—at least insofar as it was consciously identified with the idea of the avant-garde—held two dominant themes in precarious balance. The first, stemming from the demand for cultural revolution and a sense of the exhaustion of traditional academic forms, stressed the need to remake the language of the art, to explode aesthetic conventions, and to construct out of the debris a manner of speaking adequate to the Modern moment. The other theme, tied to the tradition of utopian and materialist attempts to refashion the social world, called for a political and economic transformation that would precipitate society into a life of harmony in the new industrial epoch. Both themes were permeated with historicist notions of progress, of inevitable development, and of the zeitgeist which for a brief period served to hold them in tandem without perceptible contradiction. Whether their modernity was Corbusian and idealistic or Marxian and materialistic, their common cause was to reformulate language and society together: as Le Corbusier wrote to Karel Teige in 1929, "We are all at this moment at the foot of the same wall."

The assumed interdependence of formal and social change was so strong that, in the decades since the collapse of the fragile treaty that linked them beneath the sign of postwar reconstruction, the mere promise of a new aesthetic language has been considered politically threatening. However, successive attempts to postulate political utopias have all questioned the existing language of forms. As Roland Barthes noted in his Inaugural Discourse for the Chair of Literary semiology at the Collège de France (1977), "'To change language,' that Mallarméan expression, is a concomitant of 'to change the world,' that Marxian one."

When technique is used in and for itself, as Clement Greenberg perceptively pointed out in the late 1930s, it is inevitably academic and very quickly becomes kitsch. Equally, the isolation of programmatic concerns, whether they are reformist or revolutionary, tends to create a kind of social positivism, which—whether embodied in zoning codes or five-year plans—divorces art from social change with a finality that seems to preclude any possible connection between the two. Certainly the last ten years have demonstrated the distinct separation of these two concerns which were held in unity so dearly by Modernism. Any attempt to "work on the language" has, despite its own best intentions, been consumed along with every other type of imagery. Any political stance with the slightest pretension to positive effectiveness has been forced to deny its "aesthetic" potentiality.

Architecture, seemingly caught between the endless play of formal images and the economic determinisms of property and space allocation, has responded uneasily to this condition. On the one hand, investigations committed to exploring the internal dimensions of certain carefully defined languages—both White and Gray—have proceeded. On the other hand, those who recognize only the certainty of social democratic—or at least democratic—forces that predetermine the bulk, and, ultimately, the form, have been sustained within the profession. No matter how the divide is bridged—whether by idealism, hermeneutics, or economics—the gap between modernist form and modernist ideology appears to have been reaffirmed and to be a part of the inevitable conditions of a so-called postmodern era.

The work of the Office for Metropolitan Architecture—named as if to confront the modern crisis fearlessly and head-on—has always resisted this great divide between program and form, between social text and artistic technique. From the first narrative paintings of Madelon Vriesendorp and their accompanying texts, the "conceptual project" of OMA at least has tried to weld text and image in a reciprocal dance, a dance that in its various steps mirrored the lusts, atavisms, hopes, and horrors of the modern metropolis par excellence—New York. This project has had obvious—and too often repeated—links to well-known modernist themes. The surrealist and the metaphysician were unmistakable here. They differed, however, from such avant-garde movements by virtue of a persistent irony that undermined both the positive and negative avant-garde positions of the 1920s in an almost endless play of disruptions and subversions. In the work of OMA, these techniques, borrowed from the avant-garde, were in a very real sense deployed against themselves.

Against the youth and fitness cults of the 1920s, and with full understanding of the desperate need for constructivist utopias to leave their homeland after 1932, the Floating Pool and its indefatigable swimmers move, stroke by stroke, toward the center of capitalist corruption. This is a center of realized dreams (but it has been changed in the realization) that affords in itself no salvation for the unsalvageable hopes of Modernism. Against the pale ideals of the Great Society programs stands the Welfare Palace Hotel. It is indeed a place for the characters of William Burroughs, but one that they would abhor out of scorn; it is a Grand Hotel criticized even by its guests. Against the mass housing projects of the 1920s and the rental speculations of the more recent past is a gigantic enigma—The Hotel Sphinx, dedicated to the delivery of cosmetic bliss, and composed under the sign of the "need and the impossibility of 'escape' as in the Welfare Palace Hotel."

Irony is a rhetorical figure that in its common definition operates by means of mocking—whether pleasantly or seriously—the subject: in the words of a nineteenth-century rhetorical theorist, "it seems to belong most particularly to gaiety; but anger and contempt also use it sometimes, even to advantage; consequently it can enter into the noblest style and the gravest of subjects." As a dominant figure of speech and mode of thought throughout the modern period, irony, whether naive or subtle, has permeated almost every discourse—including that of architecture. The most hopeful utopias, from Charles Fourier to Le Corbusier, were at base saturated with an ironic defense against their possible—perhaps inevitable—failure. As a technique, irony would appear empty of philosophical convictions and open to employment by almost any ideology. In itself, however, due to its unique structure—the way in which it operates on texts and images—irony is deeply antipositivist. As the historian Hayden White has noted, "In its apprehension of the essential folly or absurdity of the human condition it tends to engender belief in the "madness" of civilization itself and to inspire a Mandarin-like disdain for those seeking to grasp the nature of social reality in either science or art."

Irony is certainly the figurative mode of OMA's early works and of the specific work that, more than any other, served to give these works a coherent "program" of their own: Rem Koolhaas's *Delirious New York*. This book, with its unabashed postscript of OMA's images and texts, is equally unabashed in its choice of subject and in its formal strategies, both of which are borrowed from a long tradition of modernist work on the metropolis. In it is displayed sophisticated knowledge of all the techniques by which the modern city, as unconscious artifact, is to be transformed into the self-conscious agony of the avant-garde: the sociology of metropolis, advanced by Georg Simmel; the psychopathology of metropolis, from Émile Durkheim to Sigmund Freud; the technical ideology of metropolis, from Otto Wagner to Le Corbusier and their American counterparts; and, just as important, the modes of representation of metropolis, essayed by Baudelaire in *Le Spleen de Paris* and brought to a high art of montage in the "filmic" texts of Walter Benjamin. This "manifesto," from the hand of former filmmaker and scriptwriter Koolhaas, was predictable. What is not so obvious is the way in which these borrowings have themselves been ironically subverted, by virtue of the subjects treated. How should we laugh for example, at the spectacle of positive projects, such as that of the "Fighting the Flames" event staged on Coney Island juxtaposed to the actual fire of 1911 that destroyed Coney Island—an island created for pleasure at the expense of "the masses" and contrasting with their degradation? This is at once political irony, surrealist irony, supreme irony; but when it is juxtaposed to the future projects of pleasure and economic gain of Manhattan, it is exposed as nonironic. On the one hand are the facts of the case, set out with bold titles: "Foundation," "Fire," "End"; on the other is the juxtaposition—itself a time-honored montage technique—that throws everything, including the stance of author Koolhaas, in doubt.

Delirious New York, one might think, would make excellent, dryly humorous reading, but would not necessarily provide the foundations for any kind of positive building to be realized in the world. It would seem that the very choice of such a technique has armed the critically self-conscious writer against the fate of the avant-garde builder. We did not expect to see a Welfare Palace Hotel built on landfill—indeed, we hoped that none would be built: the irony of these projects only operated if the mental rather than the physical image remained intact.

But build OMA will, and in the recent exhibitions at the Max Protetch Gallery and the Institute for Architecture and Urban Studies there are a number of serious projects for hotels, resorts condominiums, office buildings, residences, and even prisons and parliaments arranged side-by-side with the early studies in wit. Surely these are not the stuff of irony. Yet in a subtle and intriguing way OMA has succeeded in maintaining its dominant figure, both through and by means of the subjects of its new building activity. And this time the dominance of irony is not sustained merely by the nature of the drawing and its narrative; nor are we presented with elaborate scenarios of actions side-by-side with their illustration. The drawings are exquisite, it is true, but they are not in any sense the surrealistic machines of urban wit previously painted by Madelon Vriesendorp. Rather they are ruthlessly scientific, the results of a sophisticated positive technique—that of the perspectival computer graphic. View after view cuts through the received angle of vision, simply by means of the flexibility of the machine. Analysis of sightlines, of massing, or of the movement of people and objects takes its place beside the most accurate projection of reality available. These are no longer the transformations of formalist technique, dedicated to destroying our commonplaces by the unexpected, but the realism of a natural vision, ruthlessly deployed to let us how indeed it would look.

The irony no longer resides in the shock of representation or in the juxtaposition of text and image; it is, in a real sense, embodied in the formal structure of the works themselves. In these projects, almost without exception, there is a determination to absorb the didactic form of Modern movement programmatics—the zoning code, the program itself—into the form of the building. In this process the ultimate absurdity of the juxtapositions predicated by zoning—life/work/recreation—is exploited as a formal device. Modernist classificatory codes and modernist aesthetics are presented as proposing fundamentally the same "form." Thus in the scheme for the Therma Hotel on the Bay of Gera on the island of Lesbos in Greece developed by Elia Zenghelis, the "ridiculous" separations of the different functions are intensified and emphasized as strategies in themselves. The "interweaving" of public and private in the Residence for the Prime Minister and State Guest House is similarly given a formal demonstration, as the movement of the viewer around the Rotterdam apartment blocks is incorporated in the form of the towers. Functionalism here finds its expression, but in an ironic manner. For these contaminations between text and image, program and form are not developed in order to make us comfortable about the "resolution" of a problem: the questions of "relationship" between people, ideas, and buildings that arise in the normal design problem are not overcome here in any positive way. In the scheme for sixteen villas on the island of Antiparos in Greece, the environment of Greece is not overtly protected by an appeal to roots, to the vernacular, nor is it deliberately shocked by the imposition of a modern object. Rather, what in experience seems to be the innocent result of contextualism becomes in plan, as painted by Zoe Zenghelis, a powerful exercise in Suprematism.

[...] Perhaps a key to reading these projects might be found in the apparently obvious scheme for the renovation of a "panopticon" prison at Arnhem. On one level—that is, on the level of the pictorial image—this would seem to be not more than a liberal "canceling" of the old panoptical functions of the prison, so the text of the architect tells us: the axis has cut through the all-seeing center—the heart of the disciplinary device has been torn out. The postpanoptical spirit has destroyed the panoptical one. Here we find echoes of a reading of Michel Foucault whose studies of discipline and power have strongly influenced the politics and strategies of the generation of OMA. However, this would be a vulgarization of the appeal made by Foucault to the Panopticon as a physical form. Moreover, Foucault himself resists all such reductions in favor of a generalized perception that sees in each and every act of reform a pervasive will to power. This will finds its capillary-like paths through every crack of least resistance—both institutional and environmental. The actual scheme of Jeremy Bentham's Panopticon in such a prescription is only the emblem or caricature of an all-embracing system of power, institutional from the outside, and psychological from the inside. According to this formulation, the act of OMA would simply be read as a displacement of one form of power into another form: there is no loss of energy, no effective change. A cynical spirit would even perceive the superimposition of cross over circle as a restoration of another kind of power, religious over secular. But this interpretation would ignore the fact that, for the architects of OMA, all this is known and understood; in fact, it is with these perceptions, in the space marked out by Foucault after Nietzsche, that the project has been conceived. That is why, for example, the organization of the new prison disappears underground, and operates for all the world like the prehistory of the old: it stands, so to speak, for the archaeology of the ruin itself.

Should this complicated set of negations and counternegations be interpreted as anything more than a dried-out cynicism, a loss of faith in Modernism, while employing the husks of modernist form? Should we conclude that irony, when wielded against itself, turns into nihilism, or, worse, into Postmodernism? A partial answer would be provided by the texts on which these designs rest their case: the writings of Roland Barthes and the philosophy of Michel Foucault. For it is under these signs that Modernism, in the present, continues to operate—not as kitsch, but as work.

It was Foucault who, in an early essay entitled "Language to Infinity," spoke of the transformation of myth into literature, of Homer into the Marquis de Sade, of the complete heroic work into the infinite whispering of writing, of Rhetoric into the Library. Barthes, in his meditation on the "languages" invented by Loyola to "speak to God"; by de Sade to "speak of sex"; and by Fourier to "speak of social harmony"—all impossible projects demanding new languages doomed to speak to no one—developed this perception. Both Foucault and Barthes—sensitive to the world after Nietzsche—the former by positive reflection, the latter by writing itself—have opened the possibility of what one might call a "restricted Modernism." Such a restrained art, conscious of its loss of positive ground, yet intimately aware of its own procedures, is bound to speak, even though the results are not only unpredictable, but also impossible to endow with unitary purpose.

In this context OMA refuses the positive inquiry into semantics, the structural semiotics that have characterized so many attempts to develop "true" meaning in architecture in recent years. Nor does it intend to anthropologize its productions with a false humanism, for the complete independence of image and society is affirmed. Similarly, the linguistic analogy, while affording valuable insights into the operation of signs in the classical world, no longer holds an absolute interpretative value. Even the space marked out by Nietzsche—which provided so powerful an incentive for Foucault—no longer seems for OMA an adequate space for production.

Neither "words in liberty," nor the endless play of figurative mechanisms revealed as "truth" by contemporary philosophy of language operate as effective codes for inserting irony into life's present conditions. Irony, as Søren Kierkegaard observed, is inexhaustible as technique and as figure; its effect, calculated but unexpected, is to produce results negatively. This was, of course, one of Modernism's utopias, as it attempted to reveal the reality behind appearances. But the dominance of irony was perhaps not fully realized until these utopias too had been proved barren.

ELIA ZENGHELIS, REM KOOLHAAS, ZAHA HADID

Peter Buchanan
Architectural Review 1040 (1983), 64.

"The aim of Diploma Unit 9 is to rediscover and develop a form of urbanism appropriate to the final part of the twentieth century: new types of architectural scenarios that exploit the unique cultural possibilities of high densities and result in a critique and rehabilitation of the Metropolitan lifestyle." In the 1976–77 Prospectus Rem Koolhaas and Elia Zenghelis announced the concerns that were to be central to their unit, and that remain so still today when the unit is run by their protegée Zaha Hadid.

[…] This unit carries the torch for Modernism. While not interested in rehabilitating its purist forms they preserve many of its ambitions and share such determinist notions as that architecture can/should provoke lifestyle. But instead of architecture explicitly defining a single utopian lifestyle—as some Functionalism implied—the approach is pluralist, advocating the creation of stimulating settings in which disparate lifestyles can coexist. For them the task of today's architecture is not to raze and rebuild the city, but through selective and strategic intervention to reequip it with the new facilities that will allow mass society to fully exploit the potential of our time—not least for hedonism.

What our time offers is the "Culture of Congestion." With a sufficient density of populace and with novel juxtapositions of different activities, catalytic reactions set in which spontaneously generate new and ever more exciting activities and forms of social intercourse. The architect's role is to provoke and manipulate such effects. The underlying model is, of course, Manhattan (subject of Koolhaas's book *Delirious New York*), certain constructivist projects—and perhaps the fast breeder nuclear reactor. Treating architecture and culture as intertwined, and a concern with "the masses" and the nature of an uncondescending mass culture all necessitated an historic perspective and so seminars, often on recent history, were essential components of the unit's design investigations. A way of designing and drawing evolved—or rather was taken over from OMA—that attempted to shape and depict buildings that would be graphically explicit of their role in the city and of the social instability they were intended to provoke. Typically the buildings were boldly massed as a collage of separate elements while inside these envelopes interiors were loosely defined and space and activity agitated by sensuous curves and violent graphic slashes and interpenetrations. (The resultant plans often seem neither very useable nor spatially comfortable.) The unit, like others at the AA, quickly became identified with a particular "style."

To fight off the risks of freezing into a set style, Zenghelis and Koolhaas stressed analysis of program and the elaboration of imaginative scenarios to inform the design. But no matter how analytical and theoretical an approach, it can still run the risk of collapse into being merely a consumable style. This is the central problem Hadid has had to face since taking over the unit. In a way she has chosen to fight it on its own ground and asks that if one pursues style it be done with and judged on flair and executed in a sharp black line that will not tolerate fudging. And though she also insists on the creation of urban scenarios to generate brief and program, these are already informed by an extremist's sense of style.

PURITANICAL HEDONIST
Franco Raggi
MODO 58 (1983), 26–28.

[...] **fr:** Do you like sex films?

rk: Yes, I still like them.

fr: Which do you like better, sex films or porn films?

rk: I'm not sure what you think is the difference. Maybe the difference is that sex films deal with the problem in a humorous way and porn in a serious way ...

fr: Pornography is more technical, it approaches the problem in terms of "gymnastics" and not aesthetics.

rk: Not just gymnastics, it's more emotional and existential.

fr: Okay, maybe existential, but with a sort of anatomical hyper-realism.

rk: No, that's not what I'm talking about. When I went to the US for the first time, we lived in Ithaca, there was a cinema that showed pornographic films and they changed the program every week. So I went to see porn movies once a week for a year.

fr: So as a "philologist" of this genre, can you tell me if a porn film can be interesting in terms of aesthetics?

rk: They can be very good, but especially in existential terms because they deal with the theme of the Greek tragedy; in porn, the tragedy revolves around a guy who has to get laid at all costs and in every way possible and the problem becomes very serious. [...] So his view of the world is always colored by this obsession. It's like an endless tragedy.

fr: What fascinates you about repetition?

rk: The fact that you know that something is about to happen, but you're never sure how it's going to happen. It becomes a play on infinite permutations, insignificant on their own, but not if you look at them all together.

fr: Have you ever mixed sex and architecture?

rk: Yes, in Exodus, where I divided London in two, not by a wall but by a sort of metaphorical neutral zone across the city, in which the architecture takes on separate and distinct functions at the edge of a paradox. There was a sort of Turkish bath house, and in the baths there were these niches that contained images of nude bodies taken from stills from the film I made.

[...]
fr: What is your relationship with citation in architecture?

rk: I'm perfectly aware of the fact that we are all constantly making citations, but there is a logic to citation, in the sense that it is logical to not reinvent something that's already been invented.

fr: Well, in that case, everything's already been invented ...

rk: No, let me explain. To me it's important to invest your energy precisely and only in the part of the compositional process—even if it's just a small part—that needs to be original, and originality means different from everything that has ever existed before. Everything else, which doesn't have to be original, I can "borrow" from things around me. You end up with a whole made up of indifferent citations, "relocated" citations, and various inventions.

fr: So do you think nostalgia can be a progressive philosophy?

rk: Yes.

fr: That's not very modern.

rk: I don't know, on the other hand it's hard for me to imagine what can be considered modern today.

fr: What do you mean?

rk: You tell me, you're the one who mentioned modernity.

fr: I think of modernity not in a linguistic or formal sense, but in terms of behavior. Modernity has to do with the interpretation of and the attribution of meaning to cultural tensions; in architecture, it tries to express these tensions in terms of environmental configuration.

rk: Okay, I think we try to do this too, but we try to do it in a much less innocent way. I think that after everything that's happened from 1930 to today, it's impossible to be innocent like they were back then.

fr: What's your opinion on citation and nostalgia in postmodern architecture?

rk: The most obvious contradiction is that the postmodernists claim they use citation and nostalgia to create a more communicative architecture, more familiar and understandable. I think this is a populist assertion. The actual result is that they make totally incomprehensible and alienating buildings. Incomprehensible even for me, let alone nonarchitects.

fr: Sometimes I think they're not so much alienating as embarrassing.

rk: In my life I've always been torn between a sort of puritanism and hedonism; no, not really torn, more like always striving to combine these qualities. What I find embarrassing is this one-way investment in the ornamentality of the facades. Since it isn't based on some cynical philosophy of surface treatment, the result is more stupid than it is provocative.

fr: What is your take on the contemporary city? Do you see a decline in the ability to conceive the city?

rk: No, I see a decline in the ability of architects to understand the city.

fr: What is there to understand about the city?

rk: That it has become a place of alienation, devastation, solitude and destruction. And since these conditions are real, we need to create an architecture that contains them, that doesn't ignore them, that accepts them and works with them. I don't see how architecture can modify these conditions by applying of the old concept of elegance.

fr: Do you still think of the city as the place of architecture?

rk: Certainly, because the city is by definition a generator of relationships and also because in the city every error is a new source of inspiration.

fr: What are the new sources of inspiration for architecture? In the 1920s it was the car and purism. In the 1960s it was technology and socialism. And in the 1990s?

rk: I don't know what the source of inspiration might be in terms of images, but in existential terms I have a feeling that it's a situation like "the morning after a crazy party." You know, when you're surrounded by a big mess, and everybody has a hangover headache, and you have to start all over again, sober and clearheaded …

fr: What party is it that's over now?

rk: The party of an architecture that has social and aesthetic legitimacy, with a "powerful" design. But the atmosphere after a party has its attractions and architecture can interpret it.

fr: Do you sense this same atmosphere in the fields of industrial design and interior architecture?

rk: Yes, I do. Even though I don't work in these fields, they are part of my "creative perimeter" and every once in a while I discover that there are a lot of parallels between what I think and what is taking place, for example in Italy in the field of research on the relationship between objects and the environment.

fr: How do you experience the relationship between the artificial and the natural?

rk: Maybe it helps to tell you how I live, which is half the time in London and half the time in Rotterdam. In London I live in a house in Hampstead, old but with no history, like all turn-of-the-century houses in England; in Holland I live in a typical speculative building from the 1960s, an apartment block with many floors overlooking the beach, totally artificial, and I really like it.

fr: Do you like it because when you're inside you can't see it?

rk: No, I like it because it's the physical form of a binary opposition, it's completely hopeless aesthetically. And our work always has to do with binary opposition, with the drama of the decision, and the inevitability of compromise.

[…]

fr: What is avant-garde today?

rk: I don't know.

fr: But do you think it exists?

rk: Yes, but avant-garde isn't what's famous today, because one of the characteristics of the avant-garde should be that it's not digestible, while the theory today is that avant-garde has become a sort of popular behavior, it's become acceptable. I still think it's important and possible to seek an unacceptable position for the avant-garde, or in any case a position that's in conflict with the way things are. Otherwise I don't see how we can find the inspiration to be architects; if everything is perfect, what's the point of adding anything?

PARIS X PARIS
Olivier Boissière
Domus 646 (1984), 16–30.

The plans of the socialist government in France for public building projects (above all in Paris) almost seem to have been inspired by Keynes, though it is not sure what effect they might actually have on revitalizing the national economy. Of the immediate effect there is no doubt: the curiosity and interest of the architectural world have been aroused and Paris now comes after Berlin with its great architectural competitions as one of the hot spots of architectural activity. The program was announced in March 1982 by the President of the Republic in person. It is ambitious in aim and seeks to be a model of procedure for the selection of architects.

The presidential term of François Mitterrand should see the completion of the Museum of the nineteenth century at the Gare d'Orsay, and the Museum of Science and Technology at La Villette; the construction of a new Ministry of Finance near the Pont de Bercy, and of an Institute of the Arab World at the Halle aux Vins; and of an urban park and "music center" at La Villette, of an International Communication Center, two Ministry buildings at La Défense, an opera house in the Bastille area, and a hall for popular music at Bagnolet; work will also be started on the project for the "Grand Louvre." Some program! Certain critics say it's too much, though a short time ago the same people were complaining about the lack of architectural activity in the country. The centerpiece of the whole program was to have been a 1989 Universal Exhibition, now abandoned to the regret of many. It was a risk both for the government and for the opposition: one assumes therefore that its abandonment was decided mainly for political (the worst possible) reasons. France and Paris have therefore let slip an excellent opportunity to make up for certain recent outrages (the most recent of which, Les Halles, is still in progress).

In recent years continual revision and alteration has undermined projects such as that for Les Halles (quite rightly) and La Défense. The competent authorities for these *grands projets*—the Ministry of Town Planning and Housing or the Ministry of Culture—have hedged themselves around with precautions and have tried to elaborate inalterable procedures: clear definition of objectives, detailed briefs, national, international, and invited competitions, and selection of a small number of designs from each competition to present to the President, who then makes the final decision. One might raise an eyebrow at this rather monarchical last stage: Pompidou, by accepting the choice of the Beaubourg jury, showed much more political flair. If the design had been a failure he could have escaped the consequences with honor; as things turned out, however, he is attributed the merit of its success.

[...] The park at La Villette has stirred up much more of a hornets' nest. The program for "an urban park for the twenty-first century" was farsighted and unconventional, open to inventiveness yet with precise guidelines, and with the occasional joke ("there will be no fast-food restaurants despite proximity to Boulevard Macdonald"). One could feel the enthusiasm and spirit of François Barré. Exceptionally, for this competition only, the jury was sovereign (they did not have to present short-listed favorites for a Presidential decision), and was formed, in a notable exercise in ecumenical opening by Barré, of the most important world experts in architecture and landscape art.

Fatalitas! The prestigious assembly of judges was unable to agree on a single prizewinner; they decided to reconsider all the entries once more, and so—in order better to defend their own positions (or unnerve the opposition)—they nominated nine ex-aequo first prizes, five of which were later designated by the regulations committee as completely ineligible (out of courtesy, unnamed here). At the second round, then, the uneasily reconciled jury members selected the lowest common denominator of mutual understanding, at the expense of the design by Rem Koolhaas. A great pity. Koolhaas and OMA had produced one of their most carefully considered project/programs: a park which Barré himself confided to us to be without antecedents or identifiable references: "a pure invention." Modern therefore. The rigorous plan is based on a grid reminiscent of computer circuitry, bare of any bucolic concession, the greenery in straight lines bordering on parody. The jury members probably smelt a whiff of hellfire sulphur, or rocket exhaust fumes, the crude glare of neon, the fear of bombs and fragmentation, and so quickly withdrew their support. La Villette by Koolhaas was a terrain for the children of punk and microprocessors, not for the children of those cherishing the memory of the old Front Populaire left-wing alliance. Unless they are the same. [...]

THE TRADITIONAL IDEA OF ARCHITECTURE HAS VANISHED: LA VILLETTE PARK COMPETITION

Françoise Choay

The Princeton Journal: Thematic Studies in Architecture: Landscape 2 (1985), 211–14.

According to the established order, Rem Koolhaas's project for the La Villette park could not possibly have won the competition: it was, by far, the best entry.

I was a member of the jury that failed to give him the first prize. I am glad to seize the present opportunity to proclaim that among 471 anonymous entries, the one—and only one—that immediately attracted the eye, puzzled and stimulated the mind by its strangeness and the questions it raised, was the project of that architect whose name was, I must confess, unknown to me, and whose identity had not been suspected by his fellow architects on the jury.

A serious presentation of Koolhaas's proposal would need a detailed analysis of the site and the program prior to the description of his answer to their requirements. This is impossible in the space that I have been allotted. Therefore my sole endeavor here will be to point out why Koolhaas's project, though unbuilt, must be considered an important event in the realm of building.

The program in its competitive context was almost a paradigm of the present approach of big public projects in France. This ethnically determined program also caricatured and hence unmasked conditions that were elsewhere implicit or hidden.

The program was:

a) Overinflated. In a vacant space no larger than 55 hectares one was to include:

▸ Educational facilities, such as a library; spaces for various kinds of exhibits, some permanent, such as: "an astronumerical garden comprising a radiotelescope, a sundial inspired by an Indian example, and an amateur observatory"; temporary "science clubs"; and "workshops for production and creation," hosting "group music, photo, cinema, video, model making, ... microcomputers, gardening."

▸ Sports facilities, such as: a skating rink; playgrounds; stabilized surfaces for sports and games (volleyball, basketball); play areas; "thermal baths" including saunas; squash courts; and a connected dance and music workshop.

▸ Social facilities, such as: a diversity of eating places from sophisticated restaurants to refreshment bars, picnic and party areas; plus a large natural space for strolling and walking.

▸ Commercial facilities, such as: a temporary market and permanent shops.

▸ Entertainment facilities, such as: outdoor theater and concert areas and similar sheltered areas, for both major and minor events. (This is an incomplete list.)

b) Overconstraining.

▸ Every item of the list was described in maniac detail. I shall give a single example, that of the "thematic gardens," the purpose of which was "the exhibition of plant growth with a goal to expose and inform, while avoiding any overly stated didactical character" and which should include "orchard, beehives, botanical garden with water garden, rose garden, mythical garden, scent garden, tinctorial plant garden, practical garden, wheat garden, fruit garden, weed garden, moss and fern garden, vegetable garden, underground mushroom bed."

c) Contradictory.

▸ A collage of contradictory logics, this program that addressed the free artist but left hardly any freedom to his imagination asked for a park at once: rural and urban; vegetal and mineral; closed and open; still a park yet something entirely new and innovative.

La Villette was to "review the idea of an urban park and its role in the city ... The goal is to devise successfully the concept of a park of the twenty-first century." It was to replace the former Haussmannian parks that, against the most striking evidence, were claimed to be "almost deserted and disconnected from the new styles of urban life."

The three aspects of the program can be related to various causes, the most important of which is the role played by historical perspective in our Western societies, where it permeates all social practices. This is especially true in the field of architecture, in which every new public project appears to clients and architects alike as a historical deed and a historical document. This historic quality is believed to be achieved deliberately by rational synthesis. Historicity then lies no more in a primary, spontaneous process later to be built and seen as historical by the historian's eye; rather, it results from a secondary, self-conscious process.

Moreover, the effects of this obsession with history are emphasized by the lack of communication between the civil servants who prepare the program and the architects supposed to answer it. Each speaks his own language: the former the language of computers listing data; the latter the more and more narcissistic idiom of a professional community. Only a miracle could make these two parallels meet: the La Villette program explicitly appeals to magic when invoking (postulating) a structure that would prevent the park from "becoming a hotchpotch of diverse objects."

Rem Koolhaas's answer is neither servile nor deceitful, oversimple nor fantastic; it is casual, humorous, complex, realistic, and actually innovative. It is innovative because in the present crisis of architecture—a crisis of status, form, and meaning—instead of once more proposing a new model and a new image, it proposes a method, thus exposing the gigantic blank of a gigantic program. Koolhaas's method may be used to realize the program, but also to discard it, to alter it; in other words, to discuss it. It breaks off with the totalitarianism of form and the present arbitrariness of image.

Koolhaas's project may be seen as an answer to both history mania and schizophrenia, the two present predicaments mentioned above. It makes place for the unpredictable, that is, for real time instead of an instant fake eternity and it makes place for dialogue, for a host of major and minor decisions and choices to be made and argued in the course of time.

Koolhaas's solution is casual and humorous with regard to the program requirements because it does not take them for granted, and it makes fun of how exhaustive they are. It is realistic nevertheless because it allows for each item to be realized, in the course of time, according to social demand and ... according to the availability of public funds. (The present situation at La Villette shows how realistic this provision was). This long-awaited reconciliation with real time and duration is possible only because of the complexity of the project, no longer a stable object but a system of evolving relationships. The traditional idea of architecture has vanished.

I would like to end by stressing a last, unexpected feature of Koolhaas's project: its relationship with the French garden tradition (including both the classical and the Haussmannian). Koolhaas has solved the contradictory requirement that the park be at once thoroughly natural and cultural. Greenery is used extensively. It is treated not only as a building material but almost mechanically: it symbolizes artificiality as it is made part of the general evolving system (this is achieved in part by using different kinds of vegetal earth). This dominant artificial-looking material is in humorous contrast to an almost vegetal urban furniture: vegetal here being related not to any formal resemblance but to modes of distribution. Koolhaas is paying tribute to the innovative aesthetic and unifying role given by Haussmann to urban furniture; he also calls for further creation in this—though essential—decaying field.

The verdict of the jury was inspired by fear:

- Fear of innovation and of the unpredictable, from the programmers who had been asking for it and refusing it at the same time.
- Fear by lack of understanding, from the nonprofessional members on the jury.
- Fear by too much understanding, from the same architects on the jury.

A DEVELOPMENT OF DENSE EPISODES

Bruno Vayssière, Patrice Noviant, Jacques Lucan

Architecture Mouvement Continuité 6 (1984), 16–21.

Rem Koolhaas is an architect who has succeeded in inventing his own "style" that can be perceived in each of his projects. Yet Rem Koolhaas is a paradoxical figure. When questioned, he often responds with allusions, evocations and ellipses—perhaps because, although he likes to talk, he is not so keen on giving interviews. They are an exercise with which he has never played along. On this occasion he is kindly granting us a favor. Rem Koolhaas can be considered a paradoxical figure because although he is certain about what he does not like, he has no absolute certainties when it comes to his architecture. Anxious, he does not speak in categorical assertions; it seems he is never sure of his case.

[…] Rem Koolhaas's dream is that of intellectual, "cerebral" architecture. This dream may well be very "aristocratic." In the following pages we explore the Amsterdam-North complex, where Koolhaas designed the urbanism and oversaw its construction. He is about to begin the realization of two housing buildings as well as a social center. We will see from the presentation of these projects that Rem Koolhaas's concerns are highly unusual in terms of housing types.

jl: We are in Rotterdam. You told us that you like this city a lot but you're not too keen on Amsterdam. What does this opposition mean to you? What do these two poles represent?

rk: The important thing is that I don't live in Rotterdam either. In the Netherlands, I think there's actually a conflict between Amsterdam and Rotterdam. You could say, oversimplifying a little, that Amsterdam represents culture while Rotterdam represents industry. Amsterdam is like a kind of enclave with quite a melancholic arrogance, a confidence that is hard to bear. Rotterdam, as you can see, is an abstract and characterless city. Let's say it's "neutral," it's a city where it's very easy to be anonymous. And we take advantage of that.

pn: In this opposition between Amsterdam and Rotterdam, between "culture" and "industry," you have chosen one of the two cities and by doing so set down a site for your work.

rk: Obviously, Rotterdam is also a more interesting city as far as I'm concerned because its history is that of the postwar period. There is a lot of 1950s and 1960s architecture that is very rich. Five years ago, when I came back from America, Amsterdam was a city that gave birth to a continuous architectural movement represented by Aldo van Eyck and Herman Hertzberger. For me, Amsterdam represented the epicenter of Dutch urbanism and an architecture that was, let's say, structuralist, or humanist.

It was then that I asked myself where the value of this position lay and I noticed something very simple. On the one hand, this generation of "humanist" architects explicitly or implicitly assert that their work is of interest to humanity as a whole; on the other hand, they create buildings for single mothers, orphans, students, the elderly, always for a special category of people who are vulnerable. I became concerned and spotted a danger in wanting to create types of soft gulags for particular social classes: architecture used always to want to focus on a precise group and come to its aid … there is a condescension in this aid. Paradoxically, the result is an architecture that gives rise to problems by claiming to help.

jl: In contrast, your interests seem more focused on defining an architecture that is more anonymous.

rk: Yes, an architecture that is less specific in its aims. But this problem is very ambiguous. I greatly admire this intentionally programmatic approach and I respect Van Eyck's positions; I too have always placed particular importance on programmatic issues. Only, I begin to worry when it's at risk of degenerating and as a consequence becoming a kind of prison of the precision and humanity of these buildings.

pn: When you talk about more anonymous architecture, does it correspond to a desire for freedom in a society that specializes, a society of archipelagos?

rk: Yes, but I'm finding it difficult to answer. I should admit that it's been a long time since I was last interviewed so I don't have any prepared answers. Four or five years ago, I think I would have answered any question easily. Now it's more difficult because I've realized through working that things were much more complex than I would often have believed.

[…]

bv: When we talk about the "humanist" architecture of Aldo van Eyck and Herman Hertzberger, are we talking about the sought-after concordance between space and usage, the desire to think in accordance with the specific usages that qualify this extremely complex kind of architecture?

rk: Yes, Aldo van Eyck gives the activities that take place in a building an almost mythical charge that can be difficult to bear. That's what I'm criticizing, ultimately and paradoxically from a very "humanist" perspective. It's “cruel” to treat orphans, single mothers, and the elderly in that way. I made this criticism five years ago because it was the dominant position here in the Netherlands. I saw that too much value was being placed on issues relating to categories, to social communities, and I understood Van Eyck’s insistence on injecting exotic examples, those that were outside the tradition of Western civilization.

pn: What do you mean by “injecting exotic examples”?

rk: All those examples from Africa, the example of the Dogon villages developed by Aldo van Eyck. After all, I think all that came about, particularly in the work of others, from a touristy simplification, so much so that it became dangerous.

jl: With regard to all those particularisms, do you try to put forward an idea that could be seen as approaching universality?

rk: No, not necessarily because universality worries me as well. Specificities interest me, local specificities that don’t have to lead to reproduction. What I try to avoid is that these specificities become a system or a prescription.

[...]
jl: Let’s talk about the architectural space you try to conceive.

rk: I’ve never understood what people mean by the word *space*. I think it was most revealing when I was in New York, at the IAUS. You know the Institute, on the top floor of a tower, with a large room, balconies and offices for all the intellectuals that participate in the life of the IAUS. It was wonderful! They gave me an office where I worked for a year. There was hardly anyone there. But every afternoon, about four o’clock, Peter Eisenman would come to see me to relax, smoking a fat cigar. He would come into my office saying “Koolhaas, you have no sense of space.” I would reply: “Yes, that’s right. But I’m delighted to be here as you’re going to explain to me what this concept of space is all about!” But Peter was never really able to explain it to me properly. The only way he had of making me understand was to take my hands, twist them and make a kind of onomatopoeic noise: “*crrrr* ...” Since an intellectual like Peter Eisenman couldn’t explain to me what space was, I haven’t tried to go any further in understanding something that seems to be based on animal noises. When it comes down to it, I don’t believe in it.

jl: When you say you don’t believe in space, isn’t it in fact that you don’t like enclosed spaces, architecturally qualified by targeted lighting, like Louis Kahn’s “room”?

rk: Oh, Kahn! I must admit he’s an architect I don’t understand at all. I’m blind to his concerns.

[...]
jl: The way you use walls, screens, and partitions is often very similar to that of Mies van der Rohe.

rk: Obviously. Mies is very important to me. There are no rooms in his architecture. But the irony is that I find very few of his projects exciting. I don’t like the Seagram Building; I only like the Barcelona Pavilion, the patio houses, the Berlin projects ...

bv: Isn’t it that you like removing barriers? You don’t like enclosed systems. You always need something to cross, a diagonal or a vanishing perspective?

rk: That’s true. But I can’t say anything else on this subject except “that’s true” because one day I may want to close something off. Because I think that what’s important in our case is a somewhat deliberate absence of dogmas. Our projects are very different from one another. Even if there are things that are similar, there’s still a great deal of diversity.

jl: I would like to take the example of La Villette or the urban planning project in Amsterdam. These projects are based on work that removes barriers. There are juxtapositions and overlaps in a system of bands, parallel lines that never lead directly to a specific point that determines the layout, one that closes the “composition.” Images of La Villette remind me a lot of Dutch fields, always parallel and separated by small canals, or endless rows of greenhouses that are also parallel ...

rk: Yes, that’s right. Those images of the Netherlands can be found in the La Villette project. I would never have been able to do that project without my weekly flights between Rotterdam and London. During the second phase of the La Villette competition, we created a model by defining certain parts in a very elaborate way. In our system we needed to specify particular instances that provide a feeling of serenity. Instances that for me provide compensations, compensating for the absence of space perhaps. Lots of people criticized the undefined nature of the project in terms of its space; they undoubtedly preferred projects that were full of spatial compositions.

pn: You’re now working in Europe but you spent a long time in the United States. How would you describe your journey?

rk: There’s one thing I now think was important for me and I’d like to explain. Between the ages of seven and eleven I lived in Indonesia. Not when it was a colony but after independence. My family moved there and it was like a liberation for me. Since then I've never been able to share the Dutch seriousness ... In Indonesia we lived in the stables of a large house, surrounded by a wall. On the other side of the wall was a wash house with a series of long, parallel basins. Beautiful women would wash their sheets in a very slow and erotic way. At one point a bell would ring out, it was lunchtime and the women would leave. The men would arrive, take off their clothes, urinate in the water and swim among the sheets. It was a great experience.

pn: Your first experience of a programmatic confrontation?

rk: Yes, something like that. When I was twelve or thirteen, all I wanted was to become an architect, a Brazilian architect, Niemeyer ... I seriously thought I was going to emigrate there. Then, and I don't know why, I forgot about it. I became interested in the cinema. Perhaps because I had a friend who made films. [...] After that, I left for the Architectural Association in London and my friend left for Hollywood. I continued writing scripts as a student to earn money. And when I was in America, from 1972 to 1978, I spent six months in Hollywood writing a script with Russ Meyer, the so-called king of soft porn.

[...]
bv: The cinema experience was very important for you. How did you make the transition between cinema and architecture?

rk: For me, the transition between cinema and architecture has always been very simple, very clear. The same talent or the same ability that makes it possible to write a script is very useful in architecture. You find the same issues with sequencing and "block" compositions. A script is never a story that just flows, it's a development of dense episodes composed in sequences. I think it's the same thing in architecture. In any case, let me tell you why I decided to become an architect and gave up on developing film scripts. Spending your life inventing stories struck me as very sad. It was a bit like being a jazz musician. Being a saxophonist at fifty is completely inconceivable for me. I came back to architecture, but I see it as the metamorphosis of the same being.

jl: In Amsterdam you were guided by similar ideas when you worked on your urban planning project. If you go there and walk around you can see a succession of plans; some of the diagonals would be ideal for tracking shots ...

rk: There's another thing that's like the sequences of a film. The parallel rows of housing are spaced out regularly. It might make you think that it's all the same ... But the cross row isn't perpendicular to the other rows, it's slightly askew. It creates a certain suspense, a shortening of the depth. It's not all that eloquent but it's like a film. Suspense is created by a misplaced trust and then later you find out it was premature.

[...]
bv: You're now in a situation in which you design a great many buildings. You're about to start work on your first building in Amsterdam; it will be the last building in the housing complex for which you drew up and oversaw the urban planning. Until now you've been seen primarily in terms of the projects you've designed and your writings. You're now about to start building, what do you think about this transition?

rk: I've never thought of myself as a theorist or a writer. In a very egotistical way, I've only collected the things that were useful to me for a number of reasons. The public side of my research in America is expressed by my book *Delirious New York*. But the private side of my discovery was my fascination with the way in which they did things there, the way they used materials. I was fascinated by the architect Wallace Harrison; I organized an exhibition for him during his lifetime, just before his death, at the IAUS. The exhibition was widely criticized in New York; Peter Eisenman and Kenneth Frampton, for example, were really disgusted that we had exhibited this nondescript architect. [...] We need to accept modern architecture without neurosis, as if it were almost vernacular, with its impressive qualities as a physical object. That's what we're trying to develop here, and if we succeed, we will have won, I believe. I see this as the place for the loftiest ambitions.

jl: What you admire about the UN building is how smooth, abstract, and anonymous it looks. You don't want the construction of a building to try to support a moral value; you don't want the architect's hand to be present or recognizable in every element of the building. Is that right?

rk: Yes, I find it very stressful when it's like that. If a little bit of the world can be loaded with a multitude of intentions then the rest of the world becomes a nightmare. I would also like to say that an America exists that I like a lot and find very important. It's the America of sheet rock architecture. Do you know what that is? It's an architecture of plaster panels. You can do anything with them, make whatever shapes you like using concrete guns and staplers. It's an astonishing idea. It's an architecture that is completely without complex, shame, or seriousness ... It avoids that terrible European condition that thinks inexpensive architecture is always bad, a real insult.

jl: Has this discovery led to an attraction to everyday materials?

rk: What's important is not the individual value of the material. You can build a whole range of things using the most inferior materials. You can even create a luxury space; Formica can become granite ...

bv: Are you more interested in some materials than others?

rk: No. One thing I try to cultivate when I'm drawing are my dislikes. If you start with those it becomes easier to find other things.

bv: Cultivate your dislikes?

rk: Yes, it's very simple. Everything starts for me with a fundamental disgust for concrete. Starting like that is a liberation. Concrete's like a kind of sludge for me. I also have an aversion to panel systems with joints, things that can be articulated in a fragmented way with neoprene joints. I'm not sure why but I'm allergic to them.

bv: Perhaps you see the joints as being representative of a system?

rk: That might be it. It might be because they're always trying to reveal the way architecture is made. And perhaps it's the fact that buildings speak for themselves. It's this "speaking for themselves" that bothers me. In a certain way, from Eisenman to the cheapest office building systems.

bv: Sheet rock on the other hand doesn't speak for itself?

rk: No, it only reveals the intentions of the people that make it.

bv: Are you fascinated by technology at all?

rk: That's an impossible question. I think the modern fascination with technology is a fascination with electronic chips. That doesn't mean anything; it's a fascination with nothing. I can be fascinated with what these chips can do but not with what they are.

bv: So you're not fascinated by technical objects, aircraft carriers, etc.?

rk: That's really 1960s.

bv: You don't have any pretensions to technical research then?

rk: There may be situations when it becomes necessary. Let's say if we want to produce an effect at any price ... If we had the money we may well want to research something technically. But I don't think it will ever be a quest for building itself; it will always be for the effects you might expect because architecture can communicate in this way. There are times when I can feel myself being seduced by construction effects, like the effects of language, but not really by the construction itself. That could be a rich source of irony.

THE STRATEGIES OF OMA

Bart Lootsma

Forum 3 (1985), 124–30.

This operation becomes therapy for the removal of all archimanias ...
Superstudio

It came as a surprise when it became apparent in 1983 that there were serious plans to hold a world exhibition in Paris. After Expo '70 in Osaka, no one had expected that such a spectacle could be organized. World exhibitions are, after all, mainly gigantic demonstrations of political and technological skill in which both countries and multinational companies do their best to compete as hard and tastelessly as possible. They are a sort of Cold War, disguised as fairgrounds in which the original marketplace function has been made redundant by improved communication and transport networks and smaller international exhibitions specializing in specific areas of production. After the Club of Rome reports, the energy crises and the hippie movement, such an ode to Progress seemed unthinkable.

Nevertheless, the socialist government in France obviously still expected an economic shot in the arm from an exhibition. Vittorio Gregotti was initially asked to make a design for a new world exhibition, which was to be held in 1989 on four separate sites in Paris. He produced designs for two sites on the Seine. Gregotti was once described by Dutch architect Rem Koolhaas as an Italian communist architect who wanted to build dams all over the world, and on one site in the Southwest he plans to celebrate the 200th anniversary of the French Revolution with, predictably, a dam in the Seine combined with a tight urban arrangement in blocks.

The other location for which Gregotti provided a design was the old world exhibition site around the Eiffel Tower, which was to be linked by a bridge, designed by Renzo Piano, to the deserted site of the old Renault factory further up the River Seine. This is where the actual world exhibition with its national pavilions and other festivities was to be held. Gregotti had a vision of tidy cubes surrounding the national pavilions on the Renault factory site, which is rudely bisected by one of Paris' most important and busiest thoroughfares. That was either the result of a rather naive attitude, or Gregotti just had not done his homework, because anyone who has taken even the most superficial interest in the development of world exhibitions is immediately aware that the layout has gradually become more chaotic over the years and that the countries taking part would certainly not appreciate being jammed into a cube. The most important activity at such events is, after all, to flaunt one's individuality. Fair enough: a melting pot can have its advantages. Gregotti's attitude, however, resembles that of the village policeman who, in his enthusiasm to maintain the arcadian peace in his manor, locks up drunken tourists in the summer. A pointless pursuit, because the tourists regard the village policeman as a spoilsport and seek their entertainment elsewhere, while the furious local refreshment industry sees the potential income disappear from under its nose and takes the first possible opportunity of finding someone else to defend its interests.

So the organization predictably sought someone else to make a new design for this international section of Expo '89: Rem Koolhaas. The immediate motivation was Koolhaas's entry in the competition for the Park for the twenty-first century in Paris. [...] But Koolhaas's attitude is in every respect the opposite of village policeman Gregotti; he just joins in the festivities as he had already done with his proposals for New York. It is no accident that *Delirous New York* is a manifesto in retrospect. One normally completes a manifesto before starting work. The rules are formulated, the principles by which one plans to operate when faced with a situation judged to be wrong. This was impossible in Koolhaas's New York, just as impossible as for the Calvinist Le Corbusier. All wishes and desires, however crazy, are realized without any frustration.

All that Koolhaas does, in his design for the world exhibition too, is to reflect the desires and wishes, categorizing and channeling them. The scenarios act as an aid to developing images. The strategies serve to channel them. But Koolhaas's scenarios and strategies are restricted to the site of the world exhibition itself; beyond the one site chaos reigned. The Brussels Expo '58 was reason enough to renew the whole Belgian road network and to restructure Brussels. In Paris, Koolhaas had no plans for new roads and even intended closing an important link which annoyingly bisects the exhibition site. Sheriff Koolhaas does not lock up the drunkards, but makes sure they do not end up under a car. Anything to maintain the festive atmosphere. His argument is that a world exhibition always creates traffic problems and Paris is chaotic anyway, so a bit more or less does not make any difference in this City of Congestion. It begins to resemble "dancing on the volcano." Decadence and decline are words which spring to mind. Delirious to the point of delirium. It is, after all, only temporary.

Koolhaas probably visited the Brussels Expo '58. He would have been fifteen or sixteen and it must have made a considerable impression on him. This can also be seen in the shape of the small pavilions, which he has sketched on his proposal in typically atomic style. [...] The various participants are given a territory within which they are free to do their thing, much as in the blocks of the New York grid or in the ideal model based on it, the City of the Captive Globe. While New York has a road network, the participants here have to arrange their own circulation between themselves. Koolhaas also draws other conclusions from the architecture of recent world exhibitions, especially Osaka in 1970. He argues that the architecture of the pavilions has gradually been characterized less and less by building walls, but more and more by illusions created, using electronic and projected effects. He mentions the Ricoh pavilion in Osaka as a cynical pinnacle where hundreds of crying children were projected on a circular screen. In Paris in '89 he foresees a widespread use of lasers that will evoke the most tasteless images as holograms. Koolhaas wants emphatically to dedicate Expo '89 once again to progress, a concept which in his opinion has wrongly had a negative sound to it in recent years. An ambition such as "to draw up a balance of the current state of affairs, so that all people can prepare themselves for the creation of a better world," as expounded by Brussels' Expo '58, is now out of the question. The only "message" now is the medium.

[...] By including a parody of the phenomenon world exhibition in his proposal, Koolhaas frightened off his client. I am, however, not sure that Koolhaas intended it all to be a parody. During a lecture at the Festival of the City in Arnhem in 1984, he was shocked and even annoyed that the audience laughed as if he were a satirist. If the world exhibition had gone ahead in Paris in 1989, it would certainly have been a satirical spectacle, but then probably more in the spirit of Frankie Goes to Hollywood's summer hit "Two Tribes."

A striking illustration of this is the photo of an exploding Eiffel Tower with a button in one corner. The image corresponds miraculously with the Tarot card of the Tower, which means "Fate" or "a sudden change for the worse." What does all this mean? Is the parody or satire a result of Koolhaas's approach using scenarios, in which a simplistic vision of the world is given? Is it a result of the paranoid-critical method, with precipitous action on the basis of scant details? The paranoid-critical method was invented by Salvador Dalí, and I am reminded of a television broadcast in which the Surrealist "demonstrated" that Rembrandt was in fact blind. "Look," he said, "at those scratchy drawings. And look at how a blind man feels his way with his stick." He demonstrated how, and there was no way of arguing with him. I had to laugh, there was nothing else I could do. Or maybe Koolhaas was deliberately trying to make a parody, holding a mirror up to the world. It works perfectly, but it does not help get commissions, and that must have been Koolhaas's aim. It is after all the same Koolhaas who once commented on a prize he had won for his design for the IJplein in Amsterdam-Noord, that he was so satisfied that the execution displayed "a certain normality."

It may be good to return to the origins of his use of scenarios, which forms the most characteristic feature of Koolhaas's concept of architecture. Several publications have pointed out that Koolhaas adopted this method from the Superstudio group. Superstudio is a group of Italian architects who augmented practical work in actually constructing buildings and, in design, spent a lot of time in theoretical research into architecture. Their best-known work is the Continuous Monument dating from 1970, a gigantic grid extending across the whole surface of the Earth. In 1970 and 1971 Superstudio developed a number of what they called "didactic projects," of which the most significant was The Twelve Ideal Cities. This design was published in a simplified version with three cities, in *Archithese* (1, 1972) in an article entitled: "Drei Warnungen vor einer mystischen Wiedergeburt des Urbanismus." This article presents a portrait in text and pictures of three "utopian" cities, each of them with a completely closed cosmology. One of the cities is the "2,000-ton town," a gigantic and even grid in which the individual inhabitants each have their own cell with connections for the input of food, for the output of waste matter and for their sex lives. The ceiling of the cells receives cerebral impulses which are passed on to a central computer, which adjusts the needs of the inhabitants to each other. Death no longer exists, except for the fools who rebel against this existence. The first time, the computer is lenient, but the second time, the ceiling crashes down under a weight of 2,000 tons. The cell can then be used for a new individual to be created.

Superstudio designed another eleven cities, all equally despotic and with similar scenarios. At the end of the article this all turns out to have been a test in which the readers are asked how many of the cities presented they would like to see realized. Dependent on whether all three, two or only one city are chosen, the reader is a "Zombie," a "Golem," or an "Obscene Mutant." Even those who don't want to see any of the cities realized, are not safe, because they have not realized that these were not utopias, but inevitable futures for the Western world: if you had not realized that, you were an idiot. The only way out, according to Superstudio, is "to go to the old gray-haired man on top of the mountain and to become his son." [...]

It would be wrong to take it for granted that we should regard Koolhaas's world exhibition design in the same way, as if it also had such a didactic, moralistic approach. Koolhaas's variation on the Superstudio cities, the 1972 Exodus project, is almost its complete opposite. Everything here is free and voluntary. The inhabitants of the strip are "voluntary prisoners," everyone is able to realize his or her desires and wishes, using deviant behavior as an example, "patients from four lunatic asylums who, as a therapy, depict their crazy ideas as lessons for precocious children," as Koolhaas wrote in a publication of the Van Rooy Gallery in Amsterdam. In the same way, the Exodus strip should function as an example for its London surroundings. This may appear to be a utopian attitude at first sight, but it comes down to an ironic comment on the cheerful projects of Archigram, with Koolhaas secretly hoping that the inhabitants of Exodus would become homesick for their old, familiar, boring, brown London. OMA's design for the extension to the Dutch Parliament provoked Koolhaas to state that the space surrounded by glass bricks intended for "orgies of participation" would eventually be demolished if there was no enthusiasm for participation. As Peter Sloterdijk wrote in his *Critique of Cynical Reason*: "Reality will always be different."

That may be the clue to a parallel between Koolhaas and Superstudio: this definitive end which both ascribe to utopian thought in architecture. This does not provide much insight into Koolhaas's own options on the design for the world exhibition. It is of course possible to refer back to a statement in an interview with Hans van Dijk: "The inner cities of Europe are stagnating in any case. This is something which will affect the whole of Europe. I do not regard this as a tragic process, but one with its own possibilities. *Designing depopulation* [of European inner cities] strikes me as being a correct term for what we are doing." Superstudio writes: "in accepting his role, the architect becomes an accomplice to the machinations of the system." That may be so, but do we have to be so enthusiastic about it?

It may help to return to the period when Koolhaas wrote film scripts. In 1969 he wrote the scenario for *The White Slave* with René Daalder. [...] It is a film mainly about people who are wrestling internally with their personal desires, their ideals and their morality. The fact that all these motives take turns in dominating them means that people can hate each other one minute and lay in bed together the next. "Scenes based on folk theater and romantic fiction are developed, supported by pathetic music and truly moving camera work (Jan de Bont). Clichés are pursued shamelessly only to be immediately and exaggeratedly turned against themselves, as Pinter sharpens absurd situations," according to Dutch film critic B. J. Bertina after the premiere in 1969. He continued: "People do something, they show off and have their moments of tragic realization, which could make you laugh."

It is significant that it is not the clichés in *The White Slave* which are exposed, as one might expect, but the people who consider themselves above the clichés. Koolhaas and Daalder take the clichés incredibly seriously, just as when they invited the evangelical folksinger Gert Timmerman to make the soundtrack. Clichés are presented as people's deepest and most real desires and hence beyond mockery. [...] The film was an enormous flop commercially, probably because the makers had aimed it at a large audience, while it can possibly only be appreciated by an elite film theater audience. [...] Apparently you don't have just to be an elitist idealist or a do-gooder to see your ideals come to a sticky end. [...] This is also the subversive element in the work of OMA, but someone with such a philosophy of life can no longer be an idealist, as becomes clear in the script of *The White Slave*: everything can always turn out different to expectations. "Reality will always be different." But in this case, Koolhaas is a person who takes people's desires very seriously, as revealed by his attitude. This can lead these people to experience moments of "tragic realization" when they are confronted with their own desires. This can prove to be such a shock, that people completely deny these desires. Or the desires get adjusted. [...]

FROM THE BRIDGE TO THE TOWER
Umberto Barbieri
Lotus international 47 (1985), 125–26.

[…] Designed by civil engineers W. N. Rose and Van der Tak at the same time as the urban development scheme and infrastructures for the sites to the south of the Meuse in Rotterdam, the Spoorbrug and Willemsbrug first span the Koningshaven situated between the left bank and Noordereiland, then cross the new arm of the Meuse which is 327 meters wide. While the Spoorbrug is on the traditional pattern of iron bridge with arched structures, the cross section of the Willemsbrug is a rectangular tunnel, resting on two iron girders that are supported by concrete and basalt pillars founded on piers. The entrances to the bridge are made to resemble gates to the city by imitating a neoclassical design of the Beaux-Arts type.

The image of Rotterdam at the beginning of the twentieth century is characterized by these two bridges, whose technical perfection and basic structural aesthetics are the best expression of the city's cultural atmosphere. At the start of the 1930s the film *The Bridge* directed by Joris Ivens not only confirmed this "cultural" aspect of the two structures but also their function in the collective "memory" of Rotterdam. They mark the beginning of the city's process of expansion and at the same time, by uniting the past with the future, the residential area with the port, they are an expression of the continuity of urban development.

The two bridges survived the bombing of the historical center and harbor by the Germans at the start of the Second World War: together with the tall building of the Witte Huis, the Laurenskerk, and the town hall, they were the "emotive" bases, the historical monuments on which the process of reconstruction could be founded. Although in the early plan, drawn up soon after the bombing, history and monuments still served as poles of reference for the new constructions, the "functionalist" mold that typifies Dutch town planning and architecture in the 1950s dominates in subsequent schemes, especially that of the Basis Plan, a document that still provides guidelines for intervention in the historical center to this day. The urban grid was in fact conceived and designed without taking into account those references, those nodal points, which had determined the architectural character of different periods in the city's growth. The urban road system, which goes back to the functionalist city, was based on the idea of a city center in which commerce (the Lijnbaan) and the tertiary sector dominated. Later on a stimulus was given to housing schemes of a speculative nature and the subsequent demolition of old quarters. The themes of urban renewal, which were central to the debate over the city at the beginning of the 1970s, were imposed on a planning procedure ruled by the laws of the industrialized building cycle and by the politicization of the housing problem. This resulted in the loss of urban features and buildings from the nineteenth century and of a number of architectural "fragments" that marked the historical stratification of this city. One of the first "offerings" made to the altar of functionalist ideology was the Willemsbrug, replaced by a modern motorway bridge of concrete at the beginning of the 1980s. This will be followed by the Spoorbrug, to be demolished after construction of a tunnel beneath the Meuse.

Against this background of functionalist "destruction" of the city's historical features stands the project by Rem Koolhaas in collaboration with Stefano de Martino, Kees Christiaanse, Jeroen Thomas, and G. Comello for reutilization of a 110-meter-long section of the Willemsbrug. Hence this is a project that forms part of the development of an idea of the city characterized by the use of archaeological relics. The use to which they are put is not just historical but also architectural, projecting them into the future.

So Koolhaas's challenge to the functionalist bias of Rotterdam's planners and architects is based on an architectural project in which history is not seen as "conservative restoration" but as reference and stimulus for new images. The idea of preserving one span of the old Willemsbrug is in part founded on a conception of image and memory not as static moments but as dynamic ones, in that they stimulate new technical reflection and the construction of a new urban reality. A reality in which nineteenth-century engineering is transformed into constructivist architecture, being "translated" into a "modern" language.

Thus Koolhaas has chosen from the vocabulary of architecture the very language which is most suited to the culture of this city as it has been interpreted and determined by Rotterdam's best architects, from Oud to Van der Vlugt and from Brinkman to Van der Broele and Bakema. The architectural and cultural value of Koolhaas's proposal has met with no response at the political level: the demagogy of participation and low-cost housing has proved that it holds sway within Rotterdam's Social Democratic council.

Despite being fated to remain on paper, Koolhaas's project has stimulated a new attitude toward discussion and planning, on the urbanistic level, of interventions in the city. It is no accident that the beginning of the 1980s saw a resurgence of controversy over the value of the Basis Plan and that in planning of the process of reconstruction of the old port area, the architectural project has won back a position of prominence. Koolhaas's project, along with the international event "Kop van Zuid" in which Aldo Rossi, O. M. Ungers, J. P. Kleihues and D. Walker all took part, has give risen to a new sensitivity to planning in which "the invisible city" has come back to play a determinant role in the formation of the future city.

THE SECOND CHANCE FOR MODERN ARCHITECTURE: REM KOOLHAAS

Patrice Goulet
L'Architecture d'Aujourd'hui 238 (1985), 2–9.

[...] **pg:** When and how was OMA founded?

rk: Since the Exodus project, Zenghelis and I had agreed on the idea of setting up a practice together, but at that point it was an entirely theoretical idea. He came to Ithaca, then to New York, where he taught at Columbia and where we really worked together for the first time, on a design for the Roosevelt Island competition, which we didn't win but we did receive a mention, and then I came back to London ...

pg: Your first project was the extension to the Parliament building in The Hague?

rk: Yes. We did it with Zaha Hadid, one of our students who had just graduated. She worked with us for three months.

pg: How did you do it?

rk: We discussed the approach and then split the project into three, with everyone taking care of their own section, while I took on the most because I was familiar with the context and the contacts: Zaha did the large block, in which you can see the beginnings of the typical "Hadid" style; Elia took charge of the second, lower block, in a very classical way; and, taking the route of a former canal as my starting point, I sliced up and deconstructed the existing building, cleared a courtyard, and produced the small skyscraper, something very "boring." The axonometry of Zaha, who annexed the tower, is very recognizable. The aerial view was the last drawing I did myself.

pg: After The Hague came the Dublin competition?

rk: Yes, our first project out of nothing, in nature. Our first attempt at handling nature in the same way as an urban setting: in other words, our design emerged from a very advanced reading of the site. Elia and I established the outline together. The program included two houses, one for the prime minister and another for his guests, and the site was split into a regular and rectangular space, a former kitchen garden and the remains of a romantic park. We also decided to split our design into two and worked out who would be better at each part. The kitchen garden was transformed into an American motel, and because this was the simplest and least interesting part—a simple succession of rooms in which the public elements just needed to be distributed tactically—I took care of it. Elia, with a pure logic that could be described as "very Bauhaus," worked on the most unruly part, for which you needed to be very illogical and brilliant: the residence itself, which Léon Krier always called "the two bananas" because two curved buildings intersected.

pg: Didn't you say Zenghelis had taken charge of the most classical part in The Hague?

rk: Yes, that corresponds to the other side of him ... The best way of working with him is to shut him in a room, slide the data and some blank paper under the door and then come back in the evening to collect the extremely eccentric hieroglyphics he's produced. I don't know whether it's through choice or necessity, but he always works better on his own and in complete concentration. He always finds the problem and, in a really complicated way, manages to resolve it. That's how he manages to give his characteristic density to his designs. He has mastered the art of navigating through the arbitrary and the illogical, while I always need reasons and logic. Dublin was the first OMA project to be seen through to the details—materials, structures, constructions—with a desire to match American aesthetics and expertise.

[...]
pg: Like some of OMA's drawings, the collision of words seems to be aimed at reviving ideas that seem old-fashioned, giving them new life, like "tour en barre" and "street in the air."

rk: Because I used to be a journalist, I'm very aware of the impact of the subtle change in meaning words can bring. It's a bit like at the stock exchange: the concept of the passageway had fallen really low and it was almost with a shudder that we rediscovered it and made sure we brought it back. This combination of an unintentional poetic strategy and a simple piece of linguistic pleasure counts a lot for us. We discovered the formula on which the design for La Villette is based with the same intense emotion.

pg: What formula?

rk: The equation that gives the distance to be established between the facilities. It was about rediscovering the strength of rules, something that was very dubious at that time.

pg: A return to the most elementary functionalism?

rk: We've often tested the law that says that the dustbin of history is littered with the richest ideas: the most discredited when it comes to good taste and the most innovative in terms of content. That's what is happening at the moment, for example, with the ideas championed by Team 10 or Archigram, which are seemingly completely out of date when judged formally but carefully revealed the problems that sprang up in their time.

pg: The design for Amsterdam-North was OMA's fourth project in the Netherlands?

rk: Yes. In September 1980. The City of Amsterdam was hesitating between Ralph Erskine and myself for this project, which was very funny. Erskine was the champion of participation (he had just finished Byker Wall) and I'd just said in an interview that all the good intentions of participation would degenerate into a kind of gulag in which single mothers, widows, the elderly and orphans etc. would all be grouped together. So, they had to choose between a Swede who believed in participation but didn't speak Dutch and a Dutchman who didn't believe in it.

pg: Why did they contact you?

rk: Yet again because of *Delirious New York*, which the deputy mayor's assistant liked. Through its defense of the idea of the city, the book was very controversial at a time when the Netherlands was like Cambodia under Pol Pot, so great was the frenzy of ideology, so much so that everything was done to bring the ideas of 1968 into being.

pg: Obligatory freedom?

rk: Exactly! By chance, the book came out at the same time as the decision on the Parliament building in The Hague and it was quite surprising to have this shockingly modern project on the one hand and this very dense book that wasn't even formalist on the other. The Netherlands was in the process of waking up from a nightmare and I took advantage of it!

pg: The competition for The Hague must have had a big impact as well?

rk: The press talked about it a lot, deeming it to be a scandal that our project didn't win. An association was even founded to champion our project and its members included Jan Voorberg, who came to see me and soon became a friend. When I was contacted by Amsterdam, I asked him to work with me. With incredible tenacity, it was he who relentlessly continued the dialogue, listening, discussing, explaining and making our intentions clear. He took care of the landscaping and was responsible for the superb drawing of the western section (he also worked on the landscaping for La Villette). The project was very tough. We were somehow parachuted into the middle of a group of about thirty people who had already developed a project that we had been asked, without anything being made clear, to destroy. In the end, it was the inhabitants who got our design adopted.

pg: Generally speaking, how do you manage to translate your very minimalist designs into reality?

rk: I think we manage without too many sacrifices or too much ridicule. What we design is not absurd, we're just part of a certain material and economic logic.

pg: Is your solution anything like that of Ungers?

rk: No, not at all. For Ungers, it's important that nothing should disturb the platonic side of his architecture. The design for the Dance Theater shows clearly that, on the contrary, we took a logic from the obligation to use very economical materials that would lead to a certain emotional richness, by setting them up in opposition to one another. The current problem is that our projects haven't been built yet and lend themselves to all sorts of speculation.

pg: You insist on the primacy of the program but every time you talk about a project, you start with the impact of the location!

rk: Because our attitude toward the program is always the same, so it's almost automatic for us. It's through a very advanced reading of the context that a project assumes individual characteristics.

pg: Isn't their specificity in contrast with the search for banality that is often said to lie at the heart of your interests?

rk: I don't think I've ever used the word *banal* ... Let's say that, of course, it's not banality that we're striving for but a way to succeed in working with it.

[...]
pg: Can you explain to us how you work?

rk: Firstly, you really need to understand that all of OMA's projects are the result of a collective effort, whether in Rotterdam, where there can be about twenty of us, London, or Greece. It's by talking, discussing and criticizing one another—through very little designing—that we move forward. For La Villette, it took two months, after the failure of a series of sketches, before we were able to discover, through diagrams, that the only possible solution was simply to illustrate them.

pg: And with Elia?

rk: For me, working with him means working with someone who knows me very well (and whom I know very well) and in whose judgment I have complete confidence. We use each other mutually as critics. I show him a design, he tells me what he likes and doesn't like and I do the same thing for him. We can each say whatever we want to say, we don't have any ego, and it is this climate of self-criticism that is typical of OMA.

pg: Is it indiscreet to ask you what you and Zenghelis talk about besides architecture? Film, art?

rk: Our relationship is much less intellectual. Much more friendly. Architecture is secondary even. If we had to choose whether to remain friends or partners, I would definitely choose the first solution. It's not that we have the same character though! Elia is a very bizarre being; Mediterranean and very "Wagnerian," much more serious and profound, much more possessed and crazy than me. But sometimes it's not about what we have in common but the differences that fuel an attraction. We work together in a way that's quite comical but it's not architecture that binds us most.

OR THE START OF THE END OF REALITY: ELIA ZENGHELIS

Patrice Goulet
L'Architecture d'Aujourd'hui 238 (1985), 10–14.

pg: Did you meet Rem Koolhaas at the Architectural Association?

ez: Yes, Rem was the first student to whom I had nothing to say but "Go on." He was the first to inspire rather than discourage me. I don't know what I gave him back then, other than encouragement. We were both very isolated because we didn't agree with what was going on around us. We loved architecture, which wasn't fashionable at that time, in the years that followed the events of May 1968. We didn't have the same temperament (I always have a tendency to get discouraged while he, on the other hand, is always persistent) but the same goals: we could fight together, because it was really about fighting, the irony being that today, we have to protect ourselves against the senseless and extremely oppressive flood of architecture that bombards us constantly.

[...]
pg: And you did Exodus?

ez: Yes, for him, it was a school thesis, for me a new beginning. For him, it was the fruit of his knowledge of Berlin, for me a new version of my fortress-city, with the abrupt line that separates good from evil and that everyone wants to cross to get to the oasis. Rem then left for the United States, but we continued working together.

I went to join him to give some lectures and we each worked on some theoretical projects on New York that helped us think: the Welfare Palace for him, the Hotel Sphinx for me.

pg: Why did you take Léon Krier to teach with you?

ez: I really liked the projects he published in *Controspazio*. I imagined that he lived in Italy but then I found out he was working for Stirling. I called him. He came to see me the same day with all his designs and started teaching with me the following day. We've stayed very close, even if we both think the other has gone mad. He continues to assure me he likes modern architecture and that if all modern architects were like us there wouldn't be any problems. But, alas, that's not the case! He would also like to stop us before our influence leads to "catastrophes."

pg: Does mediocrity need to be managed?

ez: It's a problem, and we're not indifferent to its arguments. I remember that an uncle I respected a lot when I was a child, someone who would have a huge influence on my life, told me that the pleasure you get from a city is not so much about the quality of its monuments but the harmony of its fabric, and that there's no point searching for something metaphysical. He also added that this pleasure could not compete in intensity or quality with that produced by painting, literature, or music. It's not wrong to say that this obsession among architects with turning every building into a work of art is a pure product of the twentieth century, but perhaps it's a natural product, a historical consequence that cannot be denied but which leads to its own problems. For me, despite everything, there is no doubt that because of its material and programmatic dimension, architecture is a more hedonistic art than the other figurative arts.

pg: Yes, it's about giving pleasure, of course, but doesn't architecture aim to express ideas as well?

ez: I would say it's more about providing a critical dimension. This is what seems important, essential even, as far as I'm concerned. I believe that this need to find a system of meaning in a piece of architecture, one that is so structured that if you move even a small part of it everything changes, belongs more to an aesthetic of thought than to architecture; this reading seems to me to result from a typically French sensibility.

[...]
pg: You clearly don't like being fashionable, but isn't the appeal of your drawings dragging you toward it?

ez: Good taste and fashion are forms of oppression that take the ability to think away from us and reduce us to a robot-like state. Our recovery of certain vocabularies that are no longer in fashion has a critical dimension for us. Because over time everything ends up becoming familiar and therefore consumable, we have to keep constantly changing the rules of the game to keep a certain dose of indigestibility in our work. We are so allergic to it that we end up loving intensely what used to horrify us. This annoys our friends a lot when they come back to us after a year and accuse us of defending something we attacked during their previous visit.

pg: But isn't this participating in consumption then?

ez: Transforming food into poison disrupts the order of things and provides for a critical dimension. As nothing is established anymore, you really have to think. It's a method similar to searching for intelligence where it doesn't exist.

pg: It's a means and not an end!

ez: Exactly, a means that serves our interests. It's about a shift that is no doubt similar to what we do with the nature we describe as idyllic when we arrange it strategically.

[...]
pg: It's striking to notice how much you both seem to always want to give a meaning to places that seem to hardly have any. Wouldn't the adjective *retroactive,* used by Rem to describe his manifesto about New York, still be entirely appropriate here?

ez: That's true. We like to find the invisible justification for what we can see. It's an obsession, and it's only afterward that we're keen to work because architecture serves to make explicit what was merely implicit before. For us, architecture has no interest or isn't possible if it doesn't give a certain intelligence to something that was, or at least appeared to be inanimate.

[...]
pg: The key word for you still seems to be *artificial*?

ez: It does indeed express one of our aspirations, the easiest to justify because it is universal. By its very essence, everything natural is doomed to disappear. We are born, we die, we disappear; only ideas, art, things that are artificial seem to offer some promise of permanence. Humanity's ultimate hope may be that it can become immortal through artificiality. Why live if everything dies and you have to start again with every birth? Things that are artificial resist this absurd condemnation and at least give us the illusion of survival and that we are a part of the continuity of an infinite existence. What other reason is there for art if it's not about managing to go beyond the moment? The question is not whether or not you like the sun, trees, birds, or anything else it would be absurd to deny the pleasure that they bring because, on that level, every discussion about nature becomes a farce. It's instead about agreeing to question whether the history of humanity, in all logic, isn't heading toward the substitution of natural with artificial, which (at the risk of becoming the victim of its own extreme oppositions) will win the definitive victory over death.

THE ECONOMICS OF IMAGINATION

Mil De Kooning
Vlees & Beton 4 (1985), n.p.

mdk: You asked the audience during your lecture on the Blaak project how familiar they were with the layout for Blom's Bastille. Then you said, "The quality of education rises in proportion to the degree to which one's knowledge of recent history is deep and that of distant history superficial." Why limit the discussion to contemporaries or spiritual forefathers?

rk: It's not really a limitation, is it? Repeat that quote again—I mean, I'm sure it's true ... (*laughter*) I wasn't arguing for superficiality with regard to the distant past and depth on recent events, absolutely not; the best education delves deeply into everything. But if I had to choose between schooling that provides a solid understanding of recent history and only a rough understanding of ancient history and an education based on the reverse, such as currently seems to be the case, then I find the former better, for the simple reason that in order to operate with any intelligence, you must at least know your history for the past twenty-five years. There are architecture students out there right now who are barely aware of it, who probably don't even know much about Aldo van Eyck. That means, at the very least, that they are blind to trends and responses, in the sense that every building is a response to its immediate predecessors or its contemporaries. If you are unaware of that ...

mdk: But isn't the reverse much more common? Students with short memories who follow the latest trendy development close on one another's heels?

rk: I haven't encountered that hardly at all, unless you're talking about very recent history, the recent recent—a Mario Botta, for example. But if you drop the name Georges Candilis at any school of architecture, it registers a total blank. I think that's dreadful. Because that means an entire link is lost and then you are, by definition, heading down a dead-end street.

mdk: Don't the choices you make in your work suggest an equally selective memory? In your submission for the IBA, you stated that both the baroque fragments and the buildings from the 1950s and 1960s "are all now equally shipwrecked." But your proposal reaches back exclusively—and this is more of an observation than a criticism—to a modernist idiom.

rk: Look, I am in one sense incredibly naive. Unlike many other people, I don't view the modern period as being concluded. I have this unshakeable feeling that no matter what we say or do, we are still living in it. I'm not polemical about it at all, although it has a polemical effect in context—one of "this guy doesn't realize that Modernism is dead." And that makes it appear as if I do realize that and thus have a much more complicated relationship with it than is actually the case. None of that takes away, of course, from the fact that I too know we are at a certain remove from it and that my work is indeed partly a comment on those historical facts. But I never feel that with the baroque and "Modernism" stranded in equal measure, the choice should be completely discretionary, just because we live in the 1980s and are thus by definition closer to the 1950s. That's actually a very trivial explanation. I do try to do something with all modern things, value all fragments equally as they are and elevate their quality to equal degrees. And also I believe that we live in a time of elevated consciousness—an excess of consciousness—which means that, unlike during the first wave of Modernism, we can never do anything spontaneously anymore. You might say that has the disadvantage of creating a certain overrefinement, but it also has the advantage of allowing you to return to these things and reap a second harvest from the meanings and potential they contained. I am very consciously aware that I perform that operation from a polemical stance, whereby I am waging a battle against the generally accepted understanding that Modernism never sought any relationship to history. I try to relativize, or even repudiate, that notion by demonstrating in the work of others—such as Mies and Leonidov—and in my own projects how, far from asserting a nonrelationship, those modernist typologies can instead engage in all sorts of connections in a very profound way that have not yet been explored. And I might add that we have no other choice, such as here in Rotterdam, but to continue to pursue these kinds of typologies.

mdk: That's true. But how are the components of the La Villette project connected to Paris? You associated those strips with the rows of greenhouses you see every week from the plane going from Rotterdam to London.

rk: That association was actually made by Jacques Lucan—an association I don't deny because it sheds light on the fact that every operation has both a ridiculous and a complicated explanation. And I find both equally legitimate. Because it is certainly true that I would fly back exhausted every Friday night slack-jawed and, utterly devoid of inspiration, observe, "Oh, that works too." But there is also just as easily a very sophisticated explanation. To me, the apotheosis of metropolitan architecture was the Downtown Athletic Club, where each floor was given over to a different program; the condition of the metropolis had been maximally exploited in the architecture, as it were. But whereas that skyscraper represented a more primitive stage of that condition, the situation at La Villette is much more subtle: there you have the metropolitan condition in its purest form, even without architecture, pure density and activity, without the obstacle of floors, all arranged in layers and blocks independent of one another, with a shared autonomy. So, there is an intelligent explanation as well, though in my experience they always go hand-in-hand. Except you never hear about both sides—or some people hear nothing but both sides! (*laughter*)

mdk: Why do you feel a kinship with Mies and not Duiker?

rk: There's probably an emotional reason for that, though I think I can explain what's behind it. What I appreciate about some of Mies's designs is their rebelliousness, which in my opinion makes him more subversive than Duiker. What Duiker built was beautiful, it was different, modern, but it doesn't raise any fundamental issues. [...] Duiker doesn't have that dimension at all. Duiker is about form and form doesn't interest me. Not really.

mdk: Such modesty regarding form, when most people are dying to get into architecture?

rk: Of course it's a witticism to some extent. I am interested in form, but my interest is in the relationship between form and event. Because I don't believe in the mythology that form has become all wrapped up in.

mdk: Maybe this Duiker business is related to your allergy to concrete.

rk: That allergy has an intellectual explanation, but there is also undoubtedly something Freudian about it. And I'm sure there's a banal explanation as well. Maybe I spent too much time as a boy playing in the mud in bombed-out Rotterdam; but now I'm not seriously trying to interpret it. What I do have against it is how lacking in character it is, by definition. And the fact that it makes stupid things possible; namely, everything. One of the phenomenal things about Mies is that his courtyard houses are modern, while still enabling an absolutely classic form of urban design—a city composed of blocks, like a Pompeii, each block a random configuration of patio dwellings. And the paradox that introduces: outer modesty and inner exclusivity.

mdk: That's where your interest in Roman architecture comes from.

rk: Definitely. But also because it makes me more interested in what's happening than in what it looks like. A Greek temple is just a Greek temple, if you know what I mean. But with the Roman architecture, you can see how the people needed relatively more utilitarian facilities—libraries and so forth—because their culture demanded it.

mdk: Maybe there's a parallel between Mies's fascination for that canvas building and yours for sheetrock architecture, that is architecture built of gypsum board. But the way it's used in your Dance Theater is not as straightforward as most American examples.

rk: Sheetrock is quintessentially pragmatic. We use it, it's true, to make an ideological statement, which is related to the overabundance of consciousness I was talking about, the nonchalance we have lost. We also use it because it is a "different" material. For the world likes nothing better than that you continue making the same thing over and over.

mdk: In his memoir, *A Scientific Autobiography*, Aldo Rossi writes, "I have always claimed that places are stronger than people, the fixed scene stronger than the transitory succession of events. This is the theoretical basis not of my architecture, but of architecture itself." You and he are somewhat similar in that, but it leads him to emphasize the difference between strong and weak elements in his structures.

rk: But he views the "events" as completely independent—"transitory." He's not at all concerned about them.

mdk: To what extent is that obsessive attention to programs not really an act?

rk: Look, what I find unique about metropolises—and here I feel that we are among the few trying to plumb this mystery—is that architecture enables activities more through its organization than through its physical appearance. It's precisely that total disconnect between program and form which is so interesting. That's what you have in La Villette too: it could easily also be a concentration camp, for instance. My goal is to provide a geological layering of activities. Naturally every operation carries its own plausibility, its own chances of success. Some efforts and proposals are sillier than others, and in general you can assume that the least silly are destined for the longest life.

mdk: To guarantee that long life, you have to be able to absorb the deterioration brought about by other processes. Mies's IIT campus is being overrun by nature and suffering as a result. Rossi, on the other hand, calculates in that vulnerability. Gallaratese can withstand much more, similar to how the amphitheater in Arles could accommodate houses. "I love contaminations," Rossi once wrote; in Gallaratese you could easily brick up a window, for example.

rk: I don't believe that for a second. Even if Rossi were trying to suggest a kind of "endless conjecture"—something we are neither claiming nor in all probability aspiring to—then I would tend to think it's only symbolic in Gallaratese. I think a change like that might be more disastrous in his case than by us. [...]

mdk: Maybe you are more reserved than Rossi when it comes to seeing architecture as a permanent gesture.

rk: I think I differ from a great many architects altogether because I believe less firmly in architecture, or rather, I have a more complex understanding of architecture—because I, as I have said repeatedly, find every empty place inherently better than any building whatsoever that could be conceived for it. I already have a sort of built-in bias.

mdk: Did you like Geert Bekaert's text on OMA?

rk: That was, of course, a fantastic article as a construction, as a reconstruction of a manner of thinking. The writing was incredibly witty: full of immeasurable irony, which may even have made the analogy to the process we follow in most of our designs: a bombardment of idealization and speculation.

mdk: The irony escaped me.

rk: Did you take it dead seriously? One thing I found particularly well done—something people seldom grasp: our almost sadistic need to provide embarrassingly simplistic answers to the most complicated questions, which somehow nevertheless do justice to the full complexity of the job—so challengingly simple that they elicit disbelief. I realize that that probably stems partly from hubris. A simplicity such that people can't accuse you of banality. That was beautifully captured.

[...]
mdk: In each project you attempt to contribute—and here's where the generalization comes in—another element to the culture of congestion, the Manhattanism, "ready to leave the mother island."

rk: At the same time I work on very calm, serene projects that won't produce congestion. The swimming pool is the complete opposite of that.

mdk: It's nothing but congestion! (*laughter*)

rk: Maybe that's another oxymoron: a ground zero of congestion (*laughter*). What I do also recognize as a shortcoming—or quality—of my mind is the strict logic it applies in argumentation, the narrative that rules out any other possible interpretations. Yet that's not entirely fair, because I am always extremely curious about other interpretations and accordingly disappointed at the shortage of them or the complete lack of any interpretation whatsoever. At the same time, I feel obliged to explain every project completely rationally, because despite everything, it has originated in part through a highly rational process. And that probably relates back to the challenging nature of that simplicity.

mdk: The programmatic content of your projects—as you yourself have noted—makes you surprisingly like Aldo van Eyck.

rk: There was a point at which I subjected Van Eyck and Hertzberger to a good deal of criticism. But after going through a transition, I discovered two things. To start with, I think anyone who puts up a building in times like these is by definition a hero. I commend even the cheapest commercial architect who manages it—conditions are truly hellish. And indeed Van Eyck, especially, has an enormous programmatic agenda and imagination and is closely aligned with what I aim for and admire—in theory, at least. So it's a combination of admiration and enthusiasm for these dimensions in his work and criticism of the content of the programs and, shall we say, the Worldview.

mdk: You said, "It's cruel to treat orphans and single mothers that way," (*laughter*) "to imbue form with an almost mythic value that must be a burden to sustain." Even if your criticism is justified, the orphans obviously aren't conscious of that worldview.

rk: Okay. But then I would say Van Eyck wields his instruments with such control that I'm convinced they *are* conscious of it. He does it with a force that cannot be ignored.

[...]

mdk: One might be justified in criticizing Van Eyck and Hertzberger for the excessive capacity they ascribe to form. You are more reserved in that respect.

rk: I believe that too. Or maybe I'm just less optimistic. (*laughs*)

mdk: Have there been any projects you don't like?

rk: Not yet. There are plenty of places I don't like, of course; with my disposition I'm heavily reliant on a density of attributes and possibilities.

mdk: Is that the reason the design for the police station is missing some of that OMA panache?

rk: Almere has several different cores. It's almost as if they present caricatures of the fashions of the times through the years—from 1960 through 1981. Theoretically, we are building a main headquarters with extensions in every core. To make it recognizable, each building will have a front face with the word "POLITIE" [police] on it in neon letters, which can be slid onto the building either straight or at an angle, depending on the location. I will concede that it has an abundance of clarity and simplicity, but it needs to be read in the context of late Expressionism brickwork in its most watered-down form. Plus, every project naturally has a certain connotation, and you never realize exactly the same interests or ambitions in every building—at least in my case. What mattered to us most here was establishing a level of professionalism such as that which existed in the 1950s and 1960s; it's an attempt to imagine what it felt like to be Skidmore.

mdk: Accoutrements such as those neon letters have a certain vulnerability, like the electric sign on Duiker's Cineac. Is that something you consider? What if those letters disappear?

rk: It would really bother me if it happened when it was new. After that, it wouldn't in fact interest me. I can even imagine it would be fine if a letter were to start flickering. Then if it went out, you might have "POLITIE" (*laughter*). That's part of the aesthetic.

mdk: That's the exact opposite of what you said about the skin of a skyscraper—its permanence.

rk: That is irrevocable: its size alone makes it a monument. It cannot have that same degree of vulnerability. I interpret your question as implying that there's a choice. But that is not usually the case. Why did Duiker need that thing? To make his building appear like more than what it was; because no one—we can assume—will be building another Notre Dame. So it's an adaptation of that; tearing down Notre Dame would cost a thousand times more than erecting Cineac. I don't think it's so horrible, anyway, if a sign like that disappears. The very beauty of the twentieth century is that instability.

mdk: So not just a "programmatic instability"?

rk: Also in terms of the permanence of materials. I don't see why you would want to fight it at all costs.

mdk: W. F. Hermans—with his geological view—talked about his hatred of squandering. That instability could be considered a form of that.

rk: You could also call it a form of economy. I build what I need and hang a label on it separately. You could easily see it both ways.

mdk: Then you are forcing reality to conform—however temporarily—to the perfection of OMA drawings.

rk: Because there is always some point at which we approach perfection. That moment works. I think it's dangerous to look at these things purely from a theoretical perspective, because the banal explanation also has a lot to do with things; the dance theater, for instance, has to be a ridiculously inexpensive building. And that invariably means it will require a lot of maintenance. Every building incorporates its own vulnerability. For one glittering instant it looks amazing. After that it becomes drab; takes on a dull look. [...]

mdk: Maybe it's also related to the fact that you don't see yourself as an architect.

rk: I never said that. I do see myself as an architect. I just don't have a complicated relationship with architecture. But it is totally different each time. Because of the budget for the Dance Theater, you just know the building won't be around in fifty years anymore. But of course I'm hoping for marble and solid gold sometime. I think the total concept absolutely depends on all of the ingredients and not an a priori mind-set. With Rossi, by contrast, you know that every civic center is going to be *the* civic center. It's an approach based on the notion of the archetypal civic center, the expectations associated with that.

mdk: But he does it in such a way that, paradoxically enough, he's a very contemporary architect.

rk: Absolutely. I'm not saying there're no surprises in his work. But he cannot escape the meaning attached to a civic center per se. There might be some dissonances or subversions of the thing itself, but he's still playing off of the archetype.

[...]

mdk: In your Blaak presentation you talked about the remediating effects that lectures can have. What has the response been?

rk: Nothing. Nothing has effect. That is exactly one of the puzzling phenomenona of Dutch architectural culture. Overwhelming and absolute silence. I have a richer, more nuanced relationship with my American, British, and French colleagues.

mdk: Is it really about communication? Does Eisenman understand what you're doing?

rk: I'm certain of it. But you happen to have mentioned someone who ...

mdk: "displays a pathological interest in others" (*laughter*) (a quote from Koolhaas's lecture). The issue of *L'Architecture d'Aujourd'hui* is the first major publication in some time. Why the hiatus?

rk: The texts for that issue were an attempt to once again get our intentions down in writing to provide a picture of what our current interests are and how they relate to the first wave of publicity, to the book: the American work versus the European phase. In the early to mid-1970s, there was this thrilling movement full of possibilities; architecture had been rediscovered. But at the moment I find it all a trampled circus of decadent robots who almost never have anything new to report. I had this instinctive feeling that it was better for us to withdraw, so as not to be drowned by it all. Besides, we are inundated with work!

LOW-INCOME HOUSING: A LESSON FROM AMSTERDAM
Mildred F. Schmertz
Architectural Record 1 (1985), 134–36.

[...] Responsible criticism of public housing's practical failures might have led to their eventual eradication, had the United States continued to build significant numbers of units for low-income people. Unfortunately, postmodernist stylistic criticism played directly into the hands of political conservatives who under President Reagan are at last succeeding in phasing out all housing subsidies. [...]

It is not the same in Holland. The Dutch Ministry of Housing is now completing 120,000 units of housing per year. [...] The total number of dwellings built in the Netherlands in 1981 was 8.2 (finished) per thousand inhabitants. By contrast, the United States in 1982 produced 4.5 per thousand. [...] Amsterdam, unlike New York City, does not have a conspicuous number of homeless people camping out on the streets. [...]

Today, Amsterdam has approximately 6,000 social housing units in construction or nearing completion. Most are new construction, the rest are being rehabilitated. Wishing to honor this accomplishment, Kees Tamboer, editor of the Amsterdam daily *Het Parool*, with the assistance of Jaap Engel, housing coordinator of the City of Amsterdam and chairman of STAWON, a foundation for architectural research in the fields of housing and the environment, organized the Amsterdam Housing Prize to be given periodically to honor outstanding architectural design and site planning in the low-income housing field. The jurors were the architectural historians Geert Bekaert from Antwerp and Francesco Dal Co from Venice, architect Ionel Schein from Paris, and myself. The jury chairman was the Dutch filmmaker Jan Vrijman.

The jury was allotted two days to visit twenty-nine preselected projects and one day to think them over before meeting to award the prize. The site visits revealed to us that the Amsterdam housing bureaus exercise many options. [...] In the infill classification the Nieuwmarkt project was outstanding. An old center-city neighborhood which had lost much of its housing in the Second World War and was to lose more by the construction of a subway underneath it, Nieuwmarkt had been slated for nonresidential redevelopment. [...] Architects Theo Bosch and Aldo van Eyck joined the struggle as community advocacy planners and helped persuade the city to keep Nieuwmarkt residential. The activists won, and Theo Bosch became the master planner of the neighborhood and the architect of some of its infill.

Juror Ionel Schein and I urged that the housing prize should go to Bosch for the sensitivity and elegance of his master plan and the architectural quality of his infill. Furthermore, it seemed to us that the housing officials of the City of Amsterdam who continue to insist that low-income people be housed in reconstituted older inner-city residential areas near their jobs deserved recognition. [...] Jurors Dal Co and Bekaert, however, wished to focus upon what the city was doing with its newer quarters, on change rather than continuity. Believing that the Amsterdam Housing Prize should not go to what they declared to be "outmoded urban forms," however skillfully reconstituted, and deeming estate planning rather than infill to be the more difficult and urgent design challenge, they argued in behalf of the mass housing project IJplein, a new town in town by the Office for Metropolitan Architecture, Rem Koolhaas's firm in Rotterdam. A goad to postmodern nostalgic pseudo-vernacularism, it reverts in style to the forms of the early Modern movement with Russian constructivist overtones (another form of nostalgia perhaps), and appears to function extremely well. Built on a former dock and shipyard site, it adjoins and has been carefully related to a turn-of-the-century Amsterdam district, is directly across the channel from Nieuwmarkt and shares the latter's proximity and convenience to jobs and services. Because the jury would not agree, its chairman, Jan Vrijman was required by the rules to cast the deciding vote. He sided with Dal Co and Bekaert, giving the prize to Koolhaas. Theo Bosch received the only honorable mention. [...]

INTELLECTUALS TALK ABOUT ARCHITECTURE

Doeschka Meijsing
Vrij Nederland,
December 14, 1985.

Returning from his daily six-kilometer run, Rem Koolhaas reports triumphantly that he's just run past the GEB site on Stadhouderskade. "It was beautiful, so empty in the dark." The municipality of Amsterdam chose his design for redeveloping the now empty property out of six submissions, or actually the design by his architecture collective OMA. For his part, Koolhaas was recently awarded the Rotterdam Maaskant Prize for his theoretical writings. [...] We're talking about the IJplein, the urban design masterplan for North Amsterdam, which Koolhaas likes to refer to as an "urban village." The plan has grown to fourteen hundred homes, on which OMA has had to work using "a cunning mix of power and powerlessness." Part of that process between client and architecture collective includes public input, which Koolhaas once said represents a form of terrorism.

dm: When you say that every architect must engage in strategy, does that mean your claim about public input was part of a stratagem?

rk: It was not a stratagem, but a way of sending a message. I said that at a point when there was a breakdown in how that input was being interpreted. One particular group had been unilaterally declared sacred in a process that included many different groups. There was a need for some pressure from another group, from our side. We are very explicit and direct and outspoken. With the IJplein, we had to make our arguments plain for amateurs. And that left us very vulnerable. When you formulate your arguments clearly, anyone can easily counter them.

dm: And what role does public opinion play?

rk: How are you supposed to know what that is?

dm: From the newspapers. When Gerrit Komrij writes that he thinks Van Gool's buildings along Weteringschans in Amsterdam are ugly. When Renate Rubinstein starts a discourse about the new ugliness.

rk: The only terms in which intellectuals think about architecture are still beautiful versus ugly. That is incredibly limited.

dm: How should intellectuals talk about architecture then?

rk: Every era gets the architecture it deserves. In the past, architecture operated on many fronts. The movements in the early part of the century, such as Constructivism, were composed of writers and poets. And architecture was a vital part of those movements. Nowadays everyone acts as if architecture stands completely on its own. It has absolutely no breadth of support. That disjunction is a true disaster. The things architects could be doing are not being supported, inspired or critiqued by an intelligentsia. Meanwhile, that intelligentsia is incapable of seeing architecture as an extension of what *it* would like. [...] What I'm interested in is the quarantining of the intellectuals. When you stop to consider that six radically different visions were submitted for the GEB building site, which occupies a fairly important location in the city of Amsterdam, a metropolitan city, and I haven't heard a single person who was able to even begin to interpret those visions. You would think that people would have something more to say about them than "beautiful" or "ugly." That lack of connection to an intellectual world is painfully evident in the Netherlands and undoubtedly the cause of a certain level of paltriness.

dm: But when writers like Gerrit Komrij and Renate Rubinstein open their mouths, they're accused by architects of not knowing what they're talking about.

rk: Of course. Architects are, as a rule, not prepared to play the game. It is a mutual loss. My complaint about the intelligentsia is that they—as they go on and on about beautiful or ugly—have absolutely no idea about the unbelievable conditions under which an architect must work. These are forces that have a much greater influence on the world than they realize. It should be the job of an architect to control the economic and political influences at work, but in many cases that is demonstrably not the case.

dm: You engage in polemics as an architect. Who are you polemicizing against?

rk: My main polemic is that whatever exists should be given amnesty; that's a fairly shocking premise for an architect to have to start from—the notion that you should take the existing situation as a source of inspiration. Take the curious situation in Paris as an example. Three gigantic building complexes have been built there, the most famous of which is probably "the hole of Les Halles." Staggering amounts of money and ideas have been poured into it. It's like an inverse Tower of Babel going down into the ground. But somehow that kind of event completely escapes the purview of the intelligentsia; architects and intellectuals don't take it seriously. That place is present, physically dominant, it is an expression of the late twentieth century in Paris, but because of their stylistic awkwardness, their ugliness, such places become invisible.

dm: What about Centre Beaubourg?

rk: That is exempt from what I'm talking about. That is architecture, and thus recognizable as such, and thus visible. But no one talks about Les Halles; no one writes about it. You don't go there, because you know it's atrocious. You might at most get stranded there while shopping. To me, these kinds of things are like Darwin's Galapagos Islands: if you were able to properly decipher and interpret them, you could unravel what's actually going on. You would obtain insight into how people live—or in how they would like to live. It could be enlightening. That is how Roland Barthes looked at social expressions, as instructive openings. Nothing like that has ever happened in the Netherlands. You have to have a capacity for temporarily switching off your judgment and using your intellect. Ask yourself the question: What does what has been placed here in terms of human expression, for example architecture, represent? How should I read it? All of these areas need words to become a reality. They have to be processed in texts, or in related plans, that delve into them or contradict them or reconcile with them.
[...]

NETHERLANDS DANCE THEATER, THE HAGUE (1982–1987): GOOD-BYE PAPER!

4

Between 1985 and 1989 the Netherlands Dance Theater (NDT) in The Hague featured on the cover of a roll call of magazines: *L'Architecture d'Aujourd'hui, Architecture Moniteur Continuité, Techniques & Architecture, De Architect, Archis, Quaderns, Architectural Record, Bauwelt*, and *A+U*. The reason for this attention was paradoxical: it was the debut of an architect who had become famous because of his struggle to be taken seriously. The desire to build, together with the fear of being shelved as a paper architect, had been haunting Koolhaas since the beginning of the decade. In the introduction to an exhibition in Amsterdam in 1980, he wrote: "In the absence of specific commissions this work belongs to the recently invented category of 'paper architecture'. [...] The past four years (alarmed by the abundance of 'theoretical' projects—an almost overflowing reservoir of unproven claims and pretensions) OMA has taken to concrete projects in which previous assumptions can be tested. Goodbye paper!"[1]

The three-dimensional start of OMA was heavily anticipated and continuously deferred—sometimes of the architects' own volition, sometimes not. OMA had built prior to the NDT: a police station was completed in Almere during the last six months of 1985, while a cheerful and tropically tinged bus stop was constructed in front of Rotterdam Central Station in the spring of 1987. Both realizations weren't successful or big enough to count as an official debut, while it took a long time to finalize the NDT. Koolhaas's contact with its financial director Carel Birnie dates from early 1980, and the development and the construction of the building were a struggle. The site changed from Scheveningen, the seaside resort of The Hague, to the city center, while Jan Voorberg, the project architect, dramatically died shortly before construction could begin. The budget was too small, but Birnie nevertheless kept raising expectations and requirements. At the final site, OMA needed to cooperate with the Dutch architects who were building an adjacent concert hall, with which the NDT would share its main entrance. Nevertheless, Koolhaas used this tormented genesis to his advantage, as it allowed him to tell exciting stories about the architectural profession, for example in the presentation of the project in 1995 in *S,M,L,XL*.

After its opening in September 1987 the NDT was one of the architectural events of the year. Numerous critical strategies were handled to either dismiss the building (as inferiorly materialized, unnecessarily striking, badly detailed, frivolous, or too American for a European inner city) or to praise it (as an exquisitely composed chameleon blending in with the environment, as an exhilarating performance in itself, or as the great building Venturi and Scott Brown wanted but couldn't build). Hubert Damisch compared the NDT to the work of French *constructeur* Jean Prouvé—a grandiose compliment that can also be read philosophically, in the sense that Koolhaas showcased architecture (against the advent of Deconstructivism) as a "construction," as a set of building materials heaped together in order to form a meaningful whole. Also in the more technical sense, the NDT was architectonic, and marked indeed the debut of Koolhaas as a building architect. As Alejandro Zaero-Polo has suggested in

2009: "In implementing the project, [Koolhaas] discovers there are efficiencies that go beyond language and concept, because they are physical. [...] There is a certain tendency to structural oddity that characterizes Rem's work, which I am sure he discovers during the construction of the Dance Theater."[2] This view is endorsed in a short text from 1992 by Stefan Polónyi, the structural engineer of the NDT, and the first important OMA collaborator in this field.

When Koolhaas presented the first project at the University of Virginia at the end of 1982, Robert A. M. Stern reacted as follows (in a conversation collected in *The Charlottesville Tapes* from 1985): "This is a joyous but very nostalgic kind of architecture. My problem with it, especially when I think of Rem and of our few encounters, is that his nostalgia is supposed to be OK, but everyone else's isn't." Apparently, in the 1980s, it had become impossible to avoid nostalgia—or the reproach of being nostalgic—to some period or another. Koolhaas turned Stern's critical remark around: OMA's work—and the NDT in particular—presented a form of professional critique, of showing colleagues how outdated, nostalgic, and illusionary their assumptions about architecture—about its nobility, its seriousness, its financial and social value—still were. With the NDT, Koolhaas did try to popularize modern architecture—in terms of formal language, conceptual genesis, and construction methods—but in a peculiar way that couldn't be interpreted as populist, since it required quite a lot of sophistication and attention to be read and understood. The Dance Theater was an iconoclastic building, made up out of images; a singular object that was almost impossible to distinguish from its environment; a piece of architecture that criticized the discipline but could not have been conceived without its conditions, traditions, and limitations; a low-cost material and technical construction that in a hyperconscious way needed to underline its cultural position; and a final exam for an architect who would remain skeptical of the profession but would also lift it to unprecedented and sometimes unsound fame.

In 2016, as a consequence of the never-ending saga of politicking around the development of the area in which it was built, the NDT was demolished. However, the disappearance of the "real debut" of OMA barely provoked public comment, possibly indicating the decreasing cultural value assigned to architecture in the Netherlands, or to Koolhaas's strained relationship with his homeland.

1 Rem Koolhaas, "Projecten uit de jaren zeventig, 7 nov. 1980 t/m 4 jan, 1981 zaal 24–25," in *Stedelijk Museum: Inhoudsopgave 1980* (Amsterdam: Stedelijk Museum, 1980), 99–100. For a full genesis of the project, see Christophe Van Gerrewey, "Good-bye Paper," *AA Files* 74 (2017), 98–111.

2 Francisco González de Canales and Nuria Alvarez Lombardero, "In Conversation with Alejandro Zaera-Polo," in *First Works: Emerging Architectural Experimentation of the 1960s and 1970s*, ed. Brett Steele and Francisco González de Canales (London: Architectural Association, 2009), 193.

A BLIND SPOT FOR SPACE
Rem Koolhaas, Rob Krier, César Pelli, Rafael Moneo, Robert Stern, Jacquelin Robertson
The Charlottesville Tapes, ed. Jacquelin Robertson (New York: Rizzoli, 1985), 178–87.

rk: [...] I'll explain the building very quickly. It consists of a stage, a backstage, and an auditorium that is used only by the company. Adjoining the auditorium is a zone containing three major studios. With these elements we had used up our cubic meters, so everything else had to be some kind of bluff. What we tried to do in the residual spaces around this inert block was to create the public life of the building, with the entrance for the company on one side and a major public space for the members. The only way of dealing with the surrounding context in this disastrous landscape was to make an enclave and resist any other connections, so basically what we did was create a wall space that makes a triangular patio at the front, which also didn't cost us anything in cubic meters. [...] The roof could be designed without expending cubic meters; on it there is a physical therapy facility, a sauna and swimming pool, a canteen, and an office slab. Between all the elements and superimposed over them is a major architectonic element, a large rectangular canopy. This produces a contrast with the existing building, and in this way articulates the strange fact of their being forced to live together. We considered it a series of walls. Thank you.

r. krier: This is exactly what I criticize in your designs. This is antispace, not formulated space.

rk: I have admitted in earlier conversations with you that I have a blind spot for space. That is a problem I am struggling with, but I think that I have so far come a long way for somebody who is so handicapped. (*laughter*)

cp: Two things strike me most strongly about your work. One is a very strong nostalgia for a world that was or that we hoped would be and isn't indeed the 1920s. The second is the constant reference to Miami Beach, palm trees, McDonald's arches, kidney-shaped swimming pools. I know that you have put all these references there deliberately, but I do not know what the point is.

rk: One thing that consoles us about this project is that it is for a resort, and resort architecture is very frivolous; at least it has to work with and compete with other elements of frivolity. But in this project we have purified these elements, or, in any case, analyzed them so that they become emblems of such enterprises without in fact being them.

rm: Much of Rem's project expresses an overall feeling that modern architecture is also popular architecture; it has this aspect of populism in that it gives us a fresh view of some very attractive possibilities in architecture. This attitude toward modern architecture as a kind of vernacular populism could be considered to be a joke. We could speak about it with a certain sense of humor. In the end I am intrigued to see how this architecture will work when it gets built. We need such proof to understand how strongly this hypothesis opposes current trends. It might be a valuable alternative for the present time. I also very much like the hand and brain behind these drawings. Overall, the importance of what Rem has done is in his investigation of the relationship between modern architecture and populism. It's not a matter of looking like Russian architecture or Constructivism or anything like that; it is something completely different.

rs: Rafael said many things I wanted to say. This is a joyous but very nostalgic kind of architecture. My problem with it, especially when I think of Rem and of our few encounters, is that his nostalgia is supposed to be okay, but everyone else's isn't. I enjoy the drawings, the tremendous jump in scale. Of course, I have been to some places like this—say, the United Nations in New York—and I don't enjoy them so much when I am there. The absence of architectural detail at any other level than what is shown here, the reliance on the diminished piece of furniture to make the place, is not very joyous when really built. This tends to be a problem of drawn architecture: the actual building is not nearly so captivating.

jr: Rem, do you consider *nostalgia* a pejorative word?

rk: Yes.

jr: Why?

rk: Not the word, obviously, but the attitude. Nostalgia has been hanging heavy in this room for two days, and this has been a very heavy, almost indigestible burden for me. What I find most nostalgic about this gathering is not its nostalgia for any particular style or any particular period, but nostalgia for an order, for a specific role for architecture, for the role of the architect as some kind of gentleman who appears and unfolds a drawing. I find that kind of nostalgia very unhealthy because it forces us to take part in these gloomy gatherings where nothing is right, everything is a mess, and we have to make beautifully noble statements. What I tried to do in this project is to show some of that. I could have said, "This place is an idiotic mess and Bakema was a fool," but in fact the site was inspiring and extremely enjoyable in a sort of perverse way; it stimulated the project.

jr: You misinterpreted my question. *Nostalgia* in its dictionary meaning is the longing for a better time or the memories of a better time, and there doesn't seem to be anything pejorative about longing for a better time.

rk: If you define it that way, I would say that this project really has no longing for a better time or the memory of a better time. It is extremely and precisely ecstatic about this time, this year, this place, this moment, and nothing else.

EXQUISITE CORPSE

Hubert Damisch
Architecture Mouvement Continuité 18 (1987), 21–22.

Rem Koolhaas plays the role of the exquisite corpse among the architects who today hold center stage on the international scene. It is surprising to realize that he was over forty years old when commissioned to build his first important building. Besides, at least at first glimpse, the program does not seem to go well with the theories of an architect whom we were all too happy to restrict to "paper" architecture. What is the relationship between the conception and the construction of the Dance Theater in Holland's capital, which has nothing of a great modern metropolis, and Koolhaas's legendary critical activity which, ten years ago, led him to publish *Delirious New York*, a masterpiece in the form of a manifesto of another modernity? How does this first achievement justify the numerous interventions and proposals presented under the acronym of the Office for Metropolitan Architecture: all expressions of a playful, satirical connotation which was not recognized for what it was (a reaction to the "project's" prevailing ideology), but which, in one way or another, in keeping with the ambitious *and* popular architectural form (I would prefer to say "public, in the sense that an opinion can be public") including "Manhattanism," as defined by Koolhaas, proposed the example as well as the formula?

We have to be careful to avoid two critical, and in fact, symmetrical temptations. One being that the project itself had nothing in common with what had previously been the main concerns expressed by OMA, the end of which bears witness to the distance that can separate dream (or fantasy, or utopia) from reality: but this is precisely the kind of opposition that Manhattanism disowns, or *defeats* (I did not say that it "deconstructs"). The other being the search for the themes and motives, even obsessions, which are dear to Koolhaas, in architecture. An architect, as one likes to say, has the right to the unconscious; however, a critic cannot play the role of psychoanalyst, unless in parody. (We would like it to be the same for architects when they start philosophizing; fortunately, Koolhaas stays away from that). More interesting to me is the critical opening imposed by this realization, or—to put it in other words—this successful transformation.

In reality, how can a building mark an instant, in this case a theater, and what's more, a theater of dance: an art whose artifice consists of making us forget that there are women (or men, or both), who dance (to paraphrase

Mallarmé)? The architect can only take note that modernity is revealed in choreographic art as elsewhere, by focusing on expression and the strength of materials.

One of the lessons of Manhattanism is that physical presence can increase in proportion to the artifice and vice versa, as seen in the Downtown Athletic Club in New York itself. It was built to be a machine to satisfy, multiply, and intensify all corporal demands. A theatrical edifice must meet requirements for performance and representation, but the architecture cannot be reduced to that of being merely a stage, or even an auditorium and its surroundings. With its gym-like studios, sauna, showers, and massage rooms, as well as its workshops and offices, the Hague theater looks like a machine that is perfectly suited to its function, of course including that of bodies that move on a stage. Not to mention the swimming pool installed at the top center of the building, like a centerpiece as well as a reference to the Athletic Club, or the house designed by Adolf Loos for another dancer, Josephine Baker, whose blackness allowed the novelty of the invasion of wilderness into the heart of the metropolis: as if the machine had a motor, or rather a battery or a generator whose energy would produce rhythmic movements of swimmers (as told in the Story of the Pool in *Delirious New York*).

At first, the Dance Theater was supposed to have been built in Scheveningen, The Hague's seaside resort, close to a casino and attached to a circus from which it might have borrowed, perhaps too well, a more vernacular, if not suburban accent. However, as it was built, the edifice in a very different location, stuck on a poorly defined median in the central part of The Hague where rows of ministries line the streets, between two boxes, one a hotel and the other a concert hall which a mere quick coat of pinkish paint can strip off its identity. The treatment of the whole as a cheap version of the Lincoln Center was avoided by Koolhaas's trick to retain the original lateral layout while pushing one of the most disparaging features of modernity to the extreme, to the point of denying the theater any facade or even its own entrance. The audience had to enter, at least in appearance, through the adjoining concert hall, without being able to decide which of the two buildings interferes with the other. There is no way to guess from the outside that the building contains anything but offices and workshops, except for the corrugated roof over the hall that looms in the background, and the cube decorated with a fresco by Madelon Vriesendorp, which corresponds to the performance area, massively dominating a building that, unlike any other, seems to show us the backside of the edifice. It looks as if the architect had rotated it 90 degrees, with the front of the building being dismantled and sealed by the neighboring building, which thereafter would be held responsible for this incongruity. Collision or forced collusion? Whatever it is, we are dealing with a type of collage, or as Koolhaas calls it, an "exquisite corpse."

If this is a collage, however, it was in no way produced with a concern for aesthetics: it was made in order to use financial and volumetric allowances in the most economical way possible. The architect chose to emphasize the theatrical machinery, including the stage, while subjecting the audience to a form of gymnastics that is not just cultural or social. As we have seen, there is no facade or monumental entrance as there should be for a Temple of Terpsichore. There is no staircase either, or luxurious salons: only a long hall that seems to separate the dance theater from the neighboring concert hall whose wall (as I mentioned before, is of a poor pink color) is left visible. The hall is crossed by acrobatic walkways which lead to a floating balcony and bar, suspended by cables, one in the shape of a sickle and the other in the shape of a bean, while the most improbable of foyers opens, or rather slightly opens, like a seashell or a primitive shelter, under the room's sloping roof, held up by diminishing columns that only after having seen them, we realize that they correspond to the underground car park over which the entire theater is built. A corridor which looks like a copy of one of Lissitzky's Prouns on exhibit in The Hague Museum, loops around to lead to the theater and down a rather sharp slope to access the parallel rows of armchairs. Although the corridor is painted white and brightly lit, the hall itself is maintained in a semidarkness increased by the black flooring and royal blue seats. The striations of the corrugated roof amplify the free-floating effect generated by the contrast between the perpendicular sides of the cube-shaped stage and the room's soft curves: as if it were important to do away with lights and purple tones that until now were reserved for an elite group that was busy talking and as interested in themselves as they were in the show, in order to provide anonymity to an unspecified public, like a movie theater, while gold is used on the stage curtain and acoustic panels.

The art of dance usually strives to make dancing appear effortless for dancers, without ever disdaining physical prowess. Among the surprises that this theater offers, and in confirmation of that which up until then remained one of Koolhaas's proposals, demonstrates that we are dealing with a builder who does not hesitate to show some of the building's construction in an area reserved for the workshops near the swimming pool. The building's coating was cut open to present under glass a few centimeters of one of the cables that ensure the rigidity of the metallic structure. When I visited the construction site in The Hague in the spring of 1987, before the drywall panels were installed, I immediately thought of Jean Prouvé. Is Rem Koolhaas's architecture nostalgic, as false naives will repeat, while others accuse him of not having any notion of space or detail? Then yes, if nostalgic means recalling that there is no space (and, in the end, no architecture) unless it is constructed, while detail is not worth anything unless it gives access to the work of the unconscious to which the architect claims to be entitled. One of the distinctive traits in Koolhaas's architecture is, precisely, displacement, meaning that detail is found where it is not expected, and always in an unpredictable form. His first construction is proof—but more than just technical proof (Le Corbusier: "Modern architecture is possible, New York proves it")—that today's architecture cannot be really interesting unless it works obstinately against—but for how much longer?—the repression of "construction," by all definitions of the term: to construct a theater is to set up a machine that will lend itself to all manners of construction, even that of an audience, adding a new meaning to this word which the epithet "popular" would not suffice to qualify. In conclusion, a detail among others: Paul Valéry once said, "In the universe of dance, rest has no place"; I am pleased that the only place where we can see the entire theater in The Hague is from a restaurant in the shape of a control tower, itself gilded and located above the entrance, where dancers and spectators will gather after the show.

A SUPREMELY UTILITARIAN BUILDING

Janny Rodermond

De Architect 10 (1987), 73–78.

[...] In his design for the Dance Theater, Koolhaas has been accused of betraying his outspoken assertions about contextual analyses. Nothing could be further from the truth. When he was finally allowed to begin on his second design—the first had been situated near the Circus theater—the site and designs for the adjoining concert hall and the Pullman Hotel were already set. It would have been pointless to plunk down yet another box amidst all those boxy volumes. It is actually through the free combination of all its separate parts that the Dance Theater sets itself off from the massive surrounding buildings.

The conical restaurant facing the Spui is ingenious. Its shape not only resolves the clash between the two theaters, but also makes the structure the centerpiece of the entire square. When viewed from the Prins Bernhard viaduct, it is also evident how the cone's shape nicely accommodates the angled line of the concert hall encasement. Koolhaas also plays adeptly to his surroundings in his choice of materials—dictated in part by the tight budget. The rear wall of basic, muted corrugated siding turns the building with its undulating roof into an abstract sculpture. The contrast between that and the reflective wall of the concert hall accords each of the two building their own value. Moreover, Koolhaas's use of a diversity of materials—stucco, unglazed and glazed brick and gold aluminium—also emphasizes the building's fragmented structure. The wall of the stage tower has a mural by Madelon Vriesendorp inspired by the activities that go on inside. The figuration in it is almost abstract, the choice of colors restrained; it is an excellent alternative to the treatment with stone originally conceived.

"Context can be everything," Koolhaas likes to say. And even the history of a design can play a role in this. The undulating roof was adopted from the original Scheveningen design. Critics have claimed that this runs counter to Koolhaas's own principles—to the extent he has any. But would the Dance Theater have been any better or cheaper with a flat roof supported by trusses? Absolutely not. It is true that the auditorium was widened from 24 to almost 34 meters compared to the first design, which means that the roof is no longer entirely self-supporting; but that single subtended beam used to solve the problem is barely noticeable.

The main purpose of the Dance Theater is to house a ballet company. The strip running parallel to the public square houses the work spaces, with dressing rooms on the ground floor, a cafeteria and a recreational space above that, costume storage, work studios and the like on the third floor, and offices on the top floor. These various functions are all evident from the facade. Sandwiched between this box and the auditorium/stage tower/backstage suite are three spacious studios equipped with heated floors and transparent ceilings.

Barely any space has been sacrificed to hallways in the building and several of the built spaces are multifunctional. The studios can be used as additional foyer space, a tuning and warm-up area for the orchestra or storage for set pieces during a production—in any conceivable variation. The large backstage area is an additional rehearsal space, as well as a recording studio, and can also be used for presenting small productions if desired. This final adaptation was kept in play at the municipality's insistence for the eventuality that the Margetheater designed by Hertzberger doesn't get built.

According to Koolhaas, the work spaces have an atmosphere of "serene abstraction," whereas in the public spaces, circles, curves and slopes have been used in both the ground plan and the cross section. These elements are then used only very sparingly in the auditorium, the undulating roof and slightly curved rear wall being the only embodiments. The nearly square shape of the auditorium provides for amazing sightlines and excellent engagement with the stage. Moreover, one is not distracted by color. The auditorium is black and has six gold-colored screens hanging on the side walls for the acoustics. The gray velvet stage curtain is also dotted with gold balls. A deep blue has been used for the chairs designed by BOA Contractors, who also styled the restaurant entry and bars in the foyer. The effect created there is of a light, festive space that makes you completely forget that this was originally a high, narrow residual space between two auditoriums. The volume of the ground floor has been expanded by enlisting the sloped area under the auditorium. Recesses on the second floor provide vantage points from which to oversee everything, as do the glass walls for looking outside. At night the glass surfaces become mirrors in which to watch all the activities going on inside on the different levels. The "balancing" sky bar on the third story, accessible via a small, somewhat wedged-in, wooden staircase, is spectacular.

A panoply of colors and materials has been deployed in the foyer. Juxtaposed against the light pink wall of the concert hall auditorium, Koolhaas has used a warm, provocative red for the auditorium wall of the theater. The columns supporting the auditorium are painted in four primary colors and the shortest is covered in gold leaf. The ground floor is tiled, the second floor has light parquet flooring and the sky bar has a metal floor stretched with canvas on the bottom, which magnifies the sense of floating in air. The various bars also seem to float thanks to the way they are lit from underneath. The smooth, simply constructed bars are also made of a variety of materials: plastic in the restaurant; brass, zinc and wood in the foyer.

During the initial performances, this wonderful whole seemed to function organically. It is astonishing to think that such an intimate, informal theater possesses the stage dimensions and facilities needed to compete on the international market for music and drama productions. Because of its spacious stage, it can literally hold its own against the Amsterdam Concert Hall or even the Metropolitan Opera House in New York.

[...] Client and architect accepted that given the many—functional—demands and lack of money, the resulting building would be utilitarian: a steel skeleton clad with various materials. Without the perseverance shown by managing director Carel Birnie, there never would have been a Dance Theater; nor would it have existed without the stubbornness and ingenuity of Koolhaas as architect. Birnie has been quoted as saying the building fits like a "perfect skin." That could refer to its organizational layout. But it goes beyond that: the building also has the perfect atmosphere and image for a unique company such as this theater. It is moreover the first dance theater in the world and the first creation by Koolhaas to be built, a building that would be a challenge for any architect because of its departure from so many of the established principles for typology, consistency, composition, construction and material use. It is not a theater in the traditional sense, but more of a workspace, functional even in its ambiance. It is structurally intriguing as well; we have not seen a roof like this since Gaudí covered his school in the shadow of the Sagrada Familla with one. Its strategic use of, for instance, corrugated sheeting and gold leaf are evidence of a controlled capacity for improvisation. The foyer is a spatial experiment with an impenetrable section and a balancing platform. Despite all this spectacle and its fragmented structure, this building is to some extent more consistent than the adjacent concert hall, which crunched such a multiplicity of functions behind its uniform shell. This building is honest in its volume construction, layout, construction and even decoration—consistent in terms of the straightforward manner in which design solutions have been conceived and applied. And yet it functions as a theater in every way, despite its lack of similarity to any existing theaters. [...]

KOOLHAAS CONTAINER

Peter Buchanan
Architectural Review 1099 (1988), 32–39.

[...] Frustrating as the tortuous route to realizing his first major public building has been for Koolhaas, it is probably also fortunate. All the reconsideration of the place and program has resulted in his most convincing design to date, in which his particular approach seems precisely apt to program and circumstance.

Those who are disappointed or dismiss the building for its lack of, or tacky, detail rather miss the point. It is misleading to judge the building in conventional architectural terms. Instead it should be seen for what it is, a decorated shed, if not quite an archetypal one, cheaply made from steel and plasterboard. And, if quite unsuited to say opera, such a fusion of shed and scenography seems, in concept as well as in its feeling of flimsy ephemerality, extremely well suited to modern dance, that quintessential celebration of the tempos and life of the modern city—particularly the fast-paced flash of the American city. Even Koolhaas's penchant for the forms, finishes and iconography of the 1950s is for once peculiarly apt; even more than the other popular arts, modern dance seems to have generated the potent nostalgia for that period, which it still exploits.

The Dance Theater is in a singularly unattractive part of The Hague. [...] In such a strange situation it has little chance to assert an architectural urban presence and indeed any hint of *gravitas* or *civitas* would be quite misplaced. Instead it advertises its presence with the mural of dancers on the fly tower (by Madelon Vriesendorp, Koolhaas's wife, a painter), the wavy edge of the auditorium roof and the giant gold ice-cream cone that accommodates the box office and cafeteria. Other than these devices the facade is quietly recessive, mainly monochrome corrugated steel and glass.

The interior is not conventionally architectural either. Rather than being spatially articulated, accommodation is, as is characteristic of Koolhaas, simply (rationally) zoned into strips. These are subdivided into the requisite areas with the seeming insouciance of chopping a sausage. Where necessary, as in the auditorium, the resulting volume is fitted out with an economic minimalism that mixes precision and looseness—in much the same way as a hall may be temporarily fitted out to great functional and illusory effect for fringe theatricals. Devoid of *poché* or any sense of architectural mass, the scenographic rather than architectural quality of this arrangement is confirmed by its dependence on artificial light for much of its drama and spatial mystery.

The dancers' common rooms are in the strip against the square, so putting the dancers' daily life on display through the slightly tilted floor-to-ceiling glazing. Below in the blank base are their changing rooms and above in the top two floors are administrative offices. In a median strip are the dance studios interrupted by a broad corridor connecting stage with shower and changing rooms, with over this route a small swimming pool and sauna. In the rear and much the widest of the strips is the auditorium and stage with its fly tower and back stage. Separating these lateral strips from the concert hall is the perpendicular strip of the foyer which, when it is next to the rear auditorium strip, reaches right to the roof and bulges sideways under the sloping floor of the auditorium.

Again the foyer is an unconventional space. The archetypal theater or opera foyer extends the street with its colonnades and street lamps inside and upwards, making progression from outside to in into a parade of people displaying themselves and watching each other. Here there is no such articulated progression. The box office squeezes entry slightly at the doors and then the foyer is just a gap between two buildings—one wall clearly belongs to the concert hall and the gallery barely touches it, while the skybar floats quite clear. Typologically the foyer is a mere alley (*West Side Story* rather than *Don Giovanni*), a slash of space that whizzes out through the glazed back wall. And when at last columns are encountered under the auditorium, they are each a different color. This denies their supportive function both by dematerializing them and by making each unique rather than a standard element in a repetitive grid.

Nevertheless, however lowly the typological model and insubstantial the columns may seem, the foyer achieves an exhilarating drama, and with remarkably few devices. There is space that soars upwards as well as rushing onward and sloshing deep under the auditorium until at last a lack of headroom restrains its bulging parabolic edge. Set against this bulge is the dynamic boomerang of the bar which counterpoints the slashing arc of the gallery edge which in turn contrasts with the more static blob of the floating skybar. This teeters structurally as well as visually, on a single beam, restrained only by a prop from the waving roof and a tie. Then, adding to these formal gymnastics, there is the singing (and singeing too) scarlet of the long wall, and last but not least the simple but dramatic use of artificial light. Particularly effective are the bright down-lit pools on the pale terrazzo floor on which the columns stand to decorous attention to accompany the thronging audience.

Unfortunately, besides the drama, but not necessarily because of it, there are some disorienting functional ambiguities about the foyer and its relationship to the auditorium. It is not at all clear how you are meant to enter the auditorium. Rather than guiding people to the ground level auditorium doors, the foyer bellies out between them, playing down their presence and keeping extended the distance from door to stage and the bottom of the ramping side aisles. And the stair to the gallery is prominently positioned, restricting access to the far entrance doors. All these suggest that the main route to the auditorium is up this stair via the gallery and down the aisles from the back of the auditorium. Yet main bar and lavatories are on ground level and the lower route is probably the more dramatic entry and so the one Koolhaas chose when showing me around.

Like the foyer, the auditorium achieves considerable drama with a bare minimalism of form and detail (and here of color too) and stark theatrical lighting. With its charcoal painted walls and ceiling and black studded rubber floor it is almost literally a black box—though not of the sort once advocated for experimental performance. The stage is behind a proscenium cut into the end wall, and while the seats are on a sloping base that seems merely inserted into the volume, independent from it and not touching the side walls, they, like the proscenium, are permanently fixed. Again there is none of the usual architectural articulation, nor any mediation between auditorium and stage, with the audience put on display in balconies and boxes that also sweep the eye forward and so integrate performer and audience in a singular event. Instead each member of the audience confronts the huge stage as if watching a cinemascope screen, a more private experience than normally associated with dance. Not having attended a performance I cannot comment on how well this works, nor whether the dance is dwarfed by the vast stage, and its huge 65ft proscenium.

Others, though, testify to the success of the theater visually and acoustically. With the lights up, the auditorium gains some color from the curves of blue velvet seating, the gold-rubbed curved plywood acoustic reflectors that project free from the side walls and the flashy gold stage curtain. These are all spotlit to surprisingly striking effect as are the wavy curves of the ceiling. This ceiling is simply the underside of the roof. Two layers of corrugated steel with insulation sandwiched between are warped over an exposed truss to rise and fall as waves out of phase with each other along either side. Cheap and very efficient structurally, the form is similar to that Gaudí used for the roof of the workshop adjacent to the Sagrada Familia. This roof highlights a crucial aspect of the building and how, despite its cheap insubstantiality, it is not an archetypal decorated shed because its outer volume is directly related to the spaces within and even expressive of their function.

Flimsy as a tin can, with its outer volume just as directly related to its inner one, and advertising its presence much as a can from a supermarket shelf does, the Dance Theater lacks many attributes conventionally associated with architecture. There is no architectural mass articulated in form and detail and so it has no corporeality or even anthropomorphism to relate to. Nor is there spatial progression with articulated meditation and hierarchies. This building is a mere container, no matter how dramatic the effects achieved by sparingly deployed scenographic elements dramatically lit. Yet all of this is what is so provocative and topical about the Dance Theater. Also, most theaters emphasize the performance areas and the performers are only seen on stage. Lacking such decorum, this building is more pop and democratic, and puts the everyday life of the dancer on show with the performance as just a periodic culmination of a life of training and rehersals.

Perhaps the Dance Theater at last vindicates Koolhaas's design ideas and his claim to all the attention he has received over the years. But it could equally be a fluke conjunction of a very particular problem and site to which his approach was well suited. Koolhaas's challenge is to meet other problems with an equally suited strategy—something he has failed to do for the housing and school in IJplein in Amsterdam. Often he will find a scenographic shed will not suffice—and something more wholly architectural is required.

FIRST POSITION
Deborah K. Dietsch
Architectural Record 4 (1988), 72.

[...] "I'm not just interested in the harmless, early phase of Modernism, but in its aggressive side during the 1950s and 1960s, when it became an acceptable, almost vernacular style," Koolhaas explains. Like Robert Venturi, whose book *Learning from Las Vegas* he admires, the Dutch architect is fascinated by popular architecture, particularly the vulgarity of commercial buildings. This interest is reflected in the improvisational quality of OMA's disjointed compositions and by the 1950s-inspired, curvaceous forms that often strike a humorous note in the firm's projects. Koolhaas's admiration for both high and low Modernism is exemplified in OMA's "La Casa Palestra," an interpretative reconstruction of Mies van der Rohe's Barcelona Pavilion as a body builder's home, displayed at the 1986 Milan Triennale. Having bent the prototype's overlapping glass and marble planes into a curved, wedge-shaped interior, the architects promoted the visceral aspects of the Modern icon, equipping it with exercise machines, a piped-in soundtrack, laser projections, and a video "history" of the Pavilion after the 1929 exhibition. OMA's faith in Modernism also extends to the urban scale, as evidenced by numerous competition entries and urban redevelopment schemes. The firm contends that the current practice of small-scale contextualism is not a realistic solution for our cities, maintaining that architects must come to terms with the "tower in the park" and other features of postwar planning in order to effectively influence future urban growth. OMA's proposal for Bijlmermeer, a 1960s housing development in Amsterdam, attempts to do just that, with new infill to increase the density and pedestrian scale of the monolithic blocks. [...]

In arguing a convincing case for Modernism, OMA has exerted an important influence on a younger generation of architects searching for models of bold contemporaneity. Two OMA alumnae, Zaha Hadid and Arquitectonica principal Laurinda Spear, have elaborated the scenographic vocabulary of their former teachers into a richer, more colorful language—going so far as to eclipse, some would say, OMA's pivotal role in the current reevaluation of Modernism. With the recent opening of the Dance Theater, however, OMA's polemical stance has finally been put to the test of real construction, and the long-awaited translation of its visions into built form validates years of academic experimentation.

Unlike those they have inspired, OMA's members assert that their resuscitation of modern ideals boldly addresses the contemporary city as it exists. "The architects of fragmentary Modernism pretend that there can never be an integration with things as they are," argues Koolhaas, metaphorically distinguishing his younger followers from OMA: "They are like observers looking at the fire from the outside. We're in an asbestos suit headed straight into the flames."

A CHAMELEON THEATER

Jacques Lucan

Beaux Arts Magazine 60 (1988), 70–75.

Rem Koolhaas is a visionary architect. This does not mean that the buildings he designs are utopian projects never to be built, designed for cities that will never exist. He is visionary because he does not delude himself, because he does not attempt to conceal the chaos that surrounds us from himself: he brings a questioning gaze to bear on today's urban realities, and, through his projects, he helps us discover them, shows them to us and gives them a presence that transcends their ordinariness.

In a way, Koolhaas is reviving the approach made by Le Corbusier in the early 1920s, when he was intent on shaking his contemporaries, waking them up and opening their eyes to the modernity of the time, choosing the title "Eyes which do not see" for three chapters in his most famous book, *Vers une architecture*.

With the Dance Theater in The Hague, Koolhaas has designed his first important building after spending ten years on dazzling designs the images of which will never fade. [...]

The Dance Theater makes the positions taken by Koolhaas a reality in explicit fashion. He sets out from the perspective of taking into account a confused environment, a site under renovation comprising heterogeneous buildings that accumulated while the design of the city was coming apart. The theater is at the foot of the tall towers of the Dutch Ministry of Justice and is just one element of an urban plan of which Koolhaas was not in charge.

Rather than trying to stick the disparate parts back together, to reorder and homogenize an incongruous whole, rather than hoping for an impossible unity, Koolhaas chose not to be ostentatious, not to evade a reality that needs to be criticized. The Dance Theater attempts to reveal new equilibriums between parts that were unaware of each other until now. The theater is not a unitary building that puts itself forward in an absolute and independent singularity; on the contrary, it is almost chameleon-like if we think of it in its different views from its different faces that respond in their own way, point by point, to the many details of the built environment.

In the final analysis, the building becomes paradoxical because it does not have the organizing presence of a traditional building, and someone who was unaware of the history of the theater's construction would struggle to tell where the intervention of its architect stopped: could they guess that the pink chequered cube of the concert hall and its large hall enclosed by dark windows, directly adjoining the Dance Theater, were not built to Koolhaas's plans but to those of another architect? The Dance Theater is the result of the desire often uttered by Koolhaas to use every detail of the context, no matter what, with intensity, refusing to sort them in moralizing fashion. This is what he calls finding a "retroactive" concept for situations that seem doomed to solitude or despair. This belief alone has already made Rem Koolhaas a profoundly current architect.

All that remains now is to go inside the building that will reveal to us spaces designed according to principles of juxtaposition and balance, spaces that retain their autonomy and whose assembling and interweaving make the theater an "exquisite corpse," as it was described by Hubert Damisch. The stage offers an extraordinary depth of almost forty meters when the surface of the set preparation workshop can be used. The auditorium boasts a thousand seats arranged in a regular amphitheater in which visibility is almost consistent for everyone: it is therefore as democratic as can be. It sits in an atmosphere of half-light, which contributes to accentuating the choice of dark blue for the seats—as opposed to the traditional red—and the brilliance of the stainless-steel ceiling that, thanks to the breadth of its curves, seems to float above the rows of seats. The foyer is like a festival of free forms arranged in space: with a balcony that is a taut arc grazing the side wall of the concert hall; with, beneath this balcony, the smooth curve of a ceiling that plunges beneath the tiered seats of the theater until it almost touches the ground; and finally, with an ovoid that soars precariously over a red beam, the "sky bar," where sophisticated drinks can be sipped in the air, and where every movement can be felt because even the slightest twitch from a customer makes the platform tremble.

All these free forms are at the limits of instability; they are as if liberated from gravity and signs. Koolhaas has thus rediscovered the questions asked by Russian Constructivists such as El Lissitzky and Ivan Leonidov, or by neo-plasticist artists. The architecture staged at the Dance Theater is a world in which tensions are extreme, just as the materials used are ordinary. This last characteristic is not only the result of a tight budget for this kind of building, but of a deliberate theoretical and aesthetic choice: a belief that emotions are not aroused by conspicuously displayed wealth but by the new and sublime use of everyday materials always available to us.

TOO MUCH CHAMPAGNE?

Olivier Boissière
L'Architecture d'Aujourd'hui 257 (1988), 28–33.

The Dance Theater may well provide an opportunity to confirm some of the positions put forward by Rem Koolhaas in his manifesto texts, as well as how they cope with the transition to concrete and construction. From this perspective, the architect as hero, destined to overcome thousands of traps and pitfalls, finds a plausible illustration: this is the third project designed and built by OMA, after the whims of real estate transported it from its holiday in Scheveningen to the center of The Hague. All this taking the small matter of seven years. But, as we were already well aware, architecture is not a gala dinner.

On a neutral block of land bordered by a raised urban highway (a main access route people say won't be around for long) and sheltered by the towers of the neighboring ministries of Defense and Justice—beside which a quite decent building by Bakema has just been pulled down to make room for a new town hall, the competition for which was won by OMA though Richard Meier was given the current work in a second phase—the urbanist and architect Carel Weeber has traced an L-shaped plan opening up a vast esplanade. A hotel unravels a Cecil B. DeMille-style stairway here, unfinished due to a disagreement between the city and hotel as to its financing and upkeep, while the concert hall and dance theater nestle against the ministerial buildings.

An uncomfortable spot indeed for OMA, rendered even more so by the constraint of having to build on a parking lot. And in such a heterogeneous context, the "transplantation" of the Scheveningen project was inopportune. Yet stripped of its showy seaside resort trappings, the theater settles into the context in a reserved but nonetheless distinctive manner: each of its three faces (the fourth butting up against the concert hall) is defined with regards to the specific situation.

The southeast face, visible from the motorway interchange when arriving, looks like a big box covered in striated black cladding, a shadow show where a résumé of the program may be read in cutouts with the sets workshop, the stage well and the auditorium surmounted by its sinusoidal roofing. The southwest face is treated in planes playing on depth and color; juxtaposed with the black cladding that takes on bronze tints in certain lights is the almost velvet-like gray coating of the sets workshop, and then the varnished black brick surmounted by the white overhang of the administrative spaces. It is almost superfluous to mention that the refinement of these processes distinguishes the theater from the surrounding constructions.

Viewed from the esplanade, the theater appears to be more composite: it has to "compose" with the concert hall that is linked to it, a big pink box squared to 45 degrees by a thin green streak and sporting in its lower half a tinted glass mask shaped like a pair of Courrèges sunglasses, with the aforementioned unfinished stairway crossing it diagonally and the dark blue curtain wall of the hotel as well as the ministry buildings forming a backdrop.

No doubt that the difficult problem has been resolved with delicacy: a low profile and an affirmation of the theater's identity by a few unobtrusive traits. The rectilinear administrative building leans slightly over a lane that separates it from the hotel, the sinusoidal line of the roofing breaks gently with the concert hall, and the theater asserts itself in two signs: a huge fresco explicitly referring to the world of ballet, done by Madelon Vriesendorp, marking out the stage well, and the trunk of a cone shaped like a control tower amusing itself with its golden coating of riveted plates. An (almost!) neutral way of setting up shop in a banally chaotic urban environment and, perhaps, of pretending not to attach any importance to it. There is no monumental entrance to make this "cultural complex" a falsely sacred place: the entry being situated at the limit of two rooms and composed of a somewhat discreet door opening to one side between the buildings and destined to constitute an intermission foyer common to them both.

[...] Although this first major building was much anticipated, there was a certain amount of apprehension: can he build, we wondered ... The answer is yes! With a budget teetering on a knife edge, Koolhaas serves up an exercise in construction in which he puts the expertise he admired in a particular kind of American architecture to the test. It is a blend of abandonment and meticulous attention: there are no details in the "Scarpaesque" sense of the word, of course, but a deft way of juxtaposing cladding panels without joins, for example, or the inconspicuous refinement of a rest area. An invisible space is treated like a work in itself (the staircase leading to the "catwalk," lit as if by Dan Flavin!), while technical details are staged with the best reasons in the world (the windows looking into the studios from the foyer shot through with cable between two layers of toughened glass). A whole series of delights greets you in the theater, events that are sensed all the better because they never appear showy: no muscles are being flexed here! There is, if you like, as much difference between architecture according to Koolhaas and certain contemporary gesticulations as there is between dance and aerobics.

Two pieces of bravura are nevertheless worthy of mention for their spectacular dimension, despite also deriving naturally from the world of entertainment. The auditorium, a huge dark cave with its dominant blues, unleashes the drama of the double curvature of the clad ceiling in all its intensity: smooth, ribbed and glistening in the half light, it makes every audience member feel like a tiny Jonah, experiencing both a shudder and a sense of divine protection. The foyer, exuberant in the richness of its textures and colors, in the expansion of its mezzanines and the focused humor of the sky bar, contributes (perhaps it is here that Koolhaas takes his revenge) to the rubbing out of the neighboring concert hall: its pink dividing wall looks pasty and vanquished, its weakness clear. During the intermission, when the floorboards tremble under the audience's feet, when the race to reach the bars is on, when the glass multiplies the reflections of the light and the movements of the crowd coming and going, ascending and descending in pleasant chaos, a moment reigns in this space that conveys a feeling of almost Dionysiac exaltation. Or perhaps it's the effect of too much champagne?

INTERPRETING THE SUPPORTING STRUCTURES OF ARCHITECTURE

Stefan Polónyi
Lotus international 79 (1993), 87.

[...] With the help of the computer we can identify the behavior and performance of any structure; this means that, in the design of a supporting structure, the importance of the capacity to evaluate it from the viewpoint of mathematical calculation is reduced. As a consequence, the supporting structure is designed on the basis of aesthetic and technical-constructive considerations as well as static ones, and the attempt to avoid the presence of secondary stresses, to which a great deal of attention was paid in the past, loses its significance. On the basis of these presuppositions, we can turn back directly to those structures, worthy of the greatest admiration, that belong to the period preceding the introduction of statics. This tendency can be seen in the return to the use of beams braced from underneath and of Polonceau trusses. These structures require a great deal more calculation than do lattice beams, especially if you want to obtain an optimal performance by means of prestressing. It is possible, however, to reduce the cost of the materials in this way.

The engineer, operating on the basis of a procedure of analysis and synthesis, and of his training founded on Cartesian principles, designs—usually—flat, additive, and orthogonal systems of beams. This type of mentality has to give way to a three-dimensional reflection on space. In fact, it is not the engineer's job to make the architect understand that what he has contrived is not feasible. On the contrary, the engineer has to show how it can be realized. [...]

Rem Koolhaas is bursting with ideas and, to some extent, only communicates them verbally. This offers the possibility of submitting to him, at the right time, a series of suitable and timely structural proposals. In 1982, for example, on the occasion of the first project for the Dance Theater in Scheveningen, roughly the following conversation took place.

rk: The cantilever roof with its large overhang, should have a very thin edge at the front, while the struts of the front beam should all be of different shapes. The supports on the far left should be set at an angle and taper toward the bottom.

sp: Then we could anchor the beam to the stage tower with one of the braces.

rk: Yes, but only on one of the sides of the stage tower.

sp: In that case, though, we will have to provide a support on the other side.

rk: No no, not that! Further along there can be a V-shaped support while, at the right-hand end, the beam can rest on the arch. It is very likely that this solution will not be adopted because of the cost, and then we will have to think of something else to solve this problem.

sp: Okay, so let's have the beam supported on the right side of the tower by a suspended pillar that rests on a main beam reinforced by struts and braces.

rk: Very good, perfect.

sp: That way everything will work fine as far as loads due to the weight of the roof itself and snow are concerned, but the roof will tend to be lifted by the wind. Consequently, the point subject to traction from above, which is to the left of the stage tower, and the point held by lower braces to the right of that have to be anchored with cables fixed to the ground or loaded with weights.

rk: Even better! Here on the left, let's attach a cone of solid steel underneath and, on the right, let's put a sphere of steel on top.

This is how the constructivist composition of the supporting structure was born. However it was not built like that. As for the roof of the auditorium, Koolhaas's only requirement was that it should not be flat, but animated. So for this roof I proposed, as a homage to Gaudí, an undulating shape made out of trapezoidal elements of sheet metal. This idea was accepted at once by Koolhaas.

Koolhaas is particularly interested in the external image, in what might be called architectonic sculpture. The realization of this aspect had been entrusted to his collaborator Jan Voorberg who, at just that time, lost his life in tragic circumstances in Brazil. So the executive plan of the Dance Theater was placed in the hands of Jeroen Thomas. Not that Koolhaas is not interested in structural aspects or details. Quite the opposite! In his view, everything had to be very simple and be related to pure construction. Which amounts to saying that he liked to draw attention to the structure. The Dance Theater presented him with the right opportunity. [...]

FIRST DECADE, SECOND HALF (1986–1989): POLEMICS IN THE PROVINCE

5

The second half of the 1980s can be properly called the Dutch era of OMA: the office made many important projects for the Netherlands, and critical reception followed suit. The relationship between Koolhaas and his native country has always been somewhat difficult, and by the end of the decade, OMA seemed ready to depart and to expand its territory, not coincidently in the years following the fall of the Berlin Wall, which initiated the next phase of globalization. The exhibition *The First Decade* in Rotterdam, from March 4 to April 16, 1989, was a true kiss-off, and a stocktaking of everything that went wrong—an overview of all the OMA projects the Dutchmen decided not to build, particularly the City Hall in The Hague and the Netherlands Architecture Institute in Rotterdam (not coincidentally, the floor plan and the concept of the latter project was reused for the exhibition—to get it built after all, no matter how temporarily). “I believe,” Koolhaas told a journalist at the opening night of *The First Decade*, “that the Netherlands would be a better place if at least some of those plans had actually materialized, and I say that with more stoicism than bitterness.”

One of those plans was made for The Hague in 1986—it was the first time in the Netherlands that architects were asked to make a proposal for a public building in collaboration with private developers. The city hall with municipal library would be located in the direct vicinity of OMA’s Dance Theater, which was under construction. The competition became the subject of an intense debate; the five proposals were exhibited between December 1986 and January 1987, but it immediately became clear there were only two contenders: OMA and Richard Meier. OMA’s project was a skyline: the program of 150,000 square meters was organized in a rectangular structure from 240 by 43 meters. Three strips with towers of alternating height were clad in different facades: concrete, a curtain wall, and a steel grid. The result was a collage of three thin slices with an ambiguous scale, preceded by a triangular public square. The project was a Hilberseimerian assembly line for real estate development, which accurately conveyed “the commercial expediency of Holland’s present Thatcherite government,” as Peter Buchanan argued in *Architectural Review*. In Dutch newspaper *NRC Handelsblad* opinion pieces were published in close succession. Geert Bekaert’s text—a plea considering OMA’s project “a hefty blood transfusion” for contemporary architecture—was copied and made available at OMA’s stand at the exhibition of projects. A petition was organized; Peter Eisenman described OMA’s proposal as “a building in ‘process’” and “the only appropriate symbolism for a major building in a social democracy.”[1] The controversy concerned the project’s modernity: wasn’t this city hall too metropolitan for The Hague? And did it still look like a city hall? As Stanislaus von Moos argued at the end of 1987 in *A+U*, “it was an architectural tribute to the Dutch metropolis.” Dutch architect Aldo van Eyck, member of the jury, agreed, and the project was selected, but in the end alderman Adri Duivesteijn overruled the decision and chose Meier.[2]

This drama was restaged in 1988 when the same Duivesteijn, this time as director of the newly established Netherlands Architecture Institute, organized a competition in Rotterdam. OMA had already started working on the project for the Kunsthal, opposite the site for the Architecture Institute, across the museum park. Again, their proposal was seemingly neutral, Miesian, reticent, and mysterious; and again Koolhaas was considered too modern. In the catalogue of the exhibition with the six proposals, it was stated without restraint: "The lack of a real metropolitan milieu in the Netherlands raises the risk that Koolhaas's buildings will amount to nothing more than the empty, wasted gesture of a provincial prima donna."[3] The rebuke did not go unnoticed, and in 1989, in an interview with Mil De Kooning, Koolhaas called it "shameless" and "unimaginable." Nevertheless, other critical attacks were made, for example when Hilde de Haan and Ids Haagsma reviewed the IJplein project in Dutch newspaper *De Volkskrant*, denouncing "Rem Koolhaas's Big, Sloppy Dreams."[4]

By the end of decade, three attempts were made to theorize OMA's approach in concepts transcending the Netherlands. Geert Bekaert referred to a text by Walter Benjamin when he called Koolhaas "the storyteller" of contemporary architecture. In an essay on Russian author Leskov, Benjamin argued that in modernity people have lost the ability to tell useful stories, from which a moral or a future-oriented lesson can be detracted. Leskov was different because he had "counsel—not for a few situations, as the proverb does, but for many, like the sage."[5] The same could be said of Koolhaas, Bekaert suggested: "this is an architecture that has outgrown the narcissistic phase, that has ceased to listen to its own voice and to talk about itself, but has become totally bound up in the world that lives in it, and because of it." In the summer of 1988 this interpretation was in a way contradicted, when OMA was selected by Mark Wigley and Philip Johnson to be part of the group of architects that would be exhibited at MoMA's *Deconstructivist Architecture*. In the catalogue, Wigley inscribed OMA in a new tradition of a "radical questioning of modernism." The notion of dirty realism, developed by Liane Lefaivre in 1989, focused on the city. Lefaivre interpreted the position of Koolhaas—together with that of architects as diverse as Hans Kollhoff, Laurids Ortner, Jean Nouvel, and Zaha Hadid, "all scavenger-poets who have introduced harsh aesthetics of urban blight into architectural lyricism"[6]—as a critical commentary on the state of the European city at the end of the twentieth century.

1 See Francesco Marullo, "Delirious Equivalence: The Hague City Hall Competition (1986)," *OASE* 94 (2015), 84–87.

2 See Wouter Vanstiphout, "Richard Meier in Holland: Black and Whiteness," *ANY* 16 (1996), 40–44.

3 Ruud Brouwers and Bernard Colenbrander, "Rem Koolhaas/OMA," in *Zes ontwerpen voor het Nederlands Architectuurinstituut*, ed. Ruud Brouwers and Bernard Colenbrander (Rotterdam: NAi, 1998), n.p. For a reassessment of OMA's project for the NAi, see Kersten Geers, "Showing Everything: Netherlands Architecture Institute," *OASE* 94 (2015), 104–6.

4 For a recent text on the IJplein project, see Christophe Van Gerrewey, "A Weissenhofsiedlung for Amsterdam," *Log* 44 (2018), 83–92.

5 Walter Benjamin, "The Storyteller: Reflections on the Work of Nikolai Leskov," in *Selected Writings*, ed. Marcus Bullock and Michael W. Jennings (Cambridge, MA: Harvard University Press, 2002), 3:162.

6 Liane Lefaivre, "Dirty Realism in European Architecture Today: Making the Stone *Stony*," *Design Book Review* 17 (1989), 18. Unfortunately, Liane Lefaivre did not grant permission for the republication of her text.

OMA AT THE HAGUE

Peter Buchanan
Architectural Review 1084 (1987), 87–91.

Rem Koolhaas and OMA entered the limited developers' competition for a huge new town hall for The Hague only when James Stirling, Michael Wilford & Associates pulled out halfway through the 16-week design period. Yet they won with what is the best, the most exuberant and much the most provocative scheme entered. Not that they are certain to build it. For in the heated debate now raging in The Netherlands, while some heavyweight commentators favor the OMA scheme, equally influential ones back Richard Meier's project arguing that it will be more profitable and more responsive to context.

This latter is an uncertain virtue. Though most of The Hague—the part one remembers and associates with Holland's capital—consists of graceful streets and squares of stucco trimmed red brick houses, the area around the site is overpowered by huge horrors built since the 1960s. Among recent works that stand out as bad even amongst the crude slabs of government ministries are: a grotesquely elephantine white metal clad State Archive by OD 205; a mean and crude hotel by Carel Weeber; and the Dance Theater being built by OMA that, like their town hall design but with none of its merits, is a compendium of American flash and tat.

[...] Meier's "contextual" response has been to stretch drab slabs along the two long sides of the block and close either end with the vapid sculptural exercises one expects of him. Opposite approaching streets and the new square on Spui he thrusts through this perimeter to open up and give access to a huge volume enclosed under a glass roof stretched between the two slabs and in which it is impossible to imagine any human activity making any sort of impression.

OMA's approach is altogether more intense and less obvious, seeming almost to be a compaction of many of the elements around it. In rather typical fashion, they have subdivided the largest rectangle they could make of the site into three strips of identical width. At the lower levels all sorts of functions are accommodated within this structural grid. Above, each strip acquires its own "skyline" as it rises into seried and staggered office slabs, each row of which is differently clad—one of the most striking scenographic images of recent times. The whole building follows the simple and consistent discipline of these strips so that accommodation can easily be rejigged both during design and after completion.

The residual site area, between this block of slabs and the hotel and dance theater, is simply treated as a sunken plaza flanked by shops below with, above and along the longest side, a row of multipurpose kiosks. At the lower level in the main block, a café and restaurant spill out into the plaza. An auditorium, exhibition gallery, pubs, amusement arcades and huge stack rooms for a municipal library fill the rest of this floor.

On the next level up (ground floor), the municipal library has a separate entrance at mid block beside the end of the sunken plaza. Further away from the plaza, past a service road that passes through the block, are shops. The main entrance to the town hall is from Spui and via a bridge over a pool into the end of the huge rectangular block. Inside, once past the threateningly looming inverted dome of the bottom half of the spherical council chamber that hangs down over the end of the bridge, are reception, cloaks and an exhibition area. A ramp drops down through an elongated well to the restaurants and exhibition areas below. Above, a pair of wells rise several floors through the base of the building.

The first well rises ten floors to bring down natural light from a three-story window beside one of the roof terraces. The other well narrows above second-floor level (on which is a gently kinked street of shops and services) to become a long narrow slot through which a continuous line of escalators climbs to connect the several levels of the library. Around the spherical council chamber are, at the appropriate levels, facilities for councillors, public and press. Above this base are the strips of office slabs whose floors flow into each other where they touch so as to give considerable choice of depth and area in which to allocate departments. The strip closest the old town is soberly faced in stone with traditional details in some sort of contextual concession to the past and the old town in this direction. The opposite strip is clad in stainless steel, perhaps some gesture to the future. The center of this huge (or is it mini?) Manhattan sandwich is faced in an abstract grid of glass, recalling perhaps the recent but now already nostalgic past of the 1950s and 1960s. This is the era the building is inspired by, as reflected in its formal vocabulary, scenographic composition and seeming flimsiness of surface.

A spate of advertisements, for different makes of jeans amongst other things, look back to this era as one of ingenuous, unspoilt authenticity. Naive the era might truly have been, but any authenticity lay largely in the fact that symbols were obvious, brash and raw in their commercialism, still unsullied by the understated sophistication of our era. (The intensity of longings and romance some ads suggest was still possible then, was probably because the objects of desire were still limited and obvious.) The appeal of this recent apparently simple past seems undeniable—the ad campaigns are rumored to be amongst the most successful ever. But though its nostalgic forms and associations of corporate commercialism have been compacted with all the ingenuity and intensity that Koolhaas identifies with "Manhattanism," this hardly seems to symbolize a *civitas* of sufficient dignity for the Dutch capital. American-style commercial tat's antithesis to any sense of *gravitas* or *civitas* seems especially poignant in a country that, at least until recently, had strong personal and architectural traditions of honesty, earnestness and an unpompous but dignified openness in its institutions. Forthright and unpompous OMA's building may be. But while it accurately conveys the commercial expediency of Holland's present Thatcherite government, which like its UK original expects public institutions to be propped up by private profits, it hardly conveys honesty, openness or dignity. [...]

A CHANCE OF A LIFETIME

Geert Bekaert

NRC Handelsblad, January 22, 1987.

[...] A plan not easily apprehended in the tedious architectural discourse of the day is that of Koolhaas. His submission shies away from what was expected, thereby elevating the conversation to the right level. Architecture once again acquires actual import. In this regard, Koolhaas's design continues the strong tradition of modern architecture in the Netherlands, following in the steps of Berlage, Oud, Duiker, Rietveld and Van Eyck, for whom architecture was a vital part of the sociocultural system and not merely a design exercise. That singular vision is what has earned Dutch architecture its international reputation. This is the opportunity of a lifetime. By choosing this plan, The Hague can emerge as a trendsetter instead of a trend follower.

The Koolhaas plan aims not to impress, but to be understood. It does not pretend to be the definitive gesture, but instead presents an extremely smart articulation of possibilities. It makes architecture exciting again. It is not the end point, but a beginning. The design makes no presumptive claims about that location in the city or the city in general, except perhaps in terms of priming and opening it up to a multitude of experiences. The design does not adapt to the site but rather gives it form. It believes in the site's potential. It radiates optimism.

In his accompanying statement, the architect puts it thus: "We did not view our task as primarily being to design a definitive building, but rather to devise a concept capable of undergoing limitless mutations without sacrificing quality, as a model that translates programmatic stability and organizational flexibility into architectural eloquence." This thinking in terms of architecture instead of in terms of a building gives birth to an uncommonly invigorating, diversified form that can allow itself every freedom of development, a form that refuses to be captured in a single representation. The form generates an inexhaustible variety of representations without ceding its identity or lucidity. It presents itself not as immutable geometry, but as an equally arbitrary and necessary response to concrete conditions that could well be entirely different tomorrow.

No other design offers that variability, that mixture of contradictions, that symbiosis of paradoxes that is so unique to today's living city. No other design is closer to reality. None is this relaxed. And in the city's cramped attempt to renew itself, it is exactly that relaxed attitude that can guarantee results.

It is to be hoped that neither public opinion nor the experts will allow themselves to be swayed by the glitter, that they will thoroughly evaluate the intrinsic qualities of each design. If that happens, then it almost cannot fail: not only will The Hague get a great city hall, but contemporary architecture will receive a hefty blood transfusion.

DUTCH GROUP PORTRAIT

Stanislaus von Moos
A+U 217 (1988), 86–94.

That the work of the Office for Metropolitan Architecture is an enigmatically Dutch phenomenon became apparent to me around the year 1983 when I was standing in front of the Congress Center in The Hague with an American colleague. We were looking at the glass tower built by J. J. P. Oud on a triangular plan. The image of that building, almost dangerously volumeless, like the transparent mock-up of an imaginary and improbable skyscraper, made him suggest that this must surely be a building by Rem Koolhaas.

The attribution was, of course, as well-meaning as it was wrong; yet it was not absurd. In this building, Oud seems to have anticipated OMA's vision of a metropolitan architecture—or rather, certain aspects of it—at a time when Koolhaas himself was still practically a child (Oud's glass tower was built 1956–1963; Rem Koolhaas was born in 1944). For in fact, seen in this context, the functionalist fairyland architecture with which OMA made its name in the 1970s looks like a conceptual extrapolation from building ideas which were realized in Holland to a greater extent than elsewhere.

Perhaps surprisingly, these building ideas seem to be again very much in the air, for Oud's tower is echoed today in the neofunctionalism of current Dutch corporate architecture. The Mies-box has been rehabilitated in Holland, the *terra santa* of the pre-postmodern resistance against it: one has only to look around The Hague's center with its office buildings of the past few years. So to return to OMA it may appear as if Holland were on the brink of overtaking with its real architecture the fictive (paper) architecture designed some years ago by OMA, as if this country had become in its quotidian building practice the theater of that almost anachronous "modern" architecture of efficiency and urban density developed in Koolhaas's book *Delirious New York*.

Nonetheless, the "official" Hague is not yet ripe for a large-scale project built by OMA itself. Imagine the following scene: the (Social Democratic) city council majority of an agglomeration the size of Zürich decides that a new city hall should be built. What do they do? They sit down with a group of potent building contractors to invite entries for an international architectural competition—among them projects by Richard Meier, Helmut Jahn and the Office for Metropolitan Architecture. The jury, in which the voice of the grand old man Aldo van Eyck was probably the most influential, awarded OMA's project first prize in 1987.

The project's *parti* is simple. In principle, the administrative tract is made up of three horizontally-square office slabs sandwiched together (not unlike the vertically-slabbed Thyssen high-rise in Düsseldorf). Subsequently, each of these three slabs has been reduced to approximately half of its volume according to the given program, so that the slabs take on the form of three parallel combs mounted one behind the other and establishing a silhouette reminiscent of an (American?) skyscraper city.

But as we have seen, office high-rises do not set the tone for the downtowns of American metropolis alone; for years now they have also formed the distant image of the Dutch capital. As one approaches the city on the highway coming from Amsterdam or Rotterdam, The Hague's diffuse skyline emerges against the horizon while one is still far away. This image is precisely what the signal-like skyline of OMA's project addresses. Thus the city hall appears as a miniature capital, a logogram of the city, relating to it just as the Palazzo Vecchio with its crenellations and tower relates to the walled ring of Dugento Florence.

Only in The Hague it is not the symbols of military power that are embodied in the city hall's skyline, but, as in a gigantic city coat-of-arm, those of finance and bureaucracy. At the same time, seen from the north and in close-up view, the whole project relates demonstratively in scale and in the form of its details to its "historical" surroundings. While the facade facing south, oriented toward an area of new buildings, is projected in aluminum and glass, the facade facing the old town is projected in natural stone: contextualism revived.

Or should a family standing posed for a family portrait come to mind when looking at the three parallel mounted silhouettes? Koolhaas, OMA's boss, seems to enjoy the hidden anthropomorphic potential of tall buildings. He also seems to like arrangements presenting a frontal view, such as the skyline of Manhattan (or Houston or Dallas) on a travel bureau brochure. Or—to remain in Holland—such as the regents of St. Elisabeth's Hospital in Haarlem in Frans Hals' famous group portrait.

Does this comparison seem farfetched? Maybe the formula "figurative architecture" overshoots the mark here anyway. For a visitor to OMA's recent exhibition in Basel, at least, what was "illustrated" by this architecture was primarily the design process itself. Impossible, in view of the three staggered combs which define the volume of the office tract, to forget the three small pieces of plastic which Koolhaas used in the exhibition videoclip to demonstrate the central idea of the complex. (In one showcase the Architecture Museum prominently displayed pieces of colored clay models as relics of the "creative process," almost as if it were a Beuys installation.)

Thus the skyline, graduated in both height and depth, appears above all as a didactic model of the project's underlying concept. The reality to which the symbolic language of this architecture relates, is not the logic of the plan (which I do not discuss here) and the history of the project developed from it. In this respect, one may speak of a "self-referential" symbolism of a kind that is characteristic for every tradition within the Modern movement wherein works reflect most strongly the conditions of their own materialization while refusing any explicit mimesis. To point out one very clear example of this approach: the buildings of Jacob B. Bakema (1914–1981) of the 1950s and 1960s, many of which could be described as teaching aids for emphatically staged design processes. In Bakema's work, these architectural orders, made transparent, are also to be understood as conceptual models for democratic coexistence. As in the case, *mutatis mutandis,* of the serial and modular orders of colors and elementary geometric shapes in paintings by Richard Paul Lohse. The Swiss painter, too, likes to explain these "open" and nonhierarchical systems as metaphors for democracy. (I am not discussing here the fact that Bakema's "architecture-urbanism" is indebted to Lohse for many a formal stimulus.) That Bakema often related buildings to people through clear formal analogies in his sketches can only be mentioned here. While his architecture is certainly not anthropomorphic, his urbanistic "group forms" display that symbolism of togetherness dear to the *Forum* generation.

These are thoughts that almost inevitably come to mind when contemplating Koolhaas's city hall project, even though in the long run it may be closer in spirit to Van Eyck than to Bakema. Indeed its comparatively small scale and almost cozy organization around an open middle are not entirely unlike Aldo van Eyck's Amsterdam orphanage of the 1960s, the archetypal "house" programmatically conceived of as a "small city."

The site of the proposed city hall is located on the edge of an urban area which bears witness to one of the spectacular bulldozer operations of the 1960s: an act of "de-urbanization" which made room for a new main train station; the Royal Library; opulent administration buildings for the Department of Justice, the Department of the Interior and the Department of Foreign Affairs, as well as for a large number of apartments. The new city hall's role was to serve as a link between this new administrative city and The Hague's historical center.

Just a few years ago this area was an unsightly *terrain vague.* Today it has become an open-air museum of urban architectural doctrines from the past twenty-five years. Undoubtedly, the sheer mass of architectural deposits which *nolens volens* reflect a dramatic chain reaction of urban architectural concepts—each superseding and actually canceling out the other—takes on something of an involuntary monumentality. First of all, the disproportionately large main train station with its flat front building, a sort of Stazione Termini, but much higher than its Roman counterpart. Surrounded as it is by incoming and outgoing ramps—laid out according to a design by Pier Luigi Nervi and on which for a long time only one bus or streetcar was seen every ten minutes—this building documents the brisk wind of the economic boom. The same is true of the Ministry of the Interior; at that time one still believed in the Ville Radieuse.

Relentlessly, however, the exorcisms of architectural "humanism" of the 1970s followed the planning sins of the previous decades. Immediately adjacent to the "monotonous" concrete plane of the main train station stand a shopping center and a hotel. The shimmering dark brown smoked glass cubes with their "loose" silhouettes are reminiscent of hill towns such as Habitat in Montreal or—to name an equally enigmatic nearby prototype—

Herman Hertzberger's Centraal Beheer insurance company headquarters in Apeldoorn (1968–1972). The hotel bar was originally christened with the name *Kash-Bar* in homage to the Dutch Team 10 architects who, in recourse to North African settlement models *(Casbah),* promised the humanization of the city. In turn, the shopping center as a whole bears the name Babylon. This too is a quotation: for was it not the painter Constant Nieuwenhuys, one of the founders of the COBRA group, who crystallized his utopian vision of a "Revolt of the *Homo ludens*" in a project called "New Babylon"? [...]

Finally comes the Department of Foreign Affairs Building immediately next to Babylon. Contrary to it, this colossal and amorphous structure is not the mere result of a "trickling down" of elements from avant-garde high culture to the sphere of commercial application. Rather, it is a piece of authorized—if late—architectonic insurrection against the "monotony" of the International Style. For, from 1959 on, its author, the architect Apon, together with Aldo van Eyck and Herman Hertzberger, had sounded the death toll for the functionalist city in the magazine *Forum*.

In Holland the speed with which the recipes of the avant-garde are absorbed by the general practice is breathtaking. Even in H. P. Berlage's or J. J. P. Oud's times, "official" planning and design policies were receptive to advanced models of thought to a degree unimaginable in other countries. In the light of this background, Koolhaas's project seems to be nothing other than the last link in a chain of urban reform models concretized as textbook examples in The Hague's inner city. As such, it incorporates what is really a farewell to the "humanist" reform strategies of the *Forum* generation while announcing a not merely ironic sympathy for the functionalist "planning sins" of the 1960s. Instead of politely ignoring the office high-rises of that decade (as Richard Meier's project does), OMA's proposal gives them meaning *post festum* as a constituent element of the existing urban skyline. Of course it is easy to see all of this in the light of Koolhaas's interest in Manhattan. He admires the UN Building by Wallace K. Harrison, the archetype of the slab-shaped office high-rises of the 1950s (project: 1949). His sympathy for the office slab is very explicit in *Delirious New York*, published in 1978. [...] Some of the large pastel studies for the city hall project are clearly reminiscent of Hugh Ferris's dramatic renderings of New York skyscrapers. The sunken plaza at the foot of the city hall building, although cozily Dutch, also has an oval skating rink—a tribute to Raymond Hood's Rockefeller Center. The globe of the city council chamber, which hangs down into the vestibule of the city hall itself, seems simultaneously to relate to Hood's News Building lobby and to Leonidov's unrealized project for the Lenin library in Moscow (1928). Or does it go back to the monumental logo built for the New York World's Fair in 1939: the spheroid monument of Modern Times *par excellence,* abstract in its stereometry *and* popular in its symbolism?

Be that as it may, in the light of Koolhaas's brilliant typological conjuring, the "evidence" of Manhattan's architecture unfolds an unexpected utopian and poetic potential. This is not the first time, of course, that Dutch architects have fixed their sights on America. Berlage's guiding light was Louis Sullivan; Van't Hoff's and Oud's was Frank Lloyd Wright. In The Hague itself Koolhaas's grandfather, the architect D. Roosenburg, built homes in the 1930s in a kind of Dutch Prairie Style—yet the cosmopolitan imagery in the city hall project is not just another variation of a private (or national) mythology.

Is the city hall project perhaps about "postmodern architecture" after all? If by this a style or an imagery of urban nostalgia is suggested, then OMA's work can only be seen as an alternative to it. Taken in a broader sense, however, the approach to history that OMA is parading is certainly "postmodern." Judging from the wide range of architectonic experience which is worked into the city hall project, one has to speak of an eclectic sensibility. Nonetheless, Koolhaas's approach to history cannot be described as mere quotation. Historical reference here takes on a hermeneutic role. Its function is not merely to allow the art historian to pinpoint *post festum* the sources of one or another among the project's formal characteristics. Rather, historical examples introduced for comparison serve as aids to the architect himself in comprehending case by case the structure (or quintessence) of a given task.

Urban analysis through the fading-in of relevant comparative material from history: the method may be reminiscent of Aldo Rossi's *città analoga* (if not, in the long run, even of Camillo Sitte). To give but one example: in a famous 1972 study, The City of the Captive Globe, a kind of fictive Manhattan is created. Set on bases like sculptures, various sacred icons of the avant-garde are laid out in rows. Among them are Malevich's Planites, Lissitzky's Prouns, Le Corbusier's Plan Voisin or Salvador Dalí's Architectural Angelus. However, the Berlin Wall is there as well. These images not only serve to furnish a private architectural walhalla, as Koolhaas himself put it. They also serve as conceptual keys for the analysis of the metropolitan status quo, helping us to look behind the mimicry of New York's architectural epidermis and offer hypotheses as to the "structure" of the situation at hand—what Koolhaas describes as the principle of Manhattanism. The procedure is not of an historical, but rather of an associative kind and Koolhaas practices it on the drawing board as well. To return to the city hall in The Hague and its perhaps extravagant analogies to Rockefeller Center: they are not intended as mere romantic quotations. Rockefeller Center is of interest in terms of certain architectural concepts—skyscraper, lobby, sunken plaza—that are believed to be adequate given the scope of the program and the nature of the site.

[...] To compare the towers of OMA's city hall project to Frans Hals's enigmatic group portrait in Haarlem may seem extravagant in the context of traditional art history; it is harmless in the context of Archigram and Superstudio and may even be pertinent if seen against the background of *Delirious New York*—even if the more or less explicit or grotesque *outré* anthropomorphism of American skyscraper architecture is not a central theme in Koolhaas's book. [...] One image, of course, is not missing from the pages of *Delirious New York:* the famous photograph of New York's architects masquerading in 1931 as the skyline of New York with William van Alen in the middle as the "personification" of the Chrysler Building (1929) he designed. A costume ball prank and nothing more? In a project for an imaginary Hotel Sphinx (1975–1976), Koolhaas himself made the "inverse anthropomorphic travesty" (Van Leeuwen) of this architectural happening the object of an architectural *capriccio.*

The hidden anthropomorphic quality of the city hall project for The Hague, as a "Dutch group portrait" following Frans Hals *and* Jacob Bakema may be an (involuntary) joke, but without this background it is unintelligible. In terms of the present state of architecture and urban design, another of its aspects is more explosive: the fact that here the image of an

American skyline is "reproduced" at a time when America's design review boards, supposedly worried about the "urbanity" of their downtown areas, require architects to build office high-rises with gabled, mansard or hipped roofs—or better yet, to crown them with Art Deco-styled pyramidal or ziggurat-shaped tops. In this respect, the OMA project represents an unusual and, even in a European context, a probably very topical "nostalgia," a postmodern hook-up to the forgotten *Sachlichkeit* of the International Style. Or: Mies van der Rohe's revenge against a Neo-Historicism that has become too opulent and too self-indulgent.

The project, to be sure, will not be realized. In spite of the clear jury decision, the city council advanced Richard Meier's design. In the eyes of those who toppled the OMA project, the skyline it represented was probably just too extravagant. What is in fact an architectural tribute to the essence of the Dutch metropolis of today was perceived as a mere manifesto of transatlantic romanticism.

STRUCTURED THROUGH EMPTINESS: MELUN-SÉNART

Christophe Bayle
Urbanisme 222 (1987), 89.

By relaunching an urban planning competition, sixteen years after its creation, the new town was reviving a political tradition of the founding act of European cities. *Me (I)*: it was with this founding statement that the history of Rome began. It is also with the character *wou*—meaning "me" or "I" in Chinese—that the team of Rem Koolhaas and Yves Bories signed their project. A way of expressing that the founding of a town needs some kind of legend. In fact, the sign *wou* means both "me" (I) and looks like the logo from Yves Bories and Rem Koolhaas's site plan. But it is thanks to the greatest of twists of fate, to which art is accustomed, that the team arrived at that point.

Starting from the idea that the town of Melun-Sénart both feared and wanted its central space in equal measure, the project offers a system of strips empty of any urbanization. This structuring through emptiness immediately creates a system of values between empty and filled spaces on the site, through property, landscape, access, visualization and identification, capable of accommodating programs of every range and status. In this context, it is the value of a site qualified in this way that authorizes, as in traditional towns, compatibilities between site and program. The strips (or voids) are the landscaping elements that can play host to large prestige programs linked to development: universities, corporate headquarters, hotels, a large stadium or a spacious luxury environment. Additional elements of complementary programs, such as student housing or production services, are located in the filled spaces, on the edge of the strips. What is interesting about this concept is that it stymies functional zoning. The possibilities for programs to penetrate one another, provided they are spacious, are mastered completely for the first time here.

Beyond the (empty) strips, we find the rest of the urbanization, in short, everything else. As far as the team is concerned, modes of urbanization change every five years. It is therefore important for the structure of the town to take this into account if it wants to assure its continued existence.

Highly innovative, Yves Bories and Rem Koolhaas's approach provides a nourishment that will interest those in charge of the layout of many new towns. After all, they are grappling with this same principle of empty strips and full sites, although for them it is about saving significant empty spaces at the edge of or inside their perimeter. The fact remains that by focusing too much on defining space through emptiness, the architects left the jury with the impression that they had only resolved half the problem. Moreover, the key idea of a town expected by the jury contradicted this proposal, which is more a principle of the continuous development of space than a program.

NOT WITHOUT A SCRATCH: POLICE STATION ALMERE

Madeleine Steigenga

Forum 2 (1987), 2–5.

In 1986 a police station was opened in Almere-Haven. It is the first realized design of Rem Koolhaas's young architectural firm OMA. The high expectations raised by the office have not been lived up to, they even lead to an anticlimax. Besides being a literal translation of the organization of the various police activities in the station, there are other aspects of the realized design which do not stand the test of criticism. The location is abominable, the concept is dead, the joke does not work, and the building is only photogenic when photographed at cruising height. The building is literally shaking, there are cracks in the walls. We have lost an illusion: Dutch architecture will not be saved by OMA either.

[...] In the design stage a number of execution problems have been disregarded. The dilatation of the facades has been designed in a strange way, as a conspicuous, zig-zagging dilatation joint instead of a "normal" vertical section. The attention demanded by this solution reduces the wall surfaces with their immaterial pretentions to dull masonry. The "architecture" of the building remains a pretention. OMA has slipped badly on the "metropolis" of Almere.

[...] OMA claims that the poor execution of the police station design is due to the fact that this central position had been taken away from them. This is not uncommon when professional principals are familiar with the ways in which designs are executed. In this way, the role of the architect is limited to that of giving aesthetical advice, partially supervising the work and checking the work drawings. The attitude of the architectural world toward this situation is one of ambivalence and varies from refusal on principle to downright acceptance. When principal, financier and builder are united in one and the same person, the architect's fear is understandable. [...]

THE STORYTELLER

Geert Bekaert

Office for Metropolitan Architecture, ed. Carolina De Backer (Antwerp: deSingel, 1988), 3–5.

If you still don't believe that architecture can tell a story, a real story, your last excuse has just been stripped away, by the work of Rem Koolhaas, of OMA—drawings or buildings—it makes no difference. In either form, this is an architecture that has outgrown the narcissistic phase, that has ceased to listen to its own voice and to talk about itself, but has become totally bound up in the world that lives in it, and because of it.

The stories it tells are real stories. One of the most beautiful is that of the police station in Almere. I am at a loss to understand why it is so seldom mentioned. Of course there is more to a dance theater than a police station, although it's not so crazy to approach a police force as a "corps de danse." But if we are to put this architectural approach to the test, the short story of the Almere police station is perhaps the most appropriate, because it is where architecture divests itself of all its charms to get down to what it really has to say.

The characteristic of a good story is that it makes you forget you are listening to a story. The reason Almere is such an awful place is that you are constantly reminded of the story there, and what's more, it is a story with no point, making everybody and everything a laughing stock, because the fiction of reality is left behind. Of course, Almere is just a town like any other town, with the bustling of people with their own personal histories, but it doesn't seem capable of giving this bustling a semblance of reality. And then, all of a sudden, there is the police station, unmoved by all that crowding and gesticulating, with the dignity of centuries of architecture upon it. Thanks to it, the place becomes a place, the town becomes a town, the people become people, life becomes life.

Nor did I know that the stories architecture tells could be so intense, so real. This is not a story of geometry, proportions, colors, forms—it is a story of reality. It cannot be retold, you must experience it. It is a local story that is all about life in Almere. But it does not go into that life—the police station could be anywhere, or anything. It would tell the same story every time, but always in a different way.

But this is not about the police station in Almere, although it too could be regarded as a public building (even if the local police force evidently does not regard it as such), like the Dance Theater and the Netherlands Architecture Institute. I just wanted to introduce it as a yardstick to measure the reality value of architecture, something like the concrete realization of the constructivist swimming pool, of which Koolhaas himself said that it was his yardstick for the authenticity of his architecture.

If we were to let ourselves be persuaded to analyze the story linguistically, we would be able to recognize in it, without difficulty, the same construction plan, the same components, the same tricks, we find in the other designs: the lines of the plan, the composition made up of fragments, the opposition of the horizontal and the vertical, the independence of the architectural elements, walls, windows, pillars, the same play of indoors and outdoors, construction and meaning, all brought together in a single arrangement, as if that was the way it should be, and no other way would do, with nothing arbitrary about it.

[...] If architecture does not tell us about itself, but about everything that is happening in and around it, there is little chance of running out of things to say. The last story is the most beautiful, the story of the Netherlands Architecture Institute in Rotterdam: architecture that dedicates its story to architecture, a cycle. The simplicity is disarming. In a single arrangement, the most diverse, contradictory functions are related to one another, without having to sacrifice their identity. Valéry would call this a "heady mixture." Whereas in the dominant landscape of The Hague the choral composition of the Dance Theater was appropriate, the disparity that is Rotterdam is crystallized in a simple figure that brings together all its surrounding without affecting its openness and diversity, a masterly move, a transparent construction, without mass, as clear as it is elusive, an eel.

The discovery lies in the inclined, triangular roof, a floating roof that changes position continuously. It supports, and is supported by, a closed black tower, the fixed point that wavers. Here too, of course, the facades are all different, but they are still just facades. With the receding angles, they act as independent transparent or semitransparent surfaces, not as an enclosure around a space. In their very precision, all the meanings turn into their own opposite, and hold both meanings together.

The roof and floor, the site, the town square, that is where it is happening, but it's happening elsewhere, too. Because the definition of one square, inside, also defines the spaces on the outside. Everything follows from the first move, developing the program with such strict logic that, without wishing or seeking to, just goes on furnishing total surprises. Buildings and fragments of buildings, real and imaginary, move in this open structure like independent personalities. But, unlike The Hague, the building itself does provide his own framework here.

The archive tower, the *kaâba*, we have already mentioned, with its mass, impenetrable, unassailable, the weigh of the past, dangerously sloping, almost menacing. And opposite, a tower of air, not oriented toward the inclined roof, but mirrored in the flat floor. Both break open the platform, the other's reflection, but also the reflection of the open, light structure and the closed, heavy, precious volume of the platform. "The platform symbolizes possession, collection and research." It is "installed in a triangular form, in such a way that it generates the remaining elements of the program." These are quotes from the architect's explanation.

I would in fact have done better to copy this explanation, because it is impossible to imagine a more correct, more significant analysis. It tells the story—in words this time—of architecture in a direct, irrefutable manner. A good story is always irrefutable. But you have to be willing or able to listen to it. A variation on a theme by Borges: "It is not necessary to be deaf or to close your ears if you do not want to listen, we hear the things from memory, as we think from memory, repeating identical stories and ideas." Rem Koolhaas's story of architecture is not a story from memory, it is not a story to read yourself to sleep with.

THE NETHERLANDS ARCHITECTURE INSTITUTE AS A SCRIPT

Herman Kerkdijk, Arthur Wortmann

Forum 4 (1988), 39–45.

[...] One of the most important characteristics of a script is that it precedes its ultimate realization: the script is there before the film. It offers a framework within which everything is still possible. That is why we do not want to look upon the design by OMA in terms of a building. Of course, all sorts of things could be said about the proposal that has been made, but that does not necessarily mean that the design has been thought out in terms of a building. What we would like to go into here, is the design as an extremely intelligent articulation of possibilities which, almost casually, has resulted in a building. Thoughts about the ultimate result, the building itself, seem to have been postponed until the very last moment. Not until then does the design take on definitive shape, not until then are the different scenes edited. "Where there is nothing, everything is still possible. Where there is architecture, hardly anything is possible."

But, paradoxically enough, a form has been created that is characterized by a certain "formlessness." This does not mean that form is lacking; after all, the design has a triangular form and not a round or rectangular form. It means that the form resists reduction to a single interpretation. This is apparent, for instance, in the way in which the building, through its simple form, meets the demands of urban development by the varied use of different kinds of glass. The facade facing the park is made of transparent glass, the facade facing the Rochussenstraat is made of white colored fiberglass, reinforced polyester and corrugated iron plate and the entrance facade is made of tinted green glass. This creates a fascinating and differentiated aspect of three facades which present an ever-changing perspective. This is reinforced by the fact that the triangular shape and the archive tower have been slightly tilted. That is why this design, despite its simple form, evokes a variety of images which appeal to a strange mixture of simplicity and complexity, predictability and surprise. Because of these contradictory experiences the design seems to escape aesthetic judgment, which, after all, still implies the moral distinction between beautiful and ugly. These categories are, as it were, neutralized in the design by the "ease" with which it can be explained in both ways, depending on taste. But Koolhaas is not interested in beautiful or ugly.

He is rather more interested in an immoral form of architecture, in which both the beautiful and the ugly are absorbed by the fascination for a kind of architecture which is open to the many possibilities that the program potentially contains. We only have to imagine the possibilities of the auditorium: when some architectural event has attracted too many people, the dividing curtain can be opened. The auditorium now becomes part of the hall. This open auditorium, together with the ramps in the hall and the space of the café on the stage, has now literally become a party hall, enabling everyone to see and hear the speaker on the landing that protrudes from the archive tower. The same holds good for the possibility to use, when necessary, the big hall and the small hall together with the room containing the permanent collection as one big exhibition space.

In short, this very susceptibility to the often unexpected and ever-changing everyday events creates a quality in the design which is typical for the living city of today. The design is like a city: it creates a rich and contradictory area of potential and everyday relations. This urban dynamism is also present in the museum concept. It is not the location that matters but the circulation. The museum is reminiscent of the modern museums with their white walls, but also of the endlessly expandable spiral-shaped museum of Le Corbusier. There is no gravitational center. There is no special place for the highlights of the collection, there is only room for a succession of highlights.

Koolhaas has been criticized for the double incidence of light in the museum part of the building. This incidence of light reminds one of houses with through rooms, the somewhat frugal Dutch version of the continuous space. Not only can this museum with the through hall be interpreted as a translation of the desired "open house" character of the institute, but also as a typically Dutch variant of the modern museum.

Because of the open character of the building, its long lines and its wealth of potential and everyday relations, we might call it an architectural theater rather than an architecture museum, a theater of architecture, a space of looking and being looked at. Let us imagine that we are in the café on the stage enjoying a drink and looking down, to one side, through the patio, into the room of the director of the institute. Koolhaas is unique in his understanding of the consequences of the program and in his ability to integrate these consequences in a design in which these possible and impossible events may simply take place. The architecture, however, need not lose its identity in these events.

At the same time, his design is a comment on the traditional ability and desire of architecture to limit these possibilities through a process of formalization and sometimes symbolization. This is not only apparent in the organization of the program, in which there are a number of obvious references to the free ground plan of Le Corbusier, but also in the way in which the black concrete archive tower is made to follow the tilt of the roof. We could ironically interpret this making fun of the law of gravity as the unsteady balance of history, from which we cannot derive any certainties. At the same time, the tilt immediately relativizes the symbolic interpretation of the tower as a tombstone.

The design is so seductive because it allows all these possibilities and interpretations. Koolhaas commentary of his design must also be understood in the light of the seductive nature of interpretation. The "silly" way in which he sometimes legitimizes certain aspects of his designs conceals his true motives. His explanation of the tilting roof is a good illustration of this: "When one drives into the city, the sloping roof on the Rochussenstraat announces the density of the center. Along the Mathenesserlaan the vanishing point of the institute marks the entrance of Boijmans Van Beuningen and along the Jongkindstraat the slope 'forces' the city dweller to the park." These and similar formulations are perhaps intended to convince principals of the logical build-up of the building, but in fact they are clever excuses for not having to reveal the true reasons, or to reason away the irrational aspects of the design.

It is in the nature of principals to demand explanations. Koolhaas could have supplied us with an interesting commentary on the theoretical background of his architecture, but the scriptwriter in him has chosen not to burden his public with this. The public does not want a labyrinth of meanings, the public wants to be entertained. This design illustrates how good scriptwriters succeed in hiding their meanings underneath the entertainment. The way in which Koolhaas legitimizes the columns in the museum is also ambiguous. If the space of the Nationalgalerie is too undifferentiated for architectural exhibitions—as Koolhaas says—the adding of the abstract system of columns is far too weak a justification. Why not make a Soane Museum, a museum like a house, with different types of rooms, each with a shape and an atmosphere of its own?

Koolhaas is not only unwilling to reveal his real motives, he also hides them behind simulated explanations. They are doubly hidden: they are secret. [...] We are allowed to interpret. We can take Koolhaas at his word, test the functionality of his plan, regard his design as a dialogue with the Nationalgalerie or as an amusing reference to Pisa. The scriptwriter remains in the background. [...]

SYNTHETIC NIGHT SKY: APARTMENT HOUSE AT CHECKPOINT CHARLIE

Alexander Tzonis, Liane Lefaivre

Memory and Invention: Architecture in Europe since 1968 (London: Thames & Hudson, 1992), 236–37.

Checkpoint Charlie Housing in Berlin is located on what used to be the American-Sector side of the border-crossing between East and West Europe on Friedrichstrasse, an important section of historical Berlin, which was torn apart by the building of the Wall in 1961. The consequences of the Wall for this location were, on the one hand, an urbanistic trauma and a mutilated city anatomy, and, on the other, a deeper functional pathology: that of a way of life involving Berlin's very special "border activity"—separations, escapes, shootings, the trading of secrets, blackmailing and, last but not least, authoritarian policing, customs and debriefing. This project was intended to facilitate such bureaucratic functions.

Historians one day will give an account of to what extent other types of "border activities" went on in the building itself. Zenghelis believes that "the program is the generator of architecture," it "provides architecture with its visual aesthetic, the action of its plan and section ... and subsequently with the sensuous materiality of its finish." Thus, in the midst of a "void" in a "landscape of hoardings, sheds, viewing towers, car movement and manning posts," Zenghelis, with the single-mindedness and diligence of a cool dirty realist, designed "an anti-monumental border facility" with no intention of beautifying or displaying any moralistic message.

The whole "frontier" universe is on ground level: a tarmac, bus concourse, control booth, with all the backstage paraphernalia. Once above the first level of the complex, the drama and the special services of the building are over. The rest of the project accommodates "normal life": housing of mixed type in accordance with the city's range of urban dwelling standards. This residential part grows vertically above Checkpoint Charlie, set back from the street and away from the view of the Wall, forming a kind of roof above and beyond its policing functions.

The iconography of the project at ground level transfers American-born, "Truman-era" roadside structures to an urban setting and reflects the fact that the bare function of the facility, stripped of its political and social connotations, is ultimately to channel vehicles in and out. Given this fact, the choice of image was easy: "US Route 1," the only original iconography of highway architecture, which, thanks to Robert Venturi and Denise Scott Brown, is properly codified, at least among architects. It is expressed here in the neon-art "synthetic night sky" and the arrows pointing to the route to be followed by vehicles, the corrugated aluminum stand and the hovering metal roof clad in polished alloy.

In an ironic vein, Zenghelis conceived that once the cold war ended, "when the city is no longer divided and the wall is replaced by a leisure zone," the facility would become a supermarket, the memory of the site and its history dissolved and reabsorbed into the market-driven vigor of the new life.

NOT-SO-DELIRIOUS MODERNISM: OMA AT MAX PROTETCH GALLERY

Jayne Merkel
Art in America 4 (1988), 27–33.

[...] OMA is a world apart from the typical celebrity architect's office in which an army of well-educated, but humble draftsmen toil away in the manner of the master. Clearly, Koolhaas and OMA are also some distance from the mainstream of today's architectural establishment where sides are chosen on the basis of style. One is either postmodern (and therefore in favor of tradition, eclecticism, figuration, the classical language of architecture and putting cities back together in coherent ways) or neomodern (and in favor of experimentation, abstraction, creating a new architectural vocabulary and deconstructing or fracturing the cityscape in places to reveal its history and functions). [...] Koolhaas uses modernist forms as an available language, a language that is not entirely used up, and one which he has molded into his own dialect, with the accents on fantasy, humor and psychological inflection.

[...] Although OMA has been in operation since 1972 and has entered—and even won—a number of important international competitions (they also had a show at the Guggenheim in 1978), they are now completing their first buildings. The Netherlands Dance Theater in The Hague opened this past fall, and the Villa dall'Ava outside Paris, a block of apartments in Amsterdam, and an art museum and a transit station in Rotterdam are all under construction. Thus, the recent showing at New York's Max Protetch Gallery of photographs of the theater, a scale model of the villa and drawings of other projects had the air of a progress report. Finally it was possible to see how the radical early ideas were being translated into sheet metal, stucco and gold leaf.

The new work is more restrained, subtle, sober, abstract and classically modern, but it is just as ironic, double-coded and occasionally delirious as the earlier projects. It is still witty and full of fantastic elements. A certain Surrealism survives. It is not as blatant, literal, comic or outrageous as it was in Vriesendorp's drawings for *Delirious New York*. Instead of the Chrysler Building in bed with the Empire State Building, there is now just a suggestion: a wavy roofline on the Dance Theater, an ovoid umbrella on the roof of the Villa dall'Ava. Arp and Miró have replaced Dalí and the Hairy Who. Subconscious semiotics have supplanted the stuff that dreams are made of.

The oeuvre is now more conventionally architectural, though one of the most impressive projects in the exhibition was an urbanistic scheme for Expo '89 in Paris (now canceled). OMA's artificial landscape is organized according to a grid which creates perfectly square "territories" for each exhibitor. The model resembles the ground plan of Manhattan, but it also recalls OMA's City of the Captive Globe of 1972, and their much-acclaimed competition entry for the Parc de la Villette in Paris, 1982–83. [...] But even in the individual buildings, the office still has the metropolis in mind. Their design for the City Hall in The Hague (1986), a $100-million complex including council chambers, various city bureaus, commercial offices and shops and a public library, was a deliberate attempt to play with the idea of urban congestion. The proposal consisted of three parallel tiers of slab towers resembling a section of Manhattan skyline in the 1950s. It was intended to provide a contrived image of crowdedness, a controlled version of urban intensity, in the already densely populated but quiet and relatively low-rise capital. Different materials and types of gridded wall treatments appear on various facades—stone on the north toward the historic district, a big stainless-steel grid on the more modern south, glass curtain walls on the inside and smaller windows toward the east and west. Each tower is familiar and subtly original at the same time. The variety that normally accrues on a skyline over time is here built into the scheme, as is an enclosed public square (a tame, European version of the frenetic mall in the middle of Helmut Jahn's State of Illinois Office Building in Chicago). Although OMA won first prize in the competition, the commission went to Richard Meier, whose version is under construction.

[...] Koolhaas's attitude in the recent work is, ironically perhaps, similar to the attitude behind the work of Robert Venturi. Koolhaas delights in complexity and contradiction, but handles both with restraint. Less is not more, but more is not more either. Venturi's first book, *Complexity and Contradiction in*

Architecture (1966), was a critique of "orthodox modern architecture," but also a prescription for a more open-minded, ambivalent approach. Like Koolhaas's *Delirious New York*, Venturi's book was filled with history and humor, talked about old and new, celebrated vernacular architecture and opened the field to high and low cultural sources. But it was primarily Venturi's dismissal of the sterility and ideological baggage of modern architecture and his advocacy of ambiguity and historical pastiche that made him, not completely willingly, the father of postmodern architecture. By the time Koolhaas came along (he is forty-two, about half a generation younger), no such critique was needed. In fact, an antidote was called for—there was a need to resuscitate certain elements of modern architecture that were being dismissed along with Modernism's overarching ideology. Just as Venturi, in the wake of urban renewal, had to point out that "Main Street is almost right," Koolhaas has had to make a case for modern architecture being "almost right." [...]

REM KOOLHAAS'S BIG, SLOPPY DREAMS: IJPLEIN AMSTERDAM

Hilde de Haan, Ids Haagsma
De Volkskrant, September 9, 1988.

An initial glance tells you something big has gone up on Meeuwenlaan in Amsterdam North. Stretched out there along the Motorkanaal, diagonal to the avenue, is a long green stucco building on slender columns—almost oppressive in its simplicity. For a moment it feels, regardless of the weather, like a summer day on holiday, when you might stumble across a classic modernist masterpiece far from home. It exudes something... Power. Self-assurance. Could this at long last be that "big statement," the "breathtaking allure" so many architects dream of?

It would almost appear so. For under the building, the oppressiveness grows. A magisterial space looms up from the practically absurd emptiness conjured by the master's hand. The nothingness of it is pleasantly manipulative, as if you have wandered into a surrealistic decor. You start to feel as if you have somehow miraculously landed in the future.

As you walk across the elevated floor, you see the entrances to the storage areas disappear into the void. A black community center slides in under the apartment building to form a tier and straight up ahead rises an oval shopping island made of glass. Is it an Edward Hopper painting? A Jacques Tati movie?

This is the world of Rem Koolhaas. His firm, the Office for Metropolitan Architecture, drafted a development plan for this part of Amsterdam North in the early 1980s that deviated sharply from the mundane plans previously drawn up by Amsterdam's Spatial Planning Department, which simply carried over the village character embodied by nearby Vogelwijk. Koolhaas had an entirely different vision. He took the site's unique location on the IJ as a starting point and wanted to exploit the views of the water and the center of Amsterdam. This resulted in a neighborhood with a very unique character, consisting partly of a series of row houses diagonal to the water and partly of light-colored townhomes and apartments surrounded by green.

Although in the local parlance people quickly dubbed it "that Koolhaas neighborhood," his role in the development had, until recently, been limited to that of planning supervisor. He was saving his own architectural contribution until the end, and that is now just about finished: a school at the western tip of the neighborhood and two residential blocks with stores, a supermarket and a community center at the eastern edge. The largest residential tower, on columns, is far and away the most spectacular.

Has Koolhaas now finally managed to create here in Amsterdam North the fascinating, inspiring world of his drawings and lectures? On the surface, it would appear so. Unfortunately one is quickly hit with a sense of disenchantment, gradually followed by disillusionment.

But why? There is so much to see, after all. It is thrilling to have Havikstraat, coming in from Vogelwijk, cut crosswise through the large building block. Not only does this inventively connect the block with its surroundings (Koolhaas and his contextualism), it also produces problems that have to be solved in clever ways. For one thing, it interrupts the rows of slender columns the building rests on. So instead of that support from underneath, the building is given a round, red load-bearing framework on the roof at that particular point that has become a landmark visible all the way from the Vogelbuurt. Another intriguing aspect is the attempt made to safeguard the large apartment block from the threat of monotonousness. It has been cut into three parts: one section with gallery flats, one with residences accessed through entryways under the building in the middle and one with entrance hall flats with landings that stick out from the facade. This gives the western face, in particular, a variegated look with ever-changing nuances.

The decision to lower the ground floor in the smaller housing block to allow for an additional building story is also an interesting choice. This resulted in groups of two two-story residences stacked on top of one another, all of which have their entryways on the first floor. The living rooms of the lower units are partially underground, with excavated outdoor spaces in front and back. It's all certainly beautiful, but running through all these observations is a constant confrontation with an underlying sloppiness, incompetence and above all haughty disdain for the users. The fact that the shop thresholds are too high, requiring awkward modifications; that the exterior of the building has been finished in plywood; that the water drainage sticks straight out of the stairwells (forming puddles on the platform under the building); that the corrugated sheeting on the doorways is already dented; that the crossover points between the platform and the lower sections are an accident waiting to happen; that the steel ornaments meant to be golden are actually the color of green diarrhoea; that there are countless piss and trash accumulating corners—oh, all of that could be glossed over. This is a grand moment in modern architecture after all, right?

But the list is endless. For instance, the empty space under that long building proves a horrible blowhole; wind force 2 is strong enough to blow the shirt off your back, which is hardly conducive to shopping. And the timber ceiling on the underside of the building that rises outward as a result of the spatial accommodations acts like a gigantic loudspeaker; that does not exactly enhance city living. The oval shop spaces have their own set of peccadillos. The architect conceived of the rear side as a solid front of corrugated sheeting. Consequently not only is there no daylight in the stock rooms; any form of outside staircase is also ruled out. Anyone in need of an emergency exit will have to jump a mere meter into the depths.

These are among the many sacrifices to the design ideal. For what is one to think of the apartment floor plans, which have been subjugated in each of the two housing blocks to an unconventional placement of giant stairwells? In the smaller building this has resulted in a situation in which the bedrooms of one apartment are directly above the living room of another; in the larger building it has created a host of impractical spaces. And what to do with a front door that has no peephole or a gallery with an open grid, and all its attendant dampness, just for the fun of it? It might be asking too much to provide people a village environment to accommodate their dreams of rustic living; city living has its own demands. But it is also asking too much to have the needs of residents subjugated to the finger exercises of an architectural visionary. The fault is not Koolhaas's, but the client's, the Municipal Housing Authority. They should have intervened, should have provided better defense; they should have inspired Koolhaas to true architectural heights.

The Municipal Housing Authority will get its payback in high maintenance costs. Koolhaas, the visionary, has put his name on the line. He now risks gaining a reputation as an architectural slob who dreams big but remains far removed from the construction site.

CONSTRUCTIONAL PURITANISM: IJPLEIN AMSTERDAM

Maristella Casciato

Domus 702 (1989), 32–39.

For some years now Rem Koolhaas has been commissioned to design increasingly important works and today one can see buildings which bear the mark of his metropolitan vision which became familiar to us after *Delirious New York*. These images offered a view of the possible future, but it also was pathetically archaic—the way the world might have been if Tatlin, not Lenin, had led the revolution. Koolhaas has a large office in Rotterdam, on the top floor of a building overlooking the harbor's urban sector. Often gigantic floating cranes moor there, their long, steel truss-like arms mingling with the silhouette of the downtown buildings. This makes his imaginative designs, which are both mechanistic and urban, plausible or even familiar.

Koolhaas designed the recently completed buildings overlooking another harbor: Amsterdam's. This project consists of a public housing complex and a small school located on the dock bordering smaller one has more open, minute volumes. This second zone is bounded by the ferry terminal for downtown Amsterdam and it consists of alternating rows of in-line residential units and "urban villas." The latter building type has been very successful in Holland recently; they are low buildings with more than one apartment per floor situated around a central stairway.

The district's other sector has a triangular layout. Here, all the units are low, parallel (mostly row) buildings separated by narrow streets and small public gardens. A triangular piazza is located in the center. A strip of greenery used as a park divides the district in two. A red asphalt pedestrian path winds through the whole complex and links the triangular piazza to the ferry terminal. [...]

In accordance with OMA's scheme, different buildings have been designed by different architects. (This plan also called for colored facades.) OMA designed the key elements for the triangular area of the site: the two residential units at the triangle's base and the small school at its apex. This portion of IJplein has a very regular appearance since it consists of a sequence of streets running perpendicular to the waterfront with row houses and their gardens on each side. All this was conceived and realized with extreme sobriety and markedly geometric simplification, almost in a return to the districts designed by the early rationalists.

The first building, located at the site's edge, is an in-line unit containing apartments on the upper four stories. The ground floor is completely open with a succession of round columns on one side. It is a covered street where a series of large containers having simple geometric forms are arranged apparently at random. They house shops and collective facilities. The second building, situated opposite the first on one of the pedestrian streets, is entirely residential and it is one story lower. The elevations are elementary, linear and repeated. The stairs animate the buildings' appearance: at the lower levels they are outside and perpendicular to them. These stairs, above all, that look like aerial piers sticking out of the buildings' bellies, give this complex the stress on separated elements which mark Koolhaas's work.

The construction quality is poor, but this is not really the designers' fault. It is due to the government's public housing policy based on cutting costs, a policy which is generating a lot of shoddy new buildings in Holland.

The school has the same spare design as the housing. It has two different units: the oblong one accommodates the classrooms and the other, housing the gym and other facilities, consists of two rectangular volumes that interpenetrate. The exterior is in galvanized aluminium and black or gray brick. This treatment gives the school the appearance of a tough and naive object so dear to Koolhaas. It is more like a metropolitan strip then a scenario from real life. But the striking thing is the forced exclusion of any attempt to mediate, to be likeable. This work is bare, cut to the bone, with the severity of a prototype or a mass-produced object, though the use of trendy colors and materials does make it a little more appealing.

On the whole, this is an emblematic example of current Dutch architecture. Caught between growing economic restrictions on public housing and the drying up of the last masters' inspiration, it seeks again that mixture of constructional puritanism great half a century ago. This exciting mixture has not been found since then.

FOR A BETTER NETHERLANDS: *THE FIRST DECADE*

Herman Selier
NRC Handelsblad, March 3, 1989.

The Boijmans Van Beuningen Museum has an exhibition opening today devoted to the work of the Dutch architect Rem Koolhaas and his Office for Metropolitan Architecture in Rotterdam. Koolhaas is probably the most famous architect our country has at the moment, but that fame stems not so much from projects that have been actually built as from his ideas and controversial designs.

In the two galleries the Boijmans has allotted to OMA, the projects built by architect Rem Koolhaas are equally represented with those never realized. They have, for example, the acclaimed competition design from 1978 for the extension of the Dutch Parliament buildings in The Hague, which, while it may not have been awarded, was imaginative enough to ensure the OMA collective's breakthrough. The firm received so many design commissions as a result of that competition that it had to find some real office space, where about twenty people were soon busy working.

In the years that followed, a pattern emerged that can be summed up in the quip—hardly flattering to Koolhaas—that every Dutch city of any significance must have an unbuilt design of his lying around somewhere. That is what happened to the plans for modernizing the Koepel Prison in Arnhem, for an apartment complex (planned height of 72 meters) on Boompjes quay in Rotterdam and for an office tower on Churchillplein and his design for the new Architecture Museum, both also in Rotterdam. There has always been a wide admiration for the spirituality of his designs, rich as they were in historical associations, while embodying a modern urban lifestyle full of uncertainties and surprises. Some labeled it yuppie architecture, but for Koolhaas it was not about "creating forms, but creating a space for life scenarios that leave open as many options as possible."

"This exhibition was an occasion for me to draw up a sort of balance sheet of ten years of work in the Netherlands," says Koolhaas on a Sunday morning in his London flat. "It is an inventory. I believe the Netherlands would be a better place if at least some of those plans had actually materialized, and I say that with more stoicism than bitterness."

People can decide for themselves what it means that the metropolitan ambitions proclaimed by Koolhaas in his models, design drawings and other visual presentations have been almost systematically renounced. One plausible thought is that the Netherlands may simply be too small for a man who obtained much of his architectural inspiration in America in the 1970s and modeled himself after utopian Russian architects such as Tatlin and Leonidov. At the moment, he is working on projects in France, Switzerland, West Germany and Japan, and when asked, he does not rule out the possibility that OMA may someday relocate abroad.

Koolhaas *has* made attempts to adapt to the limitations of the Dutch situation. Without a nearly limitless flexibility and inexhaustible patience on his part in dealing with obdurate conditions, it is unlikely that any of his plans would have been realized. The execution of his design for the Netherlands Dance Theater on Spui in The Hague came off successfully, despite complications such as the construction site being relocated from Scheveningen to the center of town and a drastic expansion of the building volume for the same budget. Although foreign critics likened it to the Institut du Monde Arabe in Paris by Jean Nouvel, which was completed in 1988, Dutch architecture critics (to the extent there is such a thing, given only the occasional review) generally had little good to say; "extremely plain on the outside and too many fanciful excesses on the inside" was their disappointed assessment.

Similar recriminations were hurled upon completion of his apartment building on Motorwal, part of the IJplein development in Amsterdam North. This time he was even accused of "sloppiness, incompetence and… haughty disdain for the users." Never mind that the building process was backed by years of public input from the future residents and the end result won a social housing award. Apparently people expected more from the man who gave architectural thinking in the Netherlands such a tremendous jolt with his book *Delirious New York* (1978).

"One disadvantage of my eloquence is, of course, that I'm constantly being hit over the head with my own pronouncements," says Koolhaas sardonically. "In the 1970s most of the architects of my generation lived in a world of almighty dreams, as if it were possible to raise entire cities and landscapes out of the ground at will. That kind of ambition only led to marginalization, to disappointment and embitterment. I have always tried to be realistic."

He talks enthusiastically about a project in Lille OMA is currently working on, which necessitated another expansion of the offices in Rotterdam by half a floor. Huge opportunities exist there thanks to the fact that it sits in the infrastructural crosshairs of the new Channel Tunnel (1993) and the TGV connection being frantically developed.

OMA is also at work in Japan, another context that deviates sharply from the Netherlands. "In the Netherlands, outside the Randstad, you can still buy an entire football field for a mere hundred thousand, but in Japan prices are so high that the building itself amounts to just a small percentage of the cost of the land to build it on," Koolhaas explains. "You could, in a manner of speaking, lay down gold floors without increasing the overall construction costs by more than a relative fraction. Those low land prices in the Netherlands almost force you to put down shit, which is then wrapped in mirrored glass so that it looks somewhat presentable. Thus we are left with architecture that is the twentieth-century equivalent of the nineteenth-century Wild West, Main Street in Utah—a false facade with nothing behind it."

When Koolhaas won the Maaskant Prize in 1986, the jury report specifically mentioned that he was being awarded the prize in part for his role in initiating a fundamental debate about the nature of modern architecture. He is still fulfilling that role as a visiting professor at TU Delft and has also been working for the past year on a new book called *The Contemporary City*, an analysis of the growth experienced by Paris, Tokyo and Atlanta in the past twenty years.

"That development might at first glance seem purely chaotic, because it lacks any form of cohesion in a classical sense. But within every form of chaos are new forms of order and cohesion waiting to be discovered. Order might only occur sporadically, in small enclaves, like little islands in a sea of disorder. That is the essence of our current Western culture and architects are well advised to accept it as their starting point. The alternative is impotence."

For the time being, the Netherlands is still stuck with him. He is building the Rotterdam Kunsthal and the Museum Park that will lead along the Boijmans Museum to the new Architecture Museum by Coenen. In Amsterdam, work is progressing on Byzantium (commissioned by project developers MBO and the Netherlands Municipal Building Fund), a complex of shops, office space and sixty-three apartments—capped by five showpiece penthouses with views of Vondelpark and Leidseplein. The most expensive of these will go for more than a million guilders. And the latest project, announced earlier this week, is a plan for a Sports Museum to be located in the Flevo polder.

His work will continue to be controversial for the foreseeable future, though. Koolhaas remains provocative because of his radical choice for an uncontrollable modern world full of discontinuities, contrasts and contradictions, a vision of the future that makes many people uncomfortable. "My scenarios imply that nothing will ever be stable again," he says. "It's a world in which you could just as well live in a hypermodern building as in a sod house. The utopists of the 1920s struggled with the problem of how their modern world could encompass everyone. That dream is long dead."

THE STIGMA OF BEING MODERN

Koos Bosma, Hans van Dijk
Archis 3 (1989), 46–51.

Just minutes after the tape recorder is turned on, Rem Koolhaas protests about the tone of the interview. "Wait a minute. What are your intentions with this interview?" Our first few questions were about the Dutch reaction to OMA's work. Koolhaas thinks the abundant attention he has generated in the media harbors a secret wish that his comments will take a controversial or shocking turn. "I have to be careful," he says. "If I feel like pouring my heart out, I'd rather do it in written texts. What I want to do with you guys is talk about the work." Koolhaas, who three years ago publicly expressed the general desire repressed by so many for the return of the architect as visionary, has been working with a dozen or so of his staff on a visionary plan for Lille. But he claims the freedom, in this discussion as well, to not be tied to visions he may have previously put forward, no matter how zealously. He is not out to illustrate theories; nor does he want to become imprisoned in insights he may have verbalized before. Despite his gift for elocution, the architect proclaims the importance of the subconscious and wants the qualities of the work to speak for themselves.

[...]
We have surmised that, after the disappointing experiences of this past year, you are starting to develop a somewhat fraught relationship with the Netherlands.

I'll put it as neutrally as possible: if you weigh the effect of our presence in the Netherlands in terms of the number of designs realized, then it is minimal. That is one of the reasons the exhibition emphasizes the Dutch work. I hope it raises questions for people when they see what we have proposed over the course of ten years and what actually became of it all.

The layout of the exhibition includes a sealed cabinet containing seven unrealized projects in the Netherlands, encircled by columns as anchorages for exhibiting your most current proposals. We interpret that as an acerbic nod to your rejected design for the Architecture Institute.

Purely coincidental. The abortion of the Architecture Institute project was, of course, a catastrophe for us. It served to amplify the implicit questions we always wondered about: What impact does our work have in the Netherlands? What reactions does it elicit—in other words, what purpose does our presence here serve?

[...]
Your comment that an architect must somehow tap into the uncontrollable forces like an accomplished surfer riding a wave is well known. But there's a very fine, wavering line between that and being helplessly dragged under by those forces. Helmut Jahn called project developers the Medici of this century; you just indicated that they are an inescapable part of the reality of any architect working today.

It is indeed a risky position. If you jump in, you will inevitably fall every now and then and be carried under. But then the role of the critic is not to merely proclaim that a building is not good or that someone has fallen off his surfboard, but to also explain what a fiasco like that says about the forces of the wave itself.

If those project developers are so dominant, how can you continue to insist that the Modernists' project can still be realized after a sixty-year hiatus?

What makes you think I want that? I never claimed that.

Certain concepts dating from the 1920s could be realized by project developers today. The question is whether those are the most interesting concepts. The north-south axis you draw in your plans for the Bijlmermeer references buildings by Le Corbusier, Mies, Libera and so forth that originated in the 1920s, even if just on paper.

You need to clearly understand what the status of a plan like that is: it is an urban planning proposal that requires some form of illustration. One of our tactics involves economizing on imagination, the point being to only have to invent what actually needs to be invented. We demonstrate the other 90 percent in the form of a straightforward selection, "the best" of the existing reservoir of ideas and realities. [...] I can't imagine conditions under which the slab and the tower, as extant elements, will become outdated.

But you are constantly positioning yourself as "modern" compared to your counterparts.

No, I am not "constantly" doing that. I've been trying for a good three years now to shake off that stigma of being modern, for the very reason that it is so casually bandied about in the Netherlands. That is also why the book I'm now writing is not about the modern city, but about *The Contemporary City*. All I am interested in is how cities are doing at this very moment. Our work will probably always carry evidence of an admiration for, or affinity with, certain architects who worked earlier in the century. But in my view our work is increasingly less "modern" in the nostalgic sense of referring back to the 1920s or 1930s. I don't know how apparent it is for the outside world, but we—at least I—have started on an exploration of entirely different matters. That means that my interest in the 1950s and 1960s should not be interpreted as an effort to revive the ambitions of the 1920s. I just want to see what happens when certain utopian ideas from that era materialize much later, under realistic conditions.

If they are robbed of their utopianism and tested in reality?

No, they're not tested; they're simply built. And I want to know what their qualities are. The United Nations building in New York is surely no test. It's just that it was built. And that forces certain qualities to come to light.

[...]
When you talk about the 1950s and 1960s, are you primarily concerned with the aesthetics or also the social context, the way in which things were planned, the regulations, et cetera?

I'm really concerned with the planning and regulations. I am not at all interested in the aesthetics, at least not as some separate aspect of the architecture. It is not as if I look at a panorama from that period and pick out a few themes. As an architect and urban planner, you are interested in all of the topics out there. You can see how certain themes were previously broached, then recklessly thrown in the rubbish bin, but also triggered extremely interesting approaches that are relevant retrospectively. That explains my interest in Team 10. The 1920s, as you may now realize, are a station I am relieved to give a wide berth and leave behind.

But what does that shift consist of? When you designed the IJplein, you deployed several subdivision methods for the terrain, perhaps as part of an experiment. You saw what was available and, to put it simply, looked at what fit where.

No, I looked at the different implications of different actions. Because everything already fit.

But if you adhere to the principles of the 1950s and 1960s, how can you even take up such a method?

I hold the same position I always have. I haven't adopted some new 1950s-based approach. The IJplein is the classic example of a commission that was not suited to us in any way, shape or form. It was so out of keeping with what we represented at the time, the things we had done and what I had said. Yet those kinds of projects, too, are incredibly interesting for an architect. Even before we started on it, we realized we would only be able to achieve a small percentage of our goals.

[...]

If you look at the projects independently, it would appear that you are working on several levels at once. Ten years ago everyone would've claimed that OMA's architecture was not spatial. Yet, the Architecture Institute and second design for the Kunsthal are incredibly spatial.

I personally thought the house in Miami was very spatial, and even the Floating Pool. But maybe that was a different kind of space. I do indeed think that our work in the last three years has acquired different qualities, based on a host of experiences—some good, others not so good. We have experimented heavily and sometimes embarked on things we couldn't really control the results of. But we learned a lot and recent experience has shown that we are able to use that to enrich our work. But I barely know what to say about all that, because I continue to believe that the subconscious plays an important role in it all. The last couple of years I've become more personally involved in the designs, in the sense that projects such as Melun-Sénart, the City Hall in The Hague, the courtyard houses and the Architecture Institute are more personal than those from the recent past. That is something I want to pursue more actively.

OMA IN HOLLAND

Mil De Kooning
Vlees & Beton 12 (1989), n.p.

mdk: While OMA's work has generally elicited a wide range of reactions in the Dutch press, a certain critical overtone has been dominating of late—a criticism related not to the work itself, but presumed pretensions ascribed to it. [...] The most direct attack is in the catalogue for the competition for the Architecture Museum: "The lack of a true metropolitan environment in the Netherlands brings with it the risk that Koolhaas's buildings will be no more than a prima donna's empty, wasted gesture in the provinces." To start with, is it not astonishing that the last comment was made by staff of the museum competition?

rk: Shameful, inconceivable. The fact that they would formulate it like that in their own catalogue four months before the competition deadline points to a level of exasperating openness. In a civilized country, you'd be able to sue them. The assertion that "the Netherlands is not the right environment" for our kind of ambition comes across to me as nothing more than an attempt to offload their guilt: whereas critics and journalists possess a sort of collective power or at least an ability to change things about the Dutch situation, they use that kind of stance as an excuse for the fact that the situation—despite their presence and input—is "intractable." They create an alibi for themselves for the fiasco they themselves are causing. My sense is that it all goes back to *Delirious New York*. That book has become my own Procrustean bed: when we create something understated, we aren't grandiose enough; when we design something grandiose, it's not modest enough. So it's like an enclosure, a limitation of our scope, both upwardly and downwardly—and it creates a no-win situation.

[...]
mdk: How much of an impact do all those opinions and sentiments, those pseudo-arguments and that rabble-rousing, have on you?

rk: One of the means by which I have managed to survive the past ten years is through an ever-growing expansion of my subconscious, in the sense that I don't want to waste much time thinking about all that. Otherwise it would lead to a complete crisis, I think. I also don't want to become especially irritated or depressed by what is said or written. Some architects believe that their friends should only write positive things about them. I don't believe that at all. Enthusiasm is usually boring. But the tricky thing is that it contributes to a myth that becomes an ever-growing obstacle. Because through a combination of not only having our ambitions as a whole declared impossible, but also being told that we are not capable of achieving or materializing the aspirations we do have, a double contradiction emerges between megalomania and incompetence, which becomes ever-more entrenched and thus ever-more complicated to overcome. And what obsesses me is that that runs counter to my own observations, namely that a project like the Dance Theater is an insanely good, cleverly detailed building—which by the way is also how foreigners view and think about it; not only was there no better way to tackle those constraints of affordability, scale, ambition, modernity and so forth, but it is in fact an active investigation into a different form of architecture, a different form of materialization, a wholesale rejection of the fetishism of the detail.

[...]
mdk: Most of the commentators are oh-so careful. Following the decision in the museum competition, Van Dijk wrote, "The choice of architect was surprising but not disappointing." I prefer Klotz, who felt the choice of Coenen over OMA was utterly scandalous. [...] I would gather that even the assurance that your project will "make history" more than any of the other submissions, offers little consolation.

rk: None at all; just the opposite. It's a disgrace! An unbelievable disgrace, a complete disaster that our project is being dropped. The deliberateness of it all, too: it's as if no one harbors any ambition whatsoever. This is the intentional evasion of a stringent contingency and shameless spurning of an opportunity.

[...]

mdk: To return to the perceived lack of metropolitanism in the Netherlands: in a conversation with former State Secretary Brokx, you talked about the unrealized potential of the Randstad in that respect.

rk: If you total up the populations of Amsterdam, Rotterdam and The Hague, alone, it comes to one-and-a-half to two million people. Around and in between, the Randstad has about six million. That means there are four-and-a-half million "lost" Dutch people, who live "nowhere" and constitute a metropolitan potential that is only presently felt in the traffic jams and congestion on the motorways—a perfect metaphor for a country that refuses to acknowledge reality, a nation that prides itself on its role as a conduit and yet is permanently blocked. It is utter nonsense to assert that a region where six million people live is "not a metropolitan environment." The Netherlands could in fact realize a different form of metropolitanism, one not necessarily accompanied by mass density and therefore by definition preeminently modern. Because the decoupling of density and mass is, in my opinion, the most important feature of the second wave of modernity, in which a growing number of media and resources will replace and eliminate architecture.

mdk: You hold up Atlanta as a model for the Randstad.

rk: That reference was relevant because the conditions are comparable. In Atlanta they have started a form of development in which the nothingness is preserved as nothingness, punctuated only by occasional moments of intensity. The thinking behind it is, among other thing, to achieve an unbelievable mass density at attractive sites—a lake, for example—each with their own autonomy, shops and so forth. The interventions might be extremely intensive but are nevertheless manifested in a discrete fashion: because of the concentration, there is a limited consumption of land, so the attractor remains intact. This to me speaks of a superior logic because it's not frustrated by all sorts of antiquated concepts. The situation in the Netherlands is the complete opposite: the renewal around the cities occurs through this constrictive system of effete growth rings. Meanwhile an absurd amount of energy is being dumped into policy and "control": entire departments devote all their resources to stubbornly attempting to control the impossible, instead of coming up with concepts for manipulating the forces actually—and irrevocably—at work. The result is that everything that is currently attractive becomes pure squalor in the shortest amount of time—like King Midas in reverse.

mdk: These were among the problems you wanted to focus attention on at *Whether Europe*, the international symposium you organized in Delft in 1988.

rk: We wanted to examine whether a new sensibility was emerging in European architecture. Then you notice that in Spain—following a decades-long Rossi freeze—

Mateo is working with analogue concepts, for instance, and a circle is forming around *Quaderns*. In France there is evidence of far-reaching explorations in certain areas—though they may still be a bit overly imbued with a tendency toward classical Modernism. And in Germany Kollhoff is developing fascinating new ideas together with students in Zürich.

mdk: It is almost as if a "front" is forming to tackle—as in the days of Giedion and Le Corbusier—the "true, contemporary problems."

rk: Interesting parallel. Some of our contact has indeed grown out of questions surrounding the need for or feasibility of building a front. Of course, we have become extremely skeptical: compared to the early part of the century, all innocence and naiveté has been lost. But even if every form of nonambiguity has been definitively ruled out, it might still be possible to once again have an ideal opportunity, at this moment, to collectively develop some targeted polemics concerning specific topics.

[...]
mdk: Overall, OMA appears to be in high demand; every municipality seems to want to work with you.

rk: There are two curves. One represents this persistent reservoir of distrust that must be overcome in ever-varying circumstances, a skepticism whose source shifts constantly—and it is exactly because of that shifting that one is forced to conclude that it is not the subjects themselves that are up for discussion, but that the distrust stems from something else: an aversion as part of a more complex whole. On the other hand, our renown in the Netherlands is starting to assume caricatural proportions and we are becoming subsumed in a system of absolute consumption. It is very rare to be asked back a second time by a municipality.

[...] At the same time, we have noticed a great concurrence between our shifting areas of interest and the things we are asked to do. Not that we are so progressive that we constantly make surprising discoveries; it's just that we very quickly apprehend what is going on, and that alone has a magnetic force. We have just been asked, for instance, for a study project concerning La Défense: Rocard has to develop a vision for the future of Paris and has invited three architects to help. It is of course unbelievable how that coalesces with our interests.

mdk: In a presentation you once called La Défense a highlight of modern urban planning.

rk: The least you can say about La Défense is that it saved Paris. Without this "refuge," the need for offices would have erupted in the city itself—with all the disruptions that would have entailed. Beyond that, I think the concept of a refuge took on an extremely convincing form: an encircling motorway within which restrictions were lifted as much as possible, with the orthogonality of the axes as the only guideline. I admire the robustness and primitiveness of that concept because it has withstood thirty years of further development and demonstrates that heterogeneous, somewhat "dubious," architecture can eventually create an increasingly convincing spectacle.

mdk: In his book *America*, Baudrillard compares La Défense to the American skyscrapers that beget one another into infinity and "battle it out within a space rendered dramatic by their very competition." By comparison "La Défense has forfeited the architectural benefits of verticality and excess by squeezing its high-rise blocks into an Italian-style setting, into a closed theater bounded by a ring-road."

rk: That is where the seeds of my interests lie: what exactly is that European modernity? Because whereas America—in the theoretical model—never has any "context" anywhere, Europe is by definition suffused in it: everywhere, all the time. Europe is doomed to greater ambiguity, to preserving a duality in which relationships are important. Relationships are completely futile in American architecture. That's what makes it so irritating to constantly be bound to *Delirious New York*. I've been working for ten years now on a similar investigation of European modernity.

[...]
mdk: Baudrillard's assertion rings of envy and fatalism: "America is the original version of modernity." Europe is "the dubbed or subtitled version" of that.

rk: That is what I have always maintained. But things are changing. I think something authentic is also taking root in Europe. Of course every circumstance contains some form of authenticity; but I think the ingredients can be read and interpreted in a different way at the moment.

[...]
mdk: Do you find the confabs with celebrity architects, such as in Charlottesville or Chicago, productive in any way?

rk: In addition to being an architect, I am also naturally a very curious individual. Those discussions are important because they allow you to monitor and understand the profession—and also for the simple reason that you meet other architects. One of the most pressing questions is "how can you continue to grow?" There are aspects that you can, and aspects that you can't control. And there is a definite connection between how you project yourself and the kind of work you get and execute. At the same time, you have the status quo: when you are young, you can do whatever you want, it doesn't matter, because you won't get any commissions anyway; then your predecessors die and you get everything—but by that point you're forty-five and set in your ways. All of that—all those phobias, all those interests—needs to thus be constantly honed. Another element is of course the irresistibility of observing confreres in action: sometimes it's shocking; sometimes it's inspirational. So there's a lot to it: the sociology of the profession.

mdk: You asked Gehry about his reaction to the numerous imitators of his work. What about for you?

rk: I feel as if the epigones have forced me permanently on the run; it truly is revolting. Here's another thing about the Netherlands: one of the things I detest most is the inflated vanity with which the architectural world boasts about how it resisted Postmodernism and thus managed to remain "daringly modern." In my view, in far and away the most cases that was the result of pure obliviousness. I am also shocked at how our work has somehow led to the formation of a school—or more particularly about the fact that it did not prove immune to it, complex enough to resist it. You could definitely see some of our present activities as a deliberate attempt to avoid schooling. The first version of the Rotterdam Kunsthal, for instance, is a project that has—to my view—a distinct absence of glamour, which is very important to me at the moment. And I find that true of our submission for the Architecture Museum, as well, actually. That too has a radicalism that makes it difficult to imitate—at least that's what you hope each time. You can see further evidence of the redirection in our work in the color palette: black-gray-white for the exterior and auditorium of the Dance Theater, for example, at a time when pastel-colored towers are popping up like mushrooms. So it's a very uncomfortable position to be in—and was one of the reasons I stopped teaching: I didn't want to train even more people in architecture. [...]

ARCHITECTURAL SPECIFICITY WITH PROGRAMMATIC INSTABILITY

Hajime Yatsuka
Telescope: The Printed City 4 (1989), 6–11.

[...] **hy:** It seems there are two approaches to modern architecture: one is to separate the masterpieces from the derivative, the other is to have interest in all phenomena. You seem to subscribe to the second view. Ugliness and beauty are not necessarily antithetical concerns for you.

rk: No, I also find tremendous beauty in the second-rate. (*laughter*) What has been very important for our own work is the point where modernity assumes the character of a popular style. I think that is becoming more and more important to us. In the 1940s and 1950s, there was a vernacular modernity that was not polemical. On the contrary, it coincided with the whole postwar reconstruction, hence it was charged with incredibly positive connotations. And for a variety of reasons: first of all because the architects were second- or third-degree Modernists, but also because they had to work at a tremendous pace to meet a really phenomenal amount of production. The work acquires not only an elemental recognisability, but also a smoothness and neutrality which I find still very inspiring. [...] If I look at the present production of myself and my contemporaries—if I look around Japan—I have the feeling that we all try to be much too interesting, too "hyper." And that there are still some clues in those works. I cannot really judge how true it is in Japan, but in Europe and America, our postures are terribly marginal.

[...]
hy: I get the impression that you dare to design neutral buildings, unlike the Dance Theater.

rk: Yeah, that's true. But now I even think it was a mistake, for instance, to have these different colors and different textures. It would have been better to have buildings that were more homogeneous, where, let's say, shadows and light were the main differentiations. But for me this building relates to the La Villette project—also returning to your earlier question about functionalist theory. I think everything now is so indeterminate that it's an illusion to believe that you can have a theory. So, what I tried to do is in either case was to devise formulas that combine architectural specificity with a programmatic instability. I think this is terribly important to try to do today. In the La Villette project we tried it in two dimensions. The City Hall is our first three-dimensional proposal in this line of investigations. So, in that sense, I consider the former close to Team 10 investigations, in terms of clustering and in terms of their research into indeterminancy. Although they never managed to give it an architectural image that could stand on its own.

[...]

hy: Would you care to sketch a rough outline of your forthcoming book on chaos?

rk: First of all I should say I find it very scary to talk about a book which is still unwritten. But the rough outline is that over the past couple of years we are increasingly confronted with architectural situations that are hardly the result of "architects" I would recognize as such or "planning" I would recognize as such. In other words, I find that amazingly large areas of the world are right now in a state of development without recognizable connection to the profession I know. A pretty astonishing situation. These very same areas are almost universally ignored by the official profession or blanket-criticized as "nothing." Hopeless, totally ugly, forget-about-it. Based on those two notions and on my own mixed feelings that it's very hard, say, when I drive around Atlanta, to actually find things beautiful or exciting—and the same goes for the *villes nouvelles* around Paris—you could go around saying everything is ridiculous there, or you could also surrender to the feeling that maybe it's a very unique landscape that is emerging there. Maybe it's a very rich field, with a lot of potential freedom for people to live and work, etc. Anyway, I was torn between different emotions, and so basically I decided to investigate further into what was behind these reactions of mine.

The structure of the book now is to take a situation in Europe. Old Paris in the center with these rings, basically, of new satellite towns. But now these satellites have more people than Paris itself; they have more area and, of course, more construction. The same with Atlanta, for the simple reason that it's the fastest-growing city at the moment in America. Then probably Tokyo or Seoul—or maybe a combination of the two—to see how ideas of the Western city and the contemporary Western idea of modernity is modified in either case. That is a very direct reason for the book. Hence it is also a polemic addressed at large sectors of my contemporaries who have a total obsession with the center of the city; who live in a fantasy that they could ever control large areas of cities and impose plans on it. I've noted that the more they become obsessed with the center, the more they reduce the chances of anybody ever being active in the center.

[...]

hy: The Atlanta episode is very interesting, especially because most young architects in Tokyo now spend a lot of time on very, very tiny buildings. Moreover, due to skyrocketting land prices, it's not unusual for buildings to last only five or even three years. This accelerated state of building in Tokyo makes for a striking contrast to classic European cities.

rk: Well, not exactly *classic* European cities anymore. That's why it's tragic that my generation invests so much energy, really. (*laughter*)

DECONSTRUCTIVIST ARCHITECTURE: THE STABILITY OF THE ONE AND THE INSTABILITY OF THE OTHER
Mark Wigley
Deconstructivist Architecture (New York: The Museum of Modern Art, 1988), 46.

The Rotterdam project on Boompjes quay is a high-rise apartment building whose base contains communal facilities, such as a kindergarten and school, and whose top forms a street in the sky along which is a hotel, with club, health center, and swimming pool. It is located on a narrow headland between the Maas River and a parallel canal, a kind of no-man's-land cut off from the city and traversed by a major road.

The building is enigmatically poised between being essentially a single slab, a homogeneous monolith (like its neighbors), but distorted by a number of towers, and being essentially a row of discrete towers, distorted by a slab. From the river, it appears as a row of solid towers against a glass horizon; from the city, as a stone slab with glass towers attached to it.

The struggle between towers and slab opens up gaps, either as a narrow slit, a huge hole in the volume, or a complete void. Whenever these gaps appear, whenever the skin is pulled back or the volumes are punctured, a system of floating floor planes is exposed. Throughout, strong horizontal lines act as a datum against which the slab and towers play. Everything shifts, except those lines: each surface, each section, each plan is different. Tension even develops between the towers in addition to that between the slab and the towers. Each of the towers has a different angle to the slab: some fall backwards, others are contained, others twist away, while some have broken free.

At one end of the slab, a pure orthogonal tower begins to detach itself. At the other end, an angled open-steel tower has escaped altogether. It is produced by taking a section of an old bridge on the site and lifting it up to form a tilted tower. Suspended between the two—the high modernist tower and the angular constructivist tower—the slab becomes the scene of a radical questioning of Modernism. It is seen to give birth to both the stability of the one and the instability of the other. But the status of the slab is thrown even further in doubt because both of the towers related to it emerge as much from the context as from the slab itself. The identity of Modernism becomes elusive; its limits are no longer clear.

THE FALL OF THE WALL (1989–1996): THE FORCES OF THE WAVE

6

In 1985 Rem Koolhaas introduced one of his most well-known metaphors in a text in *L'Architecture d'Aujourd'hui* entitled "Elegy for the Vacant Lot," introducing the project for Parc de la Villette in Paris from 1982, and explaining its similarities with the Downtown Athletic Club in Manhattan: "This architecture relates to the forces of the Groszstadt like a surfer to the waves."[1] This sentence would become dominant in the OMA reception, repeated by Koolhaas in interviews, analyzed by critics, and republished in *S,M,L,XL* in 1995. The image of the surfer became a recapitulation of architectural practice in general at the end of the twentieth century. In the era of late capitalism, it was no longer deemed possible to oppose the forces of commercialization, of growing inequality and the dominance of the free market, together with all the forms of urbanization and suburbanization it entailed. It was better to "grant amnesty to built reality," as Laurids Ortner had already indicated in 1978.[2] All an architect could do was accept the prevailing conditions in order to surf as elegantly and intelligently as possible. When the waves did get too high, and the probability of staying upright became uncertain, this was—according to Koolhaas—not necessarily a major problem for the architect. In an interview with Hans van Dijk and Koos Bosma in 1989, he commented on his surfing: "It is indeed a risky position. If you jump in, you will inevitably fall every now and then and be carried under. But then the role of the critic is not to merely proclaim that a building is not good or that someone has fallen off his surfboard, but to also explain what a fiasco like that says about the forces of the wave itself."

In this way, critics are invited not to simply dismiss the work of OMA on moral, political, or architectonic grounds, but to use its architecture as a scalpel to dissect and to criticize the evolutions in society it is trying to embody. This could cause a new architectonic liberation, and in the case of OMA, an abandonment of the reuse of modernist strategies in favor of a larger conceptual and formal renewal. The liberation from ethical obligations could also lead, however, to the spectacle of an architect struggling to maintain his dignity, while commercialization, privatization, and exploitation pullulate, and while architecture is forced to fulfill ever-increasing demands concerning creativity, attention, and iconicity. This tension may exactly have been what Koolhaas was after, and what he offered, in a nearly self-sacrificing way, to interpreters and to the outside world. The question was, of course, that of criticality: is an architect like Koolhaas simply opportunistic, or is he able to reveal problems and to clarify circumstances thanks to his complicity and overidentification?

The invitation to answer this question in depth was above all taken on in the United States. OMA was discovered by American theory, at the time enthralled by French post-structuralism. Unbuilt projects from 1989 and 1990, such as the Sea Trade Center in Zeebrugge, the Très Grande Bibliothèque in Paris and the Zentrum für Kunst und Medien in Karlsruhe, had been developed in an ambience of optimism after the fall of the Wall, in view of the European unification. In 1990 they had been written about in Dutch by, for example, Bart Lootsma and Mariëtte van Stralen as "buildings with such an absolute presence they elude semantic analysis and quality judgments"—wordings that seem to announce Koolhaas's essay "Bigness" from a few years later. In the spring of 1990 the recent production of OMA was exhibited in Paris and enthusiastically reviewed by Toyo Ito. In 1991 and 1992, however, Koolhaas presented this handful of European projects to another audience, once again crossing the Atlantic Ocean. In the US, OMA was welcomed by Sanford Kwinter, Jeffrey Kipnis, Robert E. Somol, Anthony Vidler, and literary theorist Fredric Jameson, whose short-lived infatuation with contemporary architecture more or less centered around the work of Koolhaas, which he theorized as exemplary of "the space of post-civil society." The ANY conferences, organized by Cynthia Davidson all over the world between 1991 and 2000 as a set of explosions of words and ideas about architecture, were nodes of knowledge and discussion for what can be considered as the heyday of twentieth-century theory. The work of OMA was often present at these gatherings, although it proved hard to incorporate within the infinite deconstruction of Derridean theorizing.

Another French philosopher whose ideas were often applied during the 1990s to architecture (and to the work of Koolhaas) was Gilles Deleuze. His philosophy was used—to summarize roughly—on the one hand to justify a postcritical condition in which architects were exculpated from any consciousness of guilt, and on the other hand to legitimize an increasing amount of formal, structural, and computational experimentation. An important Deleuzian in OMA's bibliography is Alejandro Zaera-Polo, a collaborator of Koolhaas who contributed to the first and the second issues of *El Croquis* devoted to OMA in 1992 and 1996. "The work of OMA," Zaera-Polo concluded, "must be seen ultimately as a strategic retreat, the cessation of ideological resistance to the developments of contemporary civilization." In 2004 Zaera-Polo described how he arrived at OMA in August 1991 loaded with "a cocktail of Deleuze's materialism and Harvey's neo-Marxist globalization theory. [...] Koolhaas was amused at my attempt to wrap in pretentious new words the stuff going on in the office." Zaera-Polo realized how working at this Dutch office involved making projects, not developing theories: "Production at OMA was remarkably nontheoretical by American standards. The pressure of deadlines did not leave much time for constructing critical arguments before diving into the blue foam."[3] Critics and theoreticians were more than prepared to vouch for these constructions.

1 Rem Koolhaas, "Éloge du terrain vague," *L'Architecture d'Aujourd'hui* 238 (1985), 46. Republished as "Elegy for the Vacant Lot" in OMA/Rem Koolhaas and Bruce Mau, *S,M,L,XL* (New York: Monacelli Press, 1995), 937.

2 Laurids Ortner, "Amnestie für die gebaute Realität," *Archithese* 17–18 (1978), 31–34. An English and Dutch translation was published as "An Amnesty for Constructed Reality" in *Forum* 1 (1986), 44–48.

3 Alejandro Zaera-Polo, "Rising Ambitions, Expanding Terrain: A Scientific Autobiography," *Harvard Design Magazine* 21 (Fall/Winter 2004), 7–8.

LATEST STOP ON A GRAND TOUR

John Welsh
Building Design 957 (1989), 2.

Any lecture by Rem Koolhaas, partner in the Dutch-based Office for Metropolitan Architecture, is likely to be crowded. His lecture at the Architectural Association last Friday night was no exception. Koolhaas rarely gives public lectures and OMA's buildings are guaranteed to be of interest. Friday's lecture had the added attraction of three new projects: the Zeebrugge Sea Trade Center, OMA's Bibliothèque de France entry, and a new museum/theater in Japan. Bedford Square pavement overflowed. The stairs and entrance hall were crowded. Perching—rather than standing—room was the order of the day.

[...] Like the other competitors, OMA had only six weeks to work on their entry for the Bibliothèque de France. The library is to be twice the size of the Beaubourg center, housing five different libraries. Changes in technology threaten to render irrelevant all printed material or traditional libraries. But against such odds Koolhaas joked that the project had to be taken seriously. At first Koolhaas and his team tried to articulate the five libraries as five separate buildings. The site, surrounded by dull expanses of the mediocre, mitigated against low-rise, small-scale blocks. Instead the team became convinced that only a rationalist approach would work: a tower with libraries stacked upon each other. The problem lay in how to articulate such a block. Koolhaas showed several early ideas and models. These, like Zeebrugge and Babel, wrapped ramps around the exterior. Then the team slowly started to articulate each library as a void. This decision left the plan of each floor quite flexible because elements could lie anywhere and book stacks would surround each void. The key to such flexibility lay in the elevator shafts that rise through the building, connecting each of the five libraries without stopping at any of the storage floors.

The eventual articulation of each library became a game. The team pursued each library's logic and aesthetics, such as the loop the loop, until a form was found. Ironically the building's plans showed a remarkable similarity to its sections. "We felt like Houdini," said Koolhaas, the relief of six weeks' hard work now quite evident. "We had liberated ourselves from the most obnoxious elements of architecture."

Koolhaas took time to discuss Perrault's winning scheme for the Bibliothèque de France. He criticized its scale which, he said, would leave visitors with a staggering 1.5 km walk around the central courtyard. He suggested that Perrault had won through words rather than deeds, his phrase "une place pour Paris, une bibliothèque pour la France" satisfying a Parisian mayor and French president in turn. [...]

Zaha Hadid, standing in for Alvin Boyarsky, had welcomed Koolhaas to the AA. She introduced her guest as many things; a friend, a teacher and even a partner for a day. "It's a pity some of the AA's seventy staff and president are not here," she added. "They might learn something from him." Coates or Cook, Fior or Herron might disagree. What Koolhaas does expose is an image of the city that has yet to be built. Until OMA has done so, Koolhaas still has the modesty and the decency to present his learning curve as a thrilling adventure of a discovery.

NOT FORMS, BUT RULES: *FIN DE SIÈCLE*, OMA AT IFA, PARIS

Toyo Ito
Telescope: The Printed City 5 (1990), 74–86.

Room 1. A forest of poles, reminiscent of Koolhaas's Villa dall'Ava outside of Paris. A grouping of video monitors is set into a wall dotted with fragmented daily imagery and catch words. One pole is emblazoned with the exhibition title *Fin de siècle.* [...] Now, on to the next three rooms ...

Room 2. An interior buried in sketches. Drawings are pasted on the large tabletop, on the window, everywhere. Also on the table are bound folios of drawings for leafing through freely.

Room 3. The city planning room, with two huge models—his Parc de la Villette and Melun-Sénart plan—planted smack in the middle and plans displayed on the wall. The Villette model, at some 9 square meters, overwhelms; Melun-Sénart is noteworthy as the key that led Koolhaas to his ideas for the French library. This was surely what started him thinking about "void spaces." He himself talked repeatedly about "filling vacant terrain with signs." The Melun-Sénart model was a delight. The surface was studded with nails and glued over with wood scraps. Wires ran across both sides, along which moved electric lights. Primitive, but a lot of fun, this model was approximately 4.5 square meters in size.

Room 4. The last room is dedicated to the architectural line-up: The Hague City Hall, Zeebrugge Sea Trade Center, Bibliothèque de France and Karlsruhe ZKM. A brilliant presentation of his development. His work really becomes exciting after Zeebrugge. Earlier works, such as the Dance Theater, utilize 1950s vocabulary while trying hard to do the ordinary, but from Zeebrugge on Koolhaas takes a turn to the dynamic.

Koolhaas himself calls his Sea Trade Center "an upside-down Tower of Babel"; to me it suggested nothing so much as a butt head post to which ships tie up. But when I pointed out the similarity [...] he put on a surprised, then stern face and denied any such intention.

An ingenious model for Karlsruhe, with a Macintosh computer concealed in the base. One side of the model is a rear-projection screen for a Hypercard random mix of slides and video segments. Inside the model is a tray of loose pachinko balls that roll around constantly.

In a word, it was an extremely interesting show. Rem Koolhaas, I discovered when we were together in Antwerp, is an incredibly poetic man. He may well be an endless source of the fantastic, but absolutely never expresses his poetics emotionally. He always makes rules in order to give himself over semiotically to his fantasies. [...]

It's as if he's built up a stock of rules by which to create. At least, it's all very conscious, as if to say let's make a rule for everything—and that's very interesting. Not forms, but rules. With a city, you just have to lay down the basic ground rules and let the architects plan out the concrete details. That's virtually what he does with his own buildings.

That and his architectural awareness of "void space." Usually we Japanese deal with voids as leftover spaces between positive bodies—that is, quite literally—but with him it's the reverse. He carves it out of solidly packed masses—very European, perhaps. Take the alcoves in classical architecture: European architectural space is filled with little pockets. He's giving us the postmodern version. It's very curious, because we tend to see the whole as void at first. But he's looking at a solid; that's why he can work that way. Marvelous. [...]

What can I say? This was shoulders above any other architect's show I've seen to date. Fun, but with impact. He even has his method down for exhibiting—he had the show up in no time.

THE CLIENT AS VISIONARY: KOOLHAAS REANIMATES THE ROLE OF THE ARCHITECT

Bart Lootsma, Mariëtte van Stralen
Archis 5 (1990), 36–42.

[...] The designs for the Sea Trade Center in Zeebrugge, the Bibliothèque de France in Paris and the Zentrum für Kunst und Medientechnologie in Karlsruhe were produced during an intense period in which OMA worked on submissions for five design competitions at once, with each needing to be delivered three weeks apart. To meet that task, the office was divided up into teams; in addition, several former staff and friends were asked to come in and assist. The decision was made to work on all five projects simultaneously, while using the atmosphere of concentration thus created to not only devise pragmatic solutions, but also subject various aspects of each group's work to reevaluation, gradually fermenting a sort of tedium in the office. This pertained in particular to the "all too easily adopted Modernism," as Koolhaas puts it, and by extension to the fact that OMA's work is so insistently associated with Deconstructivism. Because of their enormous scale, by European standards, the proposals for Zeebrugge, Paris and Karlsruhe provided the greatest hope for a breakthrough, though they were considered large not so much from a planning viewpoint as in terms of building mass. That massive scale presented a number of challenges that Koolhaas tackled thematically. The main one is that apart from the fact that a large-scale building is necessarily higher, it also grows profoundly in depth, meaning that its center becomes farther and farther removed from the outer edges. As such, the exterior of the building is no longer a direct negative form of the interior in the sense of "form following function." More importantly, the form of the building then no longer communicates anything about what is happening inside it. Koolhaas expressed this thematically in the three designs by treating the interior and the exterior in each case as autonomous projects. The second implication of such a large scale is that every layer in the building is a separate entity with its own program, so that there are no direct spatial or programmatic connections between the layers themselves. This discovery had already been made in *Delirious New York* in the chapter on the Downtown Athletic Club. There the elevator enables a mechanical connection between the layers, which means they do not need to directly border on one another. While this does away with a tremendous number of the architect's duties in favor of certain freedoms, it also eliminates a great many avenues for spatial or plastic articulation. A fourth consequence of large-scale buildings that Koolhaas points out is that beyond a certain scale or mass, architecture acquires a moral certainty in terms of its meaning; because of their very scale, these buildings have such an absolute presence they elude semantic analysis and quality judgments.

The first project in this series is the competition design for the Sea Trade Center in Zeebrugge from 1989, which won first prize as announced in late March. Now that the tunnel under the Channel is being built, the people of Zeebrugge are reassessing their port's position moving forward. They want to imbue the routine business of port operations with added value by building a terminal in the harbor that accommodates multiple functions beyond the loading and unloading of ships, a terminal moreover that as a building at the edge of the sea, straddling sky and water, could become a distinctive landmark.

Koolhaas's design tackles the traffic flows first. Cars and lorries are led into the terminal itself along an S-shaped route past a combined park and playground and a drive-through restaurant with an arcade; there, the cars, lorries and walk-on passengers are separated into individual streams for boarding the appropriate vessel. This produces a spectacular interchange of roads and bridges that forms the core structure of the building, together with the spiral car park on top. "Not only is the traffic, congestion, vehicles, parking absorbed into the whole, but this highlights its endemic charm," Geert Bekaert writes in the jury statement. "The project presents a new way of looking at the things of our time."

Above the car park is a large public facility, the floor of which also spirals upward around a huge opening. At this level, the visitor is granted a panoramic view. Higher up in the building is the lobby with restaurants, bars and a movie theater, with a screen that hangs down into the open void. Up to this level, the building is essentially built along horizontal axes. The vertical elements appear above the public facility in the form of an office tower and a hotel bordering the building along the outer wall.

Housed in the top story are a conference center, casino and swimming pool, all with a fantastic view of the sea, brought into direct contact with the elements through the large glass dome enveloping the entire thing. In this concentration of diverse programs organized in such a manner that they have a catalysing effect on one another, culminating in the spectacular scenario on the top story, the design of the Sea Trade Center retains many of the classic features of OMA's architecture. What is new for this firm, though, is the way in which this complexity is captured in a compact form that rises in the coastal landscape like a gigantic sculpture. Visually, the building eludes all the familiar typologies. The only comparable plan is that for the Globe Tower designed by the inventor Samuel Friede in 1906 for Coney Island, but never built. Koolhaas presented this design in *Delirious New York* as the ultimate essence of the idea of the skyscraper: a gigantic building—whose shape, just like the Sea Trade Center, is a cross between a bullet and a sphere—that should have dominated the New York skyline in terms of both height and volume. Planned above an underground traffic interchange, it incorporated an extremely diverse range of programs into its design, just like Koolhaas's terminal for Zeebrugge: from offices, theaters and circuses to a terrace with exquisite restaurants and a lighthouse on the roof. Unlike the Globe Tower, however, which explicitly shows its giant steel structure to the outside world, Koolhaas employs a taut skin that reveals nothing about what is going on underneath, much like some of the latest Japanese-designed gadgets.

Completely in line with the theories of Baudrillard, Koolhaas's design seduces us primarily through its "foreignness," through the frivolous spectacle that it presents in a form that evades every consequentiality and symbolic order. It is precisely through its excess of banality that the design acquires the kind of "fatal" attraction, to use another Baudrillard term, that could turn it into a tourist destination.[1] One of the more intriguing things about this project for Koolhaas, as in the next two, is the role assumed by the structure itself: it not only serves to keep the building erect, but also operates on a conceptual level. One version of the Sea Trade Center allows for the building to be quickly erected in about fourteen months, pushing the emphasis to its outer appearance. In another version it would be built entirely with traditional poured-in-place concrete, but then construction would take about twelve years, turning the building process itself into a tourist attraction, with a crew of workers who would age and become grayer as the years wore on. While that is an amusing idea, it is unlikely that this second version will be chosen. For one thing, it would leave in limbo for too long the question of whether the building was indeed becoming a "Working Babel" (the motto of the competition submission) within the context of European unification. With its ironic tone, that motto is a perfect metaphor for a building in a linguistically torn Belgium claiming to be a gateway to Great Britain. "Ach, Europe," Enzensberger would say.

This nearly Enzensbergerian irony is also what makes the design for Zeebrugge more closely affiliated with both OMA's New York period and two earlier designs for Paris than the other two competition designs. At a lecture at the Eindhoven University of Technology, Koolhaas mentioned in that regard that those projects had always been characterized by a certain remoteness. He had a sense that that distance originated from the fact that he had always remained a child of the critical 1960s in his thought processes. [...] At that same reading in Eindhoven, though, Koolhaas also stated that in these three designs, he had been able to identify with the program more than ever before and that for the first time in ages he had gotten the sense that it was indeed possible to practice architecture in a fairly straightforward manner. Asked whether that was because he himself had changed, he answered: "I think it is largely due to the assignment and to changing conditions. There is something in the air. All three of these assignments demonstrate the tremendous, concrete demand for a host of urgently needed facilities which will have to somehow be managed using the traditional arsenal of the architect and the fact that one can no longer go around constantly projecting one's own ideas on to others and forcing them into things against their will. It could be that a sort of shift is under way, reanimating the role of the architect. That makes it easier, of course, to participate actively, with less reserve or equivocality. It is related somehow to a classic European sense of optimism that it is easy to get caught up in. [...] The strange thing about that is that we thus find ourselves in visionary territory. That ambition did not originate with us but—something that has not occurred in a long time—came rather from clients who are undertaking visionary endeavors."[2]

This was particularly true of the competition for the Bibliothèque de France in Paris, more so than with the design for Zeebrugge. As one of the final major projects initiated under President Mitterrand, it is a larger-scale assignment than the Sea Trade Center in Zeebrugge, a mega-library housing five separate libraries within: a media library containing videotapes, music and every film made since 1945, along with accompanying auditoriums and theaters where the material can be presented to the public; a current acquisitions library for showcasing recent acquisitions in every domain, thus both printed and audiovisual material; a reference library with materials that are not loaned out but must be consulted on-site; a catalogue library containing as many catalogues as possible from nearly every conceivable field; and a research library. A bastion of knowledge of such magnitude must naturally also have a conference center. Meanwhile, all of the libraries require a certain amount of storage and office space and moreover Koolhaas has added his trademark touch on the roof, in the form of a fitness center, garden and swimming pool. The construction site is on the Seine, near Tolbiac Bridge. As opposed to the elongated volume implicit in the competition brief, OMA designed a large cubic volume approximately one hundred meters square (as big as Von Spreckelsen's La Grande Arche at Place de la Défense) to house the libraries, with the conference center serving as a flat plinth for it. This was aimed, among other things, at being able to compete in terms of scale with the Palais Omnisports and the new Ministry of Finance building, ensuring better traffic flow and cultivating the ambitious character being expressed in the new developments around Tolbiac.

Koolhaas did originally attempt to accord each of the various libraries its own distinct form in the design but ended up deciding to imagine the entire library as a massive block of information in which all forms of information—books, videotapes, films, manuscripts or diskettes—were treated equally. Each separate library consists of a given storage volume, a given amount of office floor space and a public area. The offices are all stacked on top of one another in a strip on the north side of the building. The rest of the building is assigned to storage space, with the public areas carved out as negative forms. Since these spaces essentially hollow out the "massive" solidity of the building, they could take on any form, independent of the other public areas and the outside structure. As Koolhaas formulates it so poetically in the project description, "Floating in memory, they are like multiple embryos, each with their own technological placenta." At the same time, they present varied spatial experiences, ranging from the conventional to the experimental. The public areas near the media library look like a couple of large boulders located under the glass floor of the giant entrance hall; the public area for the acquisitions library is shaped like a cross made out of two tubes—one with an oval diameter and the other with a square one—laid out at a slight horizontal angle, with an auditorium where they intersect;

while that of the reference library is shaped like a large spiral sweeping up through the building. The public area for the research library has been given a "scientific" form, according to Koolhaas, that of the Möbius strip: the floor becomes the wall, which becomes the ceiling, which becomes the wall again and eventually the floor—a spatial shape never used in a building before. The form is not a true Möbius strip, though; it is cut open, meaning that it is not infinite. Ironically, this makes it more like the old Loop the Loop roller coaster on Coney Island (referenced in *Delirious New York*). The reference and research libraries are connected to each other by escalators running through the catalogue area, a half sphere intersected by the glass building facade which thus affords visitors a view of Paris, with the city being cast in a somewhat Borgesian metaphor as the ultimate catalogue in the library. Elevators drilled through the building at regular intervals provide flexibility in the layout, especially for the storage areas. A special construction method was devised for the building by which the conduits and systems are not built into the floors, since that would make the building much too high, but rather placed in vertical bearing slabs with cutouts at random locations to allow for the free forms of the public areas.

The facades are made of glass that is partially screen-printed in white with a cloud pattern. This treatment provides occasional, vague glimpses of the shapes of the public areas, particularly in places where the facade acts as a window. The exterior of the library is thus an ever-changing panoply of images, especially since it also reflects the clouds in the sky or lets through sections of the illuminated interior in random spots at night. This produces an almost frivolous, immaterial spectacle—the aesthetics of "intensities" advocated by Jean-Francois Lyotard in his essay "Adorno as the Devil."[3] Lyotard criticizes Adorno's theories about modern art. He asserts that while Adorno may well have recognized that modern art had put an end to "appearances" and the sensuous, the only conclusion he subsequently drew from this was that modern art—in that process by which it was gradually eliminating itself—was increasingly being used solely to gain insight. That, according to Adorno, was the critical content of art. Lyotard rejected this with the assertion that criticism always exists in relation to something and is therefore not immanent to the work. Accordingly, he claimed, "We have to leave behind this alternative: neither appearance, *musica ficta*, nor laborious knowledge, *musica fingens*; the metamorphic game of sonorous intensities, the parodic work of nothing, *musica figura*." At the same time, however, because of the gigantic scale on which Koolhaas applies it, its inherent unpredictability and elusiveness and the way in which it absorbs the play of elements, this aesthetics becomes a "sublime experience" that rules out any form of irony. It is therefore indeed regretful that the jury decided to award the project to the French architect Dominique Perrault, whose plan, while elegantly high-tech, remains mired in the staid metaphor of four towers evoking propped-open books.

The third design in the series is the competition submission for the ZKM in Karlsruhe. This is a brand-new center meant to serve as a combined laboratory and museum with workshops dedicated to various media, where presentations can be held that link and compare both traditional (painting, sculpture and theater) and new art forms (video, photography and film). Heinrich Klotz is the driving force behind the institute. At a later point in time, moreover, the same site is slated to house a college of the arts, in addition to an Intercity hotel. The vast complex is being built on a piece of land at the edge of the city located between the rail line where it enters the station and a traffic intersection, a typical peripheral zone in other words. The planning zone is situated roughly between the baroque town design of the city center and Gropius's Dammerstock housing estate. The plan also needed to address certain urban planning issues, including ensuring vehicular access to the city, intermodal options for motorists wanting to transfer to the train and a connection under the tracks to the new development from the city center and train station. Koolhaas based his design on the situation in place and the stipulated program, which he formulated thematically as a series of opposing relationships: he positions the futuristic Center for Art and Media Technology against the Classical architecture of Karlsruhe; concludes that the station is oriented toward the city and the Center toward the periphery, with part of its program aimed at artistic research and another accessible to the public; and finally deems that the design features related to the museum program must allow for mounting both traditional and experimental exhibitions. Koolhaas included the station in his design by designating the station passageway a media museum. Visitors from the old center walk past the entire history of the media arts, culminating at the main entrance to the Center, which represents the "present day." Koolhaas calls this the x-axis of his design. The y-axis is formed by the opposition between artist and public, production and demonstration.

Approached from the station, the laboratories, workshops and artist studios are in parallel zones on the left, with media studios and theaters below; to the right is a platform with the Museum of Modern Art. The museum consists of a cube of stacked stories each housing a different function: the z-axis of the design, covering the range of styles from Classical to futuristic. Underneath is a theater equipped with the most advanced modern equipment and at the top is a traditional museum gallery with skylights. Sandwiched in between are alternating stories, some marked by a Vierendeel truss structure and others with a completely open span. The core of the building, comprising various exhibition spaces, theaters, lecture halls and multipurpose areas is bounded by four zones. On the south side is a skin encasing a robot that moves along the entire height of the building, in essence replacing the traditional flytower. The robot is built of all sorts of technical equipment which, among other things, can also be used for "electronic decor" in various galleries and auditoriums, for both theater shows and exhibitions. This machine can be seen from the motorway through a transparent facade, so that the ZKM captures attention from far off.

The circulation of the building is accommodated at either end of the city side, with a system of ramps, elevators, staircases, escalators and balconies providing a splendid view of the baroque core of the city. One of the facades is also designed to allow giant laser projections from the workshops. Finally, the offices, storerooms and toilets are located in the fourth zone in a slab.

Koolhaas's design for Karlsruhe contains elements of both the plan for Zeebrugge—the way in which traffic flows are organically integrated into the design—and the plan for the French national library—the cube form, spatial organization and facade treatment. Yet it is also an entirely different building, with a pronounced technological edge. Koolhaas has called it a machine that becomes a building. To a certain extent, the design is also more fertile and successful in terms of its symbolism compared to the former designs, through its complex relationship with the city and tremendous variety of programmatic possibilities. It is hardly a surprise, then, that the jury awarded it first prize, though they requested minor adjustments in terms of the volumes and certain details.

Where the designs for Zeebrugge and Paris were characterized, respectively, by Baudrillard's aesthetics of "a lethal eccentricity" and Lyotard's aesthetics of the "sublime," the design for Karlsruhe is characterized by the aesthetics of simulation, in terms of how projections are used to produce an architectural image, and more notably by Paul Virilio's "aesthetics of disappearance": "the aesthetic of construction is dissimulated in the special effects of the communication machines, engines of transfer and transmission; the arts continue to disappear in the intense illumination of projection and diffusion. After the age of architecture-sculpture we are now in the time of cinematographic factitiousness; literally as well as figuratively, from now on architecture is only a movie."[4] And thus via a circuitous detour Koolhaas has landed right back where he started.

1 Jean Baudrillard, *Fatal Strategies* (New York: Semiotext(e), 1990).
2 Rem Koolhaas, lecture at TU Eindhoven, November 1, 1989; interview with Bart Lootsma, Hans van Dijk and Arthur Wortmann, January 18, 1990.
3 Jean-François Lyotard, "Adorno as the Devil," *Telos* 19 (1974), 127–37.
4 Paul Virilio, *The Aesthetics of Disappearance* (New York: Semiotext(e), 1986), 64–65.

SEA TRADE CENTER ZEEBRUGGE: CONFESSION OF FAITH

Geert Bekaert
Sea Trade Center Zeebrugge (Antwerp: Standaard Uitgeverij, 1990), 13–23.

The fact that Zeebrugge is a port unlike any other, with a distinctive character determined by its situation, history, dimensions and methods, is emphasized yet again by the organization of a multiple design assignment for a new terminal: the Sea Trade Center Zeebrugge.

[...] It is already evident from the choice of architects that the organizers were not out to enhance local factors. A number of architects were chosen from the many possibilities, architects who do not directly represent a trend or a school, but whose quality of approach to architecture is guaranteed by their personal oeuvre. The port authority was by no means trying to shirk its duty as prime contractor. It wished to broaden the horizons as far as possible in order to be able to accept this responsibility with full knowledge of the facts. For those at all familiar with contemporary architecture, the names of the architects invited to participate are most significant: Tadao Ando of Japan, Santiago Calatrava of Spain/Switzerland, Norman Foster of Great Britain, Frank O. Gehry of the USA, Rem Koolhaas from the Office for Metropolitan Architecture (OMA) of the

Netherlands, Fumihiko Maki of Japan, Aldo Rossi of Italy, and Charles Vandenhove and Bob van Reeth from the Architecten-Werkgroep (AWG) of Belgium. [...] Ultimately, on April 1, 1989, five projects were submitted: those of Koolhaas, Maki, Rossi, Vandenhove and Van Reeth.

[...] The image that Koolhaas creates eludes, in his own words, the immediately recognizable and conjures up a chain of associations, from mechanical to poetic. He refers to an active Tower of Babel, thus introducing an evocation as specific as Rossi's acropolis or Maki's mirage. An interesting aspect of this project is that, like Vandenhove's project, it is not based on existing images and references, but generates its own images. Actually, it's a totally unique image of itself, or better still, not an image at all, but a reflection of the program. In this respect, it is distinctly different from the other four projects, in which the architectural form itself is endowed with explicit value. What Rossi says about his own project is even more true of Koolhaas's project: "The design can be built without particular problems, the only problem being the acceptance of its image." The most striking aspect of Koolhaas's project is its extreme compactness. Like a machine or a poem, to again use these antipodal metaphors, there is nothing superfluous about it. Furthermore, only by combining those extremes is it possible to characterize this project.

Thanks to its compactness, it creates a particularly strong, clear and mysterious symbol in the landscape, comparable to Rossi's symbol but, at the same time, its opposite. The building realistically confirms to the consequences of its situation. Like Van Reeth's project, it is first and foremost a homogenous hull which offers protection against weather and wind. It adopts the most appropriate aerodynamic shape for this, like a rock that has been worn smooth by water.

The form, strangely enough, does not rest on its heaviest side. It doesn't taper off toward the top, but expands slightly in order to attain as large an upper area as possible. And indeed, the entire construction of the hull is aimed at the light from above, both to draw it down into the entrance hall and to enjoy the play of light on the surround landscape. The entire building can be described, at first glance, as light-conditioned.

The activity around and in this strong core of the building is based on the inherent beauty of traffic. Here there is no schism between the actual facts and their poetic interpretation. The surplus value is not an added reference, but a discovery, in the literal sense of the word, of a hidden dimension. It is not created by reaction, but by sympathy. The music doesn't start on entering the building, or on the deck as in Maki's design; it is continuous.

The traffic, the bustle, the cars and the parking space are not simply included in the event; their individual charms are brought to light. The project is a new way of looking at things, and most specifically at the things of our time. The entrance winds it way, in a fluid S-form, the traffic hub which constitutes the foundation of the building. Traffic flows freely through and around the building. Traffic is the beginning and the heart of the entire event. It is not directed toward a separate area, but merges inconspicuously into the building itself. The road to the traffic hub is punctuated by an amusement park and a wayside restaurant, providing animation for both the road itself and the parking area. The hangar located here functions as a form of boundary line. Inside the dome covering the traffic hub, the whole program evolves in an extraordinarily exciting relational pattern. As with Rossi and Maki, the various parts are autonomous fragments, each of which develops from its individual function and is characterized by an individual typology.

Contrary to Rossi, however, these elements are not arranged introversively next to one another, but relate to each other in an outgoing, lively play of components. This composite play determines the entire interior, horizontal as well as vertical, circular as well as diagonal. In all its complexity, it remains clearly structured and surprising in its perspicuity. The same metamorphosis experienced by the traffic is encountered by every other function. The office is just an ordinary office, the hotel just an ordinary hotel, but everything changes because of the context in which it finds itself. An analysis of the interior shows the enormous possibilities offered by this concept: how it captures the essential qualities of the space with minimal means, while, at the same time, remaining free and allowing a myriad of interpretations. The characteristic climate of the interior, with its great breath of life and its countless activities, is continuously enlivened on the various levels by subtle contact with the exterior. This is already detectable in the arrival area and the entrance hall where the diverse program elements are announced. Above this entrance hall, one catches a breathtaking glimpse of the firmament and the expectation of a panoramic view is already born. Here too, the spatial play of the levels in their alterning patterns and usages first manifests itself.

In addition, there is the permanence of the vertical in the office towers and the hotel. The whole culminates in the belvedere, a sort of city square above the bustle with a panoramic view of the sea outside as well as the covered city below. Every level, each part, offers new surprises.

This metropolitan bustle and animation within a limited area is in perfect harmony with the activities in and around a sea terminal. It causes a celebration by means of its unusual, but extremely efficient and intelligent, staging. As already stated, this doesn't add any value, but intensifies it from within. The obviousness of the result should not blind us to the richness and the refinement of the spatial play. If references are sought, Buckminster Fuller's USA pavilion at the '67 Expo in Montreal comes to mind, as well as the large semipublic halls of numerous present-day megastructures, already referred to in the Van Reeth project, but without the ponderosity and monumentality that often characterize them. That which appears as a clear, "neutral" framework in Van Reeth's project, presents itself here as a lively, surprising and inviting game.

The project is a very direct confession of faith in the future of our contemporary culture. It makes no comment on tradition, but absorbs its vitality, a vitality that created cities like Brugge and ports like Zeebrugge.

THE MAGIC DIE WITH THE ENCHANTED CLOAK FOR THE SQUARING OF THE CIRCLE: ZKM

Frank R. Werner

Lotus international 70 (1991), 78–81.

For the moment only one thing is certain: that in the year 1994 the new complex of a Zentrum fur Kunst und Medientechnologie (ZKM), a Center for Art and Media Technology, will open its doors in Karlsruhe. Behind this terse statement is concealed one of the biggest architectural muddles of the 1980s. Or should it euphemistically be referred to as a “challenge”?

[...] Had we not only recently been presented, in Jean-François Lyotard’s legendary exhibition *Les Immatériaux* at the Beaubourg Center in Paris, with the most essential aspects of an immaterial culture of the future? That is to say a technology- and media-based culture, broadcast on a worldwide network, of our post-industrial era, and one which, as Lyotard put it, “is already beginning to go beyond its own instruments.” And had not others already pointed out the aspect of simulation in the media as a *conditio sine qua non* or, as Paul Virilio had succinctly put it: “The shift of the center of interest from the thing to its image, and above all from space to time and to the instant will eventually replace the clear alternative between reality and its reproduction with a more relativistic one: actual or virtual.”

How then was it possible for an architect to define a spatial program, not to mention an architectural form, for something that could no longer be imprisoned in concrete materials, and for which he could find neither examples to serve as a comparison nor typological precedents? Of course there were those esoteric video devices on offer from the international art market, as well as exotic experiments conducted on the synthesizer by avant-garde music. Or perhaps those quackish side shows of holography or cybernetic space from the international amusement parks ought to be used as models? What was left but to take refuge in the tried and tested strategy of the All and Nothing, in the elusively significant external shell, in the world of pure Appearance, of pure Image?

Thus at the conclusion of this competition there were numerous prizewinners, but no really conclusive project. It is worth noticing, however, that there was one curious fact: the majority of the participants had conceived the required Art and Technology Center as a long and flat horizontal bar located to the south of the station, so that as far as content was concerned the connections with the aforesaid *corpus delicti* were reduced to more or less trivial conjuring tricks of high technology. The rest was just silence.

The planning process did not receive a new impetus until the international symposia of 1988, based on an interdisciplinary approach, produced the first indications as to what should be understood by Media Center, in terms of program, space, and fittings. But the greatest sensation, from the viewpoint of cultural policy, was caused by the selection of the highly efficient director of the German Museum of Architecture in Frankfurt, Heinrich Klotz, to take charge of the foundation of the ZKM Center in Karlsruhe. In fact this appointment immediately made it clear that the new and ambitious director would not only exercise an influence over the contents of the design process that was already under way, but that he would also require an architectural form of a high level of quality for his institute, so far the only one of its kind in Europe.

Consequently in March 1989 a competition for the realization of the Karlsruhe ZKM was announced on Solomonic premises. Klotz presented a concrete program for the fitting out of premises for data-processing laboratories and art studios, film studios, an art museum, and a mass communications museum, as straightforward repositories for collections and documentation. In addition Klotz and the city authorities were asking for proposals for a college of figurative art (which was then actually built) as an extension of the ZKM, as well as a hotel complex. All the prizewinners of the first competition were admitted to the new one, and invitations were also extended (and who could wonder at the fact?) to the Reichlin/Reinhart team, Haus-Rucker-Co., and Steidle, as well as to leading figures on the scene of Deconstructivism and decomposition: Coop Himmelb(l)au, Koolhaas, Fuksas, Alsop, and Tschumi.

The outcome is well known, but its consequences are hard to evaluate. Some of the participants who, like the Reichlin/Reinhart team, attempted to handle the required program for the distribution of spaces on the basis of an ambitious formal arrangement in the tradition of Weinbrenner, had no chance of success from that outset. It seemed that what was wanted instead were spectacular "flying buildings" in neoconstructivist colors, like the ones presented by the Coop Himmelb(l)au. However their spirited and romantic collage of space-time foundered on the shoals of its excessive estimated cost. Bernard Tschumi, on the other hand, whose relatively flat and horizontal construction stuck closely to the results of the first competition, only made it into third place, ascetically confining the destructuralist sequences of the spaces exclusively to the interior of the building. Julia Bolles and Peter Wilson, the only prizewinners from the first competition who managed to gain a place in the top group of the second one, only just missed being assigned the first prize. They had the intelligent idea of defining their long, horizontal building as a "flying carpet," and then equipped their attractive filigree of spatial sequences with a series of thematically appropriate emblems. The skillful virtual stratification of their building into primary forms (walls, objects, rooms) and secondary elements (bridge, antenna, tower) at the points of intersection between public civic space and the semipublic area of the museum would probably have convinced the jury if it had not been for the project, as simple as it was enigmatic, entered by Rem Koolhaas.

Against all the rules, in fact, he had conceived his project as an extremely flat plinth, but one that, by way of compensation, was crowned by an imposing cubic structure, set at a tangent to the historic city axis. It is likely that this enormous cube, this emblem of the city, was seen by the jury and the future directors of the complex as a *deus ex machina.* Inaccessible, saying nothing and promising a great deal like a black "magic box," the cube epitomizes the immaterial aspects of the activity of the media in a way that is no less laconic than significant. Reduced to simple, primary shapes such as the circle, square, and cube, it introduces here an unexpected fluctuation of spaces exclusively in its nucleus. This is highly filtered on the outside through a structural shell that functions as a gigantic telescreen, a monumental "magic lantern" that projects onto its exterior an ever-changing array of snapshots, scenes, and videoclips of the various activities that are going on inside the building. For the jury there was no other choice: here it was, the magic die with an enchanted cloak that would be able to square the circle! Static, black, and almost invisible in a state of rest, and nonetheless capable, once activated, of penetrating into the space and profile of the city with a dynamic swirl of flashes and sparks, was it not just that spatiotemporal metaphor that had long been awaited in the subconscious? And yet this refrigerated "reactor of the media" had the romantic air of those late-nineteenth-century panoramas and pleasure pavilions that Koolhaas himself had once shrewdly analyzed in his *Delirious New York*.

At the beginning, nonetheless, one experiences a sense of disappointment. Not so much because at this early stage concepts of this sort still smack too much of the "simulation of simulation" and therefore lead too easily to absurdity on the plane of realization (as in Peter Eisenman's housing complex at Checkpoint Charlie in Berlin), but because the ZKM, which in the meantime has actually started to function, is only opening up little by little and revealing its concrete fields of work, for which Koolhaas's mutable spatiotemporal metaphor may not always be suitable. However, even if the architect's vision *in statu nascendi* were to founder, the "Adventure of the Pure Image" (to use the words of Virilio) of the future worlds of the media in the language of architecture remains and will remain with us—as well, of course, as in the archives of architectural museums.

BOOKS IN SPACE: TRADITION AND TRANSPARENCY IN THE BIBLIOTHÈQUE DE FRANCE

Anthony Vidler
Representations 42 (1993), 115–34.

[...] Only Rem Koolhaas, the ironic modernist, author of the Barthes-inspired *Delirious New York*, and runner-up in the competition for the Parc de La Villette, produced a design that might have presented serious competition to Dominique Perrault. For Koolhaas took seriously the mandate to produce a library for the electronic present, at the same time as he was concerned to reveal the limits of "architecture" to resolve the problems of information. Further, he produced an architectural solution that worked brilliantly at all levels from the symbolic to the functional. Conscious of the "precarious" venture in imagining the "ultimate library" at a moment when "the electronic revolution seems to have dissolved all that is solid," Koolhaas accepted the liberty implicit in freeing architecture from its originally solid tasks. Basing his project on what he called "technological scenarios" developed in coordination with systems analysts, he concluded that architecture as traditionally conceived will have little role in their operation. Freed from functionalist duty, he asserted, "the last function of architecture will be to create symbolic spaces responding to the persistent envy of the collectivity." Accordingly, the library is conceived like some vast three-dimensional information chip: "The library is interpreted as a solid block of information, a warehouse of all forms of memory: books, disks, optical instruments, microfiches, computers." The ironic symbolic program has thus formed solids out of the most empty of forms (information) while the public spaces (normally solid) are now dissolved into "absences of building, voids carved out of the block of information." But the solid block of information is in fact conceived as a translucent cube, luminous, and radiating the secrets of its interior to the exterior. On this outside surface, the shadows of the public spaces within are projected like ghostly manifestations—Koolhaas uses the biological analogy of "multiple embryos"—in a "specter of spatial experiences." Suspended, as in aspic, the different libraries float in the cube as if transgressing the very laws of gravity. Koolhaas has thus revised the functionalist directive to express on the outside what is on the inside, as well as turning inside-out the traditional notions of solid and void. The result is a brilliant and architecturally original evocation of the poetics and pragmatics of information technology, and by far the most successful of all the competition entries. It was also, as a member of the jury, François Chaslin, noted, "the most radical."

That, in the event, the jury selected, not a radical invention of a library of "an entirely new type," but rather the insertion of the library in a generic form that avoided architectural articulation altogether, was entirely predictable. Under the presidency of the conservative modernist I. M. Pei, champion of the transparent Pyramide du Louvre, the process sent four projects for consideration by the president of the republic: one postmodernist (James Stirling and Associates), one technologically utopian neo-expressionist (Future Systems), and one high-tech modernist (Philippe Chaix and Jean-Paul Morel), together with Perrault's scheme. Perrault's submission, according to one of the twenty-nine-member jury, had already received unanimous approval on the first day of deliberations, and the other three selected projects were, in the context of Mitterrand's choices for the preceding grands projets, hardly contenders. The sphere at La Villette, the cube at La Défense, and the pyramid at the Louvre would now be joined in this simplistic play of simple forms by the four books of the Bibliothèque, investing Paris with a series of Socialist markers, architecturally expressing the tradition of universality through primary geometric solids that were, moreover, transparent.

Koolhaas's mistake was to configure information under the sign of translucency and shadowy obscurity; the politics of the moment insisted, and still insist, on the illusion that light and enlightenment, transparency and openness, permeability and social democracy are not only symbolized but also effected by glass. Such simple wisdom, effective enough in the rhetoric of ideology, is well served by an architect like Perrault who asserts: "I dislike walls; I like transparencies." [...]

ENVELOPES AND ENCLAVES: THE SPACE OF POST-CIVIL SOCIETY

Fredric Jameson and Michael Speaks
Assemblage 17 (1992), 30–37.

[...] **fj:** What I have been struck with in the work of Koolhaas is the way it, in effect, builds an enormous envelope for all kinds of unprogrammed but differentiated activities. If you follow Niklas Luhmann's idea that modernity is characterized by differentiation, and if you suppose that there are plateaux in the rhythm of this differentiation, as I do—in other words, that the differentiation of a postmodern global information society is going to be quite different from the differentiation of an older, "modern" society—then I think one can read one feature of Koolhaas's work as an exemplification of this. But the originality of Koolhaas (as theoretician and architect alike) is that his work does not simply glorify differentiation in the conventional pluralist ideological way: rather, he insists on the relationship between this randomness and freedom and the presence of some rigid, inhuman, nondifferential form that enables the differentiation of what goes on around it (in *Delirious New York*, within the building, the elevator, and within the urban context itself, the grid of Manhattan). Koolhaas offers the picture of the imposition on the differential of a rigid, and if I may say so, contingent or meaningless structural form, a form that, like the elevator, has no internal meaning of its own, but whose function is to allow this improvization and differentiation to go on outside of itself and around itself. Thus the free spaces are enabled by the rigidity of the framework. It is almost a political paradigm in the sense that the combination of formal requirements of a certain order without content permits all kinds of forms of freedom or disorder within the interstices. I think that what's brilliant about Koolhaas's work is not only the obviously very striking nature of the buildings themselves, but also the way in which the work offers an interesting paradigm for other levels (not only for other arts) of social life, such as the political or even the ethical, the psychoanalytical, and so forth. I don't mean that one should endorse this program and draw a politics or an ethics from the success of these buildings, but it is very interesting that they do project the combination of a law and freedom that seems to be characteristic of the present time. In other words, as an ideal this interesting combination is very different from the authoritarianism of an older corporate or planned society, whether that's conceived of from the Left or from the Right, and as it might be seen to be embodied in the International Style or in the work of Frank Lloyd Wright. But it is also very different from the fantasies of an anarchism that wants to dissolve all structures and create spaces for a free play that would reinvent its structures at every occasion or at every moment. I think Koolhaas's projects offer free play only on the condition of this rigid and meaningless internal structure, and so whatever else this is, it's a very striking solution to the contemporary intellectual problem that seems to be a reaction against an older authoritarianism and, nowadays, against an older anarchist libertarianism as well.

[...]

ms: Given this new model of the space of post-civil society that you have been developing, could you draw a comparison between the kind of space you analyzed in the Bonaventure Hotel in Los Angeles and the space of these Koolhaas projects and buildings?

fj: Yes, I think that's an interesting comparison, and it's quite right to juxtapose these things and try to figure out their difference. I think the essence of what I am trying to get at by this end of civil society is clearly at issue here somehow. The point is that the hotel is still private property. We might enter it to mill around as a crowd but we're still within the authority of private property. Therefore it's a strange kind of mixture of a private space used for some form of public deployment of the private. Now the crucial thing about the end of civil society is that what used to be public is reprivatized, that is, what used to be spaces or places marked by government, and therefore by the public, somehow revert to faceless forms of private control. So that some new kind of thing comes into being that is neither the place of one's private life nor the monumentalization of collective powers. This may be related to (but I think it's somewhat different from) Hannah Arendt's notion that the public in our time was being reprivatized in the sense in which politics became personalized and people were more interested in the personalities of political figures than in their programs. Hers was a psychological diagnosis, whereas in my view the development has much more to do with mutations in the very juridical forms of property so that new entities emerge that are not covered by the previous categories. Now the crucial thing about the Koolhaas stuff, in particular, the Sea Trade Center in Zeebrugge, is that it is an interspace between all of these countries that are streaming in to merge into others. As the crossing point or arrival point for the channel ferry boats, the terminal is therefore public in a new way, and yet somehow outside of the public spaces of any of the nation states involved. It is as though Koolhaas, observing the new "culture of congestion," by way of the rapid mixture of these populations that are streaming through, somehow also offers a machine for producing this culture in a Europe that never knew it before. This somehow seems to me much more interesting in terms of future historical development, in terms of things that will happen in these categories of public or private, than the Bonaventure, which is a far more conventional building with its hotel police force and predictable categories of behavior. I would think, then, that the Bonaventure could serve as a symptom of these developments in the strong sense, whereas Koolhaas's work is a strong formal and cultural reaction: an attempt both to register these developments and in some way to make a statement about them.

[...]

ms: In the 1988 MoMA exhibition, Koolhaas and OMA were included under the "deconstructivist" rubric. What does replication offer that the decon solution does not? It would seem to have something to do with architectural realism and representation.

fj: Yes, I think that comes back to the role that the term totality plays here. I'm not sure I'd be happy with using the term realism for any of this. But if we talk about mimesis at least we can see the difference between these other two forms of contemporary architecture as opposed to the deconstructionist one, in the sense that *Learning from Las Vegas* involves the mimesis of a part of a total urban fabric, whereas Koolhaas's buildings seem to wish to stand as a mimesis of the whole macrocosm itself. I think that's why these buildings, as I suggested before, can carry certain kinds of political messages, or can include, if you like, political and social models, because they do have the ambition to grapple with the totality of the social itself.

METROPOLITAN VERNACULAR: BYZANTIUM AMSTERDAM

Paul Vermeulen

Archis 8 (1991), 17–22.

When redevelopers submitted their proposals for the former GEB property in Amsterdam six years ago, the value of the OMA plan was eminently apparent from the outset.[1] It resides in the buildings' configuration. As in all of the competing plans, Stadhouderskade was lined with fairly high buildings, except these did not follow in one continuous line from the Marriott and the AMVJ building but were at right angles to Vondelpark, thus creating a triangular transition zone along Stadhouderskade. The remaining buildings were concentrated around the property's middle axis, with a buffer of low-lying buildings on Tesselschadestraat and tine-like extensions along the park side. This differed from the other main plans in contention, which built up the edges of the site and left the center open, thereby compromising the street and the park in favor of an artificial inner courtyard. For its part, the OMA plan accorded Metropolis and Arcadia, as they are called in the design statement, their due: a cosmopolitan decor for Leidseplein and discreet, recessed terraced housing for Vondelpark.

Today that planning envelope has been filled with its built substance and the architectural merits of this Byzantium can be assessed. The first impression is one of vague familiarity: this must be a dom-kommuna such as the ones designed by Ginzburg or Golossow in the fledgling days of the Soviet Union. Yet the fact that Byzantium harks back to a heroic time in modern architectural history is not the reason I consider it to be such a successful, innovative experiment in urban architecture. What I find innovative is the strategy used to tackle the superblock model.

The term was coined by Alan Colquhoun. In his Essays in *Architectural Criticism*[2] he points to a coarsening trend affecting the urban fabric in the current age. Large-scale entities (housing and office complexes) are being developed that disrupt the continuity of that fabric in the same way that public buildings once did, without possessing or promising the metaphorical value inherent to public buildings; Colquhoun refers to it as "the lowering of architectural voltage." On the one hand, then, the superblock lacks the representational character of public buildings; on the other, the escalation of scale it introduces eviscerates the conventions of the urban fabric, conventions related to the relationship between private and public. As part of that fabric, individual homes provide variation in the public space, while at the same time being integrated into a communal context that guarantees privacy and anonymity. In contemporary cities, therefore, designers face the precarious task of providing a substitute for those conventions within the boundaries of the superblock.

The architectural strategy used in the Byzantium development to attain the opposing urban qualities of anonymity and variation is collage. A collage creates connections between heterogeneous fragments. The fragments compiled by OMA are familiar, anonymous, unsigned—the era of Ginzburg and Golossow is long past—and can accordingly be designated part of the vernacular. What rescues them from banality is their color, which accentuates their artificial and spiritual nature (the earthy tones of Amsterdam South do not work here), and the interaction with the other fragments. These are not whole, elementary objects. They have been cut out to be fit into the collage and overlap. The black structural grid of the office building is ambiguously bordered and fades behind the glazed facade. The glass meshwork reveals a second, shifted grid. The black-coated columns of the highest two stories can be seen through the strips of windows along Tesselschadestraat, which also reflect the green glass of the tower. The park side is similarly layered with solid, void, blue and lilac.

At the same time the fragments retain a certain level of autonomy, fighting for their own place in the urban theater and thereby partially canceling out the smug isolation of the superblock. The office towers on Vondelstraat and Roemer Visscherstraat rise, slender and distinguished, in the distance, dissociated from Byzantium. The wedge, a golden magnet loaded with the kitsch of the shopping street, bows toward passers-by with its overhang and shopfront. Hovering above the blueish idyll of the park (not a Rossian, Mediterranean azure but a washed-out, diaphanous blue), in the corner of the picture, as it were, lurks a golden disc, haughty and disdainful.

The collage is interlaced with codes. It has a color code made obsolete by circumstances, since the golden restaurant (gold equals commercial) became a penthouse, which saved the developers an additional elevator. The rear entrance has the same awning as the front entrance and a dash of the same green dolomite, as if smudged by giant fingerprints. The overlapping fragments and multilayered construction extend to the interior, as well. The foyers of the residences and offices, separated by a wall of black enameled glass, are complementary. The gallery housing the residences, patios and stairwells provides an unexpected glimpse of the complexity above it through a gap in the ceiling. It is also worth noting that the office lobby and apartment walkways, with their circumspect excursions into orthogonality, are unemphatically beautiful. The long wall in the offices and low, wide spans and long hallways in the apartments effect a neutral spaciousness.

The method of design whose results I hail here as innovative is obviously not without precedent. One might cite Loos's Haus am Michaelerplatz as an example—also a commercial building built on an important site in a large city after a design competition and the subject of incredible controversy. In the Looshaus, too, the urban roles of anonymity and arrogance have been assigned to disparate fragments, not domesticated by any unifying order. In terms of OMA's repertoire, I would say the precursor to Byzantium was the Dance Theater, where the questionable neighborliness of the Spui complex is recycled in an intense collage. Another recognizable element from many OMA designs is the radically independent treatment of the different facades of the building, something that was especially evident in the Dance Theater. The primary difference is that the Amsterdam building uses robust, durable materials.

Nevertheless, the detailing has been a remarkably frequent target in the controversy surrounding the building: not built to last, claims the layman; shoddy and vulgar, says the expert.[3] Residents find the finishes in their luxury flats merely ordinary and hire in interior designers, and given that not a single one of them has entrusted the design of their interior to the designers of the building, we can assume a certain level of frustration among the latter, as well, with regard to the interior finishing. Moreover, elements such as glass railings and aluminium windows unquestionably belong to the vocabulary of the developer. The standard modus operandi has not been circumvented or surpassed, and whether that was a conscious decision on the part of the designers or something imposed by the financial backers hardly matters. The detailing is standard. It is neither beautiful nor ugly; it is aesthetically indifferent. The beauty was allocated elsewhere: in the juxtaposition of found fragments, such as a tile pathway on a gravel rooftop.

1 Rob de Graaf, "Laissez faire: Planvorming voor het Amsterdamse GEB-terrein," *wonen-TA/BK* 16–17 (1985), 6.

2 Alan Colquhoun, "The Superblock," in *Essays in Architectural Criticism: Modern Architecture and Historical Change* (Cambridge, MA: The MIT Press, 1981), 83–103.

3 Max van Rooy, "Het ingebouwd verval," *NRC Handelsblad,* May 3, 1991; Peter van den Berg, Willem Ellenbroek, "Het plein van de gemiste kansen," *De Volkskrant,* April 26, 1991.

PIANISSIMO AND GENTLE: HOTEL FURKABLICK

Lucius Burckhardt

BauDoc-Bulletin 12 (1991), 5–12.

Hotel Furkablick is a precious relict of the times in which holidays were spent at one destination. If traveling and walking were for Rousseau, Goethe and Schiller a means to perceive the landscape, the railroad introduced a concentration on the destination of the journey: “this year, we go to Helgoland, to Ostend or to Mount Rigi and spent all of our holidays there.” The need to discover beautiful places has changed; areas offering many subtle impressions with only a few highlights have disappeared from the repertoire, in favor of other impressive scenes that lend themselves for this kind of experience. The Furka Pass was one of these, as a kind of derivative and sum total of older destinations such as the hamlet Gletsch and the Rhône Glacier.

Protecting and putting back into service Hotel Furkablick therefore seems an act of raising historical consciousness. No one can cross the large room of the hotel, with windows giving out to three cardinal points, without thinking of the social circles—still so close to us in time and yet so far away in experience—that spent their time here, only one hundred years ago. The landscape is seen from a point of view that can be considered typically alpine and that will never be boring thanks to the theater of ever-changing clouds that is being staged. One profits from the nice weather and the blue sky, and then a cloud approaches from Valais, hooks itself unto the hotel and conceals the landscape. Ten minutes later, a gust of wind arrives from Urseren, tears the cloudy curtain from top to bottom, snatches the clouds out of the mountains and cleans up the valley with a big whirlwind. [...]

Last year, Marc Hostettler has decided to undertake necessary transformations inherent to the exploitation of the establishment. Hostettler wanted to free the large room and turn it into the heart of his artistic operation. He needed a larger dining room, organized in the old western part of the building. Moreover, the hotel didn’t dispose of a terrace on which visitors, provided with sunscreen and anoraks, could enjoy a small lunch. And finally, it was necessary to help those motorists coming from very far who, when opening the door of their car in the cold Furka air, feel the sudden need to find solace on the hotel floors.

To be honest: I found the idea to entrust the transformations to Rem Koolhaas at first quite farfetched, a bit like shooting a sparrow with a cannon. I say it today with all the more conviction: the blow of the cannon was a stroke of genius, and the sparrow has survived. Koolhaas has revealed himself to be an architect whose thoughts belong to a rich and complex art—his interventions, when necessary, are *pianissimo* and gentle. By the way: when visiting Furka, one shouldn't forget to watch the video showing Koolhaas's first visit to the Furka Pass. Of course, he came in winter, the season in which only the experienced skiers reach the top. Koolhaas, however, arrived by helicopter, in a rain coat, with black loafers and with the suitcase of a business man. Zealously, Hostettler needed to take his shovel and broom—without forgetting to remove the icicles from the eaves—in order to make the hotel accessible.

For the visitor, the complex intervention by Koolhaas is reduced to three apparent novelties. A dining hall has been installed in the western part. The terrace isn't attached to the building, but stands a few steps away, like a table with aluminum feet next to the dining room. And finally, there is a new entrance, also at the western side, immediately giving out to the dining room. The two opposite demands of making this entry visible from far away without enlarging the existing openings in the facade have led to an elegant solution: one of the western windows has been transformed into a door (what it once used to be), and it has been equipped with an exterior wind shield that enlarges in the form of a funnel, ending up as an oversized window. For someone approaching from the west, this window seems first of all a big door, and it's only from closer by that one realizes one is entering a funnel.

The transformation has liberated the main room to turn it into the artistic center of Furk'Art. The room is without pillars, because the rooms on the three upper floors are considered together as a load-bearing structure. It can therefore be regarded as both an architectonic artwork and a technical invention. More sentimentally inclined visitors will probably notice how anonymous the service in the new dining room has become. The time of cozy evenings in the room next to the kitchen, where it became impossible to distinguish between guests and kitchen staff, is now over. [...]

HOUSING AFTER THE MACHINE AGE: NEXUS WORLD HOUSING, FUKUOKA

Sally B. Woodbridge

Progressive Architecture 8 (1991), 60–76.

The dilemma that Western architects face when asked to design a building in Japan was well expressed by Rem Koolhaas: "Should the building be as Western as possible—is it just another export—or should it reflect the fact that it is built in Japan?" The dilemma was intensified in the Nexus World project because, as Koolhaas observed, the context was not the expected chaotic jumble of buildings in an ill-defined pattern typical of most Japanese cities. Instead, the site was in an orderly new town still in the process of development on land reclaimed from Hakata Bay. Moreover, the master plan simply took a superblock and ran a street with a crank in the middle through it. Since the northwestern corner of the block had been reserved for other development, the available site was an L-shaped parcel with a slightly undulating southern edge. The perimeter was to be lined with low-rise housing blocks, a very Western idea. The "Japanese" part of it (that is, a dramatic contrast in scale) consists in plans for two 120-meter-high apartment towers in the center. These high-rises, designed by Arata Isozaki, are to be surrounded by low-rise condominiums designed by Steven Holl, Rem Koolhaas, Mark Mack, Osamu Ishiyama, Oscar Tusquets, and Christian de Portzamparc.

The mixed message of the site program is implicit in the project name, Nexus World. "Nexus" stands for the link between the present and the future, or next, world. The name cryptically expresses the intentions of Fukuoka Jisho, the developers of Nexus World. They see this community as a cultural link between rapidly Westernizing Japan and the Western world, which, at least in housing, seems to offer a good model for the future. The site itself is a nexus between the established town of Kashii and the new town on land to the west that is part of an ongoing Hakata Bay reclamation project. It comprises six condominium buildings, harbingers of the future, that contain 192 units. Constructed in ten months, the buildings are a dazzling display of handcrafted finishes and details, flawlessly executed. Is it any wonder that some of the architects featured here wish they could build all of their buildings in Japan? Japanese contractors have a reputation for meeting standards of quality in construction that are far above what prevails in the rest of the world. If anything, the contractors' performance on the Nexus World buildings surpassed the architects' already high expectations.

In part, this feat resulted from keen competition between the contractors for the individual buildings, but much of it was also due to the willingness of the contractors to work with the architects in creating finishes and details that neither had executed before. Thus, the architects' direct experience of craftsmanship broadened the scope for their talents and raised the overall quality of the project. Too bad this situation is so unusual.

Another much-discussed aspect of Nexus World is its contribution to the tradition of the building exhibition. Publicizing new architectural ideas by inviting the public to see innovative buildings originated in Europe in the nineteenth century. Most relevant to Nexus World Kashii are the exhibitions of the 1920s and early 1930s in Central Europe, where a new rationalist order augured a wholesale reform of architecture by applying industrial principles to the construction and equipment of housing. The most spectacular such exhibition was the 1927 Weissenhofsiedlung in Stuttgart. Planned by Mies van der Rohe, it featured buildings by him and his avant-garde colleagues as a built manifesto of "Enlightenment in the Machine Age." Now, after more than half a century, the Machine Age no longer seems so enlightening, and the dogmatic severity of straightforward Modernism does not manifest domestic innovation. Still, in Japan, the need for innovation in housing for the mass market has reached a crisis point. As Osamu Ishiyama put it, the Japanese live in "rabbit hutches" and "match boxes" because the public and private production processes for housing are exceptionally rigid. It is this deprivation in the midst of plenty that motivated Fukuoka Jisho to sponsor a building exhibition with housing units for Japan's middle class. The innovations explored there have nothing to do with the kind of industrial technology that informed the Weissenhofsiedlung—the Japanese already have "smart houses" that all but think for their occupants. Instead, these innovations are about comfort and delight, urbanity, and connections between the public and private realms.

"For our first project in Japan," Rem Koolhaas stated, "we wanted to introduce a new type of housing—not a conventional apartment building, not a freestanding house (that we had experimented with in Europe) but a type that could now be realized in the economic conditions of Japan. The project consists of twenty-four individual houses—each three stories high—packed together to form two blocks. Each house is penetrated by a private vertical courtyard that introduces light and space into the center." It sounds matter-of-fact, but in reality, the logic of these two buildings is enveloped in a surreal quality that makes them a fitting gateway into the Nexus World site. They have "cyclopic walls," Koolhaas's term for the girdles of licorice-colored concrete with a *faux* masonry surface. A caricature of the foundation walls of Japanese castles, they are intended as a figurative base for Isozaki's future towers as well as a means to fortify the privacy of the low-rise units in the high-rises' embrace. Koolhaas's units figuratively escape their confinement with curved roofs that billow above the walls: Three warped roof planes ripple across the top of the building like waves frozen in time.

Of all the Nexus World buildings, Koolhaas's are the most self-contained, the least tied to their surroundings. Their lyric quality is best appreciated when they are seen as a totality from a distance or from the upper floors of neighboring buildings. At night, the soft glow from the interiors suffuses the air above the black walls with a fairy-tale enchantment. The interior of each three-story house progresses from a ground-floor entrance court with white walls and a white gravel floor to a *genkan,* the place where shoes are removed and stored for future use. From here a long flight of steps ascends to the second-floor bedrooms and finally to the third, or living, floor, which Koolhaas describes as "a single extroverted space." The overall tonality is cool; the character is intensely private. Hiroshi Watanabe observed that Koolhaas has captured the Japanese taste for privacy within walls. On the sleeping floor, the bedrooms are discrete spaces entered from a minimal hallway. Although each one faces the open court, the windows are above solid wall sections that screen the occupants. Even the extroverted top floor is oriented to the out-of-doors and the sky and is less amenable to sociability within the household.

There is a monastic serenity to these houses that keeps the hectic outside world at bay. There is also whimsy in the garden, a patch of green groundcover that crowns the dome of the top floor "extra" room. From the roof deck on the opposite side of the court this sprouted dome is an amusing element on the horizon; from the main living space it presents a coy, sidelong image.

Koolhaas's buildings have the largest units and the least varied floor plans at Nexus World. They are also the most expensive, a secondary issue except that their steep stairways discourage the older and wealthier generation of buyers. Although not so suitable for families with young children—too many stairs, too many places to hide—they would seem ideal for the household with teenagers, which is also the one with the most claims on its income. If we posit an American market for these units, we could predict that few people would see themselves living in a surrealistic bastion. But Koolhaas has not designed these buildings for the faint-hearted, and the Japanese seem more open-minded than any other nationality about accepting new and unusual images in architecture. Still, the developers were stunned when Koolhaas chose to ignore his choice location on the south side of the site by giving the buildings blank walls. Yet, they agreed to his scheme with astonishing magnanimity, saying that since everyone has a different lifestyle and sensibility, a generally marketable space fits nobody's lifestyle. This is the kind of statement that developers of market-rate housing in the United States use to hype their standardized plans. Maybe Japan represents the next world.

THE REINVENTION OF GEOMETRY

Sanford Kwinter
Assemblage 18 (1992), 83–85.

Classical Greek geometry—the study of straight lines, regular solids, and restricted curves—was in essence a timeless geometry: every real shape was seen simply as the reflection or extrusion of an ideal, unchanging, and eternal form. The qualities of a circle or square were constant, based on relations between *magnitudes*; *changes*, that is, transformations and emergences, were not considered real things at all, but imperfections, degradations, perversions of a noble, even divine and pregiven mathematical rectitude.

These basic premises remained almost unchallenged until the nineteenth century, when deep transformations in the theory of time started to give way. Such transformations manifested themselves not only in the new sciences of evolution and thermodynamics but also throughout the urban literature of the latter half of the century, in Flaubert, Dickens, Engels, Baudelaire. Massive and *intensely accelerated* industrial, economic, and technological innovations had begun to transform our experience of the material and historical world: the once imperceptibly slow and stable rhythms of history that earlier furnished a kind of immobile ground for the more labile and fluid human figure began to oscillate and vary in patterns of shorter and shorter duration, effecting an epochal reversal in social and historical experience. What once appeared as a fixed and global continuum subtending human temporal experience—the historico-material assemblage, for example, known as "the city"—began to multiply, mutate, and atomize so quickly and finely that it itself could no longer be conceived as anything other than a turbulent, punctuated fluid.

This new world seemed to force upon us an entirely new—or at least different—type of geometry, one whose roots may be traced with precision through Riemann, Lobachevsky, Bolyai, and Poincaré. In certain ways it may be said that in these mathematicians there may be found a deep and precocious disquietude that surreptitiously informed so much of our own modernity: that the model of discrete, inelastic, and quantitative reason was already precariously foundering even as its most prestigious and rigorous monuments—industrial capitalism, technoscientific rationalism, urbanization—were being assembled. These were the geometries that first broke with the conveniences and classical pieties of homogeneous, linear, or isotropic space; these were the protogeometries of a new, still premature form of reason, one predicated on acausality, deformability, creative diversification, and active variability. Though it took nearly another century to reach a threshold, the crisis of geometry and reason finally arrived. Today, for the first time, a number of thinkers at the forefront of speculative philosophical, material, and cultural practice have begun systematically to extend their intuition of form to new levels, indeed, to free their intuition from three-dimensional experience, and in a bold, strange act of historical recovery, to deroute the Greeks by retuming to the still-untapped power of the pre-Socratic world: in a phrase, to recognize that processes and events have shapes of their own.

Nowhere in the architectural world today is this embrace of asymmetry, nonlinearity, and the miracle and undeniability of indeterminate and spontaneously emerging material qualities—all manifested in deep, multidimensional geometric form—so rigorously taking place as in the work of Rem Koolhaas and the Office for Metropolitan Architecture.[1] All of Koolhaas's recent work is *evolved*—rather than designed—within the hypermodern "event-space" of complex, sensitive, dynamical indeterminacy and change.[2] It would be easy, far too easy, to support such an argument purely through a descriptive analysis of the morphological data that pertain to the stunning figures and exotic massing so clearly evident in every one of his recent *building* projects: the Bibliothèque de France, the Palais de Congrès d'Agadir, the Sea Trade Center, the Karlsruhe Zentrum für Kunst und Medientechnologie. But the novel, radical figures of single buildings or building systems, however advanced these may be, and however powerful the fascination they may exercise over intellectuals, planners, and architects, simply cannot do justice to the larger, if inchoate, project of OMA, its attempt to engage the contemporary forces that both carve up and produce our modern world. Indeed, OMA seems virtually alone within today's avant-garde architectural milieu (with the possible exception of Daniel Libeskind) in venturing into the space so shamefully abdicated by architects since the progressivist heyday of the 1960s: *the space of the sociotechnical formation of collective subjectivity*; in other words, the politics of metropolitan "delirium."

Koolhaas and OMA's trajectory has always been deeply linked to the larger processes that determine social formations—economics and historical trends, aesthetic idiosyncrasy as material fact rather than moral quandary, urbanism as a collection of continually diversifying practices. Yet, especially lately, this has not been at the expense of what could well be even more critical; that is, the minutiae of the public sphere—the chaotic fluctuations of markets, governments, and libidinal economies, the velleities of opinion, fashion, and taste.

To the question, What types of structure and form are possible today to sustain a maximum sensitivity to material fluctuations simultaneously *at all scales*, to sustain continual dynamic development over time within an "envelope" (one of Koolhaas's favorite words, roughly equivalent to what Althusser used to call a *conjoncture*) that is fast becoming ludicrously narrow? OMA has ventured some of the most daring—and perhaps exhilaratingly dangerous—practical speculations to be found anywhere in late-twentieth-century culture. But most important of all, it has done this in a way that is consonant with the most compelling and fruitful intellectual developments of our age: the reinvention of geometry and the geometrization of the event.

Thus it is only in the full-scale urban projects [...] that such a claim may properly be put to test. Yet what coherent worldview do they represent and what characteristics do they share? The first, perhaps most general, principle to note is that in OMA's proposals the argument always takes precedent over the project. In other words, there is always primarily an engine, be it discursive or diagrammatic, never a design that is introduced into the urban milieu to be reconfigured. It is never a question of organizing a space at the outset, but rather of unleashing, triggering, or capturing larger and already existing processes.[3]

Second is the adamant refusal to repress either the material fact, the economic reality, or the technological brutality of rampant infrastructural systems, those vitalistic circulatory systems of all modern civilizations, capitalist or otherwise. These infrastructural systems—highways, railways, escalators, roads, ramps, elevators, stairs, mechanical and ventilation systems—are generally approached as capillaries, engravings, or developmental pathways or canalizations to be inflected, redirected, or simply followed like the surf and *mise-en-délire*.

Third, elements are gathered, classified, and distributed never as preformed spaces; objects, or functions but as statistical intensities, pure potentials or virtualities, morphic resonances as variable densities of space-time, activity, or action. The idea is literally *to program,* like a dramaturge or film director, all the pathways and accumulations of information, recalling Cagney's virtuoso microgestures or Minnelli's saturated cinematic fields. In these first three general axioms there may be discerned a very clear orientation toward evolutionary, time-based processes, dynamical geometric *structurations,* not structures per se, but forms that follow and fill the wake of concrete yet unpredeterminable *events.*

The fourth axiom has to do with a completely unneurotic belief in the possible freedoms that still lie unconfronted within the type of systems that common wisdom continues to refer to as the "artificial." Though the ethicopolitical ground here may seem shaky, many of OMA's most tenable and persuasive convictions on the subject are not. This is because instead of designing artificial environments, it deploys richly imbricated systems of *interacting* elements that set in motion rather *artificial ecologies* that, in turn, take on a genuine selforganizing life of their own. The common mistake is to miss the organicism and autopoesis of OMA's approach and to attack simplistically both the mechanistic substratum out of which its fluid, metabolic systems are made, as well as the unarguably unjust, even nefarious economic and social processes off of which they shamelessly feed. This is true, of course, of all life-forms in all states of nature (nature sustains its forms only through the ongoing violence of capture and ingestion) and is a contradiction—or an ill-stated problem that no philosophy or ideology has, or ever will, overcome.

The remaining axioms and principles follow from this latter one. All of OMA's recent urbanist work is about the setting into motion of dynamic self-regulating and self-driving informational ecologies: The idea that nonorganic systems such as urban economies, or complex public-work structures, or even small electronic networks like those used in businesses or cultural institutions might have a life of their own (indeed, even the detailed mechanics of the simplest single-cell life-forms) still in our day escapes explanation, as if it were nothing less than a form of magic. Yet in the words of René Thom—and these words might just as well be the battle cry for the architectural methodologies by which OMA almost single-handedly is ushering us into the 1990s and into the century beyond—"Is not all magic, to the extent that it is successful, geometry?"[4]

1 Intimations of these developments, in less systematic form, have certainly appeared in recent work of Peter Eisenman, Bernard Tschumi, Liz Diller and Ricardo Scofidio, and Hani Rashid and Lise Anne Couture.

2 Koolhaas, with reason I believe, has consistently and categorically rejected the pseudo-concept of Postmodernism.

3 "[Manhattan's] architecture relates to the Großstadt like a surfer to the waves." Rem Koolhaas in *ZONE* 1/2, *The Contemporary City,* ed. Michel Feher and Sanford Kwinter (New York: ZONE Books, 1986), 448.

4 René Thom, *Structural Stability and Morphogenesis* (Redwood City: Addison-Wesley, 1972).

TOKYO STORM WARNING

Albert Pope

Design Book Review 26 (1992), 17–22.

The sky fell over cheap Korean monster-movie scenery
And spilled into the mezzanine of the crushed capsule hotel
Between the Disney abattoir and the chemical refinery
I knew I was in trouble but I thought I was in hell ...
What do we care if the world is a joke?
Elvis Costello, "Tokyo Storm Warning"

Rem Koolhaas's 1978 book, *Delirious New York,* is rarely considered an argument for urban revival. It does, however stand as a product of its time as one amongst a number of polemics that emerged in the 1970s with regard to established urban models. Léon Krier's medieval city, Aldo Rossi's neoclassical city, Steven Holl's alphabetical city all developed positions against the inadequate performance of the contemporary city presumed to be driven by modernist discourse. Koolhaas's metropolis was no different in unabashedly blasting modern urban theory while proclaiming the ultimate relevance of a lost form of urbanism. The call at the end of the text for a revival of "Manhattanism" and its "fictional conclusion" reeks of a nostalgia for the architecture of the 1920s. As with so many of the other models slated for revival, "Manhattanism" became potent precisely at the moment of its impossibility. It was the irretrievable dimension of the model, like the unquestionable virtues of the recently dead, that made it so attractive as to be immune to the historical and political realities of the half-century since its full flourishing.

As the Office for Metropolitan Architecture, led by Koolhaas, has since sought to overcome these retrospective tendencies and extend the "culture of congestion" to meet present realities, another more significant "fictional conclusion" has been written for *Delirious New York*. A group of four recent publications stands as that conclusion, marking a substantive translation of metropolitan-era urbanism into the "post-architectural" world of the contemporary city. These publications document, for the first time, the extraordinary change in direction that OMA and Koolhaas have made in their recent work, which both abandons and extends the metropolitan research.

[...] The two catalogs documenting the 1990 exhibitions are the most interesting as books. They challenge the banal and reductive format of architectural publication by being banal and reductive. Both *OMA: Six Projets* and *Lille* document competition projects that each involved relentless repetitive structures, bands, grids, and repetitive floor plates, all registered layer by layer, floor by floor, to make for proto-animation "flip books." The idea is ingenious in its placement of emphasis on the banal repetitive structures that inform the projects, while simultaneously questioning the commodity status of architectural publications. (The 510-page *Six Projets* takes about five minutes to "read.") Flipping through the layers of La Villette or the remarkable sequence of plans and sections of the National Library—each drawing only a fragmented frame—yields a crude animation, a counterfeiting of movement that strangely animates each project. The written texts, all in French, are only incidental to the publication. [...]

Koolhaas has frequently referred to the forces propelling the contemporary city as a wave, and to architecture (as well as the urban subject) as being propelled by something that can never be significantly influenced. Understanding the city as catastrophe and as chaos, as the seat of an infinite density and complexity, has an obvious appeal for architecture and urbanism as well as other disciplines. Referring to Marshall Berman's *All That Is Solid Melts into Air* from 1982, Koolhaas describes these forces as a kind of maelstrom to which we, as architects, can only submit. Under a retroactive analysis, unplanned intentions often eclipse planned intentions, indicating that the greatest interest of the city develops largely as a result of insensible forces—of some invisible urban maelstrom. Because they are not the product of direct intervention these forces have traditionally been dismissed or are left unconsidered by a discourse predicated on design intervention.

Koolhaas's recurrent interest in the Berlin Wall is instructive. The division of Berlin resulted from an intense political, economic, and ideological storm that raged throughout postwar Europe, finally taking dramatic architectural form in Berlin. Seen against the brutal division of the city, the intentions of architects—their capacity to methodically intervene in the city, such as the plans of Le Corbusier,

Hans Scharoun, Alison and Peter Smithson, and Rob Krier for Friedrichstadt—appears practically negligible. The wall, while standing, represented a brutal measure against which even the best of design intentions could not avoid comparison. It is the tragically complex circumstances of its existence understood against the simplicity and singularity of its result (it is simply a wall) that has made the Berlin Wall a representative intervention of the contemporary city. Koolhaas's outrageous retroactive interpretation of the zone created by the wall "as a park run through with a Zen Sculpture" is, in this regard, significant. Through retroactive analysis, the complex social and political space is brought within the scope of architectural concern, its lack of intention notwithstanding. The return of this type of political and ideological production of space does not, however, come without cost.

If, as both Koolhaas and Le Corbusier have suggested, the city is the result of some catastrophe, then the question remains if catastrophe is the occasion for reform (as it was for Le Corbusier and other conventional urbanists, both nostalgic and utopian), or the occasion for celebration (as it was for Koolhaas in *Delirious New York*). Responding positively to the force beyond intervention may ultimately amount to bargaining with the devil. Investing the residue of an unplanned, uncontrolled process with a (positive) conceptual and ideological charge amounts to a direct attack on conventional notions of urban planning and control. It is, in fact, a celebration of the very forces that preempt conventional efforts at intervention. The inability to order—an inability to plan and design in the conventional sense—opens some new and rather difficult if not (professionally) treacherous discursive territory. [...]

The transition from the retroactive study of Manhattan to the "anti-Manhattan" of the postwar contemporary city is accomplished through the dogged pursuit of the forces of urban development. Departing from the earlier studies, these forces are associated not with a specific type of urban architecture but with an entirely different aspect of the city—the program or event. The event becomes the critical locus of urban or metropolitan investigation, and architecture is understood merely as a residue of the event. [...] The event emerges as key to the postwar condition, not as a matter of preference or choice, but as a response to the apparent dissipation of the postwar city and the dematerialization of its architecture. The powerful architecture of the metropolis was dissolved, literally, in the glass wall of the corporate slab. But while it has dissolved, it has not disappeared. [...]

In a 1991 competition for the redevelopment of La Défense, OMA produced a project whose intention was simply the recovery of an urban tabula rasa. In a series of charts, the life expectancy of each building in the development was plotted, resulting in a schedule for the evacuation of the site. Given the quality of recent construction in La Défense, that schedule proved to be astonishingly short. In less than twenty years, the majority of the site would be erased, creating a metropolitan void, a conceptual Nevada, adjacent to the center of Paris. For all of the characteristics already ascribed to "the void," the tabula rasa is now perhaps the most significant.

One is struck by the simplicity of the proposition: the possibility of a fresh start, a "new innocence," shown latent in the compromised construction of the contemporary city. The tables revealed that, owing to the short life span of the buildings, the contemporary city is distinct from any other in that the possibility of a new beginning is just below the surface. This is a palpable characteristic, perhaps the salient characteristic, of the contemporary city. Flying in the face of the largely discredited notion of the tabula rasa, the project is, in effect, a substantial recognition that one cannot not have the potential to begin again.

However, before embracing (or reembracing) the tabula rasa latent in the "the void," it is important to return the discussion to the urban storm and its chaos. While the tabula rasa may be considered a critical aspect of the Modern legacy, embracing chaos comes from an entirely different world which, for lack of a better term, must be labeled postmodern. As discussed above, the retroactive method aggressively seeks to dismantle the basic planning and design intentions of orthodox Modernism. Submitting to the urban dynamic, the maelstrom beyond control, implies not another way to intervene in the architecture of the city, but the impossibility of a meaningful intervention at all. It represents a willful and enthusiastic surrender to all that modern architecture and planning attempted to control or deny. While garden-variety deconstructivists pursue *retardataire* representations of chaos, debris, and indecisiveness, Koolhaas is methodologically courting these decidedly postmodern qualities, flirting with the dissolution of basic instrumental prerogatives (planning being not so much reinvented as finally eclipsed).

The wedding of the tabula rasa with chaos theory produces a poignant irony ("post-architectural modernity") not lost on Koolhaas. In observing chaos as most clearly demonstrated in the Japanese city, he notes that in Japan, chaos has already become an object of consumption: "Where intelligence meets masochism, chaos has rapidly become the dominant leitmotif of architecture and urbanism." He goes on to remark: "How profound or pathetic is the discovery of chaos as a new inspiration? Chaos is only beautiful or interesting in as much as it represents the *end of all deliberate intervention*. Among all the borrowings of this decade, chaos is the most paradoxical."

This paradox must of course be acknowledged in Koolhaas's own work. Before embracing the outrageous possibilities of conceptual Nevadas it would be well to remember that the category could (must) be expanded to include the work of the Royal Air Force and the V-2 on Berlin and London. It could also include the holes that "redevelopment" blasted into the heart of every American city. Is the "metropolitan void" to be understood as an unmitigated violence again to urban culture, or as a tabula rasa, a necessary fresh start? Given the polarities of chaos and utopia, we seem to be suffering from a confusion of opposites. Was the Berlin Wall a savage dismemberment of the city, or "a park run through with a Zen Sculpture?" (Which do you want it to be?) This is the paradox that Koolhaas insists we reckon with.

In this regard the persistent metaphors of an urban storm, of an architecture of debris and residue, begin to take on new associations. There is little doubt that the wreckage piling up under the feet of Walter Benjamin's "angel of history" amounts to our urban legacy. Despite the protests of a generation of postmodern architects, the storm blowing in from paradise has not abated. Koolhaas is clearly suggesting that we face the other direction and veer into the storm. Unlike his contemporaries who reproduce the pile of debris, Koolhaas modestly suggests that while we may be unable to stop the pileup, we can perhaps manage a simple clearing, whether a tabula rasa, beach, redevelopment zone, or a "runway for angels," a moment's lucidity emerging from the present urban condition, which, while perhaps uncontrollable, may at least be seen and celebrated for what it is.

THE IMAGE ACCORDING TO OMA

Karen Stein

I.D. 1 (1992), 66–75.

[...] Koolhaas and the members of his Rotterdam-based firm, the Office for Metropolitan Architecture, have [...] inspired generations of students not only with their theories of a "culture of congestion," but also by their unusual renderings of proposed structures. While their American counterparts were busy producing mathematically precise ink-on-Mylar studies, OMA has been painting in color with a childlike exuberance. OMA started out in 1975 as a partnership between two architects (Koolhaas and Elia Zenghelis) and two artists (Koolhaas and Zenghelis' wives, Madelon Vriesendorp and Zoe Zenghelis), whose paintings stood as early symbols of the OMA style. [...] In what appears in retrospect to have been an impressively planned campaign, OMA began disseminating its ideas. Koolhaas and Elia Zenghelis taught at London's Architectural Association, where they quickly developed a devoted following, and OMA participated in many high-profile international competitions, yielding a remarkable portfolio of widely published designs, none of which were built. Counterbalancing OMA's rigorous practical and theoretical plan of attack was the improvisational quality of the work itself—the collision of geometric shapes that quickly became the group's signature. And if OMA's drawings at times resembled storyboards for a motion picture of contemporary life, it's no accident: Koolhaas began his career as a scriptwriter. Although his stint in the film industry was certainly influential, Koolhaas himself prefers to look within architecture for inspiration, referring to the Russian Suprematists of the 1920s and to early proponents of the International Style. As the composition of OMA has gradually changed over the years (Elia Zenghelis established an independent office in Athens, eventually splitting with Koolhaas), so too has the nature of the work, especially the types of drawing produced. Former AA students skilled in watercolor and lithograph techniques are, however, still valuable, though often anonymous, contributors to the firm's output. (For the most part, OMA's drawings—including Koolhaas's—are unsigned.) Alternatingly irreverent, slick, childlike, haunting, cartoonish, elusive, inconspicuous, and technologically masterful, the drawings today are as varied in effect as in medium: watercolor, ink-on-Mylar, Prismacolor-on-tracing-paper, collage and air-brushing are all in the repertoire. Beyond their value as an integral step in the design process, Koolhaas realized early on that OMA's drawings could serve a further purpose. In recent years, architectural drawings have been increasingly seen as works of art in their own right, offering up-and-coming collectors an affordable alternative to contemporary artists. Intentionally or not, Koolhaas has skillfully navigated the often-treacherous intersection of art and commerce. Today, works by Koolhaas and OMA remain "consistently good sellers," according to Manhattan dealer Max Protetch, whose successful show of Koolhaas's work in the early 1980s helped tide OMA through lean years. Ironically, now that the architect is at last building at a scale commensurate with his visions on paper, he has less time to spend on theoretical projects and on drawing. Recently OMA has begun to replace the hand of the artist with the artistry of the machine. Like other large firms overseeing commissions scattered around the world, OMA is exploring the use of computer-aided design. As might be expected, the group has taken its experiments with technology one step beyond simply using the computer as an electronic pencil. For example, video cameras film rough study models, from which still shots are printed. The images, blurred and purposefully vague, create a dynamic MTV-like effect to project presentations. OMA's innovation here, it seems, is not only a graphic one. It's an implicit recognition of the increasingly complex issues, both stylistic and technological, that face architects today. For in the end, OMA's art raises the thorny question of what a drawing means: is it an actual tool of design, or merely a carefully edited representation of it?

HANS WERLEMANN

Bart Lootsma
De Architect-thema 51 (1993), 22–23.

The collaboration between Hans Werlemann and Rem Koolhaas is probably among one of the closest between a photographer and an architect. Werlemann not only photographs the buildings and models, but also designs the exhibitions and installations of OMA and is routinely listed as a staff contributor on the competition designs.

Alongside his interest in photography, Werlemann has always been fascinated by architecture. He worked for the architect Fokke van Duijn for a while, even self-handedly building a house plus studio for him. Werlemann considers architecture a "more optimistic" medium than photography, because as a profession it seeks serious solutions for complicated problems in the world.

Before zeroing in on architecture, Werlemann was a commercial photographer. He once rolled special, extra-long cigarettes to market the Belinda brand. The advertisements were so successful, the company decided to actually make its cigarettes longer. One of the last ads he shot, with Alan David Tu, was for Silk Cut cigarettes: a technically perfect studio photograph of a piece of silk with the contours of a pair of scissors raggedly cut out of it, resembling a pirate flag. Neither the product nor the brand name were shown in the photo, and the only text on the giant advertising placards hanging in the Underground was the health warning by the British health secretary in large letters. In the end, Werlemann decided that one shouldn't be making advertisements for these kinds of products and he stopped doing it.

Still, he remains fascinated by how a product can be elucidated or brought to life in an advertisement. In his studio, he keeps files of his father's collection of advertisements that were cut out from American magazines. Werlemann Senior was art director of Lintas. The collection is full of remarkable images, many of them montages or collages, that either reveal some distinct idea behind the product in a cartoonish way or almost surrealistically make an association between the product and something entirely different: whiskey with a horse, for instance. In the advertising of that time, you had almost none of the more snobbish target group or lifestyle thinking so prevalent today.

A distinctive feature of Werlemann's architectural photos is that they almost never attempt to show the architecture or the space exclusively. They are always colored by a location's use and an—often very specific—atmosphere. Nor is there much difference in the approach he uses for the maquette or the architectural photos. Werlemann sees OMA primarily as an academy or university tied directly to a practice where three-dimensional, 1:1 models are built. This helps explain his need in the photos to "generate visions of the future based on what exists," as he expresses it. He deploys a variety of tricks—small lamps, collage—in photographing the scale models in order to create the most convincing "vision" possible. He also purposely uses poor focus, grainy films and video imagery to detract from the materiality of the model. This is true of his architectural photos as well. While Werlemann may sometimes use a technical camera for those, he also regularly shoots with a hand-held compact camera and a Pentax 6×7. He calls the Pentax a "soft" camera, which then also produces "soft" slides and negative. The only benefit of its larger negative size compared to the compact camera is that the slides or negatives are better for processing afterward. Werlemann takes advantage of that for exhibitions, where the photographs might, say, be printed as bubble jet prints. With all of Werlemann's photos, you are constantly reminded that you are looking at a mechanical reproduction. The focus and color saturation of the slides is such that they would have to be slightly boosted if the photos were going to be lithographed for magazine reproduction. The finest details fall away, but then that is not what OMA's architecture is about anyway. [...]

One specific problem that arises in photographing for a firm such as OMA, with its tremendous exposure in almost all of the international magazines, is the risk of image stigmatization. That is why they took such an enormous number of totally different photos of the Villa dall'Ava and the Rotterdam Kunsthal, under a wide range of weather and lighting conditions. Ideally, each magazine is then given a different set of photographs. Since most magazines tended to choose a limited number of overview shots for the Kunsthal, for example, those kinds of photos were no longer provided at all after that.

Werlemann's fascination for the advertisements of the 1960s and need to depict futuristic visions are strongly evident in the photos he made of the Villa dall'Ava in Paris. The villa is not documented as an architectural solution for a specific commission (a house for a couple with one daughter), but as a manifesto for living in the future. Werlemann developed various scenarios for happenings in and around the villa. The basic idea is that the villa offers its inhabitants protection from the overwhelming influences and events on the outside, which only penetrate in through the media. Thus in the opposite photo, you have Jean Nouvel reading a book while TV images of war are projected onto the transparent facade in the background. In Werlemann's vision, the giraffe, too, as an endangered species, has found refuge at the home, while at the same time its delicate build provides commentary on the structure of the house itself and its setting: the giraffe is a metaphor for the Eiffel Tower.

STRATEGIC RETREAT

Alejandro Zaera-Polo
El Croquis 53 (1992), 32–51.

[...] The relevance of OMA's recent work lies precisely in the evolution from those attitudes that have developed since the economic-ideological crisis at the end of the 1960s, when avant-garde architecture was confined to a superstructural position and restricted almost exclusively to linguistic manipulations or utopian formulations. This autonomy is increasingly unsustainable when the engagement with infrastructure, in whatever meaning one may give to this term, seems unavoidable. One can detect in the recent work of OMA a questioning of traditional ideologies, a quite clear interest in ideologically insane designs. If ideology has traditionally been a form of legitimization and validation of action within the production processes, constituting a type of social cement able to provide the social processes of production and reproduction with standards and values, the idea that late capitalism requires ideological consensus to survive is questionable. [...]

The aperture of OMA's ideological diaphragm permits exposure to a whole series of specifically contemporary phenomena that can only be addressed from outside traditional political ideologies, and, consequently, the renunciation of linguistic coherence. The eclecticism of the retroactive manifesto becomes the operative basis that drives the recent production of OMA from the simultaneous rejection of ideological and linguistic coherence to the articulation of multiplicities with performative aims. OMA's architecture is crucially focused on the performative, as its validation is not grounded in functional, representational, or reproductive effects, but in operative exactness, adequacy or efficiency. Rather than posing ideological or semantic questions, OMA's effort is concentrated on material, topographic, and spatial organization. OMA's work must be seen as a strategic retreat, the cessation of ideological resistance to the developments of contemporary culture.

FINDING FREEDOMS

Alejandro Zaera-Polo
El Croquis 53 (1992), 6–31.

[...] **azp:** It seems that you accept a certain cultural and productive condition as a frame for your work. How do you articulate this acceptance in your judgments?

rk: I have an interest in professional activity. I want to build: to a frightening large extent that means basically accepting most of the time. I'm not embarrassed about that. I am certainly provoked in a very deep sense by this acceptance. It engages me. In that sense, my interest in Atlanta, for example, is ambiguous. Basically, I try to postpone the moment of judgment as long as possible to derive as many influences as possible from it.

azp: But how do you deal ideologically with this acceptance? We are talking about the possible end of public realm, of the civil society, of the humanist thought, and other arguments traditionally validated as "positive." Should this acceptance be considered as a revolutionary or as a complacent position?

rk: It is almost impossible to answer those questions. If you say it's a complacent attitude, I would say no, but what does it mean if I say no? I might be just hiding my own complacency or not being self-critical enough? It certainly doesn't feel complacent from the inside. We are seduced; we feel simultaneous glee and horror. We try to think about these contradictory emotions. In my perception of Atlanta those two things always play very strongly. A simple question: how so many mediocre buildings together can generate a fantastic architectural spectacle. Or, how can so much "badness" sometimes lead to a kind of intelligence? It's not complacency but fascination, and in fascination there is always an element of surrender.

azp: Does not this mean a certain inability to judge? Or is the lack of ideology characteristic of contemporary discourse?

rk: This is also a very artificial attitude, because of course we are full of judgments and full of moralism, but nevertheless we have the kind of instinct to explore things. Judgments make you very heavy. It's like a mountaineer who has to travel light to get somewhere. And this may be a very simple metaphor, but I still think that in the end, the inability to judge is not the right expression. I would rather talk about postponement of judgment and articulation of the problematic, which does justice to as many good and bad sides as possible. In that sense, I think that we perform a role almost as medium, exactly because—in spite of everything—we are now practitioners: we are exposed to drifts, tropisms, tendencies that suggest mutations, and I think we sense them before they become the subject of official judgments. The advantage of a nonacademic position is that we can experiment—even on ourselves. But we still "judge" all the time ...

If you look at our project for Melun-Sénart, there were explicit judgments of contemporary architecture: it is mostly *merde.* And then the further attempt to make with this *merde* something which is nevertheless respectable and exciting and intellectually tenable: a redefinition of a city. We made many judgments about what is beautiful and what is not so beautiful, what should stay and what should go, what should be shown and what should be hidden. We made judgments in terms of priorities. Of course, they are all individual judgments, and in order to preserve the purity and the freedom of the various forces at play, the issue of morality is postponed till the very last moment, or occasionally suspended. As they say in Japan: it floats. [...]

azp: How do you think that the rise of "capitalist-socialist hybrids" in Europe affects the production of architecture?

rk: It profoundly influences architectural production. Lille, for instance, is a very good example, where a socialist city, a city with a socialist majority, creates a public-private partnership where it retains 50.00001 % of the financial weight in the operation. It is a socialist administration, that doesn't have any cash, but can deliver the ground. It is therefore completely dependent on certain hypotheses about finance, which determine ultimately the shape and contents of the project. The realities are both unpleasant and intriguing.

azp: Where do you find the distinctive features of the European condition, Europe being the clearest example of this political hybridization, and how do they affect the production of architecture in comparison with the Japanese, or with the American models, or even with the straight socialist models?

rk: Well, in Europe there is still a kind of safety net underneath all these actions. In other words, at some point we can say, or our clients can say: this is going too far, I don't accept it. There is no sell-out: there remains a "political" part of the program in terms of noncommercial, communal or quasi-communal elements. There is still an ideal of balance that is probably the most typical feature of this hybrid system that you are describing. What is interesting in Japan is that it is totally capitalist and you feel this in a kind of corporate hegemony, in the absence of explicit social ambitions that the socialist-capitalist hybrids have in Europe. In Japan, there is an enormous "absence" which gives you a sense of disappointment with many things, almost a systematic avoidance of any contents. And that is very exciting: *incredible buildings that are about nothing.* They have no program, no social ambition. What is really fascinating about the present moment in Europe, about the hybrids you are talking about is their capitalist society with remnants, and sometimes very intense appearances, of social ambition. I think this is really unique; it is very difficult to say if it is real or not. Maybe it was just a kind of fiction during one or two years; an ephemeral condition, a kind of temporary euphoria: there were not too many "problems."

[...]

azp: One of the most intriguing aspects of your career is your ability to break with your past: from writer to practitioner, from Europe to America and back. [...] Your process is not evolutive, but made out of breaks. Lately you have expressed your critique of Deconstructivism, although you were part of that famous show. Which are the reasons for that critique?

rk: My criticism is basically related to my observation of the effects of chaos: the "chaos sensibility." My skepticism about deconstructivists is based on their presumption that this naive, banal analogy between a supposedly irregular geometry and a fragmented world or a world where values are no longer anchored in a fixed way. It is hopelessly visual, compositional and therefore, in a very traditional sense, architectural. And that is ultimately for me decorative. I always hesitated between exploding things and making things. And right now it is ten times more interesting to make things than to explode things, also because explosion lasts one moment, but making takes much longer. In that sense deconstruction has done everything it could do in architecture. It might have been an important way of analyzing things, to experiment, but I do not see any future for it within architecture. [...] What Deconstructivism has produced is the worst response you can possibly give, in terms of my interpretation of what the profession should do at this moment. It is wonderful as an aesthetic, or as an intellectual position for the architect, but probably not for all the other partners—the public, for instance—who are stuck in that kind of fossilized moments of "dissatisfaction" or "inability." Not very interesting and even not very bearable.

azp: You experienced also that shift from being a writer or a thinker to a practitioner—from the theoretical world to a direct involvement in the processes of production. Which is for you the articulation between both?

rk: The relationship for me between the two is incredibly strong, although I never really thought that it would be possible to be a theoretician of architecture and an architect. I always felt an architect. An architect with theoretical and literary interests, with the need to analyze the exact conditions and exact potentials of the profession. That is my interpretation of my own activities. Ultimately, I wrote *Delirious New York* to define for myself an agenda of what was interesting and what could be done. And all I can confess is that it was a painful transition: to exercise the profession is almost a bestial activity. It was only recently with the Fukuoka project in Japan and the houses in Rotterdam and in Paris that I started to feel more confident as a practitioner. Maybe, I am approximating now some of the goals that I wanted to achieve.
[...]

THE IJ-BOULEVARD OF BROKEN DREAMS

René Zwaap
De Groene Amsterdammer,
November 25, 1992.

Rem Koolhaas has a strange effect on politicians. The celebrated architect has developed a jargon that is, with all its postmodern paradoxes and dark adjurations, similar to that of Jean Baudrillard who has had a few sherries too much. Koolhaas doesn't tend to initiate simple reasonings but rather druidic incantations, meant to bring his audience in a temporary intoxication of unlimited possibilities. The core is hubris-stimulating pep talk, staged with sharp disdain for the slow thinking paths of bureaucracy and the old Dutch doutbfulness. [...]

One would think that Koolhaas exactly because of this predilection for metaphysical words and the big Napoleonic gesture would be the archenemy of the average municipal politician, who is used to operating, since time immemorial, in the lowest gear, if only to keep a semblance of control. Nothing, however, is less true: Koolhaas is idolized, certainly in the city hall of Amsterdam. Never was an urbanist so endlessly trusted by his clients, or it should be Albert Speer in the Third Reich. If Mayor Ed van Thijn and his aldermen get their way, Amsterdam will become Koolhaas-City, as soon as possible.

[...] Koolhaas's star in Amsterdam has been on the rise as soon as project developer MBO [...] appointed him in 1986 as a contemporary figurehead for an urban invasion of the capital. His first big task was breaking all kinds of taboos associated with rebuilding the ever necessitous Bijlmermeer neighborhood. [...] He did so with verve. With a sparkling presentation Koolhaas took down all the holy houses of the Bijlmermeer (such as separate traffic flows and car-free ground levels). He also designed some big urban villas in an area where up till then ragged junkies had been sleeping in lush public gardens.

In the end, nothing came of all his plans, but that was not the intention. [...] Lesser gods could start to work in his trail, as little fish in the wake of a whale. Koolhaas had become a star in Amsterdam. Mayor Van Thijn invited him time and again in his residence for confidential conversations about the future of the city.

And then came the IJ-Boulevard. It started really modest, [...] but it grew to an urban Deltaplan, with a gigantic expansion of the inner city of Amsterdam at stake. At first, the discussion centered around a clear area of about 50,000 square meters; anno 1992 the scenario for the shore of the IJ involves no less than 1,200,000 square meters, extending from Sloterdijk to the IJ-Lake, known to insiders as the IJ-Axis. Professor of social geography Willem Heinemeijer, who launched the idea of a pedestrian promenade in '82, sighed: "It got completely out of hand."

This scaling of thoughts was impossible without the effort of urbanist super cannon Koolhaas who, again engaged by MBO, drew up a "spatial scenario" for the area. And again it was Koolhaas's hocus-pocus that persuaded skeptics. He talked about an "enormous injection of possible innovation and vitality in the center," which would allow Amsterdam to join in the ruthless competitive struggle between the major cities of Europe, according to Koolhaas typical for our era. Limiting thoughts to the development of the IJ-boulevard was a mistake. What was necessary was the complete development of the northern edge of the city. He advocated a gigantic building explosion in that zone, concentrated on "islands," which would turn mass into—watch out, here comes a typical *koolhaasism*—"critical mass."

Koolhaas provided—and that was the intention of his commissioners, keen on the largest possible project—a total reevaluation of all values. He pleaded for a rehabilitation of the office. The "prefered instrument of capitalist exploitation" could, when "redefined," lead "to a new idyll." It was another way of saying that along the IJ, towers of sixty to hundred meters needed to rise up. His ideas for Central Station, according to Koolhaas "an urban mistake," boiled down to total transformation. The station needlessly blocked the contact between the city and the water, and should be accommodated under a gigantic futuristic hood, with see-through options to the IJ. All in all, Koolhaas's scenario contains a new city, complete with offices, a big shopping mall, housing and cultural services. Total desired investment: six billion guilders.

[...] All this cannot conceal that opposition against the IJ-plan is increasing. And, so it seems, entirely justified. The AWF (Amsterdam Waterfront Financing Company) is finalizing the business plan of Koolhaas's urban prophecy as we speak. At last the test of financial possibilities! Although the plan will only be published January next year, it has thrown forward its shadows. Those things the city could profit from in the context of a public-private partnership (new housing and cultural infrastructure in exchange for office space), will only be realized little by little. Take the new housing district, planned for the Houthavens: further testing reveals that because of marshy ground, these houses will be three times as expensive as usual. For the "cultural services," the problem looms of the total absence of funding. At the same time, investers are not at all crowding in front of the office of the AWF. The criticism of the first hour, namely that Koolhaas's plan will be in the end nothing but a license to sell the most attractive pieces of ground to offices and that Amsterdam will in no way whatsoever profit from all this, seems more and more justified. The question imposes itself whether this hasn't been exactly the intention of the banks involved. [...]

SOME UNFINISHED BUSINESS ON ST.-GERMAIN

Herbert Muschamp
New York Times, February 14, 1993.

At a lecture in New York last fall, the Dutch architect Rem Koolhaas began by wondering aloud why his generation has taken so long to make its mark upon the city. Koolhaas, 47, is part of the postwar European generation that came of age with the "events of May," the student upheavals that rocked Paris and other cities in 1968. For Koolhaas, '68 remains a touchstone, not for sentimental reasons, or not mainly, but because the protests revealed attitudes that, for better or worse, remain in force. To paraphrase his musings: if architects of this generation feel "marginalized," that is because they chose to occupy the margins, because they staked their identity to a stance of opposition they have yet to outgrow. No one is stopping them from crossing over their self-imposed barricades, nor is the city still the stern father's stone face. Koolhaas had a point, but does it apply to him? Unlike many of his contemporaries, he has never shrunk back from the urban center, as the name of his firm—Office for Metropolitan Architecture, or OMA—suggests.

Yet that firm retains a countercultural spirit. Based in Rotterdam, OMA is, in effect, an office of city planning without a city to plan, the self-appointed bureaucracy of some imaginary city that has replaced its bureaucrats with dreamers. Images of New York and Atlanta float through Koolhaas's built and theoretical projects like wish fulfillments for a new world. But the work remains philosophically attuned to Paris and to the role students have traditionally played throughout the city's cultural history.

Now it looks as if Koolhaas will get to add a chapter to that history. In December, he won a competition to design a new library building for the Jussieu Campus of the Sorbonne, a pivotal site in the May uprising a quarter-century ago. For this architect, it is a dream of a job, a chance to explore his generation's social mythology at its historic root. And Koolhaas's design is dream architecture: a building where space flows out of confining compartments into a high-rise full of free associations.

The location is at once a dream and a nightmare. The Jussieu Campus is on the Left Bank, where the Boulevard St.-Germain meets the Seine, not far from Notre Dame. But the campus itself is infernal. Designed in the early 1960s by Edouard Albert, it is mostly housed in one immense building, a square metal labyrinth that seems to go on forever. Within the steel walls, modular units are laid out like a checkerboard, each module enclosing an abyss of a courtyard. Outside, a strip of emptiness tries to pass for public space. Only the faceless figures that populate architectural renderings would feel at home here.

The building was unfinished at the time of the 1968 riots, when construction was suspended. The Government hoped to ward off future unrest by shifting resources—and thereby students—from Parisian schools to suburban campuses. That left Albert's building with a ragged, sawtoothed corner, which is where the new building will rise. Containing two separate libraries and facilities for student recreation, the project will mark the campus's symbolic completion. Koolhaas's "completion" is also an inversion: transparent, vertical and fluid where Albert is opaque, horizontal and stiff. Seven concrete floor slabs, with 23 feet between them, define the main levels of a square, glass-clad tower.

Instead of stacking up the floors in the usual horizontal layers, Koolhaas has made large, irregular cuts in each slab, removing a third of their floor area. Wide ramps, inserted into the cuts, slope at different angles and meet at intermediary levels between the floors. The result is the most spectacular use of the spiral form since Frank Lloyd Wright's Guggenheim Museum. Entering the building at the third-floor level (through connectors to Albert's building), students can descend to a library of scientific books or mount the ramps to one devoted to the humanities. But this wide-open space will encourage a porous relationship between its components. Reading rooms, stacks, classrooms, offices and audio-visual centers will occupy both sloping and level floors. Some slopes will form natural amphitheaters; others will be landscaped, like indoor parks. Cafés and sports areas will supplement a scheme conceived to resemble the mix of an urban street. In effect, Koolhaas has scooped up the barren public space outside Albert's building, folded it this way and that to create a continuous vertical landscape, built up the landscape to keep it constantly active, and wrapped the whole thing up in a transparent skin. University life will become visibly part of the city.

While the warping of the floor planes may seem idiosyncratic, it is not without precedent in twentieth-century architecture. Those slopes will be familiar terrain to anybody who has climbed the steps of the Metropolitan Opera House or has seen pictures of the Helicline at the 1939 New York World's Fair. Wallace K. Harrison, who designed these monuments, has been a major influence on Koolhaas, and so has Mies van der Rohe. His somewhat quixotic goal has been to forge a synthesis between these two irreconcilable figures. It is Mies that we see reflected in the library's unadorned skin of glass, in the regular rhythm of its exposed concrete columns. An interplay between the disciplined and the polymorphous is the library's underlying formal idea.

While it may seem logical to identify the structural system with science, the free-form floors with the humanities, in fact Koolhaas designs against that logic. Like the philosopher of science Gaston Bachelard, he wants to pierce the wall between these disciplines. For Bachelard, a Sorbonne professor whose influence on architecture has grown since his death in 1962, the poet and the scientist were creative beings allied against the excessive claims of reason. For Koolhaas, structure may be essential to architecture but need not dictate its form. Here, the structural grid supports an experiment to show that form can depart from regularity yet deepen its obligation to function. As such, the design converts to constructive form the explosive forces that erupted here twenty-five years ago. As James Miller observes in his biography of Michel Foucault, the student protest was more potent for being apparently aimless. It was focused beyond concrete political demands toward "the very order of things in the modern world generally."

Regularized, homogenized, rigid—that order remains on permanent display in Albert's building, though Koolhaas is mature enough to recognize the idealism it once represented. Paired with it, his building will be at once a gesture of reconciliation and a permanent act of rupture. Functionally flexible, formally indeterminate, the library is designed to show that architecture can do more than contain the mind's adventures. It can also lead minds out of containment by embarking on adventures of its own. Naturally, the students who use this building may find Koolhaas's dizzying adventure as intolerable as he found Albert's.

MAY-68-PROGRAMMING

Nikolaus Kuhnert, Philipp Oswalt

ARCH+, 117 (1993), 22–33.

We have the impression that new projects like those for Jussieu and Yokohama are a rupture in your work. It looks as if you want to break with your own history and start from scratch, by developing a more abstract architecture.

I have always had this problem of jumpiness. I find myself in a critical phase. I am now forty-eight years old, and that is a dangerous age. Look at other architects. Either you have many projects and nothing more to say or you have only one or two more projects and keep a certain measure of freshness. And that is what is happening to me. If I could choose, I would only build the library in Jussieu. I'm at it right now to decrease my office. I find the prospect of working, in the coming four years, with ten to fifteen rather than with fifty people, extremely attractive.

The project for Jussieu is astonishingly brave, when one realizes that you actually want to build it.

In 1968 I was a journalist for a Dutch magazine, and in May I went to Paris to report on the events. And I was younger, I had contacts with the Dutch group Fluxus, and with some of the Situationists. Toward '68 I always had double, partly critical attitude, but the older I get, the more I realize how much I am shaped by that, much more than I previously thought. You say it is a brave project, but I believe it is simply a shocking "May-68-Programming" to do something like that. In this way it's a very political project. Not in the least because the existing campus was an important center for Paris in '68. The project is in a certain sense a dialogue with what was going on at the time.

[...]

You collaborate with modern artists. Günther Förg is involved in the Kunsthal in Rotterdam. For the project in La Défense you want to work with Jenny Holzer. The facades for Jussieu refer to the glass igloos by Mario Merz. In which way is your work influenced by contemporary art? Do you try to connect art and science, a bit like Bernard Tschumi in the 1970s, when he tried to connect his abstract and rational concepts with the unconscious sensibility of artists?

That's one way to see it, but I would rather compare it to the method of a journalist. I don't follow art and science because I want to connect them. I simply read everything, I read *Der Spiegel* and *Stern*, *Max* and *The New York Review of Books*, I read trash but also significant things. I am an omnivore. For our age the equality of information is typical, which is both wonderful and terrible. That is why I resist to speak of specific influences. [...] We all swim in a marinade, and we don't know this marinade. [...]

How should one pursue city planning today?

We have lost the possibility to plan a city in three dimensions, to develop it as a vision, as a model. Those days are gone for good. One can no longer determine and decree, one can no longer desire to regulate processes, to modify or redirect them, when they take place anyhow. [...] For this erosion of the role of the planner and the architect, there are three reasons. First, an intellectual weakness, when it comes to thinking about the center and its meaning. [...] Of course squares, boulevards and streets are wonderful, but that doesn't mean that we, under the current conditions, can still build these wonderful places. The IBA in Berlin was a laboratory of the rediscovery of all these things, but at the same time also the first demonstration of the impossibility to turn this rediscovery into the principle for future planning. The generation of 1968 has both rediscovered and destroyed the city. [...] Secondly, there is political weakness. Politicians have no money and they are obliged to others if they want to build. When these finanical problems are finally solved, politicians are always out for consensus, but they lack the courage to take risks. [...] A third important factor is the developer. These real estate companies are acting in an increasingly primitive way; they are intuitively and untiringly resisting any attempt at integrating their schemes into a programmatic concept. Today we are no longer dealing with the citizen as a responsible resident of a city who is trying to express his role in the form of a building relating to the city as a whole. Today's developers are no longer city residents—they are multinational corporations, vagrant capitals which are prowling around, driven by a quasi-biological instinct, for investment opportunities of all kinds, even on the most vulgar levels. They are at work in Berlin, they have discovered Prague, they are already on the way to Shanghai, South China or Africa, always looking to take advantage of opportunities which present themselves. These may be logical processes, but they never create the kind of stability required for programmatic work.

[...]

X-FILLED ROOM: DUTCH HOUSE IN ROTTERDAM

Joost Meuwissen

Wiederhall 16 (1994), 56–59.

By presenting his Linthorst House as a "collage" of three dwelling types—dike house, patio house, and villa with garden—Rem Koolhaas puts all emphasis on the interior where the three types overlap, not on the exterior. In this sense the types themselves could be thought of from the start as interiors.

A dike house is a house whose stories are unclear, there being no obvious ground floor; one story simply stops while another is not really a story but turns into one. And a "villa with garden" is a pleonasm, a formula which states that where the garden begins the villa ends. Two of the three types incorporate a denial. Only patio house is used as an entirely positive term—in the sense that a patio house could be regarded as the most freestanding dwelling type, one which has least to do with the responsibilities of the natural, urban and social environment. A dike house is normally built on a dike, so that the front facade has one story and the rear facade two, with the house forming a canopy over an abyss; this can be viewed as a romantic situation because the principal facade is the tall one at the rear from which a landscape is seen but which is not itself seen and can therefore be regarded almost as an interior element.

The Linthorst House is the other way around. It has no ground floor which becomes an upper story and finally a view. The ground floor stops, ceases, but this phenomenon is barely expressed in the front facade. The floor above has an uninterrupted view on both front and back from a strip window—with a window breast at the front and extending from floor to ceiling at the rear—but the view has no direction because it is designed evenly at both sides, simply as "outside," but also because the interior elements form a sequence in the other direction, across, and do not lead one's gaze. The element that would be most suitable for this, the Mies quote, the veined, flat wall that separates the living area from the other functions, has a symmetrical position in the cross section and emphasizes the middle rather than the ends. It has been domesticated and is in wood instead of marble, so that it no longer refers to the outside but only to the inside. It does not shine either, and, sunk within itself, reflects no light except its own. Moreover, despite its flatness it is not extendable, or rather if it extends it is done by other means.

The panels which slide out at each end of the wall have no color, no texture, no light and in fact no materiality. They are pure obscurity. The veined Mies wall is extendable in the form of a negation, a denial not only of its extendability but above all of its intensity as an element of the interior of the house. The wall appears to stand, as a reference to Mies's heavy marble, but the extending panels hang, like wings, without touching the floor. The floor continues underneath unmoved and uninterrupted. When the wall extends, when it makes an evident movement, it flies away and loses touch with the floor. In this way architectural elements—wall and panel—are used to define the wall as furniture, as mere interior.

[...] The house does not give shape to a natural cohesion of day and night, as if in such a cohesion the occupants were helplessly condemned to such a natural condition, subject to a rhythm they have not chosen. The natural exterior is iconographically shut out. Asked about his experience of living in the house, the proud owner replied, "We have no curtains." This draws attention to a very Dutch characteristic of the domestic culture pursued there but is also remarkable from the security point of view given that the owner was the Rotterdam alderman responsible for finance and art and later an alderman for the port, for the world's largest port, for the sea, for a depth extending over the entire globe. The architect may describe the Kralingen area of Rotterdam as an "arcadia within the metropolis," but it is nonetheless the metropolis as both chaotic periphery and global condition.

"We have no curtains" means: we never look outside, rather in the way that on CNN the word *foreign* is banned. As it grows dark no curtains are drawn. Evening falls without evoking a tactile reaction. Dwelling does not extend to outside. The "villa with garden" has no terrraces where the floor planes of the house could extend outside and ultimately define the substratum of the garden, the earth, as the fundamental and infinite base, the natural reference for the floor planes in the house. In contrast to Mies's country houses in the 1920s, here the terrace offers no proximity from which the garden is perceived as distance. The garden is not a visual presence representing a view of a landscape. It is a purely material presence, a heap of mud burying what could have been the garden right up to the house, with little firm ground. The layout of the house refers to no natural base.

The narrow terrace running the full width of the facade without interruption, even seeming to extend under the facade as if the latter were floating above its own base, is not a floor plane reaching outside as part of a sequence of floor planes forming the transition to the garden and leading the eye outside. It is an almost mobile element that seems to move more from outside to inside than vice versa. In Mies's country houses the position of the glass facade is deliberatedly undetermined, or at any rate underdetermined, so as not to disturb the continuity of the succession of terraces. In the Rotterdam house, however, the position of the facade is underdetermined because the terrace extends along it rather than at right angles to it. The terrace functions as the virtual thickness of the facade, as its *épaisseur*, as material presence without the transparency of glass—a transparency, incidentally, which is only present from inside the house by day and from outside it by night. The consequence is that the position of the facade is really only determined internally, within the facade as an element, and not insofar as it is part of the house. In a sense the terrace could be called the margin of the facade as an item of furniture, the extension of the facade into furniture. Yet the result is that the eye is stopped, as if the absent curtains had always been closed. Besides, the glass of the garden facade shows different transparencies. It is differentiated into the colors blue, white and "natural." As the "natural" becomes neutralized as a moment of choice, any view of the garden will turn into an unnaturalistic image.

The house was conceived in the mid-1980s. Rem Koolhaas felt then that behind Modernism's puritan front lay some of the most self-indulgent experiments to be found anywhere, as if the depressing look of the Modern as a style was intended to keep the unrestrained enjoyment experienced there for itself, to keep it exclusive. So from the outset the "hidden dimensions" of the Modern were regarded as individual pleasure and not as the collective program Modernism had put forward. Nor was this individual pleasure to be derived, as if in a masochistic internalizing, from individual subjection to the discipline and punishments of the Modern programs.

[...] What immediately strikes us in the Linthorst House as a false fact is that the one Mies quotation, the veined wall, relates to the other Mies quotation, the patio, in terms which reject or intensify the quotations in favor of a much more profound phenomenon. What is missing is the extensiveness of their relation, the floor or visual plane on which or in which the elements stand in front or beside each other as if they have something to do with each other, as if the marble wall forms the ideal background for the glass wall of the patio. They are both walls and are related if only by that alone. You could say that with Mies the extension of the floor plane as an architectural feature is brought about by the equal identity of the elements that rise from it. Although they look different, they could have developed from each other, as successive stages of the same thing. In this sense the floor plane is a parallel reading direction.

But the patio in the Rotterdam house, however different its facades may be, is a three-dimensional form which as a body is modeled on the other elements. As a glass case filled with air and light, as a smaller version of the house stripped of all inside and outside, of all superfluity and all attribution of meaning, as an ideal aedicule, the patio bears resemblance to Jeff Koons's glass cases containing vacuum cleaners, but then without the vacuum cleaners because it is already clean, like an image of infinite yearning washed around by the process of dwelling. The patio has no bottom and is timeless. There is no changing of the seasons or of day and night. Snow lies there summer and winter. In the evening it is lit from below through the milk-white glass floor, from the level beneath. Then it resembles an open refrigerator, an image of unrestrained mental and physical consumption, as if the occupants were meat on display.

The patio lies above the gym to form its ceiling, as the crowning of a bodily change which can assume all shapes, regardless of whatever the original human form was. Is body building anything other than having long taken leave of an original figure? The uncovered quality of the bodies below, open to every possible perception in the privacy of a hygienic space, is continued above in an aesthetic and ideal nakedness of sunbath or moonbath, unroofed but in vitro, between glass, outdoors but artificial, not in a natural space but in a space which within dwelling is most isolated from dwelling. Above people bathe in the motto which modern architecture cherished as its dream but which, as a result of supposed puritanism, under the pressure of that same motto, it had never imagined it could realize except in a spatial—and I would almost say naturalistic, noncorporeal—fashion: light, air and space, which do not come from outside but which nonetheless fill the patio equally and completely. Modernism as a basin. As ideal transformation of the house, as house in the house, as mental house—a theme whose formula could have been derived from Ungers—the patio shows the Modern to be an aesthetic of motionless fluidity, of formless fullness and all-around completeness, of hedonistic potential, of a certain oppressiveness of light, air, and space and not of their translation into motion, space, or void. The only void in the house is the staircase, the principal element of movement through the house though without becoming a promenade. The stair appears simply as the most mobile element with its length corresponding to the dimensions of the patio, just as on the other side the length and height of the kitchen unit form an interface with the patio.

[...] The elements of the house do not reflect. The elevated rooflessness of the patio is not reflected in the normal floorlessness of the stairwell. Their relation is one of denial and endlessness. Just as the patio is a slice out of the volume of the story from whose extensiveness it frees itself, so the stairwell is a slice out of the extended floor plane of the same story, so that it is filled not with bodies or corporality but with forms, with figures, with the artificially formed human shapes that rise and descend along a voluptuous, almost trapeze-like balustrade. There is formless similarity of patio and stair in their adjacency, but their similarity is expressed in such a hidden form in the layout of the house that a comparison, to use Frege's terms, can only be one of names, not of things, not of spatiality, not of appearance, not based on identity. A synthesis of body and corporality is not brought about by figure, form or shape but only insofar as the virtual space occupied by that form or shape frees itself from the extensiveness of both body and corporality and abandons the extendability of every horizontal plane, including that of stories in architecture.

THE BLINKERS THAT MAKE THE VISIONARY

Ole Bouman, Roemer van Toorn *The Invisible in Architecture* (London: Academy Editions, 1994), 442–53.

[...] *Architecture for you is above all "petrified thought." That is presumably the reason why you have no qualms about pouring ridicule on your colleagues' lack of vision and lazy-mindedness, and the fact that they so often judge your work on the basis of purely technical criteria. Does this make sense?*

Ridicule? I never meant to sound so didactic. I think that part of our activity has to do with creating a sort of *Lebensraum,* a context in which we can do what we want or rather, to put it more modestly, what we are capable of. As far as I am concerned, then, it has very little to do with some didactic need to give people a good ticking off. What does astonish me is that the things that are self-evident to us are not so for them.

All the same, after so many years of being astonished you should now be able to spot a number of examples of the Koolhaas recipe? I would have thought that you would gradually be beginning to see certain constants in the way that you and your approach are received.

It is very difficult for me to see any constants because we have changed so much ourselves. In recent years in particular we have actually landed up in a completely different world with the result that I lead a sort of double existence. I have one life in Holland and another abroad. Life in Holland is hard and abroad it is ... certainly not easy but at least it is a completely different life. We also make different things abroad from what we make here.

That means that people's responses are also different. The financial conditions under which one has to make architecture in Holland simply don't exist abroad in our experience; that also means that a number of criticisms that may be quite legitimate here, do not apply elsewhere. As far as use of materials and detailing are concerned, our block of flats in Fukuoka in Japan, for instance, is stunning in its perfection and everyone who has seen it so far has told us so. It even won the prize for the best building in Japan in 1992! I felt that the building should have something Japanese about it but that it also shouldn't be too beautiful. For that reason we opted for a very banal polyester/polystyrene matrix that was cast in black concrete; I calculated that they would come up with such perfection that that would be enough to give it some dignity. Conditions and possibilities of this order don't occur in Holland. To give you another example: I recently tried an experiment with the Byzantium building that we designed at the entrance of the Vondel Park in Amsterdam. I invited two foreign architecture critics, Klotz and Von Moos, who did not know who it was by. I asked them what they thought of it. They both thought it was an extremely interesting building. I've never managed to get a Dutch person to react that way.

[...]
Your work still seems to take what is utilitarian very much as its point of departure; it is very project-dependent and it tries to express an idea or an atmosphere that is inherent in the project. This means that you touch on matters that in themselves don't have any direct relation with architecture, that refer rather to other aspects of our culture.

We are totally dependent on the culture; that's exactly why it's so important that we make some kind of statement about it from an architectural point of view. [...] I want to work out in detail the way that we can most effectively relate and respond to what is going on at the present moment.

[...]
Is there a moment when this processing of existing conditions becomes "fashion," or aren't you interested in that particular connection?

It is interesting to me only for my own count; the others can do what they like. For myself I always try to retain an element that is hard to assimilate. I can think of nothing worse than becoming really popular, being all the rage: we should always retain something that is difficult. On the other hand there is some very fashionable architecture that I find really attractive. I experience it as very difficult to pass any moral judgment. All I know is that I myself don't want to circulate effortlessly in those smooth circles; I need the sound of grinding cogwheels too.

[...]
We talked about bringing architecture up to date. Or rather about seeing that contemporary trends are actually incorporated into architecture as it is practiced. One of the most typical features in that project is the confrontation you get with the people who want it to be "easy" and don't look at contemporary developments that are anything but easy. You could say that architecture is an ideal medium for clearing the intellectual backlog; but you might also say that, from the point of view of its limits as a discipline, architecture is neither the only nor necessarily the best means for doing this.

I am once more, quote-unquote, seriously involved in writing. That is of course another means of expression. In the Centre Pompidou, where they now give the new media the same status as painting, there is a virtual reality project in progress. I'm taking part in it. Public appearances and teaching is in a sense a sort of sideshow. For the moment I don't get the feeling that I've hit my limits. On the contrary, I feel more and more enthusiasm for defining the territory myself. By the same token I could have been a writer and I think that that wouldn't have changed very much. For humanity, maybe, but not for myself.

[...]
If the occasion arose, could those people whom you once talked about hypothetically as being potential visionaries, also succeed in being so in the realm of architecture? Does architecture really allow one the space to be visionary?

I certainly think so. At the present time architecture has an enormous potential for influencing the course of culture. But perhaps that opportunity will only be there for a moment. Perhaps it's just a small opening that will last about four years. I'm not going to make any predictions about that.

Can you give an example of a work of architecture having had a decisive impact?

It depends what you mean by decisive. I can imagine that a building like the ZKM in Karlsruhe might have had that sort of impact on the classical idea of the museum; that the new media may be able to bring about a sort of redefinition of what architecture actually is. One of the temptations with that project was to make as great a use of the media as possible, but in the end that was of course somewhat naive because the media themselves are exposed to a sort of ongoing process of change; and for precisely that reason they need a sort of crude skeleton for them to remain viable themselves. [...]

The question of course is which came first. Isn't it rather a case of architecture being called in to give a helping hand during a certain period of historical transition?

Yes, of course! But then I never claimed to be the first in the field. On the contrary. In the 1970s and 1980s the situation was so arid that we all went round with a host of ideas that nobody wanted; we were like lovers who had been rejected. The situation is more exciting now and possibly more dangerous. In contrast with the previous decade, I get the feeling that we are now actually being called on to give some kind of coherence to a number of operations that are under way. These operations are by no means unambiguous, but at the same time it is clear as daylight that a movement is going on that is wider than architecture alone.

[...]

What do you think of the reaction of people like Siza, Ando, and Frampton in his critical writings who fall back on the notion of the "tactile." What do you think of Siza when he says: "If the world is speeding up I respond by deliberately making peaceful-looking buildings and I put the materials first"?

The Villa dall'Ava in Paris is also tactile and very physical just because it is a house. What I mean is that with regards to the body the relation is so undeniable and self-evident that tactility is almost inevitable. I also feel a great deal of sympathy with that attitude. But if you look carefully at these people you will notice a sort of speeding-up right now; Ando and Hertzberger, for instance, are adapting their own sobriety to a sort of mobility. The curious thing about Andc is that the less you see of Ando, the more impressive he is, and the more you see of him, the more it strikes you that he employs the same aesthetic regardless of the project involved—a boutique, a sort of Zen Buddhist monastery, a Protestant church or a dwelling. I hardly need to say that at a certain point it becomes hard to take him seriously.

[...] *What about your own sense of commitment?*

I thought the library in Paris was an interesting project in that it showed that there is something really quite important that still remains: that is, a large collective space where (as far as that goes "shelter" isn't the right word) fragmented humanity at any rate now and then for specific reasons can reconstitute itself; that a process of reuniting of a collective population, a regrouping can take place.

But is that still collective? Is that space not just a symbol of the impossibility of forming a new collective? Is the fact that a project of this sort is included in an exhibition with a neutral name such as Energies *(Amsterdam Stedelijk Museum, 1990) not in itself, to say the least, indicative of this anonymizing and collectivizing tendency? A certain abstraction is introduced that is subversive of collectivity in all its aspects.*

It is more an answer to the question of what *collectivity* means now. Or of how you might be able once again to give form to the collective. I think that the word *collective* is very applicable to it. I think that at the moment one question is particularly relevant: in the light of the dissolution of matter, the disappearance of the need for centralization, what roles of architecture are in any case made redundant? Apparently some of the roles remain relevant, if only through the fact that we ourselves continue to exist. That is another meaning for the collective value of our architecture: to investigate and determine the implications of our profession for the present moment in our culture.

We are beginning to run out of steam ...

I know what you mean. Have some more coffee.

DUTCH REFORMATION

Douglas Coupland
New York Times,
September 11, 1994.

In 1968, in the first grade, I built a "House of the Future"—a Space Needle-ish affair consisting of one-inch doweling Bondfasted to clumps of blocks at both ends painted in solid colors. This maison was displayed in an "Art at the Mall" show at West Vancouver's Park Royal Shopping Center. Staying modern was fairly easy back then.

That same year, 1968, was also the year I was wildly envious of the house of my friend up the street, Steven. Steven's family's house gave the impression of being coengineered by both the editors of *Sunset* magazine and the Apollo 11 design team: outward swooping walls with daisy-patterned cinder blocks; post-and-beam ceilings with cerulean blue Lucite room dividers. Plastic! Intercoms! Lava rocks! Skylights! Bamboo! It was part *2001*, part Benihana's. Even Steven's backyard treehouse was modern: built from a kit ... on stilts! It resembled, say, a house on Mulholland Drive

Julie Christie would have rented during the Los Angeles filming of *Shampoo*. Steven's house was so modern, in fact, that it contained no 90-degree angles. It made my own family's Cleaver-esque number seem like a frumpier version of Anne Hathaway's Cottage. It was hard to imagine inviting Sean Connery and Jill St. John over to our house for cocktails, while Steven's house positively exuded the aura of spies and politicians contemplating sex. Steven's house was the embodiment of newness—a term I have always used interchangeably in my mind with modernity. Now, a quarter-century later, still sensitized to newness, still jealous of the future, I ask myself where is newness currently being generated architecturally? Where is Steven's family living these days?

Lille, France, would appear to be the answer, site of the half-billion-dollar EC-funded Congreplex near the French entrance to the Chunnel. The generator of the Lille Congreplex's newness is architect Rem Koolhaas: forty-four, Dutch, tall, thin, austere and Maseratti-driving—a true Eurocitizen with offices in Rotterdam, a family in London and design projects in France, England, Italy and Germany. In person Koolhaas (pronounced, almost unbelievably, "Cool House") is charming, unassuming, and hyperarticulate. For meetings he is punctual to within fifteen seconds; if a newcomer is ninety seconds late, he begins to visibly fret. Yet in spite of his punctiliousness, his demeanor is Bondian ... James Bondian. And just what is so *new* about Mr. Koolhaas's work? A good question which receives an oddly tautological reply: the very fact that it is new.

Through a combination of circumstances, Koolhaas has bypassed the intellectual gridlock of capital "M" Modernism (as well as its "lite" version, Postmodernism), and arrived at a new polemic of formal creation. One can walk through the hundreds of thousands of square feet of his Euralille (there is a subway station, a train station, a mall, four office towers, auditoriums, and a concert hall) and not find one single reference, intended or accidental, to any previously existing architect or period. There are no witty little allusions to Mies; no casual homages to Corbu. Unlike current French architect Christian de Portzamparc, Koolhaas has no formal ties to modernist architecture and doesn't even view Modernism as a classical period style to borrow from. This is an irony given that some citizens within the architectural community give Koolhaas's oeuvre a quick squint, and declare it "Modern." It is only after deeper inspection that this notion is radically disproven. Koolhaas has always been wary of Modernism because of its increasing inability to generate "newness." He says that, "by the late 1980s it became humiliating to depend on an intellectual outburst that was almost 100 years old."

To walk within the nearly complete Euralille complex, one can taste the mythology of Europe in 1992—its sense of optimism—synthetic or genuine. As Koolhaas states, "the EC mythology's drastic interventions across the territory" and the truck-clogged conveyor-belt freeway system have turned Europe into a de facto Fordian assembly line. Says Koolhaas, "Architects, for the first time in several decades are being solicited for their power to physically articulate new visions. Once again one feels a belief in the propagandistic nature of architecture."

Euralille is absolutely new and looks and feels as though a lunar research station has crash-landed onto a small, respectable French market town. This is meant as a compliment. One gets the feeling that Steven and his family are now prowling the complex, buying protein capsules with cash cards, entering oval rooms using speech-based identification systems; transferring billions of dollars' worth of currencies from one country to another in microseconds and boarding high-speed trains to Brussels. Something is happening here. But what?

What is happening is that Koolhaas is incorporating into his work the structural processes that are informing our society as a whole—something architecture has always done—and is creating architectural metaphors for these new processes. In the 1950s and 1960s society built socialized housing and UN buildings (liberal utopianism). In the 1970s it was brutalist universities (liberal paranoia). In the 1980s it built gold-skinned unleaseable S&L wedding cakes (late capitalism). And in the 1990s it builds EC megaprojects and computer codes (postnationalism and cyberspace).

But Koolhaas also explores more subtle and pervasive forces as well as obvious political ideological forces. The future—for even the crustiest of nay-sayers—is transpiring far faster than anybody ever thought it would. Koolhaas meets this future head-on, and not simply through deconstruction, a process he considers "corny at best—an obvious, quickly tiring metaphor for fragmentation." No, Koolhaas is fascinated by processes that are unsexy on the surface, yet which alter our worldview so profoundly that the processes seem almost invisible. He believes that "architecture reveals the deepest and sometimes most shocking secrets of how the values of a society are organized." Herewith a shortlist of sixteen such influences and how they might affect my old friend, Steven.

1) Transnationalism (Steven can visit Benetton anywhere on Earth; in Slovenia he rents a Daewoo from Hertz; he requires no passport to travel within Europe.)

2) Vectorialization (Steven's FedEx parcels must pass through Memphis, even if they're going across the street.)

3) Asynchronicity (Steven uses cash machines and phone answering machines; he makes several satellite calls a day.)

4) Institutionalized impermanence (Steven and his family work within fabric-covered partitioned modular work stations for transnational corporations.)

5) Deregionalization (Steven's family has moved many times; he's not sure where his ancestors are from; he's not sure where he's really "from.")

6) The obsolescence of physical space (Steven chats nightly on the Net. During sunny weather he telecommutes. He can ride the TGV train from Paris to Lille in one hour. Soon he will be able to go from Lille to London in one hour.)

7) Rupture (Steven drives freeways and daydreams that are modern moats and walls, fencing off various segments of a city from others.)

8) Discontinuity (Steven's satellite dish captures 564 channels; he plays Nintendo for 90 minutes each day.)

9) Diversity (Steven considers himself politically correct; Steven never bothers to buy presents when he jets from place to place anymore because the same things are for sale everywhere.)

10) Arbitrariness of location (Steven figures that the highway snack and gas store can just as easily go one place as much as any other along a freeway.)

11) Nodes and clusters (Steven likes mall food fairs and Las Vegas.)

12) Drive Thru-ness and fluidity (Steven drives along the conveyor belt hyperfreeways of the new Europe and thinks of Belgium as the world's first drive-thru nation. Steven could easily drive through Belgium many times a week with Rem Koolhaas in his Maseratti.)

13) Centerless cities (Steven has visited Tokyo, Atlanta, and Los Angeles.)

14) Edge Cities (Steven has visited Irvine and Santa Clara, California.)

15) Deindustrialization (The company to which Steven subcontracts his time has now stopped actually making things. The making of things has now become somewhat beside the point—the just-in-time delivery of nonpolluting, value-added intellectual properties has become the culture's most desirable socioindustrial goal. What North American city hasn't tried to foster its own little Silicon Valley?)

16) Fiscal restraint (needs no explanation).

Rem Koolhaas lassoes all of these millennial factors and rather than feel overwhelmed by them, exploits them to achieve sublime structural and stylistic effects. Walls become doors; doors and walls vanish altogether; geographically distant rooms are lazy-Susaned, giving occupants in-your-face intimacy with each other. Roads and railways penetrate and flow through structures. Seats within auditoriums are assigned tribal clusterings of color. Koolhaas wants "to reformulate the idea of a communal facility or entity in the midst of a complete collapse of the public realm, against the homogenization of mass media, and against the erasure of necessity of place … against the triumph of fragmentation." With Lille, "its very bigness becomes an antidote against fragmentation." Koolhaas believes in the ideal of social progress. The pace of global change leaves Koolhaas unfazed and optimistic. His work eagerly reforges the broken link between technology and progress. He revels in the unexpected rather than passively anticipating agony. Perhaps Koolhaas, a Dutchman, imprinted with the nation's role as an international trading center, has fewer problems with global change that might someone of other nationality. The Dutch, as a nation of traders, has not surprisingly spawned an architect whose work responds to the silent, nanosecond transnational flows of money and ideas.

Koolhaas also notes the Dutch pride in their national trait of economy and thrift. In Europe, the architect is not the Howard Roark prima donna archetype permitted in North America. In Europe, the architect is like a plumber, and is entirely at the mercy of the client, haggling over budgets and systematically negotiating even the smallest of adhesions to the original blueprint. But Koolhaas accepts this from the beginning and actually likes "the integration of the notion of cheapness to create sublime conditions."

Koolhaas recognizes "the client as chaos" and allows the European system as it stands to be used as a creative force rather than one of subjugation and compromise. "Given European architecture's inherent buyer/seller nature, chaos simply happens. You cannot aspire to chaos, you can only be an instrument of it."

Back to home. Back to where I am from. Steven's parents divorced years ago, and his family subsequently dispersed. I have no idea who lives in the house now, but I drove by just today, and its new owners seem to appreciate what they've got and have resisted the temptation to "modernize" a fine period structure. Sure, parts of its stucco could use a power wash, but the lava rocks downstairs look as though they were only yesterday airlifted in from the Ala Moana Shopping Center—and a potted orange tree on the upper verandah seemingly dreams of some sunny 1966 afternoon in Pasadena.

Actually, Steven's house now looks sedate and established. The split-leaf maples, azaleas, and dwarf beeches out front have fully matured and soften some of the house's zingy obtuse angles. What was once extreme has become quotidian. And soon enough Steven's house may well be forgotten. It may well be torn down to make way for something newer. Where I come from on the West Coast, when we tear down a building, we have a hard time remembering what used to fill the hole. There is always an ambiguous equilibrium between sentiment and amnesia. The past is a finite resource conserved by others, but not by us. We still believe that tomorrow is always better place than today. And when we hear voices crying "New is dead, New is dead" in return, like Rem Koolhaas we cry, "long live the New!"

NOTES ON KOOLHAAS AND MODERNIZATION

Jonathan Crary

ANY 9 (1994), 14–15.

[...] Since the nineteenth century a crucial dimension of the experience of modernization has been what Manfredo Tafuri called the coming to terms with "the anguish of urban dynamism"—the precarious psychic and social accommodation to the relentless processes of destruction and creation through which the city mutates according to the shifting requirements of capitalism. But while some might want to position Koolhaas and *Delirious New York* in the context of the "melting" vision of modernity (first sketched out by Marx), he is in fact staking out a very different relation to modernization and history. Baudelaire gave paradigmatic expression to two reciprocal poles of response to modernization that have had a curiously enduring half-life: on one hand, the exhilarating experience of new velocities, the apparent freedoms of sensations of new itineraries and perceptual frontiers (exemplified by today's cyberspace cheerleaders); on the other, lament at the immense richness of what modernization had eradicated forever (for example, rain forests, tradition-based communities, epic poetry). Koolhaas's project is bound up in a deployment of historical memory that is neither paralyzed by the weight of nostalgia and loss nor dissipated in a celebratory abandonment to the kaleidoscopic momentum of technological innovation. Baudelaire's swan, doomed by the spirit of gravity, flapping its wings wretchedly in the dust of urban work sites and demolitions, has as its flip side the false lightness of the man of the crowd, surrendering to the latest rhythms and force lines of capitalist reorganization.

Working outside of this polarity, one of Koolhaas's achievements is allowing architecture to become involved in the practical elaboration of the composite lifeworlds of urban collectivities, letting his work operate as a medium between the volatile possibilities of modernization and a more enduring set of routines, patterns, and desires. If Koolhaas's work incarnates a certain cool-headed social optimism it is also antiutopian and relentlessly demystifying about notions of progress. An unflinching engagement with the history of the twentieth century, its layers of savagery, stupidity, and intellectual failure, pervades his writing.

It is possible to speak of Koolhaas's thinking as "untimely," recalling that for Nietzsche untimeliness was not about forgetting but rather about creating a new kind of historical vision, the invention of new eyes and senses with which to survey the past, the difficult acquisition of new viewpoints on how to transform human experience and activity in "the perspective of life." Clearly Koolhaas has no hesitation in exploiting new technological arrangements. Some of his projects, such as the ZKM at Karlsruhe, would be unthinkable without them. But his work, for all its impressive utilization of cutting-edge technique, is not driven by the breathless "futurism" exhibited by some of his contemporaries who believe, a priori, that telecommunications and data manipulation will be the primary components of new social environments. In his encounter with technological modernity he seems strongly opposed to the sedentary model of the individual and cellular model of the social that cyberspace modernization implies. For Koolhaas, though, it is not a question of choosing the material over the dematerialized or the tectonic over the electronic. His pragmatic strategies allow him to move fluidly between these options, based on local conditions and requirements, even if his priorities are, finally, to facilitate the creative activity of human collectivities within urban assemblages.

One of the many achievements of the Bibliothèque de France project is how it sustains a resonant coexistence of two incommensurable realms—the atopic (and sublime) domain of data storage and, nested in unmappable proximity, spaces that affirm the potency of human aggregates and flows. The inclusions of features such as communal screening rooms could seem to some an antimodernizing archaism, but it is a willful repudiation of the contention that, given a global film archive, the standard method of film viewing will be isolated individuals ordering them over modems or cable systems for home consumption. Even simply the notion of a library with a great hall to accommodate 10,000 people is an indication of how the "rationalizing" logic of miniaturization and dematerialization is interpreted with a diagramming of the library-archive form as a powerful social and communal apparatus.

The library, like his other public projects, allows a polyphony of unforeseen zones and temporalities to emerge within the unstable mechanosphere we still call the city. They produce changing configurations and meetings. Collisions, not in the sense of shock or defamiliarization but of a montage of openings of the imagination onto other possible social ecologies. To say that Koolhaas works against the sedentarization now being imposed by modernization (that is, the remodeling of the body into an electronic consumer) implies that he is committed to a certain general model of the human nervous system—the body as an integrating spatiotemporal system, whose perceptual and cognitive structures are decisively linked to motor patterns. In other words, an individual both shapes and is shaped by an environment in terms of an evolving relation between memory and sensorimotor activity. (New forms like virtual reality pose a very different model of the nervous system in which there is an indiscriminate mix of sensory and the locomotor on a flattened-out surface of digital information.) Some of Koolhaas's most provocative projects, like Yokohama, Lille, and Zeebrugge, amplify the importance of a locomotor experience of movements, trajectories, and intersections of many kinds. In spite of all we have heard about the annihilation of distance and absolute speed, these projects (involving harbors, train stations, highways, ferry boats) affirm the persistence of "outmoded" vectors and vehicles, of other relations of motion and stasis, acceleration and slowness, that coexist with hyperspeeds and instantaneity. The nineteenth-century model of the journey, as Paul Virilio well shows, has long been shattered, but for Koolhaas the routines of everyday life are still composed of unrepresentable transitive moments, of the enigmatic passages that once linked arrivals and departures, which so fascinated thinkers like de Chirico, Einstein, and Duchamp. But even if some of Koolhaas's projects, like Zeebrugge, are "terminals," they are effectively intermediary elements of larger social machines, defined by the adjacencies and intermixings that occur through them, by their effective permeability.

Delirious New York was published in 1978 just when the Western City, as a theater of modernization, began to cede its primacy to another more pervasive and placeless arena of transformation and rationalization: the digital circuitry of telematics and informatics. Obviously the city, whether in the West or the Third World, has not and will not cease to be a space of instability and mutation. But as the physical map of the city is being overlaid by another radically different set of cognitive and sensory coordinates, the cultural effects of the city's dynamism have atrophied and deteriorated in comparison with the fermentation of the first seventy years of the twentieth century (for example, as the models of theme park and movie set increasingly redefine key experiences of urban texture).

Koolhaas's work inhabits this hybrid field in which diverse and historically distinct forces of modernization both interact and operate autonomously, and his notion of the "culture of congestion" comes into play here in crucial ways. For modernization continues to generate many different and even incompatible notions of congestion—some of which hold forth the possibility of livable and workable human environments even as others are producing experiences of social segmentation and separation, such as those Toni Negri has described in terms of the consequences of Reaganism and Thatcherism in the last decade. At the same time, Koolhaas is not privileging the congestion of an image- and data-saturated environment, which is also founded on the cellurization and productive separation of human beings. One of the valuable features of Émile Durkheim's analysis of anomie was the insistence that social cohesiveness depended on the richness and flexibility of the contacts between individuals in a given society, rather than the sheer number of contacts. The computer terminal seems to open onto an abyss of potential points of contact and linkage but it is a site on which communication and sensation are reduced to a single plane of affect and energy, to impoverished modalities of exchange and interface, and to anomic forms of redundancy. Koolhaas seeks to produce congestion in which a palpable heterogeneity of social/environmental contact, psychical and sensory feedback, and kinesthetic stimulation launch the individual out of the isolation that is the lot of the modernized "interactive" and amnesiac inhabitant of the Generic City.

THE TRAJECTORY OF REM KOOLHAAS

Charles Jencks

ANY 9 (1994), 41–45.

Birth

Rem Koolhaas was born too early and too late: 1944. He missed the Second World War and couldn't catch up to the specialists in angst and ennui. His first words as he sat in his high chair at age one-and-a-half were: "What have I got in my life? I've got a rotten life." Ever since then he's had a wry, black humor. This almost connects him to the postwar existentialists, but he was too late to join the Sartre-Camus Club. His parents thought of sending him to a psychiatrist. Instead he went to Indonesia where he saw so many large rats eating the beams in the ceiling that he was cured of melancholia. After the rats, his black humor was optimistic—manically so. Rem's too early/too late condition has continued to dog him as he has continuously finished second in competitions he ought to have won (against Bernard Tschumi and Richard Meier, etc.). In the 1960s he predicted his future humiliations—which have come true.

Surfing

There are three different ways to deal with the tidal wave of history. Like the young Amsterdammer, one can try to plug up the hole with one's finger—see Prince Charles, Léon Krier, ecologists, reactionaries, protesters of all persuasions. Or, like a critic who is selective, one can attempt to channel the good water to the left and the bad water to the right, thereby becoming a moral valve. Or like a Modernist and Futurist, one can try to ride the wave in the direction it is going to see how much enjoyment, profit, and art one can get out of it. This takes considerable skill. One crashes. There are no perfect buildings, mistakes are huge, rewards great, fame ensured, ignominy likely. That's why Rem was right to predict humiliations. Surfers are like Faust. They know the bargain with the devil brings regret, but they ask for compensations: creativity, skill in surfing. Being within the hollow of the wave as it pushes, breaks, and covers one in an arc of frothy sun is always described as a peak religious experience. Bystanders love to watch surfers excel, pray, and wipe out. Rem inspires the same feelings in his lectures.

Archaeology
From his thesis at the Architectural Association—Exodus, or The Voluntary Prisoners of Architecture—to his analysis of the Berlin Wall and his La Défense investigations, he has been obsessed by the outré, the taboo, the despised, the horrible, the second-rate, the banal. He once spoke to me of his natural affinity for the "provincial item"—argyle socks. His love for the 1950s has a provincial ring to it, as does his penchant for Oscar Niemeyer, Ludwig Hilberseimer, and the "generic." In the late 1960s, when I first knew him, he was designing in the god-awful, naive boomerang style of the 1950s, those amoeboid Wally Harrison shapes that everybody hated. I didn't realize then that he liked to be "bad."

Corpse
The Villa dall'Ava is a living exquisite corpse constructed from Le Corbusier (ground floor) under Mies van der Rohe (rotated main floor), covered by Gehry materials and Tadao Ando sides. A cocktail-stick forest entry, bamboo sliding walls, frosted glass, and disgusting orange plastic fencing are parts borrowed from the vernacular and grafted onto the body.

Cosmic
Since this flat rooftop with pool with a view of Paris is worthy of Homer (as Le Corbusier used to say), I suggested to Rem it might have a fitting culmination: a sculpture, telescope, cosmic object. Anything to acknowledge the route and culmination, which is equivalent to that of the Villa Savoye. But orange plastic fencing (the temporary kind, not even Gehry's chain-link) may be there forever precisely because it is so inappropriate and awefull. Recall the surrealists' third definition of beauty.

Drawing
Bad artists, like Le Corbusier, do not mind showing their quick sketches and proclaiming them art. Since 95 percent of architects' presentation drawings are meticulous and uninventive—professional kitsch done to seduce someone—Rem has evolved his own language of working and presentation. It does not allow for refinements, shadings, nuances—the gamut of feelings evoked by the classical tradition. Look at his conceptual sketches for the Lille Congrexpo, or the perspective of what he calls the "Piranesian Space" (invoking the classical). But Piranesi did not draw like Keith Haring—none of this flat, maladroit, clumsy line. Nor did he have to build his runaway spaces in fifteen minutes. Le Corbusier and Rem do. They think and sketch the same way—fast, with invention, logic, and wildness. "Zee passion of zee initial sketch must be preserved in zee building—it never takes me more than two minutes to design one—longer spoils zee passion of zee sketch." That, or some-

thing very much like it, is the aesthetic manner and creative method enunciated by Philippe Starck.

Compositional Method II

Crazy logic. Again, like Le Corbusier (and James Stirling), Rem loves an upside-down logic, a crazy rationality which no one would think of except perhaps a mad Cartesian. This method fits surrealism to a T and is why I used to write about Rem as a Surrationalist. His Kunsthal in Rotterdam, sited half on the side of a road-bank and flat park area, inverts expectations. Any normal architect would have shown the drop in section on the elevation and would have had a clear route and entrance. Instead, Rem places a huge rectangular box over slope and plane, enters by the middle of the building on a ramp, hangs masonry above glass, changes the material—juxtaposition!—at each corner, he uses orange I-beams for ornament (Mies as ornament, how very P-M), ramp as exhibition space (how very dizzy), and tree stumps as columns (how very surreal). It works much better than customary logic. I love the statue of the bedouin and camel that graces the orange Miesian cornice. It provides just the representation and small detail needed. Rem hates it.

Representation

Like Stirling (as Colin Rowe said), Rem does not know how to "top" his buildings; he just ends them. Like most late- and new Modernists, he does not know what to represent in terms of sculpture, ornament, civic life, permanence, shared value. This might be a grave disadvantage for Rem, except most architects suffer from it too. They are confused and emasculated by agnosticism. They don't know what to put in the central square, or on the top of their building. In this sense all of Rem's buildings are unfinished.

Bigness

Rem has half-theorized this. He has not taken on "The Ivan Illich Law of Architecture" (coined by me in *The Language of Post-Modern Architecture*) which tells an architect what happens when it gets "Too Big": it usually gets more boring. Rem sometimes professes to like the boring; he likes Warhol movies and Warhol epigrams. On the other hand, his large buildings are a lot less boring than the other Too Big architects because of his method of combining disparate modernist images. The exquisite corpse saves him. Also he has discovered one truth of Bigness: new forms emerge, new organizational types.

Antecedent

Surreal superposition, Constructivists, Superstudio, Archizoom, Cedric Price. When I knew Rem in the late 1960s he complained that he always had a good idea two years too early, before the right time, when Hans Hollein or Superstudio cashed it in. Nevertheless, by staying with some ideas, Rem has found their time has come around again—this time for him. In a public lecture he once called the indomitable

Cedric Price "a Prince Trying to Turn into a Frog"; the jibe hit home, Price was mortified. Rem never forgot Price's Potteries Thinkbelt and Funpalace. They became the models for his amazing organizational wonder, Parc de la Villette. This has five layers of organization run on top of each other and through each other.

Harvard

On the faculty here, Rem also represents the establishment. Everyone knows, since Tom Wolfe has been pointing it out for thirty years, that the American cultural circuit demands a deft mixture of avant-gardism, shock-of-the-new, radical-chic, and bourgeois grace. You must be revolutionary, but not really. It's the game of American culture and its rules have been fixed, at least since the 1960s. Bernard Tschumi, dean of the Graduate School of Architecture at Columbia University, is the other example that proves the rule: if you want to climb to the top of the American establishment, get born in Europe. Peter Eisenman chose the wrong place.

Game

In American culture all good things come from the East (with the exception of Frank). Of course Rem does not really want to play this game, which is perhaps why he is winning. He wants to be a New Yorker-Londoner-Parisian-Cantabridgean. He doesn't want to be Dutch, at the moment. They have not treated him as well as he thinks they might have done. After all, he is the only Dutchman who lives in London, commutes daily, speaks five languages, and used to look like Jean-Louis Barrault.

EC-Man

Rem is the only European, the only EC-Man, I know. He commutes between three or four countries per day, speaking all the local dialects—German, French, Dutch, English, Other. I once was invited to dinner by Rem in Lille; it was seven-thirty in the evening and we were a country or two away, in Rotterdam—about 160 miles. We got in his rented car, averaged 140, and sped across borders flashing an EC identity card. Arrived at a multistar restaurant in Lille and sat down to eat amid a clientele dressed in black tie: the local socialist power structure. EC-men. They change clothes four times a day, change accents six, and slither in and out of conflicts.

[...]

THE CAMP OF THE NEW

Robert E. Somol

ANY 9 (1994), 50–55.

The camp of success—always eclectic, facile, and agreeable—proceeded to modify and to use the revolution. The camp of "the true believer" always anxious for authenticity attempted to work over the results of the revolution so as to make them strange, arcane, difficult; interesting to the few and inaccessible to the many. And both parties were prone, as advantage seemed to dictate, to employ sometimes the polemics of revolution and sometimes its forms.

Colin Rowe

In naive, or pure, Camp, the essential element is seriousness, a seriousness that fails. Of course, not all seriousness that fails can be redeemed as Camp. Only that which has the proper mixture of the exaggerated, the fantastic, the passionate, and the naive.

Susan Sontag

[...]

Rem Koolhaas often opens his lectures with a provocative black-and-white image of a drive-in, circa 1960, taken by O. Winston Link. In addition to serving as an allusion to his previous career as a scriptwriter (and subsequent role as ghostwriter of Manhattanism), the image immediately establishes Koolhaas's ambiguous relationship to architecture and his fundamental "doubt" about the necessity for architecture, an apprehension that despite ten successful years of practice continues to instigate and condition the concrete speculations of OMA. In the foreground of this initial drive-in shot, a young couple sits in a convertible as a jet speeds upward on the movie screen in the distance, from which a train seems to emerge as it passes in the night, momentarily disrupting while inadvertently defining a sea of mobile spectators. For Koolhaas, this image eloquently demonstrates that it is entirely possible "to have an immense intensity of event without a single recourse to architecture." Significantly, it also registers the extreme skepticism that he and his office share concerning the "seeming obligation of the architect to express himself only in architecture and ... of the planner to express himself always in plans, plans, and more plans."

In place of the plan (and planning), all of Koolhaas's urban and architectural projects begin with the diagram and the scenario. In this way, the image of the drive-in—as a map of cultural, generational, sexual, and technological forces and effects—can be seen to function as a diagram for Koolhaas, registering degrees of intensity, resistance, and speed. It is precisely this diagram of flows, then, that aligns with the sketch of his own abstract machine at Lille, the void "Piranesian space" which reveals the dense infrastructural lines of communication and circulation describing the affiliation of the TGV station, the highway, and the metro with "the largest parking garage in Christendom." In fact, this kind of diagram of flows and stoppages has informed most of OMA's projects, all of which share traits with the parking garage and/or the drive-in (or drive-through): for example, the IJplein housing in Amsterdam, the Kunsthal in Rotterdam, the Zeebrugge Sea Trade Center, the Center for Art and Media Technology for Karlsruhe, the Congrexpo convention center at Lille, Jussieu's Science and Humanities Library, and even the ironic Miesian "bus stop" pavilion in Groningen. All of these projects, regardless of scale, appear to be motivated more by urban (collective and situational) than by traditional architectural (individual and compositional) concerns. The spiral circulation patterns of the Kunsthal and Jussieu, for example, do not establish the interiority and self-presence of the object but register various external pressures and forces. Both capitulating to and recharging various contextual flows, the projects emerge as boxes of diverse speeds, paradoxically combining visual proximity (often from "outside") and circulatory delay ("inside").

As an attempt to displace the primary representational technique of the plan, OMA's diagrams, sketches, and cartoons function somewhat as storyboards in the cinematic sense, establishing time as a constitutive element in urban description and design. At the same time, they mimic and subvert two diverse traditions or idioms within contemporary urban analysis: the haphazard drawings of the townscape movement and the rigid statistical representations of more quantitative procedures. While the views presented in the Lille sketches forever remove the technique of the former from its "association with yachting and beer drinking," as described by Rowe, the various studies for the Puntstad and Zuidstad of the recent Alexanderpolder project deploy the banal and bureaucratic strategies of the latter to "pataphysical" ends. Through the most sober and rational of means, the density and population studies of Alexanderpolder establish a series of "what if" scenarios, broaching various cultural and political impossibilities such as filling the sacred void of the Randstad with a metropolis the size of the current Dutch population. Finally, the diagram, as described by Gilles Deleuze and Félix Guattari, elides Rowe's opposition between *physique-form* and *morale-word*: "An abstract machine in itself is not physical or corporeal, any more than it is semiotic; it is diagrammatic. It operates by matter, not by substance; by function, not by form. Functions are not yet 'semiotically' formed, and matters are not yet 'physically' formed."

While the first generation of the neo-avant-garde in the early 1960s investigated the semiotics of form (whether of the icon or the index, as with Robert Venturi and Peter Eisenman respectively), its progeny (and here Bernard Tschumi and Koolhaas are most representative) have indulged a diagrammatics of function and structure, terms in the classical triad too tainted by the failure of postwar Modernism to have been reexamined before the 1970s. In other words, the quest for autonomy in postwar architecture begins with Colin Rowe's formalism and, after passing through structural linguistics, culminates with a "hyperformalism" influenced by the thought of Jacques Derrida which marks the simultaneous triumph and collapse of the discourse of autonomy (the difference measured in the shift of formal criterion from ambiguity to undecidability). Meanwhile, the complementary trajectory within postwar architectural discourse—and the tradition in which Koolhaas's production can be largely understood—emerges with Reyner Banham, passes through the situationists, and ends with the "pragmatics" or "schizoanalytics" of Deleuze (marked by the parallel transformation in the conception of function or usage from efficiency to intensity). In other words, both Postmodernism and Deconstruction tended to focus on the semiotic and/or physical aspects of form (classically, the delight), emphasizing architecture's rhetorical, autonomous, and linguistic manifestations (whether of a traditional or unconventional nature). In his investigation or reinvention of the project of Modernism, Koolhaas has instead turned to issues of structure (including instability) and function (including the unpredictable). It is important to distinguish Koolhaas's interests, however, from other recent initiatives that have also appropriated issues of technology and use, but which (unlike Koolhaas) exhibit a resentment and hostility to questions of material-form and idea-text.

[...] It might be possible to summarize Koolhaas's project in the broadest terms as the attempt to inscribe the effects of May 1968 in architectural and urban thought and practice. This entails the imagination of a new political and collective domain (since even the city has only been envisioned in the most discrete and contained terms of interiority, with analogies to the body, the machine, or the museum); the simultaneous solicitation and subversion of models of expertise and professionalism; and an engagement in the world that requires a reinvention of the traditional rhetorics and techniques of the architectural and planning disciplines. While there have been multiple avenues through which OMA has pursued this project,[1] two significant areas of investigation at the levels of expression and content have been section and event. The first would deviate the repeatability of architecture's typological solutions (which are invariably plan-oriented), while the latter would display the predictability of planning's codified programs (which are always an attempt to structure or domesticate events). As terms which impair the plan and planning (or type and program), *section* and *event* maintain a singular connection to Koolhaas's privileged z-axis, to the cuts and coups of the vertical: that which rises (section) and that which falls (event).

The complicity of section and event can be first perceived in Koolhaas's found diagram, seen in *Delirious New York*, of Dalí's paranoid-critical method in which a vertical prop rises to reinforce a collapsing blob or bubble of desire and irrationality. As a fantastic event-section machine, Koolhaas's description of the diagram—"limp, unprovable conjectures ... supported (made critical) by the 'crutches' of Cartesian rationality"[2]—exactly predicts OMA's recent speculation for the Jussieu Library in Paris where twisted and distorted concrete planes float in and are supported by a regular steel grid. Likewise, the scenario he invents for elements of the 1939 New York World's Fair not only recalls this paranoid-critical diagram, but also serves as a powerful description of OMA's competition entry for the Bibliothèque de France *avant la lettre*: "The pavilions, mollusks without shells, look like exiled interiors of Manhattan's Skyscrapers, a collection of architectural jellyfish beached before they could reach their distant destination: the needles."[3] In OMA's Bibliothèque, the jellyfish, the five sets of public spaces in the scheme, the vertical stack(s) of the Parisian cube, arrive at their now transatlantic address, and, half a century late, are finally made critical.

While to many these fictional scenarios and cultural diagrams might seem "exterior" to the architectural discipline, Koolhaas's genius has been to return them to precise architectural models, materials, and thematics. In this way, his experiments have always revolved around the structural frame and the grid, the procedures that, more than any other, have defined modern architecture and planning. While an exhaustive examination of the diverse ways in which Koolhaas has revisited these organizing paradigms (from Le Corbusier's Dom-Ino to the grids of Manhattan and the Ville Radieuse) exceeds the scope of this essay, it is possible to suggest an "internal" genealogy for Koolhaas's work on section and event through Yve-Alain Bois's discussion of the Villa Savoye. Bois attempts to describe the protominimalist character of Corbusier's villa in terms of the picturesque, the event-filled promenade, by focusing on the elements of vertical circulation in Corbusier's work (for example, the ramp, spiral staircase, and thoroughfares, all of which bear on Koolhaas's reflections, to which he adds the elevator). For Bois, "the very subject of the Villa Savoye is the penetration of a vertical section into a horizontal grid."[4]

Here, Bois adduce what Koolhaas's projects have always exposed and advanced: that repressed within the modern "free plan" resides the nonextrudable "free section"; that a potentially thriving alliance exists between such apparent opposites as the diagrams of Le Corbusier's Dom-Ino and Dalí's paranoid-critical method; that intensive uses of the structural frame and the grid, despite their conventional limitation to the cause of plan and planning, can release counteropportunities for section and event. Finally, "internal" and "external" diagrams can no longer be distinguished in terms of form or function. Koolhaas's abstract machines locate moments of collapse as specific disciplinary traits become involved with contemporary cultural conditions, while neither serves as the rationale or representation for the other. There is simply a full body without hierarchy or differentiated organs (and this begins to account for Koolhaas's quest for refinement without resort to the detail)—a singular egg of intensities without functionally or formally detachable parts. This abolition of the detail in the case of Jussieu, with its permeable and "breathing" facade, ends by turning the entire building into a "big duct" (with the textual homonym intact), not in that it resembles a building element iconically (as, perhaps, with some of the work of John Hejduk), but as it operates as one. At Lille, the intensive use of the diagram avoids any part-to-whole economy by appearing at various scales: in the overall plan, the Congrexpo building, and the void "detail" figured at the intersection of the greatest density of circulatory flows.

Koolhaas has been able to "reinhabit the former megalomaniac ambitions of our predecessors"—and to broach the two themes central to his current work, namely invention and collective arrangement (or new camps)—largely as the result of the combined public and private development that has accompanied the formation of the "New Europe." For the first time since the war, given the unprecedented scale and magnitude of work on the continent, a polemical role for architecture has again become possible. Paradoxically, at exactly the moment when a certain type of corporate practice (largely American) was all but obsolete, the principles Koolhaas had adduced in *Delirious New York* were becoming relevant for the New Europe. If this has enabled a new political dimension and visionary role, however, it is deployed in a minor idiom, disposed with Koolhaas's typical combination of exuberant doubt and ironic arrogance. His initial response to the technical demands of the officials at Lille is enlightening in this regard: "Being marked by the events of May 1968—being part of that typical generation of vast intellectual and little operational courage—we were completely surprised that anyone would ask us such a question. We actually thought and were convinced that infrastructure and those kinds of important decisions were taken by bureaucrats and people with much more robust nervous systems than us." Nevertheless, Koolhaas and OMA are now responsible at Lille for "the largest building site in Europe," where already one million square meters has been realized.

It was with the last of François Mitterrand's *grands projets*, the Bibliothèque de France, that Koolhaas first explicitly sought "to reassert and reinvent the collective." In this first library scheme the public spaces were generated by not building, formed as the residual spaces after the technical requirements were constructed, thus realigning service and served spaces. A similar strategy was also used in the plan for the New Town of Melun-Sénart, where the first move was to delineate void bands in which building would not be allowed, leaving undefined residual islands where development could freely proliferate. Thus Melun-Sénart would not be controlled by built substance but by zones where there was nothing, which Koolhaas describes as a "method to work with our powerlessness to imagine the city." Here, Koolhaas's minor megalomania does not dream of final liberation, but looks simply for "a way out," a "line of flight" established through the analysis and solicitation of specific impossibilities. With characteristics more like the gambler than the planner, this attitude engages in obsessive calculations not with the faith or desire that they will eliminate risk, but with the expectation that they will merely intensify it. Like the obsessive but futile catalogue on "nothing" produced by Donald Barthelme, it is a form of resigned mania, perhaps the only position viable today.

At Lille, the problem was the opposite from that at Melun-Sénart. Here Koolhaas was asked to design an intense zone of the residual islands that he left specifically unspecified in the New Town plan. Unlike Melun-Sénart and the Bibliothèque, where processes of subtraction or absence figured the public realm, in both the plan for Lille (as well as the Congrexpo) and the more recent Jussieu Library, an exposed infrastructural system imagined as a folded or pliable surface would peel up and fuse to create a space for the new collective.

In related but distinct ways, while the first urban plan and library would venture the *void-becoming-figure*, the second plan and library experiment with *infrastructure-becoming-figure*. This is particularly significant in the case of Lille, for it is only due to the artificial insertion of an international infrastructure—the TGV—that this small French city will become the site of an enormous program of facilities, host to one of the colossal events of the New Europe.

The hypothesis of the Lille proposal begins with this event and Koolhaas's "future context" diagram, which suggests that the problem of the metropolis can no longer be thought within city, state, or even national lines. As with the analysis of Paul Virilio, the diagram also indicates that chronopolitics has displaced geopolitics; that distances in time are now more significant than those in space. Given the speed of the TGV and the temporal datum of an hour and twenty minutes, "Lille will be at the center of a virtual, theoretical community of sixty million people." This future context diagram, the mise-en-scène for Lille, directs a virtual city. As Deleuze and Guattari write, "The diagrammatic or abstract machine does not function to represent, even something real, but rather constructs a real that is yet to come, a new type of reality."[5] The abstract machine emerges as the inevitable corollary to Koolhaas's earlier paranoid-critical activity where "impossible" speculations were condensed and objectified through a neutral medium which allowed them to become actualized in the realm of "reality."

OMA's radicalization of the definition of site and time through the use of the "future context" technique is operative in most of their urban schemes (for example, Lille, La Défense, Melun-Sénart, etc.), as well as more explicitly in some of their architectural projects. A good example is the housing for Nexus World in Fukuoka, where Arata Isozaki's proposed towers formed the future context for the two OMA blocks, which serve as underground socles to the (still unrealized) towers. The future context diagram suggests another procedure for the emergence of a both-and-neither logic, a kind of false positivism, where, as Koolhaas writes of the paranoiac, all facts are "pointing in the same direction: the one he is going in." The future context diagram describes what could be called a *virtual immanence*, in part by suggesting that what is real or possible is currently a desert.

Consequently, just as Venturi and Denise Scott Brown read the decorated sheds of Las Vegas to "point to" the passing of Modernism, perhaps the current proliferation of ducks there (in the form of the Luxor, MGM, Treasure Island, Excalibur, etc.) reciprocally augurs a return to the modern project. In this way, Koolhaas's paranoiac processes in Lille recall the aimless, desert wandering of Bugsy Seigel (as played by Warren Beatty), who, in a moment of epiphany, envisions a new territory, a new way of occupying, due to the confluence of a diverse range of factors: legalized gambling, new technologies of transportation ("a lightning-fast train that goes from Los Angeles to Las Vegas in an hour"), the development of the Hoover Dam, which enables the delivery of water as well as massive amounts of electricity for air-conditioning and lights, and the expansion of Los Angeles as a talent pool for entertainment. When asked by a business associate how "the Hoover Dam and fucking are connected," Bugsy answers emphatically with a Deleuze-Guattarian response, "By air-conditioning!" These new forces and infrastructures—aligned in a horizontal and conjunctive fashion—make evident a teeming virtuality in the desert that reveals new possibilities and traits. The projection of a center, an oasis in the least likely of places (Lille as Las Vegas), requires a certain madness, an impossibility, that nonetheless has a compelling logic, a necessity even, when emergent forces become registered through the device of a future context and condensed as the paranoid's "false souvenir" (which, of course, is also a false memory). In Koolhaas's proposal, the activities and forms that float along a trajectory at the edge of Lille "are of a dimension for this virtual city of sixty million which may or may not exist out there and which may or may not become a recognizable entity." Addressed to a new society, the Lille scheme seeks to redefine the representational possibilities of the new collective, to coax it into existence. Despite Koolhaas's well-founded embarrassment about the deconstructivist exhibition at the Museum of Modern Art in 1988, he has actually continued the project of the Russian avant-garde without the necessity of its forms. As Benjamin Buchloh explains, the program of the modern avant-garde, and particularly that of the Constructivists and Productivists, was "not only to establish conditions of simultaneous collective viewing, but further, actually to construct representations of the masses themselves, to depict the collectivity."[6] Koolhaas's rejection of Deconstructivism, therefore, has nothing to do with an abandonment of the project of conjoining theory and politics with questions of material and form, but simply a lack of faith that any historical precedents or types will be adequate to the task. In order to register the forces and effects that have caused the metropolitan condition to expand beyond the confines of the city proper and to capture their emergent collectives, a new theory and practice of institutional types will be required. While section, event. and the future context diagram may be the tools or techniques of these collective forms, the issue of their newness may be evaluated by the effects of their becoming and betweenness.

[...] The risky possibility of operating between and in excess of various frames is taken up in several projects such as the Jussieu Library, which can be seen to operate between the purism of Corbusier and the surrealism of Dalí, and the Kunsthal in Rotterdam, which collapses the cool rationality and authenticity of Mies van der Rohe with the vital popularity and kitsch of someone like Bruce Goff. What this begins to suggest is that Koolhaas's project of the new has nothing to do with classical notions of origin and originality, but emerges as the articulation of the virtual, the channeling of existent forces and effects that can no longer be referred back to (or categorically exhausted by) a previous identity. Thus, the virtual may in fact emerge through what appears as an improper repetition. (Again, the both-and-neither experience of the paranoid is described as "the shock of recognition that never ends.") While the classical (or modern) now exists as a type by its resistance to being subsumed under any other existent type, the new as virtual emerges by becoming susceptible to too many types. Thus the "virtually new" that Koolhaas pursues by provisionally confirming contradictory models can never serve as a type itself. Curiously, but perhaps necessarily, the final elaboration of Koolhaas's version of the simulacral programs of the both and neither has begun precisely to reinhabit and reconfigure alternative postmodern discourses, particularly trajectories from Venturi and Colin Rowe, in this pursuit of the modernist untimely.[7]

In addition to expanding the definition of context, OMA has numerous affiliations to the work and thought of Venturi, Rauch, and Scott Brown. Despite diverse institutional alliances and frames, both Koolhaas and Venturi are particularly attentive to questions of information, infrastructure and circulation, the banal and mass consumption, as well as the approaches of empiricism and surrealism, and both develop a related diagnosis of (if not prescription for) the severed relationship between skin and volume or outside and inside. For instance, VRSB's large glass cube with clouds passing over its surface for California City (1971) provides an interesting corollary to OMA's more developed Bibliothèque de France. In this regard, however, OMA's nonbinary logic is again displayed as the library emerges as *both and neither* a duck and a decorated shed, perhaps an involuted shed or, alternatively, a case of "duck soup" in which the sculptural volumes are suspended in an informational matrix. In other words, VRSB's feminist (or maternal) opposition of physique-form (the heroic duck, gendered male) to information-word (the billboard or sign, gendered female) is no longer operative in Koolhaas's reconfiguration and production of new bodies. Thus the Congrexpo "egg" in no way represents the maternal or humanist birth, but diagrams merely one of several bodies without organs, a condensation of form and word, a duck which is all surface, a consistent plane or topography for the exchange and circulation of forces and information.

Always expanding the possibilities and effects evident in his early term *retroactive manifesto* (itself a form of false memory or, in Robert Smithson's sense, forgotten future), Koolhaas continues to provide a model of difference quite other than that founded by Rowe's opposition of memory and prophecy. In fact, most if not all of Rowe's dialectical terms have been rethought through his work, such as word and form, literal and phenomenal, empirical and rational, Europe and America. For Koolhaas, Europe emerges as the newer New World, a reverse colonization that steals back both the idea and the material, as it were. While Rowe was to insist on a distinction between economic speculation (American development) and ideological critique (European theory), Lille renders impossible any determination as to which pole it confirms; it is fully both and neither, realigning and short-circuiting any distinction between speculation and ideology, economics and revolt. Described by the client as "a dynamic from hell," Lille thrives as a medium or consistency; it is neither the proper copy of a previous urban model nor an ideal model that can itself be generalized. The specificity of Lille resides not in contextualism, regionalism, or expressive signature—that is, the typically static architectural forms of repetition or, more precisely, precedence—but through an active repetition, as a moment in a continuous process where the alignment of particular forces and events produces something new, reveals new traits and possibilities. Thus a form of repetition becomes the potential site for the emergence of the new: the singularity of Lille. It neither proposes the essential nor tries to represent the accidental, and so cannot reside comfortably in the realm of salvation (the necessary) or silliness (the dismissible). As Sontag concludes, "Camp involves a new, more complex relation to the serious. One can be serious about the frivolous, frivolous about the serious." It is toward this new, more complex relation to the serious—to Modernism—that Koolhaas's practice aspires. [...]

1 For example, compelling discussions of fluid or probable geometries in the work of OMA can be found in Sanford Kwinter, "The Reinvention of Geometry," *Assemblage* 18 (1992); and Gregg Lynn, "Probable Geometries: The Architecture of Writing in Bodies," *ANY* 0, May/June 1993.
2 Rem Koolhaas, *Delirious New York* (New York: Oxford University Press, 1978), 201.
3 Ibid., 227.
4 Yve-Alain Bois, "A Picturesque Stroll around *Clara-Clara*," *October* 29 (1984), 57.
5 Gilles Deleuze and Félix Guattari, *A Thousand Plateaus* (Minneapolis: University of Minnesota Press, 1987), 142.
6 Benjamin Buchloh, "From Faktura to Factography," *October* 30 (1984), 111.
7 For a discussion of the relation between the simulacrum and the untimely as aspects of the modernist project, see Gilles Deleuze, *The Logic of Sense* (New York: Columbia University Press, 1990), 265: "Modernity is defined by the power of the simulacrum. It behooves philosophy not to be modern at any cost, no more than to be nontemporal, but to extract from modernity something that Nietzsche designated as the untimely, which pertains to modernity, but which must also be turned against it—in favor, I hope, of a time to come."

REM KOOLHAAS AND IRONY

Richard Ingersoll
Casabella 610 (1994), 16–19.

There is little doubt that Rem Koolhaas is the most brilliant survivor from the generation of 1968 in contemporary architectural culture. His role until ten years ago when he started to seriously practice out of the OMA office in Rotterdam was primarily as a nonaligned satirist, known for his devastating revisions of the architectural myths accompanying the heroic avant-garde, police-state Modernism, and mass culture. The oppressive essence of the big plan and the herding instinct of consumer society were hilariously parodied in a projectual fantasy called The Voluntary Prisoners of Architecture, produced in 1972 with Elia Zenghelis. One of the great works of "paper architecture," their illustrated narrative proposed that the covetousness generated by the Berlin wall could be transmuted in the center of London in the form of a hedonist megastructure. The amusing contradiction caused by recycling the architecture of oppression to install a reign of pleasure was the sort of irony that is present in most of his later projects. In his most famous work, the book *Delirious New York*, Koolhaas succeeded in adding a new, ticklish layer to the tradition of European "americanisme," no longer an elegaic moralization of the terrifying power of the New World, but rather a gossipy scrapbook for a new mythology of retroactive avant-garde manifestoes.

[...] While Koolhaas's orchestrations of absurd contradictions makes one laugh because of an ethical sense of what is good, the author never allows himself to laugh. His relationship to the ironies he portrays is completely ambivalent. I don't think I have ever met a person who both in public and private was quite so cool and quite so unwilling to laugh. This character trait has become an operating strategy that allows a strange commitment to the moral function of laughter. Irony is a two-sided phenomenon, it divides those who understand from those who do not, and Koolhaas, never laughing but always emitting irony, never reveals which side he belongs to. While a sense of irony is absolutely necessary when confronting the paradoxes of modern life, I am not so certain it is essential in the production of architecture, and am fairly convinced that it becomes a serious flaw when applied to urbanism. Without running the risk of sounding too much like a Jesuit, I am going to propose that it is Koolhaas's use of irony that makes his architecture, despite its considerable merits, so problematic in terms of a current architectural canon.

Consider for instance his Villa dall'Ava at St. Cloud from 1991. It was built on an inclined site on the outskirts of Paris for an architecturally aware client, who evidently gave Koolhaas carte blanche and the minimal criteria to provide a pool, lots of transparency, and a statement that would "add to history." The Villa dall'Ava resumes an avant-gardist quest to push the program for dwelling far beyond the preconceptions of house, a goal that was completely understood by the neighbors, who for three years held up the construction of the house in the name of neighborhood preservation. The house is composed of two steel-clad boxes suspended at opposite ends of a long bearing wall. All of the service and collective functions are tucked into the glazed gallery spaces on the lower level. The formidable bearing capacity of the wall is supplemented with a parallel row of thick concrete columns in order to sustain a nine-meter lap pool on the roof. The incongruous pool becomes the necessary luxury that organizes the rest of the building. The fundamental irony of the pool in the sky is reminiscent of Koolhaas's earlier fantasy of the Floating Pool imagined as a vessel for exiled Constructivists to propel themselves across the Atlantic. To heighten the pool's sense of the absurd, a skirt of plastic orange fences used for construction sites has been improvised on the rooftop adjacent to the pool as a defiant balustrade to satisfy the safety regulations.

The front box, reminiscent of the horizontal volume and strip windows of Villa Savoye, is supported by sixteen steel poles that are each battered in different directions and painted different shades of gray, looking like drunken piloti. These wayward supports are an amusing provocation, whether one is familiar with Le Corbusier's problems of placing the columns in Villa Savoye or not. Koolhaas's drunken piloti mock the need for the structure that only two of the poles could fulfill in stabilizing the support offered by cantilevering the box from the wall. Although this ironic gesture was undoubtably motivated by aesthetic intuition, it might actually represent the intimation of a new approach to structure derived from chaos theory that advocates random rather than regular load supports—an unintended irony.

At the other end of the house under the other metal clad Corbusian box, an equally clever trick is performed. The full height plate glass walls of the living room, close in spirit to Mies van der Rohe's completely glazed Farnsworth House, can be slid away from the corner, leaving what would conventionally be an angle of unused space miraculously exposed and awkwardly gaping. The only partitions of the living space are created by yellow silk curtains and mechanized metal screens. The proper climate for all these exposed surfaces and the aerial pool is of course anywhere but in the drizzling damp of Paris—it is indeed hard to imagine a less environmentally suitable solution for the site. The Villa dall'Ava seems to have all the negative potential for leading a happy bourgeois life that both the Farnsworth House and Villa Savoye enjoyed: so while the exquisite spaces Koolhaas has created might join these illustrious precursors in a utopian manner as a critique of bourgeois aspirations, the design in its self-consciousness affects a cynical approach to architecture in terms of dwelling. This degree of cynicism was no doubt sanctioned by the client, an architectural publisher as concerned with the historical consequences of his patronage as with the circumstances of his own existence. The serene openness of the spaces, the beautiful combination of trendy materials, the dazzling games of transparency, and the ironic function of the rooftop pool, which even has an underwater window looking back into the house, make the Villa dall'Ava thrilling to comtemplate as space and image, but antithetical to a canon that also includes the criterion of "place."

The role of irony, so evident in the Villa dall'Ava, seems more necessary at an institutional level in Koolhaas's Kunsthal in Rotterdam, finished in 1992. This is not because the functional program for a museum calls for irony, but because the content of art in the late twentieth century is so dependent upon ironic subversion. The logo for the institution, for instance, positions the last three letters upside down as if to spell out its programmatic dedication to the negative potential of art. Who will not be amused by Koolhaas's joke when they find a vast, otherwise modern gallery space supported by gnarled tree trunks instead of steel or concrete? Other such plays with incongruous materials and bizarre inflections are fielded against a self-consciously muted functionalist structure that from some perspectives resembles Mies's very unironic Neue Nationalgalerie in Berlin. The slender tower, placed at the point of maximum congestion where a complex series of ramps converges, provides a vertical anchor to the composition in the tradition of Dutch functionalism. The tower is actually a minimal scaffold covered in parts with cheap translucent fiberglass. It serves to house the air plenums and to support a real commercial billboard. This unconventional commercial cooptation of a museum structure is supremely ironic as it insures that authentic pop culture continues not as pop art but as a form of subsidy, supporting and supported by the institution. It is in such decisions as these that Koolhaas reveals himself to have a genius similar to Andy Warhol, ambiguous as to which side of the joke he occupies. The cultural gesture could be interpreted simultaneously as a critique and an endorsement of consumerism.

The grandest irony of the Kunsthal is reserved for the area that contains the lecture hall and the lower restaurant. The concrete columns supporting the roof are tilted at a 10-degree angle so that they form a right angle with the rake of the auditorium floor. Although this is structurally permissable in a rigid concrete frame, perceptually it is profoundly upsetting since it makes the room appear to be lunging forward toward collapse, rendering the space willfully disorienting. In the restaurant below, the ceiling is carried down to less than standing height to an uninhabitable wedge of space, giving the room a squeezed sense of calculated claustrophobia. As Kenneth Frampton and others have observed, the Kunsthal is Koolhaas's finest building to date, a wonderfully complex intersection of purposeful paths within a deceptively simple square frame. Some of its success can be attributed to the harmony of the architect's ironic method with the equally ironic goals of the art community in charge of the program.

Because a significant public building is involved, however, I sense that the irony has the potential to be counterproductive. Currently, in fact, there is a dispute between the client and the architect that hints at the inherent problem. It brings into doubt the practicality of the "culture of congestion" since the converging of pathways next to the entry of the auditorium has created constant disturbances for the events to take place inside. The tendentially cynical treatment of an institutional setting, and the ironic approach to the parasitism between commercialism, culture, and public space, removed from this highly self-conscious context, is less easy to accept in the search for principles and has already shown to have fostered some egregious disfunctionalities.

As the order of architecture increases in scale the meaning of particulars is diffused. Irony on a grand urban scale is admittedly hard to achieve, and I am not quite certain that the Euralille project can be analyzed so neatly in terms of it. Koolhaas as an urbanist has been called upon to conjure up the culture of congestion for a formidable project of urban renewal that gathers the TGV train connection to the Channel Tunnel and the local trains and transportation connections, with new office facilities for an international business center and convention center—it is the sort of program that Le Corbsusier dreamed of for the Plan Voisin in 1925. Koolhaas as the master planner is one of several players, and his authority is subjected to both the municipality of Lille and the private development corporation in charge of financing the project. He essentially has inherited the role of his hero Wallace K. Harrison, planner in chief of the United Nations Complex and Lincoln Center, coordinating the designs and supplying the rhetoric of development.

Koolhaas's vision for an ecstatic environment of "interconnectedness" can only be judged at a conceptual level at this point of incompletion. The plan is for a site imposed by the mayor that straddles the historic city and the sprawling edge. This version of Koolhaas's "Contemporary City" is an attempt to synthesize elements that usually have negative or alienating connotations, such as the chaotic, multilayered transportation connections of Japan with the bulky, high-rise suburban enclaves of Atlanta. The ironic metaphor for the architect that Koolhaas has invented for the occasion is the "surfer," artfully negotiating the waves of development. The architect in this analogy merely responds to the metabolism of the market. Rather than impose a vision of preconceived utopian form on the district, the architect supposedly plays a more passive role, like American corporate architects in Atlanta, responding directly to the impulses of development in terms of square footage and cladding ideas with complete innocence. If the modernist versions of the city, like those of Le Corbusier and Ludwig Hilberseimer in the 1920s, were caught in the Weberian mandate of reflecting a "value-free" bureaucratic society of well-being, Koolhaas's proposal is value-less, with apparently few pretensions for well-being.

[...] Despite the intentions to arrive at a plan through passive means, the heterogeneity of Euralille is programmatic and even in the purposely messy presentation drawings, its diversity looks contrived. One has to ask at what point does such a method trip on its own irony and start controlling the forces; when does passive become aggressive? To design something to look chaotic like Euralille, is not the same as making a rational order for infrastructure that can then host heterogenious insertions. Rarely has such a large-scale European development (not even the Thatcherite Canary Wharf in London) resulted in such a minimal commitment to the public realm. It is one thing to say that modern technologies are eliminating the role of public space; it is another, quite ideological act, to go ahead and eliminate public space in programs that would naturally generate the need for it.

Lille will doubtlessly be transformed through this infrastructural insertion into a more cosmopolitan place, but because of its geography and cultural subordinance to Paris and London, there is no chance it will ever have the contingencies that contribute to the cultural or economic variety of congested Manhattan. On the other hand, the Lille project may be allowed to bear some of the same bad fruit as Manhattan, such as the rebuilt Penn station—a spectacular redevelopment program for delirious congestion that yielded a brutal warren of anomie. As presented, Euralille apparently will have all of the dubious charm of a mini-La Défense—a string of high-rise office towers that generate wind for a heroic plinth that shrouds subterranean layers of parking and webs of train connections.

Koolhaas should be congratulated as a satirist for helping clear away some of the more oppressive tendencies within Modernism without resorting to a reactive stance. He has created an important point of reference that could be called "Critical Modernism." His recuperation of the modernist spatial revolution, the legacy of the free plan, can be found in both the Villa dall'Ava and the Kunsthal, and it is here that he perpetuates a spirit of liberation that is truly a pleasure. In this respect there are principles and details in his work that must be remembered. He also gains all of my admiration as one of the few architects attempting to respond to the conditions of urban sprawl rather than retreat from them. Nonetheless what makes Koolhaas's work so culturally resonant as media is not his developing spatial sense but the manner in which his architectural order is infused with irony. I have tried to demonstrate that it is this reliance on irony that detracts from architectural value and provides a dubious basis for planning. I would never be able to conclude that irony is inimicable to good architecture, like a Maoist claiming that "irony is the enemy of the people." It is not the presence of irony, but rather Koolhaas's relationship to it that I find makes his work at crucial moments elude principles. The irony of Marcel Duchamp, by comparison, was almost always adaptative and rarely projectual; it was an adjustment to the incongruities that modernity had inflicted but not a reassertion of them. I cannot say the same for Koolhaas, especially as urbanist. Whether there can be any principles for architecture in an age dominated by the social, economic, and geographic flexibility of the present is ultimately an ideological question connected to whether or not one believes that architectural choices can actually enhance human existence and the process of democratic empowerment, a matter that it is currently fashionable to treat with irony. As if the question will be deferred until, for better or for worse, it is no longer a question.

WALL FRUSTRATION: OMA'S USE OF BUILDING MATERIALS

Bart Lootsma
Daidalos—Magic of Materials II, August 1995, 74–83.

The way in which Rem Koolhaas and OMA use building materials is a delicate issue. Ultimately, Koolhaas's real goal is an architecture which is physically absent, one which dissolves itself, an architecture which above all channels and stimulates processes of social group formation, and which generates scenarios, as expressed most clearly in the competition entry for the Parc de la Villette. As early as 1982, Koolhaas quoted Raymond Hood: "The plan is most significant because all of man's activities take place on the ground ..." Koolhaas interprets this statement as a plea for "a 'functionalist' architecture which is not obsessed with form, but which conceives of and creates structures for human activity in previously nonexistent juxtapositions and catalyzing combinations on the floor (meaning the surface of the earth)." Within this odd synthesis of a "back-to-nature" Rousseauism and a euphoric, anarchistic, artistic modernity are echoes of the tumultuous 1960s, the period which influenced Koolhaas most lastingly, according to his own statements.

Central to OMA's architecture is the conception of the floor as an extension of the ground. Ideally, the building is a frame composed of floors, and the floor, when extruded vertically also constitutes a continuation of the ground. In the most recent designs by OMA, the competition entries for Yokohama and for the Library in Jussieu, this attitude is also evident in the manner in which the floor slabs are developed as upwardly extended folds in the landscape. The floors are generally made in materials which recall the ground as it is usually constituted, especially wooden parquet flooring or screed (underlayment) or even better, stone. A very special preference is reserved for bare concrete, sometimes painted monochromatically, as in the Kunsthal. In earlier designs, asphalt-paved paths, accompanied by signposts, moved from the street to the interior of the building. The typical, changing contours of desert sand play a key role in the design for a congress center in Agadir. Furthermore, a number of designs use water, which can also be considered a natural material for rendering surfaces. It plays an important structural role, especially in the famous floating swimming pool as well as in some designs for private residences. I cannot recall any design or realized building by OMA that contains plush carpets, for example; probably because they would conceal or weaken any direct relationship to the ground.

Assuming this kind of fixation on the floor, it is obvious that the exterior walls as well as the other walls and ceilings become problematic. In fact, for consistency's sake, they should not even exist. And if they are ineluctable, at least the secret hope remains that they will be demolished one day. This hope already asserted itself in Koolhaas's theoretical reflections on the Berlin Wall and the resultant study Exodus. In his explanation of OMA's competition entry for the Dutch Parliament, Koolhaas explicitly expresses his expectation that, one day, the glass-block walls enveloping the rooms where "orgies of debate" had to take place would be demolished. For Koolhaas, the wall seems to be a source of frustration, although this frustration can be used productively, if necessary, to provoke resistance among the public. [...]

Employed in this manner, the wall in its stoniest form seems symbolically elevated: concrete is clad in slabs of natural stone so big that they seem hewn from heavy blocks as in earlier times. In OMA's architecture, such walls are more or less explicitly insurmountable barriers radiating restrained aggression, as in the design for the Spear House, or ceremoniously dignified authority, as on the main and rear facades of the Kunsthal. This authority is again immediately undermined by lending a seemingly floating quality to the natural stone-walls through the crude, if not filthy, black substantiality of the insulation left visible on the side, and by the almost obscene transparency of the building as a whole. In more recent designs such as the housing project for Fukuoka and the Congrexpo in Lille, black concrete walls make their appearance, their surface comprising reliefs of the stratified walls. Such walls used to surround the palaces of the Shoguns and the Emperor in Japan. They assume the appearance of brims or rustications which protect the building from the hostile outside world but at the same time make the building into an aggressive fortress.

OMA would be happiest if exterior walls were immaterial, which is basically impossible, of course. [...] In OMA's design process, the exterior wall really does often seem to be the final stroke, something which must be put off as long as possible, and which, in most cases, is executed almost incidentally, seemingly provisionally, using cheap and transitory materials such as corrugated plastic sheet and metal decking. Facade drawings are frequently conspicuous by their absence. This is also true, in a certain sense, of the competition design for the libraries in Jussieu. Their exterior walls were to be made of transparent, nonreflective glass, including some colored panes. The panes were to be broken irregularly and to overlap one another, as in some of Mario Merz's igloos. And, as in Merz's work, these broken panes of glass symbolized the vulnerability and poverty of habitation in a ruined and sundered world. [...]

The interior walls in OMA's buildings are generally less problematic than exterior walls and facades, even though here, too, the intention is to problematize and provoke. The interior walls are frequently treated like furniture, and when it comes to furniture, especially seating, Koolhaas suddenly extols a lavish, seductive corporeality and a hedonism of the type he so admired in Mies. [...] OMA found the most beautiful and poetic solution to the wall problem in the Villa dall'Ava in Paris. The residential spaces occupy a story comprising a continuous floor slab which melds into the highest part of the garden. [...] The glass walls open completely at the corner. A curtain hangs in front of the glass wall on the interior. This curtain can be drawn to define an organically curving line which can create a more intimate nook if desired. The curtain is made of heavy silk and is a bit too long, so that it tends to appear as if it had been propped up rather than merely hung; each time it is drawn, it assumes a different form. The form is thus subservient to the inhabitants' behavior, not vice versa. The seminar room of the Kunsthal also incorporates a similar curtain hung before the large glass wall; the curtain here can shade the hall and make it more intimate, temporarily changing the space's form and the character as well. When completely drawn, the curtain forms a kind of circus tent, and when open it constitutes a beautiful sculpture near to the lectern in the corner. It is perhaps a kind of tent or igloo—although not in a constructional sense, as this would designate a building that was no less static than any other architectural type. Instead, it could be understood as a flexible, provisional arrangement, as the dwelling of restless nomads—as the optimal form of architecture of OMA.

WRITING AND WORKING

Arie Graafland, Jasper de Haan *The Critical Landscape*, ed. Michael Speaks, Arie Graafland, Jasper de Haan (Rotterdam: 010Publishers, 1996), 218–36.

How did you combine the writing of S,M,L,XL *with work in the office?*

It's not easy to combine. In a certain sense our work on *S,M,L,XL* was both long-term and short-term. I say short-term because I only began in December 1992. The book was finished in 1993, but we were thinking about it long before, also with Bruce Mau. It wasn't that a quantity of material was dropped on the designer's desk after the writing, but that we already had a concept before the writing actually began. This is exceptional for a book. This was ten years after the office was founded and it was very much a component in the complete revision of the office's concept. This revision process was helped forward by the fact that while writing *S,M,L,XL* the office economy caved in, and the writing was partly to blame for it. But it came also from neglecting diverse aspects of the office. At that time I was wholly occupied with Congrexpo and the book. In fact, it was a conscious and unconscious war with the office to ensure the birth of a new configuration.

What was the office's new configuration supposed to look like?

A while before, I had already developed the idea with Cecil Balmond and some people at Ove Arup, to enter into a kind of merger with their engineering office. What was interesting about that was that we wanted to start an office which would be neither architecture nor engineering. At the last moment Ove Arup dropped out because at the highest level they were afraid of losing their identity. Which looking back, I think is a great pity, as in view of the work we now have that would have been a very sensible step rather than a provocative one. It was also inspired by experiences in Asia where many architectural practices are part of an engineering firm. Whatever, I knew I wanted to be part of something bigger. I felt kind of exhausted by my need to be involved with the office's survival, involved to an unbelievably emotional degree. That became unbearable, not in the sense of having so many mouths to feed—I've never had a problem with that, everyone who works for us knows that's not what it's about. It's more that I didn't want it to be an issue on that scale. That you didn't know from one day to the next whether you had work. Certainly, considering the ambitions we had and still have, we couldn't have gone on like that. If you can't present yourself as a continuity, you're finished.

Has that now been solved by your association with de Weger?

For the moment, yes. Through joining forces with de Weger, among other things. It's a very loose association, I should add. More an exchange of people and capacity. That gives us the flexibility to be big or small. Now, if we need a project leader for example, then there's one available. And we have the possibility of turning things down. And due to the flood of work we are now the more powerful partner, who can influence to some degree the future of de Weger.

Against the background of such matters, what is your role in the office? Not the John Portman in your book… but nor are you a process controller in a pharmaceutical company. How do you define your own role? Choreography? Is that the right word?

Yes—orchestration is another good one. Whatever the case, I am closely involved with most of the work we are now doing. As a designer, that is. But I don't regard designing as a solitary act. I think my greatest quality is staging the creative process. At all events, a situation whereby the linking, composing and questioning of certain subjects generates a special insight and special atmosphere of creativity. One thing is that we are steadily losing our fear of researching certain hypotheses. At the outset of every operation we try to make an inventory of all the possibilities, and to leave out as little as possible. We have gradually developed a highly efficient manner of testing hypotheses, namely to destruct. To put them on the rack so that they either break or they work.
[…]

FLYING THE BULLET, OR WHEN DID THE FUTURE BEGIN?

Sanford Kwinter
Rem Koolhaas: Conversations with Students, ed. Sanford Kwinter (New York: Princeton Architectural Press, 1996), 67–94.

To convert optimism into danger and to make that danger speak; this set of operations arguably has always been the core of Rem Koolhaas's architectural program, even as far back as the Voluntary Prisoners of Architecture project of 1972. Yet never has it been expressed quite so explicitly as here, in this deceptively small, manifesto-like book, which opens with just such a blunt proclamation: "Architecture is a *dangerous* profession." And although this phrase emerges modestly and deliberately at the outset, with little pretense to impress, the words do not fail, by book's end, to bring home both the dramatic affirmations and the wild defiances implicit in their message.

The Koolhaas optimism, then, is twofold: it states not only that architecture must turn away from the comfortable vanity and narcissism that continue to protect it from the hazardous realities of historical becoming, but also that architectural speculation must pragmatically refocus on "discovering [new] potential in existing conditions," on "aligning, and finding articulation for, the inevitable transformations and forces of modernization." For Koolhaas, the posture of optimism forms no less than an "obligation," indeed a "fundamental position," for any architecture. Serious architecture must actually *desire* to be dangerous.

Yet the critical question nevertheless remains: How actually to become dangerous? Seen through OMA's work, at least one answer would read in the following manner: Architecture becomes dangerous when it forgoes all that is "pregiven"—in this case fixed types and predetermined matter—when, rather, it takes the actual flow of historical conditions as its privileged materiality (not the habitual discrete domains of geometry, masonry, stone, and glass), and works these, adapts these through transformations and deformations, in order to engender and bind its form. The effect of danger derives here from the fact that this radical view of materiality is a perfectly active, fluid and mobile one: it describes a materiality that actually moves and changes as it is worked, one that envelops and releases its own spontaneous properties or traits, carries its own capacities to express itself in form—all beyond the arbitrary reach of external control. This is why for Koolhaas truly radical optimism is incompatible with utopianism: Optimism recognizes an inherent propensity or directedness in any disposition of historical things (even the posthistorical "fragments" or the passive drift of cultural "plankton" to which Koolhaas alludes), a direction or propensity that may be drawn out and followed, while utopianism remains imprisoned within the moral universe of what "ought" to be, and so can call on no materiality whatever on which to impress its chimerical shape. Optimism and danger, very simply, are affirmations of the wildness of life—of the life that resides even in places and things—while utopianism remains an affirmation of the stillborn universe of the metaphysician's *Idea:* transcendent, fixed, and quixotically indifferent to the vivid roilings of a historical world.

To follow the movements of matter, to seize the prodigious blooms of "work" that emerge "for free" at certain critical moments in matter's free and irregular flow, is to collaborate with, and actually develop, the unfoldings of a vitalist universe, to tap both its powerful inevitability and its vast, though subtle, *potential*; to merge with that fluid universe, to both guide and be guided by its unchallengeable, inexhaustible, but fully intuitable efficacy. All technology depends at one level or another on the harnessing of just these types of potential forces, although for the most part we have forgotten that that is where its power and poetry lie. Thus modern technoscience happily operates on an arid continuum of numbers (or on skillfully reduced matter-models designed to behave like a pristine, controlled numerical milieu), willfully oblivious that the flow of numbers through equations only approximately reproduces, yet certainly entirely derives from, the more primitive and far more inventive flows of real matter. Though these processes today remain largely hidden from us, the premodern "arts" of intuition—ancient (and most current) metallurgy, nautical and telluric way finding, agriculture, plant pharmacology, astronomy, medical semiotics, etc.—all depended on the ability to apprehend multiple dynamic trajectories in space-time as distinct stratifications in a single organic ensemble. The trick, then as now, is to grasp both together—both the whole and the nested passages that we moderns analytically refer to as "parts"—to know that materiality is but a continuous production of properties vigorously yet compliantly seeking to integrate into new complexes, alloys, and alliances. By manipulating the focus, viscosity, direction, and "fibrosity" of these material flows, complex natural or artificial reactions take place, and from this, the "new" and the unexpected suddenly become possible. All *techne* is at bottom the husbanding and manipulation of these fluid relations to produce new shapes of order.

Although this fluid art of variation and husbandry is by no means "lost," it is clearly no longer the province of modern thinking.[1] As the world continues to vary and flow, to aggregate, self-organize, and to rebreak apart, most modern humans operate within a gridded meta-world of abstraction, ratiocination, and the crudest approximations to nature that even the most massive number-crunching devices cannot exceed. As a result most modern architecture draws its form, not from the topological world of fluid materiality, but from the rigid meta-world of ideality, of hubristic (naive) machinism, and of dead geometry. This arrested world, blind to the dimensions of time, produces an equally blind architecture, an architecture thrown from the meta-world into the real one, like a lead boot into time's refreshing river. There are simply no corresponding hooks or currents to keep it afloat.

While almost anything workaday—though also mediocre—is possible from within such a schema, everything exceptional, all true innovation, necessarily draws from the other side. Whatever depends on rote repeatability or on a uniformity of relations in space and time to achieve its effect will find its cause well supported by the time- and material-blind world of abstract operations. The "new"—by definition that which deviates or departs from what has already appeared—is, however, the offspring of creative, material instabilities cultivated beyond the looking-glass of the grid; it seems that we cannot help but explain novelty to ourselves (although this almost certainly betrays a false consciousness) as a dispatch from a mythical "outside." But this "outside" is in fact everywhere, all around us, indeed ours for the conjuring up. In the modern world we witness it most acutely in "extreme" conditions of performance, in real-time engagement with a wildly mobile environment in frenetic material flux. All extreme sports, for example—skysurfing, bungee ballet, base jumping, BMX, speed climbing, etc.—have for an ethos the concept of *a limit that must be reached and inhabited*, a performative destination known as "the ragged edge."[2] It is not by accident that such images abound: the liminal condition is in fact a communicative interface where rational information processing (that is, planning) breaks down under the weight of too many, and too quickly shifting, variables, where it then gives way to spontaneous *material* intelligences ("intuition" in philosophy, "universal computation" in science), to the archaic way of proceeding by feel and by flow and by following the grain of the world-unfolding—to the process of *becoming material* oneself. It is said that at the edge we encounter danger, but this is just another way of saying that there we are forced to communicate critically with a great many dimensions at once.

[...] For Koolhaas, the concept of "America" has always loomed large. It not only has served enormous aesthetic ends but has played a major role in generating both the novelty and the radicality in OMA's work (especially in the primarily European context with which it has dealt), and has provided a coherent theoretical framework through which the OMA office has come to understand and harness, for speculative architectural and urbanistic ends, the volatile processes of late-capitalist modernization. For Koolhaas, America, although deeply studied and assimilated into his work, has always strategically been kept at a "dangerous"—and therefore creative—distance: it has been constituted and skillfully maintained as the necessarily ragged, mythical gateway to the destabilizing, novelty-inducing outside. Koolhaas's America (Houston, Atlanta, Manhattan) would come to represent the whoosh of matter in free action, wellspring of the new, provenance of everything that has ever carried the wishful promise of "the future"—a strange and extreme milieu—a domain of pure movement free of historical drag. It was this America that actually invented the hyper-future, precisely because only America could invent the outside of the outside. Europe invented "Amerika" as their future and outside, but America invented the new frontiers—outer space and the insane warp speed that was meant to take them there—as theirs. Speed and space were the new materials of which the future would be made.

Among architects, then, Koolhaas is the true American, for he is the only one to have attempted to engage the absolute and pure future. And yet, from where does this strange idea of a pure future come? After the Second World War, America rode a manic wave of cocksureness, not so much for having won a war as for having realized the hubristic technological achievement that made such a claim possible in the first place: the Manhattan Project and its colossal, savage product, the Atom Bomb. The American air force played a crucial role in choreographing this complex, two-year long gesture, which was said to be capable of ending all wars; its pilots had also performed brilliantly in many critical battles in both the European and Asian theaters. Returning home after the war, the flying aces were celebrated as godlike heroes, and the war masters soon decided that the sci-fi, bigger-than-real postwar future would be ushered in on their shoulders (and at the risk of their necks). To maintain America's technological (geopolitical) edge, it was decided that two fundamental space-time "barriers" would have to be torn down: a manned aircraft would need to fly beyond the outer limit of the earth's atmosphere (280,000 feet), and the so-called sonic wall—Mach1 (660 to 760 miles per hour)—the speed beyond which, it was commonly believed, any aircraft would disintegrate—had somehow to be surpassed. These linked achievements laid the foundations for what the general public would soon—deliriously—come to know as the space race.

[...] There are many ways to inhabit space, and so there are many ways to handle an airplane. In Koolhaas, I will want to claim, we bear witness not only to a remarkable architectural project traditionally defined but to the emergence of a new way of holding social and economic space altogether, for which, in architecture, there are no real precedents at all.[3] Koolhaas's work, with its fierce, stark geometries and imperious logic, is in many senses an extreme architecture, and bears philosophical and ontological kinship with all extremity (even virtual or unrealized) in all domains of cultural activity. What these extreme states and activities have in common is sudden precipitation and total blending of diverse materialities, of wild fluxes, in an organic computational ensemble that defies both predetermination and "hard," or rational, control ("If you have to think, you're dead," according to a common fighter pilot's slogan). In simpler terms, extreme activities involve the mobilization of every interacting part in a field, so that every movement of every part instantaneously changes the conditions of the unfolding of the whole. [...]

1 On husbandry or the pastoral in urban systems generally, and in Koolhaas specifically, see my "Politics and Pastoralism," *Assemblage* 28 (1995), 25–32.

2 Other extreme sports such as the triple Ironman, ultra-deep-sea diving with liquid inhalants, or unassisted oxygenless ascents to the peak of Everest are also extreme by virtue of their catastrophic use of the human body's performance envelope—pushing it to the edge of unconsciousness so that an autopilot mechanism must kick in.

3 Sant'Elia, Hilberseimer, and certain early Soviet revolutionaries are among the only figures whose work comes to mind.

DISESTABLISHMENT

Jeffrey Kipnis

El Croquis 79 (1996), 26–37.

I've seen the future and it works.
– Prince, "The Future"

It's absolutely fascinating, but utter nonsense. You say he talks about it. Where? [He opens a copy of S,M,L, XL.*] Look, the words* freedom *and* liberty *don't even appear in his dictionary, or anywhere else in these 2,000 pages that I can remember. Koolhaas is like any other architect, all he does is try to make things beautiful. He has a tougher, grittier eye than most, but he's great at it, probably the best in the world. That's why the kids loved him before anyone else, and that's why he has finally become so fashionable for the rest of us old fans. If you really want to take a chance, try writing that. But then, your articles will be too short and no one will think you are brilliant.*
– Philip Johnson

Who is that tall guy sitting next to Willy Lim?
– Tao Ho, Hong Kong architect (pointing to Rem Koolhaas at the *Anywise* conference in Seoul, 1995)

[...]

Thus far, traditional architecture criticism tends to conclude any study of an OMA project with generic praise either for the work's wit, its renewed attention to the city, its perceived reanimation of dormant social responsibilities, or its neomodern avoidance of formal excess, its cartoonishly reductive diagrams, or its cheap, even ugly, construction. Each of these judgments can be confirmed in one or another of OMA's projects, but none grasps why Koolhaas's architecture has today become the most debated and influential in the world.[1] One frustrated critic, retreating to mythic platitudes, writes, "There is no other way to put it; Koolhaas is the Le Corbusier of our times."[2]

This outbreak of critical ineptitude is all the more interesting when one considers that of his confederates—Peter Eisenman, Zaha Hadid, Daniel Libeskind, Bernard Tschumi, etc.[3]—Koolhaas has been the most single-minded in deriving his trajectory and techniques from a frank meditation on architecture rather than from contemporary philosophy or cultural theory. "For four hundred years, architectural values have arisen from the same humanist wellspring. Today, these must change," Eisenman argues, "because of fundamental new insights achieved by philsophy." "Today, these are fundamentally changed," Koolhaas argues, "because of the elevator."

One might speculate that traditional criticism's less than convincing engagement with Koolhaas's architecture arises from the fact that his designs are subtle or that he pursues an unusual cultural project. Nothing could be further from the truth. Almost without exception, Koolhaas's designs are blatantly straightforward. More importantly, one, and only one, cultural aim drives the work, from the writings to the projects and buildings, coloring each decision at every scale, from domestic to urban, from diagram to detail. That aim focuses the work into such an acute convergence that as a body it begins to constitute a treatise on the topic. That aim, so brazen that almost no one but Koolhaas ever mentions it in other than occult terms, is simply this: to discover what real, instrumental collaboration can be effected between architecture and freedom.

The failure of modern architecture to fulfill its promise as a tool able to implement democratic political form or egalitarian social theory would from the outset seem to cast a pall over such an ambition, as would the reflection by some twentieth-century thinkers such as Georges Bataille on a fundamental conflict between architecture and liberty.[4] Other doubts nag the notion of freedom itself: that it is a goal perpetually compromised by the conflict between the individual and the collective, that it is an abstraction debatable beyond resolution by competing political and philosophical theories, that it is a naiveté unable to cope with the clandestine forces of determination deployed by global techno-corporate-military economies, that it is a delusion of consumerism mobilized by masters of the mechanisms of desire, etc.

Koolhaas's work stipulates many of these doubts. His architecture offers little resistance, for instance, to the intoxications of consumer culture. But he sidesteps flagrant entanglement with those complications by avoiding any a priori, universal definition of Freedom. For Koolhaas, architecture is able, but only able, to engender provisional freedoms in a definite situation, freedoms as the experiences, as the sensations, as the effects—pleasurable, threatening, and otherwise—of undermining select patterns of regulation and authority. He goes to some lengths to demonstrate that tangible, liberating experiences supplied by architecture can be engendered in restrictive contexts. His celebration of shopping in Singapore is perhaps the most notorious example, but *Delirious New York* and his design for the Panopticon prison are also poignant case studies.

Thus, there can be no Koolhaas manifesto on Architecture and Freedom, no axioms of comprehensive emancipation through architecture, not even a consistent catalog of liberating techniques. At any point in time, his treatise consists of the collected successes and failures of his efforts to use architecture to license as far as possible a situation's real constituencies, proper and marginal.

For similar reasons, a convincing critical engagement with a Koolhaas project depends more on an assessment of the particular sensations it posits and attempts to realize than a judgment of the work against a received set of expectations and values, that is, against a prior standard, though such judgments cannot be simply abandoned. The problem that confounds architectural criticism is that at many levels—formal, material, and contextual—Koolhaas embraces traditional architectural standards perfected by the Modernists. In each project, he adjusts and suspends select aspects of these standards piecemeal to accomplish his goals, rather than attempting a total reinvention of the discipline. Koolhaas's work never resists authority; it sabotages authority from within. Thus, though his practice is thoroughly radical, it is removed from the tradition of the avant-garde, with its ceaselessly exuberant efforts to overthrow the Old and assert the New. On the other hand, in its rejection of the renewed call for the supremacy of beauty in architecture,[5] it is equally removed from the aestheticisms, such as new minimalism, that have of late gained such momentum.

Consider the precocious Kunsthal in Rotterdam, a building of striking complexity that nevertheless remains virtually unapproached, not to mention unappreciated, by criticism. An adequate treatment of this definitive work is beyond the scope of this essay, but a few remarks about it may help portray some of the issues raised. Like many of Koolhaas's works,[6] the Kunsthal is a coherent synthesis—not a collage—of several familiar modern precedents, the most conspicuous being Mies van der Rohe's National Gallery in Berlin. As is well known, Mies uses the processional at the National Gallery to extraordinary effect to situate the fragile but exalted state of art in the modern city. [...] There are several distinct entries to the Kunsthal—already a significant contrast. A major sequence begins in the park and spirals up to the galleries in a parodic organizational reversal of Mies's National Gallery. You walk up the ramp toward the deferred entry to the galleries, all the while glimpsing the galleries and lecture halls through glass. Your first encounter with the art thus occurs from a service space, and forces the art into comparison with the banal furnishings and fixture that punctuate the ramp and the lecture halls. After entering and proceeding through the galleries, you end up outside the building on a plinth of sorts, though one markedly different from that of Mies. A steel-grate platform steals the ground from under you, jutting out from the building at street level far enough to seem as if it connects to the street's surface. At the end of your journey through the Kunsthal, you find yourself in the exciting but somewhat precarious position of being slightly dizzy while standing in traffic!

At the Kunsthal art is a major performer, but one among many in the profane, animating theater of the city, not the last, beleaguered embodiment of the sacred. What then is the measure of the Kunsthal? Its perversion of a modern masterpiece? Its impertinent treatment of art? Or the refreshment it achieves through its meticulous disestablishment of an institution laboring under the weight of an increasingly irrelevant orthodoxy of experiences?

But assessing Koolhaas's experiments is rarely that simple. Take Congrexpo in Lille, often dismissed as poorly built, an attack extrapolated by some critics to suggest that the architect cannot build. An examination of the Kunsthal or the exquisite rendering of Villa dall'Ava easily demonstrates that the generalization does not hold. Nevertheless, it does pertain at Congrexpo. Already, low-grade concrete crumbles and large corrugated plastic panels at best look tacky when they are not detaching from the wall! Whether the accusation of inadequate attention to construction stands as sufficient criticism, however, is not so clear.

Koolhaas generally disdains designs that are unusually costly, especially where money is spent on exotic form or expensive material. In part, he sees such tactics as senseless extravagances, whatever other claims are made for them. Mostly, however, his contempt unfolds from self-interest. When the exorbitant costs of a building make headlines or bankrupt the client, it is the celebrities of the profession that suffer the backlash.

At Lille, frugality, but not modesty, became a theme. The town was poor and low-grade concrete readily available. All the better, because in any case Koolhaas wanted to try a huge, raw, inexpensive construction, a building, as he puts it, from "the wrong side of the tracks." The architect hoped the success of Congrexpo would be measured by the degree to which it intensified the buzz of activities, coarse and genteel—rock concerts, auto and boat shows, bathroom fixture expos, political gatherings—rather than by the quality of its construction. Why should architecture always rise above vulgarity?

[...] Though Koolhaas's architectural notion of freedom never strays far from the realm of politics, its emphasis on experience and its preference for demonstrable instrumental effect over abstract ideality situates it as much in the realm of erotics. The work often contradicts conventional wisdom on socially responsible architecture. In his influential entry for the Bibliothèque Nationale de France competition in Paris, for example, the architect proposed the extensive use of mechanical circulation, isolated reading rooms, and visual opacity to eradicate the weight of institutional presence, and to allow the building to engulf the visitor in that sometimes euphoric, sometimes menacing isolation peculiar to the city, an experience of freedom not often celebrated by social urbanists. In his project for the university libraries at Jussieu, the architect revisits Corbusian themes to generate a social setting organized less by the program than by the erotic fantasies of the voyeur.

[...] The library can be understood as a hybrid of Le Corbusier's Dom-Ino diagram and a diagram of a commonplace automobile parking structure. Le Corbusier's Dom-Ino scheme, of course, was a prototype for social housing mostly concerned with repeatable concrete construction techniques. However, it came to inhabit contemporary architecture far more powerfully as a conceptual diagram. Its implication of endlessly extendable and stackable free-plan plates skinned by a curtain wall suggested certain themes through which architecture might support an egalitarian political ideal, all more or less in disfavor today. Mass production, generic form and organization, the erasure of poché, and the evocation of an infinitely removed horizon line placed the detached inhabitant in a radically denatured slab of volume floating in an undifferentiated space.

At Jussieu, Koolhaas invaginates Dom-Ino, mobilizing it from a static diagram of infinite, equalizing solitude into a finite, fluid field of interactions, benign and otherwise. To insure adequate activity in the facility, he disobeys the brief, reducing the two distinct thematic libraries originally required into a single, generic construction, one barely recognizable as a library from a semiotic or typological standpoint.

Such radical reduction of the expectations of a given brief is characteristic of Koolhaas's recent approach to a project. More like a sadist than a surgeon, he has begun to knife the brief hacking away its fat, even its flesh, until he has exposed its nerve. The focus of these reductions is always on *disestablishment,* that is, always on excising the residues in the project of unwarranted authority, unnecessary governance, and tired convention.

Reductive disestablishment provides the crucial stratagem in each of Koolhaas's recent projects, the intellectual modus operandi by which the architect begins to transform the design into an instrument of freedom. What is a university library today but a surface on which to locate books and computers and a path to bring the public to them? What is an art museum but a version of the same organization, a surface to display the art and a path for the public to reach it? Why use two pieces of land when you can use one; why design a sculpture when all you need is a box? What is an opera house but a facility for the company to manufacture performances and a place for the public to assemble and watch them? Such reductions can nail a project with agonizing clarity, and the results can be astonishing.

[...]

1 The work's ascendancy to this position is confirmed by every standard indicator: the frequent appearance of the architect on shortlists for high-profile projects; the popularity of publications by him and about his work; the number and popularity of his personal appearances; the number of student imitations; the number of professional knockoffs, piracies, counterfeits and forgeries; the virulence of practitioners who explicitly position their own work against his; and the number of practitioners, both renowned and uncelebrated, who have openly declared a debt to him.

2 Jeffrey Kipnis, "Recent Koolhaas," *El Croquis* 79 (1996), 420–31.

3 I cite these architects as Koolhaas's confederates not so much because of any shared manifesto but by virtue of historical institutional affiliations: for example, the Architectural Association, the Institute for Architecture and Urban Studies, their participation in more recent alliances, such as the Museum of Modern Art's *Deconstructivist Architecture* exhibition and the ANY conferences, and a general commitment to pursue contemporary design as a progressive, intellectual enterprise. On the other hand, it has always been an uneasy alliance that recalls Mies van der Rohe's ambivalent fraternization with members of the Berlin avant-garde of the late 1910s and early 1920s.

4 See Denis Hollier, *Against Architecture: The Writings of Georges Bataille* (Cambridge, MA: The MIT Press, 1989).

5 See Rafael Moneo, Pritzker Price acceptance speech, Getty Center, Los Angeles, June 12, 1996.

6 Throughout his career, Koolhaas has openly shown affection for the work of Mies van der Rohe and Le Corbusier. References to these architects are often found in Koolhaas's earlier designs: Villa Savoye and Farnsworth House (and Philip Johnson's Glass House) in the Villa dall'Ava, Le Corbusier's student housing in Nexus World, Mies van der Rohe's National Gallery in the Kunsthal and Agadir.

VILLA DALL'AVA (1986–1993): A TINY BIT PERVERSE

7

Like the design for the Dance Theater earlier in the decade, the project for the Villa dall'Ava was presented by Rem Koolhaas to his colleagues, this time in 1986 in Chicago. Frank Gehry said: "I like it," and then he remained quiet. Michael Graves, Peter Eisenman, and Mario Gandelsonas were all reminded of the same modernist building that was identified, a bit later in the discussion, by Susana Torre as the House for Doctor Curutchet in Argentina, designed by Le Corbusier in 1949. Graves was, however, also puzzled by the differences between both projects, and more particularly by the way OMA had manipulated this historical ancestor, if it really was one: "Your planes wrap, and they bend, and they do what they do relative to what appears to be your own interests or whims. I think there's a loss of that tenacity in this rather frivolous object that you've made."

The house was commissioned by Dominique Boudet, Lydie dall'Ava, and their daughter, and they explicitly asked for a masterpiece of contemporary architecture —for a glass house with a pool. Boudet was a member of the French Le Moniteur publishing group, which had acquired *Architecture Mouvement Continuité* in 1983, the periodical that had been publishing projects by OMA since 1981 under the editorial guidance of Jacques Lucan and Patrice Noviant. The request of the client was for Koolhaas and project architect Xaveer De Geyter more of a welcome opportunity than an impossible challenge: they turned the Villa dall'Ava into a commentary on the modernist villa—a piece of architecture that doesn't seem to take itself too seriously but that finds exactly in this frivolity new and valuable possibilities, not only for making architecture, but also for dwelling meaningfully, humorously, and sincerely at the end of the twentieth century. Looking back at the project in 2014, Françoise Fromonot described how the Villa dall'Ava was a reinvention of the subconscious forces of modernist architecture and a "prototype for a metropolitan architecture for the present day, where the exhilarating madness of modernity can express itself anew, liberated from the depths in which it had been submerged by the functionalist superego."[1]

The Villa dall'Ava was in many ways a French project, for example, because it amended—and lifted—the typical Parisian two-bedroom apartment for the suburban site of Saint-Cloud, close to the Bois de Boulogne, about 5 kilometers from the center of Paris (and only 1 kilometer in the other direction from another house by Le Corbusier, the Villa Stein in Garches from 1927). It was an event in French architectural circles, as the many reviews show, both in architecture periodicals and cultural magazines as well as in newspapers. A photograph on the cover of the Dutch periodical *De Architect* showed Koolhaas's French colleague Jean Nouvel paying a visit. The continuation of the modernist language—"all the stereotypes of modern architecture are there, all the clichés of the avant-garde," François Chaslin wrote, "but they are shifted a little, mangled into a breathtaking mannerist collage"—in a both comical and existentialist version, did seem to match with the cultural expectations projected onto architecture: to criticize and nearly satirize the postwar bourgeois establishment and its dependence on the traditional nuclear family, without overturning or effectively threatening the conditions on which it is based. On the contrary: the Villa dall'Ava is a hedonist homage to the possibilities of suburban life, and it is too easily forgotten how much pleasure it supplies to its inhabitants, for example in the both generous and ingenious way in which the glass walls of the ground floor can be folded to the degree that they almost disappear, creating a continuum with the garden and reinforcing the structural miracle of this house with a heavy swimming pool on top. Nevertheless, some critics argued that Koolhaas may have gone too far, creating nearly uninhabitable spaces. Jean-Paul Robert wrote in *L'Architecture d'Aujourd'hui*: "This manifesto of the new age is thrown like a fierce and exultant cry in the face of our times. It says that its values are empty, like words without meaning, but which we still use." Chaslin ended his review with the suggestion that the Villa dall'Ava's "subtle hiatuses, sequences, and dissonances have been rigorously controlled by a great and extremely free artist, someone a tiny bit perverse or a little decadent perhaps, someone who laughs to himself with a serious tone about dogmas and solutions that are too well established."

And then there was, of course, the French monument par excellence—the Eiffel Tower, constructed in 1889 to celebrate the centennial of the French Revolution. At the beginning of 1991 Koolhaas started a lecture at the Rice School of Architecture in Houston by admitting how "very pretentious" the name of his office actually is: "There is, for instance, a house in Paris that we are now building, one whose swimming pool happens to be on axis with the Eiffel Tower, yet this simple fact does not make the building metropolitan, even if the French seem to think so."[2] The metropolitan character of the Villa dall'Ava might indeed not lie in the direct presence of the Eiffel Tower but rather in its representation, and in the use of this steel construction as a model for the variegated manners in which architecture can become significant. Again, Roland Barthes shows the way. In 1964 he wrote how "the Tower attracts meaning the way a lightning rod attracts thunderbolts; for all lovers of signification, it plays a glamorous part, that of a pure signifier, that is, of a form in which men unceasingly put meaning (which they extract at will from their knowledge, their dreams, their history)."[3] With a slight exaggeration, it is possible to say that the Villa dall'Ava is intended to be a kind of Eiffel Tower of late modern domestic architecture—an impossible monument for an individualized and liberal society, a form in which men put meaning extracted from architectural history, from the oeuvre of OMA, and from other cultural domains nearby. At least the many photographic images and reportages, courtesy of OMA photographer Hans Werlemann, seem to suggest so, as the Eiffel Tower is reduced to a pole star in the sky, while an abundance of seemingly uninvited elements—a giraffe, a group of generic swimmers, a chair by Le Corbusier or Mies—stimulate the imagination without satisfying it.

1 Françoise Fromonot, "The House of Doctor Koolhaas," *AA Files* 68 (2014), 85.

2 Rem Koolhaas, "Lecture 1/21/91," in *Rem Koolhaas: Conversations with Students*, ed. Sanford Kwinter (New York: Princeton Architectural Press, 1996), 12.

3 Roland Barthes, "The Eiffel Tower," in *A Barthes Reader*, ed. Susan Sontag (New York: Hill and Wang, 1982), 238.

ACCEPT BEING ALONE

Rem Koolhaas, Léon Krier, Frank Gehry, Michael Graves, Peter Eisenman, Mario Gandelsonas, Susana Torre, Thomas Beeby, Rafael Moneo
The Chicago Tapes, ed. Stanley Tigerman (New York: Rizzoli, 1987), 164–73.

rk: I decided to show a building that is atypical for Europe, in the same sense that it's atypical for America, in the sense that it's a villa. It's a villa with several intimidating factors. First of all, it's an incredibly, historically charged site, in St. Cloud, a suburb of Paris, near some of the Corbusian villas.

The site is beautiful. It slopes steeply toward the Seine. Beyond it, the Bois de Boulogne and beyond that is an incredibly panoramic view of Paris. It is surrounded by nineteenth-century houses. One of them has a superb nineteenth-century swimming pool. There is also an extremely ugly fifteenth-century-style Belgian house with a tennis court. In a sense, the context has been violated.

There was a zoning envelope that gave the site the shape of a pyramidal pretzel, which really was one of the difficulties of the project. Another difficulty was that classical Monet landscape around it. This gives you the idea of the atmospherics. Because of the difficulties posed by the site the clients had two conditions: they wanted a swimming pool on the roof, which I found very unpleasant because I wanted to do a project without a swimming pool for once. And they wanted a masterpiece, which was also very unpleasant.

[...] The house is conceived as a glass pavilion, with living space made up of two apartments—one for the daughter and one for the parents—which are connected by the swimming pool. Because the site was so small, it was very difficult to occupy it without ruining it. And, as I said, the clients wanted a glass house, while at the same time imposing a lot of conditions that made a glass house near impossible. It was a difficult issue to resolve: the incredible weight of the swimming pool resting on this glass pavilion. We did it by creating a three-story concrete wall, which had a cutout representing the glass building. Inside the glass pavilion is the structure to support the weight of the pool. [...]

lk: Are there no conservation groups in Paris who try to stop this?

rk: Yes. They had permission to build. Then the neighbors started a battle, and they lost. The house was constructed within all the laws and everything else. And they threatened to donate the site to an asylum for junkies and that was a very effective way of silencing the neighbors.

lk: Last time when you showed this I said it's very much like Monet, it's so moving that you are working now in that context.

fg: I like it.

mg: Rem, there's a house—I've been trying to remember its name. I think it's in Chile.

pe: It's in Brazil.

mg: It's in Argentina.

pe: It's south of the border, somewhere down there.

mg: It stands in a plain. It's a doctor's office in front and a house behind and a ramp in between—well, you know it. There's something in that house that describes the surface of the front building as an urban proposition on the street, a part of the street. Then there is the pavilion in the back and the ramp is the connector, obviously, between the two. But there's a planar reference in the front that makes as much as it could of the street facade, a public facade. While the pavilion in the back became more relaxed and more lyrical, it, in a sense, loosened the boundaries on the rather dense, formal facade that was on the street. But while the masses of your building make a similar composition, I don't get the urban idea here at all. I don't know whether that was a model for you, an interest of yours. I don't see how it could help being an influence in this house. But your planes wrap, and they bend, and they do what they do relative to what appears to be your own interests or whims. I think there's a loss of that tenacity in this rather frivolous object that you've made.

rk: Are you saying that you don't recognize an ambitious way of superimposing an urban and a suburban style?

mg: Well, given that there's a front building and a back building and a garden in between, which is described effectively with the pool and so on, there would be a chance to make that garden the span between the front and back building and haul out the difference between the two. But it seems to me that you weren't interested in that. Or perhaps I'm reading it in a way I shouldn't.

rk: No, it was not a particular interest of mine. But nevertheless, I feel that there are two elevations that are different in the sense that the one on the street has much more weight. The other one literally is floating or hovering above the garden, rather than making a linear progression from the street to the center of the site. It is at right angles to the street, it's a strip of a bent garden, a bent house, and a bent tarmac, which is the driveway to the garage. And so it's really not a question of two opposites but rather the exploitation of a series of parallel but contradictory conditions that interested me. And I think it's also important to include in the judgment of the house the effect of the walls of the site. They are crucial vegetal elements in the definition of the glass pavilion.

mg: Tell me something about the prophetic nature of the house. The particularly nostalgic moment that you've chosen somewhere in the 1940s.

rk: You always ask me the same question.

mg: You do it very well. I just wonder how you do that. You probably weren't even born then.

rk: Last time you also implied that it was nostalgic. Your reaction is remarkably similar, but I think that in this house, in its detailing, there is very little of that left. It's much cruder and more direct than what you say.

st: Michael was referring to Le Corbusier in La Plata, Argentina, where I had my architectural training. It's a place that I know quite well. It is a house that, as some of you may be aware of, Le Corbusier alternately claimed as author and denied as author. [...]

pe: I wanted to ask Rem a question. Four years ago we had a similar meeting and, Rem, you showed a similar project. I'm always very fond of your projects, you know. I'm predisposed. And that's why I'd probably be one of its most ardent critics. I have a sense that your work falls into the surreal category. It's my use of the term; I don't suggest that you even think your work is surreal, but if I were to categorize it—and I'm prone to make these overgeneralizations, and I apologize for the apology, but it seems necessary—I would say it's surreal. The question that I want to ask is, do you think it's possible to sustain surrealism in a world of television, an utter surrealism that seems to exist outside of the world of art? Do you think it's possible to maintain art in a surreal way, or in an effective way, as an artistic discourse?

rk: You have to explain a little more why you say that.

pe: Well, I just find the world I'm surrounded by so surreal.

rk: I understand why you call the world surreal, but why the project?

pe: Because in iconographic terms, if I were to try and place it, it seems to be articulating an energy which you might call surreal. That's why Michael calls it trapped in the 1940s. He would argue that in the 1940s it might have had an impact, which it probably would have—that's what I'm questioning. I just asked a question. I mean it as a very serious one. Do you think it's possible to be a surreal architect today?

rk: I can never answer this question with saying yes, because I don't think it's a surreal purpose at all.

pe: It's also surrealism in an earnest project.

rk: Maybe it's a series of complexities or disruptions. It is, let's say, subtle forms for a very heavy top structure in the center of a glass house. Perhaps you will sense the quality of the building doesn't derive from these forms. In fact, for me it derives from a kind of luxury which has these ambiguities as a permanent commentary.

lk: Well, you're driving on the right. You park on the terrace. Then from there, how do you go up?

rk: The staircase.

lk: From the garage, yes, but the main entrance is exactly on the opposite side. It's very confusing.

rk: There is usually an entrance at the garage to the rest of the house.

lk: But it's at the opposite end.

rk: I don't think that's an interesting question.

lk: It doesn't matter. But it is a point. The other thing is that you create a type of residence which is really an apartment on the grounds of a suburban house. On the right you have the zone that is completely unusable except for a car. It occupies the maximum amount of space for the car to get to the garage. And on the right you have a zone of grass, which is purely decorative. I don't think you can sit out there. It doesn't look as if you could.

rk: It's on the south and it has a beautiful exposure and the main garden is on the front of the house.

lk: The garden is on the slope.

rk: The garden is on the slope on the west side—a very good side for a garden.

rm: I feel quite sympathetic to Rem's work. If we go again into the meaning of language today, it seems to me that he does not rise up to the understanding that we have today of this kind of language. Of course, you will always find a certain section of the market, of the intellectual market, that will be able to understand and to appreciate your work. But I don't think that you are using the energy, either of the language itself or your own energies, in the most positive way. It seems to me that you are, at this moment, a bit arrogantly perhaps, alone, and defending a section of modernity that perhaps deserves to be defended. But it should be defended with more intensity. You are probably doing it less effectively than you could. I mean that perhaps the other editors of modernity could be Piano or Foster or Rogers, with whose work I am not as sympathetic as I am with yours. They will perhaps be using some of the weapons that are in your hands and using them in a way that is going to be much less pungent, less sharp than your work could be. I don't know if it is just the matter of its being a small house, keeping the comments on the language and on the flavor of language. I think that it affects your entire work. I would like to see your position as that of having quite an important role to play in the contemporary scene. And that is, of course, a very personal remark.

rk: It's very kind of you to be so sympathetic. In a way, you're asking something of me which I really completely resist. I think that our work is not a defense of modernity, not a defense of Modernism, it's not defensive in any case. I think it's a harvesting of some of the remnants that are left in a kind of collective consciousness. For me, it's an interesting point where modernity maybe is almost a vernacular. And if this house has any quality for me—and maybe it was a mistake to show these images that are very highly charged—it's a deliberate attempt in a way to refuse all that luggage.

rm: But, however, you see that Peter's observation about surrealism matters. I understand why Peter is calling it surreal, and it's not a pejorative word. But he's leaving you slightly out of the discussion of some problems. And I would like you to be more a party to this, to address some of the problems that some of the people are dealing with. Otherwise, it's always going to be opposite, a kind of marginal anomalous situation that doesn't address the problems that architecture seems to be working with today. I don't know if, after twenty years or forty years, people will say that you were addressing the actual problems. It seems to me that it is going to allow you to do quite interesting work but that it's always going to be a bit marginal. I don't know how much you are interested in working the margins instead of going into the middle of the fight.

rk: In spite of everything that connects us, like sympathy, I think we have a totally different perception. I mean, of what you call marginal. I don't have this impression at all. You ask me the question, "Are you interested in being a marginal figure, making some pathetic variations on the sidelines of the big stream of history?" I really don't see it's the case at all.

rm: I understand this answer very well. But it means that you should accept being alone, and being alone a lot.

RIGHT UNDERNEATH THE POOL
François Chaslin
Le Nouvel Observateur 1437 (1992), 178–80.

Rem Koolhaas is a lanky Dutchman striding out across the world, from New York to Fukuoka, from London, where he spends the weekends, to Rotterdam, where he works, and finally from Lille, where he is building the new business center between the TGV and the old town, to St. Cloud, where he has just completed the strange Villa dall'Ava. An emaciated, serious and focused beanpole, he navigates the chaotic world of international metropolises in what appears to be a hurry, constructing unusual buildings by virtue of a logic that seems impeccable to him but that is paradoxical nonetheless, and which he succeeds in steeping in a mysterious Nietzschean aura. The villa in St. Cloud, on the hillside, is located on a sloping street planted with plum trees and lined with large opulent-looking houses. These are mostly Anglo-Norman in style, made from buhrstone and light brick, with hints of a frame either beneath the heavy tiled roofs or sometimes on the ridge, standing upright like a finial, a ceramic stork. The architect of this villa has kept a stretch of old and decrepit yellow wall along the pavement, above which a strange box of undulating metallic gray sheet metal now springs up, causing a scandal in the neighborhood. Once inside the full sheet metal door, opaque to prying eyes, a curious and striking object is revealed: the box is cantilevered, supported by fifteen slender stainless-steel posts that appear to stagger. A narrow concrete path slides between them, snaking across the grass as if in a primitive suburban garden.

There is something of a kid's drawing about it, of Little Nemo's dreams, or of the set of a Spirou comic in particular. Something of this Belgian art that, since the Second World War, has valiantly maintained a taste for the 1950s-style Modernism that was snubbed in high places before coming furiously back into fashion.

There is a second iron door into the ground floor of the house, which is flat and papered with blocks of dark slate. It is a relatively tight entrance. A quarter turn to the right leads into a high-ceilinged, empty room tiled in black marble, habitable and apparently with no other particular function than being spacious. There is a metallic spiral staircase in one corner. Heck, do we really have to go up that? No. A half turn to the right is a long sloping ramp that is so narrow it needs to be negotiated in single file. It is hardly a welcome and even less so a corridor. Rather a professional space. We are in a monument, a work of art. How else would you get into it other than with a rite of passage?

On one side of the ramp, a window overlooks the emptiness of the car park. On the other side, there is a thick rustic plywood structure, part wall part furniture. Further on, you can make out a second cantilevered box covered in undulating sheet metal, this time colored a metallic salmon pink. At the end, another staircase masks the view before the living room is finally revealed. A light space, it is open entirely onto the garden but for a large yellow silk curtain that runs idly along the ceiling, allowing it to be sealed off depending on which view you want. There is more glass if you turn around, as well as opalescent walls of frosted glass, a mobile blind made from bamboo rods and another from perforated aluminium. The meagre kitchen is behind a translucent curve of pale plastic, followed by a corner for a frugal dinner at a glass table with a black stainless-steel base, set up on a balcony over the sort of empty hall that you come into as you arrive, with the spiral staircase that goes up to the little girl's bedroom.

Let's come back for a moment to the magnificent living room, ever so slightly sloping toward its huge sliding windows that open at the corner. Three cubic Le Corbusier armchairs, model Grand Confort 1925, are the only occupants. Our architect-cum-strider, who is not keen to make us lazy, thought that would suffice. We are surrounded on all sides by the view. Among the cherry trees in bloom or the autumn rain. Among the other houses, right up close, protected by their thick facades, concealed, hypocritical behind their shutters and the black holes of their windows.

While all the villas in the neighborhood have been built in the same register — near the street, garden behind — this one has muscled into the back of its plot to expand its living room, to show itself off and steal the most intimate of views from its neighbors. You would have to live there in plain sight, as if in an advert, clean and relaxed, modern if you like, with nothing to hide, stripped of the miserable secrets that make up the most ordinary of lives.

From the little girl's bedroom, to which we finally go up (exposed concrete walls and ceiling, large window-cum-show window, bright colored curtains scattered with cockatoos and plump peonies), a stepladder provides access, through a secret door, to a walkway, a ship's gangway rather, lined by three long taut stainless-steel cables like a handrail. It looks down on the neighboring plot. A folding industrial staircase leads back down into the garden, if you can be bothered to release it by its system of handles and pulleys. Another very steep staircase leads down in one go to the terrace, surrounded by a simple fence.

Astonishingly, this is where the pool is, on the roof, blue, long, in a vertiginous position, without a parapet, bordered on one side by a narrow teak pontoon. What austere and perhaps faintly exhibitionist gymnast, what abstract and vertigo-free being would dive into it, muscles flexed toward the landscape, in line with the Eiffel Tower, sticking up in the distance, far beyond the foliage of the Bois de Boulogne? Who would dive in and then stretch out, unassumingly, on the other side of the abyss, on a lawn of rare moss surrounded by and protected from the emptiness by a meagre red plastic building site fence?

From one last staircase, that of the parents, a round voyeuristic porthole looks at the murky bottom of the pool. It is all curious, or very humanist. In this house you feel both stimulated by the architecture and shaken by all that is trivial, carnal, and human within you. All too human, perhaps. Beautiful shared spaces, more monastic cells by way of bedrooms, ascetic bathrooms and hardly any storage. No past. No room here for nostalgia, mess, books, trinkets, or old clothes. No tenderness. Long-held dreams of a cellar or a loft have been banished. Everything here is strange, upside down, above your head, but this is what makes it captivating.

Stilts, overhangs, fluid interior spaces, architectural promenades, the death of the window, opaque boxes countered by moments of complete transparency, rationalism and intransigence, a refusal to withdraw and a projection into the outside world, in the open air. All the stereotypes of modern architecture are there, all the clichés of the avant-garde. But they have been shifted a little, mangled into a breathtaking mannerist collage. Their subtle hiatuses, sequences, and dissonances have been rigorously controlled by a great and extremely free artist, someone a tiny bit perverse or a little decadent perhaps, someone who laughs to himself with a serious tone about dogmas and solutions that are too well established.

SUBURBAN SUBVERSION

Jean-Louis Cohen

Progressive Architecture 4 (1992), 114–20.

Incongruous in its middle-class, suburban setting of St. Cloud, the Villa dall'Ava by Rem Koolhaas marks the welcome return of an architectural approach to single-family dwellings that has been virtually absent from France for the last fifty years. Intolerable to its neighbors, unacceptable to French planning authorities—even Le Corbusier probably could not obtain building permits for his modern houses now—the house is set on a narrow lot of some 7,000 square feet sloping down to the east, where a strict interpretation of zoning laws would have made it difficult to build any conventional structure. The irreversible prohibition of any direct views into neighboring properties led Koolhaas from the start to break—at least in appearance—with the layout of the traditional suburban Paris house.

A double-L contiguration of volumes permitted him to make use of the narrow facade on the street, with access to the yard in the rear, and with the two lower levels occupying a relatively narrow footprint. Koolhaas thus created a kind of inverted house, narrow at the base and growing broader toward the top as it gradually opens toward the sides and toward the sky. This outward expansion of the building also afforded a solution to the problem of the lap pool, which could not be dug into the earth. Instead, its trapezoidal tank is located at roof level, where it enjoys a grand prospect of Paris. The structure of the house is therefore a kind of water tower, held up by a row of reinforced concrete columms and two hollow pillars, from which the bedroom wings protrude on slender, strategically placed supports.

From the outside, this eccentric structure is only partially revealed; the rear facade of the master suite seems to float above the ground like a tin-clad Villa Savoye, though it is actually cast in concrete. Koolhaas has made secondary (or even false) supports prominent, while hiding the real load-bearing elements, and masked the concrete shell with lightweight corrugated aluminum. The clients wanted "the house of a lifetime"; through these manipulations, Koolhaas brings into question the unquestioned expectations invested in the building of a masterpiece. The Villa dall'Ava is as sturdy as a bunker, yet stripped of the semblance of enduring architecture—erudite and even respectful in its modern references, yet quite without reverence for so-called structural integrity.

From a certain vantage point, the trunk of an old tree appears to be holding up the house like a living crutch. Despite that illusion, the house is hardly contextual. The slate of neighboring rooftops may be repeated, but in the large slabs covering the ground-level walls. If indeed the preexisting houses in the neighborhood share any elements with the Villa dall'Ava, it is only indirectly, as the low brick walls and vernacular materials of the surrounding homes are absorbed into the landscape of the house through the long glass expanses of the living room.

Developed on the basis of a plan dictated by the nature of the site's topography, the Villa dall'Ava is foremost a variation on the conventions that define a middle-class house in western Paris. Its provocative challenge to the accepted stereotypes explains the neighbors' numerous lawsuits, which delayed the house's completion by nearly four years. Regardless of the success of President Mitterrand's *grands projets* program and of the boom that new architecture seems to be enjoying in public works, the French bourgeoisie is on the whole viscerally opposed to modern architecture.

The spatial principles of the Villa dall'Ava make obvious references to those of Le Corbusier and Mies, in particular to the villas Savoye and Tugendhat. But Koolhaas has also repeated the vertical division of function characteristic of the Parisian *hôtel particulier,* assigning services to the lower level, living and entertaining areas to the *piano nobile* with access to the garden, and sleeping and bathing to the upper floor. Koolhaas's use of parallel strips in the plan, some determined by structure while others are free, may also be associated with the zones and exterior margins emphasized by his compatriot Nikolaas John Habraken in his 1961 book, *Supports.*

As early as 1982, in his competition scheme for the Parc de la Villette (similarly based on the relationship between functional parallel strips), Koolhaas had been inspired by the mathematical planning methods of the 1960s. Subsequently his rational, at times severe, concern for function has been combined with paradoxically free form. In this sense, the Villa dall'Ava, conceived in 1984, is both a record of the original research efforts of OMA and a fitting, if delayed, conclusion to them. At the same time, the St. Cloud house is an expression of a certain renewal of thought and technical innovation in France. Frozen since 1945 in veneration for reinforced concrete, which was considered practically a "national building material," reflection on the construction aspects of architecture was revived only by the persistent effort of Jean Prouvé in his lightweight buildings. By the stubborn eclecticism of its framework and its exterior cladding, the Villa dall'Ava signals that a less dogmatic approach is making headway among French engineers, echoing Prouvé's work.

In fact, the work of engineer Marc Mimram, who collaborated with Koolhaas on the Villa dall'Ava, is exemplary for its appearance of lightness and its empiricism. While the reinforced-concrete construction supporting the elevated pool is self-effacing, and all but invisible from the outside, it is intrinsic to the interior, where it is incorporated into and emphasized by a long storage wall. The apparent lightness of the corrugated metal cladding veils the inversion of mass taking place in the heart of a house actually crowned by several tons of water. And it is this kind of paradoxical blend of historical allusion and structural illusion that best characterizes Koolhaas's subversive—if rationally grounded—contribution to contemporary architecture.

In his *Delirious New York* of 1978, Koolhaas proposed an imaginary floating pool in which "architect/swimmers" carried the germ of avant-garde Modernism from Russia to Manhattan. Firmly attached to the St. Cloud house, the Villa dall'Ava pool delivers its own message to Paris: a new kind of single-family house is possible only at the cost of unflinching commitment—such as the rare conviction that united Koolhaas and his clients in the face of adversity.

THE GIRAFFE AND THE ARCHITECT

Frédéric Edelmann
Le Monde, March 26th, 1992.

The Villa dall'Ava in St. Cloud was barely finished when it was already considered to be the *ne plus ultra* in both architecture and the avant-garde movement. It was built by Rem Koolhass, head of OMA and the most controversial personality in the relatively exclusive circle of world-renowned architects, which surely can mean both dreaded and appreciated. The tall, lanky, giraffe-like Dutchman was born in Rotterdam in 1944, at the end of the war. He grabbed postwar architecture like a wild but intelligent child might take his brother's blocks that were absentmindedly arranged to please his parents. Kaboom!

[...] Thus, the problem child is interested in space, in void, in a sort of elusive dialectic that allows him to simultaneously approach order and disorder. The Mayor of Lille himself had a hard time imagining what his city would be made of and no one was surprised when Koolhaas was chosen for the new International Business Center around the new TGV train station.

In architectural terms, our Dutch architect, a natural advocate for the innocence of the city, of architecture and of his own alike, appropriately began to pay tribute to the cube, as a tribute to complexity. The Sea Trade Center's cube was designed in a spirit of absence. Koolhaas imagined the intersection of a sphere, or rather an egg, and a cold, futurist cone, which has nothing to do with an ice cream cone. The cube used for his project for the French National Library was a real cube, but filled with spheres, eggs and cylinders, not unlike the areas in space explained by astrophysicists: black holes, nebulae and galaxies that seem to both ensure the unchangeable order of things and at the same time, collapse on each other, annihilating distance and time, to finally reconcile being and nothingness by the threat of an eternal judgment.

And then, to remain in France, the Villa dall'Ava was built. A tiny, impractical oblong piece of property in an elegant neighborhood, a remnant of the suburbs. It was closely surrounded by inexistent or picturesque homes. Did the sponsor understand the yoga and contortions that Koolhaas would have to use to tame the land? Or was it Koolhaas who, once he accepted the project, understood how to master this small vegetable garden? In any case, the proof is that this infinitely small piece of land became infinitely large thanks to the magic of rather simple folding (undoubtedly a tribute to Columbus's egg), of the most complex to draw and the most natural in which to live, despite the inevitable concessions made to vertigo that an old friend to Japanese-American chaos could not avoid.

The shape, if we can call it that, is one of the simplest: an elongated block, an inviting area for friends that also welcomed the small garden, which can penetrate the premises to the point of becoming one with the architecture. It is topped off with a modest-sized but genuine swimming pool that could not have been placed "outdoors." The extremities of the block rest cantilevered on two boxes dedicated to the family's privacy. The children on one side, the parents on the other, connected by extremely ingenious passages, with the addition of several components of home automation and audiovisual dialogue, as the feeling of close family is quite ambivalent (not too close, albeit not capable of being far away from one another). A few slants and curves add a soft, human feel to the entwining parallelepipeds.

Les Éditions du Moniteur, who award a series of prizes to buildings and not to persons—the expression of the best possible harmony between architect and commissioner—gave a "special out of competition prize" to the Villa dall'Ava that year. Why special and why out of competition? The Equerre d'argent, the highest award of this type at the Festival of Cannes for architecturography, went to the square des Bouleaux, a wonder of urban invention by Renzo Piano and Bernard Plattner for the Régie Immobilière de la Ville de Paris and the Mutuelles du Mans. [...] The award for first work went to the extension of the Enghien Museum, a simple, neat object by the young Bresdin, Jacquard and Pignot. Why then, in this bouquet of successful achievements, the house by Rem Koolhaas, for which the jury also wanted to recognize "unanimously the interest and originality"? Actually, the "out of competition" can be explained by the fact that the sponsor of the Villa dall'Ava belonged to the *Moniteur* group. It is, if you will, a tribute to blushing modesty. Then why the adjective "special" for this award, which bears two adjectives that are contradictory and borderline pleonastic (for can that which is *original* be without *interest*?). In fact, we know very well how much the term *interest* can be used to avoid commitment or enthusiasm for authentic originality.

However, the jury was not wrong (was it chance or intuition?) to choose these terms. Professionals are attracted to and enthused by the quality and accumulation of its cleverness, through its obvious and constant search for perfection. At the same time, professionals understand that by the use of materials and some of the decisions to break away from tradition and to dazzle create a "shelf-life date," beyond which the product will no longer be fit for consumption, trendy, just a snapshot in history.

To give just one example: the photos presented by *Le Moniteur* to demonstrate the project's interest and originality were forced to accept a genuine giraffe as main occupant of the home, next to a few distant human silhouettes. It's true that the space escapes the image—it is that fluid and taut—and the relationship between the interior and exterior are difficult to show. Note the siding—rectilinear and rectified with giraffe spots—of the "if you want it, you can have it"-type. Note the plastic orange railing directly borrowed from a worksite and without any other relationship to a giraffe than its incongruity. Finally, to mark the entrance, note the forest of stilt-like columns, all slanting sideways like a birch wood, a bamboo grove or the four legs of a miserable baby giraffe. How charming.

However, the jury was probably most troubled by the importance of historical references, although hidden by so much charm, that perhaps make the five-dimensional villa a very clever, even ingenious, application of formulas developed for other circumstances. Let's imagine Wright's house on the waterfall being forced to marry the Farnsworth house by Mies Van der Rohe on a Japanese tatami, while dreaming of the agility of a humorous, poetic construction site foreman, while preparing to buy furniture covered in giraffe skin. Would architecture designed under such circumstances be that much different?

A MODERN CONSTRUCTION

Jacques Lucan

Domus 736 (1992), 25–34.

The clients' brief was summed up in three essential points: the house must have a very open living room as a continuity of the garden; two separate bedroom-apartments, one for the parents, the other for their daughter; and a swimming pool on the roof from which swimmers can see Paris on the horizon. The site is on the St. Cloud hillside with its panorama over the Seine valley. [...] The question was: how could this plot be taken possession of without sacrificing its striking landscape qualities? How was the architecture to avoid destroying the beauty of its sloping site which must always be perceptible and felt? How would the building not impede glimpses over the hills, seeing that the land narrows in its lower part toward the street?

Rem Koolhaas made a simple choice. It consists logically in not establishing broad vertical fronts which would be an obstacle to the continuity of the relief. The house yields to this necessity by stretching its subfoundation in the direction of the slope, which flares as the site gets wider: on the ground it occupies only a thin middle trip, leaving two transparent bands on either side to hug the party boundaries. Would not the impossible ideal have been for the house to be a blade, as seems to be suggested by a single veil of reinforced concrete planted vertically on the villa's longest line, though already an ambiguous veil, horizontally rent by a glazed wall that goes on to form the glass box of the living room? On the middle strip, the subfoundation rises from the ground with its almost naturalist slate cladding: carrying the glass-box living room whose ground level exactly meets that of the garden.

Above the glass box, the two bedroom-apartment boxes are set perpendicularly to the slope and parallel to the level curves, in order to comply among other things, to the necessity for aerial views over the hill and of Paris. Being raised from the ground, the boxes let the road slip beneath them, in this way safeguarding the property depth of the two lateral strips of land. As for the swimming pool on the roof, it recaptures the orientation of the slope, ensconced as it is, between the bedroom-apartments. It is not ostentatious, indeed there is nothing to indicate its presence perched up there at the top.

Discovering the interior is to witness a multiplication and intensification of the effects achieved by the initial choices of plan. From the entrance we go up the ramp which easily follows the slope, watching the north side of the house slowly emerge. Meanwhile the horizontal glazed wall accompanies us toward the living room. No opacity is interposed to prevent us seeing the garden. The upper box of the bedroom-apartment comes forward in an overhang, the absence of any support exalting the presence of three trees whose trunks look like stilts. The underside of the box, in the same aluminium sheet as its vertical surfaces, is the ceiling of an open-air drawing-room whose perimeter has apparently vanished. The virtuality of the room's center is perhaps signified only by a few slate slabs imprinting the mark of a paved floor in process of self-effacement. After leaving the ramp, our view from the living room sweeps over the garden. But the extension of the room westwards is halted in order not to interrupt or spoil the continuity of the strip of land transversal to the slope, free from construction.

This flat end ledge in the hillside considerably augments the garden's attraction, extending the view southwards beyond the parceled limits of the site. It is there that the sliding bay-windows forming the corner of the living room can be totally opened, to let the garden into the house, or the house into the garden.

The atmosphere of the living room is calm and limpid. Coming back toward the entrance it shrinks slightly, heightening a perspective effect again emphasized by the translucent curve of the kitchen; while in the opposite direction, its nonparallel longitudinal sides have a reverse effect to the opening of the house onto the garden. The south front is not always identical: it alternates transparent or frosted glass walls in order notably to comply with standard restraints which forbid the opening of direct views over a distance of five meters from the partly intermediate boundary. This alternation modulates the light at the same time as the views: the glass box is an experiment in diaphragms; the glass becoming a veritable material for the construction of an inwardness, as the two patio houses built by OMA in Rotterdam had begun to demonstrate.

The return to the balcony on the entrance, and on the road beyond, transforms the route into a loop, allowing us in a circular way to perceive the house's closer horizons—while the distant, panoramic vistas will be discovered from the windows along the bedroom-apartments and from the accessible flat roofs.

Since the living room "space" stretches to the very edges of the plot and sometimes beyond, yet welcomes the garden so warmly into the house, Rem Koolhaas proves at the very least the pertinence and intelligence of this contextual approach. As he likes to point out, the house "surrenders" to the reasons of a site saddled with numerous standard constraints which had to be reckoned with ... and got around. The house does not oppress the land: it does not try so much to impose its law on it as to bring out the qualities of a site without ever seeking to contradict them.

Rem Koolhaas is not an adept at "subjective gestures." The objectivity of his position and the rationality of his work resides in a "bias" which he has always stated: that of an "automatic overestimate of the existent." It is based on "the most clinical possible inventory of each site," which prohibits any kind of systematism. Like every true house, Villa dall'Ava is a microcosm, but a microcosm "enlarged" to its near and far limits. It does not retreat into itself in proud isolation or stand aloof. It is camouflaged like an animal adapting to the conditions of a habitat, as was the Dance Theater. [...] In that respect, Rem Koolhaas accepts the insuperable horizon of the contemporary city, which makes any urban or suburban situation a disjointed emplacement nevertheless to be measured.

A BROKEN RELATIONSHIP

Akira Suzuki
Kenchiku Bunka 547 (1992), 142–43.

I don't know about the time of Baudelaire, but I once saw the apartment of Jean Genet on television. The steel bed, the wood-framed window. When I looked down, I saw cigarette butts smoked to stubs scattered around the floor right up to where I stood. In this small room, he sat on his bed and roamed through his fantasy world all day long. Perhaps not all day; he also spent half of every day sitting in the café that could be seen from his window.

What could an architect do here, invading the bubble of this content city life like some meddlesome tailor? Compared to the supreme bliss of a cup of coffee in the café on one's familiar neighborhood street, the philosophical ramblings of an architect would hardly be of interest.

I imagine Madame dall'Ava moving through her house, her steps as lively as a modern dancer's, every movement precise. Save for the hard floor and the level ceiling, every part of this house is transparent; any partitions and walls feel barely present. That is why Madame dall'Ava's every movement is like a performance on a stage. While getting ready for the day, she might flit through the bedroom or across the roof terrace, hop up the steps of the spiral staircase like a rabbit, disappear and then reappear on her stage again as if she was never gone at all. Surely that is how she moves through her house. Her movements and actions have drawn uncountable straight lines and arcs across the level floor, invisible to the eye but present nonetheless. I still do not know if these patterns were secretly planned out by a designer with a flair for strategy, or if the Madame engraved them there herself.

The Villa dall'Ava perches at the corner of a gentle slope in a Parisian suburb filled with rows of villas. It stands out effortlessly in a neighborhood full of splendid mansions that have all windows closed even during the daytime. However, this home is not defined by how starkly it stands out from those around it. On this slope stands a naked personification of the program of living in a city. It has been stripped of all ostentatiousness and snobbish style. That does not mean it forces an ascetic lifestyle onto its residents. A thoughtful observer will notice that the solid black floors mirror and reflect back all the activities of city life. When you ascend to the top of the ramp and the spiral staircase that winds skyward like a Moebius strip, you reach the roof and come to stand on the diving board of a swimming pool full of clear water. Beyond the opposite side of the pool, the city of Paris extends across the horizon. The Eiffel Tower rises along the axis of the pool.

That breathtaking vista immediately put me in mind of something else. Le Corbusier's mysterious appartement for Charles de Beistegui. From the rooftop of that creation, the actual Arc de Triomphe would line up with its miniature version. That little roof garden holds a collection of homages by De Beistegui to Paris. However, this man did not like to face the city head-on. He locked himself in his study instead, peeking out through a periscope that protruded toward the sky. This is an example of a Parisian with a broken relationship with his city. As a Tokyoite, however, I somehow feel that I can sympathize. [...]

I should note that Madame dall'Ava does not get stage fright in her house penetrated by gazes and noises, bombarded with input from phones and fax machines and sometimes even radio waves directly from satellites. On the contrary: her light steps become ever more refined as she lives a life of supreme self-confidence. I only found out about this later, but it turns out that Madame dall'Ava works as a psychoanalyst. During her conversations with patients, she hears about all the anxieties that plague city people. In other words, she untangles the affairs of people living in a modern city. I had been too hasty in imagining her moving through her home like a dancer. Perhaps rather than a performance for the audience that lived around her, her life was a dialogue with the city reflected as an abstract mirror image by the floor, an attempt to analyze that city?

Of course, this too is a kind of pleasure offered by the city. Or is it? I remembered a small round window, hidden at the end of the staircase that ascended toward the bedroom. It gave a view of the surface of the pool bathed in brilliant sunlight. But perhaps at night, it gives the viewer a peek at the reflection of the city of Paris in the water.

What does it mean to live in a large city? Few architects really try to get to the bottom of that question. Has an architect ever interrogated this through a residence, an office building, or a regional plan? More pertinently, has an architect every really interrogated this? In other words, what is the meaning of family? Television? Food? Conversation? Labor? A big city changes the meaning of myriad acts and actions, unavoidably transforms them until they are far removed from our commonplace assumptions. We who actually live in a city are aware of this to some degree, but we always work to forget about it. However, most architects don't seem to have noticed.

It's hard to imagine that the "works" these architects continue to produce will one day reflect those changes. The more one emphasizes the work as an expression of the self, the further away it moves from the city and all its rich narratives. Have these architects ever had a dialogue with a real city? Have they ever really wanted to feel the pleasures of a city?

At the beginning of the century, houses were programmed to be "machines for living in." Today, however, such programs no longer necessarily reflect what a house really is. The city dwellers and architects who first took note of this obvious fact are already drawing up free and uncontrolled programs for living in the city.

LIVE
Jean-Paul Robert
L'Architecture d'Aujourd'hui 280 (1992), 10–19.

You have to look at if from all angles before you can grasp this villa by Rem Koolhaas. Retrace the shock it causes from the street, in this calm and cushy quarter of St. Cloud, on this hillside looking toward the Bois de Boulogne and the distant spectacle of Paris. Its silhouette is reminiscent of an aggressive and run-down Villa Savoye, rising behind the alibi of an old boundary wall. The same features are there: a floor torn by a long window, set on a floating ground level that stands on piles. But the upper floor, capped by lacquered corrugated iron, butts brusquely against a wall that cuts it. And, once past the gate, the eye balks at the piles out of plumb, painted in differing grays to create a trompe l'oeil depth, with the pathetic little concrete path running over the lawn and weaving thru them.

So the snare is set from the start: the house is not what it appears to be, and systematically adopts—sometimes with humor, sometimes aggressively—the contrary position to what it recalls, to what we expect, or to what we imagine.

In this way, the ground floor is nothing of the sort. Because of the slope, it is imbedded *in* the ground. The real ground floor is upstairs, flush with the upper part of the garden. After the sophistry of the entrance that gives onto a room glazed full height, a ramp, like the one at Poissy, leads up there. The ramp runs along the glazed wall, which would be a facade were it not parallel to a party wall. The promenade is brief and uncovers nothing, except the living room, glazed like an aquarium and opening onto the garden that nothing really delimits. This level turns about to return to the volume of the entrance. It unfurls spaces that are fluid—too fluid—and glazed too, on the other long side. It is an open corridor, too open, a sequence of spaces accelerated by the curved kitchen wall in folded, translucent plastic. Caught and held in a state of weightlessness, the Villa dall'Ava seems to be running away from itself, as if it were on the verge of dissolving, even if it does run toward the improbable confines of an elsewhere, on the nontraced bounds of the garden, or toward the forbidden facades of its stuffy neighbors.

You have to push to understand, take one or the other of the stairways placed at either end, leading to the suspended boxes that are the two private apartments of the house. The first, on the street, is for the child. The second, for the parents, is placed over the living room. It is displaced to the other side of the wall line in an unbelievable overhang. You have to go even higher up to look at the suspended places of the roofs, the basin of the swimming pool, and the vista over Paris, which up to here the villa seems to have ignored. Everything is contrary to common sense, disconcerting. Gravity is upended: the heaviest on top, the laws of physics denied. [...]

So many delicate balances, constantly threatened by instability, are to be found among these gravitational tensions abolished by frozen movements, or interferences of directions. There is no pause, however. No static position really possible. To escape from this discomfort, you have to take refuge inside the boxes, where intimacy seems to be reserved. The play on the roof offers another illusion. The gift of the sky is factitious. Resting one's body there would mean exhibiting one's self, and, since there is no parapet, it wouldn't do to be subject to vertigo. Not for you and me then. No more perhaps than the villa itself, since nothing proves that it is a house, so thoroughly has the idea of home been evacuated.

This manifesto of the new age is thrown like a fierce and exultant cry in the face of our times. It says that its values are empty, like words without meaning, but which we still use. That there is no living, outside of the hollow of a box. No communication other than deambulation, or the dumb parade of bodies. Just as there are no walls, no windows, no above or below, no inside or outside. When nothing speaks, when nothing more is said, when anything can be done, there still remains what we desire. Making architecture for instance, and talking about it.

But is this house—which could in no way serve as a model—still architecture? It is creation, pure creation, and in this sense, it satisfies the clients who wanted—more than a mere house—to add something to history. Koolhaas's own exigency has gone beyond their dreams. Their villa is a work. Hieratic and perfect, critical and absurd, enigmatic and loquacious, like a work of art, a Donald Judd or a Tony Smith. The latter entitled one of his works—a block box—*Die*, which might be taken as an injunction. Its purely mental space could not be lived in. Similarly, the Villa dall'Ava might well be entitled *Live*. Live now, if you can!

THE IDEAL VILLA

Charles Gandee

House & Garden 3 (1992), 158–72.

Five years ago, in the dead of winter, I flew to Rotterdam, a place I would not recommend in the dead of winter, to meet Rem Koolhaas, a tall, gaunt, Ingmar Bergmanesque man who became an architectural cult hero in the late 1970s when he published *Delirious New York*, which depicted a sensuous vision of ecstatic Modernism—picture Le Corbusier on LSD, picture the Empire State Building in bed with the Chrysler Building. Although Koolhaas seemed more inconvenienced than impressed by my pilgrimage, he did oblige (somewhat grudgingly) with a guided tour of his Office for Metropolitan Architecture, best known as OMA, which included a preview of drawings and collages for a house to be built just outside Paris. The house was called the Villa dall'Ava, and at the time it struck me as the most beautiful house I had ever seen.

The Villa dall'Ava is now finished. And it is still the most beautiful house I have ever seen. The husband and wife, a publisher and a psychologist, who commissioned the villa asked for three things: a swimming pool, a lot of glass, and an architectural masterpiece. Regarding the latter, the husband told me: "We didn't want just a beautiful house, we wanted something that adds to history, if possible. So our models were Le Corbusier, Kahn. It is very difficult to find a contemporary architect of this caliber." But the publisher and the psychologist were determined. So they looked and they interviewed—in France, in Japan, in Switzerland, in Italy, in the US, and, of course, in the Netherlands. They chose Koolhaas, who responded to their four-page postinterview plea for genius with a note that read, "OK. Telephone me." Signed "Rem."

Koolhaas is like that. Lean. Abrupt. Direct. Not lacking in self-confidence. I recently caught up with him over breakfast in Paris after visiting the Villa dall'Ava for the fourth, and probably the last, time. (Now that construction is complete, the owners have sworn themselves to privacy.) I wanted to talk about the house. But Koolhaas did not. "I have an incredible fatigue with describing my own work," the forty-seven-year-old architect said with a sigh of existential impatience, and then, in impeccable French, he ordered the waiter at the Ritz to bring him scrambled eggs and bacon. I persisted. Koolhaas stuck to his silent guns, allowing only that "reaction to the house has been euphoric," a piece of news that seemed worrisome to him. (One of the other exceptions Koolhaas made to his I-refuse-to-talk-about-my-own-architecture rule was what may have been an oblique reference to the three-year-long legal battle he and his clients had to wage with the neighbors, who were less than enthusiastic about welcoming a modernist masterpiece into their traditionalist midst. "Our initial exuberance was replaced by intense determination," recalls Koolhaas, who realized his design for the Villa dall'Ava without a single concession.)

The euphoric reaction should not come as a surprise to Koolhaas. Or to anyone else, for that matter, who visited the construction site, where the graffiti covering the Belgian contractor's sign ran along the lines of "Je t'aime, Rem," with all the attendant hearts and arrows, scrawled by one enraptured admirer. After all, Koolhaas and his clients were intent on building a new Mecca for a new Modernism. The difference between the old canonical Modernism and the new Koolhaas Modernism is the difference between Coco Chanel's Chanel and Karl Lagerfeld's Chanel. (This is an analogy Koolhaas will hate, but so be it.) In other words, Modernism in Koolhaas's hands is insouciant, invigorated, enriched-celebratory. In other words, Modernism in Koolhaas's hands is the menage à trois of visual energy, spatial excitement, and an ultrasensual palette of materials and colors that demand not merely to be admired but also to be rubbed up against. If the word "modern" conjures up images of rigorous, disciplined, dry, stoic, abstract, anonymous design, Koolhaas is intent on redefining it. With images of surprise, delight, pleasure, joy, something approaching aesthetic salaciousness. As well as with images of surrealism, of course, such as the rooftop swimming pool with a view of the Eiffel Tower and, on a clear night, the Arc de Triomphe.

But down on the street there's discretion too, as the house tries to hide from public view behind a preexisting masonry wall that Koolhaas restored. Once you enter through an electronic door in the wall, however, the house reveals itself. It soars like some sort of steel and glass cubist butterfly, hovering above a massive stone plinth dug into the sloping ground. A narrow path winds through a forest of sixteen tilted steel columns—grading from black to gray to white—supporting a corrugated steel box containing a wing for the couple's fourteen-year-old daughter. The front door is carved out of the stone base, which functions as foyer and provides two routes to the living, dining, and kitchen area above: a circular stair, if you're in a hurry, or a 52½-foot ramp, if you're in the mood for something more ceremonial. Upstairs, overlooking the garden, is a glass pavilion reminiscent of Philip Johnson's 1949 Glass House, which is to say it is reminiscent of almost every house Mies van der Rohe ever designed. The difference, however, is that Koolhaas has a hand that deals in diversity rather than consistency, which explains the terrazzo floor, the perforated plaster ceiling, the built-in plywood bookcases (which double as room dividers), the luminous plastic globe encircling the kitchen. There's also the suggestion of luxe in the yellow silk curtains, which, when closed, completely transform the room: you feel as if you've gone from a fish tank set down in the middle of a garden to the inside of a ball gown. The requisite Mies daybed is perfectly positioned. As are the requisite Le Corbusier chairs. A metal stair leading up to the master suite, housed in a second corrugated metal box, interrupts the luminous space. To activate the sometimes-transparent, sometimes-translucent glass public rooms, Koolhaas installed a medley of robotized screens—made of bamboo, made of perforated metal—that function like some sort of elaborate László Moholy-Nagy construction. I asked Koolhaas if he knew Moholy-Nagy's Light-Space Modulator at Harvard's Busch-Reisinger Museum. "Unfortunately," said Koolhaas, with a Mona Lisa smile, "I know everything."

OMA MANIFESTO

Bart Lootsma

De Architect 3 (1992), 29–33.

St. Cloud is an upscale residential neighborhood at the edge of the basin in which Paris lies. The hills there provide a spectacular view of Paris, with the Bois de Boulogne in the foreground and the Eiffel Tower smack in the middle of the panorama. The neighborhood is quiet, beautiful but also a bit boring. Most of the villas date from around the turn of the century. Shutters are kept shut, and the residents, with their garden walls, hedges and guard dogs, give off the impression of wanting nothing to do with their neighbors or the rest of the world. Instead each house smugly presents itself as the center of the world, though their deterioration is evident in the peeling paint. The gardens might accommodate a tennis court or swimming pool within, the red clay or clear blue shimmering through the dark shadows of the foliage. People here have money and they use it to pay for a suburban peace right next to the city and the luxury of relaxation. "This is the life; everything else is secondary," the residents seem to be saying. "We live in the manner of our parents and grandparents." Except they are probably rarely home, since they have to work so hard in the hectic city below to meet their mortgage. That turns the neighborhood into a sort of bourgeois decor for all manner of intrigue. It is with good reason that so many Maigret novels have been set in such an environment. One house, however, rises above this hypocrisy. It is a new house, and from the street it looks like a poorly parked pile of gold luxury caravans supported by a rugged concrete structure. It is the latest project built by the Office for Metropolitan Architecture.

Architecture, what architecture? The initial impression is that no attempt has been made whatsoever to engage in architecture here, at least not in a traditional sense. The composition is wobbly, threatening at any moment to fall apart into separate pieces. There is no sign of distinction. Any references to modern architecture, such as the strip window in the tall facade to the right or the way the building floats above the landscaping, appear coincidental. More to the point, they appear to have been employed under duress—unwillingly, just because it happened to work in terms of what was wanted for the house. But that is hardly on a par with the famous examples being referenced: the villas by Le Corbusier, for example, located not far from here. "It is not about what you see," the house seems to want to say. And that gives it a disturbing aspect, something surreal that is not easy to pinpoint.

Koolhaas may well have realized in this house the most concentrated form yet of OMA's objectives, as he formulated them in 1980 in the statement "Our New Sobriety," in which he cites Raymond Hood: "The plan is of primary importance, because on the floor are performed all the activities of the human occupants." According to Koolhaas, "that formulation by ... Hood ... defines 'a functionalist' architecture not obsessed with form, one that imagines and establishes on the 'floor' (= the surface of the Earth) patterns of human activity in unprecedented juxtapositions and catalytic combinations. OMA has been concerned with the preservation and revision of this tradition of so-called functionalism ... that was a campaign of territorial conquest for the programmatic imagination so that architecture could intervene directly in the formulation of the 'contents' of a culture based on the givens of density, technology and social instability."

The client for Villa dall'Ava, as the house is called, is Mr. Dominique Boudet, a top executive at Moniteur, a construction industry publisher in Paris. He had wanted to study architecture when he was young, but his parents would not allow it, and he had dreamed for years of building a house for himself that would be an architectural masterpiece—an expensive undertaking for which he had to save up, even with his presumably above-average income. He therefore lived in a two-room flat with his wife and daughter until the house was built.

Boudet had previously bought another piece of land for which he had an architect friend of his make a design. When that did not satisfy him, he bought the present property in St. Cloud and hosted a small design competition. The results of that also failed to impress. Then he became acquainted with Koolhaas's work. In 1984 he wrote a long letter to the latter requesting that he design a house for him, a letter that, legend has it, Koolhaas answered by fax with a simple "Oui."

The further evolution of the project was not so simple, however. The client's expectations were high. He wanted a glass pavilion to make the best use of the garden and gorgeous surroundings; he wanted a swimming pool on the roof, even though that clashed with the desire for a glass pavilion; he wanted separate apartments for parents and daughter, who had suffered from a lack of privacy; he wanted the house to be equipped for the future computerization of the domestic environment; and above all he wanted the entire project to be an architectural masterpiece. An additional problem for the designers was that it proved difficult to fit the project on the narrow parcel, because the building regulations prescribed a spatial envelope with a peculiar form such as that which could only originate through bureaucracy.

Koolhaas once said he found the project rather onerous because for once he wanted to design a villa without a swimming pool and also because of the demand that it be an architectural masterpiece, something which did not interest him at the time. Together with

Xaveer De Geyter, he nevertheless produced a design that met all of the client's requirements: the living areas on one floor in a glass pavilion, with separate apartments for him and his wife and his daughter above it, separated by the swimming pool. The outer form was not dictated by the desire to create an aesthetic object a priori, but instead adheres closely to the prescribed envelope. [...] The form is thus a negative form that leaves the shape of the land parcel intact as much as possible; not an aesthetic composition, but a conceptual one, like Bruce Nauman's sculpture *Platform Made Up of the Space Between Two Rectilinear Boxes on the Floor* from 1966. And as with Nauman, the deadpan criteria produce a form with ineffable tension.

The builder was pleased with the design, it was everything he wanted, and the building permits were issued. Only then did the neighbors realize what lay in store and they attempted with all their might to prevent its construction. The project was held up in court for years, with the central argument being that according to the letter of the law, the main facade of a building was the one containing the most glass: the side facade in this case. Boudet eventually won all of the court cases, helped undoubtedly by the fact that he threatened to donate the property to a center for drug addicts if he did not get his way. The only evidence left of this battle is that some of the windows in the glass box were frosted to avoid too much direct contact with the neighbors. That does not detract from the whole, though, since the plan for that part had always been to include various retractable screens made of perforated steel, bamboo or other materials to create a facade of ever-changing transparency and thus allow for an ever-varying atmosphere in conjunction with the light falling through the foliage.

The house is much more radical than the drawings and models that had been circulating for years led one to believe. Models and axonometric drawings inevitably emphasize the object nature of the design and become imprinted onto the mind much more obstinately than blueprints and descriptions. In the absence of a material presence, then, the design appeared at first to be a late-modern Le Corbusier pastiche: the residential area lifted above damp, unhygienic ground; the first story wrapped in ribbon windows; and a rooftop garden with swimming pool to capture the sun and revel in the view. A system of ramps and stairwells appeared to function as a *promenade architecturale*. Upon closer inspection, though, all of this has only been used as the vocabulary at hand; the visual similarities are not as great as the drawings suggest and the meaning of the symbols has been altered.

The most defining element of the house as built is the ground floor. A glass-encased box provides space for the communal living functions, such as cooking, eating and sitting. The spine of the layout is a freestanding cabinet wall with wood paneling, into which random cutouts have been made. The wall camouflages the row of columns that supports the upper story together with the concrete northern wall. The kitchen is hidden behind a chrome-plated screen of transparent corrugated polyester sheeting. The dining room is situated in the "armpit" formed where this partition meets the cabinet wall. The extremely subtle, nuanced way in which the deceptively simple form of the space is sectionalized through the placement of just a few elements is incredibly clever. The architects play here with all the forms of literal and phenomenal transparency explored by Colin Rowe and

Robert Slutzky in their famous essay from 1963. Not only is the literal transparency of the glass exterior wall mutable as a result of the sliding screens, but the cabinet wall, the screen and the staircase to the daughter's apartment have been laid out in such a way that any movement through the space offers new perspectives. Noteworthy views such as of the garden or the house next door—and of course the Eiffel Tower—have been strategically framed. The view out onto the garden is panoramic; the adjacent house is glimpsed through an intimate window in the cabinet wall; and the Eiffel Tower is visible from along the stairs and above the void of the entrance foyer, making the character of the view stand out all the more.

The spatial boundaries of the sitting area are merely hinted at by the walls, being more predominantly defined by the bowl-shaped space of the garden and the underside of the story above. It is difficult to convince people who have not visited the house of the wonderful intimacy this space has. Comparisons to Philip Johnson's Glass House do not apply because that has a much more open location and ended up being placed above the lawn on a small plinth. At Villa dall'Ava the floor is on the same plane as the grass. In the summer the nearly three-meter-high glass panels can be slid away at the corner, removing the physical boundary between inside and outside. Even when closed, though, they do not truly constitute a spatial barrier: the garden and overhanging roof, along with a few strategically placed items such as the fireplace and stairwell, create vaguely circumscribed "places" to which one naturally gravitates. Next to the living room is an open-air chamber under the first-floor overhang with a similar such area suggested by the organically shaped pattern of flagstones. Other than with Le Corbusier, Johnson or Mies, there is thus a direct, sensual contact with the ground, instead of a purely visual relationship. In the evening, a curtain on a simple chrome railing can be pulled around the interior living spaces. Made of thick yellow silk and just a touch too long, with an extra heavy chain edge, it can be "fashioned" in various positions like a sculpture so the place never looks the same twice, even closed off, and the space is directly shaped by human action.

The main living floor is where the communal living activities take place, where one receives visitors and the like. But it is not custom-made for a preordained family life, or any other preordained behavior for that matter. It is a setting, one in which the decors are not predetermined, but rather materialize through the actors' interventions. Its relationship with the rapidly evolving outside world and the interrelationship with the coactors are constantly being explored and reexplored.

This unstable situation seems to be reflected in the design of the house. It is not just that the composition is in constant danger of falling apart; the building structure itself appears to be in precarious balance. The upper story balances on just a few columns; the master bedroom cantilevers out over open space; and the daughter's bedroom sits on a coppice of fragile slanted columns.

There are undeniable echoes of Le Corbusier's ideas about domestic life from the 1920s. The home is an emptiness into which the "naked man" can withdraw to meditate and reflect on the decisions to be taken in an ever-more rapidly changing world. He looks out over the city, as in all of Le Corbusier's prototypical interiors, but unlike in those designs, this house precludes any sense of harmony—in the composition, in the construction or in the organization. Much more so than in a Le Corbusier, then, the inhabitants are left to fend for themselves.

This becomes abundantly clear when we look closely at the rest of the blueprint. It shows that the individual living compartments of the inhabitants have been pushed as far apart as possible. Each can only be reached by a dedicated staircase. The parents' apartment is separated from the daughter's by the swimming pool. It contains Madam Boudet's office in addition to the master bedroom and bath, so that it almost becomes a modern boudoir. The daughter's apartment also consists of two connected rooms with a bathroom. Monsieur Boudet has his own soundproof room in the basement, where he can practice piano uninterrupted. That is the only room with no visual contact to the surroundings, the only natural light coming from a glass strip in the ceiling.

Unlike the cool, removed aesthetic of the communal spaces, the individual compartments were all given a much warmer, personalized ambiance in consultation with the owners. In Mr. Boudet's "gentleman's quarters," this takes the form of deep wooden built-in cabinets with hidden doors. Ms. Boudet's "boudoir" has a dark parquet floor. The walls are partially exposed concrete and partially covered in wood wall cabinets. The curtain is thick, like that of the living room, except made of dark-green silk. The daughter's boudoir has a light-green poured floor, the walls are a mixture of exposed concrete and extremely rough chipboard and the curtains have an exuberant design of flowers and fruit. The individual ambiance of each of these rooms is naturally amplified by the personal attributes they house: old furniture, paintings and photos, the man of the house's piano, Madame's computer and a teenage girl's accoutrements. Any individual compartment could exist entirely on its own. One could imagine the inhabitants gradually retreating more and more to their own cells over the years—something not at all inconceivable as the daughter grows up—and the glass living space becoming redundant. In such an event, the latter could essentially be easily removed, in the same way as the glass spaces meant to accommodate the "orgies of speech" in Koolhaas's 1978 design for the Dutch Parliament Extension in The Hague.

One of the most striking features of Villa dall'Ava is of course the rooftop swimming pool. Although a prominent feature in the blueprints and sections, the swimming pool is actually the best-kept secret of the house. It cannot be seen from the street and the only view of it, underwater, is through a tiny porthole in the master bedroom. The swimming pool manifests itself primarily as an inaccessible emptiness around which the house is built. It terms of volume, it nearly matches the individual apartments. The swimming pool can be reached by a narrow, hidden staircase that climbs up from the landing between the daughter's and the parents' apartments. There is also a drop staircase that can be lowered from these stairs on down into the garden. At the top, you are standing on the roof of the parents' apartment. From there, you have a gorgeous, unimpeded view of Paris and the Eiffel Tower, looking out over the swimming pool, rooftop garden and daughter's apartment, which is somewhat lower. In the evening and at night, the golden lit Eiffel Tower glows on the horizon. It is a scene reminiscent of the romantic landscapes of Caspar David Friedrich or John Martin, in which man is a mere speck in the vast, yet dangerous beauty of nature: it is sublime—except the metropolis has replaced nature here. Given Koolhaas's ideas, that is hardly surprising. In *Delirious New York* he long ago described the metropolis as a sublime natural phenomenon which is at the same time fascinating and dangerous, "the city of congestion." Unlike with Le Corbusier, the rooftop garden has very little design. It is more like the flat roof on Adalberto Libera's Villa Malaparte on the coast of Capri from 1940. A simple railing on the roof of the master apartment is all that prevents visitors from following off the edge, and the roof of the daughter's apartment has only temporary fencing such as that used by road workers. This serves to reinforce the effect of the sublime, which has been characterized as the sensation of a promenade along a cliff in the mountains.

Bathing, swimming and physical culture have played an important role in Rem Koolhaas's work from the beginning. There was a time when he included at least one swimming pool in every building he designed. [...] The swimming pool is one of his focal points for reflecting on culture as a whole. It is a place where the antitheses which have largely shaped Koolhaas's thinking—spirituality versus carnality, good versus bad, history versus future, ideals versus reality, nature versus city, Europe versus America—clash most intensely and paradoxically meld together. Indeed, he frequently resorts to oxymoronic tropes in his writing. In Koolhaas's vision, therefore, the swimming pool can be simultaneously both the polar opposite and the consummation of the congestion of the big city: "Maybe that's another oxymoron: a ground zero of congestion," he once said in an interview with Mil De Kooning. It is not Koolhaas's intention, however, to use the structure of the oxymoron to synthesize incongruous elements purely for effect. It is more as if he were constantly searching in his scenarios for an indefinable third category that might provide a way out, or better yet: an escape through the possible. It is a category that transcends the existing order, a surreal category reminiscent of Alfred Jarry's concept of pataphysics. The building and the swimming pool are like social condensers that can generate new, and hopefully unknown, forms of social behavior. Human beings, humanity, human action and the human body are central to this. In a recent article in the new American architecture journal *Anyone*, art critic Rosalind Krauss uses George Bataille's essay "The Big Toe" to demonstrate how the physical is a category that eludes the descriptive, controlling matrix of contradictions and therefore works subversively.

Many of the aspects that characterized Koolhaas's earlier, theoretical pool studies recur in a modified form in Villa dall'Ava. There is no doubt that the house is meant to be read as a built manifesto: a social condenser for the family. What the tangible results of that might be for the Boudet family remains to be seen. Villa dall'Ava will serve as a manifesto primarily in the publicity it generates. To avoid having the house exclusively presented as a classic architectural-aesthetic object in that interaction, Koolhaas developed a scenario with the photographer Hans Werlemann to be used in photographing it. This scenario deploys a series of staged scenes to highlight specific qualities of the Villa dall'Ava in a manner taken from advertising or fashion photography, although parallels can also be drawn to the early films of Luis Buñuel and Jacques Tati and to *Les Mystères du Château du Dé*, Man Ray's film in which the Robert Mallet-Stevens villa in Hyères plays a central role. The photos can be grouped into several categories. There are photos that capture the villa's aesthetic qualities under varying atmospheric conditions (compositions of light and surface); there are staged photos that pay homage to architectural role models admired by Koolhaas (such as the one with the Mies van der Rohe daybed from Philip Johnson's Glass House or the one with Jean Nouvel); there are staged photos that clearly point out the associations to Koolhaas's earlier designs and ideas (such as the scene from the Floating Pool); and there are staged photos that envision possible future scenarios in and around the house (leaving it open as to whether the events are probable or not; presumably they are holographic or video projections along the lines of the future predictions of Paul Virilio). It is the last two categories, in particular, that underscore the subversive nature of the architecture. The scene with the swimmers from the Floating Pool on the roof suddenly becomes an ironic commentary on the house. It recalls the swimmers in Koolhaas's Floating Pool who had to swim toward the Kremlin for fifty-four years in their attempt to escape Stalinism and reach the Statue of Liberty. The swimmers here are swimming toward the Eiffel Tower in order to get as far away from the city as they can: an elegant metaphor for the client who had to work in the city so hard for so many years to be able to afford a house in suburbia. Other scenes enact secret meetings of mysterious men dressed in black or simply the housecleaner at work. The most curious are the photos in which an actual giraffe appears: an endangered species in a completely artificial environment. And yet it looks right at home in the coppice of askew columns supporting the daughter's apartment: the underpass seems built to its size. In other photos, it appears to have befriended the letter carrier, as in a scene from a Tati film. Apparently, a black panther was set loose in Ms. Boudet's boudoir but it was too dangerous to photograph. Who knows? It could be true and what does it matter anyway: if we are open to it, real life is probably even more surrealistic and subversive than we can imagine. The clients, for instance, absolutely refused to allow the staged photos of naked men in the shower to be published—when that is exactly the sort of routine situation that would happen in real life.

KUNSTHAL ROTTERDAM (1989–1993): A MATURITY THAT ONE HAS LONG BEEN WAITING FOR

8

The Kunsthal in Rotterdam is the hinge on which OMA's oeuvre rests and rotates, and the first project of Koolhaas's that has been unanimously received as a masterpiece. Even the Dutch couple of critics Hilde de Haan and Ids Haagsma, OMA skeptics par excellence, had to admit in their newspaper review that "Koolhaas merges banality with chic in this brilliant design." (They ended, however, their piece somewhat sardonically with a warning: "Koolhaas has proven with the Kunsthal that he is an architect whose talents should be deployed sparingly ... very, very sparingly.") Kenneth Frampton noted in *Domus* that the "recalcitrance," by now typical for OMA, was in the case of the Kunsthal "surely indicative of a tectonic maturity that one has long been waiting for." The theoretical and critical strategies that Frampton had developed during the 1980s against Postmodernism and the loss of identity, architectonic quality, and structural honesty had not been quite compatible with the much more ambiguous position of OMA. For the Kunsthal, however, he seemed to make a one-time exception, although the praise was already withdrawn a few years later in 1997, when Koolhaas was scolded by Frampton in a digression in an essay on recent Swiss architecture: "While one may discriminate between the lyricism of Koolhaas's Villa dall'Ava in Paris and the more arbitrary formalism of his Kunsthal in Rotterdam, on balance the primary motivation remains the graphic image rather than the phenomenological presence of either structure or material."[1]

Together with the Museumpark (developed in collaboration with Yves Brunier and Petra Blaisse) and the unbuilt project for the Netherlands Architecture Institute (both in front of the Kunsthal), the building was part of an urban vision for Rotterdam developed at the end of the 1980s. It presented, shortly before the global museum boom, an idiosyncratic contribution to the debate on museum architecture and art exhibitions in an urban and public context. In terms of structure, organization, composition, and use of materials, the project challenged (indeed in a by now classic OMA tradition) many dogmas of late modern postwar architecture, particularly because of the use of ramps and sloping surfaces—elements that weren't exactly new, but that stemmed from more marginal traditions, and that were reintroduced in unforeseen ways and combinations. At the same time, the Kunsthal was developed as an explicit challenge for the office itself, as an attempt at escaping the method, the preferences, and the polemical choices that OMA had become known for during the 1980s. This shift is visible in the two versions that were made. Kunsthal I consisted of one very simple floor of 3,600 square meters with a free plan. A lifting platform in the middle—called "the robot"—would ensure flexibility and programmatic liveliness between the three levels.[2] Several reasons have been given for the abandonment of this project: the alderman of the city of Rotterdam didn't like it and was hoping for something more flamboyant and striking; the urban situation changed because OMA lost the competition for the Netherlands Architecture Institute; or Koolhaas became annoyed with the "modernist" rationality (and orthogonality) of Kunsthal I because it was too much in line with OMA's previous work, which had started creating a conspicuous amount of (Dutch) epigones.

In any case, Kunsthal II was different: Koolhaas, together with project architect Fuminori Hoshino and structural engineer Cecil Balmond, tried to establish the looseness and the mobility of the first version without the trick of the analogous robot. What occurred, more or less, is "the denial of the ground as a datum,"[3] as Peter Eisenman wrote on the occasion of the project for the Jussieu Libraries in Paris developed between 1992 and 1993—in many ways a continuation and radicalization of the Kunsthal as it was built. This means that although the Kunsthal seems—on the outside—a simple box with facades of montaged material surfaces, the interior spaces give the impression of escaping Cartesian legibility. "The relative simplicity of the Kunsthal's exterior," Terence Riley wrote while the building was still under construction, "contrasts with the spatial complexity of its interior, the main circulation path being a multilevel 'figure eight' more easily experienced than comprehended." More recently, Roberto Gargiani argued that in the Kunsthal (and more particularly, in the auditorium) "the contamination of different spaces through programmatic overlaps is encouraged, forming a new kind of architecture through functionally saturated pliable surfaces."[4]

To interpret what this meant—for OMA, for architecture at the end of the twentieth century, and for the experience of this kunsthalle and the art it should exhibit—wasn't an easy task for critics. While Bart Lootsma and Jan de Graaf argued that the building "showcases the vitality of the architectural experience instead of an architectonic concept" and Paul Vermeulen praised the almost tender "tonalities of light" in which the Kunsthal is clad, Deyan Sudjic warned that the architecture itself threatened to become a megastar, putting everything it should accommodate in its own brilliant shadow. The crucial notion might be that of fragmentation (and of the deconstruction of the totality of architecture): instead of offering a classicist and harmonious sequence of traditional and clearly delineated spaces, the Kunsthal is an assemblage of incidents and ideas, of confrontations between inside and outside, and of spatial and conceptual surprises which nevertheless, against all odds, seem to belong together. Does this mean that it still possesses a formal unity—a kind of wholeness that Koolhaas wanted to grant to an increasingly fragmented, complex, and globalizing world? Or is this building much more mimetic of the fin de siècle ambiance it was developed in, and does it offer, as Cynthia Davidson suggested in a late review from 1997, "a premonition of the possible death of form in the fragmentation of Koolhaas's architecture, toward its own disappearance in the flow of time?" With the Kunsthal, OMA quite uniquely succeeded in keeping both options open.

1 Kenneth Frampton, "Minimal Moralia: Reflections on Recent Swiss German Production," in *Labour, Work and Architecture: Collected Essays on Architecture and Design* (London: Phaidon, 2002), 330.

2 See Jacob Comerci, "The Robot of Kunsthal I," *Log* 36 (2016), 63–67.

3 Peter Eisenman, "Strategies of the Void: Rem Koolhaas, Jussieu Libraries, 1992–93," in *Ten Canonical Buildings 1950–2000* (New York: Rizzoli, 2008), 203.

4 Roberto Gargiani, "Kunsthal: Rem Koolhaas/OMA," in *The Companions to the History of Architecture*, vol. 4, *Twentieth-Century Architecture*, ed. David Leatherbarrow and Alexander Eisenschmidt (Chichester: John Wiley and Sons, 2017), 659.

A "SMITH AND BROWN" BUILDING

Terence Riley

Newsline Columbia University,

September 1992, 2.

The construction of the Rotterdam Kunsthal, designed by OMA/Rem Koolhaas and scheduled to open this year, has been virtually overshadowed by the press blitz surrounding the Villa dall'Ava in Paris and the derailment of the Karlsruhe Media Center earlier this year. This relative inattention will hopefully soon be corrected, as the Kunsthal is surely OMA's most important built work to date.

This new project provides a tangible link between OMA's urban investigations of the last decade — the Mélun-Senart, La Villette and La Défense studies — and a series of interrelated public projects: the Bibliothèque de France, the Agadir Convention Center, the newly designed Educatorium for the University of Utrecht and the aforementioned Karlsruhe project. The Kunsthal also successfully extends the ideological thread to the level of construction, something critics found lacking in OMA's earlier built projects.

The project, as approached from the city center, is first glimpsed from an "entertainment" district — a strip of seedy but docile X-rated dance bars. Diagonally opposite the bars is a large urban park, and in the distance the Kunsthal at its edge. The edge is defined by a roadway that seems too wide, too high and too fast-moving for its environs. Clambering up and down the embankments, crossing the multiple lanes of traffic and finding that distances are farther than anticipated evoke images of Los Angeles rather than European cities.

This type of urban space is familiar to OMA; most of Koolhaas's urban investigations have exploited the potential of discontinuous environments. Off the upper gallery of the Kunsthal, which is roughly on the level of the roadway, is an enormous covered terrace that engages and monumentalizes the urban edge just as the lower level responds to the park.

Like the Agadir, Karlsruhe, Utrecht, and Paris projects and most of the architecture of the urban projects, the Kunsthal is a relatively simple rectangular form in the built landscape, with only the most meager formal elaboration in relation to its surroundings. The intention seems to have been to diminish the significance of the building's form to magnify the importance of the facades as screens. In a sense, the figure of the building is transferred to the facades. At Karlsruhe one facade was to be a literal screen: a gigantic media display wall.

At the Kunsthal, the image transference is less radical; no element is as spectacular as the media wall. Yet the result is all the more accomplished. Though more architecturally articulate, the facades retain a mediated character: they amplify the building's condition to the scale of the urban environment. This is enhanced by a multitude of indeterminate materials: perforated metal screens, gratings, mottled and frosted glass, translucent fiberglass and plastic sheathings. These materials are as critical to OMA's current position as plate glass was to Mies's minimalism. The clarified humanism of the latter is replaced in OMA's work by the veiled, flickering projections of activity and space read through the building's outer membrane. The emphasis is on the fundamental difference within and without the skin rather on a universal, rationalized space.

The relative simplicity of the Kunsthal's exterior contrasts with the spatial complexity of its interior, the main circulation path being a multilevel "figure eight" more easily experienced than comprehended. The architectural detail contains yet another inversion: most evident is the simple butt-jointing of sheathed surfaces. The highly articulated ceiling of the large upper gallery is the exception. Though highly competent, the details aspire to the simplicity of the overall form rather than to the complexity of the interior space.

The classical dictum that an ideal object is ideal in all its parts seems useless in current critical discourse. Not only are we suspicious of the "ideal," we are skeptical of the relationship of any construction to its parts. But the Kunsthal displays a remarkable conceptual consistency from its urban implications to its architectural detailing. What is most remarkable is achieved by pursuing what is most obvious. There is throughout a distinct lack of moralizing and an equally distinct affirmation of the structures, methods and products of contemporary society.

Yet Koolhaas's descriptive manner should not be seen as uncritical. The object of the criticism is not the culture at large but the architectural profession itself. This internal critique is analogous to Ludwig Wittgenstein's criticism of his and his colleagues' philosophical preoccupations in the mid-1930s: "Suppose people are playing chess. I see queer problems when I look into the rules and scrutinize them. But Smith and Brown play chess with no difficulty. Do they understand the game? Well, they play it."

The Kunsthal is a "Smith and Brown" building not obsessed with the "problems" of architecture. The question remains: If OMA's recent projects are not concerned with the "problems" of architecture, of what do they speak? Again, Wittgenstein: "It seems that there is nothing intangible about the chair or the table, but there is about the fleeting human experience."

KOOLHAAS MERGES BANALITY WITH CHIC IN BRILLIANT DESIGN

Hilde de Haan, Ids Haagsma
De Volkskrant, September 17, 1992.

Even though the building was still partially shrouded in scaffolding, with some floors half unfinished and the sound of industrious construction workers echoing through the hallways, the directors of the Kunsthal in Rotterdam designed by Rem Koolhaas proudly held an official, "exclusive," preliminary viewing on Wednesday.

The new space will serve a somewhat curious function as an anonymous rental office for exposition halls. It is not a museum because it does not possess a collection; it is rather an exhibition space for housing primarily large blockbusters since existing museums, such as Boijmans Van Beuningen, cannot process such massive audiences.

The directors commissioned the architect to create an "exhibition machine." That's a nice sound bite. It's somewhat reminiscent of Le Corbusier's "house machine," with its messianic vision for a new, technologically determined future.

Led by Rem Koolhaas and Fuminori Hoshino, OMA has created an extremely captivating design at the southern edge of Museumpark. The new hall is located at one end of an axis in a park designed by OMA that runs alongside the Boijmans and connects to the future Architecture Institute. It is a gorgeous urban planning concept that openly competes with the Museumplein in Amsterdam, although the hall does have the distinct disadvantage of being set against the five-meter-high Westzeedijk.

But Koolhaas overcomes that handicap brilliantly. He uses the height difference to install a long sloping ramp right through the hall—which is actually shaped like an enormous box. This ramp serves as both a public access to Museumpark and a sinuous connecting route between the three exhibition halls. The box itself is clad partly in chic rock (Spanish travertine) and partly in black, with subtly placed, bright orange steel beams. The roof has an outlandish rectangular billboard on it as a precocious, but convincing, architectural element.

Koolhaas has delivered world-class architecture with this Kunsthal—the compelling architectural form we have been waiting for nearly in vain all this second half of the twentieth century. Of course, such extreme architecture is not necessarily a good draw. Its tremendous power could intimidate the public, whereas the clients had expressly asked for a building that would "lower the entry barriers."

Koolhaas has a gift for combining his magisterial architecture with something more accessible. The advertising tower, for instance, is executed in cheap, corrugated plastic and the cleanly designed black wall is finished in such a nonchalant manner that there's no risk of its assuming too much prominence as an architectural element.

On the inside as well Koolhaas has managed to convincingly humanize genius-like accents. Just think about it: you have to design three large exhibition halls, an additional gallery, an auditorium and a restaurant in a box that has been sawed in half so that the individual spaces can be used not only independently, but also all together for exhibitions as desired. Koolhaas has managed to link the halls together along a single hinged axis, creating an ingenious floor plan. For example the sloping floor of the auditorium is cleverly used as a sloped ceiling for the restaurant.

So it is that Koolhaas creates contemporary spaces, which he then accentuates with slanted columns. In the large exhibition halls, too, he uses sophisticated tactics to create a late-twentieth-century space: for example the columns are asymmetrical and some walls slope at a diagonal, only to be met by straight ones. He even dares to construct the floor of one of the galleries out of steel grates so that you can see directly down into the exhibition below.

This kind of modern architecture is almost too beautiful, too wonderful, too impressive for a large public, and that too is something Koolhaas realizes, prompting him, yet again, to masterfully intervene. Although the ceiling of the exhibition hall is entirely black, he manages to give it a sophisticated allure by cladding the columns in refined, hollowed-out oak and chestnut tree trunks. The unfinished trunks are outfitted with wooden boxes and hatches for accessing the cables and sockets. Steep staircases, narrow passageways, absurdly low ceilings and shabby corrugated sheeting all make visitors feel right at home.

Koolhaas is not averse to setting a column right next to an entryway or glancing against a glass wall: perfect little touches for preventing the allure of his spaces from becoming too overpowering—just as in the restaurant, where he abruptly terminates the sloped space under the ceiling. He is abundantly aware that an overly refined sightline or overly sophisticated detailing would imbue the space with too much life and thus deliberately eschews them—just as he abruptly interrupts a delicate red-tiled wall with an unruly white joint.

It takes you aback: that wall leads to a hallway to the lavatories and the opposite wall is a mighty wall of mirrors. It's almost too much beauty, but the dark recesses in the lavatories bring it all back down to earth, introducing the necessary banality into all that brilliance—just as Koolhaas had his grid-floor gallery end in a staircase you might find in an auto parts warehouse: the triumph of vulgarity.

Koolhaas has proven with the Kunsthal that he is an architect whose talents should be deployed sparingly ... very, very sparingly.

LIKE A MAGIC BOX

Bernard Hulsman

NRC Handelsblad, October 31, 1992.

"Kunsthal"—the word evokes images of Germany and large sterile boxes full of white rooms that, through their very anonymity, are perfect for all kinds of temporary exhibitions. Similarly, the new arts center in Rotterdam designed by Rem Koolhaas's architecture firm OMA, which was officially opened today by Queen Beatrix, looks at first like a box nestled up against the Westzeedijk. The building already has a nickname: the parking garage. And the fact that no fewer than six different shows are on view starting today leads one to suspect that the box is made up of a number of orthodox, nondescript spaces on the inside, too.

But upon closer inspection, Koolhaas's Kunsthal is more like a magic box than the usual arts box. To start with, all four of its facades are different. The collaged side along Westzeedijk, for example, has an "urban face," as Koolhaas puts it; the quiet side at the rear, along Museum Park, is meant to provide a "traditional contemplative museum atmosphere," with its travertine marble cladded top section and glass bottom section. As an added attraction and counterpoint, Koolhaas has placed a second, narrow, upright box on the roof to hide, among other things, the ventilation system exhaust pipes. On the inside, the building houses three exhibition halls, each with its own ambiance, as well as an auditorium and a restaurant which can be used separately. As if that were not enough, the Kunsthal is dissected by an existing street, with above that, kitty-corner to it, a "ramped street," a word not yet in the dictionary. The main entrance and box office are in fact located on this ramped street, which connects the dike to the park located five meters below. But anyone not interested in art can simply walk on through to the park, thus using the building merely as a gateway.

Even though the existing street that cuts straight through the Kunsthal is little more than a quiet service road, the confluence of drivers, cyclists, exhibition visitors and park users turns the building into a lovely example of "congestion," the accumulation of various activities in a single spot that Koolhaas has been advocating for since the start of his career in the 1970s.

In 1988, at the infamous *Deconstructivist Architecture* exhibition in New York, Koolhaas was still being presented as a representative of Deconstructivism, though he never truly felt at home in that camp of architects obsessed by uncertainty who believed that in "our fragmented world" there was only room for a "fragmented architecture." [...] The Kunsthal nevertheless has some features that might be considered deconstructivist: the steel beams installed at varying angles under the twisting overhead lights of Hall 2, the useless continuous I-beams on the roof, and most of all the slanted columns visible from the outside that cut straight through the restaurant on the ground floor and the auditorium located above it, as if gravity did not exist. Then there is the steel X between the columns on the dike side that seems to block the side entrance of Hall 2, which is also designed for independent use—a joke worthy of a Deconstructivist such as Peter Eisenman.

But the "fragmented" sections are subordinate to the whole. The Kunsthal's defining feature is the series of ramps that connect the auditorium and the three exhibition halls. They give it a tightly organized feel. After entering at the box office, visitors who tour through the building keep coming back to that ramped passage, the heart of the building. The architectural route is an experience in and of itself, gradually unveiling the complexity and abundance of the structure, and those who walk from one exhibition to another will be afforded ever-changing views of the service road, the ramped street and the sloped roof garden with real pear trees. *Promenade architecturale* is the French term for such an architectural route and it has an immediate association with the work of Le Corbusier, who was also so taken with ramps. Le Corbusier described architecture as "circulation," a definition that probably also appeals to Koolhaas.

The Kunsthal evokes other associations as well. The glass facade combined with the roof overhang along Westzeedijk is reminiscent of Mies van der Rohe's Neue Nationalgalerie in Berlin. But the most unexpected reference is in Hall I, with its five felled tree giants, which eighteenth-century classicists would undoubtedly have read as archetypical columns from the dawn of classical architecture.

It has become something of a Dutch tradition to criticize the poor craftsmanship and detailing of Koolhaas's buildings, and here too in the Rotterdam Kunsthal, he has given his critics some obvious fodder. The facade of the shipping/receiving area, for instance, is disagreeably bare and the plastic corrugated sheeting appears to have been cut with the dullest of blades in certain places. It is all intentional on Koolhaas's part. "Critics say the details are just poor. I say those aren't details. That is the quality of the building. No money, no detail, just the pure concept," he said in an interview.

Money or no money, the poor finishing of some sections detracts to some extent from the Kunsthal. It is also difficult to get used to the combination of slum materials, like corrugated sheeting, with royal varieties of stone, like travertine marble. In that sense, what Koolhaas himself says about Deconstructivism holds true: the sharp contrast is "naive and banal"; it is an overly literal and heavy-handed representation of the clash between "lofty" and "commonplace," between "high" and "low" culture.

Koolhaas has never been bothered by such criticism and will not be bothered by it now. And as long as he continues to design buildings like the Kunsthal, it does not matter. Because when the architecture is this ingenious, sophisticated and stunning, people are prepared to overlook its faults.

CONFIDENCE AND PRECISION

Kenneth Frampton

Domus 747 (1993), 38–47.

Related, as are many recent projects by Koolhaas, to the work of Le Corbusier—in this instance to Le Corbusier's congress hall projected for Strasbourg in 1959—the new Rotterdam Kunsthal is the most rigorous and exhilarating civic work that Koolhaas has produced to date. This building seems to return, by a kind of legerdemain, to that heroic moment of the Modern movement when structures were poetically inspired by their programs. Countless examples may be cited, of course. One thinks of Le Corbusier's Centrosojus or his Armée du Salut, but one could just as easily cite less familiar pieces, such as Mattè-Trucco's Lingotto works, Owen Williams's Peckham Health Centre, or the Bexhill Pavilion by Mendelsohn and Chermayeff. This sociologically modern spirit springs exuberantly to life in Koolhaas's Kunsthal, at a scale that is altogether more convincing than the Villa dall'Ava that for all its exuberance and photogenic brilliance seems willfully cramped and uncomfortable.

Here, on the contrary, one has a piece that in all probability will never photograph well; a paradoxical phenomenon that has by now become the touchstone of a rigorous architectural work. In this instance such recalcitrance is surely indicative of a tectonic maturity that one has long been waiting for. I am reminded for example of Koolhaas's remarkable AA student thesis for a Turkish Bath in Leicester Square, London, which was also a poetic proposition that stemmed, in all its essential aspects, from a tactile but minimalist treatment of its programmatic elements.

As much a social condenser as an art gallery, this work stretches back across time to recall other monuments in the architectural history of this century, above all the fertile affinity that once existed between the Dutch and the Russian avant-gardes. The architect's habitual return to this particular conjunction assumes an exceptional convincing form in this instance; firstly, because of its dramatic proximity to a land-bound dike, affording major and minor road access at two levels separated by a drop of some 5.5 meters—a displacement which in this case approximates to the height of the lower floor; secondly, because the initial avant-gardist thrust is reengaged here through a perception that chooses to render a temporary exhibition hall as an occasion for a series of set pieces, linked up to form a complex *promenade architecturale*. This last mediates between two different aspects of the urban context, namely, the dike datum carrying the principal public approach and the lower park level, that combines secondary public access with service. The aforementioned promenade, splitting the building into two unequal parts, is in effect a kind of ramped Moebius strip, and it is this unique feature that animates the entire work. Recalling the role played by a similar feature in the Villa Savoye, the lower ramp in the building, serves first and foremost to link the park on the north with the dike and main entrance situated on the south of the four-story mass. This ramp gives on to a porte cochere and from here it is but a step to enter the principal top lit gallery, one of two galleries, placed on top of each other at the eastern end of the building.

The building breaks up at this juncture into a layered and spiraling complexity; the main gallery being linked volumetrically to a lower exhibition hall, of virtually the same area, through a narrow gallery space with open metal gridded floor. Needless to say, the entire lower level is artificially illuminated throughout. It compensates for its subterranean enclosure by opening out to the park along its northern edge. Here, evoking Salvador Dalí's so-called paranoid-critical method, Koolhaas elects to clad the freestanding steel stanchions with hollowed-out tree trunks in order to suggest, through the presence of disembodied trees, a continuation of the wooded parkscape beyond. If the main exhibition space, with its ingeniously braced structural monitor lights, is to be regarded as the first set piece, then the second is this field of stripped tree trunks and the matte black ceiling they support, relieved only by a staccato pattern of neon tubes running across the ceiling, like a mechanical graphic image. Here, as in the work of Zaha Hadid, one encounters a concept that is essentially graphic rendered as though it were a three-dimensional form. Be this as it may, the theatrical character of the internal space throughout derives in large measure from the applications of decorative neon lighting close to the surface of the principal ceilings.

The building attains its apotheosis as a quintessentially modern work in the sloped lecture theater, with its canted steel stanchions and ramped stairway that gives access to the highest level of this inclined public floor. This long trapezoidal space is subtly modulated by a flanking curtain wall and by a large picture window set above the rostrum at the end of the space. All of these elements are dynamically interrelated by a draw curtain suspended from the ceiling. When drawn, this curtain forms a partially elliptical enclosure that defines the lecture theater proper as a broken egg-like volume. These obvious overt references here to Le Corbusier's Mill Owner's Building in Ahmedabad. Part reception space, part lecture hall, the transformable character of this long, inclined box has a lyrical quality, and this lyricism is carried on by the stepped ramp that gives access to the roof. The roof terrace itself is enriched by views over the city and by a roof garden planted on top of the main ramp.

The layered, liberative character of all this is inexplicably compromised by an unnecessarily schematic treatment of the restaurant at grade, for while the ceiling of this space is animated by a neon-light sculpture, built to the designs of Günther Förg, it has insufficient openings onto what is clearly intended as the restaurant terrace, overlooking the park. This is more than just an unfortunate oversight, it is rather the deliberate weakening of a marked liberative tone that is otherwise sustained with great tenacity throughout. This lapsus arises out of a position that lies oddly caught between a passionate commitment to a reengagement with the modern project in the Habermas sense and a laid-back, laissez-faire aestheticism that unlike high-tech is only too willing to accommodate the online products of the building industry as they are currently made available. This it presents to us as a kind of latter-day pop architecture (hence the studied affection for the work of Wallace Harrison) or rather as a kind of pseudodadaist honky-tonk in disguise rendered neatly subtly acceptable to hip middle-class taste.

In its particular combination of vitality and repose, of event and invent, this building serves as an autocritique of all previous OMA work. It makes one acutely aware of the conceptual knife-edge that separates rock-bottom, normative production as found from the received mannered cult of the throwaway object. This is nowhere more evident than in the extensive use of translucent plastic siding that aside from producing subtle membraceous effects, particularly when double-layered, lies oddly caught between cool craftless technique and a kind of wanton use of cheap material than in all likelihood will not stand the test of time. This ambiguous tectonic is at once provocative and difficult to read. Is it merely expedient construction or gratuitous aestheticism or is it both? Elsewhere the building together with its urban park runs through an equally polarized range of values, from decorative kitsch on the one hand to tectonic grace on the other, from a rock-glass stream that winds its way through the park to become a surrealistic parody of the water that it encloses, to a minimalist, Donald Judd–like mezzanine, cantilevered out in one corner of the main exhibition hall as a seemingly weightless concrete plane.

Despite Koolhaas's weakness for what one can only call a mannered lack of style, there is an undeniable feeling of exhilaration in this work, of confidence and precision, particularly in the luminosity of the main public space with its canted columns that seem to float before the world with inexplicable lightness. A comparable weightless energy carries one up to the roof where the flat pylon of a steel-framed service tower, covered in plastic siding and illuminated from within, flares up at night before the force of the wind. Facing out toward the ultimate sea dike and the harshness of the North Sea, one can not help but be reminded of Van Tijen at his best in his proud tower at Scheveningen or alternatively of the giant illuminated letters of the Van Nelle factory etched out on the skyline of the Rotterdam hinterland more than half a century ago. This is the Netherlands at its best and for once postmodern Rotterdam has produced a modest but vital building that is worthy of its heroic name.

IN SERVICE OF THE EXPERIENCE

Bart Lootsma, Jan de Graaf

De Architect 1 (1993), 19–34.

In the 1980s museums became architectural flagships. An architect of any stature from that time had at least one museum to his name. In tandem with a return to easel painting and sculpture in art and a revisionism of art history, the large spaces in museum architecture that afforded layout flexibility were replaced by a more traditional system of partitioned halls and galleries. After the heady 1950s and 1960s, the museum once again became a place for (historical) reflection. This was expressed in the postmodern architecture of the buildings. Despite its international fame, OMA has never built a museum. The group's most interesting contribution to the architectural discourse lies not so much in the area of historical reflection, but in staging intense experiences. Seen in that context, it seems only logical that the second cultural building OMA would build, after the Dance Theater in The Hague, would be not a museum, but an exhibition hall, the Kunsthal.

Of course Amsterdam, in all its range and depth, is and will remain the cultural capital of the Netherlands, with its historical cityscape and abundance of monuments, museums, galleries, theaters, universities and academies. It is an old garden that with each passing autumn composts the fallen leaves for new plants and flowers, whether tended or not. By comparison, Rotterdam is still largely a fallow terrain that can only be brought to life for brief or prolonged periods of time with repeated care: a field of flower bulbs. Since the Second World War, the city has had a tradition of ambitious but temporary expos and festivals. [...] All of these expos sported refreshingly unconventional exhibition design that cleverly combined education with fun and culture with technology. And all of them, except C70, were concentrated at The Park and the "Land of Hoboken," just across the Westzeedijk thoroughfare. Given that tradition, it is hardly a coincidence that the new Kunsthal is now also located there—a building intended to serve as the site of a series of temporary exhibitions and expos in the widest possible range of fields, designed by the only legitimate heir to the reconstruction architects: Rem Koolhaas of the Office for Metropolitan Architecture. Rather than an "arts center," Koolhaas prefers to call it a "palais des festivals" in the tradition of the world fair pavilions.

The commission for the Kunsthal was awarded in 1988, the year of the last large Rotterdam festival up to that point. As part of that festival, OMA designed an installation for an art exhibition in the former arrival hall of the Holland America Line, which had been serving as a provisional arts center. The first design for the Kunsthal, from 1988, follows in the technologically innovative tradition of world fair pavilions. Formally, it is a relatively straightforward concept: a flat, square, glass box—the permanent exhibition space—appears to hang from a central core, a tower. The tower contains a "robot," a kind of stage scaffolding such as one might see in the theater for holding lighting systems and so forth, but then in reverse. For whereas in a theater the stage scaffolding is intended to create an artificial world within the proscenium stage sets, while the auditorium remains unchanged, the robot is actually constantly transforming the form and function of the public space. The floor, for example, can move up and down in sections if needed to create an exhibition route of varying levels and voids, or be tilted so that different stages can be created for performances, lectures, films and plays.

The first design for the Kunsthal was part of an urban planning design drawn up by OMA in 1987 at the request of the municipality for the Museum Park, which also comprised the Boijmans Museum and a site for the Netherlands Architecture Institute, along with proposals for supplementary housing. In that design, the Architecture Institute forms the terminus of the park on the north side. The Kunsthal is set somewhat back from the road as a freestanding pavilion, so that the park on that side can remain open. The building thus creates a different landscape on each of its four sides. When OMA was invited in 1988 to submit a design for the closed competition for the Architecture Institute, on top of winning the commission for the Kunsthal, it chose to amplify and thematize the polarity between the two new buildings in its design. Koolhaas's design for the Architecture Institute also consists of a—in this case triangular and sunken—glass box with a central tower to house the archives. In the first Kunsthal design, the tower is a source of vitality; in the Architecture Institute, it's a mausoleum. The fact that the competition for the Architecture Institute was ultimately won by Coenen was therefore a double catastrophe for OMA. Not just because of the building itself, but also because the dream of a museum quarter that could compete with Schinkel's in Berlin or Semper's in Vienna dissipated like a fata morgana. As a result, Koolhaas no longer found the first design for the Kunsthal viable. [...]

The design for the Kunsthal which has now been built needs to be viewed through the lens of much more than the festival tradition, however. The art policy of the city of Rotterdam can be characterized, especially since the Second World War, as a form of measured cultural politics. During the heroic phase of the reconstruction, manpower and materials were scarce. The rebuilding of ports, office buildings and housing took precedence, and there was a lack of funding and consideration for enriching the city with impressive cultural attractions. It has only been in more recent decades that much effort has gone into rebuilding a permanent cultural infrastructure. [...] The council actively seeks to promote a unique identity within the cultural spectrum of the Netherlands. Its emphasis is on contemporary architecture, design and photography, since these art forms are well suited to the city's contemporary, dynamic image and they attract less attention elsewhere. As a result of this active, outspoken policy, the Dutch government decided in recent years to locate both the Photo Institute and the Architecture Institute in the city. It was only the Design Institute, which would have completed this new cultural trifecta, that went to indolent Amsterdam, curiously enough. Nevertheless, with the new prestigious Rotterdam Design Prize and a new wing in the Boijmans for its design collection, the city still holds a distinct advantage over the capital in the field of design activities. Besides those three types of institutes, another phenomenon missing in the Netherlands compared to surrounding countries was an arts center. [...]

The arts center phenomenon cannot be explained solely by the power of large numbers. An arts center is a place dedicated to providing an optimum, intense experience of art, other than in a museum, where building and showing the collection and historical perspective are paramount. The arts center represents living art, a museum for ancillary art; an arts center is thus far more than a would-be museum, one that lacks a collection. On the contrary: in the 1960s and 1970s there was a discernible trend of museums themselves acting as arts centers of a kind. [...] The viewer's experience took priority—among artists who poured their energy into organizing happenings and performances that could only be experienced by participating in person and among the educational services that jumped eagerly on-board. At the time, these services were preferably run by artists, as well. [...] Museums were to become centers for art where the public could meet and interact with the artists, where you could eat and take in a concert, and where art was not meant to amaze but simply offered for sale. Much has changed in the arts since that time, but the focus on an intense, dynamic *experience* has remained central for arts centers.

Nearby countries have two kinds of arts centers. The relatively smaller ones, such as the Kunsthalle Basel, the Whitechapel Art Gallery in London and Porticus in Frankfurt, exhibit the most recent developments in the visual arts, things which have not yet been picked up by museums for a higher-minded, qualitative presentation. These institutions tend to be highly reliant on a single director who sets out a distinctly personal vision and backs it conceptually. In Basel, that included in the past such legendary curators as Harald Szeemann and Jean-Christophe Ammann; in Frankfurt, Kaspar König. Rotterdam too has had Chris Dercon, heading the center for contemporary art Witte de With since 1990. That kind of specific, elitist policy is not what we should expect with the Kunsthal, however.

In addition to these small arts centers, there are a host of larger institutions, such as Martin Gropius Bau in Berlin, the Stadtische Kunsthalle in Düsseldorf, Schirnhalle in Frankfurt, the Triennale buildings in Milan, Palazzo Grassi in Venice and the recent Kunsthalle in Bonn designed by Gustav Peichl. These arts centers excel at putting together large-scale exhibitions, "blockbusters," on a famous artist, for example, by assembling pieces from various collections around the world for the first time, or which are dedicated to a particular theme, such as "The Search for a Total Artwork." These are one-off, but extremely expensive, exhibitions that stand or fall on mass attendance. They are curated by a specially compiled team of experts who work on the preparations for several years. The quality of the objects on display must therefore be absolutely unparalleled. The director's role is thus more that of manager who works in the background, unlike the situation at small arts centers.

Given all this, it seems only logical that a world-famous architect would be contracted for the building itself: in the Netherlands that means Koolhaas. Once all of those conditions have been met, the institute can operate with relatively modest government funding over the long run, and that is exactly what the Municipality of Rotterdam envisions with its "new hard-line leftist" approach. Only it would appear there was some miscalculation in terms of the initial investment. The construction budget was only a fraction of the sum spent, for example, on the Kunsthalle in Bonn—which is comparable in terms of programming—and the opening exhibitions were thrown together by the Kunsthal's staff with a limited budget in much too short a time frame—with disappointing results. It is essential that this inauspicious start be remedied as quickly as possible, otherwise the institute will quickly lose prestige, failing to generate any money and costing the city a great deal for years to come, and the public will be robbed of fantastic exhibitions. None of that can be blamed on the building, however. One problem that did affect it was that in the pursuit of funds, the construction time needed to be cut by three months, so that it's not completely finished yet. [...]

Apart from the evolving urban planning conditions, it was the programmatic orientation toward becoming a large arts center that dictated the ultimate design. It was interim director Wim van Krimpen who, upon his appointment, immediately ruled out the first design, for the "palais des festivals." On the night of November 15, 1988, he faxed over a single page of an amended schedule of requirements, the most prominent new feature of which was a significant presence for a cafeteria-style restaurant, as well as a large café restaurant on the square. Van Krimpen thought the café restaurant could also be used as an auditorium and concert hall, but that ended up being built underneath. Particularly interesting are some of the preferences Van Krimpen formulates and two fragments from a text on architecture he apparently finds relevant: "After years of being dominated by the practically lifeless dogmas of the Moderns, architecture is gradually springing once more from imagination. There is a need for a new architecture. We can no longer tolerate these stereometric, unornamented forms, whose exterior serves no other purpose than to intimate the interior's construction," states the first fragment. The second fragment posits a different kind of architecture in opposition to that, "architecture with aesthetic conviction. Their structures are more than mere instruments of use; they possess a clearly defined identity, as opposed to what I would call the horrors of contractors' modernism. People get lost in there for the simple reason that these products have neither recognizable elements nor their own look." Van Krimpen would thus appear to be expressing a clear preference for postmodern architecture. [...] One wonders whether, when he assumed his duties, Van Krimpen was aware that Koolhaas had adopted an entirely different strategy for rising above mediocrity from that of the compensatory concealment of the Postmodernists. Koolhaas ramps up the banality to such an extent—in an almost Baudrillard-like fashion—that it reaches a "dead point," a desert-like emptiness in which anything is possible once again. The surrealistic camel by Henk Visch is perfectly in place here, despite the fact that the blue square it was intended to be placed in is not being built. The Kunsthal is bare and ornament-free, an illustration of what Walter Benjamin provokingly called the "new destitution" and "new barbarism," the goal being to clean house and start anew, to seek new perspectives. The only (postmodern?) reference in the building is the overhanging profile on top of the glass facade along the front, an homage to Mies's National Gallery in Berlin. The minimalist artworks by Günther Förg and Günther Tüzina reinforce the "barbaric" aesthetic, while at the same time their subtle subjectivity highlights its implicit opulence.

The programmatic predilections formulated by Van Krimpen comprise exhibition spaces with closed walls and overhead light (possibly with embrasures near the emergency exits for looking out at the park), a café restaurant as a separately identifiable "body" and a museum path that would feed into the Kunsthal and the nature museum. It should be noted that OMA did not comply with any of these wishes—or at least only to a very limited extent. The largest exhibition space does indeed have overhead light, but also a large glass wall overlooking Westzeedijk, so that the streetscape across the way constitutes one of the space's boundaries, in a similar way as in the villa OMA built in Paris. The lower hall does not have any overhead light and also has a large glass facade that in fact allows the space to overlap into the park, an effect beautifully heightened by the fact that the columns are clad in tree trunks. To top it all off, the museum path runs straight through the building from the top to the bottom—as necessitated, according to Koolhaas, by the planning regulations. According to those regulations, the building now had to be located directly on the Westzeedijk thoroughfare, unlike the first design, as a result of which a second road runs under the building. In his own inimitable fashion, Koolhaas took this impossible situation and turned it into a theme for the building. Despite how brilliantly he managed it all, though, it is hardly surprising to learn that both he and Van Krimpen experienced the construction of the Kunsthal as a battle.

The building is brilliant: the simple box form as an illusion emanating—as with the villa in Paris—from the prescribed envelope. Just as in the first design, the four sides differ entirely from one another, in conversation with the different landscapes each faces. And the building still got its robot tower, except that it houses only the extensive climate-control system and a moving billboard. It is that billboard that gives the Kunsthal something of the "palais des festivals" originally conceived. The service road and museum path cut the box into several pieces, into which the various exhibition spaces, offices, restaurant, auditorium and workshops all seem to fit perfectly. The slanted roof over the museum path is designed like an orchard, an extension of the Museum Park. The spaces themselves are connected through an ingenious circulation system, as required for a building that must process large numbers of visitors. The circulation system is knotted around the road crossing, with the various public spaces all also separately accessible. As schematic as it sounds, that is how complex the details are, with each space retaining its own unique character as dictated by the view, the materials and the form. One spectacular feature is the auditorium, which is actually a staircase of gigantic proportions. The space can be made smaller with an enormous circular curtain, giving it an entirely different form—another aspect similar to a tactic used in the Villa dall'Ava. When it's closed, the detailing of the curtain evokes a circus tent. The sculpture gallery on two floors is also surprising, with its steel grate flooring making the full height or depth of the building palpable. The construction and detailing are not about emphasizing the schematics of the building, but rather thematizing the exceptions in the design: the wind braces in the large exhibition hall, the various engineering principles and the conflicts that emerge where beveled blocks meet. This makes it a building that showcases the vitality of the architectural experience instead of an architectonic concept, just as the programming of an arts center is meant to prioritize the intense, dynamic experience of art over historical reflection. Now we just have to wait for exhibitions that actually do the architecture justice.

PERFECT DISORDER: DETAILING AND CONSTRUCTION

Ed Melet

De Architect 1 (1993), 35–37.

Rem Koolhaas is known the world over for his qualities as a thinker and designer. There is, however, far less consensus on his capabilities as a project architect. Many critics and colleagues have singled out the detailing in his designs as particularly weak, a criticism also leveled at Koolhaas's most recent creation, the Kunsthal in Rotterdam. Yet outright condemnation seems out of place here. Although OMA is once again guilty of structural errors, Koolhaas's method of detailing has imbued the building with an extra dimension, bringing him one step closer to achieving a synthesis between design, detail and structure.

Even before they enter the Kunsthal, visitors are confronted with OMA's wondrous method of detailing. Because of a detailing fault at the head of the sloping public tunnel, an underground, inverted river has formed against the ceiling of the passageway, giving the rain an even stronger presence here than in the Museum Park. This phenomenon gives visitors the unsettling impression of being completely enveloped by water. The tone for the rest of the Kunsthal has been set.

Koolhaas: "Have you ever seen anything like it in a building? I think it happens to be one of the most beautiful things about the Kunsthal. That said, I won't pretend it was intentional. While building, we discovered that the rain was seeping along the ceiling and we thought long and hard about how to drain it off. Normally, these kinds of problems are solved. But I have something of an aversion to solutions, because they provide a semblance of certitude in this crazy world. But then we realized the rainwater did not actually trickle down anywhere. The concrete had already been treated to prevent the formation of algae, so we kept things the way they were. All we need to do now is build conduits to channel the rain water past the columns; at present, it pours down these columns and onto the ground." As a result, the floor of the public tunnel gets just as wet as the ceiling, which is further exacerbated by an incorrectly placed gutter, which discharges the excess water from the little pear tree orchard into the tunnel. Walking through the tunnel is not exactly a pleasant experience yet. The gutter was installed there as a temporary measure, because there was no more time for a definitive solution. The Kunsthal needed to open — three months ahead of schedule. These kinds of mistakes, more or less caused by the reduced completion time, will be rectified by OMA.

The way in which OMA details its buildings cannot be explained by obvious reasons such as time pressure or lack of funds. [...] However, the Kunsthal's slapdash execution comes across as too well thought-out, while what traditional builders would see as a much more polished result could just as easily have been achieved. There are examples of "unfinished" details aplenty. For some strange reason, for instance, the ceiling of Hall 3 is full of badly fitted hatches. The emergency lighting, which consists of little more than haphazardly placed bare bulbs, creates an even more chaotic picture. And then there is the amazing space of the gallery at the back of Hall 2, where the sockets were fitted too low, so part of the aluminium skirting board had to be cut out.

It looks as if no space was allowed to be perfect. Whereas Koolhaas had no choice but to furnish the Dance Theater with a minimum of details, this time the coarser detailing seems to be deliberate. Necessity appears to have been translated into vision. It is a vision that imbues the building with an indefinable tension, which arises from continuous confusion and suspense. As an onlooker, you are constantly in search of something to hold on to: something traditional perhaps or at the very least a clue as to why this style of finishing was chosen. It is only outside that this seems to be provided, in the shape of an enormous, orange-painted steel profile, which protrudes 1.5 meters across the roof overhang. It looks as if someone accidentally left it on the roof or forgot to make it to measure. Maybe the profile fulfills the same function as the filled tooth or the wristwatch that the Delvers, the makers of worlds in *Strata*, one of Terry Pratchett's sci-fi novels, gave the dinosaurs before installing the earth's next layers. Their reasoning was that once the civilizations of these worlds had produced archaeologists, it would confuse them, show them that not all is what it seems, or else they did it to deliberately distance themselves from the perfection of their creation.

Koolhaas, too, appears to have purposely inserted beacons of imperfection. [...] With that, details have become an integral part of the concept. They help visualize the social instability, maybe even the chaos. Paradoxically, this requires both a perfect execution and a special design intensity that eschews impracticable connections. If this is not done satisfactorily, then this deliberate choice can easily be mistaken for incompetence. The Kunsthal is certainly not perfect. Some of the ways in which the connections between the walls that intersect at different angles have been dealt with are particularly unsatisfactory. The most telling example of this is the detailing of the connection between the end elevation of the public tunnel and the wall of Halls 1 and 2, where multiplex boards are needed to keep the aluminium profile in the right shape. These kinds of mistakes detract from the appealing idea that details are no longer just a tiny part of the whole, but also reflections of it.

Since the Dance Theater, the construction itself has been an integral part of Koolhaas's designs; it is not used purely to prop up the building, but also to reinforce the impression of the buildings' perfect chaos. It goes without saying then that OMA's ideas about the form in which the structure must be poured are crucial. In dialogue with the structural engineer, these are tested and modified until it is unclear who actually created the resulting concepts: the architect or the structural engineer. This process places specific demands on the latter. The structural engineer is expected to be creative in his or her own right, but also see the architect as an equal discussion partner. Since 1985, Cecil Balmond of Ove Arup has served as OMA's sounding board and advisor. On the face of it, it may seem strange that this English office decided to work with Koolhaas. After all, it made a name for itself with the perfect, bordering on soulless, high-tech buildings by Rogers, Foster and Piano. However, in Koolhaas's designs structural engineering is certainly no less important than it is in those of the high-tech architects, nor is it any less bold or complex. The difference lies in the role Koolhaas ascribes to it. Whereas in Fosters's and Rogers's early work especially the structure and installations had an almost exhibitionist character, in the Kunsthal, in particular, both are virtually completely concealed. Where they are visible, they look bizarre, chaotic or mysterious.

In previous projects, too, the collaboration between Ove Arup and OMA has led to a convergence of architecture and structural engineering. The design of the Zentrum für Kunst und Medientechnologie in Karlsruhe is perhaps the best example of this. For this building, Koolhaas and Balmond entered into an imaginary discussion with the history of architecture and asked themselves whether the layout of the Centre Pompidou could be improved in order to maximize the usable part of the section. Its actual layout alternates clear heights of 3.90 meters with structural frames of 2.10 meters in height, so that in principle 40% of the section is unusable. By giving the structural frame the height of a story, Koolhaas and Balmond created a section with stories shaped by the Vierendeel girders, alternating with completely structure-free floors. Thanks to this principle, 100% of the section is usable.

Vierendeel girders were also used in OMA's first design for the Kunsthal. As a counterpart to his competition design for the Netherlands Architecture Institute, Koolhaas wanted to create an almost floating building on the other side of the Kunsthal's Museum Park. The structural problem—how can such a building be supported without undermining the underlying architectonic idea—was solved with Vierendeel girders. For this first design, Balmond compiled a structural engineering catalogue featuring lots of different types of Vierendeel girders, drawing on the largely free layout they facilitate. He devised the most banal girders, which would then be lined up in the Kunsthal. Upon entering, they could all be seen at once: a totally incomprehensible, banal jungle of structural signs. While walking around the building and looking at the girders individually, they would present a clearer picture. [...]

After it became clear Jo Coenen would be building the Netherlands Architecture Institute, the Kunsthal design was altered twice. First because Koolhaas thought such an insubstantial-looking building was misguided now that it no longer had a counterpart. Then it was changed again, because the director of the Kunsthal, Wim van Krimpen, did not like the design. But even the realized design offers perspectives that provide what look like structurally chaotic scenes. A single glance captures the steel profile of Hall 2, the enormous concrete column of the public tunnel and the sloping concrete column of the auditorium. Seen separately, the structural solutions make sense, even though the traditional is shunned in all cases.

Structurally, the Kunsthal can effectively be seen as three separate buildings. Like nearly all halls, Halls 1 and 2 are made of steel. Koolhaas would have preferred timber columns in Hall 1. But since the budget would not stretch to solving the structural and detailing problems posed by yet another material, he settled for steel profiles, which he chose to clad in hollow tree trunks. (They subsequently became the most talked about objects in the Kunsthal.) The most striking aspect of this Hall, however, is the position of the columns: the traditional, symmetrical grid has been abandoned. Since this made the span bigger than normal, the steel beams would have to be higher than Koolhaas intended. To limit this height, a steel-concrete girder was used, with the steel profile providing external reinforcement and absorbing the tensile stresses, and the concrete taking care of the compressive stresses. The bracing of the north wall as Koolhaas had in mind (that is, without really revealing the structure) presented far more problems. Balmond and Mr J. Laurens of the Utiliteits- en Waterbouw engineering firm of Rotterdam's department of public works came up with a structure in which this heavy wall is supported by cantilevers and partially suspended from the steel girder lying on the roof. This does indeed create the impression of the wall floating in air.

Hall 2, which is positioned above Hall 1, has a completely clear span. The roof is supported by truss girders, which are just about visible behind plastic. The orange wind braces shoot through the plastic, into the sky, and connect the truss girders that look like they are in another dimension. If this structure comes across as mysterious, that of the auditorium and Hall 3 looks familiar and bizarre in equal measure: familiar because it is realized in concrete, which—given its functions—is an obvious material; bizarre because the columns are slanted, as they are in a few other Koolhaas designs, including the Villa dall'Ava in Paris. Structurally, this means the introduction of an extra horizontal force, which is transferred via the auditorium floor to the stiff core underneath the public tunnel.

Koolhaas and Balmond chose to treat the separate parts of the building as autonomous entities instead of drawing on a bag of tricks to weave them together. [...] This view is a typical example of structural engineering reinforcing the architecture. The boundaries between the two disciplines have long since disappeared in Koolhaas's work, in the same way that he is now trying to break down the boundaries between detailing and design. This remarkable synthesis, in which his unusual choice of materials also plays a role and each individual element reinforces the whole, ensures that his buildings do what he thinks they should do: reflect an era.

THE MUSEUM AS MEGASTAR

Deyan Sudjic
The Guardian, January 25, 1993.

Rotterdam's new Kunsthal gallery is a building that brings to a head the argument between those who maintain that the primary role of a museum designer is to eat humble pie and defer to its contents and those who believe that a museum's special place in the modern city should be reflected in the exhibitionism of its architecture.

Designed by the British-educated Rem Koolhaas, now the angry middle-aged man of Dutch architecture, the Kunsthal is a building that appears to break all the rules of museum design. Koolhaas has deliberately set out to make the museum the primary exhibit. Rather than expend endless care on an invisible yet sensitive lighting system and on perfectly proportioned galleries that set off the contents to their best advantage, the Kunsthal shrieks for attention itself—every bit as much as Frank Lloyd Wright's supremely egotistical Guggenheim museum.

It is not really a museum at all, more an installation on the theme of the impossibility of building coherent architecture in an incoherent world. It faces on to the dual carriageway that skirts the edge of Rotterdam's academic and museum precinct, like a motorway service station. It advertises the fact that it is "modern" with its fractured black-glass facade and exposed orange steelwork, as well as a large electronic signboard. The architectural vocabulary is a loose paraphrase of Mies van der Rohe's National Gallery in Berlin. But while Mies created a building that is almost classical in its formal perfection and the precision with which it is put together, Koolhaas has deconstructed Mies's idiom, signaled most conspicuously on the exterior by his use of a giant tree trunk as a handrail. Rather than crafting space and materials in the manner of architects from the Modern movement, Koolhaas is happy to allow one space to collide with another with the abandon of runaway goods wagons. As if to show that the Kunsthal offers culture rather than lead-free petrol and a drive-in car-wash, the external advertising includes a curious sculpture of a camel on the roof, though it is a last-minute addition with which Koolhaas is unhappy.

[...] Curators and artists often rail against conspicuous architecture, which they see as belittling the art. But it is not just architects who have a different agenda. Museum directors are in the position of competing with one another to attract more visitors. As the building of the Centre Pompidou in Paris and James Stirling's Staatsgallerie in Stuttgart proved, few things are more effective than a spectacular piece of new architecture. Clearly that factor played a large part in the reasoning behind the decision to appoint Rem Koolhaas to design the Kunsthal. Koolhaas is rapidly establishing himself as one of the most provocative architects in the world and by identifying itself with him, the Kunsthal not only becomes an attraction but puts itself on the cutting edge of the avant-garde. Indeed, the Kunsthal's director wrote a brief that put as much emphasis on the café, the restaurant and the bookshop as on the gallery spaces, accepting the new definition of the museum.

Architecture is more and more a profession driven by short-lived intellectual fashion. After the overripe historicism of Postmodernism, it is the work of Koolhaas and a group of like-minded architects which is providing the impetus for the next wave. The Postmodernists sought to prettify the ugly, brute, concrete face of the modern world by putting back the mystery and charm that, as they saw it, had been lost. Hence their architecture was intended to be decorative and richly allusive. However, in too many cases that honorable intention was reduced to a skin-deep layer of stone.

Koolhaas's approach, on the other hand, is to reject all that as a sentimental evasion. He sees himself as the tough-minded new kid on the block facing up to the realities of life in the modern city. A place which is full of pathetic self-delusion, as he sees it, in its attempts to recreate the piazzas of Tuscan hill towns or the facades of Georgian England. In an uncertain, fragmented world of airports and freeways, where cities are glimpsed from cars on elevated highways, architecture has to reflect that same uncertainty and fragmentation. Equally for Koolhaas, there is no refuge to be found in treating architecture as if it were jewelry and concentrating on the gem-like perfection of the way in which a handrail wraps itself round a staircase or the manner in which a window sits in a wall.

[...] The Kunsthal's exterior is both a homage to and a subversion of Mies van der Rohe's museum in Berlin in much the same way that James Stirling paid tribute to the nineteenth-century museums of Schinkel. Koolhaas wants desperately to be modern; but he knows that modernity, in the old utopian sense, is no longer a realistic option. So what he does is to adopt elements of Mies, as well as more banal architecture from the 1960s, and filter them through his particular view of the 1990s.

CLAD IN TONALITIES OF LIGHT

Paul Vermeulen
Architectuur in Nederland: Jaarboek 1992/1993, ed. Matthijs de Boer, Ruud Brouwers, Vincent Van Rossem, Zef Hemel (Rotterdam: NAi Publishers, 1993), 90–91.

The Kunsthal is the gateway building of the museum park on the Westzeedijk. A road descends through the building, from the dike to the park. Halfway along are the ticket desks and the main entrance; lower down, you encounter the entrance to the restaurant. A second road, the parallel route at the foot of the dike, runs through the building. "I liked the vulgarity and ambivalence of this spot," wrote Koolhaas. "On one side urban, almost crudely so, and on the other side very museum-like." The crude-urban features of the new building can best be enjoyed if you take the Zeedijk in a western direction. Spontaneously recognizable in the flat profile and the advertising tower is the typology of hypermarkets and shopping malls tailored to urban freeways. The low cornice which leaves the gently sloping bitumen roof and the backs of the light streets visible, reinforce this association. The Kunsthal is primarily a hall.

If you were to construct a genealogy for the Kunsthal, it would contain, apart from Mies, the Paris Soviet Pavilion by Melnikov. Melnikov's wooden pavilion can certainly serve as a rudimentary prototype of a building which is cut into pieces by a half-covered road, has its entrance on this self-generated road and despite the chopping up into pieces, forms a spatial unity. The presence of Mies's influence is more diffuse. On the Zeedijk, the building rests upon a Miesian floating steel plateau. The use of this is all the more significant, because the space between building and ground level, which in Farnsworth House is merely Platonic, is here really exploited: the ground level twists downward and provides space for the parallel route. That is why the plateau is paved not with stone, but with grilles. Cool light falls upon the sides of the dike.

Nevertheless Mies's role seems to be that of an old friend with whom you disagree violently. Many reminders of the old master are accompanied by a critical commentary. Apart from travertine, polycarbonate slabs or roughly brushed concrete are used. A material is noble, Koolhaas appears to be saying, not because it is expensive but because of its intrinsic qualities. The main difference of opinion is about the construction. For Koolhaas this is not morally unassailable. His treatment of structure is pragmatic, opportunistic, subversive. He places columns perpendicularly on a sloping floor: the spatial logic does not necessarily follow gravity. He screws lamps into concrete columns. Five supports, all five different, shoot out randomly from the steel plateau. The big steel girders on the roof are not, as in Mies's Crown Hall, the highest truth of architecture, but the leftovers from a stabilization job, carelessly left lying on the roof.

The truth must be told. In my opinion, this Kunsthal provides the most stimulating experience produced in years by Dutch architecture. Two aspects in particular deserve unreserved admiration: the use of material and the plan. Koolhaas's constructive relativism results in an architecture of the casing which seems to be the realization of the ideas on this matter of Adolf Loos and Gottfried Semper. Semper's provocative position that textiles are the shared root of both architecture and clothing is demonstrated by the slantwise hemmed curtain of the auditorium. When closed it is reminiscent of the silk walls of Mies and Lilly Reich rolled up the ascending hem gives it the elegance of a party gown. In the second exhibition hall the steeply rising light strips seem to be notched into a tightly stretched cloth. The hammer-bars of the trusses disappear in the light, just as in Wagner's Postsparkasse the porticos in the glass roof become hazy. Elsewhere, semitransparent corrugated slabs reveal what is usually hidden: the skeleton of the wall, the movement of the lift — but they hide the windows. It is an unworldly apparition when at night the artificial light projects the windows on the slabs. Numerous observations confirm the theme even further: the building is clad in tonalities of light.

Finally, the plan. The alternation of dimensions and atmospheres, the knitting of tracks, of well-lit routes and half-hidden alleys, the junction of two public roads in the heart of the building — it makes a small city of this big building. It is necessary to climb in order to find the most picturesque panorama of this little city: the slope planted with pear trees behind which the tower rises up at an angle like a belfry. It is worthy of a postcard.

MARATHON
Andrew MacNair
A+U 287 (1994), 120–23.

[...] The Kunsthal acts as a train station without trains, an airport without planes, a terminus which is a place of intersection between ordinary people and ordinary art. Nothing stays very long. There is no library, no archive, no study center, and few permanent curators. It is part of a living art highway. A Kunsthal is an intersection on this highway: an oasis as a cultural pit stop along the world highway of space, time, and speed.

Such a hybrid of museum, gallery, and production space forms a condition and program of paradox for the Rotterdam Kunsthal: it is both a place of contemplation yet a place of action and perpetual change; it offers a space for stopping yet it's a space always on the go; it is a big container itself harboring smaller containers in transport from one port to another via container ship and container truck; it is a workhouse in a work city showing to working people the work of art, high and low art; it is owned by the state, the people, a tax-payers' pedestrian hallway yet it owns nothing, except its land and building; it is appointed, defined by the elected officials, but has no accumulating power base; it is fragile in its temporariness, delicate in its life on the edge; a cross between a shipping transfer warehouse and an exposition hall for transport and commerce. A place between entertainment and education.

[...] The Kunsthal in its most basic terms was conceived as a square crossed by two routes: one is a road running east to west parallel to the Maas Boulevard leading down from the upper level of the dike, under the building, and then up again to the Maas Boulevard dike forming a detour for cars and bikes as weil as a porte cochere. The second route is a north-to-south route leading from the Maas Boulevard dike into the front entrance of the building along a wide-open ramp through the bulk of the building volume to the main ticket booth and front entrance door and then out the back of the building. These two routes form two big, wide new roads anchoring the Kunsthal by its own fabricated crossroad. A station at an urban and rural intersection.

The crossroads divide the land of the site into four parts. One challenge stated by the architect was to make a Kunsthal of four autonomous projects yet as one whole. The building consists of four squares (the office block, restaurant and auditorium, Hall 1 and 2, and the front porch) around an intersection of the two major routes connected by a three-dimensional interweaving path of people walking along the route of an interior and at times exterior spiral pathway. The main concept of the building's organization is a continuous circuit within a four-square building.

In the most public and urban way the Kunsthal forms not only its own dialectical crossroads juxtaposing the city road to the country road, but also builds a free public interior and exterior meandering three-dimensional pedestrian pathway as a walk up to, into, through, up, down, over, under, along and against a kaleidoscopic promenade triggering a world of explicit and implicit natural and architectural overlays, overlaps, splits, intersections, echoes, ricochets, reflections, shadows, shouts and whispers charging a tight crossroad intersection with its own premeditated choreographic, cinematic phenomena as urbanism. Quite a quiet box of a building with a subtle, often mysterious, and perplexing interior maze.

[...] Halfway down the Main Street ramp, it intersects with the opposite slope of the sloping floor of the inside auditorium. At the point of shear, Bang! — a rupture occurs between these two concrete planes; the tiny ticket booth and small, almost obscure entrance door and miniature vestibule form a crunched entrance — a compressed doorway off the main street. Point of rupture equals entrance/exit: jammed into the most sensitive and critical fault line breaking the two sloping slabs and marking the only safe leap from one shifting broken land plane to the next. Entrance is a leap of faith. While impossible for the handicapped, this tiny but monumental moment celebrates notions of aberrant structure, a fundamental of contemporary deconstructivist architecture: an architecture of anxiety. The entrance is a post-disaster episode before the disaster hits, a post-earthquake model made into theory and simultaneously built into pre-earthquake practice. There is no retroactive manifesto, only hard-core evidence.

[...] Thin orange lines of wind-bracing steel tubes secure the lateral forces between the trusses in the ceiling and roof. They are structural supports. They look like thin, pen-like lines of the uniform, crisp Koolhaas Bic-Pen drawings adopted by the entire OMA office — a trace, an index of the OMA method, and perhaps a footnote about an anti-arty sensibility — yet somehow they are still mysterious skylines of some automatic, semiunconscious, unexplainable doodle.

[...] Spiraling back down and out the second half of the building walk and architectural promenade recapitulates its own genesis: The flower blooms, the flower closes. This part of the two-way time line of circulation in architecture is often ignored by architects. One of the four "Times of Architecture" — the time of the walk of the human body along the path (circulation) — includes not only entrance and path into and through a building but also includes the path back, through, along, around, and eventually back out to the outside. Here in the Kunsthal, the path down and back out is equally planned and scripted. The path down emphasizes events going up that may appear to be secondary. When going back down, they reappear under different light and perspectives. The roof garden gains literally and metaphorically much greater weight as it sinks back downhill into the inner volume of Hall 2. The tongue-balcony jutting off the bottom of the roof ramp, now on the downhill run, swings us by accelerated momentum of gravity out onto a porch balcony overhanging and overlooking the exhibition in Hall 2.

[...] The Kunsthal fulfills the dictum that Robert Rauschenberg and I discussed in New York shortly before he died. I asked him at an opening of his copperplate silk screens at the Knoedler Gallery, "What constitutes the success of a work of art?" He said, "I don't know." I said, "Take the object, cut it in half, turn it inside out and/or upside down, paint it pink, and put it on wheels." Rauschenberg smiled, leaned over and whispered ... "and spin!"

In summary, the Rotterdam Kunsthal addresses issues about the banal box, the spiral helix, the simple outside and complex inside, the endlessness of the Möbius Strip, the tango of the architect and the engineer; issues about the Dutch Culture of Ennui, the Dutch Kiss, and Dutch Rain; ideas about the time space of the four-dimensional video and video game; inhabiting spaces in-between; an architecture of the airport, flying, and jet-lag; of architecture, not-architecture, and not-not architecture; of art and not-art; of Pop, Kitsch, and Rock and Roll; of Warhol, Venturi, Mies, Leonidov, Harrison, and perhaps, an architecture of the perpetual, eternal, and sweaty jog.

HISTORY LESIONS

Cynthia Davidson
ANY 21 (1997), 36–40.

Time has to split the present in two heterogeneous directions, one of which is launched toward the future while the other falls into the past. — Gilles Deleuze

[...] I first visited the Kunsthal on a dull January day in 1997, when the orange girder that juts over one edge of the flat black roof glowed especially bright against the washed-out Rotterdam sky. Koolhaas drove me up to the street side of the Kunsthal, steering his black Maserati over the curb to park on a muddy patch of grass. We were stopped on the Westzeedijk, one of Holland's many polders, the integrity of which cannot be disturbed by excavation for fear of weakening the barrier to the sea. The

Kunsthal thus barely engages the dike, offering only the merest slab of a "levitating" platform, a kind of front porch, as an invitation to enter the building through its "front" doors. The real energy of the street front comes from the void just to the left of the platform that, yawning broadly, literally pulls visitors in. This "entrance" to the Kunsthal is a ramp that passes straight through the building, connecting the street to the park below.

Koolhaas and I descended the ramp and halfway down turned left to enter the building in precisely the same way he leads a reader through it in *S,M,L,XL*: "Approach the building from the boulevard. Enter the ramp from the dike. It slopes down toward the park. Halfway down, enter the auditorium. [Actually, enter a small ticket foyer.] It slopes in the opposite direction. A curtain is drawn, blocking out daylight. [Or not drawn, this day.] At the bottom, see a projection screen. [Or a window wall if the screen is up.] Walk down. Turn the corner. Enter the lower hall, facing the park. It is dark, with a forest of five columns. [Primitive tree trunks in a high-tech performance.] To the right, a slender aperture opens to a narrow gallery. Look up. [See the much-photographed metal grate floor.] Rediscover the ramp you used to enter. Walk up. A glass wall separates the people outside. At the top ... turn left. Enter the second hall. It is bright, with no columns. Look back. [The ceiling is all daylight from one direction, opaque from the other.] Exit under the balcony. See the auditorium but don't walk that far. Instead, turn and take a third ramp. Halfway up, grope through a small dark room and emerge on a balcony that penetrates the second hall. [A disconcerting diversion that causes you to double back.] Return to the ramp, run up, and emerge on the roof. Look down. Spiral back down to the beginning. Exit to the park. Pause. Turn the corner. Pass the restaurant underneath the auditorium. Keep going."

"Keep going" refers to one's movement around the building but could just as well refer to the "spiral" framed in the new "box" of time, for the interior tour too replays itself endlessly. This way, that way, the building aggressively demands. Dutifully I come up the glassed-in ramp from the gallery below only to find myself at crosspaths with spiral breakers, people entering the front door. What happened? Where am I? Where, even, is the so-called spiral? To ask this question assumes that the spiral is continuous and spatial, like Le Corbusier's spiral at the Mundaneum. But it is not.

The second time I visited the Kunsthal, in June, I avoided the front door question and approached the building from the back, from the park, where it is different, other, separate from my first impression. The difference makes clear the need, in Walter Benjamin's words from his *Moscow Diary*, to experience a place "in as many dimensions as possible. You have to have approached a place from all four cardinal points if you want to take it in." Benjamin's words seem especially relevant in the fragmented time of Postmodernism, the time of the Kunsthal. Sitting alone on the landscape, its four facades are each equally approachable and each completely different in material and sensibility from the others, almost as if they have been split apart from one another. Seeing each elevation is essential to knowing the building and to seeing it in relation to Koolhaas's view of time. This no longer seems like a static box but rather a series of pictures that play back in the mind. I am reminded of Jean-Luc Godard's filmic jump cut, where time between frames vanishes, no longer providing a continuous narrative sequence and momentarily dislocating the viewer with new visual information.

[...] So on my second visit I approach the Kunsthal from the Netherlands Architecture Institute, crossing the length of the park, coming upon a paved path punctuated decoratively with circles of glass, and then looking ahead at a serene glass and travertine facade. Except for the giant chimney-like signpost that projects from the roof there is no visual noise here, rather the mood is contemplative, the materials in harmony with the brick and limestone nature museum next door. The solid band of travertine seems to hover above the transparent grade level that opens views into the building. From this park view the pedestrian ramp sends out a seductive concrete tongue, mysteriously providing the only entry into what already seems open and accessible. I walk in and up the ramp, enter the auditorium, and then break the prescribed route by zigzagging into the quirky bookshop, a kind of poché wedged alongside the auditorium that provides a view into the restaurant space below the slope of seats. Out again the way I entered, I continue up the ramp to the platform that hovers over the dike. Now details begin to appear, four different column types that, in their uniqueness, can only be read as quotations from a previous time. A cruciform column, two black square columns, a white square column paired with a flat, white, perforated one. These last two are cross-braced with metal rods that, when viewed from the street, seem to cancel, or X-out, entry through the "front" door, itself a painted graphic that is more signlike than doorlike.

To see the four cardinal points I keep going, descending the access road to grade behind the dike. Here a wall is divided horizontally in half by the use of two materials: painted concrete below; seamed, semiopaque glass above. This building looks like a banal warehouse, complete with service road and delivery docks. I walk under the building on the service road until I come to the opposite, east facade, this one raw concrete above and clear glass below. The elevation is literally a section diagram, the sloping auditorium floor drawing a long line across the glass wall and separating lecture hall above from restaurant below. Cumulatively, the four elevations read as the functions of the Kunsthal: administration; education and entertainment; exhibitions; art handling and storage.

The Dutch, Koolhaas said during my first tour, think the Kunsthal is badly detailed. Compared with OMA's meticulous Villa dall'Ava in Paris or housing complex in Fukuoka, Japan, the Kunsthal does appear hastily, even arbitrarily put together with an assortment of materials. Corrugated plastic and metal mesh mix with steel and travertine, exposed concrete meets wood. It gives the box a quality of having been snapped together, of pieces, perhaps, of walls being slid into place like the walls of a De Stijl diagram. This is particularly noticeable at the corners, where thin planes of plastic, concrete, travertine, and glass intersect without one material overwhelming another. Perhaps this thinness is the cause for criticism; it feels fleeting, almost ephemeral.

At least three devices in the Kunsthal recall Le Corbusier: the ramp, or in Le Corbusier's terms, the *promenade architecturale*, the spiral, and the basic square plan. Koolhaas's debt to Le Corbusier, like that of many architects, is an acknowledged fact. For example, Kenneth Frampton, in a 1993 review of the Kunsthal published in *Domus*, suggested that the Kunsthal recalled Le Corbusier's congress hall for Strasbourg, designed in 1964. Indeed, a close examination reveals several similarities. In both, an auditorium (though on different floors) is pushed to the same corner of a square plan. At Strasbourg, a ramp for cars passes under and around the building to the roof. At the Kunsthal, a series of ramps allows pedestrians to move from the street to the roof. Le Corbusier hangs exposed concrete over glass but leaves the supporting pilotis exposed. On two facades of the Kunsthal, Koolhaas pulls in the columns and pushes the glass at grade out flush with the travertine or concrete above. But where Le Corbusier's building is a unified whole, inside and outside, Koolhaas's is fragmented. Rather than enfolding the building, Koolhaas's initial ramp is a void that allows one to pass directly through the building without entering it. In addition, the vehicular street at cross axis to the ramp cuts the building apart at grade. This tunneling through the square eats away at its formal geometry and begins to break up the ideal form of the square. Inside, the "spiral" that attempts to move through the fragmented square continuously breaks apart, sending the visitor into volumes of space before sucking him or her up again into another progression.

These fragments are the key to Koolhaas's idea of time. For Le Corbusier time is linear, narrative, the time of a unitary subject. In this sense Le Corbusier's object and subject occupy the same time. At the Kunsthal the time of the subject and the time of the object are disjunctive. Koolhaas's fragmented architectural object confuses our sense of time. This is another version of Godard's jump cut—a cut in space and time prompted by the difference in time of the viewer's movement and the movement of the object of viewing. The jump cut occurs throughout *S,M,L,XL* too. Smack in the middle of the Kunsthal story there suddenly appears a double-page photograph of cars strewn across an urban street. Is it Paris in 1968? Prague? It doesn't matter. The disruption of the Kunsthal narrative, of continuity, matters.

In 1929 Le Corbusier designed a circulation spiral in the Mundaneum, a museum for Geneva, and called his plan diagram for it "continuous circulation." As the spiral turned in on itself, the building rose in height, taking the form of the spiral itself. Koolhaas diagrams the spiral of the Kunsthal in such a way that the building too is the result of its circulation, although that process produces no recognizable form. Here, movement and form are discontinuous. The box contains the spiral, compressing and deforming it while also being fragmented by it. The spiral's ramps become thematic of the building's conflict with its confining static envelope, its form. This is also a confrontation of two different times, the static and the mobile. Koolhaas attempts to erase this dialectic because the subjective time of the experience of the viewer, which was formerly synchronic with the space and form, that is, the time of the object, is disjointed from the subject. The spiraling ramps of the Kunsthal move away from Le Corbusier's circulation systems as form-making to symbolize instead the movement of architecture from figure to flow and from an actual spiral to a spiraling affect. Now the object, like the time of Godard's jump cut, separates from our experience of it. Time is no longer, as Deleuze says, a matter of degree but a difference in kind from the space of the subject.

[...] While walking through the Kunsthal I was reminded of Richard Wagner's opera, *Der fliegende Holländer*, if only because Koolhaas's bravado suggests high flying. Senta, a ship captain's daughter, falls in love with a mysterious Dutchman who has unexpectedly sailed into the harbor and promises to leave with him the next day. In the third act we learn that his ship is but a ghostly coffin that only comes into port once every seven years. The entire narrative of *The Flying Dutchman* is based on this disruption in time, which alters the course of events. As the music spirals to a crescendo, Senta discovers her fate and then plunges to her death. Indeed there is the faint smell of death in Koolhaas's work. Is it a premonition of the possible death of form in the fragmentation of his architecture, toward its own disappearance in the flow of time?

"BIGNESS" & EURALILLE (1989–1998): I KNEW I WAS IN TROUBLE BUT I THOUGHT I WAS IN HELL

9

OMA has never truly believed in urban planning, and what little confidence they had disappeared during the 1980s. In an essay from 1992 in *Design Book Review* (covering recent books from and on OMA), Albert Pope quoted Elvis Costello's song "Tokyo Storm Warning" from 1986. The quote succinctly describes OMA's both pessimistic and thrilling worldview, prompted by the conviction that cities are uncontrollable and often absurd environments: "The sky fell over cheap Korean monster-movie scenery / And spilled into the mezzanine of the crushed capsule hotel / Between the Disney abattoir and the chemical refinery / I knew I was in trouble but I thought I was in hell / [...] What do we care if the world is a joke?"

The joke did get real when OMA was invited in 1989 to brainstorm about the future of a small, postindustrial, and not very vibrant city: Lille, 225 kilometers north of Paris, it is closer to Belgium than to the capital of France. What happened in many of OMA's projects also materialized here: a singular situation became exemplary for a period in the history of a continent. In the hands of OMA, the project for Lille became a metaphor and a test case for nothing less than the future of France, the European Union, the project of Enlightenment, the possibility of urban planning, the advancement of passenger transport, and the desirability of economic, financial, and technological progress under late capitalism. The project made explicit—or even outperformed—the economic euphoria of the early 1990s, given the hot-brained conviction that it was impossible to invest too much in finance, trade, and real estate. As Peter Newman and Andy Thornley wrote in 1995, Euralille was the penultimate case of boosterism at the center of Europe. Again, the fall of the Berlin Wall and the process of European unification (the European Union was formally established on November 1, 1993), only added to this optimism.

OMA depicted Lille as the future urban hub of Europe, as a midpoint between the capitals of the UK, France, and Belgium. The commission had a very close deadline: Euralille, and more particularly the new train station Lille Europe, needed to be ready by the end of 1994 to take up its role in the network of high-speed trains connecting London to Paris and Brussels. Koolhaas mentioned a "dynamique d'enfer," a dynamic out of hell, that forced the quite inexperienced and not very numerous members of OMA to accomplish the most ambitious, mediatized, and complicated urban development in Europe at a breakneck speed. In a condemnatory article from 2002, "The ¥€$ Man," Joan Ockman has argued how Koolhaas's "limited success in realizing anything [during the 1980s] left him utterly unprepared, at the end of that decade, for the breakthrough project of Euralille. [...] This commission required such an exponential jump in the scale of his operations that the only possible strategy was to theorize it. Out of this personal crisis of bigness came the first of his extra-large books [*S,M,L,XL*] as well as a new worldview."[1]

The essay in which Koolhaas theorized Euralille (and its architectural centerpiece, the Congrexpo—the only building of the master plan that OMA accounted for) was entitled "Bigness," first published in *Domus* in October 1994. It was written to distance OMA (again) from the fragmentation of deconstructivism, but it also opened up a possibility for architects to continue to contribute to cities, against all odds. As in the case of other essays Koolhaas wrote during these years—such as "The Generic City" or "Whatever Happened to Urbanism?"—novelty can't have been the main concern. Already in 1979, Ada Louise Huxtable ascertained in the *New York Times*: "There will be bigger building everywhere, and contrary to all predictions about the decline of urban centers, construction in big cities is on the rise." She went on to speculate that "it may also be the fulfillment of what the Dutch architect and author Rem Koolhaas has prophetically characterized as Manhattan's 'culture of congestion.'"[2] In 1996 an issue of the journal for architectural history *Daidalos* was devoted to "Bigness," although OMA was only addressed in passing. "Rem Koolhaas's manifesto 'Bigness' reveals on second reading—but not before then!—nothing fundamentally new or different," Werner Oechslin ascertained. The writings of Koolhaas had become ways of recapitulating, of sketching a "totality" or a "whole" (also a kind of "bigness") in an atomizing society, and for a discipline ever more subject to the division of labor and the fragmentation of knowledge. At the same time, "Bigness" cannot be appreciated without its built counterpart, not because it realistically illustrates Euralille or the Congrexpo, but exactly because it doesn't—or at least not completely.

The reception of Euralille was the most extreme in the history of OMA. It was praised for the optimism and the formal bravado the architects showed, but it was heavily criticized because of its financial opportunism and the inability it expressed—with the "espace piranésien" of the train station as the most obvious example—to realize what were considered scandalous dreamscapes. For many architects, the unorthodox way in which public space was organized (or disorganized) at Euralille "was akin to a renunciation or even a betrayal, the outcome of an urbanism that led to the dismantling of the European city,"[3] as Valéry Didelon argued in a recent reconstruction of the project. What also played a part was the French intellectual conviction that the country needed no other city since it already had Paris. "Is it necessary today, for whatever purpose it may serve, to step up the contrast ... as at Lille?" Jacques Lucan wondered in *Domus*. Comparisons between Koolhaas and Le Corbusier particularly enraged Jean-Louis Cohen, who wrote that OMA didn't stand "the test of the construction site" in Lille. The PR-team of Euralille published a book in 1996 (in a French and an English edition) to contradict this dominant view, with commissioned texts by Daniel Treiber, Stanislaus von Moos, and Jean Attali, who tried to counter the negative press, suggesting that "criticism has lost its bearings."

1 Joan Ockman, "The ¥€$ Man," *Architecture* 91, no. 3 (2002), 78.
2 Ada Louis Huxtable, "Bigger—And Maybe Better," *New York Times*, August 26, 1979.
3 Valéry Didelon, "Euralille: The Deconstruction of the European City," *Log*, no. 39 (2017), 129.

THINKING BIG
John Rajchman
Artforum 4 (1994), 46–55, 99, 102.

[...] **jr:** When and how did the theory of Bigness become explicit, the object of a manifesto and a principle by which to present your work?

rk: It was a very slow, inarticulate dawning, and I'm not even sure that I've fully captured it now. There was a very slow awakening to first the existence, then the potential, of Bigness. I have to say that it was actually the practice of architecture—very rarely intellectually stimulating, because of its very difficulty—that gradually imposed a realization upon us: projects like Zeebrugge, the TGB, Karlsruhe, Lille, all had as a common denominator a large scale, accumulations not only of one big program but of clusters of diversity, and a political importance that required making very visible statements and changing conditions emphatically. All these were *external* forces that forced us to realize that "something" was going on. *Delirious New York* describes the same sort of problem, but in terms of a movement that died, or did not survive the lucidity or clarity or propaganda of Modernism. I was surprised by its return. For me, Bigness is a concept that accumulates a cluster, a cloud, of issues. The combination of those issues is liberating for architecture, and maybe for other domains. It ends the obsession with history and context. By reintroducing the notion of teamwork—inevitable on that scale—it also liberates one from the narrow identification of a single architect with "his" or "her" object; it makes it less personal. It is artificial, and therefore asserts an implicit adhesion to the process of modernization, without necessarily opening a polemic about modernity. It also permitted us to polemicize with my generation of architects, with Deconstructivists, in the name of real complexity and real specificity. It allowed us to explore new definitions of collectivity after the demise of the public realm—public man—eroded by the onslaught of the media, pressures from the virtual, multiple privatizations, the end of the street, the plaza, etc. Bigness also liberates us from the obligation of the "general," which in retrospect may be the greatest weakness of Modernism—its inability to deal with, to accommodate, to theorize, the specific. But it is therefore a limited manifesto, or a "weak" manifesto. It does not prescribe, but it identifies a number of possibilities. [...]

jr: You say Bigness alone instigates a "regime of complexity" in which "programmatic elements react with one another to create new events." How does this differ from the sort of complexity Robert Venturi called "the difficult whole," or Colin Rowe the "collage"?

rk: Let's start with collage. Collage is simulated complexity: instead of a Mondrian-esque composition of slabs, you imagine a Piranesian composition of fragments. It is composed, controlled, limited—it's a purely visual complexity. The fact that it is antiutopian still doesn't make it political. It is very close to deconstructivist architecture. I think Venturi, in the 1960s, was one of the first to sense that "the whole" was becoming problematic, that it is based on a series of denials and repressions. The quality of his book *Complexity and Contradiction in Architecture* was to unleash those repressions. But he called it a "difficult whole," not an "impossible whole," and in the 1970s and 1980s the entire notion of the whole was denigrated, fragmented to the point of nonexistence. In that context, a theory of Bigness should maybe talk about the "new whole"—the whole after the crisis of the whole, a whole based no longer on exclusion or homogeneity but on cultivating the uncontrollable—a whole that does not pretend to control beyond the range of a single perspective.

jr: That brings up the matter of the influence of French theory. You're fond of repeating that its effect on architecture has been to tell us that we are not whole (Derrida), not real (Baudrillard), and not there (Virilio)—an untenable result. Does that mean we should just go back to traditional notions of holism, reality, and place in architecture? In what ways does Bigness change our thinking here?

rk: No. These theories were for architects an alibi not to deal with the essential, inherent definition of architecture: *to make*. What is both the beauty and the agony of a given profession or discipline like painting or architecture? They are like lead balls chained to the leg of a prisoner. Their essential contents are given and almost impossible to dislodge, mutate, exchange. Painters have painted since the cave man, and still put down paint. Architects still build. What Baudrillard, Derrida, and Virilio did was to offer the mirage of a miracle exit, an escape from the lead ball: "Architects, leave no traces, be *Luftmenschen*." But no, I think it's more exciting to work with and on the lead ball, patiently, like a prisoner who plots his escape: scrape lead off with a teaspoon.

jr: In this situation it strikes me that some concepts from Gilles Deleuze may be of use: the idea of an "open" or "complicated" whole prior to totality or simplicity, a sense of intense zones or "envelopes" of the real prior to what is thought possible, and the vision of an abstract, "ungrounded" movement that doesn't go from one place to another but, in Deleuze's words, "passes between points, ceaselessly bifurcating and diverging, like one of Jackson Pollock's lines." Indeed there seems something almost "rhizomatic" about your vision of out-of-control Bigness. When did you first come across Deleuze, and how did you react?

rk: When I first came across Deleuze—maybe six or seven years ago, through conversations with Hubert Damisch—I started to read the books and almost immediately closed them because of their uncanny analogies, their incredibly free-ranging speculations. I closed them, clearly, out of fear of becoming Deleuzian and a sense that maybe it was already too late. Now I have read them in small doses. It's the anxiety of influence.

jr: To deal with this uncontrollable yet open—this "rhizomatic"—sort of Bigness, one must go, I gather, beyond what you have called "merely visible," faux, "decorative" sorts of order and of disorder. What about the urban and architectural "cuts" of Gordon Matta-Clark? How did you react to them?

rk: I was fascinated by Matta-Clark. I thought he was doing to the real world what Lucio Fontana did to canvas. At the time, the most shocking, exciting aspect of his work was maybe the glamour of violation. Now I also think that his work was a very strong, early illustration of some of the power of the absent, of the void, of elimination, that is, of adding and making. I never really thought about it but maybe some of the notions of the TGB, where tunnels are drilled out of the volume of the building, go back to his operations.

[...]

jr: How does Bigness then transform the way we see and think about "public space"?

rk: It both proclaims the death of public space and finds new ways of accommodating the collective. The public realm has been surprising resilient under the onslaught of the masses, the car, the media, etc. The only thing it did not survive was its attempted resurrection. (Please note that public art died with it.)

jr: In what ways does Bigness fit with the Modernism/Postmodernism division? What do you make of European Neomodernism? Could that term describe your own work?

rk: European Neomodernism is a very unradical movement that now tries to adopt/adapt the language of Modernism to context, forgetting that seemingly the whole point of Modernism was the break from context. To the extent our work is identified with Neomodernism, which I cannot always deny—it is a weakness—I have made my affinities within Modernism clear by comparing Gerrit Rietveld to Mies van der Rohe. The abstraction of Rietveld—let's say, the Schröder House—is a Romany caravan of sublimation. Everything is reinvented, reformed, but still there. Mies is more dangerous: nothing is left when he's "done" with a subject. It's incredible at the end of the twentieth century how, on every level of discourse—populist (green), rightist, artistic—the strategies of dissociation and rupture create deep unease, as if the present were so wonderful that each change could only be a deterioration. These strategies frighten. But anticontextualism is also a matter of scale: a home that proclaims "fuck context" may be simply inept.

[...]

jr: In your piece on postcolonial Singapore, you analyze that island city as a sort of compendium of the various ideological urban plans available. As such, it may supply a model for China, where the stakes are staggeringly large—in the next forty years, China plans to move a population the size of the US and Russia combined into urban areas old and new, where, it is said, if cars are used, an oil crisis will ensue. You say that Singapore is "managed by a regime that has excluded accident and randomness." In such a regime, what happens to your proposition that "only Bigness can sustain a promiscuous proliferation of events in a single container"? How does such "promiscuity" apply to "the new Asia"?

rk: Good question, John. There are many answers. You could say, as in Singapore, that at the end of all this control there is still a city that has an unaccountable weirdness; it is bizarre, interesting. I'm not writing that piece as an accountant, describing and reconsidering controlled procedures, but rather to document the persistent unpredictability that is the outcome of each attempt to establish a regime of control. Control only expands the edge of chaos. A general reason to write about Singapore was to document a way in which modernity is now a notion hijacked, appropriated, and claimed by Asia exactly at the moment when it seemed to be both depleted and discredited "here." Through this hijacking, modernity has been resemanticized and has acquired new meanings, which so far are least visible to us who have lived longest with its embers and don't believe they can ever be reignited. But what we think of as debased has become brand new. Singapore is maybe a stamp for China, but a miniature state cannot be the model for the largest nation on earth, whose modernization may be the most dramatic chapter in the history of mankind. From Singapore, though, you can draw conclusions: history will disappear; the tabula rasa will be the norm; control will be episodic, proceeding through enclaves, so that it won't generate an overall coherence; the skyscraper—Bigness—will be the last remaining typology. You may be able to say in retrospect that the rule of Bigness—"the promiscuous proliferation of events in a single container"—will have applied to the Bigness that is China.

jr: In what ways is your "theory of Bigness" then a manifesto? How does it help say what ought to be done, the kinds of design strategies to be pursued, the kinds of urban spaces to be imagined?

rk: In *Delirious New York* I asked myself how to write a manifesto in an age disgusted with them. I think that, with a kind of postmodern ingenuity, I wrote one that annexed, usurped, laid claim to the evidence of Manhattan retrospectively—undoing the basic shallowness of the manifesto, which is its inherent lack of evidence. The "age" is still disgusted with manifestoes. I guess this book is a second "Postmodernism," an attempt to do a manifesto this time by imagining how the specific can be reclaimed—seemingly a contradiction in terms—in the case of a manifesto that talks, almost by definition, about the general.

jr: In discussing a very beautiful and striking project you did in Yokohama in 1991, you talk about "lite urbanism." Later, in an essay from this year that asks "Whatever Happened to Urbanism?," you return to the idea, connecting it to a new, lighter way of thinking about cities. What is "liteness," and how does it relate to Bigness?

rk: Maybe you can say that liteness is the residual field between individual Bignesses. It is clear that cities have undergone a permanent, spectacular process of thinning. Their configuration has become progressively meaningless, their substance increasingly insubstantial, their programs atrophied, secularized, banalized, and nonspecific. The city has become vacated, as if Gerhard Richter had taken a Rembrandt and scraped it. That is "lite." But in this condition there is a new potential: a Nietzschean frivolity. Bigness takes over some of the serious and displaced responsibilities. The public realm is now a forest of elevations.

jr: Is "liteness" then part of a new kind of thinking about the city? Is to think big to think lite?

rk: No, or at least not always. The melancholy "beauty" of Bigness is that it can perform the "old" tasks of architecture in a new way in an unrecognizable context.

BIDNESS
Richard Ingersoll
ANY 10 (1995), 5.

Probably the biggest hype in the current marketing of Rem Koolhaas is the theory of Bigness. Reinventing the futurists' metabolist frenzy, which celebrated the chaotic forces of technology and urbanization of the last fin de siècle, Bigness proposes a self-conscious acquiescence to forces that are larger than anyone can understand, let alone control. Koolhaas, in his essay "What Ever Happened to Urbanism?" concludes that since everything will be urbanism, a new modesty and a relinquishing of the myth of control are appropriate: "Redefined, urbanism will not only, or mostly, be a profession, but a way of thinking, an ideology: to accept what exists." That is tantamount to making Bigness a new legitimating term for big business (or "bidness," as we call it in Texas). I suggest that we take seriously the word *ideology* and challenge the current Koolhaas effect as the familiar bourgeois-capitalist program couched in seductively hip hyperboles such as "new newness" and "the liquefaction of program" which will probably result in some new clothes for the emperor, if not a new emperor for the old clothes.

It might sound old-fashioned, but the problem with the modern megalopolis that has become the habitat for more than half of the world's population is not how it looks but what it does to life, human or otherwise. Anomie, *atopie*, pollution, exploitation, displacement, insecurity: this is the ugliness of current urbanization—and precisely the thing that Koolhaas's new urbanism will never address. At its core the theory is wed to the type of social Darwinism to which the corporate power elite has ascribed since the emergence of Manchester, tidied up and rescripted to seem like a new "age of information" mandate for virtual Manchesters.

Modern urbanism has generally failed to create enviable plans: witness the holocaust of urban renewal, which destroyed city centers and displaced the urban poor without rehousing 90 percent of them. Koolhaas's idol, Wallace K. Harrison, and his Empire State Plaza are the most egregious offenders. The blame here lay not necessarily with the architects but with the greed of business coalitions reshaping the city of Albany, New York, exclusively in their own interests. As Georg Simmel put it so long ago, the metropolis is the site of the rationalization of relations of production. The megalopolis that has emerged during the last forty years adds another factor: the rationalization of relations of consumption. Bidness responds only where it can imagine the highest yield, and in the increasingly deregulated economy, that might be anywhere where labor is cheap or consumption high. No matter where it happens to be, the site is transitory, and labor may be divided internationally. While we can acknowledge the realistic ideological conditions of Koolhaas's Bigness, we need not view them as desirable, acceptable, or inevitable. The city still does exist, and the ancient idea of the polis, which carries the discourse of freedom, remains the city's highest goal. Freedom is not just the ability to find the perfect wave or to make the biggest profit; it entails a collective problem of negotiating the distribution of rights, services, and resources. Of course, the demographic explosion and the fluidity of contemporary production and consumption are expanding urbanism to an unprecedented scale, but there are good reasons (ethical but also commercial) to resist social Darwinist conclusions. Darwin's theory also included "mutual aid," which in terms of urbanism is much more complex than "survival of the fittest," as it provides for greater diversity. The city as infrastructure and as architectural frame is the greatest investment that a society can make, as its culture and ethos weave around this frame. Culture transmits the desire to be part of the city, to engage in its emancipatory possibilities. Bidness can at times be subordinated by this desire; otherwise Manhattan and San Francisco would have been abandoned long ago. Likewise, the protection of the environment, usually the nemesis of corporations, may acquire new economic significance as the quality of living conditions becomes more important.

I object to Koolhaas's alluring invectives purely in terms of the guiding ideology. I am not calling for the restitution of the classical city but for the creation of an open city that provides both urban frames as spaces of accountability while not inhibiting participation in the fluidity of modernity. There are many ways of achieving this, but Bigness alone is not enough.

Oriol Bohigas's recent planning experience in Barcelona, while not on the immense scale of Lagos or Kuala Lumpur, demonstrates that a strategy less savage than yielding entirely to big-business programs can succeed. Koolhaas in his enthusiasm for his own theory demonstrates an ill-informed alacrity to condemn en masse contemporary planning without considering its notable successes. The Bohigas interventions were inspired by a critique of modernist totalizing plans: "A city is constructed and controlled by its projects and works, and not by the methods consecrated by planning which are contaminated by programmatic pretensions of an unreal systematic." In replanning Barcelona, Bohigas relied on interesting parts, new areas that would be assigned architectural character to project an idea of the whole. Parks, playgrounds, new streets, public spaces, and housing were judiciously placed to imply new connections of the city's infrastructure. A building as brilliant as Koolhaas's Kunsthal might have fit right into Bohigas's strategy. The effect is that the culture of the city, the possibilities for public life, have made Barcelona even more desirable while accompanying a major modernization of its infrastructure.

Whether any architectural principles can persist in an age dominated by social, economic, and geographic flexibility is ultimately an ideological question connected to whether or not one believes that architectural choices can actually enhance human existence (and by extension protect the environment) and facilitate democratic empowerment. This issue may not be bigger than Bigness but might be better kept alive as the true discourse of the city.

BOOSTERISM AT THE CENTER OF EUROPE

Peter Newman, Andy Thornley

European Urban and Regional Studies 2 (1995), 237–46.

[...] The Euralille project exemplifies the use of large-scale property development to strengthen the local economy and international reputation of a city. Euralille is a business and office development of about seventy hectares around and above the new TGV interchange in Lille. The development has attracted worldwide publicity and, as already noted, the TGV network can be argued to have had significant effects on the geography of Europe. In its publicity the Euralille project accentuates the significance of this changing geography. Lille is claimed to be at the center of a "virtual community" of 100 million people. However, the processes of planning and developing Euralille reflect local political and institutional realities and a specifically French approach to civic boosterism.

[...] Although Lille had been designated as a Métropole d'Equilibre in the 1960s as part of a regional policy of encouraging the development of cities outside Paris, up until the end of the 1980s it had not been as successful as other, southern, cities in attracting new growth. The conurbation suffered from high unemployment and the physical signs of a lost industrial past. The complex industrial geography of the conurbation also contributed to the relative failure to develop service sector jobs in a central location. However, the new national context of the late 1980s—the Single Market, construction of the Channel Tunnel and the TGV network set a favorable background to the development of new local policies.

The political management of the conurbation changed in 1989. The strategic authority for the conurbation, the Communauté Urbaine de Lille (CUDL), established in the 1960s, is an alliance of both the bigger towns in the conurbation and smaller communes which are controlled by a range of political parties. The CUDL now groups together eighty-six communes. The communes are represented on the board of the CUDL according to their size.

Before the 1989 elections a socialist group dominated by members from the smaller communes controlled the CUDL. They showed little interest in conurbation-wide strategy. The socialists lost their majority in the 1989 elections and a new multiparty ruling alliance was forged. The presidency went to the socialist mayor of Lille, Pierre Mauroy. The practice of multiple office holding in France allowed Mauroy to be at once mayor of Lille and president of the CUDL. Mauroy's interest was in reviving his city's economy and he, together with leaders of other parties, underwrote a policy program which supported the Euralille project, but which also committed the CUDL to a range of economic development projects in other towns not controlled by the Socialist Party. Euralille became part of a strategic approach to economic development, including new industrial and distribution centers sited across the conurbation, which was linked to an idea of a distribution of functions between different towns. Lille, for example, was seen as a business center and Roubaix as a center of communications. The new program of the CUDL included social expenditure as well as economic development projects. Revisions were made to the strategic plan for the conurbation to accommodate the new development proposals.

[...] Euralille was constituted as a Société d'Economie Mixte (SEM). The use of SEMs to carry out urban development is common in French cities. A SEM is a private company conforming to company law. The basic legislation affecting SEMs originates in the early part of the century. However, the powers were redefined during the decentralization reforms of the 1980s and these changes have had the effect of encouraging local government to establish this sort of joint venture with private partners. The effect of the reforms of 1983 has been to double the number of SEMs in the ten years since. The advantages of the mixed company formula are generally seen as: the binding together of public and private partners; freedom from administrative rules and regulations, for example in recruitment of staff; and flexibility in decision-making.

[...] The president of the SEM Euralille is Pierre Mauroy. There is thus strong political direction if only indirect political accountability through the local government shareholders. Formal planning approval was the responsibility of the communes and the CUDL. After that, decision-making was passed to the SEM Euralille. Relationships between public and private sectors are negotiated through the SEM. In addition to this key role in shaping investment decisions the SEM has some direct development responsibilities—it was one of the developers of Lille Grand Palais and responsible for car parking and some other works.

Management of developers and contractors is undertaken by a small office with twenty-five staff. Most of the work on the project is contracted out to up to 1,000 staff in architectural and engineering consultancies and other companies. The SEM contracts work to French and UK technical consultants, management consultants and to the CUDL for those aspects of the project affecting the road network. SCET advises on financial management.

Work on the station was the responsibility of SNCF, and the CUDL was responsible for planning the extension of the metro through the site. Project management is thus complex, involving a variety of relationships with the developers of the constituent parts of the project and management of a range of other agencies and subcontractors. The task of Euralille is not surprisingly seen as a technical challenge of coordination and management, and its success defined in how well these challenges are undertaken.

The management process owes as much to the private sector as to public bureaucracy. There is a set of Japanese-style "quality circles"—groups of selected experts to advise on economic development, communications, and cultural developments in the project. Most important is the "circle" of "urban and architectural quality" consisting of experts drawn from architecture, journalism and government departments, at both regional and state levels, the chamber of commerce and industry, and local government. This "circle" was initiated at the start of the project and originally had twenty members chosen by the project manager. The number was increased to thirty-eight in 1993. The "circle" acts as an advisory committee. Both the project manager and the architect claim that the "circle" gives them a source of informed opinion and support in the vast and complex task of running the project. Meetings are held every two months with the participants convening on site to discuss a variety of projects within the overall scheme.

However, an important function of the "circle" is to promote Euralille among urban experts in France. Discussion about the project in the quality circle is restricted to expert opinion. Promotion of the project is integrated into its organization. This happens in a number of ways. One of the first actions of the political leadership was to secure an architect with an international reputation. Each candidate shortlisted by the president of the CUDL was given about two months to work up a half-day presentation of ideas about the project. In the choice of an architect the president sought commitment to the project before any drawing was started. The eventual choice of Rem Koolhaas and his company, the Office for Metropolitan Architecture, lends prestige to the project. In a similar way Euralille tried to encourage a hotel group to join the company, to make a commitment to the project before starting to negotiate about the details of hotel development. Getting an international hotel company onboard would encourage other international investors to risk money in the project.

The SEM Euralille has also invested directly in promoting the project. During the planning work of the project's first two years, one third of Euralille's budget was spent on information and publicity. The publicly funded Lille Grand Palais was the first part of the development to be

completed and has itself a promotional role in bringing business exhibitions and conferences to Lille. Architectural prestige, the support of experts in the "quality circle" and the nominal shareholding of foreign banks were all important in presenting Euralille as an exemplary development. In 1992 Euralille's marketing strategy won the project an award for "urban marketing." It has been argued that the primary role for the public sector in this sort of large urban development project is promotion.
[...]

BEYOND A CERTAIN SCALE, OR TITAN IN SLIPPERS?

Werner Oechslin
Daidalos 61 (1996), 16–29.

"Docti rationem artis intelligunt, indocti voluptatem." Thus, Watelet introduces his article on *effet* (effect) in the *Encyclopédie* of Diderot and d'Alembert. Indeed, the distinction between the understanding of art and its enjoyment has much to do with the question of bigness in architecture and the ways in which it has been regarded. If art's audience and the means by which art is communicated are to be accessed by the artist via the senses, then this distinction becomes critical. The mastery of an artistic medium and its calculated application is one thing; its effect on the viewer is another: "L'effet … est pour le spectateur cette volupté, ce plaisir qu'il cherche & qu'il s'attend à ressentir." The effect is delight and pleasure, sensual pleasure. And Watelet takes it for granted that this a perfectly justifiable expectation: the artist must provide such an effect. This demand, in turn, will change the rules of art itself and will unhinge its autonomy.

Boullée maintains this position with consistency. Regarding architecture he contends that it is the effect of the masses and volumes ("l'effet des corps") that governs everything else: "C'est par les effets que produisent leurs masses sur nos sens que nous distinguons les corps légers des corps massifs." But the rediscovery of Boullée's megalomaniac images in the Modern period should not cause us to suppose that his is an "aesthetics of prisms" oriented only to massing and large size. Boullée speaks of the distinction ("nous distinguons") between light and heavy bodies, regulated "par une juste application." Through the correct and fitting application (of the bodies), the desired effect is attained, the content of which is the appropriate character ("à donner à ses productions le caractère qui leur est propre"). To be sure, the exposition and application of this principle does include the discussion of buildings which seem to stretch endlessly toward heaven and thus elevate and delight us. But even this attempted analogy of form and psychological effect is already qualified in the next sentence: the constitutive principles of architecture, he says, are symmetry and order.

Since his rediscovery in the 1920s, Boullée has inspired the modern imagination precisely with respect to bigness and mass. But a more careful reading reveals that even he gave precedence to regularity, principles and order, in the best Vitruvian tradition. Still, something had changed. Toward the end of his life, Jacques-François Blondel described the buildings of his younger colleague Ledoux as disproportionate and anticanonical; Boullée and Ledoux themselves, on the other hand, claimed to have mastered the rules. "Bigger" architecture can indeed be harmonized with the old principles—over and over again. The corresponding process of perpetual change and accommodation can be continued almost indefinitely and is plainly visible in the "bigger" architecture that has actually been realized. In 1927, in the preface to Heinz and Bodo Rasch's *Wie Bauen?*, Adolf Behne writes that the big cities of the twentieth century "differ from the small towns of the fifteenth century only in scale." But then he criticizes this very thing, this continuing adherence to the rules and the adaptation of reality to them while real change is overlooked: "Bad taste is only the result of holding to an old standard in a different dimension. The prettiest house in Rothenburg enlarged eight or ten times is no longer charming." Indeed, this approach characterizes our usual response to urban growth: always a little higher, a little wider, a little deeper, but no "shift in paradigm" and certainly no architecture of rediscovered bigness!

In the first place, one should be amazed at the enduring continuity of architectural rules that focus on the mastery of bigness and not simply on bigness itself. Le Corbusier's continuing appeal to the all-powerful *ordonnance*—coupled with a warning against false American tendencies and influences—is the best example of this intention and optimism. Meanwhile, every student of architecture will assert that the American skyscraper developed from the multiplication of the number of stories inserted between base and cornice—at a ratio of three to one! A view of the whole, on the other hand, would effortlessly render the "momentous, monumental form of the skyscraper" clear, as Gropius wrote in *Internationale Architektur*. This view of the whole has, however, called attention to bigness as an architectural theme in its own right.

[...] Now the question arises anew as to whether bigness should be considered an aspect of beauty at all. "Whether the emotion of grandeur make a branche of the emotion of beauty, or be entirely distinct from it, is an intricate question," says Lord Kames in *Elements of Criticism*. In the end he decides to regard grandeur as altogether "pleasant," and illustrates his point using Shakespeare and ancient texts. "Bigness in and of itself" has now achieved aesthetic recognition: a undefined balance of indeterminate nature, but for that very reason still a conditional one. This is manifested as well in the discussion of the sublime. In his *Philosophical Enquire into the Origin of our Ideals of the Sublime and Beautiful* (1757), Edmund Burke had treated not only of "magnificence" as one of the sources of the sublime, but also of a specifically architectural "magnificence in building." "To the sublime in building, greatness of dimensions seems requisite." Greatness of dimension is thus a necessary condition for sublime architecture. (After all, one does not choose a statue of Bacchus or Pan to evoke the sublime, but rather a great, muscle-bound Hercules!) But even here, "no greatness in the manner can effectually compensate for the want of proper dimensions." Somehow it still has to be fitting or appropriate. To be sure, we are no longer dealing with an ideal, humanistic theory of proportions. The human body does not owe its beauty to proportion; its many and varied manifestations teach us otherwise.

And if anyone still thinks he can find the ratio of the body in the proportion of the head, Burke informs him: "what a fallacious standard we have chosen." Standards as well as rules are now in crisis—and bigness is set free.

[...] The architecture of the seven wonders of the world again becomes the subject of interest, and with it the "Babylonian." As Goethe stated, "the highest level of architecture is immensity." And under the title "Works of Architecture Built to Unify the Peoples," Hegel treats of that "enormous work of architecture," the Tower of Babel. In tone, this essay is not far removed from Josef Ponten's *Architektur die nicht gebaut wurde* of 1925, a time when the "Hegelites" had long since been succeeded by "Nietzschelites." Ponten began his discussion of that "Babylonian-immense, oriental-colossal idea," the transformation of Mount Athos into a giant statue of Alexander, with the following words: "As a kind of revenge on the all-too-human, on the trivial and the paltry, my love was for those architectural ideas in which the weight of the earth was the least onerous, the freest, the boldest, the largest, all of those of which the sacred word says 'let us build a tower reaching to heaven in order to amaze the peoples,' the Babylonian!"

[...] Roman bigness, Egyptian bigness—American bigness: bigness begins its victory march and allies itself with the new, young nation of America. Walther Rathenau pays tribute to it in his characterization of the "Four Nations," in the chapter on the United States of *Impressionen*: "Without strong sensual pleasure, all of their thinking is directed to the material; the fact rules the land along with its exaggeration: the sensation. To purely material men, this kind of thought and action sometimes seems fantastic. It is so only in the most concrete aspect, in the cult of dimension. Quantity and dimension are for Americans the most important thing, as they are for children in our culture; the superlative is quintessential. 'The biggest boat in the world,' 'the highest tree,' 'the quickest train,' 'the most expensive picture': to them those are things that need no interpretation. Almost all of their writers worship material data and quantities, and even religion approaches the material forms of business or medical establishments."

"Things that need no interpretation"—Quatremère de Quincy had already assessed that as advantageous, the advantage of direct comprehensibility ("indocti voluptatem"). The bigness of the skyscraper needs no explanation in order to be "grasped"—unlike an architecture whose reserved and unobtrusive order abstains from any sensationalism. Is bigness so specifically American, so counter to Western moral sublimation—or maybe just to European moralism? Le Corbusier opposes *ordonnance* to American bigness yet once more, while Gropius recognizes "the momentous, monumental form of the skyscraper," "despite its desultory plan and excess of irrelevant stylistic forms." And even Rem Koolhaas's manifesto "Bigness," reveals on second reading—but not before then!—nothing fundamentally new or different: "Beyond a certain scale, architecture acquires the properties of bigness." Correct, as was noted two hundred years ago: beyond the purview of measure and order, in pre-Grecian times, bigness becomes "pure quantity," "absolute." Koolhaas climbs Mount Everest in spirit to find this out: "because it is there."

In June 1953, after his return to Zürich from a stay in New York on a Rockefeller scholarship, Max Frisch related his American experiences in a talk entitled "Cum grano salis" at a local BSA group. He remarked that "in his home town everything had become much smaller than he remembered: the train station, the square in front of it, the little streets, the dear river with its bridges," and noted "quite in principle": "how very much scale … is a matter of what you're used to." In 1919, at the peak of enthusiasm for Expressionism, J. L. M. Lauweriks wrote an article on "The Titanic in Art" for the journal *Wendingen*. In it, he stated that while he would indeed wish for Prometheus to be unbound, he could do without Titans, or, if need be, would accept at the most one open to human interests, a "Titan in slippers."

THE SCALE CANARD

Richard Plunz

Daidalos 61 (1996), 128–31.

[…] The present global rush for the highest skyscraper boils down to fetishistic ideas about bigness which transcend all rationality, except short-term economic gain. This canard belies an underlying longer-term panic as we arrive at the final moments of the industrial era. The architectural scene accurately reflects this state of affairs. […] No wonder Koolhaas can be so enamored of the mediocrity but incredible power of Wallace K. Harrison, palace architect to the Rockefellers, and fantastic purveyor of the future. Like Harrison's, Koolhaas's work is significant as a period-piece reflection of such power; now for a second generation of postindustrial strategizing. Koolhaas fails to perceive that fighting scale with scale is a dead end. The postindustrial city is not consumptive of physical space as such: it differs from the extensive growth patterns formerly established by the industrial city, with its vast integration of factories and related infrastructure: the railyards and port facilities, for example. The current panic to reuse old infrastructure is understandable especially given the political liabilities of contraction and abandonment: hence, the tendency to fight the scale of abandonment with even more larger-scale spatial development. Nothing can be consumptive enough, however; and the consumerist nature of these programs are marginal relative to the fundamental global economic transformations which are underway. These entirely mediated environments are products of an ersatz socialism of a slightly provincial and politically ephemeral nature; "crowd-pleasing" in a phrase, for regions of labor obsolescence. Obsolescence of the social program, like the work force, is a hallmark of the last manifestation of the "city of consumption." One can imagine that in fifteen years, politicians and bankers may well be ruminating on what to do with Euralille, just as they ruminated on the same site fifteen years ago.

The culture of architecture, like the culture at large, has been nurtured on an expansionist notion of building which implies ever-increasing scale. In fact, now, the opposite process of atrophy is more and more important—"unbuilding." Today, the process of removal can be as important as that of addition, yet architects and urbanists are totally ill-equipped to deal with it, from any point of view. Scale is all that is left to the market, and "business is business," thus the deliberate dumping of obsolete technology from "developed" to "developing" nations. Within the realm of the built environment, this does not just include the relatively simple technologies of the "world's tallest" building. Far more consequential is the question of basis infrastructure. The problems facing Western urbanism, particularly in the period of postwar de-urbanization in the United States, can ill afford to be repeated on ever larger scales elsewhere. In Asia, for example, we begin to see cities which replicate the sprawl of Los Angeles or Phoenix on a scale far more vast: de-urbanization without automobiles, enforced by the ersatz socialism of centralized power in a region of labor commodification. Of course, this can be a difficult issue, especially given the ideal of the "American way-of-life" which the global power of the US media continues to promulgate. The antithesis of infrastructural investment is short-term profit.

[…]

THE TEST OF THE CONSTRUCTION SITE

Jean-Louis Cohen
Lotus international 86 (1995), 50–59.

Few urban development schemes of the modern day have been so praised before being carried out, and few have had such insistent institutional sponsors as the complex coordinated by Rem Koolhaas and brought into service in 1994. Long before the first high-speed trains reached the metropolis in the north, Euralille was made the subject of a genuine press campaign celebrating the "concept" of its architecture. Thus for a long time the real purpose of the project seems to have been more the communication of images than the realization of a program of commercial offices and public facilities at the point of connection between a nineteenth-century terminus (Lille-Flandres) and a transit station for the High-Speed Trains linking northwestern Europe with the tunnel under the Channel.

At the same time, an unprecedented development in the long history of public architecture in France, a "board of quality" was set up, under the chairmanship of François Barré and with the participation of Joseph Belmont, to oversee the implementation of the original intentions of the consultation that was held in 1988. Based not on projects, but exclusively on an oral declaration of their intentions for the site, this procedure had set Norman Foster, Oswald Matthias Ungers, Vittorio Gregotti, and Rem Koolhaas against four French teams: Jean-Paul Viguier and Jean-François Jodry, Yves Lion, Michel Macary, and Claude Vasconi, and had been carried away by the rhetoric of the Dutchman.

The political support from which Rem Koolhaas's project had later benefited had been both persistent and massive. The determination of Pierre Mauroy, the Socialist mayor of Lille and former prime minister under François Mitterrand, to get "his own" *grand projet* and to bring it to completion, in the teeth of the erosion of his electoral support and the rise of the right wing amongst the city's middle class, had been unwavering. It was combined with the decisive commitment of the Deposit and Consignment Office, a para-State banking organization directed by Robert Lion, which had been constantly involved in the policy of the *grands travaux* during Mitterrand's two seven-year terms, and in this case underwrote the financing of the operation. This support had been made even more necessary by the fact that an extraordinary range of technical means had been deployed, in particular to drain the land, where it had proved necessary to build an impermeable wall to hold back the water. The lowering of the ground water level, an action whose necessity had been disputed, had required considerable resources, which could certainly have been used in a more visible way in the budget for construction.

Much more than an act of will—or power—on the part of its architect, it seems as if Euralille belongs to the typically French family of major urban projects, such as the office districts of La Défense or of the Part-Dieu, to the east of Lyon, with which the operation in Lille has more than one point in common. These projects are characterized by the superimposition of infrastructures with a configuration of their own, before any architectural decision is made, which are then overlaid with commercial buildings and offices. The consequence of this has been the production of a dilated space, which has very quickly become obsolescent. In each case, they illustrate an architectural process that has combined, as Oriol Bohigas so rightly pointed out a few years ago, the frenzied vision of Jules Verne with the formal mediocrity of the surveyor. [...]

So the question raised by Euralille right from the start was whether the culture, intellectual capacity, talent, and energy of Rem Koolhaas would allow him to break with the past and improve on earlier experiences. The expectation that he could was based in particular on the way in which the plans for the new district would be able to draw on the analyses of the modern metropolis on which Koolhaas has been working for the last twenty years. What finer terrain on which to put them to the test, in fact, than this fringe of a city cleared of its fortifications and where the combination of underground public transport systems and high-rise constructions was almost natural? In a way it was a question of the materialization in advance of that founding cliche of Americanism, the vertical city, extending both upward and downward, and which has been one of the driving forces of the metropolitan congestion to which Koolhaas had devoted his *Delirious New York* in 1978.

Notwithstanding the laudatory tones of many French critics, the disappointment has been as great as the expectation was high. Even before the completion of the first stage, the urban spaces and buildings of Euralille have revealed that the promise of the initial sketches and the later models has only been very partially kept. Alongside the compact and well-structured whole that constitutes the center of Lille, undoubtedly one of the big French cities that has had the greatest success in containing the flight into the suburbs, the test site that Koolhaas has tackled has not gone beyond the condition of a collage in which the principles appear to be simplistic. An assemblage of constructed segments whose connections are still problematical, Euralille's relations with its neighbors are painful. While the aggression is sometimes on the part of the latter, as in the case of a bank situated next to the city whose placid vulgarity has a jarring effect, the articulation of the commercial center that leads to the area closest to the historic center of the city is feeble. Seen from the square of the old station, the district looks like a new gray object added on to the shabby vestiges of the real estate policies that followed in the wake of the railroads. On the other side of the railroad tracks, the Congress Building looks as if it has been swallowed up by the apartment buildings, in spite of the gap created by an expressway, destined, it is true, to become a quieter boulevard. On its other sides, Euralille adjoins isolated areas of a surprisingly bucolic calm, such as a stud farm separated from the station by the expressway.

There is not one of the internal articulations between the constituent parts of the operation that does not pose a problem, and the borders between the individual programs have been hacked out in the roughest fashion. Singularly inhospitable on the side facing the old station of Lille-Flandres, Jean Nouvel's commercial center constitutes a closed entity, that is half opened onto the city by a gap on the side of the station. [...] At the meeting of the low ridge of the commercial center, the Lille-Europe station, and the fairly transparent viaduct designed by François Deslaugiers, the Place de l'Europe, long dedicated to Le Corbusier, is considered to offer the only public space in Euralille that is at once open and protected. To judge by the sketches of OMA, the interaction of the different architectural orders was supposed to produce an animated urban scene on the edge of a canal. It is still difficult to evaluate its function, yet there can be no doubt that the intensity of the life that goes on there will be directly dependent on the pressure that the commercial center will exert on what is its only outlet into the open air. [...]

The two types of space associated with the new station have completely escaped OMA. This is especially the case with the "Piranesian" space in which the different modes of transport should have been projected to accompany the escalators linking the station to the subway. Entrusted to the local architect Jean Pattou, this place, which was undoubtedly the one where Rem Koolhaas's playful approach would have found its best support, has foundered in a heartbreaking regionalism. More daringly, the high-rise office blocks soar above the nave of the station in a rather empty gesture of heroism. [...]

Once the general principle of a triangular arrangement had been established, with its edges punctuated by the lines of the towers, and setting aside the Congress Building, to which I shall return later, Koolhaas's work will have consisted essentially in following up this group of projects. It is legitimate to wonder what would have happened to Euralille if the operation had not been carried out by architects like Nouvel and Portzamparc. This vulnerability of the overall choices to the personality of the architects chosen reveals just how theoretical were the rules of assembly and of definition of the relationships among the objects constructed. What we seem to find here, notwithstanding Koolhaas's declarations on urbanism, carried with a degree of self-satisfaction by certain American publications that have tended to create the image of a new Le Corbusier (such as the "Urbanism vs. Architecture"-issue of *ANY*), is a sort of renunciation of any attempt to work on the raw material of the city. At Euralille the energy seems to have been expended not on the structural elements, but on the surface of the ground or on crossings of it that were abandoned in the end. The aesthetic pleasure expressed by OMA's innumerable drawings representing slender spurs of expressways and airy footbridges suggests an emphasis on image, on the visual rhetoric of a somewhat antiquated modernity: today, happily, footbridges and slabs have been brought into question, and even demolished, in all the operations inherited from the 1960s (including Lyon-Part-Dieu ...).

What about the only building whose design and construction was left completely in the hands of OMA? Shifted to the eastern side of the tracks of the Lille-Flandres station, the ovoid volume of the Palais des Congrès, initially called Congrexpo, sums up the ambitions and reveals the limits of the specifically architectural work of Koolhaas. It is not irrelevant to point out that the building is, in its present configuration, only a figure of resignation, since the initial design was for a bridge structure spanning the railroad lines. Its isolated location, accessible by tortuous underground passages, is therefore a makeshift.

Measured by the yardstick of aircraft carriers or zeppelins in seductive graphic comparisons, the ellipse belongs without doubt to the order of Bigness on which Rem Koolhaas has been insisting for a while. Nevertheless, this scale is hardly perceptible, as the view of the building—which is segmented by the horizontal divisions of its facade—is conditioned by the infrastructures and by the neighboring buildings, like those of Albert Laprade's administrative district. Even though Koolhaas has long presented the fact that the concert hall communicates with the exhibition hall by transverse walls primarily as a functional innovation, the grouping will not be able to keep this totally theoretical promise, since the acoustic requirements of the different types of facility are contradictory. With the disappearance of the generous utopia of the program, it is on the differentiation of these spaces that the work of OMA and its partner from Lille, François Delhay, has concentrated, and this is without doubt the best that the building has to offer: a spacious Grand Palais of exhibitions communicating easily with the outside, and surrounded by well-defined halls; a complex pattern of distribution presenting a sequence of spatial experiences that causes the staircases to branch out and leads to the three meeting rooms; the effective curve of the tiers of the Zenith, the hall for rock concerts whose form generates that of the envelope, on the north side.

The semicircular structure of the Zenith constitutes, along with the section of the building faced in concrete that has been treated as if it were a caricature of ashlar masonry, the most solid part of the construction, whose exterior combines a brutalism, which will undoubtedly be incomprehensible to the people who attend congresses there, with a disturbing fragility. This impression of vulnerability to the ravages of time can also be seen in the treatment of the large congress hall and of numerous spaces inside, as if Koolhaas had preferred to ensure that his conceptual sketches and models would be preserved in a museum over giving any *firmitas* to his buildings. On this occasion his ability to create fairylands on paper is given a disappointing translation into actual constructions, which are going to age rapidly.

If the slogan of Bigness remains associated, as in this case, with an architecture verging on modern shoddiness, it is to be feared that it will prove sterile. Yet Koolhaas's interventions on smaller scales have shown his ability to approach public buildings—the Kunsthal in Rotterdam—or domestic ones—the Villa dall'Ava—in terms that are at once pertinent and refined. Unfortunately, in a project that is descended directly from the tertiary utopias of the 1960s, what we find is a certain disenchantment, a realism bordering on cynicism, in spite of the thrill of anticipation stirred up by the mass of studies and images he built up over the course of seven years.

THE VOLUNTARY PRISONER OF ARCHITECTURE: LILLE GRAND PALAIS

Jacques Lucan
Domus 774 (1995), 25–26.

A circle is a regular and closed geometric figure if ever there was one: generated from a sole point, its center. An ellipse already contains, potentially, a fissiparity: two focuses linked by a large axis, orientate the figure whose minimal complexity contains the possibility of a division. Lille Grand Palais is not a circle; it is an ellipse. Lille Grand Palais is not an absolutely unitary building because it is not centered on one program only. It is made up of three programs, which are as many slices brutally cut out of the ellipse: a rock hall for 5,500, a congress center with three auditoriums and a restaurant; and a 20,000-square-meters exhibition facility.

These programs need not have been contained in a single figure. If they are, it is because, arranged in succession and parallel to one another, they are supposed to be able to maintain relations, their contacts and rubbings, their oppositions and complementarities being likely to intensify the uses of a building once again presented as a sort of "condenser" of energies. If the three programs can in effect work independently of each other, they can also open up to one another on the occasion of more exceptional events, to create an inner depth of 300 meters. From the point of view of its overall figure, Lille Grand Palais therefore witnesses a rejection of all fragmentation. Its architecture, as Koolhaas points out, is thus "scandalously simple."

This scandalous simplicity was not however the outcome of an immediate "discovery." Before Congrexpo (the initial name of the Grand Palais) became enclosed in the form of an ellipse, he had first tried, through a number of procedures, to span, like a bridge, the pattern of roads and railways; he had subsequently designed a triangular socle that followed the lines defined by the same road and rail infrastructure bordering the site; and finally, he had mixed and overlapped the programs into a solution that did not have the radical, parallel simplicity of its final score.

The choice of the ellipse thus seems to have been the logical and ineluctable conclusion to an initially hesitant process, the project having surrendered to the negative reasons of an "uninhabitable" and thankless site. By a resolute, affirmative gesture, all compassion toward context had to be quelled. In the inextricable skein of roads and railways, a given expanse dreaded as a kind of limit situation, the Grand Palais creeps into its shell to resist all dislocation and dissolution. The ellipse is the minimal act of delimitation. Lacking the "purity" of a circle, it makes alterations and irregularities, inflexions and declensions, variations and repetitions possible.

When all is said and done, Lille Grand Palais stands in splendid isolation. Koolhaas seems blatantly to flout the architects agglutinated a stone's throw from there, on the other side of the roads and railways. Are not Jean Nouvel, Peter Rice and Jean-Marie Duthilleul, Christian de Portzamparc, Claude Vasconi and François Deslaugiers and the like, all locked in the maelstrom, in the resounding accumulation of Euralille's "triangle of stations," while he, Koolhaas, stands aloof at once free and a prisoner of his island?

It would be tedious here to dwell on the formal as much as on the technical inventions adopted by Koolhaas at Lille Grand Palais. The inventions describe an arc that reaches from the bright ideas of a do-it-yourself manipulator of ordinary materials, to the development of sophisticated technical devices necessitated notably by the large scale of the work and by the tightness of its construction budget.

As far as the DIY is concerned, we would mention for example the extraordinary 500-seat auditorium at the congress center. Its suspended ceiling is made of translucent polycarbonate corrugated slabs with a strange geometry of irregular framings. One of its lateral walls possesses a doubled glass woolfacing that is visible behind the same polycarbonate slabs. The pattern of the amphitheater lets the access corridors descend sinuously, with nonchalance, to the rows of seats, which are individually colored by a palette that creates an aleatory stippled composition.

On the sophisticated technical side, developed with Ove Arup and Cecil Balmond, we would mention, for example, the structure of the large exhibition hall, the hollow posts of which are also ventilation conduits, freeing it from all the encumbrance of outer housings. The roof frame allies beams reduced to the essential traits of their structural necessities, and small composite foliated-glued wood beams and metal trellising; with small beams that design a regularly ribbed ceiling.

By their diversity, Koolhaas's choices are thus at the antipodes of any exalted constructional prowess of the kind entailed by a large structure homogeneously covering a uniform building. It should be noted here that most of his buildings, from the Dance Theater in The Hague to the Villa dall'Ava at St. Cloud and to the Kunsthal in Rotterdam, had already accustomed us to the taste of "impurity" and its numerous surprises. And we are used by now to iconoclastic inventions that are certainly not exempt from jubilation but which are also not without unconstraint. Indeed their freedom from conventional standards of comfort sometimes borders on insolence.

For it is there that Lille Grand Palais keeps up its harsh if not aggressive appearance. In the use of materials violently stripped bare, juxtaposed and assembled edge to edge, without "details" or elements of transition or articulation. In the atmosphere deliberately formed by rugged contrasts between the three programs or, in the congress center, between the three auditoriums and the distributory and exit spaces. In a light that goes from the almost dazzling whiteness of the large exhibition hall lobby, to the almost crepuscular gray of the atrium and foyer in the congress center.

So Koolhaas looks as if he had set out to provoke, disconcert and put off anyone coming to a congress, exhibition or trade fair. Concert fans may, perhaps, be the only ones to be seduced immediately, by the exciting discomfort of the rock hall. Lille Grand Palais, by adding, juxtaposing and connecting different programs, adopting technical and constructional solutions specific to them and tailored to particular settings, is a deliberately hybrid building.

[...] In Lille, to explain and illustrate the principle of addition used for the programmatic components of Congrexpo, Koolhaas has relied this time on a cabalistic formula: Congrexpo = Z + C + E, where Z = Zenith (the name given, in France, to big rock concert halls), C = Congress and E = Exhibition. It will be noted here that this equation is of the same type as that of the "complete work" of OMA, announced a long time ago and now eagerly awaited in New York: *S,M,L,XL*, that is, Small + Medium + Large + Extra Large. For Koolhaas, additive logic has paradoxically multiplicative effects. For example, the peripheral envelope of Lille Grand Palais is defined by three types of facade (plain cladding; double skin cladding; and exceptional, "sublime" type). But these facades can be endowed with different qualities: transparency, translucence or opacity. In other words: 3 types × 3 qualities = a range of 9 possibilities of facades.

Additive logic therefore sparks a movement beyond all mechanical determinism. It becomes rapidly impossible, if not illusory, to control a multiplication of situations or architectural effects difficult to foresee. It is there that

Koolhaas describes the urbanistic logic of the Grand Palais architecture, and the creation of a potential to be developed. This is how he manages to reassert his skepticism toward architecture, or again to repeat that architectural writing rises from the unconscious, as if all questioning of this work could thereby only be lost in the unfathomable depths of a personality.

Meanwhile personality is certainly relevant here. For Lille Grand Palais, being the first truly big building built by Koolhaas, will certainly have allowed him to break through a stage in his reflections: "Bigness is ultimate architecture." For the major competitions in 1989, notably that of the National Library of France in Paris, and that of the Zentrum für Kunst und Medientechnologie at Karlsruhe, Koolhaas had already enunciated the 4 theorems, or 4 "points," of his architecture of "Three Big Buildings," or "buildings of a third type": autonomy of parts; the liberating potential of the elevator; interior and exterior as independent projects; impact "beyond good and evil." With Lille, Koolhaas adds a fifth "point," of astounding radicality, which makes the Grand Palais a veritable "objet trouvé": "Fuck context."

There is nothing to be astonished about, therefore, if the "innocence" constantly desired and claimed by Koolhaas to "rediscover the true fire of modernity," makes itself heard in ever more insistent Nietzschean accents. If urbanism must become a "Gay Science," it is that Bigness would have to do with a new sort of city that would replace the old one: "Bigness no longer needs the city: it is the city."

This affirmation lends all its significance to Lille Grand Palais and to its splendid isolation, while also allowing us to wonder whether this announcement, this prophesy of new times, is not that of an apprentice-sorcerer. To end with a parable, let us go back to the Downtown Athletic Club in New York previously evoked as a metaphor of the metropolitan condition. What did it announce? It announced, according to Koolhaas, the separation of mankind into two tribes: the tribe of those capable of utilizing all the equipment of modernity, that is, the "bachelors" of the club; and the tribe comprising the rest of the traditional human race, that is, those who do not belong to the club. One might well ask, while deaf to the accusations of unpardonable tenderness or sentimental feebleness, if it is necessary today, for whatever purpose it may serve, to step up the contrast ... as at Lille.

THIS WHOLE CENTURY

Bruno Fortier
L'Architecture d'Aujourd'hui 298 (1995), 18.

There is no doubt, in this whole Euralille affair, that it is the wise, placid mayor Pierre Mauroy who will remain the ultimate difficulty. An explanation will need to be given as to how such an affable man, who could have consolidated his domain bit by bit, ended up thinking he was in charge of a rocket ship rather than an Airbus. Such a confrontation and commotion came about that those responsible would not have been able to tell him if Jaurès was a metro station, a mathematician or an exiled *communard*, but he thought they were so sure of themselves, so devoid of any prejudice, that nothing was going to dissuade him from entrusting them with the party he had in mind.

So, why don't we all, including Mauroy, take a look at what might have happened? Was it a desire to forget, to get away from the old, protracted caress of rain on the brick that had always surrounded him? Was it the drunkenness of a leftist union that found itself united at the controls of the first TGV? Or rather the prestigious "quality circle": all those intellectuals distracting him with Pollock, intriguing him with Oldenburg, regaling him with talk of Hong Kong and the blazing city for which he had to head ... The fact remains that something got so out of control one day that old Europe, which has seen plenty of this kind of thing and has never been left behind in terms of incongruity, should have come up with—a mere stone's throw from the pinnacles of working-class Lille—the unlikeliest and ugliest, the most unexpected and without a doubt the most energetic of all the *grands projets*.

But let's get back to what happened and to the mechanism that must have been set in motion by the TGV and the gamble that one day Lille would finally wake up from its slumber. When this project began, there was an idea that time, as it was for Swift, might prove sufficiently serene that everything would be within reach. A feeling that Paris, Antwerp and Düsseldorf would eventually lay down their weapons and become principalities. A certainty that a bet needed to be made, that this great shrinkage needed to be anticipated by bringing aboard the most sophisticated institutions. Enter Jean-Paul Baïetto, on whom everything was supposed to have rested—the setting up of the operation and the likelihood of a bet already won. All the data would be available, even if there was a lack of someone to take charge, a theoretical Stravinsky. A Rem Koolhaas chosen by interview, at which it is not hard to imagine what he might have said (that Lille was a comet and that it would be the ultimate madness to stop it and that it was there, he could feel it, that everything would play out); asserting squarely, with that nutty Buster Keaton air we all know so well, that not only was he annoyed with the twentieth century but that he had never had confidence in his own projects. A perfect misunderstanding, in which, looking at the members of the jury, talking to them about the future and the times that were just around the corner, he had already assembled the planets, the flying saucers and the methods borrowed from Lissitzky, the Smithsons' Berlin and Le Corbusier…

The plans were quickly completed, as were countless models—hasty, ever-changing, in nauseating apple green, neon red and faded blue—the lively, "nice" towers that so far only Portzamparc has managed to brighten up, and all the "Piranesian wells": a metro on an air cushion, magnetic TGVs, a Renault-Espace climbing up on spirals to the shores of a project the most surprising aspect of which is that it should ever have been built at all.

Not exactly, that's true, not quite in its entirety: some towers ended up foundering, others—by Vasconi—are still under construction; the Palais des Congrès, originally a low-rise structure and bridge, has become a stranded saucer. In the end, nothing else remains of the fine layout and the breaks in perspective heralded by the ground plan. But Koolhaas will tell you that all this was foreseen and that the role of a plan, if it has to exist at all, is not to anticipate, even less to give orders, but to be the prey for dreamers who, bit by bit, will tear it apart. Form without appearance, localization without outline, the constant theorizing of which is somewhat annoying, but for which it cannot be said the current architects were not prepared. The whole secret of Euralille, everything that is strange about this great upsurging of sheet metal and signs, of cladding and angles, is that the architects who came together did not seem keen to do anything other than rub shoulders with one another. We could, of course, imagine Duthilleul sticking a peristyle outside the TGV, Portzamparc sealing up a block or Nouvel obediently respecting a line. But it is first and foremost a collage that Euralille seems to usher in, a definitive and literally unrelenting mishmash; it is not to Koolhaas the urban planner that it traces its paternity but to the fine connoisseur of modernity that he is. Familiar with "isms" and the bizarreness of the abstract, long aware of the ease with which the most straightforward of plans can break down: sowing doubt among order, interfering with the most expertly constructed analysis and opening up a Pandora's box beneath our feet. The conceptual Moriarty he has always been seemed immediately to have imagined that Deslaugiers would transform "Rue Le Corbusier" into a scarab beetle and that Portzamparc would take up the Surrealist idea of a coffin table from Matisse. Predicting that Nouvel would not hesitate for a moment to make an Olympic descent from the roof of his supermarket and that he himself would retain only from the flying saucer that Alison and Peter Smithson had once suggested the unrestrained gigantism of an object that it takes you a good minute to go past on the train. The time to see that this too is not the pure volume you might imagine, that it has nothing, really nothing, of the creamy charlotte a Saarinen or a Philip Johnson might have baked, and that it borrows from *Moby Dick* the wrinkles, scars and harpoons of a huge sperm whale these journeys would eventually ravage.

An infernal process that must have been slow and difficult to bring to a conclusion, but its result is here to see: thundering (because Lille, undoubtedly, does seem to be waking up) and unsatisfying (it takes a good dose of patience to find the foot of the Palais des Congrès behind three motorways), but, most importantly, also destructive. Between the perfect curtain wall that Portzamparc designed and the quickly dispersed undulation Koolhaas chose to use, the tower that leans, rests and takes a seat at this hypermarket where everything would be perfect (the glass, the signs, the rhythm) if Nouvel had made a screen of his roof as per his design, it is this century—this whole century—that stands up to be counted: telling us that if there are still forms left, they will no longer be ordered, that if they move us it will not be by their beauty, and that their construction, their deep armature and their stability are the very last thing that should be asked of them.

We no longer know who is right and who is wrong: us, passing behind the Palais des Congrès, jealous of a facade we would never have dared to torture to such a point, or the 1960s architects—mystics of shock concrete and demi gods of molded plastic—who would have eaten their hats if they could see the extent to which Mies could have got it so wrong.

CRITICISM HAS LOST ITS BEARINGS

Jean Attali
Euralille: The Making of a New City Center, ed. Isabelle Menu and Frank Vermandel (Basel: Birkhäuser, 1996), 184–86.

The severity with which the best French critics greeted Euralille's first constructions is astonishing. When so many voices accuse in unison, when there is so much aggressiveness, sometimes one ends up suspecting that there is an inhibition or a mental block at work. Rem Koolhaas wrote that "the desire to alter the destiny of an entire city remains taboo."[1] Criticism recoils before transgression. Euralille reflects a destabilizing force onto the conditions of judgment: that of an urban gesture which projects architecture "beyond good and evil."[2] Between conceptual advance and critical backwardness (between prophecy and hysteria), the project seeks its meaning in an era, beyond the interests of a policy of reputation, even beyond the image—because it is the failure of the image which defines/conditions the imaginary. The city is the setting of our entire culture, the resource and fund from which we draw our arguments, from which we forge our concepts. When this setting spreads out, distorts itself, becomes the direct object of our productions, the project takes over where thought leaves off, radically displacing its criteria, its passions, altering its aims ...

What then are the subjects and terms of the debate? The primary criticism concerns the scope of the enterprise as well as its public meaning: a sort of unholy alliance between architecture and politics. The energy spent in Lille recalls the era of Le Corbusier's great urban sermons. The ghost of the Soviet Palace, or the Voisin and Obus plans in Algiers hover over the Northern metropolis. Le Corbusier, as Jean-Louis Cohen long ago explained, "feels the intense need (despite his repeated failures) for a big order—sometimes also hardened by the utopic pressure/tension of big modernization projects—to carry out the major transgressions toward which his work is targeted."[3] Alain Guiheux resorts, in the exhibition catalogue *La ville, art et architecture en Europe, 1870–1993,* to the same references to cast doubt on the relevance of Koolhaas's discourse: the architect of the Universe, he who wants to teach us a lesson. [...] "Metropolitan development undermines the foundations, the mental universe of a profession ... Under these circumstances, the urban philosophy of Le Corbusier can only develop in a scenic context/setting, that of public relations projects albeit rather desperate ones." Could reality have taken a different course for this city within Lille, had we let it be molded by our preconceptions of cities such as Buenos Aires, Montevideo and São Paulo? "The imaginary world of the magician comes at the end of the metropolitan development in a flight from reality."[4]

The magic of ubiquitous thought, projects without any real territory but carried along by a fantastic desire for image, the only thing left at the end would seem to be a totalitarian dream. Euralille is accused of being utopic in terms of its goals, authoritarian in terms of its decision-making system, and badly adapted to the city's structural and recreational space. But who is in a position to judge the project? Who then—the critic, the architect or his client—fuels the debate over the ends and means of urban policy? For as soon as one moves from visionary postulates to the constructed project, the issue of judgment takes on a different meaning, the burden of proof switches sides. With its multitude of projects, sleeping partners, individual architects, the urban project, once finalized, expresses political ambition and established its primacy over the architectural project. Conversely, Euralille represents the paradox of urbanism exacerbated by architecture for having constantly sought out the formal expression of economic strategies and the aptitude of overscaled projects to constitute a new type of landscape. In such a way the urban form seems to have been identified here with constraints that tended to explode it, while the expression of the city was strenghtened over and above the paroxysm of its technical edification.

The second type of criticism is aimed at the development side of Euralille and lambasts its "contempt for the existing city." To the rejection of modern urbanism (as if we had learned nothing from it and as if our experience of the city hadn't been permanently marked by it either) can be added the incantatory evocation of the urban fabric/tissue and the traditional mix. How can the problem of the bonding between the historical city and its contemporary extension be resolved? It is in terms of functions and uses that Euralille invents an answer. In the historical city, we find spaces being put to uses that differ from those originally conceived (the lofts of New York City, the studios of Faubourg Saint-Antoine in Paris, etc.). Urban plasticity reveals itself in this aptitude for overimpression and overdetermination. Through these changing uses, the city demonstrates its capacity for absorption: it even gives ironic confirmation of this every time it manages to digest its most indigestible monuments. But there comes a time when this resource becomes exhausted, where the relationship between space and use reverses itself. The planned use then preceded the space and defines it, to the extent that signs of this mutation are written onto the plan: the plan is no longer working toward the gradual completion of the drawing; it flees following its own rules and course of action, freeing itself from interior constraints that have previously held it down.

The block plan as a segmented phenomenon [...] what counts is not its control, nor its appropriation, but rather its reshaping, its redefinition, the possibility of attributing characteristics to a territory which put it in contact with other frontiers, a new periphery. The crux of the block plan thus consists of exerting pressure on the limits, of establishing alternative vectors and speeds within a given field. However, the Euralille plan contains only directions. The only major axis is that of the TGV line, which is open but then again mostly underground. Neither grid nor slab, nor cutting by blocks, nor stratification by bands—on the contrary, a very free form, born of the positioning of the functions along the site's main boundaries. Like a line that gradually becomes thicker and thicker, branching off into several different directions, the plan rises and splits itself. The main lines divide themselves, inside as well as out: suspended galleries or overhangs along the facades of the Jean Nouvel building; intersection of the streets and the roof inside the shopping mall; intersection of the Le Corbusier viaduct with the slope of the Place de l'Europe; superimposing of the different levels of the station that overlook the tracks; the line of vision from the train windows toward the belfries of the city. The shores of the site floating along and above the major roads accentuate the impression of a city that has been designed as a cross section, as if the urban plan itself had begun to waver under the violent impact of the force that traverses it.

[...] The third criticism is inspired by constructions deemed disappointing because they are inadequately "articulated" or clustered together. Perhaps the variety or the incompatibility of architectural styles calls the traditional figure of the head architect into question, governing not only the mass plan and the volumetric envelope, but also the lines of the full-scale working diagram and the nature of the facades which were supposed to guarantee the unity of the composition. To the almighty accusation is thus added—between the lines—doubts about the ability to manage multiple architectural teams. But the clash of forms and the aesthetic discord are no more than histrionic manifestations of these "constructed characters"[5]—as jarring in their critical rivalries as Gilles Deleuze's "conceptual characters"[6]—that Rem Koolhaas seems to be making, speak here in the architectural equivalent of indirect free discourse. "In his subconscious mind, there is a reservoir of people, older or younger than himself, with stronger nerves or more primitive or more brutal instincts."[7] Buildings are like the voices of the other in the creator's mind (novelist or filmmaker, philosopher or architect), the project's progression within a vision that is openly exposed to urban polyvalence. Such would be the meaning of an architectural subject enriched by the city's contradictory cultures. The variety of projects and their coexistence within construced spaces reveal the ability to adapt to usages: here a rock concert hall, there a business school, furthermore spaces left unoccupied used as artist's studios. A hotel, some apartments, student housing, a "residence hotel." Behind the assembled facades, interstices, pathways, spaces negotiated on a case by case basis. The functional optimism on display at Euralille is perhaps what reduces the tension that has tended to spring up everywhere between urbanism and architecture. Does this spatial democracy have its own particular aesthetic? It would be found in this resistance to formal unity, and in the openly-avowed confidence in the mixing of genres, despite the fascinating shape of the overall project.

"What is important about this place," according to Rem Koolhaas, "is not where it is but where it leads and at what pace—in other words, to what extent it belongs to the rest of the world." The distance at which the Congrexpo, project centerpiece, sits (Lille Grand Palais is nothing more than a non-name for a nonloved monument) symbolizes its strategic retreat. The palais is distanced only that we might better behold its exemplary nature. What is true of the entire Euralille site is true a fortiori of this vessel, simultaneously bridge and castle. Koolhaas invents spatial devices which directly link a territorial and urban vision to an architectural system. The attempt to encompass within architecture the wealth of motivations and the apparent disorder of the innumerable functions that urban life must manage, is coupled with the intuition that it is possible to stage—spectacularly and convincingly—the technical and spatial resolution of this complexity. The nine facades of Congrexpo alone summarize this philosophy of the city, engineering and art. They are a catalog of references to civil engineering, to industrial construction, to stadium architecture, to curtain-wall cladding, to the open-air theater—but for the purpose of parodying them, of subvering them with all the jubilation of the great Constructivists. These facades are shores. In their own way, they express movement, the tendency toward self-projection into the distance.

"Beyond good and evil?" Understand: when it is impossible to decide between what results from the mass of limitations to which one is subject and what is the product of the nobility of the wished-for spaces, that is, in the hope of producing a new synthesis which is absolutely active or openly utopic, which doesn't escape aesthetic or technical compromises with functionalism, but which turns it into the target and the decisive feature in the ability to create architecture.

1 OMA/Rem Koolhaas, *Lille* (Paris: Institut Français d'Architecture/Carte Segrete, 1990).

2 An idea which is regularly taken up by Rem Koolhaas, according to which the scale of bigness radically modifies the conditions of architecture, to the point of rendering design conventions inoperable, and which henceforth only function as preconceived notions.

3 Jean-Louis Cohen, "Droite-gauche: Invite à l'action," in *Le Corbusier, une encyclopédie,* ed. Jacques Lucan (Paris: Editions du Centre Pompidou, 1987), 309–13.

4 Alain Guiheux, "L'architecture de l'Univers," in *La ville, art et architecture en Europe, 1870–1993,* ed. Jean Dethier and Alain Guiheux (Paris: Editions du Centre Pompidou, 1994), 290.

5 See Emmanuel Doutriaux, feature article on Euralille, *L'Architecture d'Aujourd'hui* 280 (1992).

6 See Gilles Deleuze, *Qu'est-ce que la philosophie?* (Paris: Éditions de Minuit, 1991).

7 Rem Koolhaas, "Urban Operations," *D: Columbia Documents of Architecture and Theory* 3 (1993), 25–57.

COMPOSITION AND OBLIQUE VIEWS

Stanislaus von Moos
Euralille: The Making of a New City Center, ed. Isabelle Menu and Frank Vermandel (Basel: Birkhäuser, 1996), 187–88.

As a laboratory experiment carried out on a 1/1 scale, this construction presents a challenge. One of OMA's objectives for this project was to highlight both infrastructure and economic dynamics (rather than dissimulating them), to produce architectural results that fully measure up to the urban ambition. This is understandable given the institutional context of architecture in France where, at least since the Eiffel Tower was built, high technology has been de rigueur, with all that this implies in terms of rapid obsolescence. Examples abound in major public projects such as airports and museums (Roissy and the Centre Pompidou), the fabulous TGV stations in the middle of nowhere, where there are four arrivals and four departures a day (as is the case at Lyon-Satolas), not to mention the gigantic office towers and shopping arcades worthy of the Houston suburbs, planted in the heart of Paris, or very nearly (the Tour Montparnasse).

Seen from outside France (my perspective happens to be Zürich, Switzerland), this experiment should be perceived—by architects in any case—as both liberating and challenging, even if it should not be taken as an example to be followed to the letter. Is it pure coincidence that the city of Zürich, which can be compared to Lille in terms of size and position, stands at the opposite extreme in terms of urban planning? It is not that the business world has lost interest, but the "gnomes" have long since understood that their hold would be that much more effective if they showed a certain degree of sensitivity to cultural heritage, and if they respected "context," environment and tradition—in short, if they presented their projects as "embellishments." This is why the Hauptbahnhof Sudwest project, that is, the massive expansion of the central station with office and other buildings which is currently in the design phase (a project which is comparable in scope to Euralille, minus the TGV), is being carried out with such extreme discretion, to avoid leaving the slightest trace on the skyline. Offices? Fine, as long as they look like apartment buildings whenever possible. In fact, the existing station already sits on a galaxy of multilevel shopping arcades. One can't miss it—like the Lille station—the difference being that it is entirely underground, that it remains nonexistent as far as the urban physique is concerned.

And what about public officials? Their role consists of ensuring that growth does not stray beyond a timid reinterpretation of what existed before the last economic boom. Contrary to the situation of the 1930s, when the city felt the winds of change and innovation, even on an urban planning level, today's consensus is cool enough to encompass left and right, pink and green, democracy within conceptual stagnation. This stagnation reflects a curious mix of ecological concerns and a sense of guilt, to which a rather touching dash of hope for cultural renewal is sometimes thrown in for good measure. Given the architectural record of the 1960s and 1970s, this state of affairs is not totally lacking in plausibility.

Assuming that the Zürich approach could, like that of Lille, signal its readiness to take things seriously, the OMA project may offer both an alternative model and a curious historical episode, a point of departure for possible futures, and an achievement that will remain both sui generis and typically French. It is unique in its romantic celebration of anarchy and expansion. It owes its elegance to an ingenious plan which takes urban givens and traffic flow patterns as a launching pad for the composition of volumes in space. The old notion of "composition" gives some idea of the abyss which exists between the impressive triangular Forum rising up from the TGV station toward the shopping arcade, an authentically urban space (a "core," to borrow the CIAM term), and the techno-futuristic obsession mentioned above.

The OMA catalog *Lille*, published by the Institut Français d'Architecture in 1990, features a series of graphics which illustrate, among other things, the aesthetic paradigms which reigned when the project was being conceived. They allow us to decipher the urban chaos that was Lille, analogous to the geometric debris that floats through space in a Malevich painting. Suprematism is without a doubt the missing link between Lille, such as it is, and the gigantic sloping platform which forms the roof of the shopping mall—a platform whose edges are pierced by the prisms of the office towers. But in its ongoing dialogue with the visual arts, OMA has not stopped at the three-dimensional design of constructions in space and time. The oblique roof does not stop at merely giving the impression of being an object that has come from elsewhere. It actually organizes the visual field for the visitor who arrives on the TGV, whose every move is planned out for him from the moment his train comes into the station, conducting him with precision across a series of view points which present the new city center in all its splendor as an urban spectacle.

OMA buildings have always been set up to be perceived above all as a series of oblique views. In the OMA catalog, the vedute has been assembled like movie stills. It is worth noting that at Euralille, the splendid spectacle that greets one upon arrival is partially lost on the traveler, if only because the windows of the TGV trains were conceived with the seated view in mind, when in fact one must stand up in order to head for the exit. Once on the platform, when one looks out across the Forum, one becomes aware of another problem that the lovely Koolhaas vedute was unable (or unwilling) to anticipate: the fact that the perception of an urban space, no matter how well organized, can be compromised by badly synchronized structural and tectonic details. For similar reasons, the "Piranesian" space which, in the Koolhaas drawings, appears to be the quintessence of the project, is finally only a parody of the renderings which prefigure it.

The most pleasant surprise for me was the enormous "ski boot" designed by Christian de Portzamparc. While it is certainly not Cinderella's slipper—after all, Lille isn't Disneyland, even though as sketched by Koolhaas the name Disneyland (next to those of Paris, London, Brussels, and Rotterdam) counts among the centers which place Lille squarely within the cultural topography of the continent. As for Jean Nouvel's dangerously nearby shopping arcade, it is an impressive urban ensemble, but its luxurient upholstery made of pearled glass does not completely succeed in erasing the sign of its original sin, which is its design. In all its splendor, it still looks to me like an enormous model kitchen. To avoid this same effect with the Congrexpo, OMA chose instead to play a game which is as subtle as it is dangerous. The ovoid shape seen in the plan invites curiosity. Its gigantic scale surpasses the possibilities of the architectural medium.

How was the bigness dilemma resolved? By the ingenious handiwork of tectonic components, access arcades, suspended staircases, sloping walls, piers leaning slightly to the left or right—in short, miscellaneous incidents and formal ruptures, constructed partly using inexpensive materials (which may not age well). All these features are both indicative of the diverse functions which are to be served and the concern to avoid compromising the overall concept. This is what, in architecture, allows "bigness" to merge with "grandeur."

AN URBAN PARADOX

Daniel Treiber
Euralille: The Making of a New City Center, ed. Isabelle Menu and Frank Vermandel (Basel: Birkhäuser, 1996), 176–78.

[...] The first indication of how Koolhaas interprets urbanism dates from the time of *Delirious New York*. Ever since, Koolhaas has considered free treatment of the interior enveloped by a silent architectural covering as a sign of metropolitan modernity. In Lille, this internal mix can be found in the Grand Palais, and even more in Jean Nouvel's shopping mall. The overriding effect that really strikes the visitor's eye is the interior space of the shopping arcades: a huge area covered by a roof which the shops never quite manage to touch. These shops are tiered, in the style of a pueblo town, and have been very cleverly arranged around a *cardo* and a *decumanus*. In line with the urban approach adopted by OMA, Nouvel has managed to produce what, for the moment, is one of the most effective segments of Euralille, even if Koolhaas's Grand Palais is considered more unusual and "contorted."

This mixing of elements fosters the strongly antiurban flavor of the steamboat image illustrated in Le Corbusier's famous book *La Cité Radieuse*, where the multifunctional city is no longer represented as an external public space, residing under a sky which for all mankind in some way interacts with what Rabelais called "the deist seigniorial manor, the dry land." Instead, we enter into the sheltered world of huge interior cities, of the type that can be seen in fantasy stories, such as science fiction comic strips. And it is perhaps not completely out of the question that regions such as ours where it rains nonstop, could in the future become metropolitan states in the style of *Blade Runner*. A highly successful shopping mall is V2 in Villeneuve d'Ascq, which is already an interior commercial city, hinging upon a long internal street, whose construction has sucked the very lifeblood out of an "upper street." Today, the latter lies dormant, with no sign of life, though thirty years ago it was conceived by its creators as being the main street of the new town. In a certain way, this "climatology" can also be found in Koolhaas, who when asked about his latest theories on the essence of a site, said: "some (of the people we dealt with) thought that as I was from the north, I would opt for a fairly convivial form of achitecture, in brick of course, whereas in fact for me the main feature of northern towns and cities is their light, their grayness: a diffuse blur, which inspires me." And yet this strongly internal vision of the metropolis comes across as an attempt to lure the latter away from the arbitrary nature of meterological phenomena.

[...] And so we gradually come to the project's main square, where the cars that pass by Le Corbusier Avenue also contribute to the overriding effect of modernity. This avenue has been raised little by little, not on pilotis, but in a new paradoxical way—on perpendicular arches—which comes across as being both a little insipid and overexpressive. Whereas in traditional stations a frontal awning allows people to wait for a traveling companion or a taxi, here a long ornamental lake (to be worked on by a designer) links the station with the adjacent park. And so here again, another urban archetype is short-circuited to be replaced by a supposedly avant-garde attraction: this isn't the only example of its kind—the beginning of the Le Corbusier viaduct, near the blue building is also characterized by such a feature, namely the video screens embedded into the wall.

What all these features share is the attentive concern to block out any conventional style of architecture—anything which could give the slightest hint of traditional design, thus cutting off all those archetypes which have governed our urban context for two millennia. According to Koolhaas, such fundamental elements which maintain a sense of continuity for urban civilization no longer exist. Instead, they have been replaced by a tendency to strive toward the artificial, a concept which OMA appears to consider as universal, and for which New York (one of the most traditional cities in the USA) was used as a kind of "testing ground." As the cofounder of the OMA, Elia Zenghelis pointed out in the 1980s in *L'Architecture d'Aujourd'hui*, "everything that belongs to nature is in essence doomed to disappearance. Only concepts, art and artificial elements can survive."

The few lines of the masterplan devoted to "basic requirements" clearly reveal the problematic nature of Euralille regarding its urban context: "The architecture should be entirely modern, compatible with its surrounding built-up environment, and adapted to the culture and climate of the north." Koolhaas has indeed endowed Lille with an emphatic, if not hyperbolic form of modernity. [...]

Even if Koolhaas has stepped back from the deconstructionist movement, he is still far from being interested in the continuity of the past. But at the end of the day, after seventy years of experimenting with modernity (and at considerable cost!), starting from scratch again, as happens in the overhyped tabula rasa, makes a mockery of the whole process. Nothing prevents an authentic form of modern expressionism from using the past as a reference point. We all know that Le Corbusier continually promoted this idea, and he was right up there with the best of modern Expressionists. Incorporating the past has never and never will condemn towns and cities to cheap imitations of previous models.

As Koolhaas expressed in his essay "The End of Inoccence," writing about his fears for the future, there is a risk of our world becoming nothing more than one of the ghost towns mentioned by Adolf Loos, an acclaimed founder of architectural Modernism. These cardboard towns were erected in the Russian countryside on the orders of General Potemkin as the Tsar passed through. Such are the consequences of a process of urbanism that smothers the fundamental concern for lasting qualities in any project: "after the Potemkin town, comes the Potemkin world."

LEAVE OLD CITIES ALONE
Ian Buruma
The New York Review of Books 19 (1996), 42–47.

[…] Koolhaas has a way with words, which includes a facility for obscuring difficult questions by enveloping them in rather glib statements. He finds it "crucial that the tradition of reinvention, which may be the most fertile, progressive Dutch tradition, is itself reinvented." Sounds good. But what precisely does he mean? What is to be reinvented? You cannot reinvent chaos or spontaneity. But you can give it scope, by an architecture that doesn't pretend to offer any lasting solutions but allows people to use it in any way they like. That seems to be Koolhaas's point about bigness. Holland is, at any rate, hopelessly unsuited for the extra large. It is in every sense a small country. So Koolhaas has followed another Dutch tradition. He continues to do what Dutchmen impatient with the cramped context of their nation have done for centuries. He crosses the ocean for adventure. That is how New York was founded. It is how he founded it again.

[…] What Koolhaas is advocating, then, it seems to me, is not the destruction of old cities to replace them with clusters of hotels and shopping malls. His argument is that old city centers will become unlivable if they are not revitalized by the shock of the new. The double act of making a fetish of the identity of old cities while adapting them to modern life puts them under intolerable strain, for there is only so much you can do to make an old city new while disguising that you are doing so. Besides, it has the perverse effect of robbing them of authenticity, of making them into fake antiques. In Amsterdam, for example, more and more houses are being demolished, except for the old facades, which are grafted onto new buildings like masks. And the sprawling peripheries of old cities are denied an urban identity because they remain just that: the despised environs of the historic metropole, which alone represents "the city."

That explains Koolhaas's vision of a new Dutch metropolis. Making the old city centers peripheral, you take the load off them and allow them to breathe. At the same time new architecture should be less apologetic, more bold in its modernity, in a word: more urban. Koolhaas is content to leave old cities alone. He is stimulated by the wastelands of cities, the neglected industrial zones, bombed tabulae rasae, and derelict suburban blocks. That is why he likes Rotterdam more than Amsterdam, and London or Berlin more than Paris. Bomb sites can be turned into new cities. Dereliction can be made beautiful. His most interesting project to date can be seen in what was one of the most wasted, peripheral cities in France: Lille.

Until recently, Lille was a melancholy dump. The textile and mining industries that once made it prosperous had collapsed, and two World Wars left horrible scars. The old city, *vieux Lille,* was a dilapidated, crumbling wreck of a place, too depressed to be romantic. Lille was a town to avoid. Then the keen French and the more reluctant British finally completed the cross-channel tunnel, or Chunnel, closing the gap between the Continent and Britain. This opened up endless possibilities, especially for an architect who likes to think of space in terms of transportation: air miles, rail links, freeways. If the tracks of the TGV (super-fast train) from London to Paris to Brussels could go through Lille, the geography of the city would change. No longer just an urban dump in France Nord, Lille would be little more than an hour away from Paris and London, a European hub of constant movement.

[...] On a walk through Euralille I came across a large group of Japanese architects, taking notes and gawking at the shopping centers, car parks, movable station roofs, office complexes, and walkways with the excitement of provincials in the big city. They were from Tokyo. And this was Lille! The astonishing thing about Euralille, and this is really the point, is how this modern development, including of course the TGV itself, has revived old Lille. Nobody lives in Euralille. It is a place to work, eat, buy, or stay overnight, a transitional city, full of commercial activity, but no neighborhoods. Old Lille, however, is now a thriving area of fine, renovated houses, excellent restaurants, attractive, well-stocked shops, and also of squares and streets teeming with life. A bold, big, modern architectural development has revitalized a dying old city. And new Euralille didn't even have to be ugly to show off the beauty of old Lille. What is striking about Euralille is not its bigness, but the intricacy and complexity of its design. The different, autonomous parts are so intertwined that the whole looks magnificent in the vast, webbed, human way of a Gothic cathedral.

[...]

THE END OF MODERN URBANISM

Vittorio Lampugnani
AMC 86 (1998), 50–55.

[…] The Euralille plan was a *Delirious New York* in miniature, a concrete emblem of the "culture of congestion" the Dutch architect saw as giving rise to the fascination, as well as to the visionary and futuristic dimension, of Manhattan. The city of the future, which Euralille was supposed to make a reality, was the city of technological hyper-urbanization.

For all that, it was in no way deprived of architectural qualities. Its metropolitan potential was not exhausted at all by this juxtaposition nor by the deliberately chaotic and disconcerting superposition of functions and interlacing spaces. On the contrary, it was highlighted by the architectural setting of these functions and spaces. The green spaces became abstract compositions and the skyscrapers were transformed into giant sculptures. The station, the centerpiece of this new metropolitan machine, formed the stage on which the show it had largely inspired was played out: the underground TGV route was exhumed and the side walls of the track torn open to form large glazed windows. In just a few minutes, these offered travelers a glimpse of the modern metropolis, whose very raison d'être was the train in which they were sitting. But most importantly, they allowed the inhabitants of and visitors to Euralille to see into the comings and goings of the high-speed trains without which the city in which they found themselves would never have sprung up.

[…] One of the characteristic contradictions of the Euralille project was that it was instigated and implemented by a socialist alliance between the State and the municipality, but with a massive input of private capital. The public authorities' power of control, guaranteed by their majority share in the capital of Euralille, could barely be felt in the final result. Instead the new city displayed the aggressive and anarchical appearance of something born out of purely capitalist interests, to which this aggressiveness and anarchy undoubtedly provided an aesthetic dimension. Whatever the case, it had been possible to build a surface area of almost 300,000 square meters in just six years, and for that purpose to channel almost four billion francs of private investment into a region that had previously been devoid of any economic interest.

The new station, through which 15,000 people pass every day and 15 million passengers per year, was, of course, completed, in accordance with the plans of the architect Jean-Marie Duthilleul in partnership with the engineer Peter Rice. Its gently undulating steel and glass roof fitted well with Rem Koolhaas's concern for transparency. On the other hand, all that remained of what was originally supposed to become a "Piranesian space" was a conglomerate of gloomy halls clumsily linked by escalators. The hollow rhetoric of the whole marked an edifying contrast with the elegant technological solutions developed by François Deslaugiers for the Le Corbusier viaduct, yet did not succeed in allowing the brachial gesture of the bridge stretched over the square and park to be forgotten.

[…] Initially eight and then six towers were supposed to line the rail tracks; due to the crisis in the office space market only two were constructed. The Lille Europe Tower and the World Trade Center, built to the southeast by Claude Vasconi, represent 40,000 square meters of office space in total. The Crédit Lyonnais tower, originally entrusted to Richard Rogers, was eventually designed by Christian de Portzamparc: 15,000 square meters of offices in a shoe-shaped tower as bizarre as it is debatable, which can be explained in part by constraints at the level of its foundations. The hotel designed by Kazuo Shinohara was not built, and the second project, by François and Marie Delhay, is currently being rethought.

The most emblematic example is that of the convention center, which Rem Koolhaas kept for himself. Its gigantic arch spanning the railway and motorway would turn out to be indefensible from not only a functional but most importantly economic perspective. Koolhaas therefore developed a new design: a flat oval, no less gigantic, with a surface area of 45,500 square meters, measuring 300 m on its largest side, no longer located above but between the railway and motorway. Koolhaas brought to life his vision of a hybrid functionality inside the colossal building: a convention hall (Congrès), a concert hall (Zénith) and an exhibition hall (Expo) are gathered under the same roof and open out onto the "Piranesian space" he was unable to create under the station. The enormous "egg" of the Grand Palais is more than a simple container to bring different programs together, it is the materialization of the concept of bigness developed by Koolhaas. As convincing as its interior may be, the building's exterior proves disconcerting: drowning in the traffic, the Grand Palais at Euralille is the symbol of the contemporary metropolis, the unconditional acceptance of the technological benefits of which (and therefore of the high-speed traffic) comes at the price of an equally unrestrained (not to say brutal) confinement of the pedestrian population.

It goes without saying that the enormous changes experienced by the outskirts of European cities since the start of the century required radically different strategies to those deemed appropriate for their historical centers. But, as Euralille demonstrates so clearly, in no way can this be a question of approving the most wretched aspects of the periphery and further heightening the inhospitable, even inhuman, nature of these in the name of an abstract aesthetic concept.

Irrespective even of the erosion and setbacks experienced by the project due to the economic situation, Euralille appears to be an archetype of the "misfortunes of virtue" of contemporary urbanism. The acceptance of major pieces of infrastructure as constituent elements of the urban landscape has made the city itself dependent on them. In this gigantic tangle of railways and motorways almost nothing remains of the structuring axes and enticing perspectives that Koolhaas had promised Euralille in his initial sketches. What could be built is tucked in timidly next to or, at best, above the peremptory routes of the traffic lanes that are not content with determining the shape of the city, they first and foremost define its function. The high-speed TGV train, expressways and slip roads with attenuated curves may well make it possible to get around at the speed of light, but as soon as they step onto the platform or park their car in one of the many unwelcoming underground car parks, pedestrians feel lost in the heart of Euralille. The Grand Palais and the Centre Euralille offer its only refuge, but require you to be a spectator, audience member, conference delegate or shopper. Failing that, it seems more prudent to seek refuge in the old town, a short stroll away.

This shortcoming should not be attributed to Koolhaas in particular but to modern urbanism in general, of which he is the most exemplary exponent. This type of urbanism, which has reached its peak with Euralille, also seems to have reached its end here. It is here that the designs of Antonio Sant'Elia, Le Corbusier and Peter and Alison Smithson find their extension and fulfillment. In the inhospitable nature of the best of the cities designed by OMA, they also demonstrate their tragic and immanent failure.

S,M,L,XL & "GENERIC CITY" (1994–1998): NO END TO REVISION

10

S,M,L,XL is—until further notice—the last book everybody dealing with architecture was and is aware of, and every architect, critic, historian or student probably has leafed through it, or can immediately recognize its spine in public libraries and private book collections. It is also the only book on architecture that got reviewed and covered in the most divergent media and publications, from *Canadian Architect* to *Architectural Research Quarterly*, from *L'Architecture d'Aujourd'hui* to the *New Yorker*, from the *Village Voice* to *The Observer*, and from *Print* ("America's Graphic Design Magazine") to *Elle, Harper's Bazaar*, and *Vogue*. The book managed to give the impression that architecture had finally succeeded in becoming a true cultural discipline and a subject that could attract profound attention, from academic circles to the popular press, not unlike the movie *Se7en* (directed by David Fincher), the novel *Microserfs* (by Douglas Coupland), the record *To Bring You My Love* (by P. J. Harvey) or the art installation *Everyone I Have Slept With 1963–1995* (by Tracey Emin)—to name some other cultural achievements from 1995.

At the same time, probably no one has read *S,M,L,XL* from cover to cover. Was it even meant to be read, or did it really emerge, as Will Novosedlik wrote, reviewing the work of graphic designer Bruce Mau, "as a kind of multimedia experiment trapped on too much paper, a rambling hypertext without a navigational device"? *S,M,L,XL* grew out of two projects: a study of contemporary cities such as Singapore, Atlanta, and Paris that Koolhaas had been working on (and talking about) since the mid-1980s, and a long-awaited monograph produced by OMA that would recapitulate their production since the early days. Understandably, it was highly anticipated, but it immediately presented different challenges, formal and theoretical, although one of the puzzling aspects of *S,M,L,XL* was the way in which it alluringly but confusingly merged content with form. It offered visual and intellectual pleasure, but how far-reaching and lasting was this delight? How could or should the glossary, running through the book and compiled by editor Jennifer Sigler, be related to the content? Was scale indeed the last remaining meaningful way of ordering architectural projects? What was the book's (and the author's) message? Could this message still be associated with traditional values and rewarding goals? Did it ask to be imitated, or was it rather a tombstone for the profession, initiating an epoch in which architecture would increasingly be reduced to decoration and design? "The only ambition that one can attribute to *S,M,L,XL* without the risk of falling into a hazardous interpretation," Catherine de Smet suggested in a late review from 1999, "is that it pretends to exist as a book, as a sustainable object—something that represents today a real challenge in the context of publishing in general, and in the architectural context in particular."[1] In a conversation with George Baird—one of countless events in the wake of *S,M,L,XL*—Koolhaas admitted: "we could not make a book that gives the impression of an overall edifice or a stable position."

S,M,L,XL succeeded in getting attention for more than three years. It was announced in 1994, with the distribution of black-and-white proof copies, but also with an OMA exhibition from November 3, 1994, to January 31, 1995, at the Museum of Modern Art in New York, entitled *Tresholds/OMA at MoMA: Rem Koolhaas and the Place of Public Architecture*, curated by Terence Riley. The show was, as Grahame D. Shane wrote in terms that apply to *S,M,L,XL* as well, a demonstration of Koolhaas's "awareness of his difficult megalomaniac situation, while simultaneously trying to distance himself, subverting the normal devices of publicity to his own ironic and poetic ends, attempting an impossible demonstration of transcendent personal independence." In conjunction with the exhibition, issue 9 of *ANY Magazine*, edited by Cynthia Davidson, was devoted to OMA and to "Urbanism vs Architecture: The Bigness of Rem Koolhaas." It would take until October 31, 1995, before *S,M,L,XL* was published—"With Rem there was absolutely no end to revision," production manager Kevin Sugden told John Shnier on the pages of *Canadian Architect*—by Monacelli Press in New York and 010 Publishers in Rotterdam. The first edition of 30,000 copies, with Koolhaas's name on the cover in yellow lettering, was sold out within months; for subsequent editions, the color of the architect's name would change. The book was reviewed by critics and theoreticians, but also by colleagues (Toyo Ito, Claude Parent) and philosophers (Richard Sennett, Fredric Jameson), and critical reception continued far into 1997, and it is in a way still ongoing.[2]

The main topic—and the main concern—came to be located in the essay "The Generic City": an analysis of the late twentieth-century urban and human condition, but also—seemingly—a farewell to human intervention and cultural or authorial difference (and thus meaning), characteristics that could also be projected onto *S,M,L,XL*. Once again, the major problem was the gap between critical analysis of the contemporary world, and the way to deal with it—let alone to change it—by means of architecture. British critic Irénée Scalbert accused Koolhaas of an "obliviousness to even the most basic social (let alone democratic) processes that make a city." German critic and urban planner Dieter Hoffmann-Axthelm noted: "As a person, he inhabits airports. Fine. It's his choice. But why does he revile the real cities, then?" Belgian philosopher Lieven De Cauter interpreted *S,M,L,XL* as a "flight forward"—as an attempt to both express and anesthetize revulsion, but also—possibly—to bring about forms of awareness or even anxiety that might, in the end, lead to change, or at least to the realization of the necessity of a different kind of living and working. It is therefore not a coincidence that the most enthusiastic reactions for *S,M,L,XL* did not come from inside the world of architecture, but from art and literature critics, who had no trouble in liberating the book from the fate and the future of the discipline. In the *New Yorker*, Brendan Gill praised Koolhaas as "a master of serious clowning, a latter-day Robert Burton," author of *The Anatomy of Melancholy* from 1621—a contradictory, syncretic book that demonstrated how "there is no greater cause of melancholy than idleness, no better cure than business."

1 Catherine de Smet, "'Je suis un livre': A propos de *S,M,L,XL* par Rem Koolhaas et Bruce Mau," *Les Cahiers du Musée national d'art modern*, no. 68 (1999), 110.

2 See for example the issue of *Journal of Architectural Education* (no. 69, 2015), devoted to *S,M,L,XL* and published on the occasion of the book's twentieth birthday. See also Gabriele Mastrigli, "The Last Bastion of Architecture," *Log*, no. 7 (2006), 33–41, which compares *S,M,L,XL* to *Six projets* from 1990.

THE ARCHITECT IS OBLIGED TO BE AN HONORABLE MAN

Hans van Dijk
Archis 11 (1994), 18–24.

[...] **hvd:** The opening pages of *S,M,L,XL* contain graphs of OMA's order book, work force and turnover. Having peaked some three years ago, they are now dropping slightly. During that period you were busy with the book. Is there any connection?

rk: After OMA had been going for more than ten years, it had a staff of sixty. Numbers like that enable breakthroughs, but also have their disadvantages. You can organize the work like a Blitzkrieg. With a force that size you can literally surmount some problems and force breakthroughs, instead of depending on inspiration. And yet those numbers require an incredible effort to keep the creative process going. That was one actor. Another was that architecture is such an addictive and exhausting occupation that it is almost impossible to combine with thinking about architecture, or with anything other than architecture. In addition, the world economy was changing, and that had financial repercussions for all architectural offices, including OMA. Lastly, I simply had the urge to write again. These four factors resulted in our downscaling the office as an economic precaution, and I could make the most of it to start on the book I had been announcing for an embarrassingly long time. If I had not written it then, it would never have been written.

hvd: You mean *The Contemporary City*, a book about Atlanta, Paris, Seoul and possibly the Dutch Randstad.

rk: I had started researching *The Contemporary City*. As I progressed, I realized that you cannot write a profound book on that subject unless you concentrate on it for years. It's not interesting to merely speculate on Atlanta. I wanted background information and realized that it was essential to research it "academically." A large office leaves you hardly any time. The research, which did not in fact reach any real conclusion, also proved to affect our work at the office. At OMA there is a close relationship between analysis—program data, books or history—and projects; it's part of a spectrum. At the same time pressure was being applied to publish a monograph. I didn't want to write a traditional monograph. So, since two books were impossible—a popular monograph and an academically sound book on the contemporary city—the combination of *S,M,L,XL* resulted.

[...]
hvd: *S,M,L,XL* contains two essays on the office building *ohne Eigenschaften*: "Typical Plan" and "Last Apples." The ground plan is still merely neutral graph paper with elevator cores, the section an alternating accumulation of horizontal zones for people and zones for concrete and ducts. Why do you devote two theoretical treatises to the building type with the least exciting program and the greatest proliferation from which an ambitious architect can gain hardly any credit?

rk: That interest in the typical plan, the neutrality and absence of character of certain types or architecture is once more connected to an aversion to determinacy. Architecture is generally described and experienced as a discipline which converts a sum of programs into a sum of forms. And the city is, in turn, the sum of that. But we have now landed in a completely different situation. By far the greatest part of the urban substance consists of open structures with a minimal, formal quality. This architecture is increasingly concerned with erasing specificity, and the city becomes an accumulation of these deliberately empty containers, programmatical voids and undefined sites to a degree never before experienced in the history of mankind. That for me was a discovery.

hvd: But a disturbing discovery. It seems as if that omnipresence of the building *ohne Eigenschaften* is a relief to you.

rk: Absolutely. I want to see demonstrable precedents for the forms of erasing.

hvd: Doesn't that mean you are siding with an old architectural tradition which concentrated on flexible plans and the "service shed"?

rk: Some of those themes do have an undeniable irrevocability. That is why we are constantly struggling with them. The Centre Pompidou has solved the problem of indeterminacy, while at the same time raising it again. I consider the Centre Pompidou, both as an emblem and in its effectuation, a highly suggestive building. It is a kind of benchmark, it makes the permanence and the solutions of the themes accessible. It seems as if no one of my generation has more affinity with it than I; in other words, no one perhaps is more old-fashioned in his basic assumptions. We have always wondered how, in spite of that indeterminacy, architecture can still be made.

hvd: *S,M,L,XL* is a hybrid book. It is a monograph, a tract and a collection of essays at the same time. It contains autobiographical revelations, extracts from diaries and academic discourses. But as a monograph it is also selective. Some projects have been omitted (such as the IJplein), others are included without further explanation, some are merely provided with a few aphorisms, others with lengthy descriptions. What criteria did you use?

rk: The theme of the book is, of course, Bigness. "Bigness" can be read as a manifesto. To some extent it is the foundation of the book. It is important that bigness goes well with local variation and specificity of components. There need not be a connection between bigness and generalizations. The book itself is an example of that. It is a paroxysm of specificity, incorporated in a massif, a composition constructed of specific elements. It was important to highlight each time those aspects which by implication could also stand for the whole. That explains the inclusion of "More?"

the chronology of the Dance Theater in The Hague. After that kind of chronology, you don't need a second one. In addition, it's the result of drastic selection. It contains nothing I don't find interesting, and everything it doesn't contain is not, to my mind, worth showing or mentioning. For instance, I found it unacceptable to show yet again all the diagrams and precedents involved in the IJplein project. That strategy, interesting as it was, could legitimize the lack of inspiration as found in Dutch Modernism.

hvd: You just mentioned the chronology of the Dance Theater. In this and other descriptions of processes and building chronicles there is a fair share of autobiography. Did you want to produce an egodocument?

rk: Quite the reverse. The book makes no claims to honesty. It is a composition, nothing else. I have my qualms about the idea of a self being present at all, and am comfortable with the thought that OMA's architecture is "me-less." But in my career I have kept on trying to be open about certain aspects of the process. It struck me as important to make the dilemmas facing architecture accessible to people in intellectual circles who were interested in the subject. If architecture is to survive it is important that it's not reduced to an outside which everyone looks at, but that insight is also given into the "inside." Of course, this is dangerous. Its close ties with the economy and with clients make architecture extremely vulnerable. The architect is obliged to be an honorable man. In the twentieth century all forms of art can permit themselves incredible liberties. A writer can easily combine his career with that of drug addict, fornicator, criminal or any other excess. The same goes for painters, scriptwriters and producers. But none of these models is possible for architects. The architect is always forced to be an honorable man, to read only honorable things, undergo only honorable experiences and live only with honorable thoughts. I thought it was important for once to give a picture of the "marinade" in which we work and which is made up, to some extent, of frivolous, explosive, sensual and dishonorable interests.

[...]
hvd: The dominant theme in the building chronicles is that of a heroic, mythical fight, with the architect's role alternating between that of Prometheus, Hercules and Sisyphus. Is that characteristic of your operation or a feature of the architect's profession in general?

rk: I don't know. There is always a direct connection between ambition and difficulties. I know from my circle of friends—Nouvel, Kollhoff, De Portzamparc, Eisenman and Hadid—that they have great battles too. But I am not concerned with the fight. Our experience in Lille was the complete opposite. There the architect and the client shared an ambition. Ultimately, the book is a plea for the clarity of ambitions. Any architectural project requires, by definition, tremendous ambition on both sides.

[...] I am convinced that an architect without a client is absolutely nothing, he just doesn't exist. One of the problems of present-day architecture is the very fact that architects are always being required to explode, in every situation, with a maximum of eloquence and energy—regardless of whether there is anything behind it. That is suspect, to my mind. I personally feel just as strong and good as the constellation projected in every endeavor. So the piece about Villa dall'Ava not only relates to the obstructions by the neighbors, but also to the incredible courage of the Boudets to take their case or rather the house's case—as far as the French Supreme Court. If the building chronicles in my book are dramatic, it is mainly because the client's role is often virtually nonexistent these days, being distributed among utterly impenetrable, impersonal and irresponsible bodies.

[...]
hvd: Rem, is it in any way conceivable that there still is an operational approach which justifies architecture and urbanism as intellectual disciplines?

rk: I don't see the book as a sign of despair by any means. It entails a subtle exploration of the world and its conditions. That's essential to an understanding of what is possible. That's also one of the attractive aspects of the paradoxical situation in which OMA finds itself. On the one hand, we have little work here, thanks to a peculiar breakdown in relations with the Dutch clientele. Yet that compelled us to undergo experiences almost everywhere else in the world. Apart from the logistic problems, this has a tremendous advantage: you must experience and examine the vast differences in possibilities in every place in the world. It's a remarkable paradox that globalization is keeping pace with balkanization. On the one hand everything seems to be turning out the same, on the other every difference is intensified and thrashed out in the minutest detail.

hvd: In this book you've deconstructed the traditional pretensions of architectural and urbanist practice so thoroughly that I see it as a symptom of the exhaustion of Deconstructivism. It's time for a new, intellectual project. Not something you formulate ad hoc with each new task, but for the discipline in general.

rk: If the role of architecture in general is being questioned, I believe critics have a bigger job here than architects. I'm so convinced of the differences that I have great difficulty formulating general standpoints. That's why it was so interesting for me to write "The Generic City," because it deals with global generalities.

But, as OMA, we can certainly formulate ambition for the medium term. At a fairly local level we have several new projects behind us which at any rate demonstrate our intentions: we have done what we have done deliberately. By cutting back at the office and concentrating on the book, we've also been able to reformulate our architectural approach. The book closes a period. But it also introduces a new one. This is necessary, because the stupidity of the architectural profession these days results in an acceleration that blocks all innovation at a certain stage. We are getting involved in bigger projects involving more money and more dangerous cultures, such as the American culture, where every mistake can lead to claims for hundreds of thousands of dollars in damages. A number of people at our office have successfully completed some big projects. The problem now is how to proceed without declining into conservatism and predictability.

hvd: Yet you too continue to be active in the world of reflection. You've been given a tenure at Harvard University. What exactly will you be doing there?

rk: I am going to Harvard on the condition that I will not be teaching design. I want to do research at the "Institute for the study of what used to be the city" that they are setting up. It is based on the phenomenon of "phantom pain," when you continue to feel pain in limbs long after they have been amputated. In the same way we can also experience "urban pain" now the city no longer exists. And maybe it's also an attempt to draw up an agenda for architects and urbanists who have to pursue their profession under those conditions and take account of the modifications and mutations it is undergoing. Providing the commissions keep coming we shall also be opening an OMA office in Cambridge, Massachusetts.

PLUMP FICTION: CONVERSATION WITH BRUCE MAU

John Shnier
Canadian Architect 11 (1995), 18–21.

For five years, Bruce Mau and his Toronto Studio, and Rem Koolhaas with his Office for Metropolitan Architecture, have been working on a project that will have a profound effect on their respective fields of graphic design and architecture. The scope of the undertaking is huge. The book is identical in length and height to a typical brick plus a mortar joint. It contains some 60,000 or 70,000 words, including 17 essays by Koolhaas and a running glossary which weaves all the way through the book, 33 projects organized by both physical and intellectual acreage into categories of small, medium, large and extra large, and over 1,100 images. The first copies of the book, published by Monacelli Press, are expected in December. A three-foot high stack of fax correspondence from Rem Koolhaas documents the Sisyphean revision process, and acts as the proxy voice for the tall, gaunt figure of the architect himself. In a crowded studio above a pastry factory in the west end of Toronto, I engaged Bruce Mau and the book's production manager Kevin Sugden in conversation, and pondered the difficulties in reviewing such an endeavor as *S,M,L,XL*.

js: There are more than a few good reasons why a review of *S,M,L,XL* cannot be written.

bm: The danger of working on something over this length of time is that you can pound the life out of it.

js: Neither I, nor Bruce, nor even Rem, for that matter, have even seen a final version of the "book." And even if I had a final copy, so much has already been written about "bigness."

bm: That *S,M,L,XL* also connects the practice of architecture to the product world, with all of the contradictions and compromises and opportunities and entanglements that implies, was certainly not unwanted or unnoticed.

js: And even if I had the time to read/experience the whole thing …

bm: This was not going to be an architectural monograph or a book about an office.

js: … there is not the space here to go into any depth on the content of this 1376-page volume.

bm: I am concerned with the movement of the "subject/object," and getting inside it, knowing it. The "object" is in fact even more than "OMA," it is an approach to creative practice.

js: But the most compelling reason against writing a review of *S,M,L,XL* is this: the book does such a thorough job of reviewing itself. Within the first few ounces of its ten-pound bulk you get an introduction which is an emotional and intellectual purge, setting a grand stage for a tour de force of supremely edited, endlessly revisited, photoshopped streams of consciousness. *S,M,L,XL* describes itself early on as a "painfully utopian enterprise." We are exposed to a range of idealism which is nearly impossible to grasp.

bm: I believe deeply in the untapped potential of books to intimately explore ideas and to reach people in new ways with those ideas, in their dual capacity as both historical record and manifesto—in their ability to project history into the future.

js: I do, however, have all the mock-ups and I have seen the first color press proofs. Still, I think to even begin to understand this much-awaited "object," you have to spend the money, haul this thing to your table, crack it open, smell it and test the binding against the heft of all that coated paper.

bm: I realized that what I had done was to create, in collaboration with Rem, a new object. [...] Graphic design is essentially a seduction. The moment you become conscious of the seduction, it ceases to function. It's no wonder that critics are not able to distance themselves in the seduction. If the work is good, they are trapped in it. There is a fine line between free movement and self-indulgence. We'll know in a while on which side of that line we finally set down.

js: Mau's skyrocket into designer orbit can probably be attributed to his work on the now famous *ZONE* book series, especially Book One. Ironically (and unlike his assessment of the anticipated public reaction to *S,M,L,XL*), *ZONE* was immediately lauded for its style rather than its content. One can only speculate on how many people who own copies of this "got to have it" item have yet to get it, so to speak.

bm: Our expertise is a capacity to incorporate a vast amount of disparate material, reformulate it around a thematic drive and create a comprehensible product.

js: Yes, and architects can be said to (try to) do the same.

bm: Except that we are more centrally concerned with directly presenting ideas.

js: Koolhaas once wrote, "I have complete horror of what happens to architects when they are really alone and how boring and important their work becomes. To fight against that incipient mania of loneliness, I have become more interested in involving other people in the designs."

bm: And he's there, in Holland, where there is a fabulous graphic designer on every corner.

js: The book's identity oscillates between form and content with a haughty ease.

bm: In previous publications of OMA work, priority has always been given either to theory or design. One thing that became clear to me working on the book is that the two are quite rigorously concurrent in Rem's method ...

js: Yet this arrogance is not altogether disturbing. Perhaps it is because here, Koolhaas has set aside the known world of architectural design and has taken up graphic design with the zeal of a dilettante.

ks: ... in a kind of hyperdance intent on action-production.

js: There is abundant evidence that the minutiae of this book have already received more attention from Rem than any detail of (his) architecture.

bm: A good place to look is the Très Grande Bibliothèque in Paris, which is the best presentation of this project that I have seen, if I do say so myself.

js: I had predicted that the project would take on the almost casually unedited form of the Japanese manga comic books. OMA's experience in Fukuoka on the Nexus World Housing Project obviously brought Rem in contact with this genre. Earlier evidence for this borrowing back of an originally Western medium—the comic book—can be seen in two, almost photocopied quality, French publications of OMA: *Six projets* and *Lille*. There are almost no words in these books.

bm: Even though the Bibliothèque project has already been published a lot, the way it is presented here casts it in an entirely different light, one in which the ideas will be brought forward with a clarity for the first time. It avoids the often intentionally opaque nature of other presentations of OMA's work, where the architecture was compelling, but the ideas were shrouded.

js: Wasn't Rem once asked to write a screenplay for Russ Meyer? Perhaps that accounts for a certain quality ...

bm: Pornographic? I hope not, I do hope however that the book exudes a subtle and sometimes not-so-subtle sexuality. I've thought of early television and the way it was so filled with raw desire.

js: Even if the weight of the book were not an issue, and I think it is, and even if the thesis on bigness postdated the notion of *S,M,L,XL*, and it did, the scale of the task itself is daunting.

ks: Starting and finishing—whenever there was a design review, I'd set out the materials in a linear fashion on the table, expecting to go through sections from start to finish, tagging problems, corrections ...

js: Sometimes you have to prepare dessert at the beginning of the evening in order to serve it at the end of the meal. In *S,M,L,XL* the order of preparation has everything and nothing to do with the structure of the object. Process is both the tail and the dog.

ks: ... this never happened. Bruce and Rem would invariably start in the middle, skip around a bit ...

js: Now there's an image!

ks: ... work to the end, then go back toward the beginning, never right back to the beginning, back to the middle, then run out of time. With Rem there was absolutely no end to revision.

js: Yeah, meanwhile it's taking a helluva long time to build it and then Tschumi's book hits the shelves, all 624 pages of it. Anyway I have this speculative fiction: some time ago, on some messy desk, in somebody's office, somewhere, at a very important institution dedicated to the dissemination of all sorts of stuff about modern (and contemporary) culture, some place in a major North American city, sat a *S,M,L,XL* dummy. Maybe a dozen people know about this dummy, and dozens know only rumor and speculation about it.

ks: Our office manager first saw Tschumi's book in New York and brought it back to the office. Maybe we'd been scooped: after all, it appeared as if Tschumi's show at MoMA would take the slot originally reserved for OMA.

js: For the record, *Event Cities* is 625 pages printed on slightly heavy paper to give it more bulk. *S,M,L,XL* is 1376 pages on considerably thinner paper ... no contest. To tell you the truth, when I saw *Event Cities*, in black and white and a little messy, I thought it had the "tidy incompetence" that I was expecting to see in the original manifestation of *S,M,L,XL*.

ks: We prefer to think of our project more as untidy competence.

js: Everyone keeps asking: "What is it like to work with Rem?"

bm: Rem and his practice were transformed by this project.

js: With other projects, Mau's involvement implies a range of participation that does not necessarily refer to partnerships or collaborations. However, on this project, his creative liaison with Jennifer Sigler at OMA and the invaluable production management of Kevin Sugden were key to the final outcome. I note, though, that the point size of both names (Rem's and Bruce's) as they appear on the cover of the dummy, are not equal. This raises the question of authorship and the nature of collaboration in the truest sense.

bm: Authorship is one of the most difficult issues of this project. At the beginning it was not even an issue. The empathy was strong, and the other contributors recognized this right away. There was never a question in terms of the division of work. We set out to make a collaborative object. To exact what is my work and what is Rem's in the book becomes really difficult. At the level of ideas, the work is Rem's, but in the synthesis of text, image, architecture, the authorship is not distillable. Once the book goes out to the public authorship becomes an issue.

js: Once information is excerpted out of the context of the project, the seduction is broke, content and form are torn from each other. Mau is not interested in taking any credit for OMA work or Rem's text in the abstract. The collaboration exists in the process and bulk of *S,M,L,XL*, but it has a precarious and fragile existence.

bm: It is heartbreaking, the kind of ruthlessness with which the public attributes things ...

js: I think that more than anything else it is a book about an office ... two offices which have dedicated themselves to not be dedicated about the way things have been done before. Dedicated enough to bring you to that moment when you know that you have achieved full artistic success ... financial and emotional bankruptcy.

bm: The ambition, which was fairly megalomaniacal, was to formulate a concept of architecture in our culture. The book will open up the definition of *architect* to reinstitute design practice in our lives and to recognize that it is a kinda messy thing. It will open up ... Well how can I get at this? One of the things that I am generally against is a tradition of "professionalism" that supports a reductionist notion of creative live.

js: One day, all the graphic designers left. Some started their own practices and are becoming famous, others went to work for interesting institutions. One day, you looked around the studio and all you saw were people who at one time or another had gone to architecture school.

bm: I think that the book will be a road map to creative practice, one that is not exclusive to the architectural field. I am aware that a number of people we know are baffled by the project. [...] For me, the most significant change is that I have realized that the avenue that has opened, and the one that I must go down, is the avenue of content development, starting from scratch and doing my own projects, to become a cultural producer, an author. To go back to a traditional practice of design, where people send me the manuscript and I design the book is just not realistic any more. I cannot imagine giving up the experiment of inventing new books. I am working on a comprehensive project with Frank Gehry, called *Frank Gehry, Incomplete*. And I'm talking with Koolhaas about our next project, *OMA, Detail*.

js: Yet, standing out—cutting at least as large a figure as the subject of all that millwork—is the producer. That's right, Bruce Mau is a producer and no longer simply one of Canada's preeminent graphic designers. In fact, the English term *graphic designer,* unlike its Dutch equivalent *typografie,* seems a subrank after publisher, editor and author ... The fax rings—another note from Rem: the R on the contents page is too far to the left ...

LEVIATHAN

Will Novosedlik
Print: America's Graphic Design Magazine 4 (1996), 90–95, 237.

[...] If nothing else, the sheer volume of the recently published *S,M,L,XL,* by Rem Koolhaas and Bruce Mau, will establish it as a towering rebuttal of the much-heralded death of print. Mau and Koolhaas have produced a leviathan that is both biblical in its length (1,346 pages) and DeMillean in its ambition. Dystopian urban fantasies, statistical babel, polemical essays, project drawings and models, detailed case studies, diaristic ramblings, garage comic book art, flashed of pornography, idiosyncractic margin gloss, and over 1,200 illustrations are assembled together between the covers of this titanic text. We may be moving from a universe of atoms to one of bits, but digital be damned: This is an unbridled celebration of all things atomic. If less is more, these guys haven't heard about it.

Dutch architect Rem Koolhaas is an iconoclast with a prodigious flair for self-promotion. [...] Canadian graphic designer Bruce Mau is no stranger to iconoclasm himself. Practicing steadfastly outside the commercial mainstream, Mau has staked out a claim as designer of choice for a range of artists, cultural foundations, architects, museums, and esoteric publishers. He is best known for his design of the six volumes of *ZONE,* a series of texts on philosophy and urbanism edited by Jonathan Crary, professor of art history at Columbia University, and Sanford Kwinter, professor of architecture at Rice University. Mau will most likely be remembered by American designers as the former art director of *I.D.* magazine, but his work on *ZONE* also garnered him assignments in the US and Europe from organizations such as the Los Angeles Philharmonic, the Getty Institute, the Carnegie International, and EMR, a German electric power authority.

It was most certainly Mau's work on *ZONE* that made Koolhaas aware of him, but he did not approach Bruce Mau Design when he initially set out to create an ambitious monograph on the work of OMA almost seven years ago. The *ZONE* books are grand in scale, philosophical in content, and diverse in imagery: three qualities which were critical to the design of *S,M,L,XL*. After reviewing several Dutch and European alternatives, OMA decided that, despite the enormous distance, BMD was the right firm for the job of designing this ambitious survey of its work.

[…] Size is thus the central metaphor of this book, and Mau plays this theme out in a number of different, masterly ways. The book's opening section, for instance, consists of sixteen pages of statistical lore about OMA. Graphs depicting quantitative data regarding the OMA workforce, its income and expenditures, staff turnover, and travel behavior are superimposed on photographic spreads of the OMA working environment. The graphs give us, in broad-stroke fashion, a clear sense of the scale of this enterprise: its international client base, its use of money, its global range of human resources. The photos show us an office which is caught up in a whirlwind of creative chaos: tables covered with the debris of model-making, bookshelves crammed with the detritus of past projects, a kitchen area strewn with the remains of a fast-food feeding frenzy—all signs of the "chaotic adventure" that Koolhaas calls architecture. These spreads articulate what he believes to be the "incoherence, or more precisely, randomness that is the underlying structure of all architects' careers."

The most interesting chart in the book is to be found a few pages beyond the opening section. It depicts credits for all the projects in OMA's history by lining up personnel on the left against projects on the right. The dense pattern of lines connecting the two sides of the chart (161 staff members to 81 projects) effectively depicts the amount of human resources allocated to each project and the workload of each staff member. The reader can easily see which projects demanded the most resources, and which staff members had the greatest amount of responsibility. The overall impression is that this is one big, busy place.

The title page and subsequent acknowledgments demonstrate that Mau is no stranger to the lessons of French book designer Pierre Faucheux, who has never been afraid to exploit the heroic (or sculptural) potential of typography. As if the sheer weight of the book isn't enough to convince you of its epic scale, its title is set monumentally across two pages, thus assuring the reader that the words of Robert Venturi have been taken to heart by the designers of this massive tome.

Perhaps the most interesting way in which Mau plays with the notion of size is in how he treats the idea of duration. Case studies are often expressed as luxuriously long photo sequences, some of which are directly followed by an equally long series of plans, elevations and sections, and others in which the two are intermingled. In this way, the underlying structure of the book is manifested as cinematic rather than literary. Picture editing becomes the principal narrative device, one that has characterized much of the earlier work of BMD, but which is taken here to the point of hyperbole. Photo sequences 40 or 50 pages long allow a depth almost never achieved in shorter books. Movement through space is expressed as a carefully scripted tour through several pictorial frames, which, taken together, leave readers with the distinct sense that they have just been to a movie rather than sitting with a book.

This kind of visual narrative has a curious effect: It creates a multiplicity of viewpoints that destroys the idea of the building as a single object. Most architectural books and magazines provide readers with a handful of key perspective photos, thus leaving them with the impression that they have a grasp of the building as a discrete entity. In *S,M,L,XL*, there is no central reference point, no single point of view. Instead, the building is presented as a mutating field of interdependent processes: political, social, aesthetic, functional and cultural. The more you see, the less sure you are of what you saw.

The reader's sense of "real" size and scale is further distorted by the fact that Mau and Koolhaas have combined case studies of projects (an architectural euphemism for buildings that were never built) with case studies of actually completed buildings. Projects are depicted by means of plans, elevations, and sections, but more importantly, as close-up photos of models. Models are photographed with the same attention to detail and at the same scale as buildings, and drawings are given the same conceptual weight as built form, thus marking the book as a homogenizing force in the depiction of both fact and fantasy.

The most blatant manipulation of size as a means of graphic expression is to be found in one of the book's central essays, entitled "Bigness, or the Problem of Large." Appropriately, it serves as the opening piece of the section headed "L" (for large) and is a discussion of the problems that occur when architecture gets beyond a certain scale. In a vaudevillian response to the subject of the essay, Mau sets the text as a 21-page typographic diminuendo beginning at 48-point and ending at 24-point. At first glance, it seems audacious, but its humor quickly fades into the design equivalent of a one-liner. You can almost hear the drum roll and the crack of the cymbal by the time you turn the first page.

While size is most certainly the central metaphor (and the central subject) of this book, there are many other uses of metaphor which deserve discussion. One sequence, entitled "Life in the Box?," takes the reader on a bottom-up circular tour of the Rotterdam Kunsthal. Each photo spread has a full-bleed shot of a stop on the tour, with a small inset that refers to the content of the next spread. In small text at the bottom of each spread, you are given directions: Go up here, turn left there, look up, turn left again, turn right, etc. The dizzying effect of this concentric movement is heightened by yet another layer of text, set in 60-point-type. The text is a passage from Samuel Beckett's *Waiting for Godot,* and the conversation is, of course, about going around in circles.

[...] Tension and juxtaposition are narrative devices that Bruce Mau has employed in many previous works. His use of them is essentially filmic, and this is most evident in his photo editing. But he has also been able to apply cinematic thinking to the deployment of graphic form. Many of his books, including this one, have exploited the effects of chromatic juxtaposition: A purple page will be positioned next to a yellow one, for instance, or a green against a blue one. In this book, a bright orange sequence is immediately followed by a metallic purple sequence. A wordless sequence of full-bleed photo spreads is followed by several pages of densely set text. A case study set in discrete columns of 10-point type is followed by one set in bold 32-point type that fills the page from side to side and top to bottom.

The most curious use of juxtaposition occurs in places where you least expect it. The reader may be caught up in an architectural narrative that is suddenly and inexplicably interrupted by a Renaissance painting, a newswire photo of some disaster, a still from a porno movie, or the front page of a tabloid newspaper. While some of these images may be understood as intellectual stimuli designed to enrich the narrative, others seem to be nothing more than capricious reflections of Koolhaas's fascination with the vernacular of obscenity. His prurience tends to dislocate rather than deepen the reader's engagement with the text.

By far, the most successful sequences in this book are the ones in which Mau and Koolhaas let the images do the talking. One of the most eloquent passages is a series of fourteen photo spreads entitled "Cadavre Exquis." In its meditation on the design and construction of the Netherlands Dance Theater in The Hague, each spread carries only one word identifying an aspect of the building's development: innocence, panic, simulation, battlefield, disbelief, approach, engagement, suspense, compression, immersion, performance, release. The relaxed pace of this passage is a welcome respite from the vigorous density of the rest of the book.

The same can be said for a 13-spread section called "Congestion without Matter," in which the reader is invited to pore over full-bleed shots of a model for the design of a vast public park in Paris. The sequence is entirely wordless, and we are treated to worm's-eye and bird's-eye views of this huge model without the distraction of Koolhaas's ideologically charged text, which tends to wing, pendulum-like, between frantic and pedantic.

Mau has used all of these devices to construct what amounts to a "Working Babel," to quote the title of one of *S,M,L,XL*'s case studies. [...] In a way, Mau's design skills sometimes provide the ice that Koolhaas skates on, glossing over his lack of interest in arguing a point, entertaining rather than informing the reader.

Will this book take its place beside other landmarks of design such as the works of Pierre Faucheux, Robert Massin, El Lissitzky, or Quentin Fiore? Inasmuch as it reconstructs the medium of print by applying cinematic techniques to the deployment of photographic, schematic, and typographic material, it is an experiment that emerges from the same tradition as Massin's *Cantatrice Chauve* and Fiore's *The Medium Is the Massage.* Its reverence for the pure visual drama of abstraction sometimes recalls the constructivism of Lissitzky. And its elastic approach to typography pays homage to the exuberance of Faucheux. It therefore can be said to extend and enrich the visual tradition of these works; but only time will tell if it shares their stature.

In its admittedly arrogant scope and exhaustive ambitions, *S,M,L,XL* will stand as an arcane anomaly in the face of print's demise as the primary medium of information exchange. In a way, it echoes and accepts that demise in its effort to reinterpret the form of the book, just as its experimental predecessors did. Like its predecessors, its substitution of visual for literary form raises more questions than it answers. It emerges as a kind of multimedia experiment trapped on too much paper, a rambling hypertext without a navigational device. [...]

KOOLHAAS GETS A FOUR-STAR RECEPTION AT AA LECTURE

Paul Finch
Architects' Journal, December 14, 1995.

Can it be fifteen years since Rem Koolhaas launched his seminal book *Delirious New York* in the basement of the Architectural Association in Bedford Square? It can; the intervening years have seen the status of the Dutch iconoclast (who lives in London at weekends) rise and rise, despite troughs and peaks in the life of his practice, OMA. It is now under the wing (while keeping its autonomy) of a large Dutch civil engineering group, following a financial crisis.

Koolhaas was his usual confident self last Friday evening, when the lecture room of the AA was packed for his slick, but not too slick, slide show promoting the ideas in his 1376-page epic book, *S,M,L,XL*. He began with a comment that it represented "modesty on a megalomaniac scale," being simultaneously a critique of his office, a collection of projects and buildings, essays, travelogues, diary notes, and, not least, an alphabetical collection of unattributed (until the end) quotes: "You don't know if they are by Philip Johnson or a hairdresser."

The comments and aphorisms came thick and fast: how the absence of mass after the Berlin Wall was demolished had, for him, become an obsessive subject; how in Japanese censorship what was not shown became more important than what was; how La Villette showed landscape doing what architecture no longer can; how every city becomes "the appendix to an airport" (the book is twice as thick as an airport novel); how Asian architecture combines infrastructure with tradition, and how a care for landscape was replacing urban ambition, as cities generally shed identity, becoming generic rather than specific.

[...] He referred to his book as "the apotheosis of specific cities." AA chairman Mohsen Mostafavi, who chaired the event, asked the best question of the evening: how does landscape meet bigness? What happens to the surface at Euralille? Koolhaas referred to the "schizophrenic condition" of contemporary urbanism, with functions housed in "giant containers or extremes of shapelessness." He sought an "engineering not based on repetition."

Asked about the future of architecture as a profession, Koolhaas said he preferred to think of architecture as "a form of intelligence ... a way of thinking about a problem." The lecture made his point.

OMA AT MOMA

Grahame D. Shane

The Los Angeles Forum for Architecture and Urban Design Newsletter, May 1995, 1–7.

The Rem Koolhaas show at the Museum of Modern Art in New York pointed to one of the key problematics of the postmodern city, which is half fused with media hyperspace and advertising simulacra. Like many of his generation, Koolhaas had intuitively understood the public relations dimension of the modernist urban project, long before the current scholarly interest in the rhetorical and staged aspects of Le Corbusier's architecture and urbanism. [...]

In Koolhaas's pioneering work the image of the city became an important visual commodity, a promotional tool ironically derived from Surrealism. At MoMA, Koolhaas began with an extraordinary reading of the section of New York City as an automatic image machine, tracking its media/publicity dimensions in a not-so-random but wandering approach to the exhibit. This sectional exploration and its dissonant simulacra are a key to Koolhaas's urban projects, which were presented on a landing outside the Architecture Gallery.

These urban projects attempt to poetically manipulate the repertoire of "Exquisite Corpses" that inhabit the postmodern city-region, strange combinations of low-density new towns, highly concentrated urban theme parks and massive shopping malls/office parks attached to highways. This imagist, *musée imaginaire* collage approach confronts its own paradoxical limitations in the "Big" three architectural projects displayed at the core of the exhibit in the inner sanctum of the MoMA Architecture Gallery.

The section of the city had a peculiar importance for the Surrealists since it cut behind bourgeois facades and revealed hidden interiors, buried canals of unseen services, providing pointers to the repressed, collective unconscious of the city. Through the section amazing and grotesque juxtapositions could be mapped, splendid opulence could be shown floating on a surface of abject poverty and filth (the Surrealists loved to tour the Parisian slaughterhouses and sewers). Normal codings could be reversed and thrown into question. At the MoMA installation Koolhaas's subversion began with the placement of a long incendiary text in the subway exit of 666 Fifth Avenue, under the street across from the museum, perhaps 100 feet below the exhibit. The text was part of Koolhaas's forthcoming volume *S,M,L,XL*, a witty and nostalgic poem to the global economy, traditional, standardized mass production, sprawling suburbs, the "generic city" of the new postmodern city-region and its alleged new center, the giant international airport (why only one?). The neat black monotype was artfully designed to avoid doors, knobs and mullions in the windows of a large empty store, a victim of the prolonged recession in New York's economy.

Reeling from the underground assault, the museum visitors could pick up the sectional trail again at nearby newsstands in the styling, fashion and women's magazines with interviews given by the architect. At street level, telephone booths carried further passionate messages from *S,M,L,XL*, spotted by AIA's *Oculus* correspondent Jayne Merkel. Philip Johnson is said to have chuckled as he paused before the monotype posters tastefully announcing the ephemeral nature of the city on nearby street hoardings. These hoardings stand in front of the derelict townhouses to be demolished for a museum extension (they are posted above the cardboard boxes in which homeless people sleep on the street). Once inside the museum the messages continued. Ascending the escalators, the visitor could look down at a model of an elegant suburban house design with a rooftop swimming pool (positioned where Koolhaas's and Kollhoff's model of Leonidov's enormous Palace of Heavy Industry project had been displayed in the Deconstructivist show). At the top of the escalators on the foyer landing, Koolhaas's voice could be heard talking about his Lille Project on a publicity videotape. The Architecture Gallery itself was filled with standard, cheaply made New York bus shelters whose large illuminated panels displayed four projects in place of the usual commercials. This surreal transposition, bringing the street furniture from the city into the windowless room, faced a blackboard, containing, in the architect's inimitable scrawl, another manifesto for Bigness in five neomodernist points, echoing the underground *S,M,L,XL* passages.

Koolhaas employed his thread of publicity as a narrative promenade woven through the section of the city up into the museum, in a gesture which attempted to recoup an avant-garde impulse of the Situationalist's random *dérive* or *drift*, long lost to manipulative commercial art and the advertising industry. The museum itself would never have employed such blatant propaganda techniques in its early drive for modern art and Modernism. This mission has changed during the 1980s as the earlier educational drive for Modernism fell away and the postmodern entertainment, mall-like aspects of art consumption were amplified in the César Pelli redesign of the facilities for a new commercialism. The abandonment of the didactic, model-filled room of projects by canonical European, modern, dead white architects (single projects by Mies, Le Corbusier, Aalto, the mummified model of Falling Water, etc.) followed the larger shift in the museum toward contemporary work with corporate and wealthy individual sponsors. The evacuation of the canonical models left a void in the Architecture Gallery which occasioned the initial publicity events of the Koolhaas show. Bernard Tschumi came to be the first contemporary architect exhibited, mysteriously beating the Dutchman to the post as he had done at Parc de la Villette. Herbert Muschamp, the architecture critic of the *New York Times*, amplified this rivalry by his negative review of Tschumi's show, positioning himself clearly in favor of Koolhaas. Shortly before the opening of his own show Koolhaas scored another publicity coup at *The Times*: a young reporter enthusiastically described the details of the architect's lifestyle in the "Living" Section. In the end, Muschamp's final review of Koolhaas was surprisingly cool. It appeared on a Friday and did not connect with the "Big" drive of the show, discoursing instead for half its length about the abstract, formal problem of placing a spiral in a cube. Muschamp preferred Peter Eisenman's tiny show on urban archaeology at the CCA in Montreal, giving it the premier slot on the Sunday after Koolhaas's opening.

The approach to the exhibition, wandering through the city section and city media, gave a clue to the organizational layering of flows and the architect's informational, imagistic vision of the city. Arriving at the landing at the top of the escalators in the foyer to the Architecture Gallery, with the crop-dusting helicopter permanently suspended overhead, Koolhaas's video presentation reinforced this emphasis. He enthusiastically argued that the space-time compression flowing along the lines of the TGV's 180 mph trains would provide the momentum to lift the decaying textile town of Lille into the ranks of the best office parks of twenty-first-century Europe. A vast model of the new complex stood close by the monitor, showing the old railway station and Jean Nouvel's triangular shopping mall, which was linked to the TGV station, positioned beside the highway system, surrounded by an enormous linear parking garage and straddled by a series of office buildings commissioned from a variety of architects. In the background loomed Koolhaas's Congrexpo, an enormous oval building located beside the highway and seen speeding by as an indistinct blur outside the architect's Masserati windshield. To judge by the photos in *ANY* 9, surrealist sectional magic was assured in the parabolic, concrete, dished roof "garden" of the vast Congrexpo building. Here the captured skyline and unusual roofscape may offer a rare and welcome respite from the circus of flows below.

The delicacy of the Surrealist's relationship with advertising and commercial marketing becomes clear in Koolhaas's delight in describing the marketing convention of Mazda salesmen in the Congrexpo building. Here hundreds of new cars and dealers could be united on stage. The architect's enthusiasm accentuated the ability of the building to host publicity events on a vast scale and manipulate time in staged simulacra, commercial urban spectacles and media circuses. The merging of Surrealism and advertising in mass marketing becomes explicit, with architecture as its largely uncritical facilitator and handmaiden. These new interior urban media spaces are places of space-time compression mapped in the network of larger global communication, marketing and transportation flows. These internalized spaces attempt to concentrate vast new mass meetings and hyper-real publicity events but have almost nothing to do with the traditional city, beside whose decontextualized corpse they are sited. Their creation is also dependent on international capital flows, in this case manipulated by the state to create a suitable real estate package, set within a larger city-region.

For Koolhaas these interior spaces are crucial components in defining the image of the postmodern city. Interior sectional revelation of surreal juxtapositions form the basis of Koolhaas's urban imagemaking in a collage of ready-made elements. Koolhaas's voice-over on the video emphasized Lille's new center as the interior, self-referential sectional excitement of the *espace piranésien*, connecting to the TGV. Here his surrealist sectional predilictions came clearly into focus. A monster, multilevel pedestrian interchange hall was dissected by escalators and overlooked by the highway, linking visually to the trains. Sectional transparency transforms urban transportation flows into a spectacle, hopefully very different from the utterly banal, state-sponsored panopticon in the circular central space of the old Charles De Gaulle Airport outside Paris. His image of hyper-concentration, although greatly miniaturized for the small provincial town, echoed his heroes of the oil-rich Rockefeller dynasty, who planned the New York Rockefeller Center in the 1920s and 1930s.

This real estate venture and public relations effort (to cleanse their name after press revelations of their unscrupulous business methods) was an economic and urban disaster according to Robert Fitch in *The Assassination of New York* (1994). The construction of Euralille demonstrated Koolhaas's skill in this tradition of urban image making, moving Lille into the postmodern commercial realm, employing largely interior, sectional, urban spaces and manipulations of the city skyline to project a positive and dynamic future.

[...] The final model on the foyer landing brought together the themes of sectional space-time compression in the center and the peripheral, "Exquisite Corpse"-layering of surreal plan analysis into one project. The project for Yokohama developed the logic of American multifunctional regional malls, whose parking lots house the cars of office workers, shoppers and cinema goers in shifts throughout the day (as at the Galleria complex in Houston). The Yokohama plan proposed a multifunctional city center based on the car parks of an early-morning fish market. [...] The perspex model of this project, illuminated by different-colored flashing lights, perhaps to represent different uses at different times, presented an image of accelerated flows and transparent connections as the postmodern city mutated hourly in section. City-media here took on the problem of the ephemeral, accelerated, compressed, sound-bite quality of the architectural and urban image in the postmodern city, as the prelude to the visitor's entrance into the inner sanctum of the Architecture Gallery.

After all this public foreplay with tentacles stretching down into the subway, arrival at the inner sanctum was somewhat anticlimactic. A blue-gray light suffused the room, reflected from the gallery walls, which were plastered with mouled gray drawings, reminiscent of construction bluelines. These drawings, mounted directly on the walls like fly-posters for rock bands on New York streets, referred to the bus shelter directly in front of them. Amongst the matrix of bus shelters stood often enormous models mounted on big bases to raise them to eye level, each shimmering perspex cube almost rivaling the black mass of the shelter. The walls were strangely uninviting. The blue-gray light reflected off the walls conspired to make the gallery feel underlit, allowing the illuminated poster panels on the bus shelters to dominate, along with slides projected onto the building facades of the model for the Kahlsruhe Center for Art and Media Technology. The facade of this building thus became the central locus, an immaterial, constantly changing flow of information and images projected on a vast urban billboard by a suspended, constantly clicking Kodak Carousel slide projector.

A large blackboard mounted floor to ceiling on the wall to the left of the entrance announced the logic of the vertical projects in the Gallery, contributing to a dark, penumbral, slightly funereal feel of the room. Unlike Tschumi's brightly lit, suspended, free-floating installations, the buildings were displayed in a very static manner like dinosaurs' bones in vast cases. Koolhaas's handwritten text on the blackboard provided further grist to the city-media machine, reechoing the theme of Bigness first broached in the subway perhaps 100 feet below. [...]

The vertical projects further developed the logic of Lille and Yokohama. "Big" buildings were cities in themselves, the Modernists' dream of the ocean liner as self-contained community, detached from place, mobile and decontextualized. The ambition of the vertical projects, as at Yokohama, was to encapsulate and replicate the life of the city within one single building envelope or enclave, providing for a shifting and changing use throughout the day and over time. Sectional and plan juxtapositions derived from the Surrealists would be engineered to give an appearance of diversity and difference, despite the enormous unifying effort which concentrated regional, even national and international flows in one space. These buildings became total, parallel worlds, a self-referential hyper-space, like the Surrealist's "Musée lmaginaire"—a largely unconscious, collective memory device or image bank which conditioned behavior for those within its confines. [...]

The sectional organization and plan juxtapositions of the tiny, built, Rotterdam Kunsthal demonstrated in miniature the promised virtues of the other jumbo-sized projects in the Gallery. Each plan cell contains one function, one image. In section the project is like a split-level ranch, connecting to the surrounding park on the lower level and highway on the upper level. A central fire safety box contains a fairly steep ramp connecting the levels and forming one cross axis. A service road passes through on the lower level parallel with the highway forming the other cross axis. The exhibition hall and auditorium are located in cells on either side of the ramp and step up in section to avoid the service road. The gallery is conventionally lit from plate glass windows, while the auditorium contains many nice lighting devices and small-scale structural displays—animating the interior surfaces as in the earlier Netherlands Dance Theater. As in that theater, a café is hidden under the slope of the auditorium floor in a beautiful, crypt-like space, lit by artificial light. The vertical fire-safety service core is extended onto the roof to carry a billboard and projection screen visible from the highway.

The sequence of larger vertical projects appeared to propose both larger boxed partitions and a more dynamic interplay between partitions and ramps in plan. In each project Koolhaas rapidly proceeds to try to break down these monster programs into intelligible distinct cells with distinct images, set within the secure perimeter of the cubic enclave. The huge model of the Très Grande Bibliothèque of 1989 nicely illustrated this strategy with its plaster-cast white programmatic elements distributed like sculpted organs throughout the section of the vast building. As at Yokohama, each plaster-cast cell contained its own distinct program and image, this time vertically layered inside the grid of Maison Domino—like library stacks, with elevator cores providing the vertical connections. The Karlsruhe project appeared to keep the boxed interior cell-image partitions of Rotterdam, but with escalators in a separate boxed zone which wandered past the vertically stacked partitioned rooms and linked outside to the nearby station. As at Rotterdam it was the exterior of the building which acted as a publicity billboard, addressing the center of the city on the other side of the railway tracks. In the library for the University of Paris at Jussieu of 1992 the vertical sectional juxtapositions were this time married to a spiraling ramp perhaps inspired by Wright's Guggenheim or Mike Webb's Sin City Project of the Archigram years (setting off Muschamp's musings). In the Jussieu project the spiral also weaves down through the podium of the miserable, existing monument to French bureaucratic Modernism in a surprising attempt to link the sterile dinosaur to its small-scale historical surrounding neighborhood.

The vertical projects demonstrated the limits of the surrealist impulse as it became imbedded in the logic of the state bureaucratic apparatus. These were totally controlled, interior environments very different from the libertarian impulse of the Situationist technique of sectional, narrative *dérive*, or the Surrealist techniques of the "Exquisite Corpse" or the "Musée Imaginaire." Slowly I began to read the penumbral lighting and funereal tone of the inner sanctum as a typically ironic performance by Koolhaas, framing the public display of these vast corpses in a temporary graveyard, a suitable resting place for such megalomaniac urban and architectural aberrations of the late 1980s and early 1990s. The tawdry bus shelters, gray walls and apocalyptic blackboard pronouncements reinforced this impression. In this suggested reading Koolhaas's use of subdued lighting and aggressive public relations skills masked a display of self-doubt, lacerating his modernist soul in public in the blue-gray haze of the Gallery, before the required arrogant display of monumental certainty.

The vertical projects also revealed the limitation of the Surrealist critique, as the projects collapsed over the edge of Bigness into either a commercial or a political quagmire. The cult of Bigness is one of centralization and standardization, once favored by modernist corporations and symbolically represented by the Rockefellers. It was also beloved by dictators in many ages, ranging from the Pharaohs to Napoleon, Mussolini, Stalin, Hitler etc. Koolhaas's preemptive defensive strikes on the theme of Bigness seek to deflect criticism from the weakness of the situation in which he finds himself. The funereal tone of the inner sanctum was no accident in a period of dispersal and miniaturization, cheap CD-ROMs, the World Wide Web and Internet, mass home computer ownership and global communication so crucial to the generic city-media machine. Paradoxically the two largest vertical projects displayed were in a direct line of descent from the megalomaniac schemes of Boullée for a gigantic Bibliothèque Nationale at the time of the French Revolution. Here all global information would be centralized, ordered by the state and disseminated to the people on a vast scale in a monumental setting. Totalitarian logic distrusted people and relied on a superior central intelligence to educate and to guide the general population like sheep, using terror if necessary.

The Surrealist's joke of the "Musée Imaginaire," a collective imaginative space of random juxtapositions based on the dream work of Freudian analysis, could be adapted to authoritarian traditions. The cult of imagery and hyper-reality could easily be manipulated to serve politicians and big business, massaging populations via the media to accept new visions of society or buy new products. Neither Surrealism nor Modernism was immune from this manipulative impulse. Salavador Dalí opted for Franco and the Church, while Aragon and others became Communists despite Stalin. Meanwhile countless advertising agencies have drawn upon Surrealist works.

Manfredo Taluri in *Architecture and Utopia* demonstrated how the utopian and dystopian impulses became integrated into the process of capitalist, industrialstate production through the dream of a central controller, a single controlling imagination or point of view. The integrating element of Koolhaas's surreal theater of operations is precisely the dream of controlling the imagination of the controller, through publicity images coordinating state and commercial planning (thus the inventory of ready-made projects devoted to postmodern diversity, malls, office parks etc.). As a media artist the architect seeks control of the urban image, which has become a commodity at play in the marketing strategies of state or private developers attempting to differentiate themselves from their competitors. Koolhaas's tomb to the unbuilt vertical projects at MoMA beautifully demonstrated his awareness of this difficult megalomaniac situation, while simultaneously trying to distance himself, subverting the normal devices of publicity to his own ironic and poetic ends, attempting an impossible demonstration of transcendent personal independence.

HISTORICAL MAGNANIMITY

George Baird
Harvard GSD News, Summer 1996, 49–50.

gb: To start us off I'd like to reprise some arguments I made about OMA a disconcertingly long time ago, in 1977, in a short essay in *AD*, before the firm became as famous as it is now. Then, as now, I was an admirer of the work, and when I reread my text, I was pleasantly surprised to discover how astute I'd been. I described four paradoxes that seemed to me to characterize their work. First, at a time when Modernism had lost much of its momentum and was being attacked and disparaged, it was fascinating to see architectural projects that so resolutely hung onto the visionary dimension of Modernism. [...] These projects were visionary and implementable, and that seemed to me unusual for avant-garde work at that time. A second paradox that interested me was the work's combination of surreal qualities, on the one hand, and commonsensical qualities on the other. The deliriousness of New York had by that time become familiar to many, and it was readable in the production of OMA. Yet here again, one could see a hard edge of common sense. [...] The third paradox was that the work seemed simultaneously puritanical and luxurious. There seemed an interesting play between sublimation and gratification, especially in the treatment of spatiality and visual surfaces. The fourth paradox was the combination of both revolutionary and evolutionary qualities: revolutionary because of its seemingly unique affirmation of the legitimacy of the metropolis as a phenomenon of modernity, which had almost across the board been seen negatively by the major figures of the tradition since the early nineteenth century. OMA's work had evolutionary characteristics as well; what struck me as interesting was the matter-of-fact adoption of propositions about building typologies that might constitute a repertoire of available programs and building types for the orchestration of metropolitan phenomena. So OMA's work seemed to me a very powerful cultural proposition. In the era of postmodernist doubt, it was affirmative; it reasserted a strong interest in building program as a component of architectural innovation. In 1977 all this suggested a provocative future, and I think we can say that *S,M,L,XL* certainly represents confirmation of this future.

rk: You began by congratulating yourself on your astuteness and consistency, so it might also be said that we have not evolved and that therefore your intelligence is only an effect of our stupidity. But you've also done something that I want to persist in avoiding, which is to look back. In a certain way, every book is both a positive and a negative project: each is the book that you want to do but also the book that you want to avoid doing. In this sense, *S,M,L,XL* is an accumulation of avoided issues and ambitions. We have avoided either looking back on our own work or giving an "official" version of it. The reasons for this are personal—one effect of the changing status of our work and also, I have to admit, of myself, is an incredible expectation, an incredible pressure, also an incredible greed, to have the various interpretations of our work and our character supported and underwritten by ourselves, to have the theoretical constructs that may exist about our work be approved or disapproved by us. In other words, we are no longer the only persons, to quote Bruce Mau, pushing the envelope of our own identity. But it seems very important to avoid being involved in this, because every definition of our work clearly limits our freedoms. And if there's any consistency, in both our work and personalities, it involves a systematic search for freedoms. I see the oppositions you describe in our work less as the unique characteristics of one office or one or more persons, but rather as some inevitable reactions to a new situation in which architecture finds itself. In our creative work, our projects, and our overall position, the cultivation of a systematic acuteness based on articulating and defining certain dissatisfactions with the profession of architecture, areas of aversion and resistance to given interpretations and descriptions, is just as important as a formal, respectful, and official reasoning. My relationship with architecture—which might be described as either traumatic or radical—began when I entered the profession, after having been involved in another profession, and found it grotesquely ill-equipped to deal with pervasive and operative conditions. Maybe it is difficult to remember how the profession was then interpreted—or maybe not so difficult. Architecture was then considered a kind of humanist profession, with a long tradition of humanist discourse, and a seemingly endless future of humanist activity. It was considered a powerful profession, the practitioners of which would play an important role in the world, and an ordering profession, skillful in improving bad and chaotic conditions—not averse to improving the world. It was a profession that regarded itself as ideological, with a certain political operationality. All those conditions were to me illusions; the certainty the profession expressed seemed to me dubious, implausible. Another important aspect of our career, simply because our firm started in the 1970s, is the whole process of globalization, which is not unique to our career, but pertains to a potential architectural career in this final part of the twentieth century. It involves a potential but also a difficulty, the difficulty of straddling a number of cultures. Europe and America have been the most important cultures for us, but increasingly the cultures of Asia play a role in the definition of ourselves and our office. In a sense, I was exposed in a drastic way to this potential of operating in different cultures. For that reason alone, your initial set of oppositions involves not necessarily the eccentric or lucid impulses of a unique individual, but rather the result, on the one hand, of this aversion to the profession and a corresponding ambition to change it, and, on the other, of the way in which those two aspects are modified by the experience of globalization.

So, for instance, if our work is visionary yet implementable, that seems to me a direct result of how, in the 1970s, you could have an experience of Europe and America simultaneously at the beginning of your career. In the most banal way, as a European, I was aware of the tendency and ability and the genius of Europeans to imagine manifestoes, but also of their seemingly corresponding weakness at implementing them; and at the same time, I had the experience in the United States of the genius of Americans in implementing their ideas, but also of their inability to articulate their visions. So in that sense, I think of our career as an intersection or hybridization of a European impulse to define, combined with the American will to implement. You talk about the surreal and commonsensical. The word "surreal" in 1977 had a much more negative meaning than now; then it seemed to connote weirdness and Dalí; and Dalí was a discredited artist. But we have seen a rehabilitation of surrealism in intellectual circles; Rosalind Krauss has showed that surrealism is, in effect, a serious attempt to create a less dictatorial relationship with a number of themes—to be less obsessed with the imposition of order on themes, to let the formless energy of those themes be manifest with minimal conscious interference from the artist. So there, again, that opposition seems to me to involve less a bold attempt to connect extremes than the awareness that surrealism has a strong relationship with rationality and with the commonsensical—a word I hate. As for our puritanical aspect—well, I would rather not comment about that because I want to have the freedom to roam in this domain as I see fit, and also, more importantly, as my clients allow me. And as for our revolutionary and evolutionary aspects—I think that my earlier statement about the misreading of the powers, the potentials, and also the definition of the architectural profession, and of the profession of urbanism, applies here as well. In my view there was an increasing gulf opening up between illusions about the profession and the drastic, accelerated developments in other domains, such as the evaporation of Marxism and of the Communist states, and also the global tendency toward the creation of ever larger organizational complexes and corporate entities. In many ways, then, the writings in *S,M,L,XL* are simply attempts, whether retroactive or prospective, to explain and argue what a redefined profession might look like.

gb: Well, one is familiar with the propensity of cagey revolutionaries to argue that they are merely the vanguard of inexorable, broad-based historical forces. I'd like to relate this question of professional efficacy to my thematic juxtapositions. I wouldn't mind trying to unpack a bit more of the European-American methodological polarity that you described. And this question of efficacy relates also to the overthrowing of the project of Postmodernism, for a conventional history of the period since the middle 1970s would see typologies regarded for a time as part of a legitimate methodology of building and urban designing, and then banished with the rebuttal of Postmodernism in the 1980s.

rk: One of the interesting things about the twentieth century is that we live in a period and a culture in which rebuttal doesn't lead to death. Architectural Postmodernism is an interesting case in point. It acquired a certain intellectual credibility and glamour, which it quickly lost. It's no longer discussed seriously in architectural schools; we have signed its death sentence. Yet if you look around, out in the world, it doesn't look as if anyone has noticed. To me this illustrates the lack of efficacy of our profession, our inability to dictate the agenda. But it also shows how professions always create an ideal explanation of movements. According to our profession, for instance, Postmodernism was an intellectual and ideological reaction to the dearth of articulation of Modernism, the inability of Modernism to establish a relationship with the past and to invent typologies that might build a city. But I think that a more accurate interpretation is that Postmodernism is simply a new architecture that can be generated at the speed that architecture now has to be generated—and here I mean architecture with a small "a"—given the incredible acceleration of urbanism in countries like China, Korea, and Thailand. In places where metropolises are being invented in front of your very eyes, it might be distressing but it is undeniable that Postmodernism is the style and method of choice; and this has nothing to do with articulation and nothing to do with reactions to Modernism. In that sense, I think that our activities in the La Défense project consisted in part of saying, in effect, "Okay, if you want to build a city with this speed, this dearth of program, this repetition of accommodation, and this unadventurousness of form, then let's accept all that and base a notion on it." I would say that our work in this way connects with that rationale for the emergence of Postmodernism. What I'm trying to do is show how every position is, to some extent, a form of grandstanding; if you are involved, as we are, in an intimate way in these processes, then you must know that what you present might be completely denied by events taking place behind your back.

gb: Rem was the first person I knew who was prepared to make a defense of the cultural production of Team 10 in the years after it had suffered radical criticism, but I hadn't realized until tonight that his historical magnanimity even extends to PoMo. But actually I think that this tendency always to second-guess the conventional reading of the moment is interesting in itself. It seems to me, insofar as one might define professional efficacy in part as the ability of architects to respond to the subconscious expectations of large populations, that Postmodernism differs fundamentally from both Modernism and Deconstructivism. Now, I would argue that one of the enduring projects of architecture for the past 100 or 150 years has been the attempt first to identify some trajectory of powerful social forces, and then to intersect or align with them so as to maximize the power of an individual or a group.
rk: I think that there may be some misunderstanding about the word *alignment.* Alignment doesn't mean, for me, that we take an uncritical position toward the phenomena that interest us. It's possible to want to respond to a tendency that seems triumphant or dominant, without necessarily being euphoric about it. In our work we try to combine criticism of a phenomenon with an ability to work within and parallel to it.

gb: Fair enough. But I was quite struck in *S,M,L,XL* by the Singapore essay, footnoted even.

rk: Why do you say "footnoted even"?

gb: There are not many footnotes in the rest of the book.

rk: But the book consists of many kinds of writing, like dreams. Footnotes to dreams would be a bit pedantic.

gb: The Singapore essay seems to point to patterns operating under the surface of an explicit discourse that has opened up many provocative possibilities. Indeed, one of the powerful moments for me in that essay was your citation of the architectural rebels of the early 1970s who attempted to bring into the Singapore architectural milieu a set of propositions which do in fact come from Team 10 and from Metabolism, and who succeeded in actually doing so, maybe to their own chagrin. And I wondered whether these citations refer to the combination of somehow both "rolling with the punches" and critically intervening that you seem to endorse. On the other hand, I have to confess to considerable disappointment with the Atlanta essay, which in comparison seemed to have a Fredric Jameson or even a Mike Davis style—or perhaps I should say a Baudrillard style—encouraging us in a slightly queasy way to enjoy how bad the place is.

rk: Well, that was certainly not my intention. The present reading of the city is as a group of buildings, streets, plazas, et cetera. But definite, even aggressive, investigations of a new relationship between architecture and the nature of what is public are now occurring. In the nineteenth century, public life was understood to involve a *very* intense urban life in the streets and relative intimacy and isolation in buildings. It is clear that such demarcations no longer exist, and that the enormity of certain buildings has forever, I think, redefined civil society. Attempts at creating new forms of civil society in those buildings are now a necessity. Our Jussieu project, for instance, manipulated the exterior, and organized it, in a sense, as an interior. [...] It occurs to me to ask you whether the book has helped you to understand our position, whether you think that the analogy between the book and the subjects works or doesn't work. Do you think it camouflages contradictions that are too strong to be hidden?

gb: I don't yet have a coherent picture of the book's intentions or results, although it's certainly informative and provocative.

rk: I hate to be childish, but that's exactly the point. This book has tried to avoid the compulsion or obligation to present a career in a formal or conclusive way. It instead tries to convey the fact that as an architect you are influenced by a number of fairly random forces, over which you have limited control. Given all this, we could not make a book that gives the impression of an overall edifice or a stable position.

LIBERATING MICRO-EPIPHANIES

Haig Beck, Jackie Cooper *UME: The International Architecture Magazine* 2 (1996), 48–49.

Just the thickness of this book alone defies its being approached as a sequential narrative. The contemporary era of information overload and overstretched schedules makes it almost impossible to undertake as a continuous and sustained project the reading of 1,344 pages. Vikram Seth's *A Suitable Boy*, at about 1,100 pages, is an epic read: his narrative as chronology, recalling the tradition of Dickens, is a way of sustaining the reader over such a lengthy text. But the first detective novel is closer in form to Koolhaas's *S,M,L,XL*: Wilkie Collins's long book, *The Moonstone*, is organized as a series of disjointed episodes that make sense only as they are brought together in the last few pages. However, unlike Collins, Koolhaas provides no resolution at the end of his book. Instead, there is a multitude of resolutions, questions, insights, paradoxes and meanings littered throughout; and they are delivered not only through the texts but also through the projects and their drawings.

Bruce Mau, the book's typographer, has equal billing on the cover with OMA; the precedence of Rem Koolhaas is signified only through color. The typography, by one of the great contemporary typographers, follows the new convention of cybergraphics, which defies rationalism. Essentially phenomenological in approach, cybergraphics establishes an emotional equivalence between type and image, lending type a similar range of expression previously belonging to images; here information is to be experienced directly and synchronically rather than gathered and processed sequentially and chronologically.

[...] Each text and project introduce a contract between reader and author: the reader must bring a critical intelligence and interpretive imagination; the author ensures that each text and project is a demonstration of a critical position or theoretical proposition. Mau's graphics and typography and Koolhaas's ordering of the material (and there is an order) generate disruptive opportunities for the reader's interpretive imagination to engage. There are clear links here to dada and surrealism. Even the very weight of the book has an effect on the reading of its cybergraphic design. The length introduces a third dimension, as it were—assuming the first two dimensions to be represented in the coincidence of typography and image, which induces the instantaneous consumption of text. This third dimension is considerable time: few could contemplate reading *S,M,L,XL* in one go; and if you consume it in short bites, it will take you months to get through. And that in itself induces a reflectivity that's missing from conventional cybergraphics.

Like all Koolhaas projects, this book has an order. And like all Koolhaas projects, it is an arbitrary and random order imposed on the project to guide its form (which helps the designer) and to induce chance conjunctions in the mind of the user/reader through the collision of orders. In essence Koolhaas first defined this approach when he identified the culture of congestion, which is at the core of his first major theoretical work, *Delirious New York*. In *S,M,L,XL* he chooses to interpose a series of orders. The first is that the projects are organized in terms of scale—hence the title. And generally these projects are set down chronologically within that framework. Koolhaas occasionally breaks his own rule. The projects and buildings span a period from 1972 to 1993.

[...] The elements of the lexicon are both unavoidable and irresistible. They provide a textual titillation, and no matter what you are reading, your eye will stray to the column running down the side of the spread. The consequence is crazy and accidental juxtapositions. In this respect the book is most like a city, offering the culture of congestion, with the lexicon providing chance encounters with strangers, heralding the opportunity for new understandings, new insights, new relationships.

[...] Like many of us, Koolhaas has had only one really very good idea. And like all really good ideas, it generates countless others. Unlike Koolhaas, most of us never work out what our good idea is or get to its essence. In Koolhaas's case, it's the theory of the culture of congestion. This is his hardcore: he believes in it implicitly. One can look at *S,M,L,XL* and the enormous range of projects and writings as the outcomes of his program of action, providing the various means by which he puts this single, simple and powerful idea to work. And what we see in his method almost parallels the cartoon parody of the Dutchman as a cool, emotionless rationalist: while Koolhaas desires the hurly burly of chance conjunctions and the collision of events in the culture of congestion, he nevertheless wants to set down a system, a mechanism for encouraging, containing, designing such a culture and such congestion. Koolhaas has remained totally focused throughout his career on this dichotomy of wanting to experience both control and chaos, for he knows that it is out of this human paradox that invention—new programs—arises. New York is his muse, with its highly organized system of gridded streets, extruded city blocks and seething urban intensity. And La Villette—in which the rationalizing system is far more complex than sketched here—becomes his method. Every OMA project follows this way of thinking: a rational system is imposed on the irrational.

[...] The central paradox that OMA engages in, the coexistence of order and chaos, can be seen in many variations—as operating between pain and pleasure, hedonism and repression, responsibility and freedom, or between the conceptual and the experiential. OMA sets out to make an architecture which continually heightens the tensions of these paradoxes, in particular the tensions between the conceptual and the experiential. It is the experiential, the phenomenological dimension of architecture, that is always the least discussed—precisely because it is to be experienced rather than conceptualized. Yet, after satisfying the utilitarian demands of a brief, it is clearly the most important of architecture's qualities. And because OMA operates in the realm of the paradox, it operates in this experiential dimension. Indeed, it is probably the most important aspect of OMA's built work. In publishing the Dance Theater, Koolhaas uses key words for each major image: Approach, Engagement, Suspense, Compression, Immersion, Performance, Release. These are all crude, raw allusions to spatial experiences. Such experiences are engendered through the manipulation of architectural space and through the choice of materials. And let there be no doubt in this regard, Koolhaas is a hedonist. Of the Welfare Palace Hotel, he notes in his description of the project the materials: marble, steel, plastic, glass—and there's acres of marble. He has no qualms using the rarest of rainforest timbers: the house in Floirac, Bordeaux uses mahogany as the preferred timber. Also in this house you can see him passing the inhabitants and visitors through a sequence of highly theatrical spatial experiences. The richest, rarest and most expensive materials can be juxtaposed against the most utilitarian, and these unexpected conjunctions bring new meanings to both. Cheap aluminium sheeting, corrugated metal, industrial glazing are suddenly featured in the most significant/special public spaces. And the rare and beautiful in turn are located in places that are essentially service areas in a building, but which people often come in contact with. So there is an equation operating here, which places together rarity and frequency, and then the utilitarian and public importance. One dimension of these conjunctions is conceptual: what do they mean? The building literally challenges the intelligence of the user to interpret. But the other dimension is the highly pleasurable frisson that comes from encountering the transgressive conjunction or location of materials. OMA makes buildings full of pleasurable transgressions and opportunities for tactile and spatial sensations. Users experience wonderful and unexpected combinations of materials: they see them, feel them, hear them. The result is a series of liberating micro-epiphanies. In OMA spaces, people are sensitized—to their surroundings, to themselves. It is not a question of just being: they are engaged, and their presence becomes a performance. And while it looks like spare and minimalist architecture, there is a generosity of space. OMA makes a stage. [...]

CLOSE TO LIFE

Florian Beigel

Architectural Research Quarterly 3 (1996), 88–90.

S,M,L,XL is a timely reminder that architecture can be life or at least can be close to life. Rem Koolhaas and his collaborators are continuing the modern experiment of openness, of space first then object, of void and its inhabitation and of communication on a larger and more complex scale than the modern pioneers. We are presented with a spectacle of congestion that sometimes assumes nightmarish proportions, into programmatic scenarios of the fantastic that embrace the uncertain, the delirious, the paradoxical and the chaotic in our metropolitan condition. The message is that it is happening anyway, and we had better work with it rather than hide our heads in the sand.

The architectural response that Rem Koolhaas proposes is interesting: “If there is to be a ‘new urbanism’ ... it will no longer be concerned with the arrangement of more or less permanent objects, but with the irrigation of territories with potential.” Master plans and other propositions of finalities are inappropriate in a situation of large scale and of flux. These territories are architectural infrastructures of varying scales waiting for inhabitation. They have what he calls an indeterminate specificity. The idea is that the order of size of such an infrastructural architecture would have sufficient unifying power to make differences in inhabitations enjoyable. Cedric Price laid the seed for these territories in his work and built a prototype of it in the form of his Interaction Centre in Kentish Town, North London, which provides a kind of urban table in part serving as a roof but otherwise open ended in its use.

S,M,L,XL is a book for architects and nonarchitects. It makes our work enjoyable and is a most welcome inspiration for the process of design. It is didactic and it contains original research and inventions in the realm of design processes among which is the current compositional technique of collaging a plan in overlapping programmatic layers. This method is clearly demonstrated in the La Villette project: named "Congestion without Matter" (signaling two key ideas in the work), it brings composition out of the cupboard and makes it accessible to critique. Also demonstrated in this project is the even more fundamental idea of composition from vertical to horizontal: the Downtown Athletic Club Skyscraper in New York with its floor spaces varied in character and program, is laid as if on the ground providing a starting point for the idea of the program stripes of the park. This procedure reminds me of Candilis's idea of "laying Le Corbusier's Unité on the ground" in order to give a starting point for his group's design for the Free University in Berlin.

The postscript part of the book, titled "Unraveling," describes the winning competition design of two libraries for the Jussieu University in Paris. Incisions are made into the ground plane which is subsequently unraveled upwards to produce a continuum of sloped planes which could be described as a vertically extended landscape with cultivations of bookshelves and reading tables—Scharoun's idea of the reading landscape of the Berlin National Library drawn to higher levels.

The section titled "Darwinian Arena" describes the competition design development for the ZKM in Karlsruhe. Every floor is specific in this large box and with the aid of the story-high Vierendeel truss structures every other floor level is liberated from structure. I think this design—a collaboration with a structural engineer with an interest in chaos theory, Cecil Balmond of Ove Arup & Partners—applied for the first time the Vierendeel girder to multistory construction in this way. The effect is astonishing. The Vierendeel truss is a most architectural truss as it is free of diagonal members because of the bending stiffness of the joints and truss members. It could be described as a set of flying columns. The theme and the variations of the truss in the Karlsruhe design are an essay in making spatial specificities by the architectural and engineering team, not an exercise in structural acrobatics. I haven't seen a multistory construction with such a high degree of sectional variation before, although there are traces of it in Le Corbusier's work.

None of the projects is really a building. They are more fragments of city space, which might be described as outside-inside inversions. They are not fragments of a traditional European city. They are pieces of a more open city with a flowing space, perhaps fragments of what Scharoun, talking about his Berlin Hauptstadt Competition of 1957 and the Baroque city of Prague, has called *citylandscape*, in which urban space is compared to geological formation.

[...] The relationship of fullness and emptiness is a central concern in the work. It operates at a range of scales. In the Euralille project an entirely new city, straddling the new TGV station, has been inserted into Lille close to the historical center. The relationship between the two is made very clear through the void of the *Triangle des Gares* between them. Having designed the relationship, OMA leaves fullness to others and enjoys the charge and the freedom of the void. [...] Lille is a rare European example where the relationship between the old city and the new is so uplifting.

Rem Koolhaas's preference for the poetry of the in-between, its programmatic scenario and his tendency to leave architectural things to the process "of what is happening anyway," explains perhaps a certain relaxedness if not disinterest with and in materiality and building. The approach relies heavily on the art of collaging readily available materials and components (the method of building a 747 aircraft), on good catalogue collection and selection, on good technology transfer, on good and sympathetic contractor designers and most of all on sympathetic and capable engineers. What would Congrexpo be without Ove Arup & Partners? There is a conspicuous absence of technical documentation in the book apart from the conceptual notes and sketches by Balmond. The way OMA's material choices are informed by their concept of void can only be deduced from the photographs, which are often so cinematic that deduction is hard work. One is also sometimes left wondering about lifecycle planning.

Koolhaas's project diaries, dreams and nightmares give this book a warm touch and demonstrate how close architecture can come to life. He manages with these accounts to make us feel it is all worth while although it can be miserable, traumatic, infernal and sometimes very lonely. Rem Koolhaas never made a secret of his suspicions about architecture. "Architecture is mean, urbanism is generous"—his open urbanism to be exact. I would describe him as a landspace architect operating from S to XL. Visiting the Kunsthal in Rotterdam last year, I found a series of internal and external information gardens, arranged between the dike and the low land (a symbolic place for Holland), and between the traditional brick urbanism at the upper level and the 1920s experiment at the lower end of the gardens (a collaboration with the late French landscape architect Yves Brunier, who died much too young). My steps quickened and I was going on my toes. The sloped floor was fascinating. It had been a long time since I had felt freshened and awakened like this when visiting a new building. There is a collage painting full of wonder about this project in the book.

It is time that OMA and others are allowed to build in this country to help lift the tired traditionalism and myopia that is burdening us. After all many of the ideas originate from this country.

BRAVE NEW BOOK

Irénée Scalbert
Architectural Research Quarterly 3 (1996), 90–91.

The most obvious fact that distinguishes Rem Koolhaas's latest book is its bulk: 1376 pages in all. Coming from an author for whom bigness has value in itself, this bulk is appropriate, provocative and faintly predictable. [...] In one sense, it is the first volume of an *oeuvre complète* and supersedes previous publications by OMA. But only to a point: the balance is heavily weighed in favor of illustrations and visual pleasure, often at the expense of descriptions. Lay people should enjoy the book, as long as understanding the projects is not among their priorities. The book will be of more value to the cognoscenti, and above all to the converted for whom the mix of oracles, flash graphics, slices of modern life and memorable model photography will be tantamount to the voice of the master.

S,M,L,XL falls uneasily between the models of an *oeuvre complète,* a coffee-table book and a bible of which, give or take half an inch, it adopts the standard format. A comment by a young and well-known architect, to the effect that his problem is how to keep the book away from himself, underlines the force of its cult appeal and gives a hint of its probable success. From this perspective, the choice of Bruce Mau as book designer and his creditation as coauthor are consistent. Mau established his reputation with the design of *ZONE.* In this fashionable reader's digest, a few extracts by Deleuze, Virilio and others (too short for assessment but long enough to feed polite conversation) confer respectability on a host of derivative writings and eye-catching snapshots of modern life and "critical" art. Mau's varied and effective use of typography, color and photography inserts was to a large extent responsible for the success of the magazine. Much the same devices were reused in the design of *S,M,L,XL,* with greater licence and imagination. This is not to suggest that OMA's work is derivative and second-rate: quite the opposite is true. Rather, that contents, as in *ZONE,* come to depend on the form of the book, and not the reverse.

Provided the form is attractive—and it is—this order of priorities has advantages. Reading becomes easy, quick and pleasurable, affording a methodical person the rare satisfaction of ploughing through 300 pages in a single evening. Yet "reading" seems a strangely inappropriate word for a book that is mostly pictorial. The downside is that the surfeit of visuals belies the thoughtfulness which one knows, or rather guesses, informs most projects, and diminishes the authority which these and the texts might otherwise better command. As the book encourages browsing from page to page as one might "graze" from one TV channel to another, irritatingly, it also presumes standards of understanding among readers that are well below those which presided over the conception of projects.

However impressive, presentation will regularly frustrate goodwill and intelligence. For example, the reader will learn nothing about Congrexpo, Lille's new conference center, save that it is big. Its plans are difficult to read in themselves. Lacking annotations, they will be incomprehensible to specialists and mystifying to lay persons. Other projects, like a town planning exercise for Yokohama, fare worse in spite of marginal comments, so much so that some readers will suspect a hoax produced in one or two sleepless nights on a photocopier and a scanner (this last scheme gets twenty-eight pages).

The structure of the book imitates the section of a skyscraper which may one day be recognized as an architectural paradigm, as insistent in OMA's work as the hut or the concrete frame was in the work of others. Projects and articles are intermixed throughout the four sections which correspond to the categories announced in the title: from Small for housing, to Extra-Large for urbanism, with everything else in between. Occasionally, inserts are included, like floor tenants for whom one has a vague curiosity yet whom one chooses to ignore: surgeons operating on Lenin's corpse, an ad for men's underpants, banal images of sex or nudity, etc. In addition, a primer of more than a thousand quotations scans the margins of the book in alphabetical order, from Abolish to Zone Ratio. Ranging from the profound to the amusing via the merely indifferent, happily free of pretentiousness, it conveys both the random variety and the impressive openness of OMA's intellectual mind cast.

Present in the dictionary-like layout of the book, Koolhaas's interest in the typical recurs in many ways, most explicitly in two essays entitled "Typical Plan" and "The Generic City," extolling the virtues of the absence of specific qualities in commercial office planning and in the modern urban landscape respectively. It is reinforced by a professed disaffection with formalism that is shared among some architects of his and subsequent generations. No project better illustrates this disposition than OMA's competition entry for the Très Grande Bibliothèque (TGB) and its sequel, the ZKM building in Karlsruhe (OMA's best designs since the proposal for the park of La Villette). It is engaging that Koolhaas can hardly refrain from airing his own enthusiasm for these projects, describing an early sketch drawn for the former by an assistant as "astonishingly absurd, astonishingly beautiful." Both designs testify to a remarkable inventiveness that proceeds not so much to break every conceivable rule, but from an almost palpable and hugely invigorating desire for unchartered experiments, sustained by a euphoric pride alluded to in the double-spread insert of Tiepolo's heavenly Apollo and the Continents.

These projects which became rightly famous convey, today still, an intimation of liberating, buoyant creation, bubbling up from within the deep sea of historicism. Like Rauschenberg who once erased a drawing by de Kooning before offering it as art, Koolhaas, with heroism rather than humor, attempts to reinvent architecture by shedding his designer self. In the TGB project, he makes use of a "strategy of the void," and seeks to define spaces from the inside out alone, in an imitation of functionalist method. Hence the monumental cube proposed for the Bibliothèque circumvents deliberate signification. Its facades, according to the architect, "merely represent four out of an endless series of possible cuts" or sections, and the public rooms are "carved out" or "left out" from the "neutral" void of storage and service spaces. Koolhaas's will to escape the "unbearable task" of making form, this "sad mode of simulating invention," has a curious outcome. The plans of both the TGB and the ZKM building are a precise reversal of the "typical plan." The service areas which, in a commercial skyscraper, were located in the center of the plan, are now wrapped around the periphery. Besides enforcing an unwitting specificity, most noticeably in the interior of the TGB—the envelope can no longer be the container of residual and therefore neutral spaces—this arrangement offers the very real disadvantage of removing usable spaces away from natural light (this disadvantage was largely circumvented by Richard Rogers in the Lloyds building). At this point, two questions arise. Is not Koolhaas's much advertised dedication to program constrained and eventually contradicted by his desire to demonstrate a feature recognized in the New York skyscraper and later enshrined in his "theory" of bigness: namely the divorce between appearance and performance, between envelope and space? Further, could not OMA's escape from formalism be, not so much a new dedication to program (which could hardly differ from old-fashioned functionalism), but formalism turned on its head, a search for formlessness? The answer to both questions is, I think, affirmative. Yet this Möbius-like quality of Koolhaas's argument amplifies rather than denies the haunting, absurd and epic poetry of his quest for nonform, that is the thread running in and out of sight through an imperfect and sometimes scary *oeuvre*.

As for OMA's urbanism, its singular merit is to draw attention to what architects and planners cannot do. Not without reason, Koolhaas argues that "the most progressive architects have an emotional interest in perpetuating backwardness, and a corresponding degree of bitterness at the success of policies whose failure they predicted and whose attractions they underestimated." "What if we simply declare that there is no crisis—redefine our relationship with the city not as its makers but as its subjects, as its supporters?" While *Delirious New York* was largely descriptive, Koolhaas now makes regular prescriptions about what the city is, and what the architect must not do. His views have become hardly different from Jean Baudrillard's, though they have little of the latter's sophistication, sensibility and poetry. The Postmodernism that shapes what Koolhaas dubs the Generic City, or the city without qualities, "is a new form of professionalism, ... a technical training that creates a new unquestioning, a new efficacy in applying new streamlined dogma." "All resistance to Postmodernism is antidemocratic." It (Postmodernism) creates a "stealthwrapping around architecture that makes it irresistible, like a Christmas present from a charity." Any takers?

The architect is not merely content with abandoning the city to what he describes in the context of New York as "collective forces"—a notion which assumes that the will of developers like, say, Donald Trump, is at one with the will of the silent majority. He further argues that "the serenity of the Generic City is achieved by the *evacuation* of the public realm." What this seems to involve, in physical terms, is the elimination of "what the French [with Koolhaas's approval] call *la merde*" (or shit), of what he elsewhere describes as "plankton" and once as "improvised hovels" (referring—is the architect aware of it?—to the houses of the largely Algerian population of Nanterre).

This "merde" is to be replaced with a "post-architecture" of bigness which, all considered, is not so different from the megastructures dreamt of in the 1960s, save that it will be built by the private sector. As a foreboding of this future, public consultation is granted two lines of text in the book section on Euralille, and the essay on the Generic City includes a mere seven lines on the subject of politics. Notwithstanding the enormity of Koolhaas's courage and ambition, his obliviousness to even the most basic social (let alone democratic) processes that make a city, and his possibly deliberate naiveté concerning real estate are not the most endearing attributes of his brave new book.

THE MASTER BUILDER
Martin Filler
New York Times Book Review,
March 17, 1996.

[...] Much of the size of *S,M,L,XL* stems from an apparent desire to add bulk to Mr. Koolhaas's relatively small body of built work—fewer than twenty executed schemes since the founding of his firm, the Office for Metropolitan Architecture, in 1974. But though Mr. Mau carries off arresting effects here and there, the high percentage of pages given to labored attempts at mimicking electronic media obscures an understanding of Mr. Koolhaas's achievements, which are of exceptional quality.

Over the past decade, countless architects have been the subjects of monographic catalogues deemed necessary as sales brochures to win clients. The author and the designer of this summary of Mr. Koolhaas's output (arranged chronologically within the four size categories of the title) do everything they can to divert attention from the fact that this volume is not much different in intent from, say, the collected works of Gwathmey Siegel & Associates. Perhaps afraid that readers will be daunted from advancing into the depths of this silver-covered brick of a book, Mr. Koolhaas runs a "dictionary" in the margins throughout. Words from *Abolish* to *Zoom Ratio* are commented on in a high-low mix of quotations by authorities ranging from Charles Baudelaire and Arnold Schwarzenegger to Jacques Derrida and Tammy Faye Bakker. By turns portentous and sophomoric, this self-conscious device seems more suited to a high school yearbook.

During the late 1960s and early 1970s, Mr. Koolhaas studied at the Architectural Association, the London school then in the forefront of design counterculture. Its heady experiments at fusing technological advances and superscale cityscapes with the gritty immediacy of Pop Art had a formative influence on him and are still readily discernible in his projects. Megastructures are a particularly recurrent obsession for him, even though urban planners everywhere now prefer the intimate human scale. For example, Mr. Koolhaas's unexecuted Sea Trade Center of 1989, meant to be erected in Zeebrugge, Belgium, would have been an eighteen-story "working Babel" (in the architect's term) combining ferry docks, garages, offices, a hotel, movie theater, restaurant and casino. Its bulbous form is reminiscent at once of a lunar landing module and a tumescent cephalopod. [...]

Equally indicative of the author's Architectural Association origins is the look of this book. The London-based Archigram group, which popularized the AA style, published its pamphlets twenty-five years ago in an explosive graphic mode meant to convey a breakaway energy conspicuously lacking in corporate Modernism. A wild jumble of grainy xerography, homemade cartoons, purloined typefaces and multicolored inks and papers, those ephemeral handouts were thrown together with a bravura abandon that undercut the pomposity so prevalent in the architectural profession. *S,M,L,XL* aims for a similar antiestablishment spontaneity. But with its high price, lavish production values and chic juxtapositions of violent news photos, pornographic outtakes, cheap advertisements and fine-art reproductions, it is closer in spirit to the deluxe boxed CD sets of aging 1960s rock stars.

Mr. Koolhaas has always been an astute social observer; that is one reason his architecture has a compelling presence that transcends the empty stylistic concerns of many of his peers. His ability to penetrate and interpret even arcane human interactions is evident in this book's most sharply drawn segment, "Learning Japanese," a poem based on his experiences during the design and construction of his Nexus World Housing complex of 1991 in Fukuoka, Japan. This is a highly perceptive account of what it is like to do business with the Japanese. The inflexible scheduling, interminable meetings, convoluted negotiations, evasive locutions, micromanagement of details, ritualized hospitality and insuperable dominance of the group over the individual are all portrayed with pinpoint accuracy. No chauvinist, Mr. Koolhaas (who maintains homes in London and Rotterdam) observes that "Japan equals England in surgical manners, also in insular self-love."

A pragmatist to the end, he includes a haiku dedicated to the patron of his Fukuoka apartment development. Reflecting his gratitude at receiving work during a global recession, he writes, "Japanese client / gulp of melted snow / in Superdry desert." This is one visionary determined not to have his dreams confined to sleep or consigned to paper.

EXHILARATION IN DEFEAT

Jean-Claude Garcias

L'Architecture d'Aujourd'hui 304 (1996), 59–61.

Aesthetic categories have the capacity of freely trickling down through the centuries, serving the most contradictory types of mindless thinking or the most absurd systems. That is doubtlessly the case of "On the Sublime," a theory by Cassius Longinus from the third century, reinterpreted by Boileau to serve the quarrel between the Ancients and the Modern thinkers, pirated during the Age of Enlightenment by the politician Burke, and recently borrowed by an ingeniously dry wit, Rem Koolhaas. In a book that significantly borrows its title from English ready-to-wear sizes, our Dutch Buster Keaton glorifies *Bigness, Sublime Bigness,* and claims to prove that oversized and unfettered projects, such as La Défense, Singapore and Euralille, provoke more sublime emotions than programs that are fractioned and more or less rational. *Big is beautiful.* [...]

It is true that the discussions of sublime held by reactionaries at the end of the eighteenth century referred to elitist hobbies—painting, landscaping, poetry—while Koolhaas, the neo-situationist, writes about urban development and architecture, the living environment of the masses on a global scale. Although supported by new technologies, a new approach to space and a new order of social forces, the reasoning remains fundamentally the same. Albion's economic take-off, improved suspension for horse-drawn carriages and the extension of the Grand Tour enabled young lords to admire the awe-inspiring beauty of the Alps. Industrial decentralization, globalized architecture and thousands of kilometers traveled by jet revealed Atlanta's convulsive beauty to Koolhaas. (In thirteen years, he covered 360,000 kilometers by plane and spent 305 nights in hotels; as always with Koolhaas, these statistics can be read in two ways: literally for businessmen and as a parody for his friends and colleagues.) The resurrection of the Sublime during the Revolution revealed a new sensitivity to the savage beauty of landscapes. It also owes much to the fear of social brutality: "French ideas" and Terror, slave uprisings, Frankenstein. During a conference in 1790, the painter Reynolds described the Sublime as a rapture of thought: "The sublime in Painting, as in Poetry, so overpowers, and takes such a possession of the whole mind, that no room is left for attention to minute criticism. The little elegancies of art in the presence of these great ideas thus greatly expressed, lose all their value." Shenstone, another of Burke's friends, pushes the concept even further: "Large unvariegated, simple objects have the best pretensions to sublimity." This is exactly what Koolhaas states two centuries later, with the addition of distance: "An operation such as La Défense is composed exclusively of mediocre, ordinary buildings which are both ugly and complete failures. However, the group as a whole has a certain bigness, and on certain days, when looked at from a certain angle, it appears positively, absolutely magnificent." While Burke's reactionary nonsense on the Sublime has lost its ability to do harm, the same cannot be said of Koolhaas's theory: cynical or hopeless, it is perfectly adapted to the current system of globalization, collective amnesia and leveling. It is also laced with humor and intelligence, which makes it even more difficult and urgent to refute.

There are thousands of ways of approaching *S,M,L,XL*. The easiest would be to consider it as the *press book* of all *press books*, the absolute communication weapon. For a tolerable price and recoverable on sales in successful in bookshops, Koolhaas and OMA have a definite advantage over all other agencies on the planet. How can a dowdy collection of photocopies from a small agency weigh in against this two-kilo bound edition? How can one not notice the difference between his avant-garde model and business sales brochures? After having received such an *objet d'art*, what minister or promoter can afford to not invite OMA to participate in a bid? However, we can also trust the author and the editor, and consider *S,M,L,XL* to be some sort of novel, the *Ulysses* of architecture. [...]

S,M,L,XL is thus a book-world, like *Pantagruel*. It is somewhat similarly organized, with a false heterogeneity. Convinced that "incoherence ... is the underlying structure of all architects' careers," Koolhaas merrily combines theory, practice and references: a primer with 1,200 extremely varied quotations, since they run from John Lee Hooker to Louis Marin, from Deleuze, Bellow, Starck quoted by Boissière, Debord, Trump, Virilio and Koolhaas, where *Delirious New York* is mentioned more often than all of OMA's buildings. We could even call it a constant recycling of Koolhaas's greatest success: *Delirious New York* has full page, black and smoky white reproductions, to the point where the naive reader wonders if he should not start (re)reading it. After ten pages, he understands that he has fallen into the trap: "in our society," it has become impossible to distinguish the original from the copy, primary from secondary, meaning from nonsense. [...] But like Hamlet's madness, Koolhaas's incoherence is not lacking in method, and the very trendy-looking book is really a camouflage for something more traditional: the Bildungsroman of an intellectual architect, the *Sentimental Education* of a tortured soul. Because the most motley collection of texts printed in the most diverse fonts, the most disparate assortment of plans and project photos, the odds and ends of models or the most insane references all keep telling us the same thing.

Beginning in 1972 (or '68?), young Rem found his niche, his trademark: emigration from the interior, satisfying alienation or happiness in despair. When others were getting high on nostalgia or shooting-up with modernity, Koolhaas was tripping on the loss of meaning. *S,M,L,XL* begins with his graduation from the Architectural Association in 1972. Struck by the "stirring beauty" of the Berlin Wall, Koolhaas proposed to reproduce it in the heart of London around a rectangular vacant lot. The "negative magnet" was supposed to attract "Voluntary Prisoners strong enough to love it," or "thrilled with the feeling of freedom produced by the architectural confinement." We know that Koolhaas is the all-time champion of oxymoron and that his favorite metaphor is that of voluntary servitude or happiness in slavery, a type of *Story of O* at the metropolitan level. But this paradoxical way of thinking, which is more like the French comic character, the sapeur Camember, French author and humorist, Alphonse Allais, and French psychoanalyst, Doctor Lacan, than Swift, Flaubert or Debord, leads him to deny any possibility of architecture resisting the chaos of merchandise: since the mysteries escape us, let's pretend to organize them; things being what they are, they can only get worse and that's a good thing; the more boredom there is, the more the individual is liberated; brutality alone can save civilization. [...] Such is the red and black thread that runs through the 300 pages. For example, there are hilarious travel notes from Singapore, whose Minister of Arts and

Information was said to have stated: "We must seriously tackle the problem of *fun* if we want to remain competitive in the twenty-first century"; or Atlanta, where the Marriott atrium designed by the unfortunate Portman, is described as the exact architectural equivalent of Jean-Paul Sartre's statement that "hell is other people." [...] The projects that are presented are usually better known, except for a "Small" one like the model apartments in Fukuoka, a "Medium" project like the Agadir hotel, and an "Extra Large" project on the Yokohama seafront. [...] The small Spear house does not appear. A copyright problem?

We can understand that there is much disillusionment in these perpetual provocations, and that all of this cynicism could well hide a heart of gold. It remains to be known why Koolhaas is constrained by so many tongue-in-cheek contortions, bitter irony and polite despair, of which the psychological cost is undoubtedly nonnegligible. Why is he so eager to force a laugh? So as not to cry? The task of criticism is of course not to analyze the fashionable architects, but the reasons for which their idiosyncrasies can spread like wildfire. In the case of Koolhaas, an initial lead would be that of dark humor as an analgesic. The systematic use of paradox in his writings and projects enables both him and the architects who read him to bear the pain of the failure of Modernism. Or put more simply, to resolve, at least symbolically, all of the contradictions which made the great moderns fall on their faces and break their necks: democracy-enlightened despotism, quantity-quality, avant-garde-entrenchment. Koolhaas may thus be accomplishing a common mourning process, by producing the antidote capable of persuading decision-makers and builders that urban problems exist more in their heads than in reality. It is more difficult to convince those who live in the favelas, in Val Fourré or in the Bijlmer. [...]

In the same psychological vein, we might claim that Koolhaas's worship of the void stems from the fact that he has less need for meaning than others, that he feels a bitter joy at seeing it fade, or that he refuses the traditional role of the architect as a purveyor of meaning and social ties in a society that no longer wants anything to do with them. A process that is not without suffering, examples of which could easily be found in Le Corbusier. It is significant that the only "revealing" text in a book that is so perfectly controlled is the story of a nightmare at the beginning of XL. Koolhaas tells how, with his associate Voorberg, he dreamt that he lost his balance on a slippery dock (in Holland?) before falling from a dizzying height into a small meadow where a crowd was picnicking (the Netherlands again?). And despite the hopeless efforts of Koolhaas-Icarus to avoid falling on anyone, he landed on a baby's head. Should we see this as self-criticism of the *surfing* theory, which states that the architect cannot resist the wave of scale and Bigness, but *surfs* on it? Another clue as to the origin of Koolhaasism might be the fear and negation of provincialism. It is probably not a coincidence that the cantor of ultra-architectural laissez-faire hails from a hyper-democratic country where the welfare state reigns. If the theoretician of Chaos and Bigness resides in a small, flat, rural country where everything (apparently) has been bathed in polder water and bureaucratic-Calvinist oil for centuries. Or if the inventor of slogans such as "Bigness fucks context" and "Bigness strips architecture of all ethics" is a compatriot of Fabritius and Vermeer, the painters of poetic daily life. We could say of Koolhaas that he intentionally refuses to become a Dutch artist, that he travels the planet to escape from the "flat country," that he is striving to stand out from the hippies in wooden shoes and the Gouda cheese-porters in their hats. The love for Chaos and Extra Large may well only be the flip side to the hatred for rows of tulip bulbs, Friesian cows and windmills. Importers of Koolhaasism in the already chaotic places such as the peripheries and French low-housing areas would do well to notice before deconstructing spaces that are yet to be built. It should also be noted that Koolhaas's theoretical work is directly written in English, including the drafts for the agency reproduced in the book, which speaks volumes about his desire to escape provincial status.

[...] Again, like Le Corbusier, Koolhaas dreams of urban history that is reduced to architecture, at the expense of economic and social life, and for the greater happiness of the innovators. Let us add in case of failure (a change in the majority in Lille?) the architect may always blame incoherence, chance, political imperialism or conservative populations, and wear the rags of a misunderstood genius.

Let us repeat that there is cynicism and suffering, commonplaces and intuitions, conformism and situationism in *S,M,L,XL*. Koolhaas starts from the despair-ridden acknowledgment according to which certain forces (decentralized capitalism, mass tourism, the private car, the retreat into the private sphere) are devastating city centers, which were formerly oases with relative order. These forces are also creating pockets of chaos in peripheral areas which in time become the "Generic City." But from this analysis, which might be globally qualified as leftwing, the author draws strangely defeatist conclusions, since he recommends not to resist the barbarian tide but rather to ride it like a surfer on a wave. This carries something like a policy of the worst to come, which increases tensions or pushes contradictions to the absurd. Worse still, there is a kind of exhilaration in defeat, in the renouncing of secular urban culture. Koolhaas can then close the loop of the Sublime Bigness. The movement at the end of the century (the car that races onto the access ramp, the TGV that sideswipes the mountain) plays a role that is quite close to that of a ha-ha! Invented by English landscape artists in the eighteenth century, the recessed landscape area visually joined the grounds of a castle with the surrounding countryside, while creating a physical separation. By knocking down a wall on the grounds and replacing it with a ditch, William Kent convinced the gentry that "all of Nature is a garden." By traveling the globe in a jet and the *Großstadt* in a limousine, Rem Koolhaas saw that all architecture is chaos, of which he had no problem convincing the decision-makers: it is always a question of widening the perspective, of increasing the scale of surrendering to Bigness. While the unfortunate neo-classics of modernity are reluctant to restore a "human" scale to programs that have gone mad, Koolhaas and the chaotics take note of the terrifying Bigness of the order, and beautifully theorize what a previous generation considered to be the hideousness of capitalist monopoly. However, I must say that thanks to Koolhaas, we have had a good laugh.

KOOLHAAS IN 2-D

Brendan Gill
The New Yorker,
February 12, 1996.

What sort of architect bent upon producing a lively book about his work and thought would choose to give it the weight and shape of a block of granite—a miniature tombstone? The answer, in two words, is Rem Koolhaas, who in his oddly entitled *S,M,L,XL* demonstrates that he is no less gifted as a writer than he is as an architect. He also demonstrates that he possesses an attribute rare in both occupations: an invincibly merry view of life, based on the assumption, if I read him correctly, that since everything is bound to end badly, we should take care to have a particularly good time along the way. With that intention, Koolhaas has become a master of serious clowning, a latter-day Robert Burton. The same sunny temperament that led Burton to write *The Anatomy of Melancholy* has led Koolhaas to write this entertaining anatomy of architecture. He carries out the task as if on a tightrope, where maintaining a balance between opposing forces leads to frequent contradiction—and in Koolhaas's opinion the more contradictions the better. Having described with evident satisfaction his designs for houses, office buildings, museums, parks, and entire neighborhoods, Koolhaas disconcertingly notes that whatever an architect attempts to achieve in order to improve the built environment is likely to fail. In Koolhaas's view of the profession of architecture, winning is hard to distinguish from losing. In either event, on one goes: the seduction of the tightrope remains.

With a relish for outwitting expectations, Koolhaas has called his book *S,M,L,XL* in order to emphasize not subject matter but, like a sweater salesman, size: small, medium, large, extra-large. He has organized the book's contents according to the scale of his architectural projects, ignoring chronology, tossing in obiter dicta wherever it has pleased him to do so, and providing along the margin of nearly every page of text a curious alphabetical grab bag of quotations from diverse sources. The first entries under "A" are by Susan Sontag, Tama Janowicz, James Gleick, Tennessee Williams, Henry Miller, and Ludwig Wittgenstein, but Baudelaire, Derrida, and

Arnold Schwarzenegger also put in welcome appearances. “The book can be read in any way,” Koolhaas boasts, asserting an analogue with the fact that “incoherence, or more precisely, randomness, is the underlying structure of all architects’ careers.” He seems to be signaling to us that his volume—weighing more than five pounds and containing thirteen hundred and seventy-six pages of words, drawings, and photographs—need not be granted the awe commonly bestowed on so strenuous an autobiographical effort. Although a chart in the opening pages of the book indicates that the success of his firm, which he calls the Office for Metropolitan Architecture, has been attained at the cost of his flying hundreds of thousands of kilometers and spending more than three hundred nights in hotels all over the globe, he has borne these traveler’s burdens lightly, and why not? Personally and professionally, he has been having great fun: labor and play have been one.

[...] Koolhaas at fifty-one, in mid-career and with much of his promise fulfilled, is quick to acknowledge that *S,M,L,XL* is the product of many helping hands—the flying Dutchman is not flying solo. He shares credit on the cover with the celebrated Toronto graphic designer Bruce Mau and the Office for Metropolitan Architecture, and on the title page with Mau, OMA, Jennifer Sigler (editor), and Hans Werlemann (photographer). The block of granite that I spoke of proves to be not a tombstone but a cornerstone—the base of an immense edifice of Koolhaasian fact and fancy, reaching exhilaratingly skyward.

All those kilometers of travel, all those nights spent in who knows what hotels have yielded an ample harvest. OMA structures are to be found scattered throughout Koolhaas’s native Netherlands and in France, Japan, and Switzerland. Like any architect seeking to break new ground (a metaphor that comes close to being literal), Koolhaas has on his drafting board innumerable projects that have yet to be realized—projects that were entered in competitions and then failed to win, or were prepared for exhibitions that never took place, or were commissioned by clients who found that they couldn’t afford to build them. For Koolhaas, as for Frank Lloyd Wright, the ideal client is one whose relationship to his architect is that of a dog to his master, and for whom financial ruin wears the rosy hue of a sacrifice well worth making. As one might expect, the unbuilt projects are more revealing of the radical, chance-taking directions that Koolhaas has striven to pursue than the projects that, embodying compromises known only to him, meet with ready acceptance. It is in this fashion, among others, that an architect may be said to be simultaneously winning and losing. Prudently, in public he manifests a calculated equanimity—the smiling mask that conceals despair and that architects have worn for centuries, in order to preserve their self-respect as they abase themselves in pursuit of the next job.

A voluptuous superfluity of full-color photographs and drawings characterizes *S,M,L,XL*, and has the sorry effect of making Koolhaas’s prose less accessible to the reader than it would be on an ordinary printed page. We have the designer of the book to thank for this problem. Mau is known for, in the jargon of the day, pushing the envelope, and in the present case he has all but exploded it. One must dive deep into the maw of Mau to fetch up precious snippets of Koolhaas biography and to sample a rich variety of Koolhaasian ruminations. The sheer physical gorgeousness of *S,M,L,XL* greatly increases the usual difficulty of judging architecture from photographs. A building is designed and constructed to be viewed in three dimensions, and its appearance on paper in two dimensions creates an initial distortion. A further distortion—the degree of intervention on the part of the photographer, including his manipulation of light and shade and his use of a parallax-correcting lens—can never be accurately ascertained. In the case of contemporary architects, the difficulty is heightened by intentional distortions of perspective, which are a feature of their designs, and which architects of the past, following the Beaux-Arts tradition, would have considered the work of madmen. A photograph of a building designed by the classicist John Russell Pope—the National Gallery of Art, say—is comparatively easy to "read" and criticize; photographs of buildings by Koolhaas are optically incomprehensible, however much sense they may make in actuality. I drifted at ease—I could not possibly have marched through the surrealist pictorial wonderland of *S,M,L,XL*, and I felt as if I were drifting through the blue gardens and tawny castle courtyards of a Maxfield Parrish mural. Hard as I may have wished to pass judgment on a given project, I was often unable to tell whether the pictures were of a model or of the real thing, much less whether I found the project, in either case, admirable. Again and again, I was tempted to shout "Hurrah!" at one or another of Koolhaas's airy, zigzag, deconstructivist ingenuities, but were they really airy, were they zigzag, were they in fact ingeniously deconstructivist? Sternly, I would attempt to withhold my hurrah, but in vain: a whiff of the insidious Koolhaasian joie de vivre (bottled, it would be called Essence of Magus) would leap up from the page and render me mindless.

BIG IS NOT ALWAYS BEAUTIFUL

Robert Harbison
The Architects' Journal, February 8, 1996.

S,M,L,XL, Rem Koolhaas's new book, is more like a building. Once installed, it is not that easy to move. First irony of many: the first letter of the behemoth's title stands for small. Many of its 1,344 pages contain recycled material, the most glaring example being the treatment of *Delirious New York,* the book that launched his career and is mentioned more times in these pages than all his buildings put together. *Delirious New York* is given nine double-page spreads in the form of dingy gray photographs of its pages, one per page. This is a joke carried on so long that we begin to think we are actually expected to read it in this unattractive form. The point being, something Koolhaas relishes, that we live in a world where primary and secondary, authentic and derived, are no longer easy or even possible to keep straight.

Although the book contains everything—the Complete Works and more—it moves at an unnervingly rapid pace, as if afraid of being caught with its feet on the ground. So hundreds of ideas appear and disappear, each present for a tenth of a second until the reader feels like some poor sleepless creature startled by the slightest sound.

The subject of the book is not hard to define. It is not the ones proclaimed on the back cover—the contemporary city, or the state of architecture at this moment in history. No, the subject is really the mind of Rem Koolhaas and its medium is principally words. I view the modernist form of *S,M,L,XL* as camouflage for this monotony in the central material. The result is visually centrifugal but intellectually centripetal and reiterative. Various texts printed in different typefaces, sizes and layouts look like raw materials or notes toward a synthesis as yet unrealized. But the message, though relentlessly "new," has been present from the beginning in all Koolhaas's utterances since his student days. The first text is his final student project at the Architectural Association, written in 1972. I assume it is printed complete; in any case, it is remarkably long and remarkably clever. Kicking off from the Berlin Wall, it proposes an architecture-free swathe cut through the center of London, which will act as a kind of negative magnet sucking people into its void.

Already we find that contented, even triumphant alienation which is Koolhaas's trademark. He gets high on the loss of meaning, perhaps because he senses he needs it less than other people. All his later theories about the city are arguments in favor of the void. Cities are losing their identity, and this is a good thing. Boredom is increasing in modern urban conditions, which liberates the individual (whose individuality fades) into a wider realm of choice—he/she can opt for meaninglessness, or sometimes for meaning.

To understand the appeal of such ideas to their author we would need to become psychologists. At bottom, they give one a way of coping with pain, or at least of resolving contradiction. They are a powerful analgesic soothing us with the idea that all our problems lie in our conceptions. The most interesting item on these themes is the early piece about the Berlin Wall, and the weakest is the last, summary essay on the Generic City. In between comes a revealing piece on Bigness, but I would not like to try to find this, or anything else here, in a hurry. Flipping through the book is a bit like that humiliating experience which follows when you have thrown something out by mistake—you become a sifter of debris.

The Berlin Wall piece contains the astonishing statement that, having read and heard about it, when Koolhaas came in sight of the wall he found it "heartbreakingly beautiful." Needless to say, beautiful is not a word you will often find him employing. I put this statement alongside another earlier in the same piece where Walt Disney is called a "twentieth-century genius," which is about the most unqualifiedly positive remark he makes about anyone.

In both instances there is a love of paradox and of standing received categories on their head, which is one of Koolhaas's intellectual trademarks. Love of paradox is fine in a journalist, whose memorable formulations can be left behind after they have served their purpose of jolting sleepy minds awake. But the syndrome is treacherous in an architect, for jokes which will not go away are no fun.

The other main weapon in Koolhaas's mental armory is the confident global generalization based on only one case or a few bits of data. Because one panoptic prison has been subverted by later use, he concludes that "changes in regime are more powerful than the most radical architecture—a conclusion both alarming and reassuring for the architect"—and a conclusion false as often as it is true. The biggest conclusion ever drawn in this way by Koolhaas—that Lille sits at the center of a virtual urban agglomeration of 70 million people—seems silly to me but has convinced some of my friends. It is no surprise that the megalomaniacal mayor of Lille has bought this fantasy, but what can make anyone else believe that London and Lille are not really distinct any more?

Bigness fascinates Koolhaas in the form (among others) of the 250,000 air miles he has clocked up in the past thirteen years. Heidegger's gnomic "nearness remains absent" runs through my head, and Emerson's scorn for travelers who forget that wherever they go they take themselves with them. It is true that these two are not exactly apostles of modernity. But if modernity takes everyone where it has Koolhaas—"Bigness makes architecture amoral," "Bigness fucks content"—then we need to head in another direction.

ARCHITECTURAL INCIDENTS REPLETE WITH FANTASY

Toyo Ito
A+U 314 (1996), 131–33.

A sudden, entirely unforeseen event like the Great Hanshin Earthquake is not all that common in contemporary society. Most incidents are waiting to happen in society, and the surface phenomena we perceive every day anticipate them. However, in the enormous, complex environment that is the city today, the manifold phenomena we perceive are like a snarl of vine whose main stem or root cannot be distinguished. Most people today have abandoned the troublesome task of searching for that main stem or root. Indeed, many find a society whose structure or overall image cannot be discerned agreeable. They accept and idealize this complex condition, which they label "chaotic" or "fractal."

However, there are persons who do not accept such a condition—careful, calm individuals who painstakingly search for the main stem even in a hopelessly entangled jungle of vine. When their sharp-edged knife severs a certain stem, black blood starts to flow copiously from the cut. That is the moment when a phenomenon becomes an incident. [...] What they have in common is the way they first come to light. They always appear first in mass-circulation weeklies as topics that pique the interest of readers in an unsavory way. They begin as scandals. Coverage in more respectable media [...] comes much later, and it takes even longer for high-minded justifications for rooting around such as the pursuit of social justice to be voiced. Disclosures made at great risk are the only effective means of getting to the heart of a case. That is why reporters who are otherwise extremely rational and careful [...] boldly put their lives in danger.

Rem Koolhaas is a reporter who transforms architecture as social phenomena into scandalous incidents. Rem is the only architect of this type in the world.

The sundry buildings constructed in the world are erected in accordance with the political and economic principles prevailing in their respective societies. To that extent they exist within society and are incapable of becoming incidents of any kind. As long as a litany of stock phrases—such as public accessibility, airiness and functionality, safety and ease of maintenance, and friendliness to senior citizens and the weaker members of society—is recited, architecture is accommodated, uneventfully and harmlessly, by society.

However, architecture can become a scandalous incident at any moment if an architect chooses to wield a sharp analytical instrument in the manner of a skilled investigative reporter. Architecture may appear at first glance to be a product of the pursuit of social justice or truth, but it can suddenly be shown to be full of hypocrisy, profligacy and superficial appeals to nostalgia. For that to happen, an exposé must be brazen.

Rem, it seems to me, is drawn to the photographs of Nobuyoshi Araki because the photographer too cuts through to the heart of the matter. Araki has long taken pictures of incoherent landscapes in cities such as Tokyo and the young girls who live in them; that is, cities of unmitigated flatness, cities that lost any character of place long ago, cities whose historical identity has disappeared behind a veil of uniformity and the people who, through life in such spaces, have lost all individuality or become completely expressionless. Araki has taken it upon himself to uncover the power of life and sex that is latent in such emptiness. Instead of seeing possibilities in a world that is highly expressive and clearly individualistic, full of confidence and truth, he attempts to confirm contemporary reality in the Eros latent in a world that is its complete opposite. Unless one takes a scandalous approach, characterlessness and emptiness simply continue to proliferate, unchanged.

Though he lives in Europe, or precisely because he lives in Europe, Rem has always made it a point to visit cities without a history or without much identity. He has wandered about Manhattan and Tokyo and more recently has shifted his focus to metropolises such as Hong Kong, Seoul and Beijing. Like Araki, Rem has shown an interest in the lives of expressionless people in cities without individuality, that is, generic cities. He visits cities that are past their prime like Manhattan and Tokyo. He is probably in search of some confirmation amid the emptiness of cities that have already seen their best days, or perhaps it would be more accurate to say that he visits such cities to confirm that there is indeed nothing to search for.

"Where there is nothing, everything is possible," declares Rem. "Where there is architecture, nothing is possible." Few architects have created as many projects that ought to have been realized but were not. There have been many competitions where his proposal addressed the issues most clearly but failed to win, and there have been many competitions that he has won with proposals that ultimately failed to see the light of day. The proposals remained unrealized, not because they were too costly or because there were conflicts with the client or the local government over the program. Rather, the proposals remained unrealized because they ignored the aesthetic, artistic and social values of architecture itself. His proposals have always been architectural incidents and scandals.

S,M,L,XL, which was published in collaboration with Bruce Mau, is a casebook of incidents he has been witness to in cities throughout the world—little incidents, middling incidents, big incidents and especially big incidents. No connections are provided. Nothing regional or chronological necessarily relates the incidents. This publication, which is 1,344 pages long, may be arranged like a book, but it more closely resembles a television news show, edited according to scope of topic. It is composed in a way that makes it more suggestive of electronic media than the videos and CD-ROMs on which the collected works of architects are nowadays introduced.

The scene of an incident might be shown in extreme close-ups of a limited area or as overhead shots of the city from a helicopter in which the scene is only a spot. They are quite different from photographs of architectural details or the contexts of buildings. They are more like shots of a camera closing in on the splattered bloodstains or the scattered shoes and glasses on a street or images from a helicopter circling over the scene of an incident. The more the world becomes uniform and flat, the more new media proliferate. In a generic city, one encounters the same space no matter where one goes. The only way such a space can be changed into a place that is unique in the world is to cause an incident. The incidents Rem instigates are stimulating and scandalous. It is as if he were smashing with a metal bat outdated aesthetics and morals still cherished by architects.

Rem creates projects with the speed of a rapid-fire gun. I once called him a "fantasy-making machine." He seemed to produce architectural projects one after another in phlegmatic and nearly automatic fashion, as if he were a sort of pitching machine. That is how I still think of him, but today I would probably use the word "incident" instead of "fantasy." Several years have passed since I made that remark, and now his projects are more like media and incite in more scandalous ways, like a knife thrust deep into the body of society. They are architectural incidents replete with fantasy.

XXL: REM KOOLHAAS'S GREAT BIG BUILDINGSROMAN

Fredric Jameson

Village Voice 19 (1996), 17–19.

Quantity has had a bad name for some time, despite Engels's first law of dialectics (or was it Hegel's? or Stalin's?)—the transformation of quantity into quality. Whatever is good about this or that individual big thing always seems to get explained by reference to some other feature, and not its sheer magnitude. Meanwhile, sheer numerousness—multiplicity as such—is often filed away in some other category, as though demography were not subject to the same thought processes as Mount Everest or the Pacific Trench. Yet the face of Deng Xiaoping, intent and pedagogical, on the inside endpaper of Rem Koolhaas's impressively square and massive new tome reminds us that lots of people are fully as "sublime" in Kant's sense as mountain ranges, giant hotdogs, nonstop dancing records, or the age of the universe.

As its title suggests, *S,M,L,XL* is something of a manifesto for bigness, as well as being a rewriting of *Learning From Las Vegas* in an utterly new nonhumanist idiom. But bigness is so familiar and banal that it doesn't seem to explain anything any longer: to solve the mystery of Koolhaas's work—buildings as well as books—by saying that it is big (or great) simply because he wants to think big and build big constructions—simply because he wants to promote bigness—is not very satisfying somehow. Could you have a small thought of bigness, for example? Or can you think big by the mere taking of a thought? Strange reflections that end up having some family likeness to the ontological proof of the existence of God (who exists simply because "existence" is a necessary component of your idea of His perfections in the first place).

It would be as misleading to describe *S,M,L,XL* as a record of the achievements of Rem Koolhaas's Office for Metropolitan Architecture as it would be to call it a marvelous picture book (albeit of non-coffee-table format); although there is a little of both those things in it. Perhaps—not really about architecture at all in the first place—it is a bravura performance by the invisible camera-man (Bruce Mau), who has chosen Rem's work as the pretext for his own delirious (and very satisfying) bookmaking. But you might equally well think of it as an architectural autobiography, or even (on the other hand) a cunning exercise in planned chaos (among other things, many other things, a book without an index or table of contents!).

There runs through it the institutional thread all the disciplines are supposed to have learned to respect. In this case, what is the architectural profession today? Is architecture in some radically new kind of crisis? How to characterize the role or mission of the architect today (after Modernism, for example)? A nonarchitect may well initially be more interested in the architect's point of view on daily life: not so much what the architect does as an architect (the opening shots of office space production or project graphs do that, however) but rather what the world looks like narratively and novelistically when it is an architect who is moving through it (indeed, the cover tells us that *S,M,L,XL* is a novel: which is just about as misleading as the other characterizations I tried out at the beginning of this paragraph). Not the architect as hero, as in Ayn Rand: but the architect's experience of the passing or insignificant detail. Are the reading notes Rem's own (or OMA's), for example? Is one supposed to read dutifully through all of these? They are, to be sure, all very interesting; but they are there essentially to give you something else to do with yourself when the principal business of the page, visual or textual, has lost your attention for the moment. As in Rem's buildings, these are among the multitudinous other things, large or small, that are also supposed to be going on, and that we mistakenly call—which I have mistakenly called—"chaos," but that we had also better no longer call "complexity" either, since that is too formal and modernist a word for the way we live now or the way Koolhaas thinks we ought to reconcile ourselves to living: although "reconcile" is surely too mild a word for what he has in mind.

At any rate, whatever the point of view this "architectural novel" happens to confront, the focus is not on beautiful buildings or on epiphanies, rather, there is a separation between two dimensions, on the one hand the microcategories of noneventful everyday time. The novelist or dramatist normally uses space as a stage or scene for an Event to happen in. Here, spatiality not being reserved for the unusual or exception, we need a different set of categories: "Nothing ever happens here, yet the air is heavy with exhilaration."

On the other hand, a macronarrative that we are asked to learn: getting the contract! Competition, the program, whether we win or lose out ("Dear Diary, do we want to win this competition or not?")—it is the success or failure plot of the bestseller, the privileged narrative form of the market and big business, yet here oddly inflected in a variety of new directions. The book is a success story; OMA does finally go to Lille, the small projects barrel forward into twenty-first-century urbanism. Yet the really stupendous things here are "failures" unbuilt (at least so far): the Sea Trade Center, the Très Grande Bibliothèque, the Karlsruhe Art and Media Center, each unfolding over fifty or sixty pages, according to a new type of narrative form—the description of the project, a slide show in real life that becomes something better than a film within a book itself while at length, a conception of the City begins to evolve in which the building of buildings like this slowly ceases to be the Ayn Rand type of "success" to the degree to which this enormous manifesto finds itself scandalously arguing for the wholesale tearing down of everything every twenty-five years or so, at which point the competitions, getting the contract, etc., stop looking like the architectural specification of some more general success-or-failure story (what they might have looked like in Zola, for example), and now somehow seem on the point of offering a new paradigm altogether that we do not yet seem fully to understand or to imagine the application of. To put it another way, this is a vanguard operation without the avant-garde vision or mission; a powerfully future-oriented material imagination without a future in any traditional sense of the word; Dystopia as Utopia, perhaps, but at an intensity that dissolves the usual overtones or connotations of both those words all at once.

At any rate this is no conventional narrative or logbook of projects; rather it envelops and includes all those, along with cartoons, collages of images, journal entries, and even narrative "myths" of the Platonic type. Like its predecessor, *Delirious New York* (published in 1978; and this year reissued, but without its delirious illustrations, and also cannibalized in part within *S,M,L,XL*), it wishes to be a "retroactive manifesto" that rewrites the past according to another, hitherto unnoticed, only recently excavated, agenda, a rediscovered Habermasian "unfinished project" that can now be pursued and continued. Yet it is also a record of the discontinuous historical situations that succeed each other as convulsively as small-medium-large and unexpectedly turn a past into the anticipation of what used to be an impossible future. This is the face of bigness, about which Koolhaas has said that he wrote it up historically in the US because there was no conceivable possibility of putting it into practice in an ancient Europe and small-scale Holland: suddenly, with the new Europe and a new posturbanistic urbanism, the aesthetic that had been "cryogenically" preserved like a time capsule in *Delirious New York*. [...]

Besides Manhattan, however, there are two other significant influences on this act of the spatial imagination: the Berlin Wall and John Portman's Atlanta, alongside which—as the slide show of what are already more momentous than individual buildings expands into dimensions that wish to displace and cancel ordinary conceptions of city space or urbanism as such—full-dress essays make their appearance, on Singapore or La Défense, on the Bijlmermeer housing development in Amsterdam or on globalization as such.

Globalization is indeed the other crucial historical force of which *S,M,L,XL* wishes to be the document and the record, if not the symptom: Mies's travels and exile, here fantasmatically narrated as the adventures of the material components of the Barcelona Pavilion through the vicissitudes of the War years—the evocation of Japan as the space of otherness and construction beyond Europe or the US—these are still relatively static expressions and evocations of a new global situation that consists in sheer relationship, in action at distance, in overlapping global force fields, or international "gene splices," as Koolhaas himself puts it. Architects today work in a frenzy of international travel (Michael Graves's forty buildings in Japan are indeed offered as something of a prototype for chaos itself), but at that level, we have to do merely with an interesting biographical fact, or an exhausting one, as the case may be. It is the sheer existence of Japan or the US that changes the situation of the architectural new Europe, whether you travel to them physically or not, whether or not you sample their cultural styles (in fact, Japanese megastructures of the 1950s and 1960s are detonators as crucial for Koolhaas as the New York skyscrapers about which he has so eloquently and pointedly written). We cannot (yet) map out the interrelationships of late capitalist globalization with anything like the figurative distinctness of the older modernist foreign affairs.

[...] It is this "lesson of bigness" that *S,M,L,XL* now extrapolates into urbanism itself, or rather the former urbanism: for here what is effaced is precisely that tension constitutive of the whole architectural tradition hitherto—the incommensurability between thoughts about an individual building and thoughts about the urban fabric as a whole, if it really ever was one. Koolhaas has many outrageous things to say in this spirit, which ought to scandalize us; which need to be scandalous or we will not be getting our money's worth. If you don't see how the proposal for a Lite Urbanism undermines all the classical values we have been trying to associate with what remains of the city, then these texts have gone flat and the projects themselves stand littered about us like so many open bottles of stale beer.

The projects are not the answer, for one thing; and to point to the artistic grandeur of the Sea Trade Center or the Très Grande Bibliothèque as a consolation prize for what Koolhaas proposes to do to the city in general would amount to a containment and a neutralization of this text and its virulence: a trivialization dressed up in the art appreciation trappings of yesteryear.

The attack on humanism has lost its programmatic appeal in recent years (except for Jesse Helms); but perhaps we can revive it one last time in order to measure the enormity of the destruction Koolhaas proposes and the ideological achievement of his thoughts of bigness here taken to their logical conclusion. To be sure, Le Corbusier (in his Plan Voisin) rehearsed the sheer triumphalism of the modernist New by suggesting that "Paris" might be scraped away (Rem's expression) and replaced by several rows of gigantic skyscrapers. The supreme impertinence was also a Pyrrhic victory: "the notion of a new beginning—starting from scratch, the tabula rasa—had been taboo ever since Le Corbusier's operation closed the book on the question of the new beginning for generations to come." The coming into being of La Défense now changes the picture insofar as it saves rather than destroys Paris (Rem dixit: "each 'eyesore' realized there has prevented an invasion of the center"). But now comes the subversive proposal: "How many of these buildings deserve eternal life? We analyzed this question in numerical terms and discovered that if we laundered the site in five-year increments by simply erasing all buildings over the age of twenty-five, vast areas would gradually be liberated" (older buildings "of merit" or "of sentimental value" being preserved "as a kind of twentieth-century acropolis").

We need to be attentive to the language here: "vast areas would be liberated." The emphasis finally, and the radical innovation being staged here, lies in the idea of the "area"; not the prospect of putting some newer building in the place of a still fairly new one (and then of repeating the process twenty-five more years down the line) but in the laying open of a strip or a band ("the beach beneath the sidewalk," as the students of May 1968 liked to put it, in a wall slogan dear to Koolhaas), a band or strip that can then coexist and be dramatically juxtaposed to strips or bands of different textures and characteristics, as in the rotations of medieval agriculture. It is a design and a program that OMA then dramatically proposed to carry out in their idea for a new city at Melun-Sénart. [...]

Suggestive formal ideas, these—and surely it is the idea of new forms that we crave, and whose short supply tends to be masked by the profusions of late capitalism and the postmodern (a word used only once here, although very affirmatively). But we have to chasten this aesthetic excitement with the reminder that for Koolhaas the City of the future is not the new Rotterdam or the sight line out from Napoleon's Arc de Triomphe: it is Singapore, along with the prophecy of innumerable Asian neo-cities of the future, patterned on the Singapore model. This is the sense in which East Asia is to *S,M,L,XL* what the domain of the American skyscraper was to *Delirious New York:* even Koolhaas's terminal notation about the island city-state ("Singapore mantra: don't forget to confirm your return flight") authorizes us to mix in a quotient for grimness here. It is a grimness we need to retain for the final summing up of this multipaged journey, the supreme manifesto on the so-called Generic City in which it is affirmed, among other things, that the contemporary airport is the exemplary microcosm of the new urban form, as well as "its strongest vehicle of differentiation." Those who follow contemporary fashion in denigrating the "placelessness" of the contemporary airport (along with the contemporary motel) will find this just the right note to approach the concentrated scandal of "The Generic City," which has a whole checklist of impertinences in store for us. "The Generic City presents the final death of planning. Why? Not because it is not planned ... but its most dangerous *and* most exhilarating discovery is that planning makes no difference whatsoever." "Each Generic City is a petri dish—or an infinitely patient blackboard on which almost any hypothesis can be 'proven' and then erased."

The infinite sequence of these hypotheses is in and of itself the richness of the Koolhaas/OMA conception of chaos, which the Generic City is designed to liberate. Anything goes: we have been liberated by the grid or the band, Rimbaud's Commune revised: "Il faut être absolumment postmoderne." But to do so means not abolishing history (for I fear that *S,M,L,XL* is history in the making, as they say), but the nostalgia for history: "Regret about history's absence is a tiresome reflex. It exposes an unspoken consensus that history's presence is desirable. But who says that is the case? A city is a plane inhabited in the most efficient way by people and processes, and in most cases the presence of history only drags down its performance." Fair enough, and a Utopian reminder to boot. Probably we will all need a little time to decide if this is the way we really want to wake up out of the well-known "nightmare." What is undeniable is that the authority with which Koolhaas speaks (in so many different graphic voices) springs from the resonance of a future within these projects and ideas. Is OMA an avant-garde movement, and have we not been taught (ever so recently) that a belief in innovation and in the future, in the *Novum*, is a characteristic of Modernism and of avant-garde movements, which is no longer available to us?

Most recently, the tired regret about history without a future has been countered by enthusiasm for a future without history. My own feeling is that the enthusiasm needs to be separated from the theory (which is generally only the former's rationalization) and examined in its own right. The tangible words and theories of works that we are offered here can only enhance and intensify the activity of the observer. Koolhaas offers us lessons in how to break down the doors of impossible situations, how to turn dilemmas and contradictions into sources of new productivity. We need be in no hurry to classify OMA's projects as a style or an aesthetic (particularly since it was the end of those things that spelled the dilemma and the block in the first place); let us first read this big book as the mimesis of radical choice, decisiveness, cutting through the knots, inventing new solutions—that is: as a story that must always exhilarate.

REM KOOLHAAS SIZES UP THE FUTURE

Herbert Muschamp
New York Times, March 3, 1996.

By a happy coincidence, Rem Koolhaas's new book, *S,M,L,XL*, arrived just as the magnificent Mondriaan show was ending its run at the Museum of Modern Art. One couldn't ask for a better symbol of the passing of modern art's baton than the fortuitous dovetailing of these two events. Mondrian, the pioneer abstract painter, ended his career with *Broadway Boogie-Woogie*. Koolhaas, the flying Dutchman of contemporary architecture, began his career with *Delirious New York*, a 1978 book that paid a comparably ecstatic tribute to Manhattan's fascinating rhythms. For a brief moment this winter, it seemed that the Dutch still held sway over this tiny, as yet untamed New World island.

Too bad New York hasn't staked its claim on Koolhaas. A week after the publication of his new book, MCA, the media giant, announced that it had given Koolhaas his first American commission. As master planner for Universal City, MCA's Los Angeles headquarters, Koolhaas will supervise future development on a 415-acre site that already includes offices, production studios and a popular theme park. It's a dream job for an architect whose work is vibrantly alert to the impact of media on architecture.

Koolhaas, who is 51, has been tantalizing his admirers for some time now with his precarious balance between dreaming and building, but in recent months the architect has been piling up evidence of his determination to build. Euralille, a major trade and convention center in northern France for which Koolhaas provided the master plan, has enabled him to build on the urban scale that has long captivated his imagination. Thanks to an association formed last year between his office and a Dutch engineering firm, he is now designing rail and highway projects in Germany and the Netherlands. *S,M,L,XL*, published by Monacelli Press, is a record of Koolhaas's voyage from visionary to practitioner, a stunning, bloated 1,344-page collection of the architect's writings and designs. The title describes the organization of its contents. The collection starts off with Small projects (private houses, short essays) and builds up to Extra Large urban plans. But the word "organization" fundamentally misrepresents the volume's peculiar, loopy structure. Koolhaas calls the book a novel. I'd call it jazz, a series of riffs on architecture between Koolhaas and Bruce Mau, the graphic designer responsible for the book's dazzling visual style.

Photographs and plans for completed buildings, renderings of unrealized projects, diary jottings, favorite quotations, reports on urban development in Asia and the United States, cartoons, aphorisms, movie stills: the book's topics spill into one another, as if to represent the unexpected connections of Koolhaas's thinking. Fragments of a screenplay, for example, are printed over pictures of an art museum in Rotterdam completed in 1991. Construction shots of Congrexpo, Koolhaas's convention hall in Lille, are interrupted by a reproduced tabloid headline: "The World Ended Eight Years Ago: We are all in the afterlife, says top researcher." The effect of this overlapping technique is to suggest that Koolhaas's individual projects and thoughts are less significant than their complex interweaving. The book is not a shapeless mess. Its loose, improvisatory framework suggests a model for thinking about the design of cities. The interwoven topics, the quirky juxtapositions, even the autobiographical entries add up to a strangely convincing way to reckon with the void left by the collapse of modern city planning.

The gist of Koolhaas's argument is this: By the time his generation entered architecture school, modern city planning was dead. Instead of thinking in terms of master plans, architects turned to "interventions," small-scale projects that don't threaten to shred the urban fabric. This thinking would be adequate had urban development adhered to the small scale advocated by Jane Jacobs and others. But it hasn't. Instead, cities have become increasingly dependent on projects of ever more colossal scale: convention centers and hotel complexes, sports stadiums, shopping malls, office campuses.

Koolhaas argues that instead of opposing such projects, architects should begin to develop theories about what he terms Bigness. They should learn how to use the large-scale project, like Euralille, as a contemporary urban force. Otherwise, they, and the city, will lose the opportunity to realize its creative potential.

Bigness? I can hear Lewis Mumford spinning in his grave. Isn't this merely the latest demonstration of architects' capacity to rationalize their dependence on the economic status quo? Could be. But Koolhaas is also offering a much-needed critique of the architectural status quo for its failure to deal creatively with the forces he's talking about. New York, for instance, has become addicted to contextualism, a formula for making new buildings look like old ones. There's nothing inherently wrong with this approach. Koolhaas is right to insist, however, that contemporary urban development calls for a fresh approach. Contextual architecture, in whatever period style, compels architects to think within a nineteenth-century framework of ideas. This is not an alien framework for central cities like New York, which are, after all, products of nineteenth-century industrialization. Period revival designs like those at Battery Park City have been useful exercises for educating architects about that framework.

But those exercises are powerless to guide the city into the future. When we read reports like the one just issued by the Regional Plan Association on the economic slippage of New York, we should be alert enough to make the connection between that slippage and the timid buildings our architects have been turning out. In both cases, we're witnessing a collective failure of creative vision. The city envisioned by Koolhaas is the ultimate form of what Umberto Eco called "the open work," an art object deliberately left unfinished by the artist so others can interact with it. Jazz lovers won't have any trouble with this concept, but even those who view the city as a built boogie-woogie may doubt that spontaneity and improvising are enough to insure the city's vitality.

And, of course, they are not. Spontaneity is not going to clean the air in Mexico City; improvisation is not going to rejuvenate New York's out-of-date transportation system, and Koolhaas's ideas, small or large, printed or built, won't suffice to insure the city's future. Koolhaas is speaking as a member of a specialized profession whose practitioners are largely restricted to the design of individual buildings. *S,M,L,XL* is a record of one architect's attempt to give his buildings a more contemporary urban dimension. The record shows that Koolhaas is also a contextualist, but in a fresh, inventive way. His brand of contextualism has little to do with making new buildings match the look and scale of old ones. It is concerned with designing forms that evoke the larger forces reshaping cities today: the global economy, advanced communications, the collapse of regional differences within a shrinking world.

The book's unwieldy size is a metaphor for this enlarged urban context, while its jazzy, free-form contents reflect an artist's intuitive response to it. Obviously, architects have no direct control over the global forces to which cities are increasingly subject. Koolhaas thinks more could be done to activate architecture as a creative force. Electronic money, high-speed trains, cellular phones: on an imaginative level, these could all be seen as instruments for spirited improvisation. Why not let buildings riff?

THE DRAMA!

Claude Parent
AMC 70 (1996), 54–55.

Who is Rem Koolhaas? It would take a very clever person indeed to provide an answer to such a question. An antiestablishment artist. A preacher inspired by architecture. An incontinent agitator. Or a nostalgic in search of a lost Eden. It is far from easy to understand the many facets of a man whose very physique helps maintain the mystery and multiply the questions.

But for me, he is first and foremost the man of *Delirious New York*. Those two limp skyscrapers—lying naked on a bed as if after an improbable coupling, while the arm of the Statue of Liberty brandishes her torch impassively on the nightstand as if to light the postcoital cigarette—have always had me caught between derision of the despair and the dramatic message of an architecture of the future.

This synthetic history wants for nothing. Neither the New York skyline seen from above, nor the bedside rug in the form of an urban tapestry, nor the light of its protective beacon, nor perhaps even the moon and its reflection in the picture hanging behind the crumpled pillows. The tattered first name at the top of the poster hovers above the city as if to organize the drama.

The drama! But what drama? The drama of the city and its painful process of decomposition that haunts the minds of twentieth-century architects, ultimately the source of all crises. It is here that the image takes over for Koolhaas, not to dazzle us with a pertinent demonstration of his architecture, nor to convince anyone who will listen of its legitimacy or authenticity, nor even to lead us into believing that he is the greatest, only and best architect in the world, but to prepare the ground for architecture; or perhaps in other words, to open the way for architects by resolving all these crises. As much for himself as for others, for all others, his preparatory work ensures that there is no way at all architecture can continue to be neutral or formulaic, or, and most importantly, keep copying itself ad infinitum.

In a contrary dialectic, he proceeds essentially as we see him in *S,M,L,XL*, by telescoping formulas and images. He does not communicate, he does not lower himself to trying to make his audience understand or to becoming consumable, he destabilizes before he steps in.

It almost sounds like a military tactic, advanced bombing before an assault by the armored divisions and infantry, were Rem Koolhaas's advanced action not instead culturally constructive. The tidal wave of images opens the mind by ridding it of any dregs, removing the scales from the eyes that made it impossible to see before striking what might be called the final architectural blow. This method allows its perpetrator to avoid scandal while at the same time keeping the recipient, whomever they may be, from cultural rape.

After, but only after, this time has been taken to prepare the previously purified ground from any ancestral anxiety, Rem Koolhaas's in-depth work can begin, a work of extreme sensitivity and expressive intensity, revealing the hidden meaning in each illustrated idea.

There is something cryptic behind this, and those who are not prepared, those who do not want to analyze every last detail risk merely scratching the surface and only taking a superficial view from this experience. And yet, the interesting thing about Rem Koolhaas's attitude lies precisely in the coexistence of an extremely intellectualized discourse and a reading that is directly accessible to all, a coexistence carried, of course, by the kaleidoscope of images and the telescoping effect this generates. This abuse of collage cannot be taken simply as a Surrealist manifestation but rather as a strategy, covering as it does not only the discourse but also the way in which architecture is understood.

Beyond the ambiguity, formal aggression, destabilization or search for the universal credo and customs of thoughts, these images contain a need for rupture that is the only way to give architectural modernity back an imperative freedom. Breaking current codes in order to liberate surprise is part of this process of preparation.

Mining the ground to make it open to freedom of thought merely appears to be a contradiction that often makes Koolhaas's work hermetic on first reading. The fact that in the XL section of his book, on page 864, the Bijlmermeer comes after a colored catalogue from the *Aktuelle slip-boutique* seems to me not only devoid of aggression or a desire for scandal, but conversely the mark of a perfect logic, of the logic of Rem Koolhaas.

The same is true of the Villa dall'Ava in St. Cloud, France. There we find a complex and sophisticated approach, an almost excessive dynamic of the interior space, a break from the exterior volume in accordance with the movement of its inhabitants. We also find a highly ambiguous contact with the ground, which is both anchored and at other times laid onto a site that has barely been grazed. But the language, the choice of language offers a surprise, a desire to break with the thread of understanding grasped in the interior.

Nothing could be better translated than by an absolute desire for naiveté. The more knowledgeable, peremptory and efficient we are the more we seem to give up on the language of "clumsy" simplicity. Naiveté in the use of corrugated sheet metal with oversized ribs out of keeping with the surface to be covered. Naiveté in the framing of the rectangular windows that fit almost homothetically into the surface of the wall. Naiveté in the incongruous borrowing of Japanese bamboo to support an enormous cantilever. Naiveté in the green roof terrace around the Californian blue of the pool, the Mexican rubble-work garden wall, the huge Neutra-style windows open to the tireless curiosity of the neighboring pavilions. It is all there, however, in the deliberate choice of naiveté in a language itself distributed as if in a collage the size of a house or even a city.

We must be wary because this false naiveté, or rather this affected naiveté, this intentional antiplasticity one could say, is a vocabulary and a means of communication. As such this language cannot be imitated or generalized as simple or parochial. As such we have the right to wonder if this architecture precedes a global movement or if it will merely be seen by history as a brilliant and essential transition toward a future modernity. This architect lives in the drama, expresses the drama, and on every page of this book manifesto flushes out the "terrifying beauty of the twentieth century," which we refuse to see because it makes us suffer, concealing it from ourselves.

We must be wary because Rem Koolhaas is more than capable of making this terrifying beauty blow up in our faces. He is even preparing the ground for us. We must be wary because in Frankfurt, Zeebrugge and Paris, with the spiral ramps of the Jussieu Library, Rem Koolhaas has laid his first foundations. And in Lille, in his Palais des Congrès, he has already shown up some brand-new works of architecture as old-fashioned. He who wants to be naive is not naive …

EVERYTHING AND NOTHING AT ONCE

Bart Eeckhout

NWT 4 (1996), 26–33.

1. Introduction **1.1** I find myself in the ballroom on the third floor of the palazzo first built for Pasquale Revoltella in Trieste and then converted into a museum. Light and dark hardwood floors in classical symmetrical figures. Marble walls, flamed gray and soft yellow, with Corinthian pillars in burgundy. All around Second Empire chairs in red velvet with drooping tresses. High above a frieze alternating female figures in bas-relief and pastoral paintings of pink, chubby, wingless putti illustrating the ways of humankind: farming, fishery, science, dancing ... A gilded coffer ceiling with recessed portraits of the nine muses, again in the guise of putti, this time with wings. Voluptuous chandeliers. In this nineteenth-century space, organized around the commonly shared myths of a culture, allegorically overdetermined, readable like an open book (and closed like a bourgeois fortress), I sit down and open the pages of *S,M,L,XL*, Rem Koolhaas's new book. A consciously dramatic gesture on my part, a maneuver with which I want to shore myself up against Koolhaas's own dramatic practices. **1.2** Pasquale Revoltella was a meat trader who rose to the position of director of the local Lloyd and vice president of the Compagnie Universelle du Canal de Suez, responsible for the construction of the Suez Canal. Between 1854 and 1857, a palazzo was built for him, intended to become a museum after his death. The city of Trieste officially remembers this Revoltella as a generous culture-loving philanthropist. But to others his wealth was founded on business practices for which today we'd be inclined to use the term "meat mob": Revoltella is supposed to have specialized in selling the same cattle twice over. Does this have anything to do with architecture? Somehow it does. Every building that presents itself outwardly as architecture contains simultaneously an invisible story of wheeling and dealing, of politics and strategy, a story that remains hidden behind a luxurious facade. The "corrosive impact" of politics and economy on architecture is among Koolhaas's favorite themes. **1.3** The museum offers me another inroad into the book, by setting up such a conspicuous contrast between nineteenth- and twentieth-century architecture. From bombastic halls and salons, I walk seamlessly into a recent extension, designed by the prominent Italian architect Carlo Scarpa. All of a sudden, I'm inside a labyrinth. Passages between spaces become confusing, cobbled staircases disorient, everywhere are corners, cut-out planes, abrupt see-through perspectives. The walls, floors, stairs acquire an "abstract" quality: monochrome white, off-green, light brown, or beige. The rooms continue up to the roof of the former house, where an extra Legoland of stairs, volumes, and footbridges has been puzzled together. Gone are all the allegories, the transparency, containability, readability. How do you find a language to talk about this? **1.4** During two periods in his life, James Joyce was a teacher at the Scuola Superiore di Commercio Revoltella—a second bequest by the same benefactor—in Trieste. After the First World War, the institute was slowly converted into the University of Trieste. An irrepressible lover of puns, Joyce turned it into the "revolver university." Joyce, revolvers: a starting shot. **2. Literature** **2.1** If there's one writer in the twentieth century who can stand model for exploding the form and contents of the novel, it's Joyce. Not that there wasn't a tradition: from the outset, the novel was a quintessentially indeterminate genre, which loved to test its own limits and subvert its own laws. (Could *Tristram Shandy* really be called a novel?) But Joyce became the undeniable modernist culmination of this tradition: *Ulysses* and *Finnegan's Wake* are experiments with everything you can try out in written form under the umbrella of "novel." **2.2** March 13, 1996, at the Bijloke concert hall in Ghent. On stage: Rem Koolhaas, unadorned, no slides or architectural scale models, just talking about his new book. The hall, about 1200 seats, is sold out; tickets have been circulating on the black market. Koolhaas is taken under siege by a platoon of Flemish architects and experts. Shrewd as a fox, he sidesteps traps, makes pirouettes, remains elusive. Occasionally, he makes his own short sally: "Why am I being questioned here exclusively by people who work in architecture, whereas my book is a novel, after all?" One panel member desperately tries to reassure Rem the book indeed reads like a Dostoevsky. Dostoevsky, seriously? What on earth gave him that idea? **2.3** The press file, it appears, which includes the following quote from *Vogue*: *S,M,L,XL* "might be billed as an epic in the great tradition of Tolstoy or Dostoevsky." Oh well, fat book, Dostoevsky, tell me about it. The things you can achieve by putting on the back blurb, "This massive book is a novel about architecture." **2.4** A novel about architecture? I know novels with architects as protagonists, say, *Paradise* by Donald Barthelme. Barthelme offers a slightly better point of comparison than Dostoevsky: himself the son of a not unimportant architect (who built a house inspired by Mies's Tugendhat in the middle of the Texan desert) and one of the prime inventors of Postmodernism in American literature. But what Barthelme serves up in his novel—though it may be experimental, cut up into fragments, and full of hilariously clashing registers—still remains quite simply fiction, a screwball story about an architect who flees to New York and goes to live in a *ménage à quatre* with three women. No, Koolhaas is still something else entirely. **2.5** With permission, let's call on Jacques Derrida instead. In an interview, he once characterized literature as the institute "où l'on peut tout dire"—in which you can say both *everything* and *anything*. It's the perfect legitimation for Koolhaas's book. At 1376 pages, *S,M,L,XL* strikes us first and foremost by its patent unwillingness to select. This is a book in which Koolhaas wanted to say *everything*: the designs his architectural firm, the grandly named Office for Metropolitan Architecture, has come up with during its first two decades, collected according to scale in the four categories indicated by the title, and represented at sundry stages of their development; the essays, manifestoes, notes, scribblings Koolhaas has turned out over the same period; a barrage of quotations culled from just about anywhere; graphs, tables, even engineering calculations. The result has, as an American reviewer described it, "the weight and shape of a block of granite." **2.6** But besides everything the book also offers anything—or flirts with that possibility all the time. This is especially the case with the "dictionary" of citations (actually put together by Jennifer Sigler, the book's editor) and the countless incongruous pictures that are allowed to interrupt every "narrative" at any moment and in the best of collage traditions. The hundreds of citations build a postmodern *summa* of their own, with famous sayings by all the great of the earth—say, Freud, Darwin, Marx, Lucille Ball, Derrida, Arnold Schwarzenegger, Wittgenstein, Heidegger, Superman, Nabokov, Joyce (sure enough), Ms. Edith Creed Bunker ("Best Teacher of 1946"),

Nietzsche, Foucault, Van Kooten & De Bie ("Dutch comedians"), Frank Lloyd Wright, Marilyn Monroe (about Brigitte Bardot: "I find her charming"), Barthes, a housewife who had her name changed into Elvis Presley, Aristotle, Fred Astaire, and yes, even Dostoevsky. The spliced-in pictures are no less excessive: a bombed skyscraper, Russian surgeons around Lenin's mummy, an eye that is being cut open (a still from Buñuel and Dalí's *Un Chien Andalou*), overturned and burned-out cars in a Parisian street during May 1968, a set of ads for twelve types of men's underwear, a collection of sex ads from *Penthouse*, a tabloid page proclaiming that the world ended eight years ago after a nuclear war (the merciful God has wiped that memory for us), the ceiling of the Sistine Chapel, queuing voters in South Africa, a T cell being attacked by the HIV virus. (It won't be a coincidence that Koolhaas is a metropolitan thinker and that the catalogue is the literary urban form par excellence.) This practice has about all the effects discontinuity and juxtaposition can trigger: irony, recognition, reinforcement, relativizing, distraction, confusion, irritation, indifference. It's impossible to determine how much intentionality needs to be ascribed to each of these effects. "The book can be read in any way," the introduction provocatively announces. What is certain is that Koolhaas detests readers who want to be taken by the hand. Those who don't want to make the effort to be as creative and inventive as he tries to be, who don't want to start reflecting and theorizing in turn on questions of signification, style, coherence, complexity, should have bought a coffee-table book instead. *S,M,L,XL* is a workpiece, also for the reader, a think tank wishing to reproduce in the reader/spectator the same uncertainties, disappointments, and ecstasies inherent in the architect's life. **2.7** The philosopher Bart Verschaffel during the debate at the Bijloke: "This is a dangerous book, because most architects are terrible readers; they just flip through pages and look at the pictures." Verschaffel is right: with this book, you have to put up an intellectual fight. **2.8** "To put up a fight." Earlier I already wrote, "to take under siege," "a platoon of architects"—it sounds almost like war. Or is that what it is for Koolhaas? Here is a sample of his style (don't worry too much about the contents): "Liberated from its atavistic duties, urbanism redefined as a way of operating on the inevitable will attack architecture, invade its trenches, drive it from its bastions, undermine its certainties, explode its limits, ridicule its preoccupations with matter and substance, destroy its traditions, smoke out its practitioners." The Greek word for war is *polemos*. Koolhaas's favorite genre is the *polemic*. To this end, he makes use of an astonishing, sometimes deafening arsenal of rhetorical weapons. **3. Rhetoric** **3.1** "Architecture is a hazardous mixture of omnipotence and impotence." That's the first sentence of the introduction, the first example also in a nearly endless series of one-liners, paradoxes, oxymorons, and aporias. Only a few lines down, for instance, we hear about the book, "Its epic scale is both arrogant and hesitant. It tries to deflate and reflate architecture—to destroy and rebuild." The both-A-and-not-A tactic is one of Koolhaas's best-loved weapons. Like deconstructionists, he writes with both hands: "Bigness is where architecture becomes both most and least architectural." Already in *Delirious New York*, his previous book from 1978 that turned him into an international cult figure almost overnight, he took delight in wielding this weapon. Manhattan's skyscrapers were described there as, among other things, "both architecture *and* hyper-efficient machines, both modern *and* eternal." **3.2** There may well be no other architect in the world who is able to spout epigrams and aphorisms with such ease and such a gift for provocation: "Where there is nothing, everything is possible. Where there is architecture, nothing (else) is possible." "More important than the design of cities will be the design of their decay." "What Las Vegas is to late capitalism, the Bijlmermeer is to the Welfare State." "Just as *The Man Without Qualities* haunts European literature, 'the plan without qualities' is the great quest of American building." "This century has been a losing battle with the issue of quantity." "More than ever, the city is all we have." "Tourism is now independent of destination." Keep rinsing your mouth; just a little more, it won't hurt. "Postmodernism is the only movement that has succeeded in connecting the practice of architecture with the practice of panic." "Japan equals England in surgical manners / also in insular self-love." "Architecture, with all of its messy complexities, is notoriously resistant to explanation, hostile to revelation." "Nietzsche lost out to Sociology 101." **3.3** There's no shortage of images, metaphors, and similes in this book either. Let's just return to that single-page introduction, the final sentence: "*S,M,L,XL* is a search for 'another' architecture, knowing that architecture is like a lead ball chained to a prisoner's leg: to escape, he has to get rid of its weight, but all he can do is scrape slivers off with a teaspoon." Here's a novelist at work, and he has a preference for brilliant hyperboles. The globalization of the architectural profession he likes to call "the final installment of the Promethean soap opera," the latest urban landscapes "this Wagnerian *ur*-soup," and the average American skyscraper "the equivalent of atonal music, seriality, concrete poetry, art brut; it is architecture as mantra." Go ahead and rinse again. **3.4** Another conspicuous characteristic: the ellipsis, especially of verbs. Koolhaas most enjoys piling up sentences as if they were building blocks—flashes of inspiration without action, recorded in a way befitting his lifestyle: fast, economical, efficient, to the point. History likewise tends to progress in shocks for him, from incident to incident, idea to idea, zeitgeist to zeitgeist. Is this the architect's doodling habit? Or is that bricklayering style the product of an essentially spatial imagination? **3.5** The seduction exerted on Koolhaas by language (not even his native tongue), the verbal fireworks he so easily ignites, is a danger not to be underestimated. Language is, after all, a lot more malleable and woollier than solid matter. It may be fun to be able to talk insouciantly of "the hedonistic science of designing collective facilities that fully accommodate individual desires," but what does this "science" entail, and how do you put it into practice? It's impressive to be able to say about a housing complex in Fukuoka that "the centrifugal substance of modern architecture is condensed to generate urban form," but does it mean anything? Does it help our perception of these houses? Does it legitimate their existence and form? In a handwritten comment on a design for the Villa dall'Ava in Paris, we read, "The best way to represent it would be to take the house as a frame to describe its environment. *It is not an object!*" The house isn't an object but a frame for its surroundings: how far can you go with such idealizations? Somewhere Koolhaas writes about "systematic *idealization*—

a systematic overestimation of what exists, a bombardment of speculation that invests even the most mediocre aspects with retroactive conceptual and ideological charge." But he himself indulges in this tendency with a vengeance. A conceptual architect who is able to juggle with language in such a dazzling manner is not an innocuous person. **3.6** Koolhaas the conceptualist is a master theoretician who is able to write a manifesto for everything (anything?). If architects are essentially hirelings, then Koolhaas is the supreme ghostwriter. Just read his "meditation" on the "Typical Plan," the default of the average American skyscraper. What Koolhaas performs there is a dizzying feat of tapdancing, impossible to still to anything resembling a personal position, a proper ideology. In his brilliant manifesto for "The Generic City," there is a fleeting mention of "an infinitely patient blackboard on which almost any hypothesis can be 'proven' and then erased, never again to reverberate in the minds of its authors or its audience." Koolhaas knows himself through and through, and he possesses an almost euphoric feel for cynicism. **4. Authorship**

4.1 The author is dead, so we know, long live the writers' collective. *S,M,L,XL* has "a hybrid authorship" (the postmodern shibboleth "hybridity" is all over the place). On the cover, we find the names of OMA, Rem Koolhaas, and Bruce Mau; on the title page, in an outsize font, those of Jennifer Sigler (editor) and Hans Werlemann (photography) are added. **4.2** The Romantic individualism of the author is at odds with the daily activities of an international architect. In his manifesto for Bigness, Koolhaas explicitly rejoices in this: the bigger the project, the less the architect is "condemned" to stardom, the more he is connected through "a web of umbilical cords" with specialists from other disciplines. "Like mountain climbers tied together by life-saving ropes, the makers of Bigness are a *team* (a word not mentioned in the last forty years of architectural polemic)." **4.3** On its back, the book is called "a free-fall in the space of the typographic imagination," referring to the contribution by Bruce Mau, a designer from Toronto. Visually, *S,M,L,XL* is indeed as challenging, excessive, heterogeneous, shrewd, dazzling, and confusing as Koolhaas's own texts. With a lot of postmodern flair, the layout plays around with the limits of good taste, with frivolities and kitsch. Mau doesn't hesitate to make the text partly illegible at times: the dizzying and satirically self-undercutting list of facts and figures about the Congrexpo in Lille has to battle it out with an imposturous background picture of the Eiffel Tower. On one occasion (p. 1212), illegibility is near-complete when black letters are printed on a well-nigh perfectly black picture—that must be a production error. **4.4** Ultimately, *S,M,L,XL* is a hypertext that doesn't want to speak its name, a collection of multimedia materials that belongs on an electronic carrier. So why did it become a book, after all? We are left guessing. The attachment to books as a format may well be the last nostalgia of an antinostalgic architect. **5. Narrative Form**

5.1 A book that experiments with language and image must try out different narrative forms as well. Much as *Ulysses* invented a new form almost chapter by chapter, Koolhaas (assisted, no doubt, by Jennifer Sigler) continuously looks for ways of telling his story differently. In addition to analytical essays, manifestoes, and pamphlets, we thus also find drily enumerating chronologies, parable-like inventions, travel notes in the form of a poem and seemingly grafted on Roland Barthes, a comic strip in black and white, a book-within-the-book, diary notes (addressed in the postmodern manner: "Dear Diary"), a bedside story, a narrated dream. **5.2** One of the more fascinating narrative experiments takes us through the Kunsthal in Rotterdam, which opened in 1992. Photo after photo, we walk through this ingeniously complex building, accompanied merely by walking instructions in a tiny font and, in big letters, flashes of absurd dialogue. In that dialogue, we quickly recognize the hand of Samuel Beckett—*Waiting for Godot*—and promptly the questions bubble up. Isn't this a misunderstanding? Can the structure and the appearance of a building make you laugh like the absurd hopelessness in a dialogue by Beckett? Is a walk through the idiosyncratic spiral of the gallery as senseless and circular as the talking-for-the-sake-of-talking by Beckett's characters? Is it just as full of unexpected turns? Indeed, may an architect to whom millions of public funds have been entrusted sport a Beckettian worldview? Now the citations and pictures of the spaces merge in surprising manners, then they part again abruptly and we're being provoked by the claim that the past fifty years have consisted of nothing but blathering. The last picture carries as final instruction, "Keep going." The building as perpetuum mobile. **5.3** That the invention of new forms may be liberating, I'm able to ascertain myself when I embark on this review essay. I decide to copy the format used by Koolhaas for "The Generic City," and immediately things become possible that previously seemed not to be: to gather an unmanageable chaos of experiences and ideas, to juxtapose disparate elements, to create the illusion of construction, structure, and logic, to intersperse bon mots. **6. Style** **6.1** The variation in ways of writing and narrative forms is no coincidence: in his architectural work as well, Koolhaas harbors a deep distrust for anything resembling a style—a proper style to which his work might be reduced. He refuses to retreat into habits, well-tested systems and formulas, which can then be repeated and monetarized endlessly, like a signature placed over and over again. That stubborn search for renewal—stepped up since the latter half of the 1980s—not only commands admiration, it sometimes also delivers the most astonishing results. Conceptual architects aren't only dangerous because they have ideas; they are also indispensable because they have ideas. **6.2** "No proper style" doesn't mean there's no method in this madness. The countless designs, models, and pictures do bring a number of recurring characteristics and ingredients to light: the consciously heterogeneous collage of forms and materials, the cultivation of irregularity, asymmetry, unpredictability, the injection of seemingly arbitrary components that work against synthetic legibility, the tendency to go underground, the usage of cool, hard textures, of stylistic citations (a few times Mies), the preference for a forest of thin steel pillars (which enable glass exteriors and thus the dismantling of the "facade"), stylized corrugated iron, curtains replacing interior walls, swimming pools on roofs. Yet none of this suffices to be called a style. The surprise at each new design remains greater than the predictability or recognizability. You're not getting used to anything. **7. Paradigms** **7.1** As a theoretician, Koolhaas has the uncanny ability to identify the architectural paradigms of our age. This already became obvious in the design with which he graduated from the London Architectural Association in 1972 and in which much of what has become topical since then (Americans locking themselves up in "gated communities," the experiment with Biosphere II, the issue of virtual reality) are intriguingly adumbrated. Early, too, was the Berlin Wall, impressively discussed as an embodiment of "architecture's true nature," and a prison in Arnhem, which made the principle of the panopticon instantly relevant again. **7.2** Paradigmatic as well is the mind-boggling, downright Kafkaesque history of a pavilion Mies once designed in Spain—a history that summarizes in a handful of pages how much architecture, when push comes to shove, can be the powerless victim of social and political events, how much buildings can be neutralized time and again to sheer matter and use value. **7.3** There is a razor-sharp analytical report about Atlanta as a textbook example of the postmodern American city (more even than Los Angeles) and the influence on the city of John Portman ("undoubtedly a genius in his own mind"). The report takes us into architectural firms that think nothing of designing an entire skyscraper in a single day—and of changing the design completely the next day, if necessary. **7.4** In an extensive, lucid study of the city-state of Singapore ("a mini-Sparta"), Koolhaas proves again, unnecessarily, his skill for synthetic thinking and his ability to detect, against all postmodern dogmas, the metanarratives of our time. In thirty years' time, the autocratic regime in Singapore has replaced the old city by an entirely new one, "a unique ecology of the contemporary," and Koolhaas predicts that in this city today the future of China is being prepared.

8. Program **8.1** From metanarratives to a proper ideological program is but a small step. Here's the introduction again: *S,M,L,XL* is "a painfully utopian enterprise" whose purpose is to arrive at "a new realism about what architecture is and what it can do." **8.2** Utopia is a word Koolhaas generally prefers not to use. The megalomaniac meliorism of modernist architects ended in dismal failure, and the disenchantment over what Koolhaas's own generation of May 1968 has achieved returns like a leitmotiv. Those 68-ers built "the largest generation ever, caught in the 'collective narcissism of a demographic bubble,'" and he reproaches them for their escape into paralyzing sophistication. "Our amalgamated wisdom can be easily caricatured: according to Derrida we cannot be *Whole*, according to Baudrillard we cannot be *Real*, according to Virilio we cannot be *There*." **8.3** "The only legitimate relationship that architects can have with the subject of chaos is to take their rightful place in the army of those devoted to resist it, and fail." By the end of the 1980s, when OMA found itself grappling with three gigantic projects at the same time (a new terminal in Zeebrugge, Mitterrand's Bibliothèque de France in Paris, a center for art and media technology in Karlsruhe), it dawned on Koolhaas that theories such as Derrida's, Baudrillard's, and Virilio's merely crippled him, while they were being overtaken left and right by reality. Out of the blue, "to our own consternation, Bigness emerged like a sudden iceberg from the mist of deconstructivist discourse and imposed itself as a political, economic, artistic necessity." **8.4** *Bigness*—it's one of those recalcitrant, slippery concepts Koolhaas loves to belabor. "The absence of a theory of Bigness—what is the maximum architecture can do?—is architecture's most debilitating weakness. Without a theory of Bigness, architects are in the position of Frankenstein's creators: instigators of a partly successful experiment whose results are running amok and are therefore discredited." The worldwide emergence of mega-buildings and totally new or renewed urban areas has gone on without a program, without a developed vision. The result is that the technocrats of architecture reign supreme; whoever doesn't appreciate their work retreats grumbling into a corner or acts up as a haughty intellectual. As a defender of modernity and modernization (but not of Modernism), Koolhaas, by contrast, sees it as his duty to dirty his hands, to participate in this worldwide process, and, in the full awareness of the futility of his endeavors, to influence it. **8.5** Such influence means, among other things, that the discipline of urbanism has to be reinvented. While cities around the world are growing out of proportion and the urban condition is spread everywhere as a way of life, urbanists have castrated themselves. "A profession persists in its fantasies, its ideology, its pretension, its illusions of involvement and control, and is therefore incapable of conceiving new modesties, partial interventions, strategic realignments, compromised positions that might influence, redirect, succeed in limited terms, regroup, begin from scratch even, but will never reestablish control." **8.6** And suddenly there's that treacherous rhetoric again. Urbanism today can consist only of "the staging of uncertainty," "the irrigation of territories with potential," "discovering unnameable hybrids," "an ideology: to accept what exists." Koolhaas still wants to be visionary but doesn't know anymore exactly how to do so. He wants to keep up the visionary pose, but without concrete contents. He refuses to forsake the social and artistic obligation to invent the future, but simultaneously wants to keep that future as open as possible. He wants to design sites that never really take form, can forever be changed again. The paradox isn't his literary weapon for nothing. **8.7** How typical is this attitude for our fin de siècle? Is Koolhaas a dramatic example of the disenchanted, hopeless intellectual who continues to act against all odds? Does he absolutize freedom and the future as endless mutation? **9. Coda** **9.1** A few years ago, in a discussion with American students, Koolhaas remarked, "There is an unbelievable overestimation of the power of architecture in terms of the good it can do, but even more, in terms of the bad it has done or can do." **9.2** Is there a comparable overestimation of the good a book can do (and even more of the bad it can do)? The first critical comments on *S,M,L,XL* disagreed in this respect. To some the book affords a euphoric reading and viewing experience that stands apart from the social laboratory and intellectual provocation it also wants to offer. Koolhaas is no more, in that case, than "a master of serious clowning." Others take the book very seriously. Like the prominent Marxist critic Fredric Jameson, they try to perform their own pirouettes around the text: "this is a vanguard operation without the avant-garde vision or mission; a powerfully future-oriented material imagination without a future in any traditional sense of the word; Dystopia as Utopia, perhaps, but at an intensity that dissolves the usual overtones or connotations of both those words all at once." **9.3** Is it a novel? An autobiography? An analysis of the postmodern architectural condition? A playground? A View-Master? A manifesto? An apology? "A rewriting of *Learning from Las Vegas* in an utterly new, nonhumanist idiom" (Jameson)? It's all of this and nothing of this. It's everything and nothing at once, a book sui generis that has had to invent itself first.

FREE FALL
Terence Riley
L'Architecture d'Aujourd'hui 304 (1996), 57.

S,M,L,XL by Rem Koolhaas and Bruce Mau is not only one of the latest in a long line of books about architecture but it also expands a smaller and historically more influential subset: like Palladio's *I Quattri Libri dell'Architettura*, Claude-Nicolas Ledoux's *L'architecture*, and Frank Lloyd Wright's *Wasmuth Portfolio*, *S,M,L,XL* is an architect's publication, wherein not one but two texts exist. The first is the graphic text of the author's architectural work; the second a literary construction which seeks to position the former in a theoretical framework, Unlike its predecessors, *S,M,L,XL* achieves a level of complexity beyond the standard architectural treatise, gyrating between the universal and the personal, the manifesto and the documentary, autobiography and *Weltanschauung*. More of an anthology than a single literary effort, the book contains Koolhaas's early writings, such as *Delirious New York* published originally in 1978 and reproduced in *S,M,L,XL*, shorter texts and lectures written during the 1980s, such as "Imagining Nothingness" and "The Terrifying Beauty of the Twentieth Century," as well as more recent works. It is the last that are the most interesting as interpretations of Koolhaas's architecture, though his earlier writings provide substantial and important prologue.

The appeal of the later writings is that they were written during the midst, and in the aftermath, of the flowering (or deflowering) of Koolhaas's professional practice, which has included such important constructions (and near constructions) as the Kunsthal in Rotterdam, the Villa dall'Ava, the Zentrum for Media-Technologie project for Karlsruhe, Fukuoka Housing and the mammoth urban and architectural works in Lille. Particularly, the essays "Bigness," "Generic City" and "Singapore Songlines" reflect a professional and theoretical synthesis—each meta-reflections on architectural theory wrapped in experiential analysis returning to theory once again. As such the essays can be read as both a portrait of a contemporary architectural practice, as well as a blueprint for Koolhaas's trajectory into the next millennium. The relationship between the architecture and the architectural text in this beautifully designed and joyously oversized 1,344-page tome is a positive one.

Marvelously produced, *S,M,L,XL* subsumes the tension that has existed between architecture and its media reflections ever since Frollo's prediction that "the book will kill the edifice." Victor Hugo's character might have been more accurate had he not predicted the demise of architecture but the end of architecture's hegemony over the proliferation of information. Nonetheless, even Hugo could not have predicted the evolution of other media, the photograph and the film, which would in turn infringe on their predecessors as well as each other. Yet, even as these new media developed, it might be said that they also, each in their own way, paid some form of homage to architecture. The traditional book's systems of structure and substructure bindings, chapters, and pages, are made evident in its frontality and rigid sequence, reminiscent of the neo-classical facade and ritualized movement enfilade.

Given its convenient immobility, it is no wonder that the first cameras were also so quickly focused on architecture and more importantly, how quickly they were refocused on the spaces between the architecture, the city streets, reproducing the sensations of depth that had so long been the province of architectural creation. With regards to film's relationship to architecture, there are probably no two creatures more interchangeable in the modern imagination than the architect and the director. Each, to some degree, self-invented, insisting on complete control over setting, movement, light, mood—the totality of sensory experience.

In this view, *S,M,L,XL* is not so much a book itself but a space in which the media creations of architecture—the book, the photograph, the film—collide, mutate and reinvent themselves. Koolhaas's instinct for constructing architectural images with the printed word is mirrored in Mau's instinct for the way in which the word appears on the page. The jumbo type faces in Koolhaas's essay "Bigness" convey as much gravity (and levity) as such inventions can bear. Mau's contributions to *S,M,L,XL* do not end with the books' design layout. Part of the real joy of the book is the quality and craft of its production, which Mau supervised at the printer's plant in Italy. The pages devoted to the Zeebrugge project feature both positive and negative images rendered in a silky flat metallic ink, portraying the architecture in such away as to suggest we are seeing the project for the first time. In the section on the Villa dall'Ava, the distinction between the reproductions of the black line architectural drawings and the reproduction of Koolhaas's red Bic-pen annotations is so sharp that it seems as if the architect has inscribed each book personally. These and other craft pyrotechnics can cause the reader to overlook the high quality of what are typically more standard printing features—beautifully rendered four-color images, halftones, duotones abound; literally, hundreds of them.

If the camera's frequent relationship to architecture is a simple documentary tool, Hans Werlemann's photos of many of Koolhaas's projects are evidence of the vacuity of standard "architectural photography." Werlemann's work is not subservient to Koolhaas's; on the contrary, he uses the architecture as fodder for his own subjective invention. Werlemann avoids the vacant, arid shots which typically portray architecture as some sort of full-scale maquette in favor of, what might be called, both extremely stylized casualness and an extremely casual stylishness. His portraits of the two Villas with Patios are less a formal rendition than a study of the multiple visual realities caused by the momentary and ever-changing interplay of light on reflective surfaces. In portraying the Villa dall'Ava, Werlemann takes a different tack, staging photos which achieve a sense of easy stylishness with more than a little tongue-in-cheek. Three divers, in identical bathing suits, are poised at the roof-top pool, part Spartakiad and part Hollywood movie. In a nighttime sequence, a giraffe elegantly and inexplicably visits the house, its splayed legs mimicking and adding to the redundancy of the forest of pilotis under the Villa's upper level.

Koolhaas's interest in film predates his activity as an architect. His brief career as a film writer has, however, had a lasting effect on his work and, in many ways, on *S,M,L,XL*. Rarely does Koolhaas portray his work as a product but as an event. The Voluntary Prisoners of Architecture, Koolhaas's diploma project of 1972, remains an important example of this cinematic approach to architecture. Certain aspects of the book's design achieve the same effect: the surimposition of text from *Waiting for Godot* over an unfolding series of images of the Kunsthal mimics the ethos of the film, with dialogue driving the experiences and architecture creating the mood.

If the thesis that the book, the photograph and the film are somehow indebted to architecture is accepted, *S,M,L,XL* represents an incredible achievement in momentarily realigning their various trajectories toward presenting a comprehensive view of Koolhaas's architectural work. Yet, that accomplishment alone would encompass only, what must be called at this moment in history, the traditional media. In this line of thinking, contemporary mass media, with its imperceptible structure and formless sensibility, is seen as an invention conceived wholly outside of the influence of architecture. This paradox of contemporary architecture culture is noted by Koolhaas: "Our amalgamated wisdom can be caricatured: according to Derrida we cannot be Whole, according to Baudrillard we cannot be Real, according to Virilio we cannot be There—inconvenient repertoire for a profession helplessly about being Whole, Real and There." Perhaps, then the real accomplishment of *S,M,L,XL* is its success in approximating this paradox. The book is, in the authors' words, "a free fall through typographic space"; an unstructured series of coherent, though randomly accessed, events within a system whose logic is too vast to easily comprehend. Without mimicking the tropes of cyber-technologies, the book approximates both their limits and potential benefits while remaining stupefyingly Whole, Real and There.

THE DIALECTICS OF SCALE

Richard Sennett
Harvard GSD News, Summer 1996, 45.

S,M,L,XL, Rem Koolhaas's new book, asks designers to think big. Although commercial architects don't need such encouragement, socially conscious architects do. The culture of the Left since the 1960s has emphasized smallness. Small is the dimension of *gemeinschaft*, of face-to-face relations in communities where people know each other. Small is also the dimension that least risks damaging others when designing their dreams. Koolhaas, though aware of the virtues of *gemeinschaft* and modest intervention, thinks they won't suffice, because a city is more than a village, and because small, self-effacing gestures leave only faint traces on the built environment.

I can't critique the architectural forms through which Koolhaas seeks to reverse the cultural sensibility of the small, but I would like to comment on the sensibility itself. In the 1960s the politics of small scale were defined in the writing of Jane Jacobs, who believed that thinking small would help prevent the kind of large-scale, official, impersonal planning practiced by power brokers like Robert Moses. Local needs, concerns, and experience would be the grit jamming the machinery of power; large couldn't accommodate small.

In the 1970s Jacobs continued to believe in small-scale resistance to Moses-scale planning; indeed, she elaborated an alternative theory of development based on local initiatives. Although she was my mentor when I began studying cities, I soon lost faith in the ability of "small" to counter "big"; even the best examples of local action seemed gestures easily crushed by large corporations or consigned to the oblivion of "appreciation" by liberal bureaucrats. Small scale seemed also to miss what urban studies is all about culturally; the genius loci of a city is impersonal, public culture—culture on a large human scale. And yet Jacobs continued to speak to me, as to many others, as the voice of conscience: social relations, like trust or mutual commitment, are personal rather than impersonal, face-to-face, local.

The opposition between large and small scale became a source of ambivalence among many left-wing urbanists: while our sensibility favored the small, our analysis led us in the opposite direction. By the 1980s Manuel Castells believed in the justice, but no longer the efficacy, of grass-roots protest; David Harvey had come to doubt the possibility of basing an urban socialism on neighborhood life. Ambivalence about scale among radical urbanists reflected a larger uncertainty on the Left: distrust of liberal "policy wonks," but also loss of faith in spontaneous popular movements; a desire to organize, but no new plans.

Then capitalism surprised us: it changed the dialectics of scale. In the last decade, the economy became as big as possible—global—while operating ever more flexibly on the local level. Information technology, world financial markets, the "reengineering" of work—all make this connectivity possible. And the politics which suits this new phase of capitalism has also changed the dialectics of scale. The state apparatus has divested itself of social responsibilities, just as big corporations are shirking obligations to their employees. In the new political economy, localities are free to manage—without sufficient money or skills—problems of poverty, aging, and schooling in any way the community sees fit. Central structures profit from localization.

Thus has the political economy connected small, medium, large, and extra large. Distinctions of scale, rather than oppositions, function like the different stops and registers on an organ. Because the political economy has changed the dialectics of scale, it would be foolhardy for urbanists to imagine that local and national, city and suburban, or (in another social register of scale) *gemeinschaft* and *gesellschaft* would continue to operate as oppositions. New problems of scale face us instead: what is the relation of economic networks to the size of cities? In an age of global communication, do cultural qualities like urbanity still depend on the physical experience of crowds, as in the time of Walter Benjamin? Does it make sense, ethically, to link qualities like modesty to local behavior in an age when the "local" serves the ideological function of a dumping ground? Indeed, is the scale of human settlement at all relevant to the practice of radical politics?

These are the sorts of questions those of us who care about the physical environment need to confront now. Perhaps when we do so, we will be better able to participate in architectural discussions about scale and have something to say about the politics of building small, medium, large, or extra large.

AN INCOMPLETE ENCYCLOPAEDIA

Jeremy Till

Artifice 4 (1996), 18–27.

Architects—All imbeciles. Always forgetting to put the staircase in.
Gustave Flaubert

Bigness

It is the fate of all seminal works (as *S,M,L,XL* is destined to become) that they are reduced to memorable tags. Thus: BIGNESS. Koolhaas thrusts forward the concept of Bigness as the way first to unravel and then to reform architectural practice. As a word, Bigness is insolent, ugly and, at first sight, disarmingly banal—all qualities that have been associated with the built work of the Office for Metropolitan Architecture. As with the architecture, it is these very qualities that will make the concept liable to unthinking appropriation and to easy dismissal. One can anticipate a rash of truly bad projects being legitimized through recourse to Bigness and, conversely, one can see a theoretical overturning of the concept by spotlighting the inherent (and magnified) poverty of such projects. It is in the nature of any polemic that it lays itself open to deliberate misreading. Le Corbusier's "Architecture or Revolution" is not to be taken as a direct choice, but as a provocation against which to measure action. To accept the word *Bigness* at face value is a misunderstanding that ignores the liberating potentials that the concept offers. Bigness is not to be read simply as a matter of physical scale, but as a catalyst that precipitates sets of complex and uncontrollable urban interrelationships. In a different context, Koolhaas describes how the Berlin Wall "forever severed the connection between *importance* and *mass*." The book itself neatly identifies the dilemma of Bigness. It is big, the beauty of its bulk rendering it a desirable object. But beyond this superficial aesthetic reading, the book also has the qualities of Bigness. The different modes of representation (narrative, photojournalism, poetry, diary, polemic, drawings and so on) accumulate to give fluid readings of the subject in which "the elements react to create new events." Such an interpretation demands an act of faith in which not every page is seen as equal to another. Whole portions of the book are there as background (parking lots of ideas, both good and not so good), places (as in the city) of banality from which the more charged moments emerge. It is only in cross readings, and in the interstices of the book, that the full alchemical potential of Bigness is released.

Catalogue
S,M,L,XL: a catalogue *irraisonné*.

Contagious
S,M,L,XL was launched in London on December 8, 1995. On December 12 a quote from the book appeared written large on one of my student's presentations. A nasty little rash. The book is in danger of becoming a major source of theoretical infection, contagious polemic lifted from a healthy host to invade less robust bodies. Koolhaas's astonishing use of language—the book is worth reading for its linguistic force and delight alone—makes him particularly susceptible to quotation. I suspect that the book is destined to remain largely unread but used as a fetishized source of fragments for the millennium, the intellectual equivalent of a European bathroom catalogue. Such pillaging may be consistent with Koolhaas's own reappropriation of cultural references to structure his work, but the danger is that misses the full force of Koolhaas's and Bruce Mau's brilliant interweaving of the fragments into something far greater than the sum of the parts.

Freedoms
In an interview with Koolhaas, Alejandro Zaera-Polo identifies the work of OMA with a series of freedoms. Freedom from ties, freedom from structures, freedom from ideologies, freedom from models ... always freedoms FROM. Koolhaas is at his best in *S,M,L,XL* in identifying the shackles that have tied architecture. His critique, often caustic, is always to the point and is used as a method of dialectically reformulating his own position. So, if context is seen as the artificial imposition of an idealized historical continuity, then "Fuck Context!" If rationality is seen as a corrupted reworking of type in the name of authenticity, then subvert the concept through the tactic of random "typological bombardment." However, this dialectical working leaves an aporia in which the newfound freedoms FOR are never identified. To some extent, this avoidance is consistent with Koolhaas's rejection of the Modernist's belief in the programmatic determinacy of architecture, but it inevitably leaves him in an ambivalent ethical position. Koolhaas defends the postponement of judgment on the grounds that it allows him to assimilate as many influences as possible. A strength of *S,M,L,XL* is in the experimentation and speculation that this postponement has enabled, unburdened by the pious stance of the liberal humanist. This may be acceptable to a point, but with the essay "Singapore Songlines," and the associated postscript "The Generic City," that point is passed. Where Manhattan was the spirit that drove *Delirious New York*, Singapore is the spectre that haunts *S,M,L,XL*. Where his love for Manhattan comes through every line of the previous book, here Koolhaas can only summon up a morbid fascination for Singapore and Atlanta. And yet he needs these two cities to drive his train of thought. Atlanta supplies the model of deurbanization and flux which challenges the stability, centrality and order of the decaying Eurocentric city. Singapore supplies the uniquely Asian megastructure which captures the qualities of Bigness missing from the "lobotomized modernism" he identifies in the early stages of the island's development. While the authoritarian

regime of Singapore is introduced at the beginning of the article, the main thrust of the piece is the tracing of an architectural genealogy. It is as if the recourse to a detached architectural mythology (a traditional methodology that Koolhaas scrupulously avoids elsewhere) relieves him of the responsibility of making judgments about the political conditions that have produced this particular urbanism. The piece ends with an ominously convincing prediction that Singapore's urban (and by association political) model will become the blueprint for Asian city-states of the future. Koolhaas ends with the glib statement, "Two billion people can't be wrong." The point is that two billion people can't be wrong because they are not allowed to be wrong, and this fact alone demands positioning on the part of the architect.

Hero

S,M,L,XL presents a sustained assault on the notion of architect as hero. Koolhaas kills off the already sickened holy cows of architecture—the fetish of detail, the iconic status of the single building, the imposition of order and the delusion of control through form. This critique represents a paradigm shift for architecture. The book makes uncomfortable reading as it consistently undermines the assumed "truths" that have sustained the myth of architecture for so long. Like a cornered animal acutely conscious of its own mortality, the threatened establishment of architects lashes out at Koolhaas with derision, as in the miserable dismissal of OMA's built work on the grounds that it is "badly" detailed. Such stupidity overlooks the fact Koolhaas is being cruel to be kind, because underlying the whole venture is an intense love for architecture. He yearns to resuscitate the discipline in a new mode. With the operations of the profession placed within the wider context of a system of forces beyond their direct control, Koolhaas argues that the profession must move into a postheroic stage. At Lille, he orchestrates this through the role reversals that are imposed on the chosen architects. Portzamparc, master of high culture, is given a brutal office block. Nouvel, spender of big bespoke budgets, is given an unremittingly cheap, generic, shopping center. In a moment of inconsistency in this playful miscasting, OMA give themselves a building full of the potential of Bigness. This points to the difficulty of reconciling the postheroic position with Koolhaas's now stratospheric status and with the sometimes invasive immodesty of the OMA operation, which the book plays a major role in promulgating.

Intelligence

S,M,L,XL is both clever in its self-conscious structuring, but also the work of a formidable intelligence. Koolhaas's achievement is to manifest this intelligence in both the writing about buildings and the making of buildings, so that each act continually informs and modifies the other. There are clearly other intelligent people operating in this field, but generally these can be divided into those theorists who build—in which case the architecture is seen as illustrations of the theory—or those builders who theorize (often after the event)—in which case the theory is seen as a legitimation of the architecture. In *S,M,L,XL* Koolhaas occupies an indefinable middle ground between the two positions, inventive and provocative, as both thinker and maker.

Unfettered by the demands of practice, *S,M,L,XL* reasserts the extraordinary importance of critique and speculation in reforming architectural culture.

Koolhaas
The authorship of the book is presented, on the one hand, as hybrid—Rem Koolhaas, OMA (itself an amorphous body) and Bruce Mau—on the other, it resonates with one identity, that of Koolhaas. In the end, the power of the word persuades me to refer to a single author, Rem Koolhaas, even though it pains me in so doing to apparently ignore his collaborators. Alex Wall's miraculous painting of Parc de la Villette is but one of many unaccredited examples where the manifest contribution of individuals is too conveniently subsumed under the guise of OMA—for which we now read Koolhaas.

Manifesto
Architectural culture is always hungry for manifestoes. We have waited thirty years since Rossi's *The Architecture of the City* and Venturi's *Complexity and Contradiction,* two manifestoes with which *S,M,L,XL* will inevitably be compared. Where *Delirious New York* (which partly filled the gap) was firmly subtitled "a retroactive manifesto," the status of *S,M,L,XL* is less obviously identifiable. To a certain extent, it is a working through of the issues identified in the first book, the fulfillment of an unrequited love, but it does not provide such a direct model for action, possibly because of the undesirability of looking to Atlanta and Singapore (Manhattan's successors) as exemplars. Rossi and Venturi both used theory to lead directly to architectural production, drawing on history to give a certain legitimacy and determinacy to their respective methods. In contrast, Koolhaas is fundamentally suspicious of the instrumental use of theory and of any recourse to historical authentication. The determinist nature of previous manifestoes is replaced with a conscious indeterminacy. For this reason, *S,M,L,XL* should not be taken as a prescriptive manifesto. Rather, it structures a way of thinking with which to react to the radical contingency of architectural practice.

Power(less)
"Architecture relates to the forces of the Großstadt like a surfer to the waves." With this image, Koolhaas summons up the powerlessness of architecture, always alert to the shifting, relentless forces which shape our cities, but unable to order them. There is a sense of relinquishment of control to these external influences and in this an abrogation of responsibility to make judgments. The ultimate manifestation of Tafuri's despair at the fragility of architecture in the face of capitalism. Yet, there is also something heroic in the figure of the surfer. Against this background of powerlessness, Koolhaas retains an almost touching faith in the promise of modernity and the power that architecture may have in contributing to that promise. This resonates with Marshall Berman's *All That Is Solid Melts into Air,* a clarion call for a revitalization of the imaginative possibilities of modernity. While Berman's uncritical and unspecific acceptance of these potentials has been noted, there is an underlying

optimism in his account which is absolutely compelling. And so with Koolhaas. In the most lyrical writing in the book ("Whatever Happened to Urbanism"), he calls for the "irrigation of territories with potential … the creation of enabling fields … the urban is about to become a major vector of the imagination." The architect (or rather urbanist) seizes the winds and spins and releases their energies. While I may profoundly disagree with Koolhaas that this is a neutral act, I cannot help but be moved by the urgent forces of his book. Reader as surfer.

Practice
Traditionally, there is theory and there is practice. Two worlds, ideally one guiding the other. Purified concepts leading to inevitable disappointment when their products are tainted by the disorderliness of the profession and the city. At a stroke, *S,M,L,XL* dissolves the distinction between theory and practice. Throughout the book we are reminded of the vicissitudes of practice, the loss of innocence, the three stages of an architect ("elation, suspense, disappointment"), the joys of collaboration, the furious frustration of collaboration, willful clients with all the power, willing clients with no power, the impossibility of order. Faced with this "chaotic adventure" of practice, it is inconceivable to formulate a determinist theory of architecture, and the two terms *theory* and *practice* elide. The book itself stands on the junction. Its complexity and scrupulous attention to making suggests a building project. Its freedom to speculate and ability to edit suggests a theoretical project.

Theory
See practice.

Zed
Always difficult to find a sensible word beginning with zed.

CLEVER CALCULATION

Tetsuzo Oshima
Kenchiku Bunka 593 (1996), 143.

A long-awaited book has finally made its way to Japan. This volume is sure to become this year's best-selling foreign book on architecture. In any case, the world (and Japan in particular) is in the throes of a Koolhaas-boom. Architects young and old are following in Koolhaas's footsteps, so architectural magazines now publish one Koolhaas feature after the other.

It's not hard to figure out why. On the one hand, there is the end-stage phenomenon of a modern language that has been consumed into exhaustion. On the other hand, there is pressure brought on by the increased sophistication and disparity of capital and technology. This pushes expression ever further along the path of virtualization, leaving us with a reality that merely serves to support the autonomous motion of images and competes with their outstanding performance. On this stage, Koolhaas is a well-known player who boasts unique talents and a tenacious intelligence.

As thick as the Bible, that greatest bestseller of all time, this autobiographical album that you can start reading from any page is not only a codex of works; it also represents an architectural theory. The book may be XL in format (at 1,344 pages, it weighs about 2.8 kilograms), but its contents are XS, just as readable and accessible as a comic. The writer seems to have approached this omnibus with the mind-set of an editor. When readers who entrust themselves to the comfortable "fluctuations" of the book finally emerge from the forest of images it presents, they will find themselves contemplating a vision of Koolhaas ready to do battle.

In a relaxed atmosphere of interactive communication, readers can acquire through experiential learning design methods that used to be available only to the pupils of strict master architects. Spaces emerge not from the accumulation of writing, but from editing and trimming. Badly diseased cities flicker through scan lines, straightening to whisper, "I am not ready to be thrown away."

But the reader should take care. This book may be a manual for accepting the dark reality of our times, but also an idol that consciously mutilates the sources of our thinking. The urban surfer who rides the rough waves of ideology is the author, and the reader (you) is always just a spectator, a bumpkin. The lack of focus that appears reflected on these magazine pages is actually the product of thorough concentration and clever calculation. The reader should be aware that it is Koolhaas himself who mined valuable hints from the Modernism he ridicules.

In this age when the whole world is seemingly shrouded in a sort of soft-focus fascism that is more elaborate and powerful than Nazism, inevitably brought on by the extreme tendencies of the media and capital, as Koolhaas stitches up the gaps formed by the chronic diseases arising from the internal contradictions of the metropolis, one should not mistake for cries of ecstasy the howls that arise from his preordained marginal position as a Dutchman—marginal not compared to the Western European mainstream, but marginal to the margins, like Japan.

Still, this book is fascinating. How fascinating? Undisputedly, more fascinating than Koolhaas's buildings.

LEADING US ASTRAY

Koos Bosma

Planning Perspectives 12 (1997), 115–18.

[...] Koolhaas seems to want to convince the reader that the end of the art of printing is nigh. His book should be regarded as an incunabulum: a preliminary state of the video disc. Assembling the book must have been a real chore. As Koolhaas's *alter ego*, Bruce Mau designed every page separately and carefully considered the relation between text and image in each case. The result is an overwhelming looseleaf book, which evokes associations with a crammed trunk. On the waves of chance the viewer surfs the layers of meaning of the visual material. The introductory pages are illustrative: spatial graphics, statistics about the size of Koolhaas's army of slaves, their ethnic origins, incomes and expenditures and the number of nights our hero spends annually in hotels are projected on photographs of the work spaces of OMA. Quasifacts, curiously depicted, but also presented with much aplomb, pop up in the book at various places like advertisements. For example, the dramatic fact that the writing of this weighty tome (1,344 pages) endangered not only the quality of the regular urban planning production, but even the continued existence of OMA, cannot be deduced from the financial graphs. However, it would seem to be a temporary depression, as at the beginning of 1996 OMA won the brief to make a master plan for the renewal and expansion of the MCA complex in Universal City (Los Angeles), the heart of the entertainment industry. As Koolhaas already has a chair at Harvard, OMA is opening an office in Boston, to add to Rotterdam and London.

Although the image dominates the text, the old-fashioned reader is still given some solid ground beneath his feet. According to Koolhaas, the exuberant size of the book makes every arrangement random. It is therefore loosely structured according to the scale of the projects, thus giving concrete expression to the book's title. In addition, the reader finds an alphabetic series of headwords from Koolhaas's extremely personal encyclopaedia which is littered with quotes from others, an intriguing analysis of the developments of some big cities (Atlanta and Singapore) and—the principal part—project descriptions with evaluations added later, in which, sometimes with barely contained emotion, the fate of the projects is contemplated.

Compared with the abundance of Koolhaas's visual erudition, the number of substantial texts is somewhat meagre. Once again he proves himself a supple thinker who is capable of reducing simple rationalizations to absurdity with casual arguments. His amoral quest for a new realism is based on an analysis of contemporary urban developments, particularly in continents other than Europe. His studies of Atlanta and Singapore seem to have pointed the way here. It is precisely this quest which makes him wary of the organizing ambitions of architecture and urbanism. His comments on contemporary urbanism are harsh, but have a certain basis: the tasks confronting the cities and the conditions under which they are growing cannot be tackled with classical concepts. It is necessary to look for new forms of planning, even if Koolhaas himself does not know which ones.

[...] In "Generic City," where Koolhaas leans heavily on the French author Marc Augé's 1992 concept of *non-lieu*, the thesis put forward is that urban identity, interpreted as a crystallized historical essence and embodiment of a collective shared past, is an outdated stance. The concept of "identity" can no longer serve as context for contemporary interventions in, and expansions of, the cities. As shown by efforts to preserve historic city centers, for example, identity centralizes. With a sharp growth in population there is proportionally less and less identity to share. In addition, he states that the more history is abused, the less meaning it has. The stronger the identity, the more we feel locked up, and the more we resist expansion, interpretation and innovation.

In the canticle of Generic City Koolhaas sings the praises of the serenity of fragmentation: all authenticity is banished, planning plays no role, the public domain is absent and there is an endless repetition of the same simple module. The only context is a free style of infrastructure, buildings and nature. Leisure time is killed with shopping. In the Generic City, the buildings do not have a formal relationship with each other. It is the unattached city without identity, without center and without historic layers, whose only point of orientation is the central airport. Future archaeologists will not come across the genius loci of Generic City in their excavations: not even a "site." Generic City is the city without characteristics. This hilarious essay, a logical reductio ad absurdum which disturbs by teasing out general trends to their conclusion, can easily be put into perspective if we take the rhetorical angle out of the discourse. The apocalyptic story of the end of the classical city is drenched in dynamism and change, apart from the fundamental thesis: everything is fluid except the crystallized substance of identity. Nowadays, this thesis no longer has adherents, even among preservationists.

If we trace the successive levels of scale of Typical Plan, Bigness and Generic City, we get a parable of unbridled neoliberalism—a consumer world without cultural ambitions. Authenticity has become impossible in a world which is made of surrogates. Who are the exclusive producers of this hollow space, this collective emptiness, this extended nonplace which, according to Koolhaas, precisely due to its lack of definition, offers optimal opportunities for unexpected happenings? Does the noble savage play the lead role here? Are Koolhaas's strategies and subversive poses capable of dealing with the tendencies he analyses? As we know, he uses a limited number of patterns of thought and design, within which everything in principle is possible. Unlike many critics, he is not opposed to the tendencies identified but wants to get to the bottom of them and exploit them as programmatic possibilities. With OMA as "fantasy machine" he will always look for the unique solution, as behooves the artist. Nevertheless we see, especially on the urbanism scale, a repetition and refining of the principles of organization with which he began his career: the spatial strip in Exodus and a fascination with large-scale architecture which evokes uneasiness, the Berlin wall as totem and taboo, graphic demonstration of the power of architecture and cruel incision in the city.

This monumental demonstration of an oeuvre can be interpreted as a highly personal quest in the urban jungle. As a treatise which contributes to the practice of the designing professions its only contribution is a few analyses, with a strong personal tint, of the current urban condition. The scale, the eruption of images, the jungle-like structure and the willful extremism of the separate texts only allows random associations, but no generalization. Nor does Koolhaas believe in that and he does not want to allow himself to be pinned down. His media strategy is constantly leading us astray. In fact, the teeming merry-go-round of images, this exhibition of Koolhaas's archives, never transcends the level of a display of his own thinking. For him, for now, Bigness seems to be the strong elixir against the fragmentation brought about by the increase in scale. The crucial question naturally is whether or not this is not a masochistic provocation: pouring water into the sea.

The adventurous exhibitionism with which Koolhaas has assembled his largely unbuilt oeuvre into a stout book inevitably invokes the idea: look at what mankind is missing. That is indeed the case. At the same time we know that his media strategy is illusionism. Certainly in the age of Generic City when the noble savage is undermining the star architect, the best work of Koolhaas and his creative machine is that which will never be built. It will never again be as beautiful as in this book.

CAN ONE SERIOUSLY SPEAK OF CITIES LIKE THIS?

Dieter Hoffmann-Axthelm

ARCH+ 132 (1996), 76–77.

[…] As far as style and tone are concerned, we are dealing here with the literary genre of the manifesto. This is where the deliberately literary, the montage, the lightning transition from exact observation to pseudo-metaphorical, the fragmentary, the breathless, the renunciation of any clarification or explanation originate from. To that extent, what is at issue is the nth futuristic manifesto. This newest Koolhaasian manifesto demands once again the abandonment of any intellectual commitment to objectivity or concreteness, place, identity, knowability, resistance, difference, rupture; instead, it demands yet again more speed, more forgetting, more arbitrariness, more derailment. This much one knows if one has read anything by Koolhaas before or heard anything about his work. But the tone that is set here is something else again. The manifesto self-destructs in the same measure that it unfolds over the course of a given number of pages. In light of the feigned rational order of the chapters and theses numbered progressively, it disintegrates into unalloyed, consciously brutal caprices merely pasted together—or rather, caprices in the sense that Goya employed them, intellectual phantoms which look so much like the world that we know—that the manifesto, that is, the advance notice of the future and Koolhaas's own role as successor to Marinetti, Breton, Duchamp, Scheerbart and so on, championing the civilization of the new order, renders itself basically superfluous. It is not that the manifesto does not take itself seriously. But it does not master its literary technique. It alternates so wildly between satire and proclamation, between cynicism and euphoria, that one notices that it is out of control. It is not so much that the text shifts deliberately; rather it is grimacing involuntarily because it is collapsing under the weight of that which it has taken upon itself. For, when it comes to the point, what exactly is Koolhaas manifesting? The meanness and malevolence of the cities that await us, or the beauty of indifference, of Generic Cities, in which any variety of baseness, social, economic or aesthetic, can be cultivated at will, unhindered in its inventiveness by any kind of intellectual scruples, architectural bonds, typologies or genres, social planning, building codes, lamentation about the public sphere and so on and so forth. Grimace means: the genre of the manifesto and the author's intention are at odds with one another. By no longer being able to distinguish between them—and he does not want to, either—Koolhaas destroys the demonstrative sense of the manifesto genre, which says that the present is bad and the future has to be quite different; therefore, let us demolish the present. If, however, the future is already that which constitutes the present, then the only use for the persuasive power inherent in the genre can be to direct that banal sandwiching together of present and future, that is, the impossibility of change, hope and so on, against those who have not yet understood, who do not want to understand that there is nothing more to change. If the present day is right, the entire emphasis of the text thus turns, in complete identification with the aggressor, against those intellectuals who have not yet progressed that far—a manifesto in the Service of the Status quo, against the retrograde, wrongheaded people who still speak of a city that has long been inexistent, both in Japan and in Singapore, but in Europe and the United States too.

It seems to me that the reason for the Koolhaasian speed is to be discerned more clearly in this distorted, satirically derailed text than in any other that I have read to date. Because it has reached such lightning speed here, accelerating from zero to one hundred and immediately running up against the outermost wall that a European can run up against, that of voluntary loss of identity, something of his motivation is revealed, both in the midst of it and beyond it. From a town planning perspective, it is a manifesto of a receptive and architectural media culture utopia—but if it is a utopia, then it is one in a thoroughly modern sense, that of a future obviously already burnt-out. Hope feeds on despair. The hope is to be rid at last of this damned European fixation on loss and mourning for destroyed identity and to become one with that which is global and up-to-date: to be able to say "yes." To this extent, the utopia of being generic is a globalized new edition of Venturi's *Learning from Las Vegas* with Far Eastern colors—whereby Venturi is particularly interesting as a comparison because as an architect, he has refused the consequences of his intellectual position and cannot endure Las Vegas and Levittown, either as an architect or as a consumer. Koolhaas performs his European mourning for the loss of identity of the cities much more cleverly and ruthlessly. He knows, in view of the example of Venturi, that one cannot separate intellectual position from architecture if one wants to be quit of the suffering that he is combating. But of course he is suffering too. Only someone who is suffering from it can describe so cuttingly the loss of identity of the old city centers and celebrate the nonidentity of the periphery. It is for this reason alone that he fails so flagrantly in his attempt to make the global city convincing for himself as the beautiful city, the interesting, creative, rich city, which produces above all architecture. It is precisely for this reason that, continually accelerating, he plays the role of the champion of civilization of a new age of nonidentity, when homesickness has been overcome. What is sad about the present text is that Koolhaas runs away and ahead so quickly that he has already arrived; he cannot offer us anything that he has withheld any more, no scraps of utopia are left, no scraps of possible future fulfillment, nothing but the present itself. Why should we make any effort then? It is sufficient to let everything go on as it is. What is left then has nothing to do with the city, it is the salvaging of architecture as a field of aesthetic activity, as billboard.

Can one seriously speak of cities like this? Many of Koolhaas's metaphors are apt, but somehow he loses sight of the main issue. In the satirical universe of the city caprice that Koolhaas designs point by point, neither real cities nor real people appear. As far as the built aspect is concerned, it is only partial domains, fragments of cities, and as regards those who live there and use the city, the lived city, we are dealing basically with city idiots, with celluloid people, with city dwellers who, as cockroaches or mice, sweat panic, chaos, blood and sperm on elaborate film sets. There is no such city, either in Europe or anywhere in the developing countries. Bombay and Calcutta are not absurd. They are like the other gigantic cities in southeast Asia, Africa, Central or South America, cities of tremendous social strength, in which masses of humanity—for whom there is no basis of existence anywhere else any more—survive, economically and socially, under an incredible pressure of poverty. The European cities bear no resemblance whatsoever to these tropes. We have the absurdity of the hollow touristic centers and those of the airport settlements; in the larger centers, we have the short-circuiting of center and periphery upon which Koolhaas's whole videoclip is based. But it is only by filmic means, through continual cutting and isolating and concentrating, that the spectacle of the city that is pending has been evoked. The real city areas, selfishly overtaxed, but also defended, lie between center and periphery. There, city for city, millions of people transform the program of globality and locality, of difference and simultaneity into everyday lives which have many flaws, but with nothing absurd about them. But Koolhaas does not live in these cities. He lives and works in the center and the periphery, at megamalls. As a person, he inhabits airports. Fine. It is his choice. But why does he revile the real cities, then? Why does he despise the stupidity of urban political decisions, the stupidity of tourists? If he is the only one to whom the new global city is present, and who is really up-to-date as a planner, why does he still have the problem that it would be more reasonable to plan everything as the Professional, Rem Koolhaas, proposes year by year? Basically, then, Koolhaas is not polemicizing at all against the rest of us who have not yet got so far, but against himself. Doing violence to himself in the process, he has ruthlessly identified with the new instant city, and yet he cannot come to terms with the fact that these Asian global cities just grow like wildfire, and not in the style of the functionally and aesthetically organized space of Piranesi that Koolhaas projects onto the real globalized cities. He too is frustrated, he too is not on contract to all the world city councils, he too is not listened to, he too is fighting on the losing side of reason. Why is he straining to be the forerunner? Come back, sit down with us on the benches in the waiting rooms of political and administrative ignorance, and let us reflect upon the reason for these stupid benches.

In conclusion, a judgment of taste. The person who leans so far out of the window obviously wants to be seen in erotic underwear, or at the very least, reviewed in the feuilleton style. Koolhaas's project of making his dilemma of the overtaking of the global plausible through aesthetic acceleration has failed—at least as text: exaggerated speed, the commercial art of the filmmaker—he should relinquish his dream of writing screenplays.

FLIGHT FORWARD

Lieven De Cauter

Archis 4 (1998), 28–34.

[...] In his attempt at viewing the Generic City simultaneously as it is *and* from an optimistic perspective—both as ineluctable fate *and* as opportunity—Koolhaas does away with all nostalgia. He points up how history, despite its absence, has become the biggest industry of the Generic City, and how tourism expands in direct proportion to the destruction of the past. But again he reverses the roles: it is not this destruction, but the false nostalgia for the past that draws scathing remarks from him. In a city without qualities and history, people seem doomed to regress to a Disneyfied, simulated version of a collective memory. Koolhaas coolly notes that in the Generic City no real individual memories exist, only memories of memories, faint *déjà vus,* a "generic memory." History, he notes in a reference to Marx, does not return as a farce but as a service.

[...] So much for our visit to the "post-city" of the future. The vision is an uncanny one, and Koolhaas's detached, lucid, occasionally witty description conveys the alienation well. But it is and remains: the end. The disconcerting thing about the essay, and by extension about the whole book, is that Koolhaas depicts this hereafter of the city, of urbanity, perhaps even of the very idea of sociability, this postmortem society, with an ironic, sometimes sarcastic, but ultimately cheerful view, and that he even defends it as a treasure trove of possibilities, as the right way to go, as a new paradigm. In the Generic City, reverse gravity reigns supreme: evaporation is the rule, the centrifugal attraction of the void and the periphery, eventually resulting in centerless agglomerations. First there was the delirium of New York, but now the "culture of congestion," once so strongly promoted by Koolhaas, has been superseded by what we might term a "culture of evacuation." Like a prophet, but without any of the prophet's pessimism, Koolhaas has an eye for the latest developments. He has accepted Dr. Faustroll's Law—the law of antigravity, of universal evaporation, of growing unreality.[1]

If we compare the generic urban condition with its traditional counterpart, one thing stands out. Whereas the classic metropolis used to be a scene entered by the masses, the Generic City is the place where these same masses have disappeared from the scene again. This absorption of the masses and virtualization of the public domain is summarized by Koolhaas in the final sequence of his essay in a dramatic, almost touching image: that of a spectacular Hollywood movie which shows a mass of people appearing in a market, but with the sound switched off and played in reverse. This links the Generic City to a media society: much as the Generic City entails an "evacuation" of the public realm, the "place" of the audiovisual media is that of a simulated public realm.[2] The so-called disappearance of the masses looks like an unavoidable side effect of the end of the industrial age: the masses are a product of the modern metropolis which disappears again in the postindustrial era. Gone is the dream of dissolving the materiality of buildings through the creation of transparency, gone is the dream of a new collectivity: in its stead we witness a renaissance of the interior. The dream which enthralled both the political utopians and the artistic avant-gardes—a dream detected by Walter Benjamin from the nineteenth-century arcades down to Le Corbusier and that exerted its hypnotic spell a final time in 1968—has been shattered. As with nineteenth-century interiors, which were inspired by a defense against the industrial city, against the real world of production and exploitation, people return to the paradisaic island of the new interior. Instead of the languorous shimmer of palm trees and carpets, of upholstery and chinoiseries, we now have cyber-cocooning in the blue lagoon. Design provides the streamlined and polished if ultimately vapid synthesis between the bric-à-brac of a bourgeois culture of plush and the transparency, rationality, and functionality, the cheerfulness and lightheartedness of the historical avant-garde. The modern antithesis has been, in Hegelian terms, sublated. The designer house of weekly sections in newspapers is Utopia realized, according to the formula: the uninhabited island + the network = paradise. Hell, by contrast, is "paradise unplugged." Hypothesis: the growing success of ideal home exhibitions, of ditto television programs and glossy magazines, is directly proportional to the growing number of homeless people.

[...] The nineteenth-century arcade to which Walter Benjamin ascribed the dream of a new public sphere that would cancel the distinction between public and private has been transformed into the "air-conditioned nightmare" of hotel atriums, of closed, artificial spaces and esplanades that are only accessible via car parks (as in La Défense, Las Vegas, or LA). There is a topicality to Benjamin's *Passagen-Werk* that its author could not have anticipated, for the mixture of interior and exterior which so characterized the arcade—an ambiguity that sparked Benjamin's project—now takes its postmodern form in new spaces that produce a new kind of sequestered public realm. The withdrawal from a threatening outside world, which to Benjamin's mind was typical of the bourgeois interior, has definitively vanquished what he called "the *plein-airism* of the revolution." Postmodern flânerie has been domesticated: it takes place in new, large inner spaces, in shopping centers or malls, piazzas, atriums of office buildings or hotels, dramatized transit zones like those of new airports, and so on—empty spaces or voids that do no more than facilitate the individual delectation of a grand architectural decor. The postmodern versions of the arcade—the shopping center, the mall, the artificial piazza, the transit zone, the atrium—are increasingly generating a new urban paradigm, that of a virtual urban condition. These are all spaces that have definitively come down on the side of the interior. People seem to have given up on the street, on the world outside.

The fantasy of a covered city that Benjamin quotes from an early-nineteenth-century *Vaudeville* has acquired a new, slightly sour taste: "You know, they are thinking of covering all the streets of Paris with glass. Imagine the lovely hot greenhouses this will produce: we will be living like melons."[3] In light of this quotation, history today appears as a remake of a science fiction classic, *The Body Snatchers*, in which an invasion of plants devitalizes mankind. And this, too, Koolhaas knows. By the end of his long essay on Singapore, he announces point-blank that "the third millennium will be an experiment in this form of soullessness." Dr. Faustroll's Law all over again: the soul, that most ephemeral element of cities, is the first element to be surrendered to the attraction of the void and to the forces of inverse gravity.

The city without qualities, nevertheless, is and remains a scenario of doom. Or at least, it would be absurd to raise these new, generic cities with their virtuality to a norm for older, "specific" cities. The third millennium must not become an experiment in soullessness; mankind must do all it can to avert this encroaching catastrophe. Even Koolhaas's own Euralille is an exercise in soullessness. He himself describes it as "a Freudian flight forward." But can an architect afford this kind of cheerfulness and lucidity as theorist without turning into a cynic as practitioner? Or is the cynicism of Koolhaas the author a mere mask, the cool look of an architect in shades, behind which a pragmatical moralist hides?

[...] Koolhaas hopes to "realize" idealism (that of the Modern Movement) by immersing it in a bath of no nonsense—the bath of his own explicit antihumanism. But in reality, he is only idealizing realism. Thus, he regresses to the opposite of what at first sight he appears to be arguing for. An "exhausting bombardment of idealization with which we [try] to maintain a marginal advantage vis-à-vis our own increasing revulsion" is not only tantamount to a (retroactive) idealization of the existing, but also to a denunciation of all idealism, to a strategy that elevates "realism" to a holy doctrine. And all of this to stay one step ahead of his own revulsion.

Koolhaas's method logically follows from his view on modernity. [...] He clearly wishes to see the utmost degradation, the debasement, the fury of destruction, as an opportunity. Destruction is accompanied by a kind of liberation, if only in the form of relief, the ditching of ballast. This desperate hope is reflected in both his reasoning and style—in his parentheses, for example, the dialectical kink in many of his sentences, in which statements are inverted. Two examples from "Singapore Songlines" must suffice. After the dictum that "the third millennium will be an experiment in this form of soullessness," he adds the parenthesis "(unless we wake up from our thirty-year sleep of self-hatred)." And a few lines down: "Singapore is a city without qualities (maybe that is an ultimate form of deconstruction, and even of freedom)." His ambivalence toward a runaway modernization becomes readable in these and similar moments of "dialectical" reversal. Is Koolhaas perhaps a crypto-Messiah who secretly operates according to the most daring cabbalistic topoi: "Israel asks of God: When will you redeem us? He replies: When you have sunk to the lowest step, in that hour I will redeem you."[4] In more modern, neo-Marxist terms: in the extremest reification, salvation is under way. Or does nothing else remain of this mental operation today but a gamble? OMA as Russian roulette?

Koolhaas sees through the process of destruction, but his lucidity offers only two outcomes: Realpolitik and hedonism. On the subject of urbanism, he writes in "What Ever Happened to Urbanism?": "Redefined, urbanism will not only, or mostly, be a profession, but a way of thinking, an ideology: to accept what exists." What else does this mean than the freedom to swim along with the current of disastrous developments? On hedonism, he writes: "Contrary to modern architecture and its desperate afterbirths, this new architecture is neither authoritarian nor hysterical: it is the hedonistic science of designing collective facilities that fully accommodate individual desires." This quotation comes from his 1972 graduation project, Exodus, or the Voluntary Prisoners of Architecture, a polemical design for a hedonistic concentration camp that cuts through downtown London.

But behind his method, there is also his Credo: "maybe all these arguments are in the end mere rationalizations for the primitive fact of simply liking asphalt, traffic, neon, crowds, tension, the architecture of others, even." Koolhaas the confirmed urbanite, the Baudelairean flaneur who enjoys the density, the clash, the confusion of the metropolis: a likable image in view of his other statements, but not convincing. This Baudelairean Credo is at odds with his method. He appears all too willing to join others in abolishing this city, whose end he ordains, for instance by assimilating and defending the developer's logic (à la Portman). That is where an idealization of architectural *Realpolitik* takes you: the importation of this American logic into Europe.

[...] The wreck of the Medusa: "After the shipwreck in the Mediterranean of the *Medusa*—a military vessel—the soldiers/castaways were left on their raft with only barrels of wine, guns and ammunition. In a premature and drunken panic they began to cannibalize each other on the second day of their journey. Saved on the 7th day of the shipwreck, they could easily have survived without eating anything at all."[5] This anecdote becomes to Koolhaas an allegory: "This monumental expression of 'loss of nerve' corresponds to the premature panic and loss of nerve about the Metropolis in the present moment of the twentieth century." A revulsion of doom-mongering and of what he calls "the practice of panic" typifies Koolhaas's texts. Under no condition does he want to collude with the convergence of architecture and such a practice of panic. But does this not result precisely in a panicky (which is to say, also, a frightening) architecture? Is this not what causes him to worship Bigness?

[...] What is the aesthetic secret of this big/grandiloquent architecture? The sublime, of course. Edmund Burke defined the sublime as that which somehow produces terror. He summed up his reasoning as follows: "The passions which belong to self-preservation, turn on pain and danger; they are simply painful when their causes immediately affect us; they are delightful when we have an idea of pain and danger, without being actually in those circumstances; this delight I have not called pleasure, because it turns on pain. Whatever excites this delight, I call *sublime.*"[6] Therefore, Burke wrote, "Whatever is terrible, with regard to sight, is sublime too." For buildings to be sublime, according to Burke, the one and only condition is "greatness of dimension." But "Designs that are vast only by their dimensions, are always the sign of a common and low imagination." Applied to our present day and age, this is equal to saying that, when all meanings have evaporated, all styles become untenable, all solutions unreachable, there is only one answer: size. Extra-large sizes always work. They are overwhelming and produce the elation of the sublime. The new architectural complexes are machines that exist just for the kick and—wholly in accordance with Burke's description—exclude any real danger, the outside, the real city. At least as an author, Koolhaas appears to opt for a spectacular architecture, for architecture as spectacle. Not an architecture of panic for him, but an architecture of terror as delight.

[...] In Koolhaas's book, the absence of violence is striking. The Generic City is quiet, "sedated," and of "an eerie calm." The Bronx and the *banlieue* do not enter into the picture. (Why not? Hypothesis: The absence of violence in the book is related to the latent violence of the book itself.) What is the connection between the latent or manifest violence of the decaying inner cities and slums, and the trance and tranquility of the Generic City? Perhaps Paul Virilio can help us here. Of course, Virilio's geopolitical fantasies on the Cold War and on how cities were being sacrificed to the two remaining strategic centers, Washington and Moscow, have turned him into something of a laughingstock. Nevertheless, on the topic of cities he did have momentous things to say, even if they were steeped in the double forte of his heroic and prophetic tone. After all, he is the first to have pointed out the transformation of the city into an airport. In his view, however, violence is exactly ubiquitous. He sees the city as a transit zone, a place of speed and hence of violence, of migration.[7] It is impossible to get a correct picture of the Generic City without putting Virilio's vision alongside, or better even under, that of Koolhaas.

For Virilio, the politics of space (territory, defense, urbanism) is being replaced by a politics of time (transport, communication, speed, networks). The cocoon-like interior and the atrium are capsules in a politics of time that rules a world with a minimum of bodily space. So what happens when the city begins to look like an airport? In abstract terms, the answer should be: we have then, by definition, reached the age of the politics of time. In other words, farewell to the politics of space. Space does not much matter anymore, which is why the city everywhere is becoming the same. The Generic City is the product of the network and thus of the politics of time.

Perhaps in a premature extrapolation of his own lifestyle, Koolhaas observes that the in-transit situation is increasingly becoming a generalized way of life. He omits to mention that this mobility (driven by Virilio's "vectors of speed," that is, cars, trains, airplanes) also generates violence. There is a huge difference between legal and illegal migration, between arriving in Business Class on a Concorde and as a stowaway on a tanker. The airport lounge and the nearby transit camp for illegal immigrants are worlds apart. But there is a convergence: the world's population is ever more subject to delocalization, as are today's industries. This delocalization is a source of violence, both because of the speed with which it is associated and because of attendant phenomena like exclusion, incarceration, collision, ghettoization, alienation, lack of rights, xenophobia.

In light of the Generic City, a CIAM pronouncement in "A Short Outline of the Core" (1951) acquires a prophetic overtone: "If new towns are built without a core they will never become more than camps."[8] Is the Generic City a camp? It is, says Giorgio Agamben. In his opinion, more and more people fall outside the status of communal life (*bios*) and into the status of unmediated life (*zoe*). This unmediated life is outlawed; it is governed by the logic of the camp. A camp is not a prison, not a legal institution, but a territory outside the law, an enclave within but especially outside society. And it is a place where anything can happen, even the most inconceivable horrors (not so much because of human cruelty or the barbarity of ideological indoctrination, but simply because of the legal structure of the camp itself). Transit zones, too, are extraterritorial (hence duty-free). They are potential camps (like the camps for illegal immigrants). Perhaps Agamben, despite the appearance of gross exaggeration, is not far from the truth when he proposes that the concentration camp, rather than the city, provides the paradigm of contemporary biopolitics.[9]

On a geopolitical scale, the ever-growing refugee problem is the only evidence to support the hypothesis that an "in-transit condition" is becoming universal. We must take Koolhaas's question seriously: "Is the contemporary city like the contemporary airport?" But we should be willing to consider the airport in its totality, that is, not only its lobbies and lounges, its catering services, cargo companies, and tour operators, but also the nearby transit camps. Only then do we obtain a true picture of the Generic City. [...]

Postscript: The Tragedy of the Architect

My entire analysis of Koolhaas's thinking may be based on a misunderstanding. What Koolhaas is out to offer is not a critical theory, one might argue, but a provocative framework for practice. My stubborn mistake would then be based on the fact that I read him as a theorist rather than as an architect. Maybe so. Yet I believe such a reading strategy to be necessary, since Koolhaas is almost as influential as a theorist than as an architect. And the architect interferes with the impartiality of the theorist. In a recent interview, Koolhaas has put his cards on the table in a rare moment of candor. To the question "You do not imagine a return to the traditional city?" he replied: "I think that it is necessary to be very modest. Nothing is ever sure, and it may be that in twenty years the need to recreate the city as it was before will be rediscovered. As an architect, the difficulty I have with the existing city is precisely that this city exists. It is still part of the mythology of our profession that we have to change things, because one cannot make a contribution to a work of architecture without changing the situation, the contexts, or the city. There is, deep down in my activity as an architect, the ambition to change things and an awareness of the inevitability of this. From this perspective, it is impossible for me to stick to the conventional city—at least as an architect."[10]

The candor is disarming. The answer explains the entire strategy of retroactive idealization, as a rationalization of the position of the architect, who will and must build. There is even an element of tragedy in it: the architect is irrevocably on the side of modernization and "postmodernization" (and thus also of transcendental capitalism). He must move ahead and help organize the destruction of the traditional city. As an architect he is, by the very definition of his profession, forced to engage in a flight forward, even if eventually he can see no other solution but to think faster than his own revulsion.

1 Dr. Faustroll is the inventor of pataphysics (the science of phantasmagoric solutions to real problems and of real solutions to phantasmagoric problems). This character from Alfred Jarry formulates the hypothesis that the most fundamental physical law is not that of gravity—a law according to which everything is attracted by mass and hence by a center, that everything evolves concentrically with respect to the massiveness of the middle—but conversely, that everything wants to disappear and go up into smoke, that all molecules strive to disperse in the open air. This law of pataphysics is used by Baudrillard as the point of departure for the umpteenth installment in his series on hyperreality, his *essai fleuve* on simulation (see Jean Baudrillard, *L'illusion de la fin* [Paris: Galilee, 1992]: occurrences tend toward their own unreality. Baudrillard talks of the unreality of political events: the Gulf War, the fall of the Berlin Wall, the democratization of the Eastern bloc. To him, these are no longer real historical events, but events that immediately go on strike and refuse to participate in world history any longer.)

2 See Marc Holthof, *De digitale badplaats* (Leuven: Van Halewijck; Amsterdam: De Balie, 1995), 78–79. Bart Verschaffel reaches an analogous conclusion about the evaporation of the public domain in his text on the network: "De kring en het netwerk," in *Figuren/Essays* (Leuven: Van Halewijck; Amsterdam: De Balie, 1996), 105–20. He was the first also to point me to the seminal essay on "The Generic City" and to Koolhaas's book in general (as well as to its riskiness). For an inspiring discussion of the book, see Pieter T'Jonck. "Bij *S,M,L,XL*: het interieur zonder eigenschappen als ruimte van de verbeelding," *DWB* 1 (1997), 76–91.

3 Quoted in Walter Benjamin, *Das Passagen-Werk,* Vol.1, ed. Rolf Tiedemann (Frankfurt am Main: Suhrkamp, 1983), 104.

4 Gershom Scholem, *Über einige Grundbegriffe des Judentums* (Frankfurt am Main: Suhrkamp. 1970), 135.

5 The scene appears twice in the book, once as a photographically reproduced quotation from *Delirious New York*, once as an entry in the "dictionary" of quotations and fragments that runs through the book like a litany. We may suppose, therefore, that it amounts to a sort of Koolhaasian *ur-scene.* We should note also how in Koolhaas's project for Welfare Island the gigantic plastic version of Géricault's Medusa serves as an entertainment for rich tourists staying at the Welfare Palace Hotel, who can go visit the larger-than-life sculpture by boat at night, after a visit to the theater formed by the inverted bow of a sunken *Titanic*. An instance of Koolhaas's rowdy, sardonic humor.

6 Edmund Burke, *A Philosophical Enquiry into the Origin of Our Ideas of the Sublime and Beautiful,* ed. James T. Boulton (London: Routledge and Kegan Paul; New York: Columbia University Press, 1958).

7 Paul Virilio, *L'horizon négatif: essai de dromoscopie* (Paris: Galilée, 1984).

8 "A Short Outline of the Core: Extracts from Statements Prepared during the 8th Congress of CIAM," in *The Heart of the City: Towards the Humanisation of Urban Life,* ed. Jacqueline Tyrwhitt, Josep Lluis Sert, and Ernesto N. Rogers (Nendeln: Kraus Reprint, 1979), 165.

9 See Giorgio Agamben, "Qu'est-ce qu'un camp," in *Moyens sans fins: Notes sur la politique* (Paris: Christian Bourgois, 1995), 47–55. See also his book *Homo sacer: Le pouvoir souverain et la vie nue* (Paris: Seuil, 1997), 195.

10 Odile Fillion, "Atlanta, Paris, Singapore: Interview with Rem Koolhaas," *Lotus international* 84 (1995), 120.

THE DAY AFTER
Alejandro Zaera-Polo
El Croquis 79 (1996), 9–25.

[...] **azp:** Your work is very well considered among both practitioners and academics, which was perhaps encouraged by certain structural conditions in Europe that facilitated operation between the two domains. Now, when these conditions have vanished, you are splitting your activity into two fronts: speculative research in the academia, and a more pragmatic, technically and financially efficient professional structure. It is as if you were creating a scale model of the schizophrenic condition of the American professional system, where people are determined to either speculate in the academia or to practice under incredibly strict legal and financial laws that make the production of breakthroughs very difficult.

rk: No, it is more related to the work of the architect itself. It can be so relentless, so simpleminded, so primitive in its almost bestial conditions, that you need another domain to sustain it, to keep freshness. That is why I started *S,M,L,XL*, mostly to have another life. My relationship with the university is not to create financial stability but to create a platform which allows us to abstain from commercial work. We have twenty cities in China at our doorstep that we all turned down. I do not believe at this moment that those could be legitimate projects. Although I find it fascinating, I do not believe in what is going on in China at this moment. It is very destructive and will be utterly regretted. In retrospect, the university allows us to develop research without the distortion of the commercial interest that architecture inevitably brings in its wake, the obligation to "do something."

[...]
azp: *S,M,L,XL* presents and unfolds your architectural practice through an incredibly rich and complex set of affiliations, which is very rare in the conventionally factual description of architectural publications. This seems to be a logical conclusion of a long-term attempt to redefine the role of the contemporary architect by dissolving the "original creator" and inspired "subject" into a character that "surfs" in an ocean of banality, bureaucracy, politics, business ... The most striking aspect of the book is that, in spite of your past attempts to erase architectural subjectivity, it has a very intense autobiographical content, almost as if you were now trying to reconstruct the subjectivity of the architect in the middle of all these harsh determinations.

rk: After a while, I noticed that too. In the beginning, I was alarmed and tried to resist. I infinitely prefer the apparent discretion of the ghost writer. But then I had to admit that *S,M,L,XL* is partly a book about experiences. I had proclaimed the legitimacy of surfing. [...] I felt I had to describe how it felt and where it ended. The main ambition of this book is accessibility and demystification; in the first place of architecture, and I sensed that I could not go all the way if somehow I did not include myself in the demystification, in the exposure. If architecture is problematic, I am part of it, whatever my attempts to disguise it.
[...]

APPENDIX

1975

Eisenman, Peter, Peter Chermayeff, Paul Rudolph, and Eberhard H. Zeidler. "Remment Koolhaas, Laurinda Spear: Award," *Progressive Architecture* 1 (1975), 46.

1976

Ween, Camilla. "Fiddling While New York Burns," *Architectural Design* 10 (1976), 630.

1977

Baird, George. "Les extrêmes qui se touchent," *Architectural Design* 5 (1977), 326–28.

Frampton, Kenneth. "Two or Three Things I Know about Them: A Note on Manhattanism," *Architectural Design* 5 (1977): 315–18.

Porphyrios, Demetri. "Pandora's Box," *Architectural Design* 5 (1977), 359–64.

1978

Blake, Peter. "Delirious New York," *New York Magazine*, December 18, 1978.

Boissière, Olivier. "Ou l'efficace rejoint le sublime ...," *Architecture intérieure créé* 168 (1978), 7.

van Dijk, Hans. "Rem Koolhaas interview," *wonen-TA/BK* 11 (1978), 17–20.

Fremont-Smith, Eliot. "Skyscraper Madness," *Village Voice* 43 (1978), 123–24.

Goldberger, Paul. "Guggenheim Unveils Surrealist City Views," *New York Times*, November 17, 1978.

Hermans, Willem Frederik. "New York's Delirium," *Het Parool*, December 2, 1978.

Hershkovits, David. "The Human Metropolis," *Soho Weekly News* 8 (1978), 48, 75.

Millstein, Gilbert. "Architectural Extravaganza," *New York Times*, December 24, 1978.

van Rooy, Max. "De ghostwriter van Manhattan: Architect Rem Koolhaas interpreteert New York," *NRC Handelsblad*, November 17, 1978.

1979

Aubry, Yves. "New York délire," *Zoom, le magazine de l'image* 60 (1979), 126.

Balet, Marc. "Rem Koolhaas, Architect," *Andy Warhol's Interview* 2 (1979), 29.

Banham, Reyner. "Manhattalgia," *New Society*, April 12, 1979, 98–99.

van Bel, Willy. "The Sparkling Metropolis: OMA at the Guggenheim," *Skyline* 5 (1979), 3.

de Bruijn, Pi. "Een Steen van Rosette uit de 20ste eeuw," *De Volkskrant*, March 27, 1979.

Constantine, Eleni. "OMA: The Sparkling Metropolis," *Progressive Architecture* 1 (1979), 24.

Dupont, Pascal. "Quand New-York voulait être communiste," *Les Nouvelles Littéraires* 2668 (1979), 36.

Goldberger, Paul. "He'll Take Manhattan," *New York Review of Books* 10 (1979), 15–17.

Gurda, Paul. "Delirious New York," *Journal of the American Planning Assocation* 3 (1979), 371.

Harris, Robert R. "Delirious New York," *The Wilson Quarterly* 3 (1979), 161–62.

den Hollander, Jord. "Rem Koolhaas over symbolen in de architectuur," *De Architect* 3 (1979), 58–59.

Huxtable, Ada Louise. "Bigger—And Maybe Better," *New York Times*, August 26, 1979.

Ingersoll, Richard. "Book Review: Delirious New York," *Concrete* 2 (1979), 3.

MacNair, Andrew. "Delirious New York," *Journal of Architectural Education* 4 (1979), 32–33.

Pam, Max. "Rem Koolhaas: 'In feite is de Bijlmer een uitgestelde polemiek tegen New York,'" *Vrij Nederland*, March 10, 1979, 17–19.

Pinnell, Patrick L. "Remifications: Delirious New York," *Skyline* 6 (1979), 8.

Pommer, Richard. "Delirious New York," *Art in America*, May/June 1979, 19.

Starr, S. Frederick. "Delirious New York," *Architectural Design* 5–6 (1979), 136–39.

1980

Chaslin, François. "Délire à lire," *Macadam* 15–16 (1980), 16.

van Dijk, Hans. "OMA's utopisch realisme," *NRC Handelsblad*, December 5, 1980.

Jonker, Gert. "Een bruuske uitbraak uit de Nieuwe Hopeloosheid: Tentoonstelling werk van Rem Koolhaas c.s.," *Bouw* 24 (1980), 24–25.

Kroon, Ben. "'Een gat in de bebouwing vind ik soms mooier dan de opvulling.' Rem Koolhaas: vaarwel papier," *De Tijd* 325 (1980), 46–49.

Meuwissen, Joost. "Overgeaccentueerde architectuur in Stedelijk Museum Amsterdam," *NRC Handelsblad*, December 29, 1980.

Munday, Richard. "Book Review: Delirious New York," *Transition* 4 (1980), 46–48.

Peake, Cathy, Grant Marani, Ian McDougall, and Richard Munday. "The Pleasures of Architecture Conference: Interview with Rem Koolhaas," *Transition* 4 (1980), 14–18.

Spring, Bernard P. "Big Apple Is Cut Open in Five Revealing Books," *AIA Journal* 4 (1980), 78, 80, 82.

Tschumi, Bernard. "On Delirious New York: A Critique of Critiques," *International Architect* 3 (1980), 68–69.

Voorberg, Jan. "Tweede Kamerprijsvraag: pleidooi voor Koolhaas," *wonen-TA/BK* 13 (1980), 2–3.

1981

Baird, George. "A Letter from Canada," *International Architect* 4 (1981), 3.

Chiatkin, William. "Tonight at Noon: Delirious New York, Rem Koolhaas," *Architectural Association Quarterly* 13 (1981), 58

Filler, Martin. "Harbingers: Ten Architects," *Art in America* 6 (1981), 114–21.

Griffin, Margot. "Competition for the Irish Prime Minister's Residence," *International Architect* 4 (1981), 6–8.

Lampugnani, Vittorio. "Avant-gardes architecturales 1970–1980," *L'Architecture d'Aujourd'hui* 213 (1981), 8–13.

Maxwell, Robert. "Introduction to New Work of OMA." In *OMA: Projects 1978–1981*, ed. Robert Maxwell, 3–7 (London: Architectural Association, 1981).

Metcalf, Andrew. "Graves, Koolhaas and Baird in Australia: A Letter from Australia," *International Architect* 4 (1981), 2–3.

von Moos, Stanislaus. "Rotterdam lädt Leonidow ein: Zu neueren Arbeiten des Office of Metropolitan Architecture," *Archithese* 5 (1981), 57–62.

Noviant, Patrice. "Rem Koolhaas: Un européen sans humour," *Architecture Mouvement Continuité* 54–55 (1981), 59.

Rodermond, Janny. "Interbau Berlin 198 (4). Koolhaas's Berlijns Pompeï," *De Architect* 6 (1981), 41–53.

Sudjic, Deyan. "Enter the Prophets of New Sobriety: Deyan Sudjic Spoke to OMA's Superstars," *Building Design* 549 (1981), 2.

1982

Beck, Haig. "Towards an Architecture of Congestion," *Express Extra* 2 (1982), 3.

Bekaert, Geert. "De Odyssee van een verlicht ondernemer: Rem Koolhaas," *wonen-TA/BK* 13–14 (1982), 50–57.

Dettingmeijer, Rob. "De sarcastische ontwerpen van OMA: Rem Koolhaas buit tegenspraken uit," *De Groene Amsterdammer* 43 (1982), 14.

van Dijk, Hans. "Het bezwijken van tegenstellingen," *wonen-TA/BK* 13–14 (1982), 12–49.

———. "Rem Koolhaas: Architectonic Scenarios and Urban Interpretations," *Dutch Art + Architecture Today* 12 (1982), 20–28.

Goldberger, Paul. "Exhibit Points Up Views on Context of a Building," *New York Times*, March 28, 1982.

Kloos, Maarten. "Van droomland tot polderpeil: OMA en het haalbaarheidsonderzoek naar eigen utopieën," *De Volkskrant*, June 25, 1982.

Maas, Tom. "Rem Koolhaas tegen historiseren: het moderne bouwen is nog niet uitgeput," *NRC Handelsblad*, February 12, 1982.

Meuwissen, Joost. "Delirious Rotterdam," *Plan* 2 (1982), 8–9.

Reijnders, Tineke. "'We hebben systematisch geweigerd de bewoners te onderschatten': Rem Koolhaas, conditionerend architect," *De Groene Amsterdammer* 43 (1982), 14–17.

Rodermond, Janny. "Bestemmingsplan ADM-terrein Amsterdam: Jan Voorberg: 'Door ons enthousiasme blijft het lukken,'" *De Architect* 10 (1982), 84–95.

Rothuizen, William. "'Wij proberen de feiten achteraf in een verband te zetten': Architect Rem Koolhaas," *Haagse Post* 22 (1982), 48–51.

Sorkin, Michael. "Drawing Conclusions," *Village Voice*, April 20, 1982.

Vidler, Anthony. "The Irony of Metropolis: The Office for Metropolitan Architecture," *Skyline* 5 (1982), 18–21.

———. "Delirious New York, Rem Koolhaas," *Architectural Association: General Studies: Projects Review*, 1982, n.p.

Wissing, Sander. "Licht in duisternis," *Hard Werken* 10 (1982), 47.

Zwinkels, Kees. "Koolhaas's ontwerp voor uitbreiding van de Tweede Kamer," *De Architect* 5 (1982), 49–54.

1983

de Boer, Hubert. "Het uur der waarheid: De juryuitslag voor de theorie en tegen het landschap," *Contour* 2 (1983), 24–29.

Buchanan, Peter. "Elia Zenghelis, Rem Koolhaas, Zaha Hadid," *Architectural Review* 1040 (1983), 64.

Cook, Peter. "Highlights of Recent History," *Architectural Review* 1040 (1983), 32–46.

Raggi, Franco. "Edonista-Puritano: Colloquio con Rem Koolhaas," *MODO* 58 (1983), 26–28.

Rodermond, Janny. "Het park van de 21e eeuw: Prijsvraag Park La Villette te Parijs," *De Architect* 3 (1983), 44–49.

Vreuls, Paul. "IJpleinproject: Hoe breng ik stad en dorp bij elkaar?" *Weekmedia*, August 10, 1983.

Wilson, Peter. "The Park and the Peak—Two International Competitions," *AA Files* 4 (1983), 76.

1984

Boissière, Olivier. "Paris X Paris," *Domus* 646 (1984), 16–30.

Bouman, Tonnis, Herma Hekkema, and Tjalling Visser. "Koolhaas: Interview: Een kijkje in de keuken van OMA," *Contour* 2 (1984), 4–13.

De Giorgi, Manolo, and Agata Torricella. "Atlante comparato dell'architettura contemporanea: Rem Koolhaas," *Modo* 69 (1984), 47.

Macgowan, Tempe. "The Parc de la Villette, Paris: Twentieth-Century Theory for the Twenty-first Century Urban Park?" *Landscape Australia* 1 (1984), 29–35.

Rodermond, Janny. "Lichtvoetig OMA-ontwerp voor Danstheater in Scheveningen," *De Architect* 4 (1984), 33–37.

———. "De stad als kunstwerk of als banaliteit? IJplein en Venserpolder," *De Architect* 10 (1984), 45–55.

Vayssière, Bruno, and Patrice Noviant. "L'indétermination et la foi," *Architecture Mouvement Continuité* 6 (1984), 30–31.

Vayssière, Bruno, Patrice Noviant, and Jacques Lucan. "Amsterdam-Nord: Rem Koolhaas: Entretien," *Architecture Mouvement Continuité* 6 (1984), 16–21.

Zwinkels, Cees. "Kwaliteit sluitpost van goedkoop cultuurbeleid: Gezamenlijke huisvesting RO/NDT in Den Haag," *De Architect* 4 (1984), 24–32.

1985

Barbieri, Umberto. "From the Bridge to the Tower: A Project by Rem Koolhaas, OMA," *Lotus International* 47 (1985), 125–26.

Barbieri, Umberto, and Ronald Van Duivenbode. "Costruzione e progretto," *Casabella* 516 (1985), 12–13.

Bekaert, Geert. "Rem Koolhaas en de bespreekbaarheid van de architectuur," *Muziek en Woord* 133 (1985), 34.

Brandolini, Sebastiano. "Il Teatro Olandese di Danza all'Aja," *Casabella* 516 (1985), 4–9.

Buchanan, Peter. "Rotterdam Rationalists," *Architectural Review* 177 (1985), 35–36.

Choay, Françoise. "La Villette Park Competition," *Princeton Journal: Thematic Studies in Architecture: Landscape* 2 (1985), 211–14.

Emery, Marc. "OMA," *L'Architecture d'Aujourd'hui* 238 (1985), 1.

De Giorgi, Manolo. "OMA." In *Nouveaux plaisirs d'architectures: Les pluralismes de la création en Europe et aux Etats-Unis depuis 1968 vus à travers les collections du Deutsches Architekturmuseum de Francfort*, ed. Jean Dethier (Paris: Centre Georges Pompidou/CCI, 1985), 57.

Goulet, Patrice. "La deuxième chance de l'architecture moderne: Entretien avec Rem Koolhaas," *L'Architecture d'Aujourd'hui* 238 (1985), 2–9.

———. "Ou le début de la fin du réel: Entretien avec Elia Zenghelis," *L'Architecture d'Aujourd'hui* 238 (1985), 10–14.

Kaal, Ron, and Tom Rooduijn. "De onmogelijke architectuur van Rem Koolhaas," *Haagse Post* 50 (1985), 40–51.

Kloos, Maarten. "Chique samenklitten op 'n knooppunt: Koolhaas maakt GEB-terrein Amsterdam tot luxe-eiland," *De Volkskrant*, September 7, 1985.

Koolhaas, Rem, Rob Krier, César Pelli, Rafael Moneo, Robert Stern, and Jacquelin Robertson. "Dance Theater The Hague." In *The Charlottesville Tapes*, ed. Jacquelin Robertson, 17–87 (New York: Rizzoli, 1985).

De Kooning, Mil. "De economie van de verbeelding: Rem Koolhaas in gesprek," *Vlees & Beton* 4 (1985), n.p.

Kuitenbrouwer, Jan. "Wat een creatieve verhuizing!" *De Volkskrant*, June 8, 1985.

Lootsma, Bart. "The Strategies of OMA," *Forum* 3 (1985), 124–30.

Meijsing, Doeschka. "Rem Koolhaas: 'Ik ben architect geworden uit een soort gêne voor vrijblijvendheid,'" *Vrij Nederland*, December 14, 1985.

Rooduijn, Tom. "Het belang van het niets bij Koolhaas," *NRC Handelsblad*, September 30, 1985.

Rutten, Jan. "Rem Koolhaas: 'Congestie voor mij interesssanter dan hoogbouw,'" *Bouw* 4 (1985), 21–24.

Schmertz, Mildred F. "Low-income Housing: A Lesson from Amsterdam," *Architectural Record* 1 (1985), 134–36.

Zwinkels, Cees. "Lintas-kantoor te Amsterdam: Een villa binnen het World Trade Center," *De Architect* 7–8 (1985), 34–37.

1986

Bosma, Koos. "Van individuele dressuur naar collectief tijdverdrijf: Renovatie van de Koepel in Arnhem," *De Architect* 5 (1986), 85–90.

Bossière, Olivier, and Dominique Lyon. "Entretien avec Rem Koolhaas," *Cahiers du CCI. Architecture: récits, figures, fictions* 1 (1986), 79–84.

van Dansik, Donald. "Bijlmer en Uithof door het OMA geanalyseerd: Studies voor de vitalisering van de stedebouw," *De Architect-thema* 25 (1986), 25–31.

Kuhnert, Nikolaus, and Patrice Goulet. "Die erschreckende Schönheit des 20. Jahrhunderts," *ARCH+* 86 (1986), 34–43.

Zanoni, Tomaso. "Precedent and Invention: Design in the Field of Tension: Rem Koolhaas: Project for the Parc de la Villette (1982–1983)," *Harvard Architecture Review* 5 (1986), 180–83.

1987

Barbieri, Umberto. "Teatro di Danza, L'Aia," *Domus* 689 (1987), 44–55.

Barbieri, Umberto, and Mirko Zardini. "Due progretti per il Municipio dell'Aja," *Casabella* 539 (1987), 39–41.

Bayle, Christophe. "Structurés par le vide: Mélun-Senart, Rem Koolhaas et Yves Bories," *Urbanisme* 222 (1987), 89.

Bekaert, Geert. "Een kans om te grijpen: Koolhaas's ontwerp voor het stadhuis in Den Haag," *NRC Handelsblad*, January 22, 1987.

Boekraad, Cees. "De invloed van Mies van der Rohe: Gesprek met Rem Koolhaas," *Archis* 3 (1987), 28–29.

Boissière, Olivier. "Rem Koolhaas, architecte visionnaire, solitaire et singulier," *CITY* 37 (1987), 78–83.

Bollerey, Franziska. "… immer wieder eine Mischung von Verführung und Ungeniessbarkeit ins Spiel bringen: Ein Gespräch mit Rem Koolhaas," *Bauwelt* 17–18 (1987), 627–33.

Buchanan, Peter. "OMA at The Hague," *The Architectural Review* 1084 (1987), 87–91.

Damisch, Hubert. "Cadavre exquis: Théâtre nationale de danse, La Haye," *Architecture Mouvement Continuité* 18 (1987), 21–22.

de Graaf, Rob. "Strip, torens en villa's: De plannen van OMA voor Amsterdam Zuid-Oost," *Archis* 11 (1987), 30–35.

Groothoff, M. C. "Contrast muziek- en danstheater een verademing: Spuitheater Den Haag geopend," *Arcade* 1 (1987), 8–19.

Haijtema, Arno. "De torenmassa's moeten in de lucht kunnen verdampen," *De Volkskrant*, January 31, 1987.

Hubeli, Ernst. "Metropolitane Erzählungen: Rem Koolhaas, Architekturprogrammatik und Projekte vom Office for Metropolitan Architecture," *Werk, Bauen + Wohnen* 5 (1987), 37–39.

Koolhaas, Rem, Léon Krier, Frank Gehry, Michael Graves, Peter Eisenman, Mario Gandelsonas, Susana Torre, Thomas Beeby, and Rafael Moneo. "Villa dall'Ava Paris." In *The Chicago Tapes*, ed. Stanley Tigerman, 164–73 (New York: Rizzoli, 1987).

Looise, Wijnand. "Inspraak IJplein," *OASE* 17 (1987), 35–37.

Rodermond, Janny. "Nederlands Danstheater: Een uitermate utilitair gebouw," *De Architect* 10 (1987), 73–78.

Rutten, Jan. "Niet vasthouden aan fictie van groene hart: Brokx praat met Koolhaas," *Bouw* 17 (1987), 10–12.

Schilperoord, Joop. "Dimensionierung und Detaillierung eines Schalendaches am Stationsplein in Rotterdam," *Deutsche Bauzeitung* 10 (1987), 48–50.

Schreuder, Arjen. "Nieuwe balletzaal in democratische en frivole stijl: Nederlands Dans Theater krijgt na dertig jaar improviseren een passend onderkomen," *NRC Handelsblad*, August 14, 1987.

Steigenga, Madeleine. "Not without a Scratch: Police Station Almere," *Forum* 2 (1987), 2–5.

Vermeulen, Paul. "Appareils instables pour la mégapole: L'architecte Rem Koolhaas," *Septentrion* 3 (1987), 44–47.

Zanoni, Tomaso. "Wettbewerbsprojekt Stadthaus Den Haag, Dezember 1986," *Werk, Bauen + Wohnen* 5 (1987), 40–45.

1988

Abrams, Janet. "Delirious Visions," *Blueprint* 44 (1988), 32–36.

Van de Beek, Johan. "Woontorens OMA markeren omslag in Groningen: Grootschalig element aan verbindingskanaal," *De Architect* 12 (1988), 73–77.

Bekaert, Geert. "The Storyteller: On the Work of Rem Koolhaas." In *Office for Metropolitan Architecture*, ed. Carolina De Backer, 3–5 (Antwerp: deSingel, 1988).

———. "De Nederlandse architectuur in quarantaine," *NRC Handelsblad*, August 26, 1988.

Bernauer, Markus. "Steinerne Erlebnisräume, oder: Eine Stadt ist kein Biotop," *Oberländer Tagblatt*, March 31, 1988.

Boissière, Olivier. "Amsterdam, le IJplein de Rem Koolhaas et de l'OMA," *L'Architecture d'Aujourd'hui* 257 (1988), 12–20.

———. "La Haye, le théâtre de la danse," *L'Architecture d'Aujourd'hui* 257 (1988), 28–33.

Buchanan, Peter. "Koolhaas Container," *Architectural Review* 1099 (1988), 32–39.

Dietsch, Deborah K. "Modern Romance: Eight Projects by the Office for Metropolitan Architecture," *Architectural Record* 3 (1988), 94.

———. "First Position: Dance Theater in The Hague," *Architectural Record* 4 (1988), 72.

van Dijk, Hans. "Ambitie op zoek naar een 'kritische massa': OMA's Nederlands Danstheater in Den Haag," *Archis* 4 (1988), 36–43.

———. "Destabilized Utilitarianism." In *Architecture in the Netherlands. 1987–1988*, ed. Hans van Dijk, 108 (Deventer: Van Loghum Slaterus, 1988).

Gandee, Charles. "Fancy Footwork: Dutch Architect Rem Koolhaas Makes a Stunning Debut with His Netherlands Dance Theater," *House & Garden* 4 (1988), 38.

Goulet, Patrice. "Trente ans après: Entretien avec Rem Koolhaas." In *Les années 50*, ed. Jacques Demarcq, 474–77 (Paris: Centre Pompidou, 1988).

de Haan, Hilde, and Ids Haagsma. "De grootse, slordige dromen van Rem Koolhaas," *De Volkskrant*, September 9, 1988.

Hollenstein, Roman. "Verfechter einer metropolitanen Architektur: Rem Koolhaas und sein OMA-Team im Architekturmuseum Basel," *Neue Zürcher Zeitung*, March 19, 1988.

Huygen, Frédérique. "Dance to the Music of OMA," *Blueprint* 44 (1988), 34.

de Jong, Jaap. "Interview met Rem Koolhaas: Rotterdam, 27.11.87." In *Architectonische Studies* 5, ed. Luuk van Duin, 109–12 (Delft: Delftse Universitaire Pers, 1988).

Kerkdijk, Herman, and Arthur Wortmann. "The Diary of an Architect," *Forum* 4 (1988), 39–45.

Klotz, Heinrich. "OMA: Parc de la Villette," *Journal of Architectural Theory and Criticism: International Union of Architects* 1 (1988), 67.

Leupen, Bernard. "Het IJplein in de traditie van de moderne woningbouw," *De Architect* 3 (1988), 51–59.

Loriers, Marie-Christine. "Rem Koolhaas: Sur la crête de la vague moderne," *Techniques & Architecture* 380 (1988), 76–77.

Lucan, Jacques. "Rem Koolhaas: Un théâtre caméléon," *Beaux Arts Magazine* 60 (1988), 70–75.

Mangin, David. "Point de vue: l'OMA n'est ni un nouvel OSA, ni un OVNI," *L'Architecture d'Aujourd'hui* 257 (1988), 20–21.

Martin, Louis. "Architectural Theory after 1968: Analysis of the Works of Rem Koolhaas and Bernard Tschumi" (master's thesis, Massachusetts Institute of Technology, 1988).

Merkel, Jayne. "Not So Delirious Modernism," *Art in America* 4 (1988), 27–33.

von Moos, Stanislaus. "Dutch Group Portrait: Notes on OMA's City Hall Project for The Hague," *A+U* 217 (1988), 86–94.

Philips, Patricia C. "Rem Koolhaas: Max Protetch Gallery," *Artforum* 5 (1988), 148–49.

Postel, Dirk Jan. "Werk in uitvoering: Woningbouw van OMA op het IJplein," *De Architect* 6 (1988), 68–75.

de Ranitz, H., and A. F. M. van Gils. "Musiktheater, Tanztheater—Den Haag," *Internationale Licht Rundschau* 1 (1988), 25–31.

Rodermond, Janny. "Zes ontwerpen voor een architectuurinstituut," *De Architect* 7 (1988), 29–41.

Vermeulen, Paul. "Office for Metropolitan Architecture zoekt punt van Archimedes," *De Standaard*, November 7, 1988.

Verwijnen, Jan. "Rem Koolhaas ja OMA," *Arkkitehti* 5 (1988), 30–43.

de Vreeze, Noud. "Een Koolhaas als sales promotion," *Archis* 12 (1988), 6–7.

Wigley, Mark. "Apartment Building and Observation Tower." In Philip Johnson and Mark Wigley, *Deconstructivist Architecture* (New York: The Museum of Modern Art, 1988), 46.

Zwinkels, Cees. "Woningbouwfestival Den Haag," *De Architect* 4 (1988), 66–71.

1989

Barbieri, Umberto. "Due progetti per l'Istutuo di Architettura olandese," *Domus* 707 (1989), 43–49.

Blundell Jones, Peter. "Von der gefährlichen Schönheit und der surrealistischen Schönheit," *Bauwelt* 1–2 (1989), 40–48.

Bosma, Koos. "De architect die leegte bouwde: OMA's stedebouwkundige concepten binnen het krachtenspel van de verstedelijking," *Archis* 3 (1989), 46–51.

Bosma, Koos, and Hans van Dijk. "'Ik ben nu al zeker drie jaar bezig om dat stigma van het moderne van me af te schudden, juist omdat het in Nederland zo gemakzuchtig wordt beleden': Interview met Rem Koolhaas," *Archis* 3 (1989), 46–51.

Breton, Gaelle. "Théâtre de la danse: La Haye, 1987: Rem Koolhaas, Pays-Bas." In idem, *Architecture Thématique: Théâtres*, 54–63 (Paris: Editions du Moniteur, 1989).

Buchanan, Peter. "New Movements in Tranquil Holland: Rem Koolhaas: A Risky Bet," *Arquitectura & Vivienda* 19 (1989), 83.

Casciato, Maristella, and Aldo Aymonimo. "Edifici residenziali e scuola, IJplein, Amsterdam," *Domus* 702 (1989), 32–39.

Cervelló, Marta. "'I've Always Been Anxious with the Standard Typology of the Average Architect with a Successful Career,'" *Quaderns d'arquitectura* 183 (1989), 78–104.

Cousin, Jean-Pierre. "Cinq hôtels pour Euro Disneyland," *Architecture intérieure créé* 232 (1989), 118–33.

Dagenhart, Richard. "Urban Architectural Theory and the Contemporary City: Tschumi and Koolhaas at Parc de la Villette," *Ekistics* 334–35 (1989), 84–92.

Emery, Marc. "Koolhaas: Puritaine banalité," *Architecture intérieure créé* 228 (1989), 98–102.

Fisher, Thomas. "In the Dutch Modernist Tradition: Villa in Kralingen," *Progressive Architecture* 12 (1989), 86–89.

Fortier, Bruno. "La Grande Ville: Entretien avec Rem Koolhaas," *L'Architecture d'Aujourd'hui* 262 (1989), 90–93.

Iden, Peter. "Auf der Suche nach der Figur," *Bauwelt* 1–2 (1989), 34–38.

De Kooning, Mil. "OMA in Nederland: Rem Koolhaas in gesprek," *Vlees & Beton* 12 (1989), n.p.

Lefaivre, Liane. "Dirty Realism in European Architecture Today: Making the Stone *Stony*," *Design Book Review* 17 (1989), 17–20.

Leupen, Bernard. *IJplein: Een speurtocht naar nieuwe compositorische middelen* (Rotterdam: 010Publishers, 1989).

Lucan, Jacques. "Auf dem Kamm der Welle," *Bauwelt* 1–2 (1989), 50–53.

Metz, Tracy. "Rem Koolhaas: Nederland mist respect voor de architect," *Avenue* 1 (1989), 63–65.

Mik, Edzard. "Rem Koolhaas, de architect met de hamer," *Het Parool*, March 25, 1989.

Polito, Salvatore. "Teatro di Danza a L'Aja," *L'industria della costruzioni* 218 (1989), 58–61.

Rodermond, Janny. "Controle in dienst van contrast: Stedebouwkundig plan van OMA voor De Uithof," *De Architect* 11 (1989), 111–15.

Selier, Herman. "Voor een beter Nederland: De architectuur van Rem Koolhaas," *NRC Handelsblad*, March 3, 1989.

Wagner, Susanne. "Welle überm Tanztheater," *art* 3 (1989), 127.

Welsh, John. "Latest Stop on a Grand Tour," *Building Design* 957 (1989), 2.

———. "Double Dutch," *Building Design* 964 (1989), 18–24.

Yatsuka, Hajime. "'I Combine Architectural Specificity with Programmatic Instability,'" *Telescope: The Printed City* 4 (1989), 6–11.

1990

Bekaert, Geert. *Sea Trade Center Zeebrugge* (Antwerp: Standaard Uitgeverij, 1990).

Boudet, Dominique. "Karlsruhe: centre des arts et des technologies: Entretien avec Heinrich Klotz," *AMC* 8 (1990), 12.

Boyer, Charles-Arthur. "Dessiner: Entre indétermination et spécificité: Entretien avec Rem Koolhaas," *L'Architecture d'Aujourd'hui* 269 (1990), 34–39.

Emery, Marc. "L'architecture est-elle toujours innocente?" *Le Figaro*, March 20, 1990.

Fisher, Thomas. "Three Recent Projects," *Progressive Architecture* 4 (1990), 123–25.

———. "Logic and Will: IJplein Urban Design and Housing," *Progressive Architecture* 3 (1990), 96–100.

Garcias, Jean Claude. "Tragico ed esilarante: l'effeto Koolhaas in Francia," *Casabella* 570 (1990), 29–32.

Graafland, Arie. "Bouwkunde Delft, Rem Koolhaas en de moderniteit." In *Hoe modern is de Nederlandse architectuur?*, ed. Bernard Leupen, Wouter Deen, and Christoph Grafe, 71–86 (Rotterdam: 010 Publishers, 1990).

———. "Beckett en Duchamp in Manhattan: Koolhaas's diagnose van de moderniteit in New York." In *Hoe modern is de Nederlandse architectuur?*, ed. Bernard Leupen, Wouter Deen, and Christoph Grafe, 111–23 (Rotterdam: 010 Publishers, 1990).

Ibelings, Hans. "Architecture as a Catalogue of Solutions." In *Architecture in the Netherlands: Yearbook 1989–1990*, ed. Ruud Brouwers, 70–71 (Deventer: Van Loghum Slaterus, 1990).

Isasi, Justo. "De hormigón y gresite: Rem Koolhaas en Rotterdam," *Arquitectura Viva* 12 (1990), 52–53.

Ito, Toyo. "Toyo Ito Reviews Rem Koolhaas Exhibition," *Telescope: The Printed City* 5 (1990), 74–86.

Jencks, Charles. "Rem Koolhaas's National Dance Theater in The Hague." In idem, *The New Moderns: From Late to Neo-Modernism*, 274–75 (London: Academy Editions, 1990).

Lootsma, Bart, and Mariëtte Van Stralen. "De opdrachtgever als visionair: Koolhaas blaast de klassieke rol van de architect nieuw leven in," *Archis* 5 (1990), 36–42.

van der Meijden, Juliette. "Rem Koolhaas: de Brasília ao futuro," *Projeto* 133 (1990), 34–46.

Melis, Liesbeth. "OMA's antwoord op Kleihues: Woongebouw bij Checkpoint Charlie," *De Architect* 5 (1990), 33–39.

Metz, Tracy. "Kruising tussen bol en kegel: Prijsvraag voor passagiersterminal in Zeebrugge," *NRC Handelsblad*, March 23, 1990.

———. "Challenge for the Chunnel," *Architectural Record* 11 (1990), 13.

Meuwissen, Joost. "Rem Koolhaas in Europa," *Kunst & Museumjournaal* 3 (1990), 44–49.

Neumeyer, Fritz. "OMA's Berlin: The Polemic Island in the City," *Assemblage* 11 (1990), 36–53.

———. "Metropolitan Interface: OMA's Projekt für Euralille," *Archithese* 1 (1990), 44–48.

Polito, Salvatore. "Edifici residenziali ad Amsterdam," *L'industria delle costruzioni* 222 (1990), 20–25.

Vermeulen, Paul. "Metropolitane architectuur: Projekt-Koolhaas voor Zeebrugge," *De Standaard*, April 28, 1990.

———. "Rem Koolhaas à Paris," *Septentrion* 3 (1990), 64–65.

Verwijnen, Jan. "Patiotalo Rotterdamissa," *Arkkitehti* 2 (1990), 44–45.

Wortmann, Arthur. "Afscheid Koolhaas in teken van moed en wanhoop: Symposium in Delft," *Archis* 6 (1990), 6–7.

Zaera, Alejandro. "Conceptual Evolution of the Work of Rem Koolhaas." In *Rem Koolhaas: Urban Projects (1985–1990)*, ed. Josep Lluis Mateo, 52–62 (Barcelona: Quaderns d'Arquitectura i Urbanisme, 1990).

Zardini, Mirko. "Tanztheater in Den Haag, 1987," *Werk, Bauen + Wohnen* 3 (1990), 32–37.

1991

Allain-Dupré, Elisabeth. "Lille: Une métropole européenne," *AMC* 19 (1991), 32–37.

———. "L'intelligence cumulative: Entretien avec Rem Koolhaas," *AMC* 19 (1991), 42–43.

Burckhardt, Lucius. "Furka 1991," *BauDoc-Bulletin* 12 (1991), 5–12.

Chenu, Laurent. "Déplacer les montagnes: À propos de la transformation de l'hôtel Furkablick par l'Office for Metropolitan Architecture," *Faces* 21 (1991), 80–85.

Delendas, Nicos. "An 'Electronic' Bauhaus: A Project by Rem Koolhaas," *Tefchos* 6 (1991), 98–107.

Goetz, Joachim. "Eine Provinzstadt auf dem Weg zur Metropole: Projekt für ein Business-Zentrum in Lille," *Baumeister* 11 (1991), 36.

Hubeli, Ernst. "X, Y und Z: Zentrum für Kunst und Medientechnologie in Karlsruhe," *Werk, Bauen + Wohnen* 78 (1991), 2–7.

Huisman, Jaap. "Byzantium, Amsterdam." In *Lelijk gebouwd Nederland: De 50 grootste missers*, 50–52 (The Hague: SDU, 1991).

———. "Winkelcentrum IJplein, Amsterdam." In *Lelijk gebouwd Nederland: De 50 grootste missers*, 90–91 (The Hague: SDU, 1991).

Lootsma, Bart. "Body and Soul, ofwel Superman brengt redding: Het zwembad bij Rem Koolhaas," *De Architect-thema* 42 (1991), 36–43.

Lucan, Jacques, ed. *Rem Koolhaas OMA* (Princeton Architectural Press: New York, 1991).

———. "Rem Koolhaas, une machine qui devient bâtiment," *Art Press* 12 (1991), 112–14.

Morteo, Enrico. "Rem Koolhaas: Housing in Fukuoka," *Domus* 730 (1991), 33–42.

Rodermond, Janny. "OMA in Lille: TGV aanleiding Europees centrum," *De Architect* 44 (1991), 28–37.

———. "Byzantium mist arrogantie: Driedimensionale collage van OMA," *De Architect* 7–8 (1991), 44–47.

van Rooy, Max. "Het ingebouwd verval," *NRC Handelsblad*, May 3, 1991.

Vermeulen, Paul. "Metropolitan vernacular: OMA's Byzantium in Amsterdam," *Archis* 8 (1991), 17–22.

Vidler, Anthony. "Transparency (and the Très Grande Bibliothèque)." In *Anyone*, ed. Cynthia Davidson, 231–39 (New York: Rizzoli, 1991).

Werner, Frank R. "The Magic Die with the Enchanted Cloak for the Squaring of the Circle: ZKM," *Lotus International* 70 (1991), 78–81.

Woodbridge, Sally B. "Housing after the Machine Age: Rem Koolhaas in Fukuoka," *Progressive Architecture* 8 (1991), 60–76.

Wortmann, Arthur. "De congestie tot staan gebracht: Koolhaas ontwerpt parkeergarage voor Den Haag," *Archis* 4 (1991), 18–21.

1992

Adolf, Steven, and Tracy Metz. "Charismatisch scenarist van de stedelijke ruimte: Profiel van Rem Koolhaas," *NRC Handelsblad*, August 31, 1992.

Casadio, Mariuccia. "Rem Koolhaas, Architect: For the Advancement of Urban Pleasures," *Andy Warhol's Interview* 1 (1992), 59.

Chaslin, François. "Un rationalisme paradoxal: Entretien avec Rem Koolhaas," *L'Architecture d'Aujourd'hui* 280 (1992), 162–65.

———. "Sous la piscine exactement: Architecture: la Villa dall'Ava à Saint-Cloud," *Le Nouvel Observateur* 1437 (1992), 178–80.

Chemetov, Paul. "Le chaos debout," *L'Architecture d'Aujourd'hui* 280 (1992), 161.

Cohen, Jean-Louis. "Suburban Subversion: Villa dall'Ava," *Progressive Architecture* 4 (1992), 114–20.

Doutriaux, Emmanuel. "Euralille, entre ville et banlieue, une métropole sur l'intervalle," *L'Architecture d'Aujourd'hui* 280 (1992), 94–95.

Drathen, Doris V. "Wohnen zum Staunen," *Architektur & Wohnen* 3 (1992), 31–36.

Edelmann, Frédéric. "La girafe et l'architecte: Rem Koolhaas et la Villa dall'Ava," *Le Monde*, March 26, 1992.

Fisher, Thomas. "Euralille, Lille, France," *Progressive Architecture* 2 (1992), 100–101.

Gandee, Charles. "The Ideal Villa," *House & Garden* 3 (1992), 158–72.

Garcias, Jean-Claude. "Le chaos et le chahut," *L'Architecture d'Aujourd'hui* 280 (1992), 158–60.

Großklaus, Götz. "Der Würfel als mediales Tor," *ARCH+* 112 (1992), 22.

de Haan, Hilde, and Ids Haagsma. "Koolhaas verbindt banaliteit en chic in briljant ontwerp," *De Volkskrant*, September 17, 1992.

Hulsman, Bernard. "Kunsthal lijkt wel een toverdoos," *NRC Handelsblad*, October 31, 1992.

Jameson, Fredric, and Michael Speaks. "Envelopes and Enclaves: The Space of Post-Civil Society (An Architectural Conversation)," *Assemblage* 17 (1992), 30–37.

Kwinter, Sanford. "The Reinvention of Geometry," *Assemblage* 18 (1992), 83–85.

Leupen, Bernard, and Christoph Grafe. "Een metropolitane villa: OMA's Villa dall'Ava in Parijs," *Archis* 1 (1992), 12–21.

Lootsma, Bart. "Manifest van OMA: Villa dall'Ava in Parijs," *De Architect* 3 (1992), 29–33.

Lucan, Jacques. "La Villa dall'Ava, construction moderne," *Le Moniteur Architecture* 28 (1992), 26–29.

———. "Villa dall'Ava, Parigi," *Domus* 736 (1992), 25–34.

de Maeseneer, Martine, and Dirk Van den Brande. "Sea Trade Center at Zeebrugge: A Working Babel," *Architectural Design* 7–8 (1992), xiv–xix.

Menard, Jean-Pierre. "Paroi translucide: Villa dall'Ava, Hauts-de-Seine, OMA Rem Koolhaas architectes," *AMC* 32–33 (1992), 84–85.

Nio, Ivan. "De congestie van Rem Koolhaas," *Rooilijn* 2 (1992), 34–39.

Pedretti, Bruno. "Lunario dell' architettura 4: l'interprete parassita," *Casabella* 592 (1992), 31.

Pijbes, Wim. "New Kunsthal Opened in Rotterdam," *Museum Management and Curatorship* 4 (1992), 421–24.

Pope, Albert. "Tokyo Storm Warning," *Design Book Review* 26 (1992), 17–22.

Riboulet, Pierre. "Composition ou décomposition," *L'Architecture d'Aujourd'hui* 280 (1992), 160–61.

Riley, Terence. "Urban Constructions: Rotterdam Kunsthal," *Newsline Columbia University* (September 1992), 2.

Robert, Jean-Paul. "Villa dall'Ava à Saint-Cloud," *L'Architecture d'Aujourd'hui* 280 (1992), 10–19.

Rykwert, Joseph. "America sogna Europa: Europa sogna America," *Casabella* 586–87 (1992), 33–35.

Schmidt, Nina. "Sieg der Provinz: ZKM-Projekt, Karlsruhe," *Baumeister* 8 (1992), 9.

Schneider, Sabine. "Kunsthalle in Rotterdam: Trügerische Transparenz," *Baumeister* 11 (1992), 40–45.

Stein, Karen. "The Image According to OMA," *I.D.* 1 (1992), 66–75.

Sudjic, Deyan. "Tough Kid on the Block," *Blueprint* 85 (1992), 16–18.

Suzuki, Akira. "This Is Not a House: Villa dall'Ava," *Kenchiku Bunka* 547 (1992), 142–43.

Tzonis, Alexander, and Liane Lefaivre. "The Netherlands Dance Theater." In idem, *Memory and Invention: Architecture in Europe since 1968*, 182–85 (London: Thames & Hudson, 1992).

———. "Apartment House at Checkpoint Charlie." In idem, *Memory and Invention: Architecture in Europe since 1968*, 236–37 (London: Thames & Hudson, 1992).

Uhlig, Günther. "Dieser Würfel darf nicht fallen," *ARCH+* 112 (1992), 20.

Vermeulen, Paul. "Een visionair plan voor Rijsel," *De Franse Nederlanden* 17 (1992), 37–45.

Vincendon, Sibylle. "Grandes idées pour un trois pièces," *Libération*, January 24, 1992.

Watanabe, Hiroshi. "Aislamiento colectivo: Las viviendas japonesas de Rem Koolhaas," *Arquitectura Viva* 23 (1992), 10–13.

Weibel, Peter. "Zum Rem Koolhaas—ZKM Gebäude," *ARCH+* 112 (1992), 21.

Wislocki, Peter. "Kool Sophistication: Villa dall'Ava," *Architects' Journal*, March 11, 1992.

Zaera, Alejandro. "Finding Freedoms: Conversations with Rem Koolhaas," *El Croquis* 53 (1992), 6–31.

———. "Notes for a Topographic Survey," *El Croquis* 53 (1992), 32–51.

van der Zijl, Annejet. "Rem Koolhaas: De droeve tegenstrijdigheid van een wereldberoemd architect," *HP/De Tijd* 43 (1992), 30–41.

Zwaap, René. "Waterhoofd: De IJ-boulevard van kapotte dromen," *De Groene Amsterdammer*, November 25, 1992.

1993

Arroyo, Eduardo. "Do Nomads Dream," *a+t* 2 (1993), 19–21.

Chaslin, François. "Una casa de ensueño: Rem Koolhaas y Villa dall'Ava," *Arquitectura Viva* 31 (1993), 32–37.

Colenbrander, Bernard. "Het labiele wereldbeeld." In *Architectuur in Nederland*, ed. Ruud Brouwers, Hans Ibelings, and Arjen Oosterman, 34–36 (Utrecht: Stichting Teleac, 1993).

Davidson, Cynthia. "Rem Koolhaas: Why I Wrote *Delirious New York* and Other Textual Strategies," *ANY* 0 (1993), 42–43.

van Dijk, Hans. "Principles of Metropolitan Architecture: OMA's Kunsthal in Rotterdam," *Archis* 1 (1993), 17–27.

Dijkstra, Rients. "Stedebouw achteraf: Het Souterrain van OMA," *De Architect* 10 (1993), 42–51.

Doutriaux, Emmanuel. "Le Kunsthal de Rotterdam," *L'Architecture d'Aujourd'hui* 285 (1993), 6–14.

Frampton, Kenneth. "Kunsthal in Rotterdam," *Domus* 747 (1993), 38–47.

Giovannini, Joseph. "Rem Koolhaas Kunsthal," *Architecture* 9 (1993), 86–89.

Graafland, Arie. "Koolhaas en de 'City of Flows': Koolhaas's ontwerpconcepten en de IJ-oeverplannen van Amsterdam," *OASE* 35 (1993), 43–55.

Ibelings, Hans. "A New Exhibition Machine for the City," *Abitare* 317 (1993), 189–96.

Koekebakker, Olof. "Minimaal overgeven en maximaal schrapzetten: Rem Koolhaas en de Nederlandse architectuur," *Items: Tijdschrift voor vormgeving* 3 (1993), 46–53.

Kuhnert, Nikolaus, Philipp Oswalt, and Alejandro Zaera-Polo. "Die Entfaltung der Architektur: Rem Koolhaas in Gesprächen," *ARCH+* 117 (1993), 22–33.

Lootsma, Bart. "Hans Werlemann," *De Architect-thema* 51 (1993), 22–23.

Lootsma, Bart, and Jan de Graaf. "In dienst van de ervaring: KunstHAL van OMA in Rotterdam," *De Architect* 1 (1993), 19–34.

Melet, Ed. "De perfecte wanorde: Detaillering en constructie Kunsthal," *De Architect* 1 (1993), 35–37.

Metz, Tracy. "Show Piece: Kunsthal Rotterdam," *Architectural Record* 3 (1993), 66–73.

Michel, Florence. "Koolhaas Kunsthal," *Architecture intérieure créé* 252 (1993), 100.

Muschamp, Herbert. "Some Unfinished Business on St.-Germain," *New York Times*, February 14, 1993.

Polónyi, Stefan. "Interpreting the Supporting Structures of Architecture, with Rem Koolhaas," *Lotus International* 79 (1993), 87.

Slessor, Catherine. "Lille Revival," *The Architectural Review* 1159 (1993), 72–75.

Sudjic, Deyan. "The Museum as Megastar," *The Guardian*, January 25, 1993.

Vermeulen, Paul. "Clad in Tonalities of Light." In *Architectuur in Nederland: Jaarboek 1992–1993*, ed. Matthijs de Boer, Ruud Brouwers, Vincent Van Rossem, and Zef Hemel, 90–91 (Rotterdam: NAi Publishers, 1993).

Vidler, Anthony. "Books in Space: Tradition and Transparency in the Bibliothèque de France," *Representations* 42 (1993), 115–34.

Wortmann, Arthur. "The Museum Park, Rotterdam: An Arbitrary Selection of Prestige Objects," *Archis* 1 (1993), 28–39.

Yashiro, Masaki. "IJplein Housing, Urban Design," *Process: Architecture* 112 (1993), 24–27.

Zerboni, Monica. "Hotel Furkablick, an Art Nest," *Abitare* 322 (1993), 210–12.

1994

Arcidi, Philip. "Rem Koolhaas in New York: Pump Up the Volume," *Christian Science Monitor*, December 22, 1994.

Balmond, Cecil. "El huevo mecánico: Luces y cubiertas en el Congrexpo de Lille," *Arquitectura Viva* 39 (1994), 42–45.

Bouman, Ole, and Roemer van Toorn. "Architecture at Remdom; The Blinkers that Make the Visionary: A Conversation with Rem Koolhaas." In idem, *The Invisible in Architecture*, 442–53 (London: Academy Editions, 1994).

Cisar, Hana. "Koolhaas, le doute consacré," *L'Architecture d'Aujourd'hui* 296 (1994), 18.

Cornubert, Christophe. "Ein offenes Fenster: Die Fassade der Bibliotheken von Jussieu in Paris," *Deutsche Bauzeitung* 6 (1994), 152–57.

Coupland, Douglas. "Dutch Reformation," *New York Times*, September 11, 1994.

Crary, Jonathan. "Notes on Koolhaas and Modernization," *ANY* 9 (1994), 14–15.

van Dijk, Hans. "A Centripetal Exodus: OMA's Euralille—An Interim Report," *Archis* 10 (1994), 36–47.

———. "The Architect Is Obliged to Be an Honorable Man: Interview with Rem Koolhaas," *Archis* 11 (1994), 18–24.

Edelmann, Frédéric. "Euralille ou le génie de la transfiguration," *Le Monde*, September 21, 1994.

Fernández-Galiano, Luis. "Megamorfosis: Piano y Koolhaas, dos estrategias," *Arquitectura Viva* 39 (1994), 17–19.

Filler, Martin. "The REM Cycle," *Harper's Bazaar* 11 (1994), 194–99.

Fillion, Odile. "Interview de Rem Koolhaas." In idem, *La ville: Six interviews d'architectes*, 28–37 (Paris: Publications du Moniteur, 1994).

Gandee, Charles. "REM Cycle," *Vogue*, November 1994, 330–35, 383–84.

Garschagen, Oscar. "Ode aan de grootschaligheid," *De Volkskrant*, November 4, 1994.

Graafland, Mark. "The Town Planning of the Office for Metropolitan Architecture," *Topos* 9 (1994), 113–22.

Hulsman, Bernard. "De provocatie van het Spartaans bordeel: Rem Koolhaas als de Johan Cruijff van de architectuur," *NRC Handelsblad*, June 6, 1994.

Ingersoll, Richard. "Rem Koolhaas e l'ironia," *Casabella* 610 (1994), 16–19.

Jencks, Charles. "39 Steps to Surfing, or the Trajectory of Rem Koolhaas," *ANY* 9 (1994), 41–45.

Joffroy, Pascale. "Formas de lo urbano: Un palacio de congresos de Koolhaas en Lille," *Arquitectura Viva* 39 (1994), 30–41.

Kwinter, Sanford. "The Building, the Book, and the New Pastoralism," *ANY* 9 (1994), 16–22.

Lootsma, Bart. "Le Grand Palais: Das neue Kongreßzentrum in Lille," *Bauwelt* 44 (1994), 2454–61.

Luchsinger, Christoph. "Komprimierte Infrastruktur: Euralille 1989–1994," *Werk, Bauen + Wohnen* 11 (1994), 18–35.

MacNair, Andrew. "Marathon: Kunsthal by OMA/Rem Koolhaas," *A+U* 287 (1994), 120–23.

Meade, Martin K. "Euralille: The Instant City," *Architectural Review* 1174 (1994), 83–86.

Melet, Ed. "Aantasting van de architectuur: Detaillering en akoestiek Grand Palais Lille," *De Architect* 12 (1994), 52–57.

Meuwissen, Joost. "X-Filled Room: Rem Koolhaas's Linthorst House, Rotterdam," *Wiederhall* 16 (1994), 56–59.

Michel, Florence. "Koolhaas: Lille-Grand Palais," *Architecture intérieure créé* 261 (1994), 96.

———. "Construire la ville à partir des infrastructures: Entretien avec Rem Koolhaas," *Architecture intérieure créé* 262 (1994), 88–89.

Mönninger, Michael. "Plankton der Vorstädte," *Der Spiegel*, November 21, 1994.

———. "Rem Koolhaas," *du. Die Zeitschrift der Kultur* 11 (1994), 74–75.

Moore, Rowan. "Reason in Hell," *Blueprint* 112 (1994), 19–22.

Muschamp, Herbert. "Rem Koolhaas's New York State of Mind," *New York Times*, November 4, 1994.

Nygaard, Eric. "Dirty Realism: Nye arbejder af Rem Koolhaas," *Arkitekten* 13 (1993), 426–32.

Parsons, Spencer. "Tourist's Eye-View: Euralille," *ANY* 9 (1994), 16–22.

Rajchman, John. "Thinking Big: Johan Rajchman talks with Rem Koolhaas," *Artforum* 4 (1994), 46–55, 99, 102.

Rodermond, Janny. "Bigness; het probleem is de oplossing," *De Architect* 12 (1994), 32–41.

Rouillard, Dominique. "Exodus, ou les prisonniers volontaires de l'architecture." In *La ville, art et architecture en Europe, 1870–1993*, ed. Jean Dethier and Alain Guiheux, 436–37 (Paris: Editions du Centre Pompidou, 1994).

Scharfenorth, Heiner. "Rotterdam setzt Zeichen," *Architektur & Wohnen* 2 (1994), 106–15.

Somol, Robert E. "The Camp of the New," *ANY* 9 (1994), 50–55.

Speaks, Michael. "Not the Last Word: Monster of the New," *ANY* 9 (1994), 60–62.

Sudjic, Deyan. "Chunnel City," *Blueprint* 108 (1994), 23–27.

———. "Lille in Steel," *The Guardian*, June 7, 1994.

———. "A Cool Head in the Midst of Chaos, Rem Koolhaas Has Been Arguing for a New Approach to Architecture for Years," *The Guardian*, June 21, 1994.

Tilman, Harm. "Vruchtbare reductie van de complexiteit: De stedebouw van Euralille," *De Architect* 12 (1994), 22–31.

Tromp, Jan. "Architect tussen modder en mythe," *De Volkskrant*, November 19, 1994.

Vermeulen, Paul. "The Terrible Beauty of the Twentieth Century: A Portrait of Rem Koolhaas," *The Low Countries* 2 (1994), 223–28.

Vidler, Anthony. "*S,M,L,XL*: A REM-based Program for Interactive Architecture," *ANY* 9 (1994), 58–59.

Wortmann, Arthur. "Mystery House: A Villa by OMA," *Archis* 11 (1994), 33–40.

1995

Bonami, Francesco. "Towards a Cyberspacial Urban Terrain: Interview with Rem Koolhaas," *Flash Art International* 182 (1995), 86–89, 128.

Brandolini, Sebastiano. "Progetti Extra Large," *Casa Vogue* 270 (1995), 118–23, 132.

Buchanan, Peter. "Crossroads of Europe: Euralille," *Architecture* 1 (1995), 68–70.

Cohen, Jean-Louis. "'Bigness' and the Test of the Construction Site," *Lotus International* 86 (1995), 50–59.

Cohn, David. "Delirious: OMA at MoMA," *Bauwelt* 1–2 (1995), 8.

Le Dantec, Jean-Pierre. "Le spectacle continue …," *Techniques & Architecture* 418 (1995), 6–7.

Devolder, Anne-Mie. "Le Grand Palais of Congrexpo: Het nieuwe Congrescentrum in Rijsel," *A+* 134 (1995), 52–56.

Doutriaux, Emmanuel. "Euralille, onder controle gehouden uitzinnigheid," *A+* 132 (1995), 66–69.

Downey, Claire. "Euralille: Crossroads to Twenty-first-Century Europe," *Architectural Record* 3 (1995), 89–91.

Finch, Paul. "Koolhaas Gets a Four-Star Reception at AA Lecture," *Architects' Journal*, December 14, 1995.

Fortier, Bruno. "Lille au trésor," *L'Architecture d'Aujourd'hui* 298 (1995), 18.

Fromonot, Françoise. "Gros plans," *L'Architecture d'Aujourd'hui* 298 (1995), 85.

———. "The Art of the Ellipse: Interview with Rem Koolhaas," *L'Architecture d'Aujourd'hui* 298 (1995), 85.

Garcias, Jean-Claude. "Euralille: Ces mystères nous dépassent, feignons de les organiser," *Le Bulletin d'Informations Architecturales* 183 (1995), 7–8.

Giovannini, Joseph. "Der radikale Prophet," *Architektur & Wohnen* 5 (1995), 106–17.

Huisman, Jaap. "Een boek als een wolkenkrabber," *De Volkskrant*, December 15, 1995.

Hultin, Olof. "Arkitekt: OMA," *Arkitektur* 3 (1995), 32–37.

Ide, Takeshi. "A Private Message to Friends, or Koolhaas in Tokyo," *Kenchiku Bunka* 590 (1995), 2.

Ingersoll, Richard. "Dear Editor: Bidness," *ANY* 10 (1995), 5

Irace, Fulvio. "Land Station: Euralille," *Abitare* 336 (1995), 75–83.

Jodidio, Philip. "Promethée déchaîné," *Connaissance des arts* 514 (1995), 98–107.

Ketcham, Diana. "Dramatic Entrances," *ARTnews* 11 (1995), 228–30.

Lamarre, François. "Menace sur la ville," *d'Architectures* 60 (1995), 26.

Latham, Ian. "The Surreal City: Rem Koolhaas at Euralille," *Architecture Today* 55 (1995), 19–25.

Liftin, Eric. "Sizing Up the City: Rem Koolhaas," *Metropolis* 1 (1995), 91–95.

Lootsma, Bart. "Wall Frustration," *Daidalos—Magic of Materials II*, August 1995, 74–83.

Lucan, Jacques. "The Voluntary Prisoner of Architecture," *Domus* 774 (1995), 25–26.

Marques, Marie. "Promenade de quartier," *d'Architectures* 60 (1995), 19–21.

———. "François Delhay. L'homme de l'ombre," *d'Architectures* 60 (1995), 28.

Merkel, Jayne. "In the Galleries: Rem Koolhaas," *Oculus* 1 (1995), 11.

Mertins, Detlef. "Open Contours and Other Autonomies: Sea Terminal." In *Monolithic Architecture*, ed. Rodolfo Machado and Rodolphe el-Koury, 54–55 (New York: Prestel, 1995).

Mitchell, Emily. "City at the Crossroads," *Time*, August 14, 1995.

N.N. "The Delirious Dutchman," *New Yorker*, January 16, 1995.

Newman, Peter, and Andy Thornley. "Euralille: 'Boosterism' at the Centre of Europe," *European Urban and Regional Studies* 2 (1995), 237–46.

Plagens, Peter. "Cool Hand Koolhaas: A Hit Book from a Hot Architect," *Newsweek*, January 16, 1995.

Rambert, Francis. "Koolille: Radical et experimental," *d'Architectures* 60 (1995), 18–19.

Riley, Terence. "Light Construction: Bibliothèque Nationale de France." In *Light Construction*, ed. Christopher Lyon, 12–15 (New York: MoMA, 1995).

Robert, Jean-Paul. "Euralille, fiction de ville," *L'Architecture d'Aujourd'hui* 298 (1995), 14–15.

Rodermond, Janny. "Rem Koolhaas: Nederland moet eerst een crisis in de politiek oplossen voor er sprake kan zijn van intelligente stedebouw," *De Architect Thema* 61 (1995), 45–47.

Schmertz, Mildred F. "Koolhaas Urbanism Exhibited in New York," *Architecture* 1 (1995), 24–25.

Shane, Grahame D. "Rem Koolhaas and the Postmodern City," *Los Angeles Forum for Architecture and Urban Design Newsletter* (May 1995), 1–7.

Shnier, John. "Plump Fiction: Conversation with Bruce Mau," *Canadian Architect* 11 (1995), 18–21.

Speaks, Michael. "Artificieel modernisme: De kritisch-paranoïde methode bij OMA," *De Architect* 9 (1995), 34–36.

Straus, Cees. "Rem Koolhaas te groot voor de wereld," *Trouw*, December 16, 1995.

Treiber, Daniel. "OMA at Euralille: Anguished Modernity," *Casabella* 623 (1995), 18–33.

Vermeulen, Paul. "Magnet and Arena: Euralille Horizontal: Superblocks by Nouvel and Koolhaas," *Archis* 11 (1995), 46–51.

Vine, Richard. "Post-Delirium," *Art in America* 4 (1995), 35–41.

1996

Aymonino, Aldo. "Rem Koolhaas/ OMA: Biblioteche Jussieu a Parigi," *Architettura Intersezioni* 3 (1996), 48–52.

Baird, George. "Conversation with Rem Koolhaas," *Harvard GSD News* (Summer 1996), 49–50.

Beck, Haig, and Jackie Cooper. "Review: *S,M,L,XL*," *UME: The International Architecture Magazine* 2 (1996), 48–49.

Beigel, Florian. "*S,M,L,XL*," *Architectural Research Quarterly* 3 (1996), 88–90.

Bideau, André. "Koolhaas's Katharsis," *Werk, Bauen + Wohnen* 83 (1996), 45–52.

Buruma, Ian. "The Sky's the Limit," *New York Review of Books* 19 (1996), 42–47.

Confurius, Gerrit. "New York, Chicago, Hongkong, Kuala Lumpur, Euralille," *Daidalos* 61 (1996), 110–26.

van Dijk, Hans. "An Anonymous Architect-Hero Is Something to Be: *S,M,L,XL* Treatise on the Undecidable," *Archis* 7 (1996), 64–65.

Douke, Hiroshi. "The Bible of Urban Architecture," *Kenchiku Bunka* 593 (1996), 143.

Eeckhout, Bart. "Alles en niets tegelijk," *NWT* 4 (1996), 26–33.

Filler, Martin. "The Master Builder," *New York Times Book Review*, March 17, 1996.

Forgey, Benjamin. "Heavy Thinking on the State of the City: Two New Books Foresee Very Different Futures," *Washington Post*, February 10, 1996.

Fox, Stephen. "BIG," *Cite: The Architecture and Design Review of Houston* 35 (1996), 34–35.

Garcias, Jean-Claude. "Koolhaas et le Sublime: *S,M,L,XL*," *L'Architecture d'Aujourd'hui* 304 (1996), 59–61.

Gardels, Nathan. "The Generic City: Singapore or Bladerunner? Interview with Rem Koolhaas," *New Perspectives Quarterly* 3 (1996), 4–9.

Gill, Brendan. "Koolhaas in 2-D: An Architect Collects His Thoughts and Works between Covers," *New Yorker*, February 12, 1996.

Graafland, Arie. "Artificiality in the Work of Rem Koolhaas." In idem, *Architectural Bodies*, 39–66 (Rotterdam: 010 Publishers, 1996).

Graafland, Arie, and Jasper de Haan. "A Conversation with Rem Koolhaas." In *The Critical Landscape*, ed. Michael Speaks, Arie Graafland, and Jasper de Haan, 218–36 (Rotterdam: 010 Publishers, 1996).

Halley, Peter. "Artificial Pleasures: Rem Koolhaas's Eurolille," *Frieze* 26 (1996), 11–14.

Harbison, Robert. "Big Is Not Always Beautiful: *S,M,L,XL*," *Architects' Journal*, February 8, 1996.

Hoffmann-Axthelm, Dieter. "On Generic City," *ARCH+* 132 (1996), 76–77.

Imorde, Joseph. "Furkablick," *Daidalos* 62 (1996), 92–93.

Ito, Toyo. "Architectural Incidents Replete with Fantasy," *A+U* 314 (1996), 131–33.

Jameson, Fredric. "XXL: Rem Koolhaas's Great Big Buildingsroman," *Village Voice* 19 (1996), 17–19.

Kipnis, Jeffrey. "Recent Koolhaas," *El Croquis* 79 (1996), 26–37.

Koekebakker, Olof. "De macht van Bigness: *S,M,L,XL*, het megawerk van Bruce Mau en Rem Koolhaas," *Items: Tijdschrift voor vormgeving* 2 (1996), 50–53.

Kwinter, Sanford. "Flying the Bullet, or When Did the Future Begin?" In *Rem Koolhaas: Conversations with Students*, ed. Sanford Kwinter, 67–94 (New York: Princeton Architectural Press, 1996).

Lagrange, Thierry. "De maat is vol: *S,M,L,XL* en de interesse van OMA," *Andere Sinema* 132 (1996), 60–63.

Latham, Ian. "Double Vision: A Villa by Rem Koolhaas," *Architecture Today* 69 (1996), 49–55.

Levinson, Nancy. "Rem Koolhaas: Reluctant Star," *Graphis* 304 (1996), 68–75.

Lootsma, Bart. "Groningen Starspangled: Public toilet by Rem Koolhaas and Gro Bonesmo." In *A Star Is Born: Groningen: The City as a Stage*, ed. Bart Lootsma and Hélène Damen, 12–13 (Bussum: Thoth, 1996).

Luscombe, Belinda. "Making a Splash: Rem Koolhaas Shows What Can Happen When a Visionary Finally Gets to Put Up a Building or Two," *Time* 15 (1996), 48–50.

MacCarthy, Fiona. "Size Matters: Fiona MacCarthy Deconstructs the First Architectural Novel," *The Observer*, February 18, 1996.

Maclaren, Gordon. "Harbison Cannot See Koolhaas's Intention," *Architects' Journal*, February 15, 1996.

Menu, Isabelle, and Frank Vermandel, eds. *Euralille: The Making of a New City Center* (Basel: Birkhäuser, 1996).

Meuser, Philipp. "Toilettenanlage in Groningen," *Bauwelt* 39 (1996), 2237.

Müller, Alois Martin. "Stadtroman, Bildfreude," *Hochparterre* 6 (1996), 35.

Muschamp, Herbert. "Rem Koolhaas Sizes Up the Future," *New York Times*, March 3, 1996.

Novosedlik, Will. "Leviathan: *S,M,L,XL*: A Book by Rem Koolhaas and Bruce Mau," *Print: America's Graphic Design Magazine* 4 (1996), 90–95, 237.

Oechslin, Werner. "Beyond a Certain Scale, or: Titan in Slippers?" *Daidalos* 61 (1996), 16–29.

Oshima, Tetsuzo. "The Bible of Urban Architecture," *Kenchiku Bunka* 593 (1996), 143.

Parent, Claude. "*S,M,L,XL*," *AMC* 70 (1996), 54–55.

Pearson, Clifford A. "Asian Cities: Is 'Generic' the Wave of the Future?," *Architectural Record* 3 (1996), 19–20.

Plunz, Richard. "The Scale Canard," *Daidalos* 61 (1996), 128–31.

Riley, Terence. "Chute libre: *S,M,L,XL*," *L'Architecture d'Aujourd'hui* 304 (1996), 57.

Robert, Jean-Paul. "Une oeuvre, quelque part aux Pays-Bas," *L'Architecture d'Aujourd'hui* 304 (1996), 78–79.

Scalbert, Irénée. "*S,M,L,XL*," *Architectural Research Quarterly* 3 (1996), 90–91.

Schnell, Angelika. "Schalten und Falten," *ARCH+* 132 (1996), 78–79.

Schumann, Ulrich Maximilian. "Super-Rem's Rache," *Archithese* 3 (1996), 67.

Sennett, Richard. "The Dialectics of Scale," *Harvard GSD News*, Summer 1996, 45.

Stuttaford, Genevieve. "Nonfiction—*S,M,L,XL*," *Publishers Weekly* 4 (1996), 54–55.

Tabet, Marco. *La terrifiante beauté de la beauté: Naturalisme et abstraction dans l'architecture de Jean Nouvel et Rem Koolhaas* (Paris: Sens & Tonka, 1996).

Till, Jeremy. "An Incomplete Encyclopaedia: Rem Koolhaas and *S,M,L,XL*," *Artifice* 4 (1996), 18–27.

Wortmann, Arthur. "Grand Palais in Lille," *Baumeister* 4 (1996), 44–49.

Zaera-Polo, Alejandro. "The Day After: A Conversation with Rem Koolhaas," *El Croquis* 79 (1996), 9–25.

1997

Bevan, Robert. "To Get Rich Is Glorious," *Building Design* 1312, June 13, 1997.

Bosma, Koos. "*S,M,L,XL*," *Planning Perspectives* 12 (1997), 115–18.

Davidson, Cynthia. "Koolhaas and the Kunsthal: History Lesions," *ANY* 21 (1997), 36–40.

Goto, Takeshi. "The Reversible Sublime: A Theory of Rem Koolhaas," *Kenchiku Bunka* 610 (1997), 157–61.

Puglisi, Luigi Prestinenza. *Rem Koolhaas: Trasparenze metropolitane* (Torino: Testo & Immagine, 1997).

Röthlisberger, Markus. "Die erschreckende Schönheit des 20. Jahrhunderts, oder: Rem Koolhaas und die 'Neuerfindung' eines Berufsverständisses," *Archithese* 3 (1997), 56–59.

Saunders, William S. "Rem Koolhaas's Writings on Cities: Poetic Perception and Gnomic Fantasy," *Journal of Architectural Education* 1 (1997), 61–71.

Sen, Itziar. "Kunsthal: Rem Koolhaas." In *The Architecture of Museums*, ed. Francisco Asensio Cerver, 120–27 (New York: Hearst Books International, 1997).

Tardits, Manuel. "Rem Koolhaas in Euralille: Between Utopia and Reality," *Kenchiku Bunka* 608 (1997), 152–53.

T'Jonck, Pieter. "Bij *S,M,L,XL:* Het interieur zonder eigenschappen als ruimte van de verbeelding," *DWB* 1 (1997), 76–91.

Wang, Jun-Yang. "Piranesi, Koolhaas, and the Subversion of the Concept of Place," *Nordic Journal of Architectural Research* 2 (1997), 7–23.

1998

Buchanan, Peter. "Netherlands Now: Rotterdam and Rem," *A+U* 336 (1998), 6–8.

De Cauter, Lieven. "The Flight Forward of Rem Koolhaas," *Archis* 4 (1998), 28–34.

Lampugnani, Vittorio. "Euralille: Une microhistoire critique," *AMC* 86 (1998), 50–55.

INDEX OF PERSONS

EDITOR Christophe Van Gerrewey
EDITORIAL ASSISTANCE Stéphanie Savio
COPY EDITING Keonaona Peterson
PROJECT MANAGEMENT Alexander Felix, Regina Herr
PRODUCTION Heike Strempel

LAYOUT, COVER DESIGN AND TYPESETTING Jenna Gesse
COVER OMA/Rem Koolhaas, Alex Wall, The Pleasure of Architecture, 1983 (OMAR/HNI, Rotterdam).

PAPER Magno Volume, 150 g/m² and 115 g/m²
PRINTING Beltz Grafische Betriebe GmbH, Bad Langensalza

LIBRARY OF CONGRESS CONTROL NUMBER 2019942856

Bibliographic information published by the German National Library
The German National Library lists this publication in the Deutsche Nationalbibliografie; detailed bibliographic data are available on the Internet at http://dnb.dnb.de.

ISBN 978-3-0356-1974-4 (Hardcover)
ISBN 978-3-0356-1977-5 (Softcover)

e-ISBN (PDF) 978-3-0356-1981-2

P.O. Box 44, 4009 Basel, Switzerland
Part of Walter de Gruyter GmbH, Berlin/Boston

9 8 7 6 5 4 3 2

www.birkhauser.com